Texas

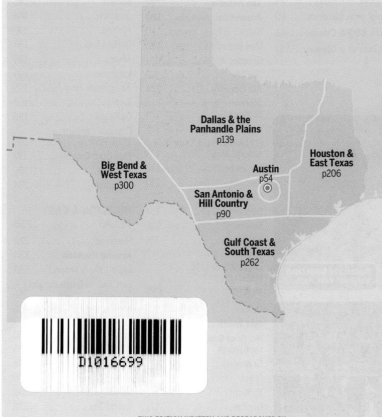

Dallas & the Panhandle Plains
p139

Big Bend & West Texas
p300

Austin
p54

Houston & East Texas
p206

San Antonio & Hill Country
p90

Gulf Coast & South Texas
p262

THIS EDITION WRITTEN AND RESEARCHED BY

Lisa Dunford,

Mariella Krause, Ryan Ver Berkmoes

PLAN YOUR TRIP

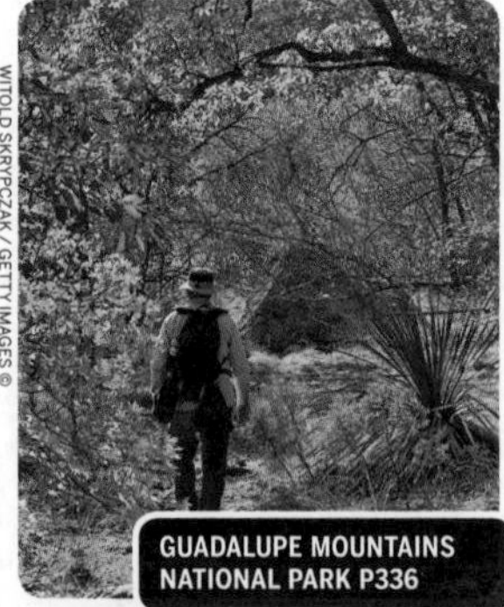

GUADALUPE MOUNTAINS NATIONAL PARK P336

BUCKHORN SALOON & MUSEUM P95

ON THE ROAD

Contents

UNDERSTAND

SURVIVAL GUIDE

SPECIAL FEATURES

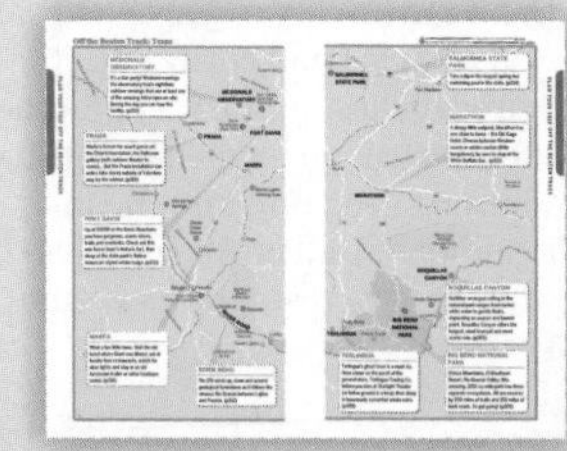

Welcome to Texas

A darn sight bigger than a whole heap of countries, Texas is largely diverse: big-city lights to small-town simplicity; white-sand beaches to high-country hikes.

Now That's Country

Country is as much about a way of life as a place. Slowing down, taking the rural, farm-to-market back roads; steppin' out in polished boots and starched blue jeans for a Saturday-night dance under the stars; doin' nothing more on a Sunday afternoon than floating down a lazy river... Life in the country lopes along. Even if most Texans now live in urban areas, they're influenced by the state's agricultural, roping-and-riding heritage – and they escape to the country just as often as they can.

Fun Foods

There's just something about eating a big pile of brisket off a butcher-paper 'plate'. Don't dare ask for a fork; real 'Q is for fingers only. And great barbecue is not the state's only fun food. At festivals, rodeos and fairs much of your meal can be served on a stick, from corny dogs to fried PB&J sandwiches. In Austin and other cities the food-truck phenomena continues. And we haven't even dug into the ubiquitous Mexican food, Dallas' fine upscale dining or the foodie-fave restaurants around Houston.

Cities & Towns

Bright lights, big cities? Check, Texas has them. Dallas and Houston both boast rich arts and culture districts to explore by day, as well as active nightlife. If you really want to party, Austin is the place – with endless live-music concerts and an outdoorsy, alternative vibe. San Antonio may seem a bit more sedate, but once evening falls on the Riverwalk there's a fiesta every night. City life is fun, but don't stop there. Texas also has countless small towns with brick-building–lined courthouse squares, landmark cafes and eclectic shops to explore.

As Big as All Outdoors

We know you've heard, but Texas is big... really BIG. More than 261,000 sq miles, in fact. That's larger than Germany, England, Scotland, Ireland, Northern Ireland, Belgium and the Netherlands combined. And it ain't all just tumblin' tumbleweeds. Barrier islands with windswept dunes and public beaches stretch down 367 miles of coastline. In the west, three mountain ranges top more than 7000ft; Big Bend National Park is the state's primary trekking and rafting destination. And to the northeast, soaring pine forests and sinuous, cypress-lined bayous are perfect for hiking and kayaking.

Why I Love Texas

By Lisa Dunford, Author

Crisscrossing the state in the 22 years I've called Texas home, I've learned that there isn't much I don't love: hiking to a riverside hot-spring hot tub made out of adobe ruins and peering across to Mexico from Big Bend; two-stepping in a giant, family-filled tent with the man who would become my husband at the Refugio county rodeo; listening to Ray Price sing 'Crazy Arms' at John T Floore's Country Store... And the folks here are just as friendly as can be; seems like each time I visit a new place, I come away with new friends.

For more about our authors, see page 392

Above: Bluebonnet wildflowers, Hill Country (p124)

Texas

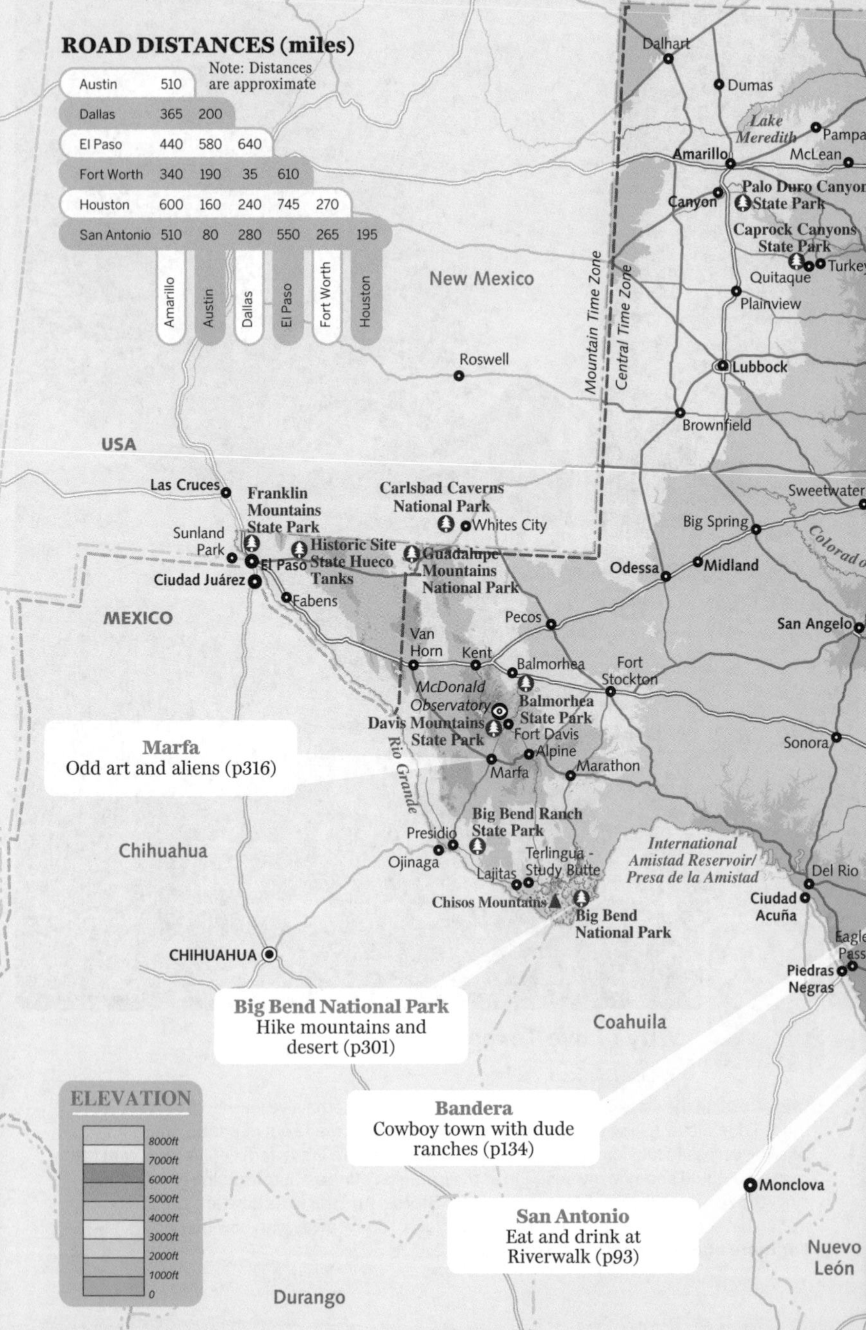

ROAD DISTANCES (miles)

Note: Distances are approximate

	Amarillo	Austin	Dallas	El Paso	Fort Worth	Houston
Austin	510					
Dallas	365	200				
El Paso	440	580	640			
Fort Worth	340	190	35	610		
Houston	600	160	240	745	270	
San Antonio	510	80	280	550	265	195

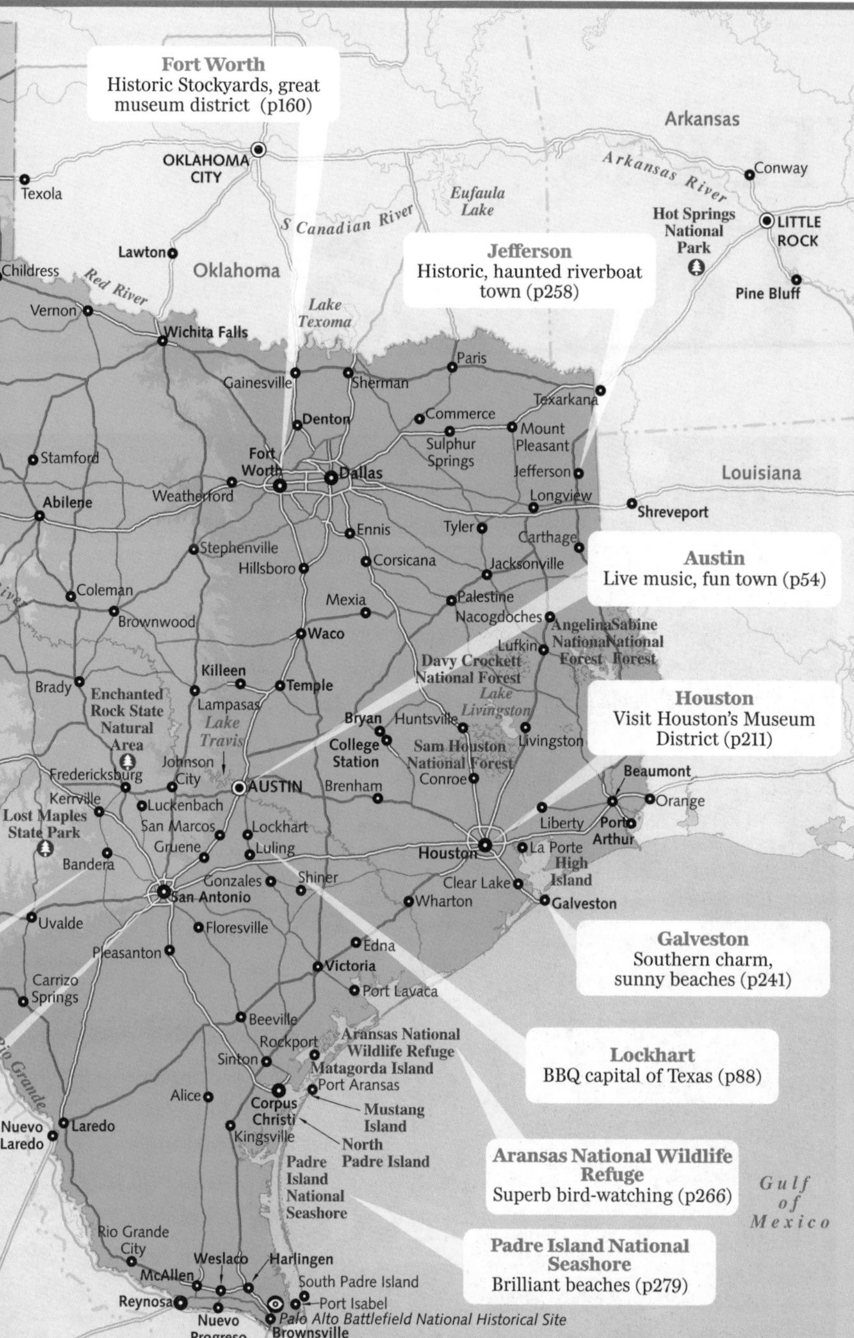

0 200 km
0 120 miles
Fort Worth
Historic Stockyards, great museum district (p160)
Jefferson
Historic, haunted riverboat town (p258)
Austin
Live music, fun town (p54)
Houston
Visit Houston's Museum District (p211)
Galveston
Southern charm, sunny beaches (p241)
Lockhart
BBQ capital of Texas (p88)
Aransas National Wildlife Refuge
Superb bird-watching (p266)
Padre Island National Seashore
Brilliant beaches (p279)
Arkansas
Oklahoma
Louisiana
OKLAHOMA CITY
LITTLE ROCK
AUSTIN
Texola
Lawton
Childress
Vernon
Wichita Falls
Conway
Pine Bluff
Hot Springs National Park
Arkansas River
S Canadian River
Red River
Eufaula Lake
Lake Texoma
Gainesville
Sherman
Paris
Denton
Commerce
Sulphur Springs
Mount Pleasant
Texarkana
Stamford
Fort Worth
Dallas
Jefferson
Abilene
Weatherford
Longview
Shreveport
Tyler
Carthage
Ennis
Stephenville
Corsicana
Hillsboro
Jacksonville
Coleman
Brownwood
Mexia
Palestine
Nacogdoches
Waco
Lufkin
Angelina National Forest
Sabine National Forest
Davy Crockett National Forest
Killeen
Temple
Brady
Enchanted Rock State Natural Area
Lampasas
Lake Travis
Lake Livingston
Bryan
College Station
Huntsville
Livingston
Sam Houston National Forest
Conroe
Johnson City
Fredericksburg
Kerrville
Luckenbach
Brenham
Beaumont
Orange
Lost Maples State Park
San Marcos
Lockhart
Liberty
Port Arthur
Gruene
Luling
Houston
La Porte
High Island
Bandera
Gonzales
Shiner
Clear Lake
San Antonio
Wharton
Galveston
Uvalde
Floresville
Pleasanton
Edna
Victoria
Carrizo Springs
Port Lavaca
Beeville
Rockport
Aransas National Wildlife Refuge
Sinton
Matagorda Island
Port Aransas
Alice
Corpus Christi
Mustang Island
Rio Grande
Nuevo Laredo
Laredo
Kingsville
North Padre Island
Padre Island National Seashore
Gulf of Mexico
Rio Grande City
Weslaco
Harlingen
McAllen
South Padre Island
Reynosa
Port Isabel
Nuevo Progreso
Palo Alto Battlefield National Historical Site
Brownsville
River

Texas' Top 25

Live Music in Austin

1 In the airport, at the grocery store, in a record shop or at an actual bar or nightclub – a concert might take place anywhere in Austin (p54). To say that this is the 'live music capital of Texas' is to promote truth in advertising. Austin country classics such as Dale Watson or Kelly Willis may be some of our favorites, but you can also rock out, get the blues, go punk, dig rockabilly or turn alternative any night of the week. You name it, you can hear it here. Left: South by Southwest Festival (p68)

The Alamo

2 A small chapel and a long barrack don't seem much to remember the Alamo (p93) by, but that doesn't deter 28 million San Antonio visitors from paying homage annually. Never mind the tacky tourist attractions nearby and the fact that the site is now dwarfed by its big-city surrounds. A few hundred Texas freedom fighters battled and died here during the 13-day siege of this fortified mission by Mexican forces, a fact that still stirs the feisty independent spirit of locals and underdog-lovers alike.

REDFERNS VIA GETTY IMAGES ©

2

ETHEL DAVIES / GETTY IMAGES ©

Big Bend National Park

3 You knew Texas was big, but did you know that it has a national park (p301) larger than Rhode Island? Out in way-far-west Texas, the Chisos Mountains (7825ft) provide an excellent place to take a hike. But then so, too, does the Chihuahuan Desert or the Rio Grande Valley. Having three distinct ecosystems in one vast and remote parkland provides something for everyone. But plan ahead – the mountaintop lodge has limited accommodations, and campgrounds fill up quickly in spring and fall.

Sixth Floor Museum, Dallas

4 The 6th floor of the old Texas School Book Depository, looking down on Dealey Plaza: Lee Harvey Oswald stood here almost 50 years ago and fired the shots that killed John F Kennedy. Or did he? This museum (p146) investigates the dark ambiguities that swirl at the heart of the tragedy. Through video, audio clips and interactive exhibits, you relive moment by moment the events that transpired on that day, as well as looking into the lead up. History – powerful and bittersweet – is alive here.

3

WILLARD CLAY / GETTY IMAGES ©

4

RICHARD CUMMINS / GETTY IMAGES ©

JORGE GONZALEZ / GETTY IMAGES ©

State Fair of Texas

5 When the weather finally cools down in October, it's festival season around the state. None is more iconic than the State Fair of Texas (p153). Although Big Tex, the 50ft-tall cowboy that welcomed fair-goers from 1952 burnt down in 2012, there's still North America's largest Ferris wheel, a midway full of carnival rides, livestock and other animal shows – plus all those crazy fair foods to try. The corny dog debuted here, as did fried butter. Our favorite? Deep-fried Oreos.

Shopping

6 Whatever you're shopping for, you can find it in-state. Fashionistas love Dallas (p157) and Houston (p230), which are both known for their upscale Galleria malls that host top designers. Funkier finds are to be had at Austin's many vintage outlets (p81). Around old town squares in rural Texas, you're likely to find a whole variety of area antiques. For Mexican arts and crafts, the Mercado (p99) in San Antonio is surprisingly authentic; and then there's Laredo (p298), where the products are made just across the border.

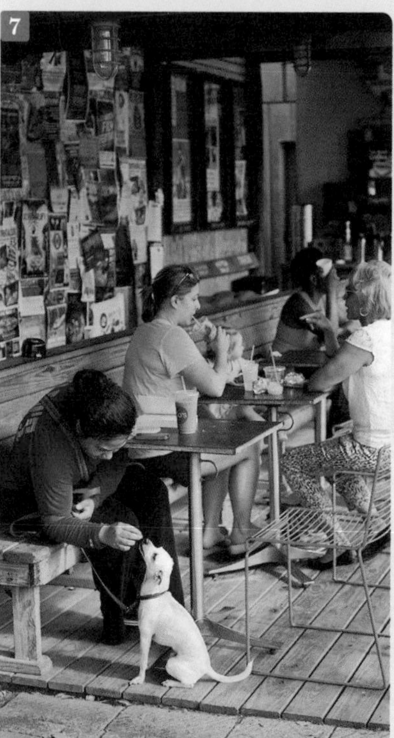
7

JULIA ROBINSON / REUTERS / CORBIS ©

8

RICHARD CUMMINS / GETTY IMAGES ©

9

RICHARD STOCKTON / GETTY IMAGES ©

Austin's South Congress

7 Just below downtown, South Congress Ave (p62) epitomizes the 'Keep Austin Weird' movement. A heady mishmash of everything we love about town, the street is lined with funky thrift stores and boutiques, locally owned restaurants, cool food trailers, lively bars and a hip couple of hotels – without a single Chili's or Starbucks in sight. In the surrounding residential area, the neo-modern environmental-standard homes and the little old arts-and-crafts bungalows (one or two turned B&B), add heaps of charm to the neighborhood. Top left: Jo's Coffee (p74)

Houston Museum District

8 Sure, the world-class Museum of Fine Arts Houston and the Houston Museum of Natural Science make their home here. And there are smaller, more specialized museums focusing on topics such as the weather and the Holocaust. But the star of the neighborhood really is the Menil Collection (p211). One of the country's top privately owned museums, the complex contains everything from 10,000-year-old antiquities to abstract art. The representation of modern artists, such as David Rothko, is particularly impressive. Top right: Children's Museum of Houston (p222)

Padre Island National Seashore

9 A narrow ridge of sand dunes backs the 70-mile-long protected coastline at Padre Island National Seashore (p279). To say this place is windswept is an understatement. Bird Island Basin, on the lagoon side of park's barrier-island home, is a mecca for windsurfers. While the first mile or so of beach south of the visitor center is usually busy, it doesn't take long to walk away from the crowds. If you have a 4WD vehicle, 60 miles of beach is open for you to explore.

San Antonio Riverwalk

10 Cafe after bar after restaurant after bar: the Riverwalk (p91) is a mighty entertaining experience. Located below street level, stone footpaths that follow the downtown riverbank are lined with places to eat and drink the day away. Outdoor stages host frequent events and there are hotels aplenty to rest your head. Follow the sidewalks further and you get to peaceful natural stretches on the way out of the city. Take a cruise along the canal or a tour during Christmas-light season to get the full festive effect.

Hill Country

11 Slow down and take a scenic country drive through the Hill Country (p124). Meander through the green rolling hills covered in live oaks, climb up to a vista and cruise down a curve. In spring the roadsides and fields are colored with Indian paintbrushes and Texas bluebonnets. But all year you'll find a tiny old Texas town, a tranquil ranch or a vineyard around the next bend. Stop to sit in a river or enjoy a pie in an old cafe. This is Hill Country small-town Texas life at its best.

High School & College Football

12 How to sum up Texans' affection for football (p362)? Obsession might just cover it. At the corner cafe on a Saturday morning you'll hear 'em hotly debating last night's game – and they're talking about local high school ball. College rivalries are even more heated, whether you're chanting on your feet as the '12th man' (p240) for the Texas A&M football team or signalling 'hook 'em horns' for the University of Texas. Game day is party time, whether at home or on a tailgate in the stadium parking lot.

Luckenbach

13 With a permanent population of three, you can't really call Luckenbach (p130) a town. What remains today is a cluster of Old West–era buildings that typify Texas country charm. Grab a Shiner Bock beer and listen to guitar pickers and singers under the giant live oak tree. In colder weather, musicians move inside the general store (p130), which is also the post office and a saloon. If you're lucky there will be a Friday-night dance on at the 1880s hall. And yes, Willie Nelson and Waylon Jennings have played here.

JOHN ALBRIGHT / ICON SMI/CORBIS ©

STEPHEN SAKS / GETTY IMAGES ©

STEPHEN SAKS PHOTOGRAPHY / ALAMY ©

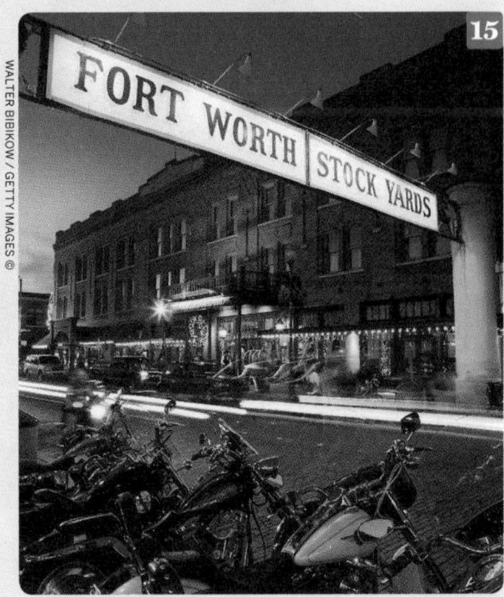

WALTER BIBIKOW / GETTY IMAGES ©

Barbecue

14 The best beef brisket has a visible pink smoke ring around the edge, testament to the fact that it takes hours and hours of cooking under precise conditions to produce the juiciest cuts. From Tyler to Temple, Texans know their barbecue. They eat it at home, at famous hole-in-the-walls or bought from a roadside smoker. It's in central Texas that you'll find the state's unofficial BBQ capital, Lockhart (p88), with three of the most lauded meat market–style joints in the state. Top right: Kreuz Market (p88)

Fort Worth Stockyards

15 Wander into the Old West at the Fort Worth Stockyards (p161), where you can drink at the saloon bar after a mini cattle drive comes through town. The old steam train that was once used take the herds north now offers tourist rides. It sure is fun to watch the kids, and some adults, get their pennies flattened on the wheelhouse rail. In addition to Western shops, the district has several in-theme restaurants and bars. Conquer both the mechanical bull and the two-step at Billy Bob's, one of the world's largest honky-tonks.

Aransas National Wildlife Refuge

16 The south Texas coast is reknowned for its bird-watching, with hundreds of species congregating along its marshy coastal plains. But its premier site is the Aransas National Wildlife Refuge (p266). It is home to the only naturally migrating flock of whooping cranes in the US. These 5ft-tall white birds with red crowns would be noteworthy anyway, but what's incredible is that the population has risen to more than 250 from its lowest point in 1941 when just 15 birds remained. Below: Whooping cranes

Galveston

17 Hurricanes have not been able to destroy this beguiling bit of Old South on the Gulf Coast. The Victorian neighborhoods of Galveston (p241) still stand, and shops and restaurants have come back to the century-old, downtown Strand District. Tour an 1800s tall ship, and learn about the town's heyday watching local films. On the flip side of the island, sandy stretches of beach beckon. Surf-bum bars and condo rentals make beach life easier. When little ones get bored, you can take them to mid-island amusement parks. Bottom: Tall ship Elissa (p242)

16

17

18

RICHARD T. NOWITZ / CORBIS ©

19

WITOLD SKRYPCZAK / GETTY IMAGES ©

20

DENNIS COX / ALAMY ©

Piney Woods

18 No one thinks of soaring pine forests when they say Texas, but that's exactly what comprises most of the northeast, aka the Piney Woods. The cypress swamps of Caddo Lake State Park are an excellent place to start exploring. Nearby, you can shop among the old downtown buildings and stay in a B&B at the riverboat town of Jefferson (p258). Other old towns abound, or you can go hiking in one of the region's four national forests and one national preserve. Top left: Caddo Lake (p260)

Marfa

19 Alien lights, an obsession with the Texas film classic *Giant*, and a renowned modern-art installation or two: Marfa (p316) is nothing if not out there. This west desert outpost attracts an interesting mix of artists and rugged individualists. The number of New Yorkers here may surprise you, but then so might the replica Prada store in the middle of nowhere. Stay at the old Hotel Paisano, where James Dean and Elizabeth Taylor once did, then head out to the lights-viewing platform at 2am to see if you can spot anything mysterious. Top right: Hotel Paisano (p318)

Bandera Dude Ranches

20 Finding places to rope and ride is surprisingly difficult in Texas. Not so if you head for Hill Country. The area around Bandera (p134) hosts more than a dozen dude (or guest) ranches. Don't expect cattle drives; do expect daily horseback rides, hay wagons, swimming holes, rodeos and at least one chuckwagon breakfast or outdoor barbecue per stay. Although everything's included in the experience, be sure to take time to trot into town where there are daily activities and two of the best cowboy bars around. Above: Dixie Dude Ranch (p135)

21

DENNIS MACDONALD / GETTY IMAGES ©

22

DANITA DELIMONT / GETTY IMAGES ©

23

DANITA DELIMONT / GETTY IMAGES ©

Route 66

21 OK, so the Texas stretch of the Mother Road doesn't amount to much, considering it's only 178 miles long. But Amarillo (p199) is a worthy guardian of the route, with timeless roadside attractions such as the Big Texan Steak Ranch and Cadillac Ranch, a series of old spray-painted Caddies planted nose down in the dirt. There's also the McLean Devil's Rope barbed wire museum, which produces a detailed map of the road's Texas attractions. The best part may be riding through the region's pancake-flat plains – the definition of an open road. Top left: Big Texan Steak Ranch (p203)

Texas Bluebonnets

22 Starting every March, the roadsides of Texas erupt with color: red Indian paintbrushes, yellow and red Indian blankets, pink evening primrose, yellow brown-eyed Susans… But the bluebonnet is Texas' state flower, and easily the star. Entire fields turn a vibrant bluish-purple for a couple of weeks, sending families flocking to take pictures among the blooms. Hill Country (p124) and Washington County (p236) are the usual picture-taking sites, but you can also find 2ft-tall bluebonnets in Big Bend and fields full of flowers as far north as Dallas.

World Birding Center

23 More than nine splendid bird-watching sites roost under one umbrella organization in the Rio Grande Valley. Texas' position on the central migratory flyway and the valley's southern locale makes this both a stopover and wintering grounds for transient species. The 760-acre Bentsen-Rio Grande Valley State Park (p295) acts as the center headquarters for sites along the border all the way to South Padre Island. Pick up maps and a bird-watching list, and then test yourself. How many of the 600 reported species can you spot?

NASA's Space Center Houston

24 Cape Canaveral may be where rockets and shuttles launch, but the trip planning and astronaut training take place outside Houston in Clear Lake. The Johnson Space Center's official visitor center and museum, Space Center Houston (p234), lets you learn about NASA's history through films and exhibits, and then try your hand at key astronaut skills. A tram tour leads you through some of the actual working parts of the complex, including space-walk labs and the original mission control. Upgrade your tour and you can even eat with the astronauts.

Guadalupe Mountains National Park

25 High country splendor in west Texas, the Guadalupe Mountains (8749ft; p336) may be one of the state's best-kept secrets just because they are so darn far from anywhere. Make the journey and your reward is stunning hikes and excellent fall color, especially in McKittrick Canyon. The mountains sit among an exposed fossil reef, so amateur geologists should take note. Others can just enjoy the historic ranch and 80 miles of trails and scenic drives located throughout the park. Bottom: Guadalupe Peak (p338)

24

COSMO CONDINA / GETTY IMAGES ©

25

WITOLD SKRYPCZAK / GETTY IMAGES ©

Need to Know

For more information, see Survival Guide (p369)

Currency
US dollar ($)

Language
English

Visas
Visas are not required for citizens of Visa Waiver Program (VWP) countries, but you must request travel authorization from ESTA (p375) at least 72 hours in advance.

Money
ATMs are widely available. Credit cards are normally required for advance hotel reservations, and car rentals. Tipping is essential, not optional.

Cell Phones
Cell-phone reception can be spotty in rural areas. Only foreign phones that operate on tri- or quad-band frequencies will work in the USA.

Time
All but two far-west Texas counties are in the Central Time Zone (GMT/UTC minus five hours).

When to Go

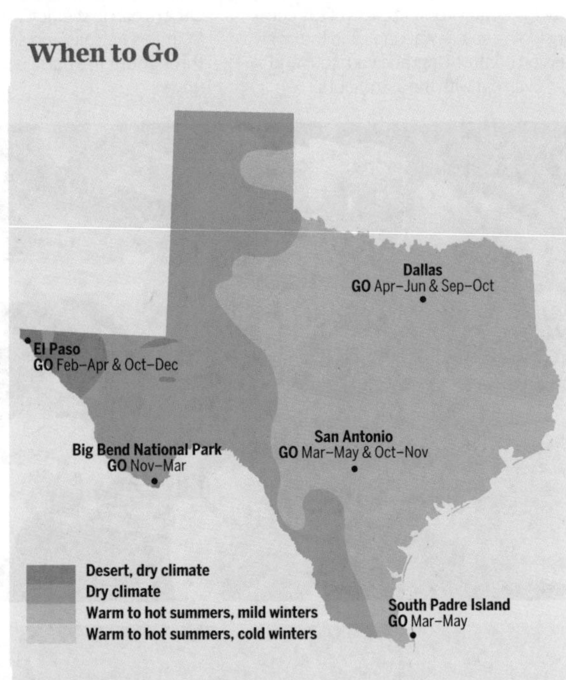

High Season
(Jun–Aug)

- Kids are out of school, so attractions are busiest.
- Temperatures will be stiflingly hot outside, but everywhere inside has air-con.
- Prime time for beaches, lakes and rivers.

Shoulder
(late Mar–May)

- Best time of year to travel: the weather is less intense, everything is still open.
- This is when most festival planners throw events, including rodeos.
- A second shoulder season lasts from September through early November.

Low Season
(Dec–Feb)

- Some theme parks and such closed for the season.
- North Texas occasionally freezes, south Texas rarely does.
- Christmastime festivities statewide.

Useful Websites

TravelTex (www.traveltex.com) State's official tourism website, where you can request the huge *Texas Travel Guide* and search through tons of info.

Texas Monthly (www.texasmonthly.com) Glossy mag with great writing about Texas, dining and shopping guides; all available online.

Lonely Planet (www.lonelyplanet.com) Research destinations, get fellow travelers' advice, post questions and much more.

Texas Highways (www.texashighways.com) Travel magazine with extensive festival and event listings.

Texas Parks & Wildlife (www.tpwd.state.tx.us) A complete guide to Texas' outdoor recreation and environment.

Important Numbers

Most, but not all, numbers require you to dial the area code even when you are within the city.

Country code	☎1
International dialing code	☎011
Emergency (ambulance, police & fire)	☎911
Directory assistance	☎411

Exchange Rates

Australia	A$1	$0.92
Canada	C$1	$0.97
Euro zone	€1	$1.33
Japan	¥100	$1
NZ	NZ$1	$0.80
UK	UK£1	$1.55

For current exchange rates see www.xe.com

Daily Costs

Budget: less than $120

- Campground or dorm bed: $15–22
- Basic motel room: $60
- Pizza or take out: $6–10
- Car rental and fuel: $40

Midrange: $200–300

- B&B or better quality motel: $90–150
- Restaurant meals and food-truck takeout: $40–60
- Car rental and fuel: $40–50
- Museums and sight entry: $15

Top End: over $350

- Upscale hotel: $180–300
- Restaurant meals and fine dining: $100–140
- Car rental and fuel: $40–50
- Museums, shows, major attractions, theme parks: $40–60

Opening Hours

We've listed individual opening hours in reviews, below are generalities. Sight and activity hours vary throughout the year and may decrease during the shoulder and low seasons.

Banks 9am–5pm Monday to Friday

Restaurants 11am–2pm and 5pm–10pm

Cafes 7.30am–8pm

Nightclubs 8pm–2am

Shops 9am–6pm Monday to Saturday, 11am–6pm Sunday

Arriving in Texas

Austin-Bergstrom International Airport (p84) Taxis to town (20 minutes) cost $25 to $30, shared-use shuttles $14; the limited bus service is only $1.

Dallas/Fort Worth International Airport (p158) Taxis to central Dallas (25 minutes) cost $40 to $60, shared-use shuttles $17; the Trinity Express train from downtown, and shuttle to the terminal, costs $2.50, but doesn't run weekends.

Houston George Bush Intercontinental Airport (p233) Taxis cost about $50 to downtown Houston (30 minutes), shared-ride van shuttles $25; the Metropolitan Transit Authority runs a limited bus service ($1.25) to downtown, but it takes an hour.

San Antonio International Airport (p118) A taxi ride to downtown (15 minutes) costs $25 to $30, a shared-ride shuttle is a few bucks cheaper. Via runs a regular bus to downtown (35 minutes) for $1.20.

Getting Around

Unless you plan to stay exclusively in central Dallas, downtown in San Antonio or Austin, or along the light rail corridor in Houston, you will need a car.

Car Easy to rent at any airport, at in-town locations and even in suburbia.

Public transportation Extremely limited outside big cities; not comprehensive even within.

For much more on **getting around**, see p376

If You Like...

Dance Halls & Honky-Tonks

You'll find most old dance halls on some rural route in central Texas; but honky-tonks can be anywhere there's music, a bar and sand for the dance floor.

John T Floore Country Store You can't beat Floore's for atmosphere. Willie Nelson played here regularly back in the 1950s; sometimes still does. (p115)

Gruene Hall Texas' 'oldest' dance hall and still one of the most popular. Weekend nights the dance floor is always packed. (p121)

Billy Bob's Texas Think rhinestone cowboy: barn-size dance floor, numerous bars and live indoor bull-riding weekends. (p170)

Broken Spoke George Strait used to swing from the wagon-wheel chandeliers here. Chow down at the restaurant then boot-scoot in the hall. (p77)

Arkey Blue's Silver Dollar Saloon This darn tiny basement club has been entertainin' folks since the 1940s. (p135)

Luckenbach Dance Hall An 1850s German *tanzhalle* that helped put Luckenbach on the map; outlaw country stars played here in the 1970s. (p130)

Texas History

Texas was once a republic of its own, and it has a good number of sites linked to the independence period.

Alamo Heard of this little fortified mission? Davy Crockett and about 150 other Texas independence fighters died defending it. (p93)

Mission Trail Before US settlers arrived, the Spanish colonized the territory of Tejas. Tour four 1700s missions built south of San Antonio. (p103)

Goliad The battle at Goliad preceded any Alamo fighting; today you can visit the Spanish mission, fort and battlefield. (p270)

San Jacinto Battleground State Historic Site Learn about the last battle in Texas' war for independence, then take an elevator up to view the site. (p235)

Washington-on-the-Brazos Tour the site where the declaration of Texas independence was signed and experience an 1850s living-history farm. (p239)

Small Towns

Jefferson Take a riverboat ride and tour a haunted house (or two) in this Southern belle of an east Texas town. (p258)

Waxahachie The historic downtown district here is filled with early Victorian, Queen Anne and Greek Revival beauties. (p175)

Gruene Shop in late-1800s wooden buildings, step out on the state's oldest dance floor, then sleep in a historic house inn. (p121)

Brenham You scream, I scream, we all scream for Blue Bell ice cream! Tour the factory and the town's fun-and-funky shops. (p236)

Fort Davis A scenic route leads to this mountain town, a base for hiking, star-gazing and Old West museums. (p313)

Nacogdoches Follow the azalea trail through stately neighborhoods and around the red-brick buildings of the historic courthouse square. (p255)

Wildflowers & Garden Trails

Blooming seasons start from south to north; roughly expect bluebonnets from late February into April, azaleas late March through April and roses beginning in May.

Lady Bird Johnson Wildflower Center Get a primer on wildflowers at a botanical garden named for the first lady who beautified state highways with them. (p63)

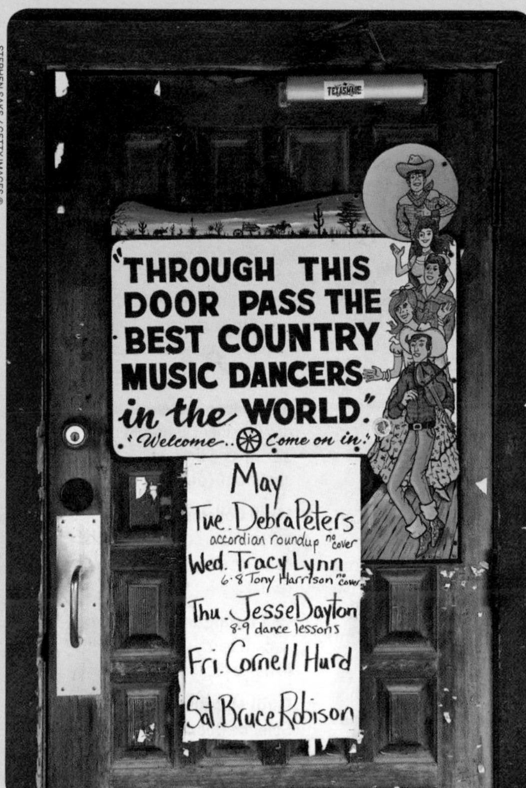

(Above) Broken Spoke (p77)

(Below) River Road and the Rio Grande, Big Bend Ranch State Park (p312)

Wildseed Farms You're guaranteed to see gorgeous fields in full bloom come spring at this garden center and show farm. (p126)

Azalea Trail Follow set routes through leafy neighborhoods bursting with azaleas during Nachogdoches' annual festival. (p255)

Tyler The rose capital of Texas has a 14-acre municipal garden and puts on a heck of a rose festival. (p256)

Cowboy Culture

Dude ranches Cowboy up and learn to rope and ride at one of many local dude ranches near Hill Country State Natural Area. (p135)

Fort Worth Stockyards National Historic District Watch a miniature re-creation of a longhorn cattle drive down main street in the historic Stockyards. (p161)

King Ranch Tour a small portion of one the world's largest ranches (it's bigger than Rhode Island). (p280)

Houston Livestock Show & Rodeo Three weeks' worth of nightly barrel-racing, bronc-busting, bull-riding action. (p220)

Cowboy Poetry Gathering Get back to the days when cowboys entertained themselves with poetry and ate chuck-wagon breakfasts. (p319)

National Center for American Western Art The details of the Old West depicted in oil and bronze. (p131)

Cowboys on Main Weekends, the little false-front town of Bandera hosts Western entertainment on the square. (p134)

The Offbeat

Orange Show for Visionary Art A wacky art car parade, a beer-can-covered home, and a maze-like orange house curated by visionaries in Houston. (p211)

Marfa Alien lights, minimalist art exhibits and a fake Prada store – in the middle of nowhere, west Texas. (p316)

International Bowling Museum Crazy-colored shoes, pitchers of beers, strikes and spares are celebrated here. (p175)

Chicken Shit Bingo Really. Beer-swilling country folk bet on where the poop will land while listening to live music. (p78)

Stonehenge II Stone monoliths and Easter Island–like statues stand outside the Hill Country Arts Foundation in Ingram. (p131)

National Museum of Funeral History Brush up on your embalming tricks and celebrate the Day of the Dead. (p215)

Buckhorn Saloon & Museum A kitschy monument to old Texas ways and taxidermy; look for the two-headed calf. (p95)

National & State Parks

Big Bend National Park Both the Chisos Mountains and Chihuahuan Desert are located in this 1252-sq-mile park. (p301)

Padre Island National Seashore The 70 miles of sandy coastline are a haven for more than 350 bird species. (p279)

Big Thicket National Preserve Cypress swamps, desert sands, hardwood forests and coastal plains together in one amazing area. (p252)

Enchanted Rock State Natural Area A pink granite dome rising 425ft just calls out to be climbed. (p129)

Palo Duro Canyon State Park Second in size only to the Grand Canyon, Palo Duro is quite a surprise on the Panhandle Plains. (p198)

Guadalupe Mountains National Park High-country hiking in far northwest Texas; fall colors in McKittrick Canyon are stunning. (p336)

Beaches

Few beaches along the Texas coast are organized. Mostly you'll find undeveloped acres, where you're allowed to drive. (Yes, drive. The 'roads' near the tide line even have speed limits.)

Matagorda Twenty-two miles of wonderfully deserted, white-sand beaches waiting for you to venture out and stake your claim. (p263)

South Padre Island Spring break central: there are 23 beach access points within this city's limits. (p284)

Stewart Beach A family beach with sponsored activities, such as sand-castle-building contests. (p243)

Padre Island National Seashore Wild and windswept; you need 4WD to access most of the protected beach. (p279)

Crystal Beach Residential community where you can escape the tourist hordes and kick back with locals only. (p249)

IF YOU LIKE... SPRING-FED POOLS

Take a dip in Barton Springs Pool (p63), the icy cool spring in Austin, or at Balmorhea State Park (p314), where the 25ft deep water is 75°F year round.

Museums

Bob Bullock Texas State History Museum Fancy, high-tech displays and theatrical exhibits tell the story of Texas. (p57)

Sixth Floor Museum Relive the day President John F Kennedy died, inside the building he was shot from. (p146)

Menil Collection One of the best private collections in the country; strong on modernists. (p211)

USS Lexington Tour a retired aircraft carrier, complete with foldable planes. (p271)

Perot Museum of Nature & Science One of the state's newest museums, with earth-friendly architecture and interactive exhibits. (p150)

Museum of Fine Arts Houston Impressive permanent exhibits and world-class rotating shows. (p214)

Bird-Watching

Aransas National Wildlife Refuge The last remaining wild flock of whooping cranes (250-plus strong) winters here. (p266)

South Padre Island Birding & Nature Center Shorebirds make themselves right at home among the sand dunes. (p285)

High Island Migratory species shelter among the trees when inclement weather threatens their travel plans. (p249)

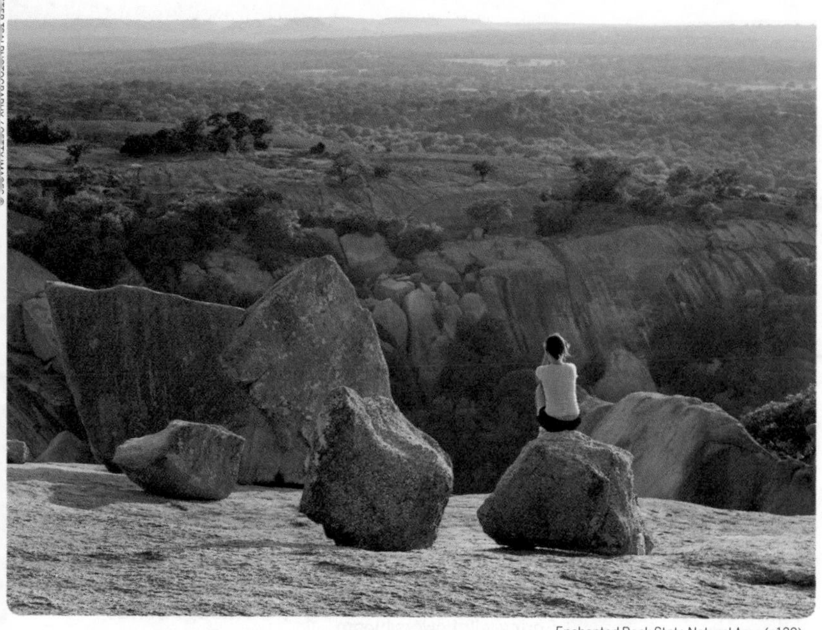

Enchanted Rock State Natural Area (p129)

Anahuac National Wildlife Refuge Snow geese, whistling ducks and other waterfowl winter here by the hundreds, sometimes thousands. (p249)

Bentsen-Rio Grande Valley State Park Headquarters of the World Birding Center in the Rio Grande Valley. (p295)

Scenic Drives

Galveston to Corpus Christi, TX 35 Cruise through small towns and across marshland and bays. (p267)

River Road, Big Bend Snake up and down along the edge of the Rio Grande. (p312)

TX 207, Panhandle Plains Enter the Palo Duro canyonlands and cross over the Red River. (p198)

Washington County Take the rural route, past bucolic ranches and in spring, bluebonnets. (p207)

Fort Davis Ascend into the Davis Mountains amid gorgeous, rocky scenery. (p314)

Wineries

Sandy soil and cool nights make the Lubbock area the state's most conducive to grape growth. But in recent years cottage wine industries have popped up everywhere.

CapRock Winery A stunning, mission-style tasting room that has served the plains for more than 25 years. (p195)

La Diosa Cellars This wine bar in Lubbock sells its own, and other Texas wines. (p193)

Becker Vineyards A much-decorated winery with an impressive underground cellar in Hill Country. (p127)

Kiepersol Estates Taste site-grown varietals with your dinner, then spend the night at the luxe B&B upstairs. (p257)

Pleasant Hill Winery Frequent hosted events attract the locals from nearby Brenham to this east-central vineyard. (p237)

IF YOU LIKE... KEMP'S RIDLEY SEA TURTLES

During late summer you may be able to participate in a hatchling release at Padre Island National Seashore (p279); otherwise, visit Sea Turtle Inc (p285) a successful rescue and breeding program.

Month by Month

TOP EVENTS

State Fair of Texas, October

South by Southwest, March

Houston Livestock Show & Rodeo, February

Fiesta, April

Marfa Lights Festival, September

February

Rodeo season starts in big and small towns across the state. Cool, not cold, weather in Big Bend means it's a great time to hike.

Houston Livestock Show & Rodeo

Starting in late February or early March, the three-week event (www.rodeohouston.com) attracts about 2.5 million visitors. Tour the animal shows, shop for Western gear, see the cowboys rope and ride – then watch a different top-name singer perform nightly (think George Strait or Beyoncé).

Mardi Gras

(www.mardigrasgalveston.com) For 12 days every February Galveston does its best New Orleans imitation, hosting two dozen parades, even more concerts and five masked balls. Events are admittedly a bit tamer here, the first Sunday is usually coined 'Family Gras'.

March

Spring wildflowers bloom, spreading from south to north. The weather across the state is mild, making this a great time to stop by.

South by Southwest

One of the music industry's biggest annual events (SXSW; www.sxsw.com). A couple thousand performers, and a couple hundred-thousand visitors, besiege the city for five days. The fun doesn't stop there; a concurrent film festival and techie show stretch the festivities to two weeks.

Spring Break

The spring break weeks vary across Texas, but they all fall in the month of March. South Padre Island is the biggest party, by far. But other beaches, like those in Galveston, also host events.

Cowboy Poetry Gathering

Relive the cattle-drive days out in the far west Texas town of Alpine. Start the morning with a chuck-wagon breakfast and watch the old hands twirl their six-shooters and recite witty, trail-inspired verse (www.texascowboypoetry.com).

Nacogdoches Azalea Trail

Each spring the historic east Texas town of Nacogdoches outlines more than 20 miles of routes (www.nacogdochesazaleas.com) through the brilliantly blooming azaleas of the region.

April

Bluebonnets generally peak in Hill Country from mid-March to mid-April, so take a rural Sunday drive. Several towns around the state host festivals, while it's still cool enough.

Fiesta San Antonio

Mariachi music, parades, live concerts, dance performances, carnivals, food and craft shows... San Antonio knows how to throw one mammoth, multicultural party (www.fiesta-sa.org). It lasts 11 days every

April and benefits area nonprofits.

Main Street Fort Worth Arts Festival

The visual arts, including fiber arts, sculpture, mixed media, leatherwork and painting, are at the heart of this four-day festival (www.kerrville-music.com), but the performing and culinary arts aren't forgotten. Stop at the Wine Experience tent to sample Texas' finest.

May

Kerrville Folk Festival

An 18-day-long folk-music festival kicks off every May in Kerrville. More than 100 songwriters perform during the event. Camp at the ranch site and you'll be privy to many more private pickin'-and-singin' circles.

Houston Art Car Parade

The self-billed 'largest art parade in the world' is also Houston's largest free event (www.thehoustonartcarparade.com). Imagine giant sharks and Dr Seuss mobiles motoring down the road and you have an idea of all the wacky fun.

July

Independence Day celebrations abound. Even if you don't attend formal firework displays, you may see some; many counties allow private fireworks.

Shakespeare at Winedale

For four long weekends starting in July, the University of Texas hosts a Shakespeare festival (www.utexas.edu/cola/progs/winedale) at the open-air historical complex outside tiny Round Top, Texas. Both the Bard's comedies and dramas are well represented.

September

Labor Day marks the official end of summer high season, but things aren't really cooling off yet; the heat lingers until October everywhere but in the mountains.

Marfa Lights

One long weekend in September the tiny west Texas town of Marfa takes to the streets to party (www.marfacc.com). Arts vendors, a 5K run and nightly dances are just some of the fun.

October

Finally some temperature relief. Toward the end of the month Halloween takes over with theme events and haunted houses. Amusement parks reopen to host fright-nights.

State Fair of Texas

Having a corny dog here (www.bigtex.com) is a rite of passage for Texas residents. Fun foods (deep-fried PB&J, cheesecake on a stick...) are a big attraction, but so is the tallest US Ferris wheel, carnival rides and livestock exhibits.

Austin City Limits

Locals much prefer this three-day music festival (www.aclfestival.com) in Zilker Park to the insanity of SXSW. Though lower key, the more than 100 musical acts that take the stage are pretty darn impressive.

Oktoberfest in Fredricksburg

Residents celebrate their town's German heritage in a big way one long weekend (www.oktoberfestinfbg.com) every October. Polka bands play, schnitzel and sausage is served and there's plenty of beer – more than 50 varieties are available.

Sand Castle Days in South Padre

For more than 25 years artists have been turning sand into sculpture on South Padre Island. Events take place over one long weekend (www.sandcastledays.com) in October and include live concerts, arts-and-crafts sales, and a juried sandcastle-building contest.

December

Almost all of December is a festive season: Christmas light shows, town festivals and decorated hotel events all say that Santa is on his way.

Dickens on the Strand

One weekend every December Galveston transforms into Victorian London during its annual Christmas festival (www.galvestonhistory.org). Costumed performers and even the 'Queen' show up to celebrate.

Itineraries

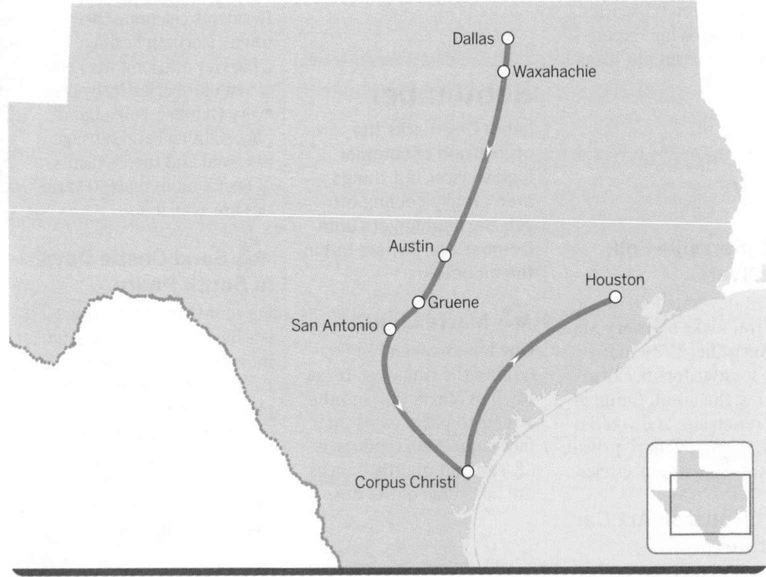

Texas' Greatest Hits

So you want to do it all but are short on time? Start with three days in **Dallas** (p140). See the JFK assassination sites downtown and eat in trendy Uptown, then the next day trip out to the historic Fort Worth Stockyards. Heading south out of town on day three, stop in cute little **Waxahachie** (p175) for a bite before spending two nights in **Austin** (p54) listening to live music and watching the bats fly.

Stop for a night in the Old West–era town of **Gruene** (p121), to dance at one of the state's oldest halls, before continuing on to **San Antonio** (p91). In two days there you can explore the Alamo and Riverwalk. Then **Corpus Christi** (p271) is just a three-hour drive south; it's a good base to kick back for a couple nights and hit the beach at Padre Island National Seashore or Port Aransas.

Afterwards it's time to turn north for three nights in **Houston** (p207). NASA's Space Center Houston is a not-to-miss attraction, as is the museum district. For a third day's excursion, hikers could trek out to Big Thicket National Preserve; history and sunshine lovers should see Galveston.

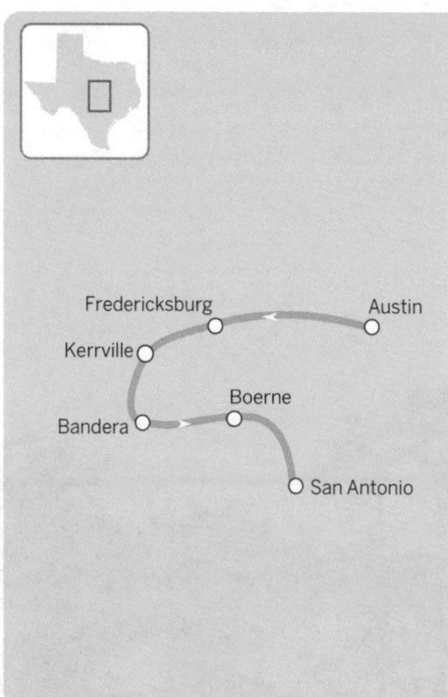

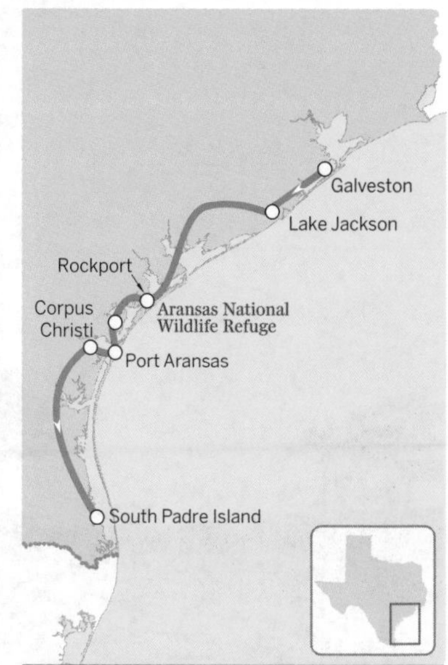

Austin, Hill Country & San Antonio

Start your Hill Country adventure with two days in **Austin** (p54). Don't miss the Texas State History Museum, a splash in Barton Springs Pool or eating along quirky South Congress Ave before club-hopping.

Next, head out for the countryside to spend two nights in the German town of **Fredericksburg** (p125); area activity choices include a visit to the Texas wine country, a climb up Enchanted Rock or a musical pilgrimage to Luckenbach.

Enjoy the wandering road, and wildflowers in spring, as you meander south. Skirt the Guadalupe River and lunch in **Kerrville** (p130) before overnighting in the cowboy town of **Bandera** (p134). A trail ride at a local dude ranch and a drink at the 11th St Cowboy Bar are must-dos.

Take time to go antique hunting (or to go caving) in **Boerne** (p135) on your way to three nights in **San Antonio** (p92). There you can follow Mission Trail and eat Mexican food to your heart's content. One night make sure to catch a live local act outside of town at John T Floore's Country Store in Helotes or at Gruene Hall near New Braunfels – now that's country.

Coastal Texas

Trade the cities for sunny beaches, small museums, historical towns and some of the state's best bird-watching. Begin in **Galveston** (p241), spending two days admiring the turn-of-the-20th-century mansions, exploring the state park and dining and shopping on the Strand.

Follow the coast south, stopping at the fun little Sea Center Texas aquarium and hatcheries in **Lake Jackson** (p267). Then make your way down to **Aransas National Wildlife Refuge** (p266), the best bird-watching site on the Texas coast. Stay a night nearby in the seaside town of **Rockport** (p268); in season boat tours depart from here for the endangered whooping crane's feeding grounds.

Spend a couple of nights at the coastal fishing town of **Port Aransas** (p276), near the outlet to Corpus Christi Bay, and explore **Corpus Christi** (p271) or Padre Island National Seashore, or just laze on a local beach.

Four more hours south finds you for the last two nights in **South Padre Island** (p284). Be sure to stop at the Birding & Nature Center there, as well as trying beachfront horseback riding or water sports.

SUPERSTOCK / GETTY IMAGES ©

Top: Caddo Lake (p260)

Bottom: Galleria (p158), Dallas

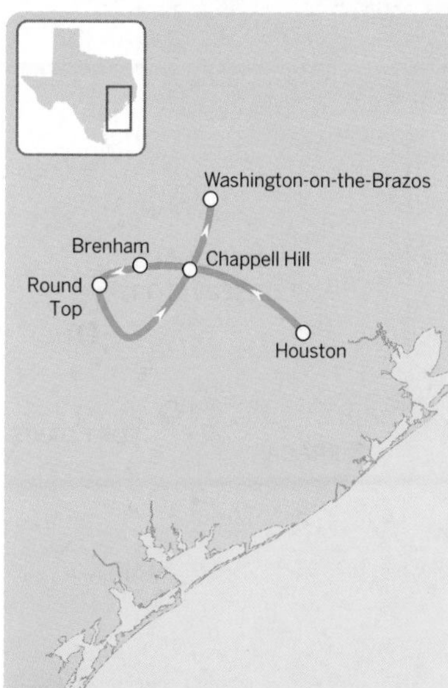

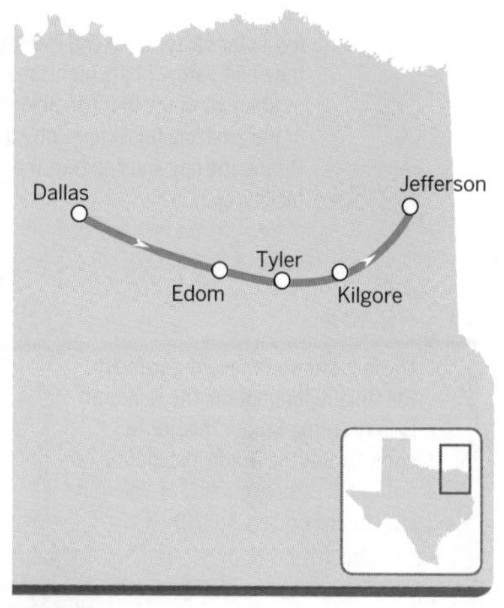

Houston & East-Central Texas

Ah, big-city life. Spend three days immersed in culture and fine food around **Houston** (p210). Check out some of the many arts and sciences exhibits in the Museum District, then prowl the eclectic Montrose neighborhood for your evening meal. While in town don't miss catching a show in the Theater District or have a night out clubbing on Washington Ave. After you've eaten, drank and shopped yourself silly, escape to the country for a few days.

Book into a B&B and spend the next two nights in the small town of **Brenham** (p236), home of Blue Bell ice cream (yes, you should tour the factory). From there you can explore the tiny towns of the region, stopping at famous Royer's Cafe in **Round Top** (p238) or checking out the lavender farm in **Chappell Hill** (p239). To the north is the historical site and museums at **Washington-on-the Brazos** (p239), where the Texas Declaration of Independence was signed. While you're in the area, don't forget to eat some of the Czech-resident-inspired *kolaches* (sweet-bread pastries stuffed with savory or sweet filling).

Dallas & Northeast Texas

Spend two days museum-hopping in **Dallas** (p141). Be sure to take a break for shopping and dining in the Bishop Arts District, or for braving the huge Galleria megamall.

Then it's time to head east for small-town pleasures among the pine forests. Be sure to detour down FM 279; the 8-mile stretch of road from Ben Wheeler to **Edom** (p257) has a surprising number of cafes, artisan shops and live music in the evenings. You can spend the night in nearby **Tyler** (p256), which is an especially good idea if it's spring and the azaleas are in bloom – or if you want to see a tiger sanctuary.

From there continue east, pausing for lunch and to see the Rangerette Showcase & Museum and the old oil derricks in the little town of **Kilgore** (p258). Spending three nights in **Jefferson** (p258) allows you to peruse the historic town and take excursions. Choose from a canoe ride or a swamp-boat nature trip on sinuous Caddo Lake or a drive to Tex Ritter's hometown Texas Country Music Hall of Fame in Carthage.

Off the Beaten Track: Texas

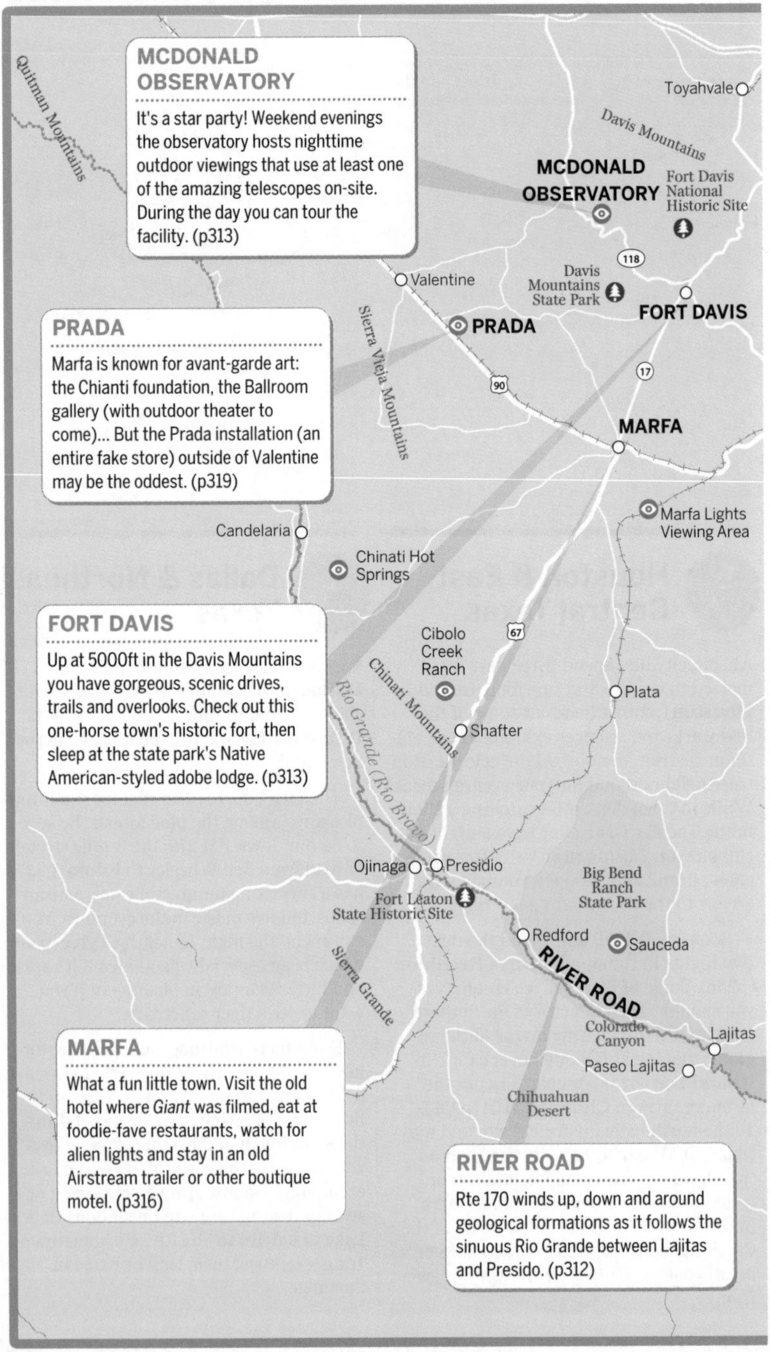
MCDONALD OBSERVATORY
It's a star party! Weekend evenings the observatory hosts nighttime outdoor viewings that use at least one of the amazing telescopes on-site. During the day you can tour the facility. (p313)
PRADA
Marfa is known for avant-garde art: the Chianti foundation, the Ballroom gallery (with outdoor theater to come)… But the Prada installation (an entire fake store) outside of Valentine may be the oddest. (p319)
FORT DAVIS
Up at 5000ft in the Davis Mountains you have gorgeous, scenic drives, trails and overlooks. Check out this one-horse town's historic fort, then sleep at the state park's Native American-styled adobe lodge. (p313)
MARFA
What a fun little town. Visit the old hotel where *Giant* was filmed, eat at foodie-fave restaurants, watch for alien lights and stay in an old Airstream trailer or other boutique motel. (p316)
RIVER ROAD
Rte 170 winds up, down and around geological formations as it follows the sinuous Rio Grande between Lajitas and Presido. (p312)
Quitman Mountains
Toyahvale
Davis Mountains
MCDONALD OBSERVATORY
Fort Davis National Historic Site
118
Valentine
Davis Mountains State Park
FORT DAVIS
PRADA
Sierra Vieja Mountains
17
90
MARFA
Marfa Lights Viewing Area
Candelaria
Chinati Hot Springs
67
Cibolo Creek Ranch
Chinati Mountains
Plata
Shafter
Rio Grande (Rio Bravo)
Ojinaga
Presidio
Fort Leaton State Historic Site
Big Bend Ranch State Park
Redford
Sauceda
RIVER ROAD
Sierra Grande
Colorado Canyon
Lajitas
Paseo Lajitas
Chihuahuan Desert

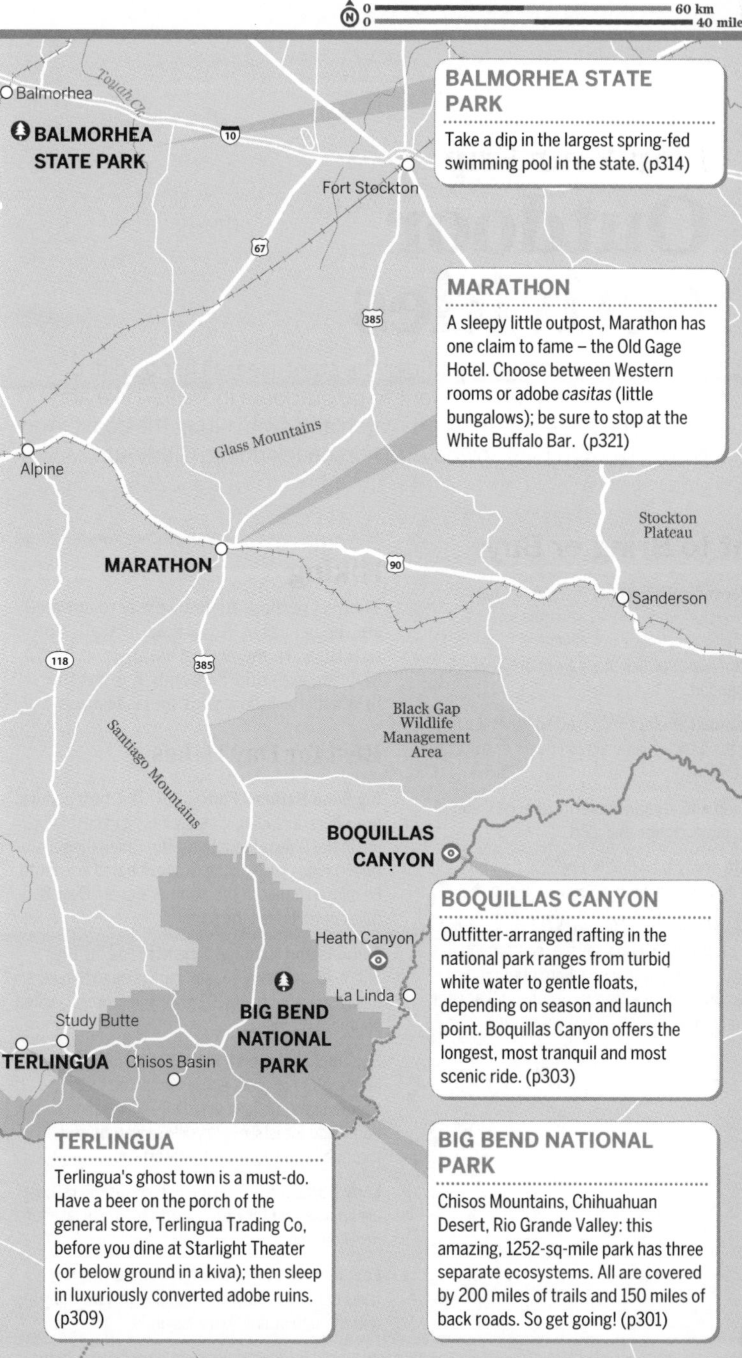
0 60 km
0 40 miles
Balmorhea
Toyah Ck
BALMORHEA STATE PARK
10
Fort Stockton
67
385
Glass Mountains
Alpine
MARATHON
90
Stockton Plateau
Sanderson
118
385
Black Gap Wildlife Management Area
Santiago Mountains
BOQUILLAS CANYON
Heath Canyon
La Linda
BIG BEND NATIONAL PARK
Study Butte
TERLINGUA
Chisos Basin
BALMORHEA STATE PARK
Take a dip in the largest spring-fed swimming pool in the state. (p314)
MARATHON
A sleepy little outpost, Marathon has one claim to fame – the Old Gage Hotel. Choose between Western rooms or adobe *casitas* (little bungalows); be sure to stop at the White Buffalo Bar. (p321)
BOQUILLAS CANYON
Outfitter-arranged rafting in the national park ranges from turbid white water to gentle floats, depending on season and launch point. Boquillas Canyon offers the longest, most tranquil and most scenic ride. (p303)
TERLINGUA
Terlingua's ghost town is a must-do. Have a beer on the porch of the general store, Terlingua Trading Co, before you dine at Starlight Theater (or below ground in a kiva); then sleep in luxuriously converted adobe ruins. (p309)
BIG BEND NATIONAL PARK
Chisos Mountains, Chihuahuan Desert, Rio Grande Valley: this amazing, 1252-sq-mile park has three separate ecosystems. All are covered by 200 miles of trails and 150 miles of back roads. So get going! (p301)

Plan Your Trip

Outdoor Activities

You may not need to sleep under the stars like trail hands did, but there's plenty of reason to want to go outdoors in Texas. Hike and camp at the state's parks, bird-watch and swim along the coast. And if you do want to play cowboy, go horseback riding. Giddy-up!

What to Bring or Buy

Long-sleeved shirt Parts of Texas leave you exposed to the sun for hours at a time; a button-down shirt made out of vented, sun-protectant material, like those from Columbia, is recommended.

Water sandals Protect your feet: whether it's for a day at the beach, hiking across rivers or traction while Jet Skiing.

Sunscreen and sunglasses A must even if you're stepping outdoors for a second.

Mosquito spray You wouldn't believe how big those little buggers get here. Hiking, along the coast, heck...everywhere: be prepared.

Orange clothing We can't say we recommend it, but if you're hiking in season where hunting is allowed, embrace this universal symbol for 'I am not a game animal so please do not shoot me.'

Hiking

There is perhaps no better way to appreciate the beauty of Texas than by trail. Note that the extreme heat of summer, at late May through mid-September, is not the best time to follow your foot's desire.

Best for Day Hikes

Big Bend National Park (p301) The most popular trails here, including Window View and Lost Mine, are in the Chisos Mountains. But Chihuahuan Desert hikes such as the Grapevine trail are not to be missed either (if the weather's cool). Over 200 miles of trails lace the park.

Padre Island National Seashore (p279) The entire 70-mile-long coastal park is open to hikers; hardy souls (with a 4WD) favor the scarcely visited southern 60 miles.

Big Thicket National Preserve (p252) At the intersection of Texas ecosystems, the Kirby Nature Loop can take you past soaring pine and hardwood forests, over cypress swamps and through sandy dunes with desert cacti.

Lady Bird Lake (p66) One of the state's prettiest urban hike-and-bike trails skirts the town lake for nearly 10 miles.

Lost Maples State Natural Area (p132) Hiking trails here take you into rugged limestone canyons and through prairielike grasslands.

- Palo Duro Canyon State Park (p198) Follow the steep and rugged Upper Canyon Trail past the canyon cliffs and bluffs.

Camping & State Parks

Texas' state parks are by far your best bet for camping. More than 60 of the 90 parks have campgrounds with electrical and water hookups; many even have wi-fi. Some parks also, or only, have walk- or hike-in tent sites – one has a canoe-in site. Booking ahead is always recommended. Campground fees range from $10 to $25 per night, cabins cost anywhere from $50 to $150. To make reservations online, log onto http://texas.reserveworld.com. Each park holds its own individual attraction; following is a list of some of the best.

- To be riverside, try Guadalupe River (p136) or Caddo Lake.
- For a mountain high, Davis Mountains (p315).
- Sleep by the sea at Mustang Island (p279).
- Looking for leafy? Lost Maples (p132).
- Go remote in Palo Duro (p198).
- Love bird-watching? Bentsen-Rio Grande Valley (p295) is for you.
- Caddo Lake, Davis Mountains (p315), Balmorhea (p314) and Bastrop (p86) are among the parks that have Civilian Conservation Core (CCC)-built cabins or lodging.

Rock Climbing

Rock climbing has become increasingly popular around the state. Perhaps the best Texas rock climbing is at Hueco Tanks State Historical Park (p335), although access is curbed to preserve the prehistoric rock art. Also in west Texas, Franklin Mountains State Park (p325) has 17 mapped climbing routes. The Hill Country west of Austin is another popular area, especially Enchanted Rock State Natural Area (p129) north of Fredericksburg. Indoor climbing gyms are found in most major Texas cities; they are a good place to learn before attempting to climb real rock outdoors. The Texas Mountaineers' website

WILDERNESS HIKING & CAMPING

To get far off the beaten path, you'll need to be prepared. Longer hikes require GPS or the appropriate United States Geological Survey (USGS) Quadrangles, also known as 7.5 minute maps, which are available through http://topomaps.usgs.gov. Remember to take plenty of water and tread lightly; pack out anything you pack in.

Texas' preeminent wilderness experiences are at Big Bend and Guadalupe Mountains National Parks, both in the state's western half. You can go far at South Padre Island National Seashore too, but remember there is no shade and no freshwater available. Note that at the time of writing, sections of the 126-mile Lone Star Trail were closed indefinitely. Whenever heading into the backcountry, map out your route and be ready to show it to park rangers. Permit requirements are as follows.

Big Bend National Park

- Available inperson only, at all visitor centers
- $10 for overnight, use at designated sites only
- 14 consecutive nights possible

Guadalupe Mountains National Park

- Available from Pine Springs Visitor Center
- Free
- Three consecutive nights allowed

Padre Island National Seashore

- Available from Malaquite Campground, Bird Island Basin and at South Beach
- No fee on North or South Beach
- 14-day permits

Top: Hiking, Boquillas Canyon (p307), Big Bend National Park

Bottom: Rafting the Rio Grande (p303)

(www.texasmountaineers.org) lists climbing sites and classes.

Cycling & Mountain Biking

Car-crazy Texas is only friendly to road cyclists in some places. Cities such as Austin and Fort Worth have developed good bike trails, but in many instances road riders will be sharing space with street traffic and extreme caution is necessary.

For urban excursions, Austin has a number of good trails, including those in Zilker Park (p62) and at Lady Bird Lake (p66). In Fort Worth, Trinity Trails (p165) run riverside for 35 miles. Katy Trail (p153) is only 3.5 miles, but passes through some nice neighborhoods in Dallas. McAllister Park (p104) will give you a taste of Hill Country cycling but is only 7 miles from downtown San Antonio.

In west Texas you'll find a good variety of road cycling under not-too-crowded conditions, especially around Fort Davis. The Davis Mountains State Park (p313) also has mountain biking. Big Bend Ranch State Park (p312) has the only 'Epic' ride, as categorized by the International Mountain Biking Association.

In the Panhandle Plains, the 64-mile Caprock Canyons Trailways (p196) is an excellent multiple-use trail with many bridges, fenced railroad trestles and a 1000ft tunnel.

For more on cycling and mountain biking, check out the Activities page at Texas Parks & Wildlife (www.tpwd.state.tx.us).

Water Sports

Kayaking & Canoeing

Texas' estuaries, streams and rivers are ripe for exploration by canoe or kayak, and numerous parks make good bases from which to set off. The lagoons and canals of the long Intracoastal Waterway system are ideal for sea kayaking.

If a place has good kayaking and canoeing conditions, there is usually some savvy entrepreneur around to rent you the gear. Prices tend to run from $25 to $60 a day. For more on paddling activities in state parks, check out Texas Parks & Wildlife (www.tpwd.state.tx.us).

Best Places to Kayak & Canoe

Caddo Lake (p260) Mist-shrouded waters, Spanish moss draped from every cypress tree: Caddo Lake is a moody and beautiful place to weave in and out of narrow bayous, around islands and through swamps.

Rockport & Fulton (p268) The coastal estuaries are prime paddling territory. Several local companies also offer kayak ecotours.

South Padre Island (p284) Sea-kayaking action off the coast of the state's prettiest beaches.

New Braunfels (p120) Inner-tubing down the Guadalupe River (with cooler in tow) may be the most popular way to go, but kayak and canoe rentals are also available.

Goose Island State Park (p267) Kayaking along the calm inlets of this marshy island allows access to Aransas Pass National Wildlife Refuge.

Bastrop State Park (p86) Paddle a calm section of the Colorado River.

Surfing

For many, 'Texas surfing' is an oxymoron. But local aficionados will argue that it is not as bad as surfers from elsewhere have heard. Long-board surfers, in fact, will have a fun time here on most days; the longer the board, the more rideable the Gulf's mush (3ft or lower). The key to riding little waves is timing, luck and patience. When a hurricane warning sounds, local surfers run towards the water instead of away from it.

The coastline south from Port Aransas is all somewhat surfable. The best surf is found furthest south, at South Padre Island, where there's a chance of catching some waves with good ground swell. Board rentals are readily available in Port A, Corpus Christi and South Padre. Mustang Island State Park, on Padre Island near Corpus Christi, is an especially popular surfing spot.

Windsurfing

If Texas' waves are unreliable, the wind is not. Constant coastal breezes, coupled with shallow bodies of water sheltered by the barrier islands, make for great windsurfing conditions. Rentals will usually run you between $55 and $75 per day. Top spots, with rentals, include the following:

Padre Island National Seashore (p279) Bird Island Basin, off the Laguna Madre, ranks as one of the top windsurfing spots in the US. Lessons available locally.

South Padre Island (p284) The lagoon side of the island is popular with windsurfers, and rightly so. Numerous outfitters provide gear and instruction.

Tubing & Rafting

From the classic Rio Grande white-water trips at Big Bend to lazy tubing on the Guadalupe River near New Braunfels, Texas offers both wild and mild river adventure. The extensive Texas section online at RiverFacts (www.riverfacts.com) outlines all the white-water paddling in the state.

Rio Grande Rapids up to Class IV alternate with calm stretches on the Rio Grande in the five canyons of Big Bend National Park (p301). A river trip here can last from several hours to several days, traversing the impressive Boquillas Canyon. Outfitters offer complete row, eat and sleep tours. Some also have multisport tours that also include hiking or biking. Early spring and autumn usually have the best weather and water conditions.

Guadalupe River One of our favorite things in the world is floating down the Guadalupe (or the Frio, or the San Marcos) in a inner tube, cold beer in hand. You can rent tubes in New Braunfels (p120) or at Kerrville-Schreiner Park (p131). The former has frequent return shuttles. Outfitters will even rent you tubes with reinforced bottoms to put your cooler in.

San Marcos River This spring-fed river is always cool, but not always flowing much. When it is, rent tubes from the Lion's Club (p122) in San Marcos.

Colorado River Bastrop River Co (p86) rents tubes and provides return shuttles for two- to eight-hour floats on the Colorado.

Boating & Jet Skiing

Texas actually has a lotta water and locals love to get out onto area lakes, rivers, bays and the Gulf by motorboat and Jet Ski. Rental options are a bit limited, but they can still be found. Boats and Jet Skis both start at $60 to $80 for the first hour, but the rate goes down for additional time.

Clear Lake Outside Houston, the marinas of the Clear Lake act as the city's water recreation central. Rent Jet Skis from Pinky's Kayak Rental (p234), charter a sailboat with Windsong (p234) or take a ride on the Beast at Kemah Boardwalk (p235).

Corpus Christi Buzz around the relatively protected bay. Rent Jet Skis and boats at places such as CC Fun Time Rentals (p274).

Port Aransas Off the northern tip of Mustang Island, outside Corpus, you can get into some serous Gulf swell. Rent three-seater Jet Skis at Woody's Sports Center (p277).

South Padre Island Numerous water-sport outfitters rent both boats and Jet Skis. Beachside concession stands also offer banana-boat inner-tube rides.

Lake Travis Rent a boat from Lakeway (p89) and explore one of the richest coasts in Texas. After admiring the Austinites' mansions, find a marina restaurant to stop at for refreshment.

Fishing

Towns all along the coast provide access to charter fishing in the Gulf of Mexico; here anglers hunt for everything from red snapper and wahoo to shark and big-game marlin. From the piers and jetties along the coast you can catch redfish, flounder, and speckled and sand trout.

Best Places to Fish

Port Aransas Fishing is big business here. Arrange a four- to eight-hour charter with outfitters such as Deep Sea Headquarters (p277).

(North) Padre Island Shore fishing is popular among Corpus Christi locals; you can have Padre Island Safaris (p280) organize a surf-casting trip or charter a boat for a trip in and around the National Seashore.

South Padre Island (p284) Wander the docks and talk to the skippers along the piers on the lagoon side of South Padre; you'll soon find one who offers the boat charter of your dreams.

Rockport Look for fishing-boat charters along Rockport Harbor (p268).

Galveston Charter fishing outfits (p241) line up along Pier 19 on the bay side of Galveston Island.

Licenses

A fishing license is required for all anglers older than 17. A one-day, all-water license is

$11 for Texas residents, $16 for nonresidents. An entire year costs residents $30 and nonresidents $68. Texas Parks & Wildlife licenses are sold online and at sporting-goods stores, such as Academy, at bait and tackle shops and at some park offices.

Diving & Snorkeling

Diving in the Gulf of Mexico is challenging and not recommended for beginners. The most interesting sites are located 40 or more miles offshore, where the water is very deep and divers are subjected to open-water waves and weather conditions.

Muddy water and heavy plankton growth make the coastal areas of Texas no good for snorkeling, despite the shallow waters and calm conditions. If you want more details on Texas diving and snorkeling, www.divetexas.com is a good information source.

Horseback Riding

Few images are more iconic than a cowboy on horseback riding across an open plain, but in this big ol' state you can also gallop seaside, in the mountains or at a full-fledged dude ranch. Rides typically last one to two hours (from $35 to $115), but longer tours are often available.

Note that while both of Texas' national parks (Big Bend and Guadalupe Mountains) have trails that allow horseback riding, neither has horses available for hire. If you bring your own, do some route planning before you get the required permits at the respective visitor centers. If you are interested in going for a ride, try one of the following:

Bandera (p134) Several of the more than dozen guest ranches in Bandera offer day rides. If you want to re-enact your own version of *City Slickers*, sign up for a multiday, all-inclusive dude-ranch experience, which includes: horseback rides, hay rides, cowhand activities, meals and lodging (from $120 per person, per day). Some of the places have swimming holes or pools to cool off in.

Old West Stables (p198) Take an hour-long trot through stunning Palo Duro Canyon.

South Padre Island Adventures (p285) A morning or a sunset ride on the beach is a great way to start or end a day.

YO Ranch (p134) Not just any ol' boring cow ranch, YO is home to exotic game like wildebeest and oryx. You can't ride those, but you can ride horses on the property.

Big Bend Stables (p310) Trail rides take you not through the national park but through the similar west Texas terrain around Terlingua.

Lajitas (p312) The equestrian center here arranges hour-long trail rides and overnights at a nearby ghost town.

Bird-Watching

Texas has nearly 600 documented bird species – over 75% of all species reported in the US. **Audubon Texas** (☎512-306-0225; http://tx.audubon.org) has loads of additional information on birding in the state, as does Texas Parks & Wildlife (www.tpwd.state.tx.us). The latter publishes full-color, interpretive guide-like Great Texas Wildlife Trails maps, which are available from their website and some park ranger stations and visitor bureaus. The Coastal Birding Trails maps are the best, but all of the regional series note local avian species.

West Texas Keep your binoculars peeled for peregrine falcons, golden eagles, cactus wren and road runners at Guadalupe National Park (p336) and Davis Mountains State Park (p313). In the Chisos Mountains of Big Bend National Park (p301) you may spot the rare Colima warbler in its only US nesting site.

Rio Grande Valley The preeminent winter bird-watching location. Headquartered in the Bentsen-Rio Grande Valley State Park (p295), the World Birding Center has nine different locations across the Valley and on the far southern coast. For a complete list of associated sites, see p269.

Lower Gulf Coast Shore and seabirds such as herons, egrets and roseate spoonbills inhabit the Gulf Coast year round. Migratory species, including numerous waterfowl, overwinter here as well as in the Valley. Aransas National Wildlife Refuge (p266), breeding ground to the endangered whooping cranes, is undoubtedly the star site.

Upper Gulf Coast The area from Galveston to Port Arthur attracts water-related species. Sometimes large numbers of migratory species drop in to High Island sanctuaries such as Boy Scout Woods (p249). Anahuac National Wildlife Refuge (p249) is always a good birding spot.

Padre Island National Seashore (p279)

Plan Your Trip

Travel with Children

With beaches for building sand castles, state and national parks for outdoor exploring, museums for fun and learning – and amusements for when your child needs a little more action – Texas is an ideal family destination. Locals love little cowpokes, so expect a warm welcome here.

Best Regions for Kids

San Antonio & Hill Country

Historic sites with activity books, plus theme parks make San Antonio especially family friendly. In Hill Country, Kerrville and New Braunfels serve as launch points for river tubing.

Gulf Coast & South Texas

Beaches line the southern Gulf Coast: some have diversions, some star nature herself. Corpus Christi is home to the USS Lexington Museum, a big aquarium and a bayfront promenade.

Houston & East Texas

Galveston Island, with its organized beaches, pleasure pier, water park and amusements, offers much fun. An hour away, Houston's Hermann Park contains a zoo, a natural-history museum and a train ride.

Dallas & the Panhandle Plains

The zoo, aquarium and science museum in Dallas all attract young attention. Nearby in Arlington, a theme park and a water park don't hurt either.

Texas for Kids

There's not too much to worry about when traveling in Texas with your kids – as long as you keep them covered in sunblock.

Necessities

Breastfeeding and changing Breastfeeding in public is accepted when discreet. Many public toilets have a baby-changing table, and gender-neutral 'family' bathrooms may be available at airports, museums etc.

Dining It's more than fine to bring kids along to casual restaurants, which often have high chairs and children's menus.

Lodging Most motels and hotels offer rooms with two double beds, which are ideal for families. Some also have roll-away beds or cribs that can be brought into the room for an extra charge. Some hotels offer 'kids stay free' programs for children up to 18 years old. Note that most bed and breakfasts do not allow children under 12 to stay.

Supplies Baby food, formula, soy and cow's milk, disposable diapers (nappies) and other necessities are widely available.

Health & Safety

Though hopefully not needed, medical services and facilities in Texas are of a high standard. Urgent Care facilities can handle minor emergencies and cost much less than hospital emergency rooms.

Texas law requires that children under the age of eight, or under the height of 4ft 9in, ride in a federally approved child safety seat. Every car-rental agency should be able to provide one ($10 per day), if you request it when booking in advance.

Note that while Texas' beaches are great, many allow driving on the beach and children will need to be monitored closely.

Discounts

Children's discounts are available for everything from museum admission to movie tickets. The definition of a 'child' varies, but usually means those between two and 12. Under two is generally free.

Domestic airlines don't charge for children under two that are carried on your lap. Others must have a seat.

Children's Highlights

Museums

➡ **Houston Museum of Natural Science**
A giant new dinosaur hall, hands-on chemistry experiments, butterfly house and planetarium. (p211)

➡ **Dallas World Aquarium**
Fourteen water ecosystems brought to life. (p149)

➡ **Perot Museum of Nature and Science**
Loads of interactive fun: travel through space or design your own robot in Dallas. (p150)

➡ **San Antonio Children's Museum**
Two floors of dress-up, crawl-around, role-playing fun. (p102)

➡ **USS Lexington Museum**
Tour a retired aircraft carrier, complete with foldable airplanes, in Corpus Christi. (p271)

➡ **Moody Gardens**
Three glass pyramids in Galveston contain a greenhouse, an aquarium and science exhibits. Outside there's a beach and a boat ride. (p243)

Beaches

➡ **Stewart Beach**
Family beach in Galveston with umbrella rentals, snack stands and organized activities. (p243)

➡ **Isla Blanca County Park**
The southern-most beach on South Padre Island; numerous concessions and facilities. (p283)

➡ **IB Magee Beach Park**
Part of 18 miles of beaches in the coastal village of Port Aransas, near Corpus Christi; facilities available. (p276)

➡ **Padre Island National Seashore**
One of the longest stretches of undeveloped seashore in the US; limited facilities, near Corpus Christi. (p279)

Parks & Rivers

➡ **Big Bend National Park**
Junior rangers have extensive trail choices here, but it's far from anything else. (p301)

➡ **New Braunfels**
Take a family float down the Guadalupe River, then splash things up at the local water park. (p120)

➡ **Hermann Park**
Ride paddleboats on the lake and a train around this park in Houston; also home to a zoo. (p215)

➡ **Barton Springs**
Cool off in a spring-fed pool in the center of Austin. (p63)

Amusements

➡ **SeaWorld – San Antonio**
Ride the rides, see the sea animal shows, then splash around at the nearby water park. (p101)

➡ **Six Flags Over Texas**
Thirteen roller coasters are only a small sampling of rides at the state's largest amusement park; outside Dallas. (p174)

➡ **Schlitterbahn**
This Texas-size water park has three locations: South Padre Island, Galveston and this original in New Braunfels. (p120)

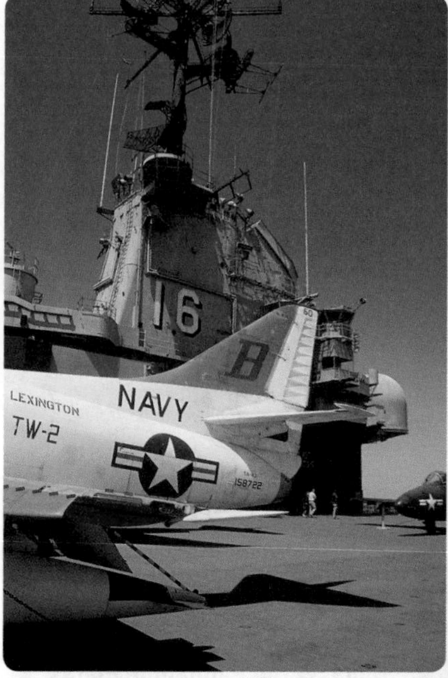

USS Lexington Museum (p271)

Planning

When to Go

Be warned, most of Texas gets quite hot in summer and attractions will be crowded. Spring has much nicer weather. Texas schools' spring breaks cover all the weeks in March, so book ahead during that time.

What to Pack

Don't forget the sunscreen. Many of Texas' best activities are outdoors and the sun can be brutal here. Count on needing mosquito spray at some time. If you're going to a beach or a river, be sure to bring water shoes to protect sensitive little feet.

Useful Resources

➡ **Travel with Children** By Brigitte Barta et al; offers all-around information and advice.

➡ **Family Travel Files** (www.thefamilytravelfiles.com/locations/texas) Vacation-planning articles, tips and discounts.

➡ **Travel Texas** (www.traveltex.com/trip-ideas.aspx) Tourist board trip planner with family-friendly ideas.

Salt Lick Bar-B-Que (p76)

Plan Your Trip

Texas BBQ & Cuisine

If American cooking could be summed up as combining generous portions of homegrown foods with foreign sensibilities and techniques, Texas spins this into a cuisine that is uniquely its own. Highlights include Texas-style barbecue, authentic Mexican fare, creative Tex-Mex dishes, down-home Southern comfort food and Gulf Coast seafood.

Tastes Born in Texas

Corn Dogs

Cornbread-batter-dipped hot dogs on a stick were created in 1948 by Neil Fletcher for the State Fair of Texas; Fletcher's still sells 'em there; now available with jalapeño cornbread too.

Shiner Bock

The state's favorite amber ale came to be when Kosmos Spoetzl brought Bavarian brewing to Shiner, Tx, in 1914. Available countrywide, Shiner Bock is still brewed at Spoetzl Brewery.

Chicken-Fried Bacon

You may have heard of steak coated and deep-fried like chicken, but the taste (and heart-attack factor) was taken to new heights when Sodolak's, near Bryan-College Station, started cooking bacon the same way in the early 1990s.

Dr Pepper

A pharmacist in a Waco drugstore–soda shop invented this aromatic cola in the 1880s. Taste the original sugarcane formula at the first bottling plant, Dublin Dr Pepper.

Barbecue

Make no bones about it – Texas barbecue is an obsession. It's the subject of countless newspaper and magazine articles, from national press including the *New York Times* to regional favorite *Texas Monthly*. Some of central Texas' smaller towns – Lockhart and Elgin, to name only two – maintain perennial reputations for their smokehouse cultures, and routinely draw dedicated pilgrims from miles around.

No self-respecting Texan would agree with another about who has the best barbecue, since that would take the fun out of it. But most do see eye to eye on a few things: brisket is where a pit master proves his or her reputation; seasoning is rarely much more than salt, pepper and something spicy; and if there's a sauce, it's probably made from ketchup, vinegar and the drippings of the wood-smoked meat.

The best Texas barbecue often comes from famous family dynasties that have been dishing up the same crowd-pleasing recipes for generations. Telltale signs that you've located an authentic barbecue joint include zero decor, smoke-blackened ceilings, and laid-back table manners (silverware optional). At most places, you can order a combination plate or ask for specific meats to be sliced by the pound right in front of you. Of course, there are variations on this nowadays, but in Texas, where barbecue baiting is a bit of a pastime, some swear this down-home style is the only way.

However you like it – sliced thick onto butcher paper, slapped on picnic plates, doused with a tangy sauce or eaten naturally flavorful right out of the smokehouse barbecue pit – be sure to savor it...and then argue to the death that your way is the best way. Like a true Texan.

History

The origins of central Texas barbecue can be traced to 19th-century Czech and German settlers, many of whom were butchers. These settlers pioneered methods of smoking meat, both to better preserve it (before the advent of refrigeration) and also to tenderize cuts that might otherwise be wasted.

Credit also goes to Mexican *vaqueros* (Spanish-speaking cowboys), especially in Texas' southern and western borderland regions, who dug the first barbecue pits in about the 16th century, then grilled spicy meats over mesquite wood. African Americans who migrated to Texas brought with them recipes for a 'wet' style of barbecue, which involved thick marinades, sweet sauces and juicier meats.

Somewhere along the way, slow-smoked barbecue crossed the line from simple eating pleasure to statewide obsession. Maybe it's the primal joy of gnawing tender, tasty meat directly from the bone, or the simplistic, sloppy appeal of the hands-on eating experience. Whatever the reason, dedicated barbecue eaters demonstrate nearly religious devotion by worshipping at the pits of Texas' renowned smokehouses.

Cook-Offs

There are people who will travel the entire state of Texas to sample all the various permutations of barbecue. But if your time's a little more limited, you can always try one of the many organized cook-offs around the state. Amateurs and pros alike come together for the noble joint cause of barbecue perfection and, if they're lucky, bragging rights. Cook-offs generally start on Friday afternoon so the pit masters have plenty of time to get their meat just right before the judging on Saturday, even if it means staying up all night. (You can't rush these things.) Once the judging is complete, the public is invited to swoop in and judge for themselves.

One of the largest events is the **Taylor International Barbeque Cook-off** (www.taylorjaycees.org), held in late August in Taylor (northeast of Austin), with up to 100 contestants competing in divisions including beef, ribs, pork, poultry, lamb, seafood and wild game. If you can't make that one, a quick search on www.tourtexas.com will lead you to events such as the Good Times Barbecue Cook-off in Amarillo or the Wildfire Barbecue Cook-off, Car Show & Festival in Bowie.

Otherwise, check out the calendar on the **Central Texas Barbecue Association** (CTBA; www.ctbabbq.com) website, where you can also read the incredibly detailed rules that competitions must follow ('CTBA recommends the use of a Styrofoam tray with a hinged lid and without dividers or the best readily available judging container that is approximately 9 inches square on the bottom half').

BLOOMBERG VIA GETTY IMAGES ©

Beef ribs, sausage and Shiner Bock beer (p122)

Ingredients

In today's Texas, barbecue recipes are as varied as central Texas summers are long. Most folks agree on the basics: slow cooking over a low-heat fire. A cooking time of up to 12 or 16 hours isn't unheard of – anything less and you're just too darn impatient. It allows the meat to be infused with a rich smoky flavor of usually hickory or pecan in the eastern part of the state, oak in central Texas and mesquite out west. (Mesquite was considered all but a weed until someone realized how nice a flavor it lent to wood chips.)

The Meat

Texas barbecue leans heavily toward beef – a logical outgrowth of the state's cattle industry – and most signature dishes come straight from the sacred cow. The most common is beef brisket, a cut often used for corned beef. With a combination of patience, experience and skill, a seasoned pit boss can transform this notoriously tough meat into a perfectly smoked, tender slab of heaven. Even tougher cuts of meat enter the smokehouse and emerge hours later, deeply flavorful and tender to the tooth. Sliced thin and internally moistened by natural fat, a well-smoked brisket falls apart with the slightest touch and can rival more expensive cuts for butter-smooth consistency.

Carnivores seeking a more toothy challenge can indulge in beef ribs – huge meaty racks that would do Fred Flintstone proud – or relax with a saucy chopped-beef sandwich. Word to the wise: if you need to stay presentable, think twice about the ribs, which tend to be a full-contact eating experience (even as part of a three-meat sampler plate).

Lone Star State cattle worship stops short of excluding other meats from the pit. The noble pig makes appearances in the form of succulent ribs, thick buttery chops and perfect slices of loin so tender they melt on the tongue. In recent years chicken has shown up on the menu boards, mainly to provide beginners with a non-hoofed barnyard option. Traditionalists, however, stick with the good stuff – red meat and plenty of it.

Every self-respecting barbecue joint will also serve sausage. Texas hot links, the peppery sausage of regional renown, is created with ground pork and beef combined with pungent spices. Although it's not technically in the barbecue family, sausage is cooked over the same fire so has the same smoky flavor. If nothing else it makes an excellent meat side dish to go alongside your meaty main dish.

The Rub

Everyone knows that the word 'barbecue' is usually followed by the word 'sauce.' But not so fast, there. Good barbecue is more than just meat and sauce. The other key component is the rub, which is how the meat is seasoned before it's cooked. There are wet rubs and dry rubs. A dry rub is a mixture of salt, pepper, herbs and spices sprinkled over or painstakingly rubbed into the meat before cooking. A wet rub is created by adding liquid, which usually means oil, but also possibly vinegar, lemon juice or even mustard. Applied like a paste, a wet rub seals in the meat's natural juices before cooking. This key step is just as important as the slow cooking in getting the flavor just right.

The Sauce

Wisdom about barbecue sauce varies widely from region to region and sometimes joint to joint. There's huge debate over what kind, how much or whether you need it at all. In Lockhart, Kreuz Market's meat is served without any sauce at all, and it's so naturally juicy and tender you'll agree it's not necessary. But excellent sauce-heavy barbecue is divine as well. We'll leave it up to you to make up your own mind.

Texas barbecue sauce has a different flavor from other types – that's why it's Texas barbecue, y'all. It's not as sweet as the kind you'll find gracing the tables of barbecue joints in Kansas City and Memphis – more a blend of spicy and slightly sweet. There are thousands of variations and no two sauces are exactly alike, but recipes are usually tomato based with vinegar, brown sugar, chili powder, onion, garlic and other seasonings.

Lambert's (p73)

The Sides

Side dishes naturally take second place to the platters of smoked meat. Restaurant-style sides usually include pinto beans, potato salad or coleslaw, while markets sometimes opt for simpler accompaniments like onion slices, dill pickles, cheese slices or whole tomatoes. (If your meat is served on butcher paper, don't worry the sides will come in a bowl or on a plate.)

Etiquette

The first question that comes to most people's mind is, 'How do I eat this without making a mess?' You don't. Accepting the fact early on that barbecue is a messy, messy venture will give you the attitude you need to enjoy your meal. One coping mechanism is to make a drop cloth of your napkin. Bibs haven't exactly caught on in the barbecue world – this is a manly meal, after all – but tucking your napkin into your shirt is never frowned upon, especially if you didn't come dressed for it.

Which leads to another question: How does one dress for barbecue? First off, don't wear white. Or yellow, or pink, or anything that won't camouflage or coordinate with red. At 99% of barbecue restaurants (the exception being uppity, nouveau 'cue) you will see the most casual of casual attire, including jeans (harder to stain) and shorts, and maybe even some trucker hats.

Whether you eat with your hands or a fork depends on the cut of the meat. Brisket and sausage are fork dishes, while ribs are eaten caveperson-style. (It also depends on the restaurant. Kreuz Market doesn't offer forks. As the owner famously says, 'God put two of them at the end of your arms.')

If you're eating with your hands, grab extra napkins. Ah, heck, grab extras anyway. You might also be provided with a small packet containing a moist towelette, which will at least get you clean enough to head to the restrooms to wash up.

A final thought on etiquette: if you're at a restaurant that uses a dry rub and you don't see any sauce, it's probably best not to ask – it would be a bit like asking for ketchup to put on your steak.

Where to Eat Texas BBQ

West Texas & Panhandle

- KD's Bar-B-Q (p181)
- Rib Hut (p331)

Central Texas

- Black's Barbecue (p88)
- County Line Smokehouse (p110)
- Kreuz Market (p88)
- Lambert's (p73)
- Salt Lick Bar-B-Que (p76)

Texas BBQ

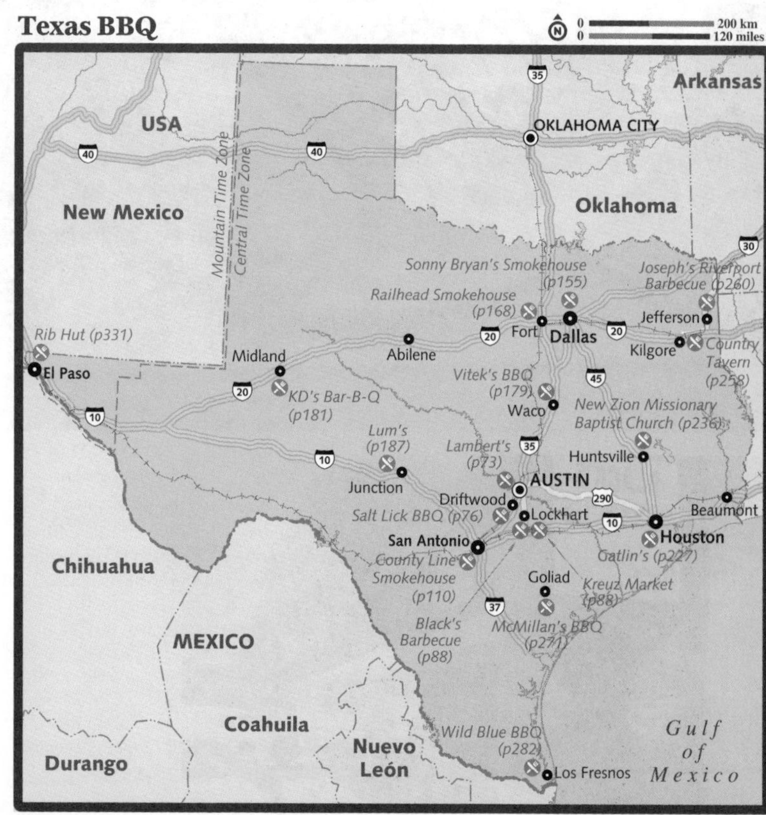

JUPITERIMAGES / GETTY IMAGES ©

GOSS IMAGES / ALAMY ©

Top: Enchiladas

Bottom: Black's Barbecue (p88)

COBBLER OR PIE?

What? You're full already? Well, just let your belt out a notch, because you've got to try the dessert. You might be off the hook if the restaurant doesn't serve sweets, but nothing follows a plate of barbecue like some hot peach or blackberry cobbler with a scoop of ice cream. (If you're feeling dainty, you can just go for the ice cream.) If you're not familiar with cobbler, picture a deconstructed fruit pie without a bottom crust. Fruit and sugar are cooked together on the stovetop then layered into a baking dish with dough on top.

Of course, a pie always works, especially if it's a pecan pie made from locally grown pecans, and chocolate cake would not be frowned upon, either, but cobblers are a classic. As a bonus, since they're seldom mass-produced, you're likely to get something made fresh in house.

- Vitek's BBQ (p179)
- Sonny Bryan's Smokehouse (p155)
- Railhead Smokehouse (p168)
- Lum's (p187)

East Texas

- Gatlin's (p227)
- Country Tavern (p258)
- Joseph's Riverport BBQ (p260)
- New Zion Missionary Baptist Church (p236)

Gulf Coast

- McMillan's BBQ (p271)
- Wild Blue BBQ (p282)

Mexican

While Californians may disagree, many people feel that Texas has the best Mexican food in the USA. Considering the miles and miles of border Texas shares with Mexico, it's no surprise that the culinary influence is widespread throughout the state.

Mex or Tex-Mex?

A regional variation on Mexican food, Tex-Mex includes Americanized versions of Mexican dishes, as well as American dishes with a Mexican twist. Don't spend too much effort trying to sort the two; there's a lot of overlap and, unless you're eating at a restaurant that serves 'authentic' or 'interior Mexico' dishes, you're probably going to have some Tex sneak into your Mex.

Staple Dishes

Mexican and Tex-Mex staples are often variations on a theme: take some sort of tortilla, whether soft or deep-fried, and put meat on it or in it, whether chicken, beef, pork or seafood. Then you top it with cheese, whether melted or not, and maybe some lettuce, sour cream, salsa and guacamole. The result? Burritos, tacos, enchiladas, nachos, fajitas and tostadas. Almost universally, a Tex-Mex main will be served with beans and rice on the side.

Menu Decoder

Breakfast burritos Eggs and either refried beans or bacon rolled in a soft tortilla.

Chile relleno A mild pepper stuffed with a ground-beef mixture and then fried.

Empanada A small pastry with savory or sweet fillings.

Gorditas Fried corn dough filled with refried beans and topped with sour cream, cheese and lettuce.

Huevos rancheros Fried eggs on tortillas, covered in salsa.

Menudo A heady stew of jalapeños, hominy and tripe (beef stomach) that's a traditional Mexican hangover cure.

Migas Eggs scrambled with broken tortilla strips and cheese.

Salsa Spanish for 'sauce' – made with chopped tomatoes, onions, cilantro (coriander) and chilies.

Tamales Corn dough stuffed with meat, beans, cheese, chilies or nothing at all, wrapped in cornhusks and steamed.

Margaritas

Drinking

The quasi-official soft drink of Texas is iced tea – almost always served unsweetened. If you want hot tea, specify that or you'll wind up with iced tea instead. Soft drinks are the same as everywhere in the world, but a local favorite is Dr Pepper, invented in Waco. Bottled drinking water is widely available, although tap water in Texas is usually fine to drink.

The strictly enforced drinking age in Texas is 21, and it's illegal to drive with a blood-alcohol level over .08%. Carry a driver's license or passport as proof of age. Minors are not allowed in bars and pubs, even to order nonalcoholic beverages.

Beer

Texas has been a little slow in building up its microbrew culture, though there is one excellent and widely available commercial brand, Shiner. You will find a good selection of out-of-state microbrews and specialty brews in larger cities, where pubs routinely have dozens of beers available.

If a bar advertises 'long-necks', it's just a standard 12oz beer served in a long-necked bottle.

Wine

Texas has two major viticulture areas, which are home to the state's most celebrated wineries: the High Plains surrounding Lubbock and the Hill Country west of Austin and San Antonio. Popular varietals are Cabernet Sauvignon, Merlot, Chardonnay and Pinot Noir.

Hard Liquor

Tequila is the most popular 'round these parts, if for no other reason than it's the main ingredient in margaritas. The unofficial state cocktail of Texas, margaritas are made with tequila, lime juice and triple sec, then served either on the rocks or frozen, in a glass with a salted rim. A few restaurants stake their reputations on specialty flavors, such as mango or watermelon. Don't knock 'em 'til you've downed at least one.

Regions at a Glance

In a vast and varied place like the Lone Star State, it should come as no surprise that you can have just about any experience your little ol' heart desires here. If you're looking for outdoor adventure, the Gulf Coast and west Texas have it in spades. Dallas and Houston are your ticket to big-city culture. Simpler, small-town pleasures await outside metro areas everywhere, especially in northeast Texas, Hill Country and east-central Washington County. If you want to eat, drink and be entertained, San Antonio and Austin have you covered. The trouble may be deciding exactly what you want to do.

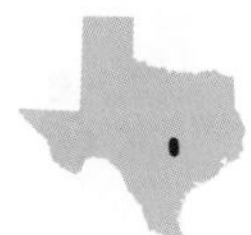

Austin

Music
Outdoors
Food

Live Music

Fun an' funky Austin has something going on every day of the week. Live music runs the gamut from local country to alternative and avant-garde.

Parks & Greenbelts

Take a dip in a natural spring pool, hike and bike along Lady Bird Lake or rent canoes or kayaks in Zilker Park. A big part of Austin's attraction is to be found outdoors.

South Congress Ave

Explore Austin's 'weird' side on South Congress Ave, where you can stay at an upscale, Zen motel; eat at wonderfully independent cafes and food trailers; and shop for vintage clothes or a new tattoo.

p54

San Antonio & Hill Country

Culture
History
Small Towns

Tex-Mex Mix

The state's Hispanic heritage is on bright and colorful display in San Antonio. Munch Mexican food to your heart's content before you tour the *mercado* (market) or listen to mariachis on the Riverwalk.

Remember the Alamo!

Although small, the site of the historic siege of the Alamo should top any visitor's list. Four more old Spanish missions (1720 to 1756) lie south of town along Mission Trail.

Hill Country Towns

Winding roads and rivers lead past old towns set among the rolling hills. In the spring brilliant wildflowers carpet the hills and dales.

p90

Dallas & the Panhandle Plains

Arts & Entertainment
Museums
Outdoors

High & Low Culture

Dallas and Fort Worth have incredible museums and arts districts. But they also have low-ball fun such as fried cheesecake and mechanical bull-rides.

JFK Sights

The stellar Sixth Floor Museum examines the facts and theories surrounding the assassination of President John F Kennedy. Other JFK-related sights include Dealey Plaza and the Kennedy Memorial.

Amarillo

Amarillo's classic Mother Road (Route 66) stops include the Big Texan Steak House and Cadillac Ranch. South of town, Palo Duro Canyon is the only break in the pancake-flat Panhandle Plains.

p139

Houston & East Texas

Museums
Food
Small Towns

Modern Art

Houston has several world-class museums. The Museum of Fine Arts Houston is certainly not to be discounted, but the modern-leaning Menil Collection is one of a kind.

Foodie Favorites

The food scene in Houston is hot. You might dine on inspired organic creations at Haven, French-Tex fusion at Philippe's or see what chef Monica Pope is up to at Sparrow Bar & Cookshop.

Piney Woods

Leave the city to explore the Southern belle towns set among soaring pine forests up in the northeast. Tyler is the rose capital of Texas, Nacogdoches the oldest (maybe), and Jefferson boasts the most ghosts.

p206

Gulf Coast & South Texas

Coastal Towns
Beaches
Bird-Watching

Seaside Fishing Villages

Towns such as Matagorda, Rockport and Port Aransas may all be home to harbors and shrimp-fishing fleets, but you'll also find sea-themed shops, boat tours and quaint accommodation.

Padre Island

The largest of Texas' barrier islands, Padre Island stretches 113 miles. In the north near Corpus Christi, commercial and residential areas with beaches give way to the pristine 70-mile-long Padre Island National Seashore.

World Birding Center

Nine individual sites scattered along the Rio Grande Valley make up the World Birding Center. Interesting year-round, winter is when the most birds come to roost.

p262

Big Bend & West Texas

Outdoors
Scenic Drives
Small Towns

Big Bend Hiking

Big Bend National Park's more than 200 miles of trails are the highlight of Texas hiking. Tromp up mountains, trace riverside trails or explore the Chihuahuan Desert.

Davis Mountain Driving

Though not as tall as neighboring ranges, the Davis Mountains provide an excellent opportunity for scenic driving. Wind your way up to the McDonald Observatory for the most comprehensive views.

Tiny West Texas Towns

Each quirky little west Texas town has an individual claim to fame: Fort Davis is Old West–inspired; Marfa a funky artist's escape; and Terlingua is a repopulated ghost town.

p300

On the Road

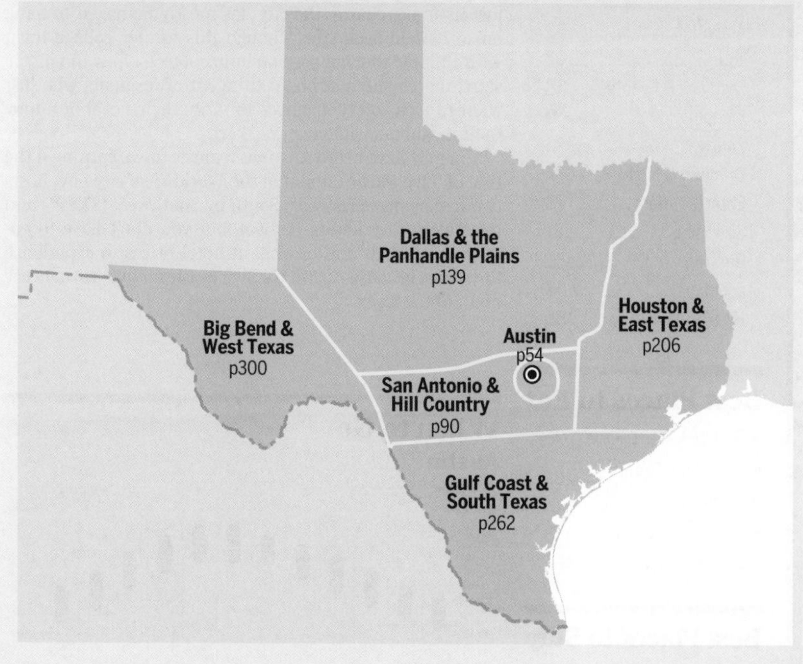
Dallas & the Panhandle Plains
p139
Big Bend & West Texas
p300
Austin
p54
Houston & East Texas
p206
San Antonio & Hill Country
p90
Gulf Coast & South Texas
p262

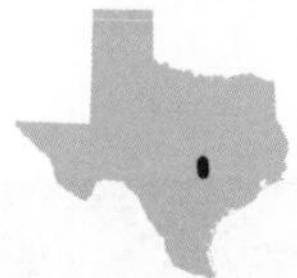

Austin

POP 820,611

Includes ➡

Best Places to Eat

- Salt Lick Bar-B-Que (p76)
- Amy's Ice Cream (p75)
- Uchiko (p75)
- Salty Sow (p76)
- Güero's Taco Bar (p74)

Best Places to Stay

- Hotel San José (p70)
- Heywood Hotel (p70)
- Driskill Hotel (p70)
- Austin Motel (p70)
- Adams House (p71)

Why Go?

You'll see it on bumper stickers throughout the city: 'Keep Austin Weird.' And while old-timers grumble that Austin has lost its funky charm, the city has mostly managed to hang on to its laid-back vibe. Though this former college town with a hippie soul has seen an influx of tech types and movie stars, there's still a strong contingent of residents who just want to focus on their music or write their novel or annoy their neighbors with crazy yard art.

You may have heard Austin is a music town, earning it the title of 'Live Music Capital of the World.' The city now hosts two major music festivals, South by Southwest (SXSW) and the Austin City Limits Festival, but you don't have to endure the crowds and exorbitant hotel prices to experience the scene, because Austin has live music all over town every night of the week.

When to Go

Austin

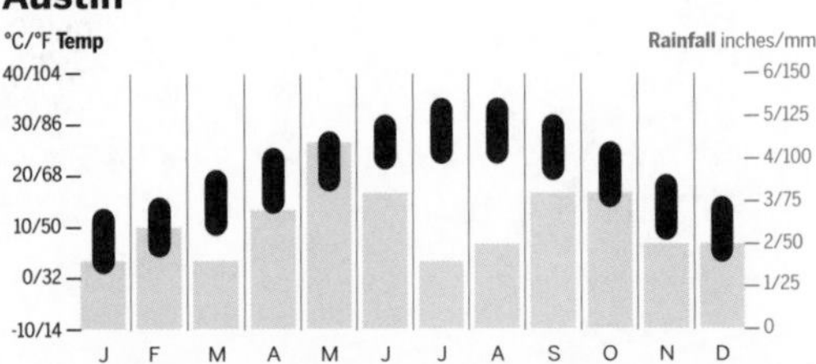

Mar & Apr Wildflowers and mild weather make this the perfect time of year to visit.

May & Jun The weather is hot but bearable, and everything is still green for the most part.

Sep & Oct You won't see any fall foliage, but temperatures will have cooled by now.

Plan Ahead: South by Southwest

If you're planning on coming for the citywide takeover that is SXSW – whether the music festival, the interactive festival, the film festival, or any combination thereof – planning ahead can save you a significant amount of money, not to mention a lot of headaches. The most affordable option is to buy early-bird tickets before mid-September, and the price goes up approximately once a month until it's showtime. Hotel rooms get booked up months ahead of time, so go ahead and look into places to stay the moment you think you might want to go. (If you're not sure, at least make a reservation somewhere that will allow you to cancel, lest you end up on someone's floor.)

FOOD TRAILERS

From epicurian Airstreams to regular old taco trucks, food trailers are kind of a big deal in Austin, and wandering from one to another is a fun way to experience the local food scene. Because of their transient nature, we haven't listed any of these rolling restaurants, but since they travel in packs, we can tell you where they tend to congregate.

➡ **South Austin Trailer Park and Eatery** This seems to be a rather settled trailer community, with a fence, an official name, a sign and picnic tables.

➡ **East Austin** This area has its own little enclave, conveniently located right among all the bars on the corner of East Sixth and Waller St.

For Kids

➡ Dinosaur Park (p88) A nature trail lined with full-sized dino replicas, 12 miles east of the Austin airport.

➡ Zilker Zephyr (p68) Take a ride around Zilker Park on a miniature train.

➡ Barton Springs (p63) Cool off in this ginormous natural pool with icy-cold water.

➡ Texas Memorial Museum (p59) More dino fun on the University of Texas campus, this time in the form of a flying pterosaur skeleton.

➡ Austin Children's Museum (p68) A new and much larger space equals more fun for the little ones.

BEST PHOTO OP

Snap a pic against the backdrop of the giant vintage-postcard mural on the side of Roadhouse Relics (1720 S 1st St) that reads 'Greetings from Austin, Capitol of Texas.'

Fast Facts

➡ **State Capital of Texas**

➡ **Area code** ☎ 512

➡ **Area** 265 sq miles

What's New

➡ Formula 1 Grand Prix (p69) A new multi-million-dollar track means an onslaught of international visitors in November.

➡ Firehouse Hostel (p69) Finally! A hostel in downtown Austin, right across from the venerable Driskill Hotel.

➡ Roy G Guerrero Disc Golf Course (p66) A brand new course to replace the beloved (but closed) Pease Park course.

Resources

➡ **Austin CVB** (www.austintexas.org)

➡ **Austin360** (www.austin360.com)

➡ **Austin Chronicle** (www.austinchronicle.com)

➡ **Austin City Links** (www.austinlinks.com)

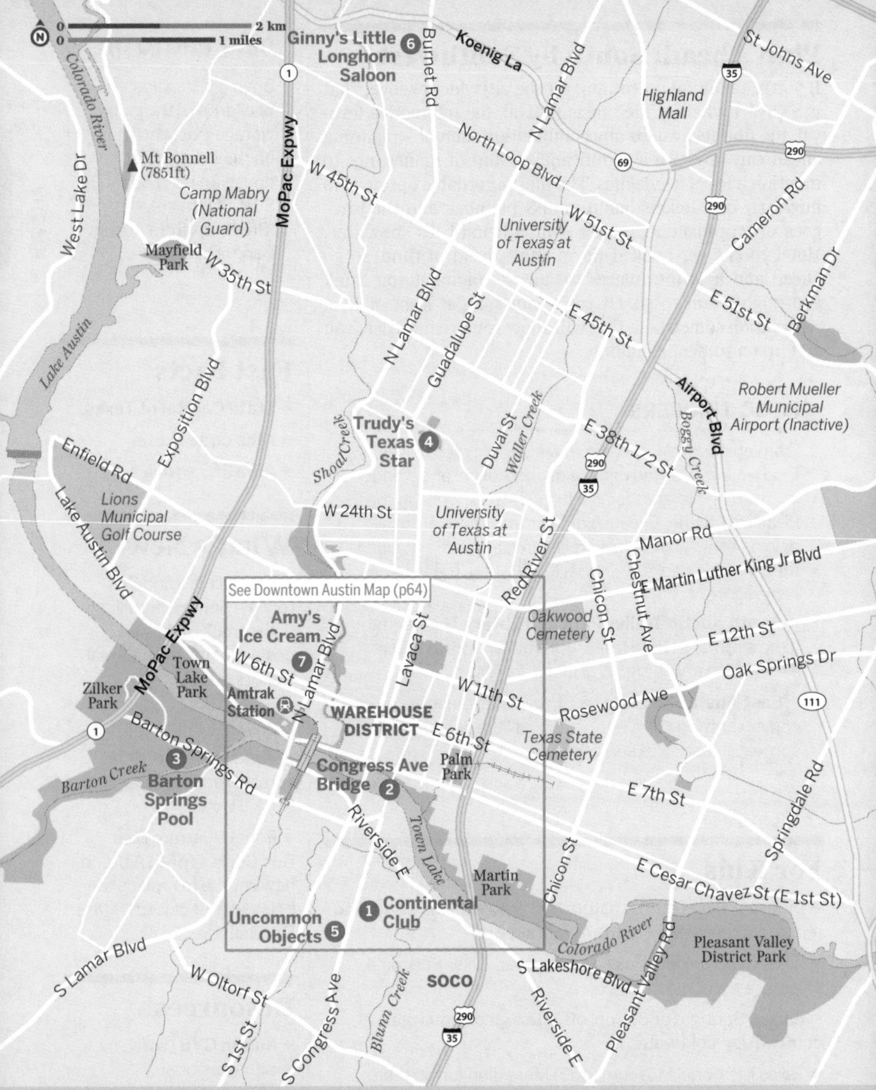

Austin Highlights

❶ Catching a local band at the **Continental Club** (p79) or one of the other hundreds of live-music venues around town.

❷ Watching the nightly exodus of America's largest urban **bat colony** (p63) under the Congress Avenue Bridge in summer.

❸ Jumping into the icy waters of **Barton Springs Pool** (p63) for instant relief when the heat is too much.

❹ Enjoying a margarita at **Trudy's Texas Star** (p75): frozen or on the rocks, plain or with a sangria swirl, they're practically perfect.

❺ Browsing booth after booth of oddities, treasures, memorabilia and tchotchkes at **Uncommon Objects** (p82).

❻ Going honky-tonkin' or playing chicken-shit bingo at **Ginny's Little Longhorn** (p78).

❼ Creating your own perfect blend of ice cream plus toppings at **Amy's Ice Cream** (p75).

History

Things happened quickly in the early days of Austin. In 1837 – just one year after Texas had won its independence from Mexico – settlers founded the town of Waterloo on the banks of the Colorado River. By 1939 the town had been chosen as the state capital and renamed Austin, after Stephen F Austin, a man who had colonized the area and come to be known as the Father of Texas.

The city experienced its first boom after the arrival of the Houston and Texas Central Railroad in 1871, and by 1900 the town was thoroughly modern and had a beautiful new capitol building that was the largest in the US. (In fact, when it opened, it was the seventh-largest building in the world.)

Fast forward to the 1990s, when the tech industry brought another boom. With a well-educated populace (thanks to all those University of Texas grads who never could quite bear to move away), Austin attracted major tech companies. It wasn't all UT grads fueling the movement: Michael Dell founded his computer company in his dorm room in 1984 and promptly dropped out of UT.

Between tech types, UT students, musicians and politicians, Austin has a near-constant influx of new residents, and recent estimates have 150 or so people moving to Austin each day. Things are constantly changing in the capital city, for better or for worse.

Sights

Downtown

Downtown Austin is an orderly grid. The main north–south artery is Congress Ave, with Cesar Chavez St running east–west. Most downtown streets are one way, including 6th St, a major westbound thoroughfare, and southbound Guadalupe St (pronounced *guad*-ah-loop locally, despite what you might have learned in Spanish class). Downtown is chock-full of entertainment options, including the bars of 6th St, music venues on Red River, and the more upscale Warehouse District.

Texas State Capitol HISTORIC BUILDING

(Map p64; ☎512-305-8402; cnr 11th St & Congress Ave; ⏰7am-10pm Mon-Fri, 9am-8pm Sat & Sun) FREE Built in 1888 from sunset-red granite, this state capitol is the largest in the US, backing up the ubiquitous claim that everything is bigger in Texas. If nothing else, take a peek at the lovely rotunda and try out the whispering gallery created by its curved ceiling.

Self-guiding brochures of the capitol building and grounds are available inside the tour-guide office on the ground floor. From here you can also take one of the interesting 45-minute guided tours offered daily (schedules vary; call first or show up and try your luck). The green sprawl of the capitol grounds and its monuments are worth a stroll before or after your tour.

Want to see government in action? Take a seat in the 3rd-floor **visitors balconies** overlooking the House of Representatives and Senate chamber galleries, which are open to the public when the state legislature is in session (odd-numbered years from mid-January through May or June).

Free two-hour parking is available inside the Capitol Visitors Parking Garage, entered from either 12th St or 13th St.

Bob Bullock Texas State History Museum MUSEUM

(Map p64; ☎512-936-8746; www.thestoryoftexas.com; 1800 Congress Ave; adult/child 4-17yr $9/6, Texas Spirit film $5/4; ⏰9am-6pm Mon-Sat, noon-6pm Sun) This is no dusty old historical museum. Big, glitzy and still relatively new, it shows off the Lone Star State's history, all the way from when it used to be part of Mexico up to the present, with high-tech interactive exhibits and fun theatrics. Allow at least a few hours for your visit.

Ground-floor exhibits re-imagine the Native American experience and later arrival of French Jesuits, Spanish conquistadores and other frontier settlers. Upstairs, visitors trace the revolutionary years of the Republic of Texas, its rise to statehood and economic expansion into oil drilling and space exploration, even Western movies and homegrown music from Bob Wills to Buddy Holly to the Big Bopper.

The museum also houses Austin's first **IMAX theater** (check website for listings; adult/child four to 17 years $8/6) and the **Texas Spirit Theater** (adult/child four to 17 years $5/4), both of which offer discounted combination tickets when bought with a museum admission. The Texas Spirit Theater is where you can see *The Star of Destiny*, a 15-minute special-effects film that's simultaneously high-tech and hokey fun.

Museum parking is $8.

AMOA-Arthouse MUSEUM

(Map p64; ☎512-453-5312; www.amoa-arthouse.org; 700 Congress Ave; adult/under 18yr $5/free; ⌚11am-7pm Tue-Sat, noon-5pm Sun) The love child of the Austin Museum of Art and the Arthouse has a cool new downtown space and a freshly hyphenated name. AMOA-Arthouse focuses on rotating exhibits representing fresh new voices – both in its main gallery, the Jones Center, as well as the museum's original home at Laguna Gloria (3809 W 35th St).

Located on the shores of Lake Austin, Laguna Gloria is an Italianate villa built in 1916 – the former home of Texas legend Clara Driscoll. It still serves as a rotating exhibition space, plus the grounds are nice for a wander.

Mexic-Arte Museum MUSEUM

(Map p64; ☎512-480-9373; www.mexic-artemuseum.org; 419 Congress Ave; adult/under 12yr/student $5/1/4; ⌚10am-6pm Mon-Thu, to 5pm Fri & Sat, noon-5pm Sun) This wonderful, eclectic downtown museum features works from Mexican and Mexican American artists in exhibitions that rotate every two months. The museum's holdings include carved wooden masks, modern Latin American paintings, historic photographs and contemporary art. Don't miss the back gallery, where new and experimental talent is shown.

The museum's gift shop is another draw, with killer Mexican stuff that's pricey if you're heading south of the border but reasonable if you're not.

University of Texas Campus Area

The University of Texas cuts a huge swath of land through the area just north of downtown; look for the main tower and you'll know you've arrived. Even if you're not an alum or a Longhorn at heart, the area is home to several worthwhile museums.

University of Texas at Austin UNIVERSITY

(Map p60; www.utexas.edu; cnr University Ave & 24 Ave) Whatever you do, don't call it 'Texas University' – them's fightin' words, usually used derisively by Texas A&M University students to take their rivals down a notch. Sorry, A&M, but the main campus of the University of Texas is kind of a big deal. Established in 1883, UT has the largest enrollment in the state, with over 50,000 students.

Notable buildings on campus include four excellent museums and the Texas Memorial Stadium, home of the Texas Longhorns football team. But none define the UT campus as much as the UT Tower. Standing 307ft high, with a clock over 12ft in diameter, the tower looms large, both as a campus landmark and in Austin history as the perch that shooter Charles Whitman used during a 1966 shooting spree. On a more cheerful note, it now serves as a beacon of victory when it's lit

AUSTIN IN...

Two Days

Start your day at the **Bob Bullock History Museum**, then pop in to the **Blanton** right across the street. In the afternoon cool off at **Barton Springs**, where you can work up an appetite for Tex-Mex at **Trudy's**. After dark, plug into Austin's live-music scene along **Red River** or in the **Warehouse District**.

On day two, take a tour of the **Texas State Capitol**, then head to South Congress for lunch at **Güero's** followed by shopping and people-watching. If it's summer, make your way towards the Congress Avenue Bridge to witness the nightly exodus of America's largest urban **bat colony**. End your evening with some Texas two-stepping at the **Broken Spoke**.

Four Days

On day three, it's time for a road trip. Head out of town to **Lockhart** for some Texas-style barbecue, then go on to **Gruene** for antique shopping and an evening at Texas' oldest dancehall.

The next day, check out a couple of the smaller **museums** around town – whatever strikes your fancy – then enjoy some outdoor time at **Lady Bird Lake** or the **Lady Bird Johnson Wildlife Center**. Make dinner a moveable feast by roaming the **food trucks**.

orange to celebrate a Longhorn win or other achievement.

The tower's observation deck is accessible only by **guided tours** (☎512-475-6633; per person $6), which are offered frequently in summer but only on weekends during the school year. Advance reservations are recommended, although standby tickets may be available at the Texas Union's front desk.

Want to see some Big 12 football or other college athletics while you're in town? The **UT Ticket Office** (Map p60; ☎800-982-2386, 512-477-6060; www.texasboxoffice.com; Bellmont Hall, 2100 San Jacinto Blvd; ⌚9am-6pm Mon-Fri, 10am-4pm Sat) is your source for all things Longhorn.

Blanton Museum of Art MUSEUM

(Map p64; ☎512-471-5482; www.blantonmuseum.org; 200 E Martin Luther King Blvd; adult/child $9/free; ⌚10am-5pm Tue-Fri, 11am-5pm Sat, 1-5pm Sun) A big university with a big endowment is bound to have a big art collection, and now, finally, it has a suitable building to show it off properly. With one of the best university art collections in the USA, the Blanton showcases a variety of styles. It doesn't go very in-depth into any of them, but then again you're bound to find something of interest.

Especially striking is the permanent installation of Missao/Missoes [How to Build Cathedrals] – which involves 600,000 pennies, 800 communion wafers and 2000 cattle bones.

Lyndon Baines Johnson (LBJ) Library & Museum MUSEUM

(Map p60; ☎512-721-0200; www.lbjlibrary.org; 2313 Red River St; adult/child 13-17yr/senior $8/3/5; ⌚9am-5pm) A major renovation has brought the museum into the new millennium with interactive exhibits and audiovisual displays. Fortunately, they didn't lose the hokey, animatronic LBJ that regales visitors with the president's recorded stories – although they did stir some controversy when they changed him out of his ranch duds into a suit much more befitting an animatronic of his stature.

There are some fascinating mementos from the 36th US president, including his presidential limo and gifts from heads of state ('Why, thank you Chiang Kai-shek, for this lovely Chinese tomb sculpture!'). The museum also provides insight into the events of the 1960s, including the Vietnam War, the Cuban Missile Crisis and the assassination of President Kennedy. Don't miss the 8th floor for a look at a replica of Johnson's Oval Office, and an exhibit on Lady Bird Johnson, the president's wife.

Harry Ransom Humanities Research Center MUSEUM

(Map p60; ☎512-471-8944; www.hrc.utexas.edu; 300 W 21st St; ⌚10am-5pm Tue, Wed & Fri, 10am-7pm Thu, noon-5pm Sat & Sun) FREE The fascinating Ransom Center is a major repository of historic manuscripts, photography, books, film, TV, music and more. Highlights include a complete copy of the Gutenberg Bible (one of only five in the USA) and what is thought to be the first photograph ever taken, from 1826. Check the website for special online-only exhibitions and the center's busy events calendar of author readings, live music, lectures and more.

Texas Memorial Museum MUSEUM

(Map p60; ☎512-471-1604; www.utexas.edu/tmm; 2400 Trinity St; ⌚9am-5pm Mon-Fri, 10am-5pm Sat, 1-5pm Sun) FREE We all know how kids feel about dinosaurs, and this natural-history museum is the perfect place for them to indulge their fascination. Look up to see the swooping skeleton of the Texas pterosaur – one of the most famous dino finds ever. This impressively humongous Cretaceous-era flying reptile has a wingspan of 40ft and was recovered at Big Bend in 1971.

There are other exhibits too, focusing on anthropology, natural history, geology and biodiversity. Upstairs, you can glimpse taxidermic examples of a Texas soft-shell turtle, a Mexican beaded lizard and other critters, but most of the exhibits are like something you'd find in the dusty attic of an eccentric great aunt.

Elisabet Ney Museum MUSEUM

(Map p60; ☎512-458-2255; www.austintexas.gov/department/elisabet-ney-museum; 304 E 44th St; donations welcome; ⌚noon-5pm Wed-Sun) A German-born sculptor and spirited trailblazer, Elisabet Ney lived in Austin in the early 1880s, and her former studio is now one of the oldest museums in Texas. Filled with more than 100 works of art, including busts and statues of political figures, the castlelike building made from rough-hewn stone is reason enough to visit.

Three of Ney's better-known works reside in the state capitol, but the artist considered her greatest legacy to be a sculpture of Lady Macbeth. The Smithsonian owns the original, but you can see a replica of it here.

Austin

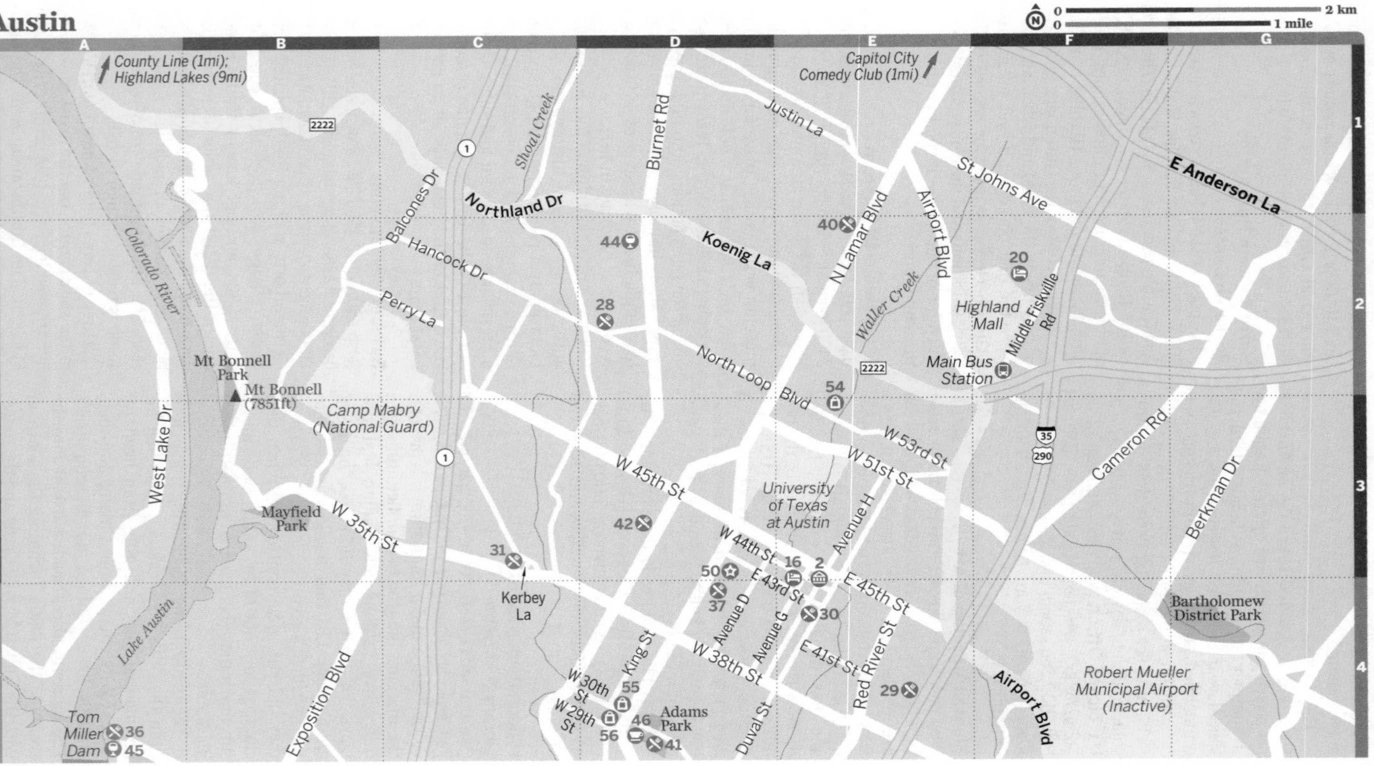
County Line (1mi); Highland Lakes (9mi)
Capitol City Comedy Club (1mi)
2 km
1 mile
Colorado River
Lake Austin
West Lake Dr
Mt Bonnell Park
Mt Bonnell (7851ft)
Camp Mabry (National Guard)
Mayfield Park
W 35th St
Exposition Blvd
Tom Miller Dam
Balcones Dr
Hancock Dr
Perry La
Shoal Creek
Northland Dr
Burnet Rd
Koenig La
Justin La
N Lamar Blvd
Airport Blvd
St Johns Ave
E Anderson La
Waller Creek
Highland Mall
Middle Fiskville Rd
Main Bus Station
North Loop Blvd
W 53rd St
W 51st St
W 45th St
Kerbey La
University of Texas at Austin
Avenue H
W 44th St
E 43rd St
E 45th St
Avenue D
Avenue G
E 41st St
Red River St
W 38th St
King St
W 30th St
W 29th St
Adams Park
Duval St
Cameron Rd
Berkman Dr
Bartholomew District Park
Robert Mueller Municipal Airport (Inactive)
Airport Blvd
2222
1
35
290
2
16
20
28
29
30
31
36
37
40
41
42
44
45
46
50
54
55
56

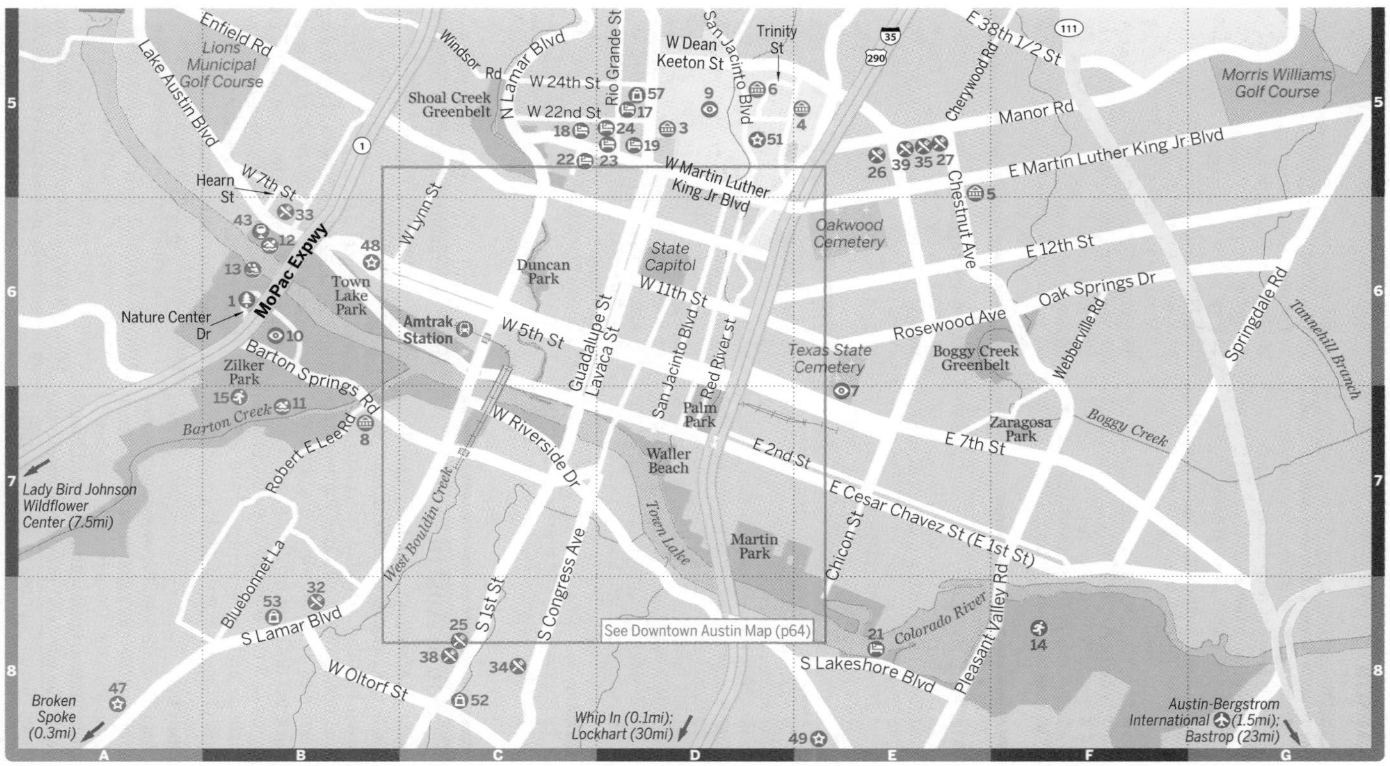

Enfield Rd
Lions Municipal Golf Course
Lake Austin Blvd
Windsor Rd
N Lamar Blvd
W 24th St
W 22nd St
Rio Grande St
W Dean Keeton St
San Jacinto Blvd
Trinity St
35
290
E 38th 1/2 St
111
Cherywood Rd
Morris Williams Golf Course
Shoal Creek Greenbelt
57
17
9
6
4
18
24
3
19
51
22
23
1
Manor Rd
26
39
35
27
E Martin Luther King Jr Blvd
Hearn St
W 7th St
33
43
12
13
MoPac Expwy
48
W Lynn St
W Martin Luther King Jr Blvd
Chestnut Ave
5
Oakwood Cemetery
E 12th St
State Capitol
Duncan Park
Town Lake Park
1
Nature Center Dr
10
W 11th St
Oak Springs Dr
Amtrak Station
W 5th St
Guadalupe St
Lavaca St
San Jacinto Blvd
Red River St
Rosewood Ave
Texas State Cemetery
Webberville Rd
Boggy Creek Greenbelt
Springdale Rd
Tannehill Branch
Zilker Park
Barton Springs Rd
15
11
Barton Creek
Robert E Lee Rd
8
W Riverside Dr
Palm Park
7
Zaragosa Park
Boggy Creek
E 7th St
E 2nd St
Waller Beach
Lady Bird Johnson Wildflower Center (7.5mi)
West Bouldin Creek
Town Lake
E Cesar Chavez St (E 1st St)
Martin Park
Chicon St
S Congress Ave
Pleasant Valley Rd
Bluebonnet La
53
32
S Lamar Blvd
25
S 1st St
See Downtown Austin Map (p64)
21
Colorado River
14
38
34
S Lakeshore Blvd
W Oltorf St
52
47
Broken Spoke (0.3mi)
Whip In (0.1mi); Lockhart (30mi)
49
Austin-Bergstrom International (1.5mi); Bastrop (23mi)
A
B
C
D
E
F
G
5
6
7
8

Austin

Sights
1 Austin Nature & Science Center B6
2 Elisabet Ney Museum E3
3 Harry Ransom Humanities Research Center D5
4 Lyndon Baines Johnson (LBJ) Library & Museum E5
5 Museum of Natural & Artificial Ephemerata E5
6 Texas Memorial Museum D5
7 Texas State Cemetery E7
8 Umlauf Sculpture Garden B7
9 University of Texas at Austin D5
10 Zilker Botanical Garden B6

Activities, Courses & Tours
11 Barton Springs Pool B7
12 Deep Eddy Pool B6
13 Lady Bird Lake B6
14 Roy G Guerrero Disc Golf Course F8
15 Zilker Park B7
Zilker Park Boat Rentals (see 11)
Zilker Zephyr (see 11)

Sleeping
16 Adams House E3
17 Austin Folk House D5
18 College Houses Cooperatives C5
19 Goodall Wooten D5
20 Habitat Suites F2
21 HI – Austin E8
22 Inn at Pearl Street C5
23 Mansion at Judge's Hill D5
24 Star of Texas Inn D5

Eating
25 Bouldin Creek Coffee House C8
26 El Chile E5
27 El Chilito E5
28 Fonda San Miguel D2
29 Freebirds World Burrito E4
30 Hyde Park Bar & Grill E4
31 Kerbey Lane Café C3
32 Lick B8
33 Magnolia Cafe B6
34 Magnolia Cafe South C8
35 Mi Madre's E5
36 Mozart's Coffee Roasters A4
37 New World Deli D4
38 Polvos C8
39 Salty Sow E5
40 Threadgill's Restaurant E2
41 Trudy's Texas Star D4
42 Uchiko D3

Drinking & Nightlife
43 Deep Eddy Cabaret B6
44 Ginny's Little Longhorn Saloon D2
45 Hula Hut A4
46 Spider House D4

Entertainment
47 Broken Spoke A8
48 Donn's Depot B6
49 Emo's East E8
50 Hyde Park Theatre D3
51 UT Ticket Office D5

Shopping
52 Amelia's Retrovogue & Relics C8
Antone's Records (see 55)
53 Austin Art Garage B8
54 Blue Velvet E3
55 Buffalo Exchange D4
56 Toy Joy D4
57 University Co-op D5

South Austin

South of downtown and Lady Bird Lake, South Congress is an offbeat and oh-so-Austin neighborhood that was pretty marginal just 25 or so years ago. Tourism types nicknamed it SoCo, which has somewhat stuck, but the locals mostly still call it South Congress. S Congress Ave is the main thoroughfare and the epicenter of the action; most of the rest is residential.

Zilker Park PARK
(Map p60; ☎512-974-6700; www.austintexas.gov/department/zilker-metropolitan-park; 2100 Barton Springs Rd) This 350-acre park is a slice of green heaven, lined with hiking and biking trails. The park also provides access to the famed Barton Springs natural swimming pool and Barton Creek Greenbelt. Find boat rentals, a miniature train and a botanical garden. During busy summer weekends admission is $5 per car.

Zilker Botanical Garden GARDENS
(Map p60; ☎512-477-8672; www.zilkergarden.org; 2220 Barton Springs Rd; 7am-7pm during daylight savings, to 5:30pm the rest of the year) FREE These lush gardens cover 31 acres on the south bank of the Colorado River, with displays including natural grottoes, a Japanese garden and a fragrant herb garden.

You'll also find some interesting historical artifacts sprinkled about the site – kind of like an outdoor architectural museum – including a 19th-century pioneer cabin, a cupola that once sat atop a local schoolhouse, and a footbridge moved from Congress Ave.

Umlauf Sculpture Garden MUSEUM
(Map p60; ☎512-445-5582; www.umlaufsculpture.org; 605 Robert E Lee Rd; adult/under 6yr/student $3.50/free/1; ⏰10am-4pm Wed-Fri, noon-4pm Sat & Sun) If the weather's just too perfect to be inside a climate-controlled building, stroll the open-air Umlauf Sculpture Garden, located near Zilker Park. Within the sculpture garden and the indoor **museum**, there are more than 130 works by 20th-century American sculptor Charles Umlauf, who was an art professor at UT for 40 years.

East Austin

East Austin is on the rise, and although it has traditionally seen few visitors, it has a rich history as an African American neighborhood, with roots stretching back to the 19th century.

Texas State Cemetery CEMETERY
(Map p60; ☎512-463-0605; 909 Navasota St; ⏰8am-5pm daily, visitor center 8am-5pm Mon-Fri) Revitalized in the 1990s, the state's official cemetery, Texas State Cemetery, is the final resting place of key figures from Texan history. Interred here are luminaries including Stephen F Austin, Miriam 'Ma' Ferguson (the state's first female governor), writer James Michener and Lone Star State flag designer Joanna Troutman, along with thousands of soldiers who died in the Civil War, plus more than 100 leaders of the Republic of Texas who were exhumed from other sites and reburied here. Self-guided-tour brochures are usually available from the visitor center. The cemetery is just north of E 7th St.

Greater Austin

Lady Bird Johnson Wildflower Center GARDENS
(☎512-232-0100; www.wildflower.org; 4801 La Crosse Ave; adult/child 5-12yr/student & senior $9/3/7, higher during peak spring flowering; ⏰9am-5pm Tue-Sat, noon-5pm Sun) Anyone with an interest in Texas' flora and fauna should make the 20-minute drive to the wonderful gardens of the Lady Bird Johnson Wildflower Center, southwest of downtown Austin. The center, founded in 1982 with the assistance of Texas' beloved former first lady, has a display garden featuring every type of wildflower and plant that grows in Texas, separated by geographical region, with an emphasis on Hill Country flora. The best time to come is in the spring (especially National Wildflower Week in May), but there's something in bloom all year.

Activities

Austin has quite a few places to play outside, including Zilker Park, Lady Bird Lake, and creekside parks and greenbelts throughout the city. You can get just about any information you might need from the **City of Austin Parks & Recreation Department** (☎512-974-6700; www.austintexas.gov/department/parks-and-recreation; ⏰8am-5pm Mon-Fri). Check its website to find everything from municipal golf courses to tennis complexes to cemeteries.

Swimming & Boating

Barton Springs Pool SWIMMING
(Map p60; ☎512-867-3080; 2201 Barton Springs Rd; adult/child $3/2; ⏰9am-10pm Fri-Wed mid-Apr–Sep) Hot? Not for long. Even when the

THE SWARM

Looking very much like a special effect from a B movie, a funnel cloud of up to 1.5 million Mexican free-tailed bats swarms from under the **Congress Avenue Bridge** (Map p64; Congress Ave; ⏰Apr-Nov, around sunset, best viewings in Aug) nightly from late March to early November. Turns out, Austin isn't just the live-music capital of the world; it's also home to the largest urban bat population in North America.

Austinites have embraced the winged mammals – figuratively speaking, of course – and gather to watch the bats' nightly exodus right around dusk as they leave for their evening meal. (Not to worry: they're looking for insects, and they mostly stay out of your hair.)

There's lots of standing room around parking lots and on the bridge itself, but if you want a more leisurely bat-watching experience, try the TGI Friday's restaurant by the Radisson Hotel on Lady Bird Lake, or the Lone Star Riverboat or Capital Cruises for **bat-watching tours**.

Downtown Austin

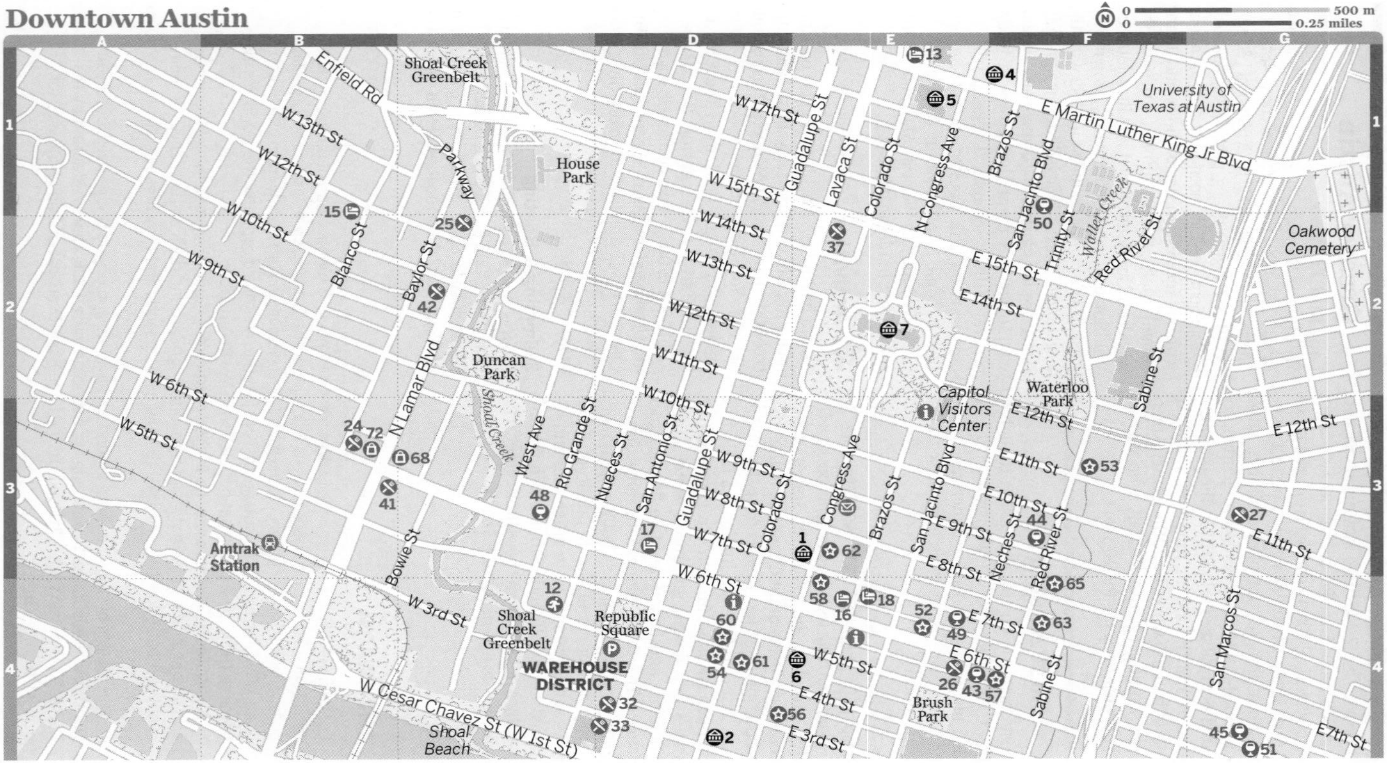
0 500 m
0 0.25 miles
A
B
C
D
E
F
G
1
2
3
4
Shoal Creek Greenbelt
Enfield Rd
W 13th St
W 12th St
W 10th St
W 9th St
W 6th St
W 5th St
Parkway
House Park
Blanco St
Baylor St
N Lamar Blvd
Duncan Park
Shoal Creek
West Ave
Rio Grande St
Nueces St
San Antonio St
Guadalupe St
Lavaca St
Colorado St
N Congress Ave
Brazos St
San Jacinto Blvd
Trinity St
Waller Creek
Red River St
W 17th St
W 15th St
W 14th St
W 13th St
W 12th St
W 11th St
W 10th St
W 9th St
W 8th St
W 7th St
W 6th St
W 5th St
W 3rd St
E Martin Luther King Jr Blvd
University of Texas at Austin
Oakwood Cemetery
E 15th St
E 14th St
E 12th St
E 11th St
E 10th St
E 9th St
E 8th St
E 7th St
E 6th St
E 4th St
E 3rd St
E 12th St
E 11th St
E7th St
Capitol Visitors Center
Waterloo Park
Sabine St
Congress Ave
Colorado St
Brazos St
San Jacinto Blvd
Neches St
Red River St
Sabine St
San Marcos St
Amtrak Station
Bowie St
Shoal Creek Greenbelt
Republic Square
WAREHOUSE DISTRICT
W Cesar Chavez St (W 1st St)
Shoal Beach
Brush Park
1
2
4
5
6
7
12
13
15
16
17
18
24
25
26
27
32
33
37
41
42
43
44
45
48
49
50
51
52
53
54
56
57
58
60
61
62
63
65
68
72

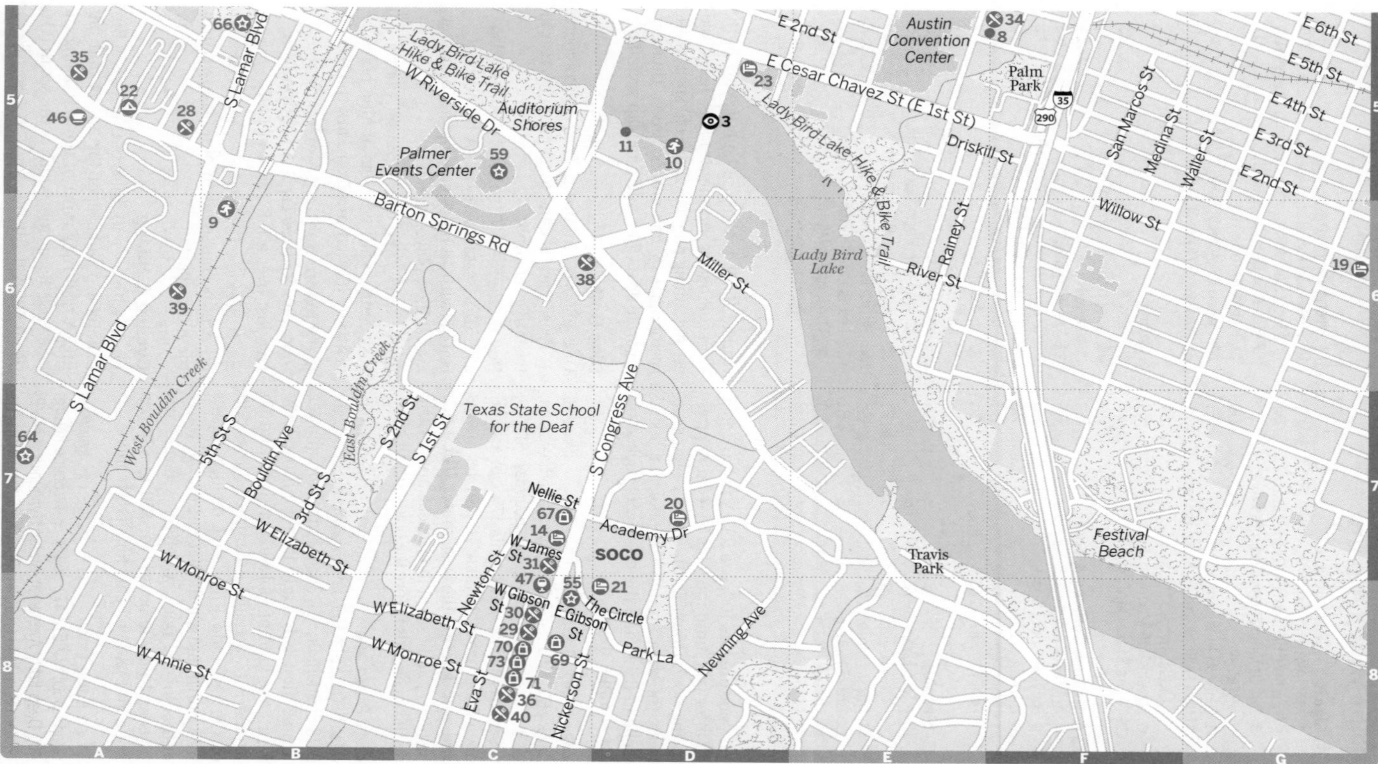

E 2nd St
Austin Convention Center
Palm Park
E 6th St
E 5th St
E 4th St
E 3rd St
E 2nd St
San Marcos St
Medina St
Waller St
Willow St
E Cesar Chavez St (E 1st St)
Driskill St
Rainey St
River St
Lady Bird Lake Hike & Bike Trail
Lady Bird Lake
Lady Bird Lake Hike & Bike Trail
W Riverside Dr
Auditorium Shores
Palmer Events Center
Barton Springs Rd
Miller St
S Lamar Blvd
S Lamar Blvd
West Bouldin Creek
East Bouldin Creek
5th St S
Bouldin Ave
3rd St S
S 2nd St
S 1st St
Texas State School for the Deaf
S Congress Ave
Nellie St
Academy Dr
SOCO
W James St
Newton St
W Gibson St
E Gibson St
The Circle
Park La
Newning Ave
W Elizabeth St
W Monroe St
W Elizabeth St
W Monroe St
W Annie St
Eva St
Nickerson St
Travis Park
Festival Beach

Downtown Austin

Sights

1 AMOA-Arthouse E3
2 Austin Children's Museum D4
3 Bat Colony Under Congress Ave Bridge D5
4 Blanton Museum of Art F1
5 Bob Bullock Texas State History Museum E1
6 Mexic-Arte Museum E4
7 Texas State Capitol E2

Activities, Courses & Tours

8 Austin Ghost Tours E5
9 Bicycle Sport Shop B6
10 Capital Cruises D5
11 Lone Star Riverboat D5
12 Mellow Johnny's Bike Shop C4

Sleeping

13 AT&T Executive Education & Conference Center E1
14 Austin Motel C7
15 Brava House B1
16 Driskill Hotel E4
17 Extended StayAmerica D3
18 Firehouse Hostel E4
19 Heywood Hotel G6
Hotel San José .... (see 47)
20 Hotel St Cecilia D7
21 Kimber Modern D8
22 Pecan Grove RV Park A5
23 Radisson Hotel & Suites D5

Eating

24 Amy's Ice Cream B3
25 Austin Java Company C2
26 Chez Nous E4
27 Franklin BBQ G3
28 Green Mesquite BBQ & More A5
29 Güero's Taco Bar C8
30 Hopdoddy Burger Bar C8
31 Jo's Coffee C7
32 La Condesa D4
33 Lambert's D4
34 Moonshine Patio Bar & Grill F5
35 Shady Grove Restaurant A5
36 South Congress Cafe C8
37 Texas Chili Parlor E2
38 Threadgill's World Headquarters C6

temperature hits 100, you'll be shivering in a jiff after you jump into this icy-cold natural-spring pool. Draped with century-old pecan trees, the area around the pool is a social scene in itself, and the place gets packed on hot summer days.

Zilker Park Boat Rentals CANOEING
(Map p60; ☎512-478-3852; www.zilkerboats.com; 2201 Barton Springs Rd; per hour/day $12/40; ⏲9am-dusk) This outfit rents 17ft canoes and open-deck ocean kayaks. It also has maps and will describe the best routes. The price includes paddles and life jackets; arrive early on the weekends before the boats are all gone.

Lady Bird Lake CANOEING
(Map p60; ☎512-459-0999; www.rowingdock.com; 2418 Stratford Dr; ⏲6:30am-8pm) Named after former first lady Lady Bird Johnson, Lady Bird Lake kind of looks like a river. And no wonder: it's actually a dammed-off section of the Colorado River that divides Austin into north and south. Get out on the water at the Rowing Dock, which rents kayaks, canoes and paddle boards for $10 to $20 per hour, and paddle boats for slightly more.

Deep Eddy Pool SWIMMING
(Map p60; ☎512-472-8546; www.deepeddy.org; 401 Deep Eddy Ave; adult/under 11yr/junior $3/1/2; ⏲8am-8pm Mon-Fri, 10am-8pm Sat & Sun) With its vintage 1930s bathhouse built as part of the Works Progress Administration, Texas' oldest swimming pool is fed by cold springs and surrounded by cottonwood trees. There are separate areas for waders and lap swimmers.

Disc Golf

Disc golf is big in Austin. The popular course at Pease Park is gone for good, but great alternatives abound:

Roy G Guerrero Disc Golf Course (Map p60; 517 S Pleasant Valley Rd) A brand-new course with 18 holes suitable for beginners and skilled players alike.

Zilker Park Disc Golf Course A fairly easy course with two sets of nine holes, centrally located in Zilker Park (p62).

Mary Moore Searight Metropolitan Park (907 Slaughter Lane) A South Austin fave just over a mile west of I-35.

Bartholomew District Park (5201 Berkman Dr) A hilly course north of downtown near the old airport.

Cycling & Hiking

Lined with over 10 miles of trails, Lady Bird Lake is a popular spot for hiking and biking. A trail runs most of the way along the lake's northern side, which is the south edge of downtown Austin. You can also hike or

39 Uchi A6
40 Vespaio C8
41 Whole Foods Market B3
42 Wink C2

Drinking & Nightlife
43 Casino El Camino E4
44 Club de Ville F3
45 East Side Showroom G4
46 Flipnotics A5
Hideout Coffee House & Theatre .... (see 58)
47 Hotel San José C8
Malverde .... (see 32)
48 Opal Divine's Freehouse C3
49 Rusty's E4
50 Scholz Garten F1
51 Violet Crown Social Club G4

Entertainment
52 Alamo Drafthouse Cinema E4
53 Austin Symphony F3
54 Cedar Street Courtyard D4
55 Continental Club C8
56 Elephant Room D4
Esther's Follies .... (see 57)
57 Flamingo Cantina F4
58 Hideout Coffee House & Theatre E4
59 Long Center for the Performing Arts C5
60 Lucky Lounge D4
61 Oilcan Harry's D4
62 Paramount Theatre E3
63 Red Eyed Fly F4
64 Saxon Pub A7
65 Stubb's Bar-B-Q F4
66 ZACH Theatre Center B5

Shopping
Allen's Boots .... (see 71)
67 Blackmail C7
68 Book People Inc C3
Lucy in Disguise .... (see 73)
69 Stag C8
70 Tesoros Trading Co C8
71 Uncommon Objects C8
72 Waterloo Records B3
73 Yard Dog C8

mountain bike for almost 8 miles along the Barton Creek Greenbelt, which can be entered near Barton Springs Pool.

If you head out to the Lady Bird Johnson Wildflower Center, plan some extra time to ride or skate the great 3.2-mile **Veloway track** (www.veloway.com; 4898 La Cross Ave; dawn-dusk) FREE nearby. The track runs clockwise, and no walking or running is permitted.

Tours

The downtown **visitor center** (Map p64; 866-361-87836, 512-474-5171; www.austintexas.org; 209 E Sixth St; 9am-5pm) has information and brochures for many of the following city tours.

Boat Tours

With a dock on the south shore of Lady Bird Lake near the Hyatt, **Lone Star Riverboat** (Map p64; 512-327-1388; www.lonestarriverboat.com; adult/senior/child 2-12yr $10/8/7) runs one-hour cruises on its double-decker paddle-wheel riverboat at 3pm each Saturday and Sunday, March through October. The company also offers nightly sunset bat-watching trips on its 32ft electric cruiser from March through October. See its website for parking tips.

Between March and November, **Capital Cruises** (Map p64; 512-480-9264; www.capitalcruises.com; adult/child/senior $10/5/8) offers competitively priced lake excursions

BEWARE OF THE GODDESS

She stood atop the Texas State Capitol for nearly 100 years, a star in one hand, a sword in the other. When the **Goddess of Liberty** was removed from her perch and lowered by helicopter as part of a capitol restoration project in 1985, no one had seen her up close since 1888. And, well, *wow*. How to put this? She was not a handsome woman.

Not only was she badly weathered, she was just drop-dead ugly, with hideously exaggerated features meant to be appreciated from 300ft below. She was also 16ft tall, so no one had the nerve to tell her. After making a cast for her replacement, they restored her to her former, er, beauty and put her on display at the Bob Bullock Texas State History Museum (p57), where you can have a face-to-face with the woman people for decades could only admire from afar.

and bat-watching trips that depart from a dock near the Hyatt at 208 Barton Springs Rd.

Austin Duck Adventures (☎512-477-5274; www.austinducks.com; adult/3-12yr/senior & student $26/16/24; ⏰check website for schedule) utilizes amphibious British Alvis Stalwarts, which start at the Visitors Center, parade around the state capitol, roll down Congress Ave and 6th St, then splash into Lake Austin. Tour guides provide a few entertaining historical tidbits along the way.

Driving Tours

For an interesting alternative to your stereotypical, run-of-the-mill bus and van tours, try **Texpert Tours** (☎512-383-8989; www.texperttours.com; per hour $80), led by affable public-radio host Howie Richey (aka the 'Texas Back Roads Scholar'). Historical anecdotes, natural history and environmental tips are all part of the educational experience. A three-hour tour of central Austin takes visitors to the state capitol, the Governor's Mansion and the top of Mt Bonnell.

Train Tours

The **Austin Steam Train Association** (☎512-477-8468; www.austinsteamtrain.org; adult $30-45, child $20-35, senior $27-42) runs seasonal weekend day trips. The *Hill Country Flyer* (six-hour excursion) and *Bertram Flyer* (three-hour excursion) steam trains go from Cedar Park north of Austin into the Texas Hill Country, with special themed entertainment runs, such as murder mysteries.

For a shorter, cheaper miniature-train ride, check out the Zilker Zephyr (p68) in Zilker Park.

Walking Tours

One of the best deals around are the **Historic Walking Tours** (☎866-361-87836, 512-474-5171; www.austintexas.org; ⏰9am Tue & Thu-Sat, 11am & 1pm Sun) FREE of downtown Austin, which leave from the capitol's south steps. Tours last between 60 and 90 minutes. Make reservations at least 48 hours in advance either online or by phone through the visitor center.

Austin Ghost Tours (Map p64; ☎512-853-9826; www.austinghosttours.com; adult $20) take visitors on tours of haunted buildings and streets in areas including the Old Pecan Street District or the Warehouse District. Downtown ghost tours last 90 minutes, usually departing around 8:30pm from the Moonshine Patio Bar & Grill, on Red River St.

Festivals & Events

Hotel rates soar and locals flee during SXSW and F1, so plan accordingly. For a complete list, check with the Austin CVB (p84).

South by Southwest MUSIC
(SXSW; www.sxsw.com; single festival $625-1150, combo pass $900-1600) One of the American

AUSTIN FOR CHILDREN

Austin is kid friendly, thanks to the casual south-central Texas lifestyle. In addition to the listings below, check out Zilker Park for outdoor fun and the Texas Memorial Museum on the University of Texas campus.

Austin Children's Museum (Map p64; ☎512-472-2499; www.austinkids.org; 201 Colorado St; admission $6.50, child under 12 months free; ⏰10am-5pm Tue-Sat, to 8pm Wed, noon-5pm Sun) Kids can try their hand at running a ranch, ordering a meal at the Global Diner and hanging upside down beneath a bridge, just like the real Austin bats. At time of writing, construction had begun on a brand-new facility at 1830 Simond Ave that will double the exhibit space, so check the website before you visit.

Zilker Zephyr (Map p60; ☎512-478-8286; 2201 Barton Springs Rd; adult/senior & child under 12yr $3/2; ⏰10am-5pm Mon-Fri, to dusk Sat & Sun) Trains on the Zilker Zephyr miniature railroad make the 25-minute, 2-mile ride along Barton Creek and Town Lake year-round. They leave the depot near the playground every hour on the hour weekdays and every 30 to 40 minutes on weekends.

Austin Nature & Science Center (Map p60; ☎512-327-8181; www.austintexas.gov/department/austin-nature-science-center; 301 Nature Center Dr; donations requested; ⏰9am-5pm Mon-Sat, noon-5pm Sun) In the northwestern area of Zilker Park, this center has exhibitions of native Texan mammals, birds, reptiles, amphibians and arthropods that have been injured and nursed back to health here. There are also outdoor nature trails lined with native plants, where you'll see bats, butterflies and birds.

music industry's biggest gatherings has now expanded to include film and interactive festivals. The city is absolutely besieged with visitors during this two-week window in mid-March, and many a new resident first came to Austin to hear a little live music. Also see box on p80.

Eeyore's Birthday Party CULTURE
(☎512-448-5160; www.eeyores.com; Pease Park, 1100 Kingsbury St) FREE Perhaps no other annual event proves Austin's offbeat flavor so completely. This event in late April, started during the hippy-dippy 1960s, has maypole dancing, live music and even a birthday cake for the namesake melancholy Winnie-the-Pooh character. You'll feel silly if you *don't* wear a costume.

Old Pecan Street Spring Arts Festival STREET CARNIVAL
(☎512-825-2634; www.oldpecanstreetfestival.com) A downtown arts-and-crafts street fair in early May with live rock, country, Latin and world music and kids' carnival rides along E 6th St.

Austin Pride PARADE
(www.austinpride.org) Austin's gay pride celebration in September is one of Texas' largest, with block parties, music and a parade.

Austin City Limits Music Festival MUSIC
(ACL; www.aclfestival.com; 3-day pass $200-225) Move over, SXSW. This growing October festival is a favorite with the locals and is gaining swiftly on the March event, with over 100 pretty impressive acts filling the eight stages in Zilker Park. Tickets usually sell out months in advance.

Austin Film Festival FILM
(☎800-310-3378, 512-478-4795; www.austinfilmfestival.com) Hollywood and independent filmmakers and screenwriters flock to this multiday event held at various venues in mid-October.

Formula 1 Grand Prix RACE
(www.formula1.com) A brand-spanking-new racetrack means a city besieged by F1 fans during this high-octane weekend in November.

Sleeping

There's no shortage of rooms, until major events come to town, such as SXSW, the Formula 1 Grand Prix, the ACL festival and the Thanksgiving Day football game between UT and Texas A&M. At these peak times prices skyrocket and rooms are booked months in advance. At other times, choose accommodations as close to downtown as you can afford.

Chains litter I-35, and while they may not offer the best Austin experience, there are deals to be had through online travel discounters.

WHAT THE...? MOONLIGHT TOWERS

Keep an eye out for Austin's moonlight towers. All the rage in the late 1800s, these 165ft-tall street lamps were designed to give off the light of a full moon. Austin is the only city in which these historic triangular metal towers topped by a halo of six large bulbs still operate. Fifteen burn bright around the city: how many can you spot?

Central Austin & Downtown

For the most part, downtown hotels come with downtown prices, but they do keep you close to the action.

★**Firehouse Hostel** HOSTEL $
(Map p64; ☎512-201-2522; www.firehousehostel.com; 605 Brazos St; dm $29-32, r $70-90, ste $120-145;) A hostel in downtown Austin? Finally! And a pretty darned spiffy one, at that. Opened in January of 2013 in a former firehouse, it's still fresh and new, and the downtown location right across from the historic Driskill Hotel is as perfect as you can get.

Brava House B&B $$
(Map p64; ☎512-478-5034; www.bravahouse.com; 1108 Blanco St; d $139-179, ste $159-250; P) Located right downtown, this B&B has two lovely rooms and three spacious suites, each one with different things to offer: choose a canopy bed in the Moroccan-style Casablanca Room, a claw-foot bathtub in the Garbo Suite and tons of space in the 650-sq-ft Monroe Suite.

Extended StayAmerica BUSINESS HOTEL $$
(Map p64; ☎800-398-7829, 512-457-9994; www.extendedstayamerica.com; 600 Guadalupe St; d $100-130; P) This extended-stay hotel has an excellent downtown location, walking distance to tons of bars and restaurants. Suites are a little on the bland side but

include a kitchenette stocked with utensils, and the weekly rates ($85 per night) are a great excuse to hang out in Austin a while.

Other locations around town will net you even better rates, if not the same easy proximity to everything you'll love about Austin.

Radisson Hotel & Suites HOTEL **$$**
(Map p64; ☎800-395-7046, 512-478-9611; www.radisson.com/austintx; 111 E Cesar Chavez St; d $169-239; P ❄ 📶 🏊) Bats? Yes, bats. This is a great place from which to watch their nightly exodus from under the Congress Avenue Bridge. It puts you right on the water and upstairs from the hiking and biking trail around Lady Bird Lake.

★Heywood Hotel BOUTIQUE HOTEL **$$$**
(Map p64; ☎512-271-5522; www.heywoodhotel.com; 1609 E Cesar Chavez St; d $179-249; P ❄ 📶) Befitting its up-and-comer status, Austin's East Side (formerly 'The Land that Lodging Forgot') finally has a hotel to call its own. The Heywood is a seven-room gem that puts equal emphasis on design and comfort. The contemporary furnishings create a serene and sophisticated oasis, and the rooms are designed for privacy.

★Driskill Hotel HISTORIC HOTEL **$$$**
(Map p64; ☎800-252-9367, 512-474-5911; www.driskillhotel.com; 604 Brazos St; r $199-299, ste $300-900; P ❄ 📶) Every city should have a beautiful old historic hotel made out of native stone, preferably built in the late 1800s by a wealthy cattle baron. No generic hotel decor here; this place is pure Texas, from the leather couches to the mounted longhorn head on the wall. (Not to worry: the elegant rooms are taxidermy-free.)

A bit of trivia? LBJ and Lady Bird had their first date here. Valet parking is a lofty $28 per night.

South Austin

South Austin has lots of interesting options, and the ones clustered around Congress Ave still keep you plenty close to downtown.

Pecan Grove RV Park CAMPGROUND **$**
(Map p64; ☎512-472-1067; 1518 Barton Springs Rd; RV sites with full hookups per day $35-40, per week $220-250; P 📶) The name says it all. Located in a shady grove of pecan trees, this pleasant RV park is exceedingly well located. It's smack dab in the middle of town and just steps away from the ever-popular Shady Grove Restaurant. Your RV never had it so good.

HI – Austin HOSTEL **$**
(Austin Hostel; Map p60; ☎800-725-2331, 512-444-2294; www.hiusa.org/austin; 2200 S Lakeshore Blvd; dm members/nonmembers $22/25; @ 📶) Just 2.5 miles from downtown, this 47-bed hostel is located on a shady street right on the shore of Lady Bird Lake. Two-story views of the water from the sunny great room – complete with fish tank, guitar and comfy couches – might make even nonhostelers consider a stay.

The facilities are clean, tidy and cheerful. And with 24-hour access you can enjoy it at your leisure – although they do ask that all jam sessions end by 11pm.

★Hotel San José BOUTIQUE HOTEL **$$**
(Map p64; ☎512-444-7322; www.sanjosehotel.com; 1316 S Congress Ave; r with shared bathroom $95-145, with private bathroom $165-285; P ❄ 📶 🏊) Local hotelier Liz Lambert revamped a 1930s-vintage motel into a chic SoCo retreat with minimalist rooms in stucco bungalows, native Texas gardens and a very Austin-esque hotel bar in the courtyard that's known for its celebrity-spotting potential. South Congress has become quite the scene, and this hotel's location puts you right in the thick of it.

★Austin Motel MOTEL **$$**
(Map p64; ☎512-441-1157; www.austinmotel.com; 1220 S Congress Ave; r $84-139, ste $163; P ❄ 📶 🏊) 'Garage-sale chic' is the unifying factor at this wonderfully funky motel that embodies the spirit of the 'Keep Austin Weird' movement. Each room is individually decorated with whatever happened to be lying around at the time, and with varying degrees of success.

Take your chances, or handpick your room from the website, which has a picture of each and every one. Poolside suites are huge, and No 138 is especially cheery.

Kimber Modern BOUTIQUE HOTEL **$$$**
(Map p64; ☎512-912-1046; www.kimbermodern.com; 110 The Circle; r incl breakfast $250-295; P 📶) Staying in one of the five rooms at the architecturally adept Kimber is like staying in a minimalist art museum, with lots of white space accented by splashes of color. But the patio – now that's a different story altogether. If the rooms feel sterile, just step outside and relax under the insanely sprawling live oak.

Hotel St Cecilia BOUTIQUE HOTEL **$$$**

(Map p64; ☎512-852-2400; www.hotelsaintcecilia.com; 112 Academy Dr; ste $295-900; P ❄ ☎ ≋) The hustle and bustle of South Congress melts away the moment you cross over onto the serene lawn graced by a 300-year-old live oak. Choose from a suite in the Victorian-style house (c 1888) furnished with the perfect blend of modern, vintage and artistic touches, a studio in the main building, or one of the sleek poolside bungalows.

A splurge, to be sure – but if you have the time to stick around and enjoy it, this place really gets under your skin.

University of Texas Area & Hyde Park

Your best bet for finding a bed and breakfast, with several located around the southwest corner of campus. Hyde Park was Austin's first suburb and sits just north of campus.

Habitat Suites HOTEL **$**

(Map p60; ☎800-535-4663, 512-467-6000; www.habitatsuites.com; 500 E Highland Mall Blvd; ste incl breakfast $89-139; P ❄ @ ☎ ≋) Locally owned and ecofriendly, this quiet place is tucked away just north of downtown, away from the hustle and bustle. The furnishings may be slightly past their prime, but practical travelers will get a lot for their money here.

The property feels like an apartment complex, both inside and out, which means plenty of room to make yourself at home. You won't go hungry, either: rates include a hot breakfast and hospitality hour, and all suites have full kitchens. Traveling with the family? Spread out in a two-bedroom suite.

College Houses Cooperatives DORM **$**

(Map p60; ☎512-476-5678; www.collegehouses.org; r per person $25) During the summer when (most of) the students have gone home, the empty rooms in the seven student coop houses are quite the bargain, and they keep you centrally located near the UT campus. The planning window is short, however: you have to give them 48 hours' notice, and they don't take reservations more than a week in advance.

Goodall Wooten DORM **$**

(Map p60; ☎512-472-1343; 2112 Guadalupe St; s & d $35; ❄ @) A private dorm near UT, 'the Woo' generally has rooms available mid-May to mid-August, and sometimes has space for travelers at other times of the year. Just the basics – expect sheets and toilet paper, but no decor – but each room has a small refrigerator. Cash only.

Adams House B&B **$$**

(Map p60; ☎512-453-7696; www.theadamshouse.com; 4300 Ave G; d $129-139, ste $169; P ❄ ☎) On a quiet corner in historic Hyde Park, the Adams House will have you feeling like a local resident in no time. The welcoming guestrooms have hardwood floors, high ceilings, wooden shutters and antique beds, all the better to make yourself at home.

During the week, guests can help themselves to a continental breakfast, and on the weekends get a full breakfast served in the dining room. Although there's no pool on site, it's just down the street from a city pool that's open during the summer months.

Mansion at Judge's Hill B&B **$$**

(Map p60; ☎800-311-1619, 512-495-1800; www.mansionatjudgeshill.com; 1900 Rio Grande St; d $159-399; P ❄ ☎) This stately building is hands down the most photogenic B&B in town. Weekend guests might have to fight their way through wedding parties or bridal photos – an unavoidable side effect of staying in a historic mansion with beautiful grounds – to get to their antique-clad rooms.

Inn at Pearl Street B&B **$$**

(Map p60; ☎512-478-0051; www.innpearl.com; 1809 Pearl St; d $175-215, ste $225; P ❄ ☎) This is a preservationist's dream come true. The owners picked up this run-down property, dusted it off and – well, they more than dusted it off. They completely restored it and decorated it in a plush European style.

The rooms come in a variety of flavors and are located in two separate buildings – Victoria House or Burton House – so check the website to find one that suits.

Star of Texas Inn B&B **$$**

(Map p60; ☎512-477-9639; www.staroftexasinn.com; 611 W 22nd St; r $95-225; P ❄ ☎) The buttercup-yellow building in the bustling West Campus area started as a private residence, spent some time as a fraternity house, and has now been outfitted with claw-foot tubs and Victorian furnishings. The wraparound porches might sag a bit, but they're a gracious place to sit a spell.

If the main house is full, they can set you up at Austin Folk House, their sister property just down the street, or in their newly opened but unimaginatively named Building 2, which sits just behind the main house.

Austin Folk House B&B $$

(Map p60; ☎866-472-6700, 512-472-6700; www.austinfolkhouse.com; 506 W 22nd St; d $95-225; P 📶) One part gallery, one part B&B, the Austin Folk House has colorful and whimsical folk art in every room and up and down the halls. The rooms are comfortable (though some are a little fussy) and it's right in the bustling West Campus area.

AT&T Executive Education & Conference Center HOTEL $$$

(Map p64; ☎512-404-1900; www.downtownaustinhotel.com; 1900 University Ave; d $189-249; ❄ 📶) This swanky hotel on the UT campus is perfect for alums who want to relive their college days but in much higher style. References to UT abound, but the motif is so subtle that nonalums would never notice – think burnt-orange accent walls, historical campus photos and leather headboards (sorry, Bevo).

Greater Austin

Emma Long Metropolitan Park CAMPGROUND $

(☎512-346-1831; 1706 City Park Rd; tent/RV sites with hookup $10/20, plus entrance fee per car Mon-Thu/Fri-Sun $5/10; ⏲gates open 7am-10pm daily; P 🐾) The only Austin city park with overnight camping, 1000-acre Emma Long Metropolitan Park (aka 'City Park') on Lake Austin, 16 miles northwest of downtown, has good swimming, sunbathing, fishing and boating. Get here early as it fills quickly and doesn't take reservations.

Eating

Barbecue and Tex-Mex are the mainstays, but Austin also has many fine-dining restaurants and a broadening array of world cuisines. For hot tips on new restaurants, pick up the free alternative weekly *Austin Chronicle,* or *Xlent,* both published on Thursday. Downtown eateries are a real mixed bag, serving tourists, business folks, politicians, artists and night-owl clubbers. South Austin, Hyde Park and East Austin have lots of interesting choices. Around the UT campus area, prices drop – but often so does food quality.

Central Austin & Downtown

Whole Foods Market MARKET $

(Map p64; www.wholefoods.com; 525 N Lamar Blvd; sandwiches $6-9, mains $6-15; ⏲7am-10pm; 📶) The flagship of the Austin-founded Whole Foods Market is a gourmet grocery and cafe with restaurant counters and a staggering takeaway buffet, including self-made salads, global mains, deli sandwiches and more.

Austin Java Company CAFE $

(Map p64; ☎512-476-1829; 1206 Parkway; mains $6-10; ⏲7am-11pm Mon-Fri, from 8am Sat & Sun; 👪) Uniquely Austin, this restaurant disguised as a coffee shop has a relaxed atmosphere and tons and tons of good, cheap food to choose from. There are five other locations in town, but only this one has a large bug on the roof, left over from the building's days as a Terminix office.

KEEP AUSTIN WEIRD

Bumper stickers and T-shirts insist upon it, but are they succeeding? Check out www.keepaustinweird.com to find out what's odd right now. In the meantime, here's a sampling of the things that set Austin apart:

- Eccentric storefronts on S Congress Ave and North Loop Blvd.
- Eeyore's Birthday Party (p69), an annual festival where weirdness reigns supreme.
- The **Cathedral of Junk** (☎512-299-7413; 4422 Lareina Dr), a climbable backyard sculpture that turns discarded items into art.
- The homegrown **Museum of Natural & Artificial Ephemerata** (Map p60; www.mnae.org; $4), open eight days a year.
- Master Pancake Theater or any other offbeat event at Alamo Drafthouse (p81).
- Chicken-shit bingo at Ginny's Little Longhorn (p78).
- December's crazy Christmas lights on 37th St east of Lamar.
- A disproportionate but well-deserved local obsession with dive bars.

Texas Chili Parlor TEX-MEX $

(Map p64; ☎512-472-2828; 1409 Lavaca St; mains $5-10; ⏱11am-2am) Ready for an X-rated meal? When ordering your chili, keep in mind that 'X' is mild, 'XX' is spicy, and 'XXX' is melt-your-face-off hot at this Austin institution. There's more than just chili on the menu; there's also Frito pie, which is chili over Fritos. Still not feeling it? There's also burgers, enchiladas and, of course, more chili.

Moonshine Patio Bar & Grill AMERICAN $$

(Map p64; ☎512-236-9599; www.moonshinegrill.com; 303 Red River St; dinner mains $11-21; ⏱11am-10pm Mon-Thu, to 11pm Fri & Sat, 9am-2pm & 5-10pm Sun) Dating from the mid-1850s, this historic building is a remarkably well preserved homage to Austin's early days. Within its exposed limestone walls, you can enjoy upscale comfort food, half-price appetizers at happy hour or a lavish Sunday brunch buffet ($16.95). Or, chill on the patio under the shade of pecan trees.

La Condesa MEXICAN $$

(Map p64; ☎512-499-0300; www.lacondesa.com; 400 W 2nd St; small plates $7-16, mains $18-26; ⏱dinner Mon-Wed, 5-11pm Thu & Fri, 11am-11pm Sat, lunch & dinner Sun) Here in slacky Slackerville, decor is often an afterthought, but La Condesa came along and changed all that with an eye-poppingly gorgeous space that's colorful, supermodern and artsy, with a dazzling mural taking up an entire wall. If you find their dinners to be a little spendy, come for brunch (in the $10 to $14 range).

Chez Nous FRENCH $$$

(Map p64; ☎512-473-2413; www.cheznousaustin.com; 510 Neches St; lunch $8-19, dinner mains $20-37; ⏱lunch 11:45am-2pm Tue-Fri, dinner 6-10:30pm Tue-Sun) This classic Parisian-style bistro has been quietly serving excellent food since 1982. Low-key and casual, Chez Nous is as unpretentious as they come, and has made many a French food lover *trés heureux* (very happy), especially with its three-course menu du jour for $28.50.

★ **Lambert's** BARBECUE $$$

(Map p64; ☎512-494-1500; 401 W 2nd St; mains $14-42; ⏱11am-2pm & 5:30-10pm) Torn between barbecue and fine dining? Lambert's serves intelligent updates of American comfort-food classics – some might call it 'uppity barbecue' – in a historic stone building run by Austin chef Lou Lambert. Sides are extra, so be prepared to spend. Or, come early and nosh on half-price appetizers at happy hour (5pm till 7pm).

> **WORTH A TRIP**
>
> **DETOUR: TEXAS BARBECUE TRAIL**
>
> They call it the **Texas Barbecue Trail** (www.texasbbqtrails.com): 80 artery-clogging miles' worth of the best brisket, ribs and sausage Texas has to offer, stretching from Taylor, Texas (36 miles northeast of Austin) down to Luling, passing through Elgin and Lockhart along the way. Marketing gimmick? Perhaps. Do our stomachs care? They do not. If your schedule or limited appetite make driving two hours and eating at 12 different barbecue restaurants unfeasible, make a beeline for brisket in Lockhart, or if it's hot sausage you crave, Elgin is your best bet.

Wink FUSION $$$

(Map p64; ☎512-482-8868; 1014 N Lamar Blvd; mains $17-33; ⏱6-10pm Mon-Wed, 5:30-11pm Thu-Sat) Date night? At this intimate gem hidden behind Whole Earth Provision Co, diners are ushered to tables underneath windows screened with Japanese rice paper, then presented with an exceptional wine list. The chef-inspired fare takes on a nouveau fusion attitude that is equal parts modern French and Asian. For a special splurge, try the five-course ($68) tasting menu.

South Austin

With more variety than any other neighborhood in the city, South Austin is a sure-fire choice for any appetite. Reservations are recommended for top-end restaurants.

★ **Hopdoddy Burger Bar** BURGERS $

(Map p64; ☎512-243-7505; www.hopdoddy.com; 1400 S Congress Ave; burgers $6-12; ⏱11am-10pm Sun-Thu, to 11pm Fri & Sat) People line up around the block for the burgers, fries and shakes – and it's not because burgers, fries and shakes are hard to come by in Austin. It's because this place slathers tons of love into everything it makes, from the humanely raised beef to the locally sourced ingredients to the fresh-baked buns. The sleek, modern building is pretty sweet too.

Lick ICE CREAM $
(Map p60; www.ilikelick.com; 2032 S Lamar Blvd; ⏲12:30-10pm Sun-Thu, to 11:30pm Fri & Sat) While we've always been suckers for Amy's Ice Cream, we couldn't help but be wooed by Lick's creative flavor combinations, like coconut and avocado, or roasted beet and fresh mint, all made with local, seasonal ingredients. Dairy-free and vegan options available.

Jo's Coffee SANDWICHES $
(Map p64; ☎512-444-3800; www.joscoffee.com; 1300 S Congress Ave; sandwiches $5; ⏲7am-9pm Sun-Fri, to 10pm Sat; 📶) Walk-up window, shaded patio, plus great people-watching... throw in breakfast tacos, gourmet deli sandwiches and coffee drinks. Stick it in the middle of hopping South Congress, and you've got a classic Austin hangout.

Bouldin Creek Coffee House VEGETARIAN $
(Map p60; ☎512-416-1601; 1900 S 1st St; meals $5-9; ⏲7am-midnight Mon-Fri, 8am-midnight Sat & Sun; 📶🖊) You can get your veggie chorizo scrambler or organic oatmeal with apples all day long at this vegan-vegetarian eatery. It's got an eclectic South Austin vibe and is a great place for people-watching, finishing your novel or joining a band.

Green Mesquite BBQ & More BARBECUE $
(Map p64; ☎512-479-0485; www.greenmesquite.net; 1400 Barton Springs Rd; mains $6-11, kids' plates $5; ⏲11am-10pm) As its T-shirts say, Green Mesquite has been 'horrifying vegetarians since 1988.' This inexpensive, low-key spot has lots of tasty meat, pecan pie, cold beer and a shady outdoor area that's lovely on cool days.

Polvos MEXICAN $
(Map p60; ☎512-441-5446; 2004 S 1st St; breakfast $5-8, mains $9-16; ⏲8am-11pm) Fun, festive and just a little divey, Polvos serves central-Mexican food that always packs in a crowd. Try some of the dozen or so salsa varieties with one of the fierce margaritas.

Magnolia Cafe South AMERICAN $
(Map p60; ☎512-445-0000; www.themagnoliacafe.com; 1920 S Congress Ave; mains $5-11; ⏲24hr) This outpost of the original Westlake cafe attracts a mix of artists, surfers and bleary-eyed club-hoppers.

★Güero's Taco Bar TEX-MEX $$
(Map p64; ☎512-447-7688; 1412 S Congress Ave; mains $6-15; ⏲11am-10pm) Oh, Güero's, how we love you. Why must you make us wait? Well, clearly it's because of the three million other hungry people crammed into your bar area. Still, we'll try to be patient, because we love the atmosphere lent by the century-old former feed-and-seed store, and because we have an obsessive craving for your chicken tortilla soup.

Shady Grove Restaurant AMERICAN $$
(Map p64; ☎512-474-9991; www.theshadygrove.com; 1624 Barton Springs Rd; mains $7-12; ⏲11am-10:30pm Sun-Thu, to 11pm Fri & Sat) 'Do you want inside or out?' Really, what kind of question is that? We came for the shady patio, like everyone else. Outdoors under the pecan trees is prime real estate for enjoying everything from chili cheese fries to the vegetarian Hippie Sandwich.

Threadgill's World Headquarters SOUTHERN $$
(Map p64; ☎512-472-9304; www.threadgills.com; 301 W Riverside Dr; mains $8-15; ⏲11am-10pm Mon-Thu, to 10:30pm Fri & Sat, 10am-9:30pm Sun) Taking home cooking to a gluttonous new level, Threadgill's lets you choose from a ridiculously long list of vegetable sides – something you just don't get at home. Pair your meatloaf or chicken-fried steak with spinach casserole, butter beans, mac 'n' cheese (not technically a vegetable, but still) and classic mashed potatoes and gravy.

Uchi JAPANESE $$$
(Map p64; ☎512-916-4808; www.uchiaustin.com; 801 S Lamar Blvd; sushi & small plates $3-22; ⏲5-10pm Sun-Thu, to 11pm Fri & Sat) East and West collide beautifully at this top-notch South Austin sushi joint run by owner and executive chef Tyson Cole. The sleek interior would feel right at home in LA, and the sushi is every bit as fresh and imaginative as what you'd get there.

Vespaio ITALIAN $$$
(Map p64; ☎512-441-6100; 1610 S Congress Ave; mains $19-32; ⏲5-10:30pm Tue-Sat, to 10pm Sun & Mon) This cozy Italian restaurant gets high marks for its fresh, authentic, seasonal menus. You can always go the pizza or pasta route, but the critics' favorites are usually found among the *specialitas della casa.*

South Congress Cafe MEXICAN $$$
(Map p64; ☎512-447-3905; www.southcongresscafe.com; 1600 S Congress Ave; brunch $9-17, mains $14-28; ⏲10am-10pm Mon-Fri, 8am-10pm Sat & Sun) The stylish side of Tex-Mex can be found at this hoppin' little cafe, which

I SCREAM, YOU SCREAM

Short of jumping into Barton Springs, there's no better way to cool off than at **Amy's Ice Cream** (Map p64; ☎512-480-0673; www.amysicecreams.com; 1012 W Sixth St; ⊙11am-midnight Sun-Thu, to 1am Fri & Sat). It's not just the ice cream itself, which, by the way, is smooth, creamy and delightful. It's the toppings – pardon us, *crush'ns* they call 'em – that get pounded and blended in, violently but lovingly, by staff wielding a metal scoop in each hand. Mexican vanilla bean with fresh strawberries, dark chocolate with Reese's Peanut Butter Cups, or mango with jelly beans if that's what you're into. With 15 flavors (rotated from their 300 recipes) and dozens of toppings, ranging from cookies and candy, to fruit or nuts, the combinations aren't endless, but they number too high to count. Look for other locations on Guadalupe St north of the Universtiy of Texas campus, on South Congress near all the shops, or at the airport for a last-ditch fix.

seamlessly combines a vintage space with modern architecture. Come for half-price appetizers during happy hour from 3pm to 6pm weekdays; stay for dinner.

University of Texas Area & Hyde Park

Avoid the bland, student-oriented fare that crowds Guadalupe St (aka the Drag). There are still plenty of cheap eats in the UT area.

Kerbey Lane Café AMERICAN **$**
(Map p60; ☎512-451-1436; www.kerbeylanecafe.com; 3704 Kerbey Lane; breakfast $5-8, lunch & dinner $7-12; ⊙24hr;) Kerbey Lane is a longtime Austin favorite, fulfilling round-the-clock cravings for anything from gingerbread pancakes to black-bean tacos to mahimahi. Try the addictive Kerbey Queso while you wait. (It has vegan queso too!) There are several other locations around town, but this location in a homey bungalow is the original and has the most character.

New World Deli SANDWICHES **$**
(Map p60; ☎512-451-7170; www.newworlddeli.com; 4101 Guadalupe St; sandwiches $5-8; ⊙9am-9pm Mon-Sat, 10am-5pm Sun) Fans of the sandwich will be delighted with the offerings at New World, whether they're after a sloppy joe, pastrami on rye, or curried chicken salad on wheat – all of which are made with New World's amazing, fresh-baked bread, and all of which will raise the bar on what you'll expect from any future sandwiches you encounter.

Freebirds World Burrito MEXICAN **$**
(Map p60; ☎512-451-5514; www.freebirds.com; 1000 E 41st St; burritos $5-8; ⊙10:30am-10:30pm Sun-Thu, to 11pm Fri & Sat) Burritos – and nothing but – are why you come to Freebirds. Each one is custom-made under your watchful eye, with a boggling number of combinations of tortilla, meat and toppings. For a place with kind of a rock-and-roll atmosphere, the staff is surprisingly friendly and helpful.

Trudy's Texas Star TEX-MEX **$$**
(Map p60; ☎512-477-2935; www.trudys.com; 409 W 30th St; mains $7-12; ⊙4pm-2am Mon-Thu, from 11am Fri, from 9am Sat & Sun) Get your Tex-Mex fix here; the menu is consistently good, with several healthier-than-usual options. But we'll let you in on a little secret: this place could serve nothing but beans and dirt and people would still line up for the margaritas, which might very well be the best in Austin.

Hyde Park Bar & Grill AMERICAN **$$**
(Map p60; ☎512-458-3168; www.hpbng.com; 4206 Duval St; mains $8-13; ⊙11am-10:30pm Sun-Thu, to midnight Fri & Sat) Look for the enormous fork out front to guide you to this homey neighborhood haunt. The diverse menu has plenty of options, but no matter what you choose, we must insist that you order the batter-dipped French fries, which is what this place is famous for.

★Uchiko JAPANESE **$$$**
(Map p60; ☎512-916-4808; 4200 N Lamar Blvd; small plates $6-22, sushi rolls $9-14; ⊙5-10pm Sun-Thu, to 11pm Fri & Sat) Not content to rest on his Uchi laurels, Chef Tyson Cole opened this North Lamar restaurant that describes itself as 'Japanese farmhouse dining.' But we're here to tell you, it's hard to imagine being treated to fantastic and unique delicacies such as these and enjoying this sort of bustling ambience in any Japanese farmhouse. Reservations are highly recommended.

East Austin

East Austin's ethnic eateries are worthy of notice, especially if you're already sightseeing in the neighborhood. This area is majorly up-and-coming, especially on 6th and 7th Sts. Look for new bars and restaurants in the blocks just east of I-35.

★Franklin BBQ — BARBECUE **$**

(Map p64; ☎512-653-1187; www.franklinbarbecue.com; 900 E 11th St; mains $6-13; ⏲11am-2pm Tue-Sun) It only serves lunch, and only till it runs out – usually well before 2pm. Don't wait till you're hungry to find out whether it's worth the insane amount of hype; in fact, just try not to be hungry, period, because there is usually a long line of people waiting before it even opens.

When your moment of glory arrives, go for the two-meat plate, or nab all you can for a feast to enjoy later. (Just be quick about it. The people behind you are starving.)

El Chilito — TEX-MEX **$**

(Map p60; ☎512-382-3797; www.elchilito.com; 2219 Manor Rd; tacos & burritos $2-6; ⏲7am-10pm Mon-Fri, from 8am Sat & Sun) If you want quick, cheap and easy, this walk-up taco stand (with a big deck for your dining pleasure) can't be beat. You've got to try breakfast tacos while you're in Austin, and this is a good place to get them.

Mi Madre's — MEXICAN **$**

(Map p60; ☎512-322-9721; www.mimadresrestaurant.com; 2201 Manor Rd; tacos $2-4, mains $6-10; ⏲6am-2pm Mon & Tue, to 10pm Wed-Sat, 8am-4pm Sun) *Barbacoa*, chorizo and *adobado* are just a few of the authentic Mexican specialties here. In fact, it was recommended by a friend who said the *barbacoa* was just like his grandma used to make. Praise doesn't come much higher than that.

★Salty Sow — AMERICAN **$$**

(Map p60; ☎512-391-2337; 1917 Manor Rd; small plates $8-12, mains $12-18; ⏲4:30-10pm Mon-Thu, to 11pm Fri & Sat) Behold the porcine wonder! This snout-to-tail restaurant advertising 'swine + wine' offers a thoroughly modern take on down-home cooking, including plenty of choices in the nonpork category.

Once you step inside, the modern farmhouse atmosphere makes you forget it's housed inside a dowdy cinderblock building. We especially love the patio when the weather allows.

El Chile — TEX-MEX **$$**

(Map p60; ☎512-457-9900; www.elchilecafe.com; 1809 Manor Rd; lunch $8-11, dinner mains $11-15; ⏲11am-9pm Sun-Mon, to 10pm Tue-Sat) Let the comfy red chairs on the patio scoop you up for half-price appetizers at happy hour. Grab a spicy, orange-infused Chilango Margarita, or stay for enchiladas and other *especialidades*.

Greater Austin

Reservations are essential at the top-end places.

Magnolia Cafe — CAFE **$**

(Map p60; ☎512-478-8645; www.themagnoliacafe.com; 2304 Lake Austin Blvd; mains $5-11; ⏲24hr) In Westlake, opposite Deep Eddy Cabaret, this casual, all-night cafe serves American and Tex-Mex standbys such as *migas*, enchiladas, pancakes and potato scrambles. It gets absurdly crowded on weekends.

Whip In — INDIAN **$**

(☎512-442-5337; www.whipin.com; 1950 S I-35; mains $6-13; ⏲11am-3pm & 6-10pm Mon-Fri, 10am-3pm Sat & Sun) It started as a convenience store on a frontage road. Then the beer and Indian food started to take over. Now it's half Indian restaurant and half beer store, with a few groceries still hanging around to keep it confusing. Would we mention it if the food (breakfast naan and 'panaani' sandwiches) wasn't awesome? We would not.

★Salt Lick Bar-B-Que — BARBECUE **$$**

(☎512-858-4959; www.saltlickbbq.com; 18300 FM 1826, Driftwood; mains $11-20; ⏲11am-10pm; 👪) It's worth the 20-mile drive out of town just to see the massive outdoor barbecue pits at this parklike place off US 290. It's a bit of a tourist fave, but the crowd-filled experience still gets our nod. BYOB. Hungry? Choose the family-style all-you-can-eat option (adult/child $19.95/6.95).

Threadgill's Restaurant — SOUTHERN **$$**

(Map p60; ☎512-451-5440; 6416 N Lamar Blvd; mains $8-15; ⏲11am-10pm Mon-Sat, 10am-9:30pm Sun) Kenneth Threadgill's original restaurant and hootenanny palace in North Austin is where Janis Joplin once performed.

County Line — BARBECUE **$$**

(☎512-346-3664; 5204 FM 2222; mains $12-23; ⏲11am-9pm Sun & Mon, lunch & dinner Tue-Sat) Unless you have an enormous appetite, there's no need to splurge on the all-you-can-

COFFEE CULTURE

Austin's a laid-back kind of town, and there's no better way to cultivate your slacker vibe than hanging out, sipping coffee and watching everyone else doing the same. Most places offer light meals in addition to caffeinated treats. Here are a few of our favorites:

Bouldin Creek Coffee House (p74) Very representative of the South Austin scene, with a great vegetarian menu to boot.

Hideout Coffee House & Theatre (p80) Despite its downtown location, it has a near-campus vibe and damn fine brews.

Flipnotics (Map p64; ☎512-480-8646; 1601 Barton Springs Rd; ⏱7am-midnight Mon-Sat, 8am-11pm Sun) This is a good place to nurse a hangover or just chill with a cigarette on the back porch.

Mozart's Coffee Roasters (Map p60; ☎512-477-2900; 38255 Lake Austin Blvd; ⏱7am-midnight Mon-Thu, 7am-1am Fri, 8am-1am Sat, 8am-midnight Sun) Out on Lake Austin you'll find a great waterfront view and a sinful dessert case.

Spider House (Map p60; ☎512-480-9562; 2908 Fruth St; ⏱10am-2am) North of campus, Spider House has a big, funky patio bedecked with all sorts of oddities. It's open late and also serves beer and wine.

eat meals. Most of the combos and platters of delicious ribs, brisket and sausage are – truly – all you can eat. We love the lakeside location (enjoy a beer on the dock while you wait) and the lake-lodge decor.

Fonda San Miguel MEXICAN **$$$**
(Map p60; ☎512-459-4121; 2330 W North Loop Blvd; mains $16-25; ⏱5:30-9:30pm Mon-Thu, to 10:30pm Fri & Sat, 11am-2pm Sun) The gorgeous building is drenched in the atmosphere of old Mexico, with folk-inspired art, and this place has been serving interior Mexican cooking for over 25 years. The Sunday brunch buffet is an impressive event but, at $39 per person, you'd better come hungry to make it worthwhile. Note that the last seating is one hour before close.

Drinking & Nightlife

There are bejillions of bars in Austin. The legendary 6th St bar scene has spilled onto nearby thoroughfares, especially Red River St. Many of the new places on Sixth St are shot bars aimed at party-hardy college students and tourists, while the Red River establishments retain a harder local edge.

We can't tell you the best dance club in town, because on any given day, it just closed down last week. (Its clientele was probably too busy seeing live music.) Your best bet is to pick up the free *Austin Chronicle* for fresh listings, or wander Sixth St or the Warehouse District and follow the thumping beat.

That said, if you are ready for a little Texas two-steppin', there is only one place you should dream of going: the **Broken Spoke** (Map p60; www.brokenspokeaustintx.com; 3201 S Lamar Blvd; ⏱11am-midnight Tue-Thu, to 1am Fri & Sat). This is country-and-western nirvana – a totally authentic Texas dancehall that's been in business since 1964. Here you'll find dudes in boots and Wranglers two-stepping around a crowded dance floor alongside hipsters, college students and slackers; many consider it an essential Austin experience. (You'll know you've arrived when you spot a big old oak tree propping up an old wagon wheel out front.)

Downtown

Opal Divine's Freehouse BAR
(Map p64; ☎512-477-3308; 700 W 6th St; ⏱to midnight Sun-Tue, to 2am Wed-Sat) Named for the owner's grandmother, a woman who supposedly enjoyed 'good drink and a good card game,' this breezy and spacious pub serves microbrews, imported lagers and almost 20 types of tequila.

Scholz Garten BEER HALL
(Map p64; ☎512-474-1958; 1607 San Jacinto Blvd; ⏱ to midnight Sun-Thu, to 2am Fri & Sat) This German *biergarten* has been around forever – or at least since 1866 – and its proximity to the capitol building has made it the traditional favorite of politicians. (Writer O Henry was also a fan.)

Malverde BAR
(Map p64; ☎512-705-0666; 400 W 2nd St; ⊙10pm-2am Thu-Sat) Handcrafted specialty cocktails and DJs set the tone for this swanky upstairs bar (it's right above La Condesa restaurant). The outdoor patio with artful plant formations is a great place to watch the city below.

Red River

Casino El Camino BAR
(Map p64; ☎512-469-9330; 517 E 6th St; ⊙11:30am-2am) With a legendary jukebox and even better burgers, this is the spot for serious drinking and late-night carousing. If it's too dark inside, head for the back patio.

Club de Ville BAR
(Map p64; ☎512-457-0900; 900 Red River St; ⊙to 2am Mon-Sat) Before Red River was even a scene, Club de Ville was there serving cheap drinks in a space decorated with mismatched retro furniture. And that's not to mention its cool, leafy patio – one of downtown's best places to imbibe outdoors.

Around Austin

Get out of downtown to enjoy a wide variety of tippling opportunities.

★**Ginny's Little Longhorn Saloon** BAR
(Map p60; ☎512-407-8557; 5434 Burnet Rd; ⊙5pm-midnight Tue, 5pm-1am Wed-Sat, 2-8pm Sun) This funky little cinder-block building is one of those dive bars that Austinites love so very much – and did even before it became nationally famous for chicken-shit bingo on Sunday night.

★**Hotel San José** BAR
(Map p64; ☎512-444-7322; 1316 S Congress Ave) Transcending the hotel-bar genre, this one is actually a cool, Zen-like outdoor patio that attracts a chill crowd, and it's a nice place to hang if you want to actually have a conversation.

★**East Side Showroom** BAR
(Map p64; ☎512-467-4280; 1100 E 6th St; ⊙5pm-2am) With an ambience that would feel right at home in Brooklyn (in the late 1800s), this bar on the emerging east-side scene is full of hipsters soaking up the craft cocktails and bohemian atmosphere.

Violet Crown Social Club BAR
(Map p64; 1111 E 6th St; ⊙5pm-2am Mon-Fri, from 7pm Sat & Sun) It's dark. It's loud. At first glance it's not terribly inviting. But damn, the drinks are cheap, making this a popular spot on the East Sixth circuit.

Deep Eddy Cabaret BAR
(Map p60; ☎512-472-0961; 2315 Lake Austin Blvd; ⊙noon-2am) This great little neighborhood bar is known for its excellent jukebox, loaded with almost a thousand tunes in all genres. Yep, it's a dive, but a top-rate one.

Hula Hut THEME BAR
(Map p60; ☎512-476-4852; 3825 Lake Austin Blvd; ⊙11am-10pm Sun-Thu, to 11pm Fri & Sat) The hula theme is so thorough that this restaurant feels like a chain, even though it's not. But the bar's sprawling deck that stretches out over Lake Austin makes it a popular hangout among Austin's nonslackers.

☆ Entertainment

Austin calls itself the 'Live Music Capital of the World,' and you won't hear any argument from us. Music is the town's leading nighttime attraction, and a major industry as well, with several thousand bands and performers from all over the world plying their trade in the city's clubs and bars. Most bars stay open till 2am, while a few clubs stay hoppin' until 4am.

You can get heaps of information on the city's whole entertainment scene in the *Austin Chronicle* or the *Austin American-Statesman*'s *XLent* section, both out on Thursday. *XLent* has an ultrastreamlined 'Club Listings' chart that lets you plan your evening's entertainment at a glance, but the *Chronicle*'s night-by-night encyclopedia of

CHICKEN-SHIT BINGO

We love Ginny's Little Longhorn Saloon any old time, but for a uniquely Austin outing, you've really got to experience the Sunday-night phenomenon known as chicken-shit bingo. Beer-swilling patrons throw down their bets of $2 per square and wait to see what number the chicken 'chooses,' with the whole pot going to the winner. The chicken doesn't seem to mind, and most Sundays local favorite Dale Watson keeps everyone entertained while they wait for the results to drop.

listings often includes set times (handy if you'd like to hit several venues in one night), plus music critics' picks and local gossip to really plug you into the scene.

Advance tickets (which may be cheaper) for major venues are sold through **Star Tickets** (☎800-585-3737; www.startickets.com); it also handles some performing-arts and sports events.

Live Music

Music is a proud tradition in this part of the state, where you can see any kind of musical performance, from a four-piece bluegrass band kicking out jug tunes to a lone DJ spinning the latest trance grooves. The area's unique prominence on the country's musical stage can be traced all the way back to the German settlers who immigrated to the area in the mid-1800s, as well as to the rich musical heritage Texas has always shared with Mexico. Austin's modern sound first took shape in the early 1970s at a barn-like venue known as the Armadillo World Headquarters.

Today, most live-music bars and clubs have a mix of local and touring bands. On any given Friday night there are several hundred acts playing in the town's 200 or so venues, and even on an off night (Monday and Tuesday are usually the slowest) you'll typically have your pick of more than two dozen performances. Often there are two or three bands per venue each night. Cover charges range from $3 for local bands to $15 or more for touring acts. Music shows often start late, with the headliner starting anywhere from 9pm to midnight, though a few clubs offer music as early as 4pm, and doors almost always open half an hour to an hour before showtime. Showing up at the last minute or fashionably late may result in not getting in. If you want to get started early, most places have a happy hour (4pm to 7pm).

Although the part of Sixth St between I-35 and S Congress Ave has become more of a frat-boy-and-tourist scene, there are still a few venues for dependably great live shows, especially as you head west of Congress. West of Congress Ave, the Warehouse District is more about sexy salsa spots and swanky martini bars, but you'll also find a couple of decent live-music venues.

Many of the venues we recommend are Austin institutions. If you want to experience Austin's music scene but aren't sure where to start, any of these are good bets.

★Continental Club LIVE MUSIC
(Map p64; ☎512-441-0202; www.continentalclub.com; 1315 S Congress Ave) No passive toe-tapping here; this 1950s-era lounge has a dance floor that's always swinging with some of the city's best local acts.

Stubb's Bar-B-Q LIVE MUSIC
(Map p64; ☎512-480-8341; www.stubbsaustin.com; 801 Red River St; ⏰11am-10pm Mon-Thu, to 11pm Fri & Sat, to 9pm Sun) Stubb's has live music almost every night, with a great mix of premier local and touring acts from across the musical spectrum. Many warm-weather shows are held out back along Waller Creek. There are two stages, a smaller stage indoors and a larger backyard venue.

Saxon Pub LIVE MUSIC
(Map p64; ☎512-448-2552; www.thesaxonpub.com; 1320 S Lamar Blvd) The super-chill Saxon Pub, presided over by 'Rusty,' a huge knight who sits out the front, has music every night, mostly Texas performers in the blues-rock vein. A great place to kick back, drink a beer and discover a new favorite artist.

Emo's East LIVE MUSIC
(Map p60; ☎512-693-3667; www.emosaustin.com; 2015 E Riverside Dr) For nearly 20 years, Emo's led the pack in the punk and indie scene in a crowded space on Red River St, and now it's got some shiny new digs (and a whole lot more space) out on Riverside.

Red Eyed Fly LIVE MUSIC
(Map p64; ☎512-474-1084; www.redeyedfly.com; 715 Red River St) On Waller Creek near Stubb's is the Fly, an anchor on the Red River scene. There's live music nightly, plus pool tables, a jukebox and extreme neon that bathes everyone in a creepy red glow.

Lucky Lounge LIVE MUSIC
(Map p64; ☎512-479-7700; www.theluckylounge.com; 209a W 5th St) Head for this no-pretense spot for early shows (usually starting around 8pm) with no cover charge. And check out that neon sign and mod '60s decor.

Cedar Street Courtyard LIVE MUSIC
(Map p64; ☎512-495-9669; www.cedarstreetaustin.com; 208 W 4th St; ⏰4pm-2am Mon-Fri, from 6pm Sat & Sun) Forget the dark and crowded club scene; this sophisticated courtyard venue serves martinis along with jazz and swing.

Elephant Room LIVE MUSIC
(Map p64; ☎512-473-2279; www.elephantroom.com; 315 Congress Ave; ⏰4pm-2am Mon-Fri, from

8pm Sat & Sun) This intimate, subterranean jazz club has a cool vibe, and live music almost every night. The cover charge stays low, mostly free except on weekends, and there are happy-hour shows at 6pm weekdays.

Flamingo Cantina LIVE MUSIC
(Map p64; ☎512-494-9336; www.flamingocantina.com; 515 E 6th St) Called 'the last place with soul on Sixth,' Austin's premier reggae joint prides itself on its good Rasta vibes and bouncy dance floor. Seat yourself on the carpeted bleachers for good views of the stage.

Donn's Depot LIVE MUSIC
(Map p60; ☎512-478-3142; www.donnsdepot.com; 1600 W 5th St; ⏱2pm-2am Mon-Fri, from 6pm Sat) Austin loves a dive bar, and Donn's combines a retro atmosphere inside an old railway car with live music six nights a week, including Donn himself performing alongside the Station Masters.

Comedy Clubs

Hideout Coffee House & Theatre COMEDY
(Map p64; ☎512-443-3688; www.hideouttheatre.com; 617 Congress Ave; tickets $6-13; ⏱shows usually Thu-Sun) The hipsters' Hideout is a small coffeehouse–theater space that rubs shoulders with the big theaters on Congress Ave. Shows here feature live improv with plenty of audience participation. The box office usually opens half an hour before showtime.

Esther's Follies COMEDY
(Map p64; ☎512-320-0553; www.esthersfollies.com; 525 E 6th St; general admission/reserved seating $22/27; ⏱shows 8pm Thu-Sat, plus 10pm Fri & Sat) Drawing from current events and pop culture, this long-running satire show has a vaudevillian slant, thanks to musical numbers and, yep, even a magician. Good, harmless fun.

Capitol City Comedy Club COMEDY
(☎512-467-2333; www.capcitycomedy.com; 8120 Research Blvd, Suite 100; ticket prices vary; ⏱shows 8pm daily, plus 10:30pm Fri & Sat) Far from downtown, Capitol City hosts national headliner comics. Mondays are often reserved for local talent.

Performing Arts

Austin has an active local theater scene, and a number of national and touring troupes find an excuse to stop off in the Capitol City as well. Check the *Austin Chronicle* or *XLent* for performance schedules.

Paramount Theatre THEATER
(Map p64; ☎512-474-1221; www.austintheatre.org; 713 Congress Ave; ⏱box office noon-5:30pm Mon-Fri, 2hr before showtime Sat & Sun) Dating from 1915, this old vaudevillian house has staged everything from splashy Broadway shows to stand-up comics to classic film screenings.

ZACH Theatre Center THEATER
(Map p64; ☎512-476-0541; www.zachtheatre.org; 202 S Lamar Blvd; ⏱box office noon-7pm Mon-Sat) Often reprising popular Broadway and off-Broadway hits, this theatre now has three venues: **Topfer Theatre** (202 S Lamar Blvd),

SXSW: SOUTH BY SOUTHWEST

For five nights in mid-March tens of thousands of record-label reps, musicians, journalists and rabid fans from around the country descend on Austin for South by Southwest (p68), a musical extravaganza that attracts a couple thousand groups and solo artists from around the world to 90 different Austin venues.

Though SXSW started out as an opportunity for little-known bands and singers to catch the ear of a record-label rep, it has since become a wildly popular industry showcase for already-signed bands. Add to that a hugely popular interactive festival, as well as a more subdued but still well-attended film festival, and you've got a major international draw that takes over the city and sends most of the locals into hiding for two weeks every spring.

You can buy a pass for just one of the three festivals, or go all out and buy a combo pass. However, what you can't do any more is buy a single-day pass. But this is one of those times when preplanning can save you a lot of money: early-bird tickets are on sale through mid-September and they can save you hundreds of dollars; then, the price inches up each month until the walk-up rate takes effect.

Too much hoopla? Come in October for a slightly more mellow experience at the **Austin City Limits Festival** (p69), an outdoor music festival at Zilker Park.

GAY & LESBIAN AUSTIN

With a thriving gay population – not to mention pretty mellow straight people – Austin is arguably the most gay-friendly city in Texas. The **Austin Gay & Lesbian Chamber of Commerce** (www.aglcc.org) sponsors the Pride Parade in June, as well as smaller events throughout the year. The *Austin Chronicle* (p84) runs a gay event column among the weekly listings, and the glossy *L Style/G Style* (www.lstylegstyle.com) magazine has a dual gal/guy focus.

Austin's gay and lesbian club scene is mainly in the Warehouse District, though there are outposts elsewhere.

Oilcan Harry's (Map p64; ☎512-320-8823; 211 W 4th St; ⏲2pm-2am Mon-Fri, noon-2am Sat & Sun) Oh, yes, there's dancing. And oh, yes, it's packed. (And how are you supposed to dance with all those people in there?) As much as the girls wish it were a mixed crowd, this scene is all about the boys. Sweaty ones.

Rusty's (Map p64; ☎512-482-9002; www.rustysaustin.com; 405 E 7th St; ⏲4pm-2am Wed-Sat, from 2pm Sun, to midnight Mon) A gay bar with a Texas twang. Rusty's hosts poker nights, karaoke nights, and, yes, country-dancing nights. Check the website to see what's going on.

Whisenhunt Stage (1510 Toomey Rd) and **Kleberg Stage** (1421 W Riverside Dr).

Hyde Park Theatre THEATER
(Map p60; ☎512-479-7529; www.fronterafest.org; 511 W 43rd St) This is one of Austin's coolest small theaters, presenting regional premieres of off-Broadway hits and recent Obie (Off-Broadway Theater Awards) winners. Its annual FronteraFest presents more than 100 new works over five weeks at venues around town.

Long Center for the Performing Arts PERFORMING ARTS
(Map p64; ☎512-474-5664; www.thelongcenter.org; 701 W Riverside Dr) This state-of-the-art theater opened in late 2008 as part of a waterfront redevelopment along Lady Bird Lake. The multistage venue hosts drama, dance, concerts and comedians.

Austin Symphony PERFORMING ARTS
(Map p64; ☎512-476-6064; www.austinsymphony.org; ticket office 1101 Red River St; tickets $19-48; ⏲box office 9am-5pm Mon-Fri, 2hr before showtime performance days) Founded in the early 20th century, the city's oldest performing-arts group plays classical and pop music at numerous venues throughout the city. The main performance season runs from September to April.

Cinema

Check the free *Austin Chronicle* weekly for movie reviews and cinema showtimes.

Alamo Drafthouse Cinema CINEMA
(Map p64; ☎512-476-1320; www.drafthouse.com; 320 E 6th St; admission $10) Easily the most fun you can have at the movies: sing along with *Grease,* quote along with *Princess Bride,* or just enjoy food and drink delivered right to your seat during first-run films. Check the website for other locations.

Austin Film Society CINEMA
(AFS; ☎512-322-0145; www.austinfilm.org) Frequent classic and independent film screenings at venues around town. *Slacker* director Richard Linklater was an early promoter and Quentin Tarantino is now on the board of directors.

Spectator Sports

The whole town turns burnt orange during UT game weekends, especially during football season, when the fiercely loyal Longhorn fans are downright fanatical. (They're not flipping you off: it's probably just the two-fingered sign for 'Hook 'em Horns.') For tickets to any university-sponsored sporting event, contact the UT ticket office (p59).

Shopping

Not many folks visit Austin just to shop. That said, music is a huge industry here and you'll find heaps of it in Austin's record stores. Employees are usually fairly knowledgeable and will likely be in a band themselves. The best stores let you listen to just about anything before you buy, and will carry the bands you see around town.

Vintage is a lifestyle, and the city's best hunting grounds for retro fashions and furnishings are South Austin and Guadalupe St near UT. (For more vintage-fashion options than those listed below, check out www.vintagearoundtownguide.com.)

For a complete list of art galleries and happenings around town, visit www.inthegalleriesaustin.com, or pick up an 'In the Galleries' brochure at any gallery.

On the first Thursday of the month, S Congress Ave is definitely the place to be, when stores stay open until 10pm and there's live entertainment; visit www.firstthursday.info for upcoming events.

★Uncommon Objects VINTAGE
(Map p64; ☎512-912-1613; 1512 S Congress Ave; ⊙11am-7pm Sun-Thu, to 8pm Fri & Sat) 'Curious oddities' is what they advertise at this quirky antique store that sells all manner of fabulous knickknackery, all displayed with an artful eye. More than 20 different vendors scour the state to stock their stalls, so there's plenty to look at.

Book People Inc BOOKS
(Map p64; ☎512-472-5050; 603 N Lamar Blvd; ⊙9am-11pm) Grab a coffee and browse the shelves of this lively independent bookstore across the street from Waterloo Records.

Yard Dog ART
(Map p64; ☎512-912-1613; www.yarddog.com; 1510 S Congress Ave; ⊙11am-5pm Mon-Fri, 11am-6pm Sat, noon-5pm Sun) Stop into this small but scrappy gallery (it's right next door to Uncommon Objects) that focuses on folk and outsider art.

Blackmail CLOTHING
(Map p64; ☎512-376-7670; 1202 S Congress Ave; ⊙10:30am-7pm Mon-Sat, 11am-6pm Sun) Black is the new black at this color-challenged store that unites Goths, punks and urban sophisticates. That means gorgeous black dresses and guayabera shirts, black-and-silver jewelry, black beaded handbags, black shoes and even minimalist black-and-white home decor.

Allen's Boots ACCESSORIES
(Map p64; ☎512-447-1413; 1522 S Congress Ave; ⊙9am-8pm Mon-Sat, noon-6pm Sun) In hip South Austin, family-owned Allen's sells rows upon rows of traditional cowboy boots for ladies, gents and kids. A basic pair costs from $50, while somethin' fancy runs a few hundred dollars.

Stag CLOTHING
(Map p64; ☎512-373-7824; www.stagaustin.com; 1423 S Congress Ave; ⊙11am-8pm Mon-Sat, to 6pm Sun) Embrace the art of manliness at this stylish SoCo store that's just for the guys, or for girls who are shopping for guys.

Waterloo Records MUSIC
(Map p64; ☎512-474-2500; www.waterloorecords.com; 600 N Lamar Blvd; ⊙10am-11pm Mon-Sat, from 11am Sun) If you want to stock up on music, this is the record store. There are sections reserved just for local bands, and listening stations featuring Texas, indie and alt-country acts.

University Co-op SOUVENIRS
(Map p60; ☎512-476-7211; 2246 Guadalupe St; ⊙8:30am-7:30pm Mon-Fri, 9:30am-6pm Sat, 11am-5pm Sun) Stock up on souvenirs sporting the Longhorn logo at this store brimming with school spirit. It's amazing the sheer quantity of objects that come in burnt orange and white.

Austin Art Garage ART
(Map p60; ☎512-351-5934; www.austinartgarage.com; 2200 S Lamar Blvd; ⊙11:30am-6:30pm Tue-Sat, noon-5pm Sun) This cool little independent…well, we hesitate to call it a 'gallery' because that would needlessly scare some people off. Anyway, it features some pretty great artwork by Austin artists. (Hey, Joel Ganucheau: we're fans.) Check out the website to catch the vibe, and definitely check out the 'gallery' if you like what you see.

Lucy in Disguise VINTAGE
(Map p64; ☎512-444-2002; www.lucyindisguise.com; 1506 S Congress Ave; ⊙11am-7pm Mon-Sat, noon-6pm Sun) Colorful and over the top, this South Congress staple has been outfitting Austinites for years. You can rent or buy costume pieces, which is this place's specialty, but you can also find everyday vintage duds as well.

Amelia's Retrovogue & Relics VINTAGE
(Map p60; ☎512-442-4446; www.ameliasretrovogue.com; 2213 S 1st St; ⊙noon-5pm Tue-Sat) Austin's queen of vintage high fashion, Amelia's brings together *Vogue*-worthy dresses, retro '50s bathing suits and other old-school glamour for both men and women. It's a favorite with film-industry folk.

Blue Velvet VINTAGE
(Map p60; ☎512-452-2583; www.bluevelvetaustin.com; 217 W North Loop Blvd; ⊙11am-8pm Mon-Sat, noon-8pm Sun) Western wear, vintage T-shirts

and even oddities such as all-American bowling wear hang on the racks at Blue Velvet, where you'll find an equal number of men and women eyeing the goods. Summer fashions are stocked year-round.

Buffalo Exchange CLOTHING
(Map p60; ☎512-480-9922; 2904 Guadalupe St; ⏰10am-9pm Mon-Sat, 11am-8pm Sun) The Austin branch of this nationwide used-clothing chain has an impressive selection of vintage clothes and shoes for men and women, including Texas styles and Western wear.

Antone's Records MUSIC
(Map p60; ☎512-322-0660; www.antones.com; 2928 Guadalupe St; ⏰10am-10pm Mon-Sat, 11am-8pm Sun) North of UT, legendary Antone's was founded in 1972 and has a well-respected selection of Austin, Texas and American blues music (with plenty of rare vinyl), plus a bulletin board for musicians, and vintage concert posters for sale.

Toy Joy TOYS
(Map p60; ☎512-320-0090; www.toyjoy.com; 2900 N Guadalupe St; ⏰10am-11pm Sun-Thu, to midnight Fri & Sat) Just north of campus, this colorful toy store for grown-ups and big kids is an exuberant repository that's packed floor to ceiling with fun. The store will move to 403 W 2nd St from late 2013.

Tesoros Trading Co HANDICRAFTS
(Map p64; ☎512-472-5050; 1500 S Congress Ave; ⏰11am-6pm Sun-Fri, 10am-6pm Sat) Browse folk art and crafts from around the world, with a heavy Latin American influence of metalwork, jewelry, colorfully painted handicrafts, the Virgin Mary, and Día de los Muertos.

Domain MALL
(☎512-795-4230; www.thedomainaustin.com; 11410 Century Oaks Tce; ⏰10am-9pm Mon-Sat, noon-6pm Sun) Stores like Neiman Marcus and Anthropologie line the streets of this upscale outdoor shopping center in far northwest Austin.

Barton Creek Mall MALL
(☎512-691-3500; www.simon.com/mall/barton-creek-square; 2901 S Capital of Texas Hwy; ⏰10am-9pm Mon-Sat, noon-7pm Sun) This is a standard indoor mall offering in southwest Austin.

Arboretum MALL
(☎512-338-4437; 10000 Research Blvd; ⏰10am-6pm Mon-Sat, noon-6pm Sun) About 20 minutes northwest of downtown, the Arboretum is a parklike collection of high-end stores, including Sharper Image and Restoration Hardware.

Orientation

Austin is bordered by highways. The main thoroughfare is I-35, running all the way from Dallas to the north, through the east side of downtown, and south to San Antonio. The other major north–south route is MoPac Expressway (locals just call it 'MoPac') on the west edge of town. Lamar Blvd runs parallel between the two and is a handy way to get around town. What most folks consider 'in town' is bounded by Hwy 183 to the north and Hwy 290 (also known as 'Ben White Blvd') to the south.

Information

The bulletin boards found outside coffeehouses, cafes and grocery stores are a great source of news about local events, special activities and classified ads.

DANGERS & ANNOYANCES

Common sense and awareness usually ensure problem-free travel in Austin. Some folks may tell you that anywhere east of I-35 is dangerous, but while there is some truth to that, overt or covert racism – this is a predominantly African American and Latino part of town – may exaggerate claims of danger.

One major complaint is drunken college students letting it all hang out on 6th St. It's a party atmosphere (imagine a small-scale Mardi Gras happening every weekend), and if you're drunkenly counting your cash and appraising your jewelry in an alley at 2am, you're as likely to encounter interest here as anywhere else. Transients and panhandlers congregate downtown near Congress Ave, especially from 4th through 7th Sts. Keep your wits about you when returning to your car at night, or hail a taxi (or a pedicab).

Austin natives claim they live in the allergy capital of America, and at any time of year visitors are likely to sneeze and wheeze along with the rest of the city's denizens. If you're at all susceptible, especially to pollen or mold, bring proper medication.

EMERGENCY

Emergency Animal Hospital & Clinic (☎Northwest Austin 512-331-6121, South Austin 512-899-0955)

Police (☎nonemergency 311, 512-974-2000)

INTERNET ACCESS

Free public internet access is available at any public-library branch; call ☎512-974-7301 for hours and locations. Downtown, **Faulk Central Public Library** (☎512-974-7400; 800 Guadalupe St; ⏰10am-9pm Mon-Thu, 10am-6pm

Fri & Sat, noon-6pm Sun) has dozens of wired terminals. Many coffee shops around town have free wi-fi. Try **Hideout Coffee House & Theatre** (Map p64; ☎512-443-3688; 617 Congress Ave; ⏰7am-11pm Mon-Thu, to 1am Fri & Sat, 8am-10pm Sun; 📶) right downtown, or join the mass of UT students at the 24-hour **Bennu** (☎512-478-4700; 2001 E Martin Luther King Jr Blvd; ⏰24hr).

MEDIA

Newspapers & Magazines

Austin American-Statesman (www.statesman.com) The respected daily newspaper. Publishes *XLent*, a supplemental what's-on guide with restaurant and entertainment reviews, every Thursday.

Austin Chronicle (www.austinchronicle.com) Free alternative weekly with independent coverage of local politics and the lowdown on the Austin music, food and performing-arts scenes.

Radio

Most of the following stations do live-streaming broadcasts online, so you can eavesdrop on Austin before you arrive.

KGSR 93.3 FM (www.kgsr.com) 'Radio Austin' is an eclectic station that airs lots of local talent; check out the 'Lone Star State of Mind' broadcasts from 10pm until midnight every Sunday.

KOOP 91.7 FM (www.koop.org) Austin's community-radio station has excellent local flavor and multicultural programming; Jay Robillard's ever-popular The Lounge Show spins 'hi-fi kitschy fun' from 10am until noon on Saturday.

KUTX 98.9 FM (www.kutx.org) Long-running shows such as Eklektikos (9am till noon weekdays) and Twine Time with Paul Ray (7pm till 10pm Saturday) focus on central Texas music (not to be confused with the all-news station KUT 90.5).

KVRX 91.7 FM (www.kvrx.org) The UT student-radio station shares its bandwidth and sensibilities with KOOP.

MEDICAL SERVICES

Check the *Yellow Pages* for dentists offering emergency care; some keep extended office hours or stay on call overnight.

Brackenridge Hospital (☎512-324-7000; 601 E 15th St) Downtown Austin's central emergency room.

Seton Medical Center (☎512-324-1000; 1201 W 38th St) A major hospital near the UT campus.

Seton McCarthy Community Health Care Center (☎512-324-4930; 2811 E 2nd St; ⏰9am-6pm Mon-Thu, 9:15am-4:30pm Fri) Seton's nonemergency clinic charges on a sliding scale. This location is east of downtown, but there's also a South Austin location (☎512-324-4940; 3706 S 1st St; ⏰9am-6pm Mon-Thu, 9:15-4:30pm Fri).

Walgreens (☎512-452-9452; 5345 N I-35, at Cameron Rd; ⏰24hr) Pharmacy.

MONEY

ATMs accepting most network and credit cards are easily found, except in the most popular nightlife areas, where privately owned ATMs (look for them inside convenience stores or often right on the street) charge exorbitant transaction fees. **Bank of America** (☎512-542-9799; 515 Congress Ave; ⏰9am-4pm Mon-Thu, to 5pm Fri) exchanges foreign currency and traveler's checks. There are exchange booths at the airport too.

POST

Downtown Austin Post Office (Map p64; 823 Congress Ave; ⏰8:30am-5:30pm Mon-Fri) Call ☎800-275-8777 to locate other branches.

TOURIST INFORMATION

Austin Visitor Information Center (Map p64; ☎512-478-0098; www.austintexas.org; 209 E 6th St; ⏰9am-5pm) Helpful staff, free maps, extensive racks of information brochures and a sample of local souvenirs for sale.

Capitol Visitors Center (CVC; Map p64; ☎512-305-8400; www.texascapitolvisitorscenter.com; 112 E 11th St; ⏰9am-5pm Mon-Sat, noon-5pm Sun) Get oriented with self-guided-tour booklets for the state capitol and grounds at this office on its southeast corner. It also has Austin information and maps of the entire state.

USEFUL WEBSITES

Austin360 (www.austin360.com) Inside the Austin *American-Statesman's* encyclopedic city guide, search for absolutely anything Austin-related (watch out for occasionally obsolete information).

Austin Chronicle (www.austinchronicle.com) Austin's local alternative weekly newspaper has comprehensive guides to live-music venues, restaurants, outdoor activities and the arts.

Austin City Links (www.austinlinks.com) The mother lode of Austin-related links covers everything from honky-tonk dance halls to Shakespearean theater festivals.

ℹ Getting There & Away

AIR

Opened in 1999, **Austin-Bergstrom International Airport** (AUS; www.austintexas.gov/airport) is about 10 miles southeast of downtown. It's served by American, Continental, Delta, Frontier, JetBlue, Southwest and United-Lufthansa Airlines.

A nice welcome to the city, the airport features live music by local acts on some evenings near the center of the departures level. You can also sample food from Austin-based restaurants, including Amy's Ice Cream and Salt Lick Bar-B-Que, or buy some last-minute CDs from the Austin City Limits store. The airport's only big drawback is its lack of lockers, so plan to keep your carry-on bags with you.

BUS

The **main bus station** (Map p60; 916 E Koenig Lane) is served by **Greyhound** (☎512-458-4463; www.greyhound.com) and the **Kerrville Bus Co** (☎512-458-3823; www.iridekbc.com). Capital Metro bus 7-Duval (www.capmetro.org) will deliver you from the station to the UT campus or downtown. Buses leave from here for other major Texas cities frequently; there are also some rather pricey services to the nearby Hill Country.

CAR & MOTORCYCLE

Driving Distances

Austin to Dallas 200 miles, 3½ hours

Austin to Fredericksburg 80 miles, one hour and 40 minutes

Austin to Gruene 45 miles, 55 minutes

Austin to Lockhart 30 miles, 40 minutes

Austin to San Antonio 80 miles, one hour and 20 minutes

TRAIN

The downtown **Amtrak station** (☎512-476-5684; www.amtrak.com; 250 N Lamar Blvd) is served by the *Texas Eagle* that extends from Chicago to Los Angeles. There's free parking and an enclosed waiting area but no staff. Fares vary wildly.

Getting Around

TO/FROM THE AIRPORT

Ground transportation from Austin-Bergstrom International Airport can be found on the lower level near baggage claim. A taxi between the airport and downtown costs $25 to $30. Capital Metro runs a limited-stop Airport Flyer (bus 100) service between the airport and downtown and the UT for just $1 each way, with departures every 40 minutes. Check with **Capital Metro** (CapMetro; ☎512-474-1200; www.capmetro.org) for exact schedules. It takes at least 20 minutes to get downtown from the airport, and 35 minutes to reach the UT campus.

SuperShuttle (☎512-258-3826; www.supershuttle.com) offers a shared-van service from the airport to downtown hotels for about $14 one way, or a few dollars more to accommodations along N I-35 and near the Arboretum mall.

BICYCLE

A grand bicycle tour of greater Austin isn't feasible, due to interstate highways and the like, but cycling around downtown, South Congress and the UT campus is totally doable. There are also miles of recreational paths around the city that are ideal for cruisin'. Check www.austintexas.gov/bicycles for a route map.

Say what you will about Lance Armstrong, you can still count on him to find you a pretty good bike. Located right downtown, **Mellow Johnny's Bike Shop** (Map p64; ☎512-473-0222; www.mellowjohnnys.com; 400 Nueces St; day use adult $30-50; ⏰7am-7pm Mon-Fri, 8am-6pm Sat, 8am-4pm Sun) is coowned by the disgraced seven-time Tour de France winner. It rents high-performance bikes as well as commuter bikes, and offers free guided bike rides (check the website for a schedule).

Looking for something a little more casual? The cool thing about **Bicycle Sportshop** (Map p64; ☎512-477-3472; www.bicyclesportshop.com; 517 S Lamar Blvd; per 2hr from $16; ⏰10am-7pm Mon-Fri, 9am-6pm Sat, 11am-5pm Sun) is its proximity to Zilker Park, Barton Springs and the Lady Bird Lake bike paths, all of which are within a few blocks. Rentals range from $16 for a two-hour cruise on a standard bike to $60 for a full day on a top-end full-suspension model. On weekends and holidays, advance reservations are advised.

CAR & MOTORCYCLE

Getting around Austin is easy enough, but the main consideration for drivers – other than rush-hour gridlock and what people from other towns consider crazy drivers – is where to leave your car when you're not in it.

Downtown, the best deal is at the **Capitol Visitors Parking Garage** (1201 San Jacinto Blvd). It's free for the first two hours, and only $1 per half hour after that, maxing out at $8. Other downtown garages and lots are fairly abundant. They usually charge $1 to $2 per hour, with a daily maximum of $8 to $10.

The state-operated parking garage at 4th and San Antonio Sts is free after 6pm, and fills up quickly. Other downtown garages and parking lots typically charge a flat fee of around $6 or so after dark. People also park for free under I-35 at the east end of 6th St, but you can't depend on it being available (or legal).

Parking meters usually cost 25¢ for 15 to 20 minutes, but gone are the days of free downtown street parking on nights and weekends. Downtown meters now run 8am to 6pm Monday to Wednesday, 8am to midnight Thursday and Friday, and 11am to midnight Sunday (although outside of downtown metering still stops after 6pm and on Sunday). Elsewhere around Austin, you can find free on-street parking, but pay careful attention to posted permit parking and time limits.

Day or night, finding a spot around the UT campus can take a while. Free visitor parking is available outside the LBJ Library, but from there it's a long, hot walk across campus to the UT Tower and other sights. Parking spots on Guadalupe St are both timed and metered. Otherwise, your best bet is to search for free parking in the residential streets west of Guadalupe St.

PUBLIC TRANSPORT

Austin's handy public-transit system is run by Capital Metro (p85). Call for directions to anywhere or stop into the downtown **Capital Metro Transit Store** (323 Congress Ave; ⌚7:30am-5pm Mon-Fri) for information. Regular city buses – not including the more-expensive express routes – cost $1 for adults and 50¢ for students and are free for seniors. There are bicycle racks (where you can hitch your bike for free) on the front of almost all CapMetro buses, including more than a dozen UT shuttle routes.

TAXI

You'll usually need to call for a cab instead of just flagging one down on the street, except at the airport, at major hotels, around the state capitol and at major entertainment areas. The flag drops at $2.50, then it's $2.40 for each additional mile. Larger companies include **Yellow Cab** (☎512-452-9999), **Austin Cab** (☎512-478-2222) and **Roy's Taxi** (☎512-482-0000).

Human-powered bicycle taxis, or pedicabs, are available downtown on 6th St and around the Warehouse District, usually from about 9pm until after 2am from Wednesday to Saturday evenings. The drivers, who are typically young students or musicians, work entirely for tips, so please be generous.

AROUND AUSTIN

Bastrop

Just 30 miles southeast of Austin lies the quintessential small town of Bastrop. With 131 buildings listed on the National Register of Historic Places, Bastrop has earned the title of 'Most Historic Small Town in Texas,' but it's the redevelopment of the cute historic center that makes it a fun place to spend a day or two. The happening little burg has first-Friday art walks from 5pm to 8pm and even has its own app for visitors – proof that 'small town' doesn't mean 'behind the times.' Check out the **Bastrop Visitor Center website** (www.visitbastroptx.com) to learn more.

In 2011, following the hottest, driest summer on record, a massive wildfire that raged around Bastrop County became the most destructive Texas fire on record. Fortunately, the town itself was spared, though a lot of the surrounding countryside was scorched.

Sights & Activities

Bastrop Museum & Visitor Center MUSEUM
(☎512-303-0904; www.bastropmuseumandvisitorcenter.org; 904 Main St; ⌚10am-5pm Mon-Sat, 1-4pm Sun) FREE Stop by for walking-tour maps and brochures, and take a whirl through the museum while you're at it. At time of writing the museum had just moved in and staff were still working hard to fill all that space with items like a shiny, red, old-timey Bastrop firetruck from 1904. But big plans were afoot, which will eventually include an admission charge.

Fisherman's Park PARK
(1200 Willow St at Farm St) FREE The best reason to visit this park on the banks of the Colorado River is the splash pad, a children's play area with water features you can run though, stand in or sit on. It not only keeps the little ones cool but fills them with glee as only getting good and wet during a hot Texas summer can.

Care for a stroll? The lovely **June Hill Pape Riverwalk** connects this park and nearby **Ferry Park** with a half-mile path.

The Crossing SQUARE
(601 Chestnut St) ,A smattering of shops and restaurants within an old-timey village outfitted in country rustic, with a windmill, barrels full of flowers, and rusty old tractors and trucks adding to the ambience. It's just a block from downtown Bastrop and set on the Colorado River.

Bastrop State Park PARK
(☎512-321-2101; www.tpwd.state.tx.us/state-parks/bastrop; adult/12yr & under $4/free) This beautiful state park was hit hard by the 2011 wildfires, which affected 96% of its nearly 6000 acres of forest. Fortunately, they were able to save the historic cabins built by the Civilian Conservation Corp in the 1930s, and the hiking, swimming and golfing continues. The scenic 12-mile drive through the park on Park Road 1C will let you glimpse both the destruction and the regrowth. It's 1 mile east of Bastrop on Hwy 21.

Bastrop River Co CANOEING
(☎512-988-1154; www.bastroprivercompany.com; 601 Chestnut St; paddle trips year-round $40, tube rental May-Sep $15; ⌚daily summer, by appointment winter) The Colorado looks mighty inviting. Grab a canoe, kayak or tube and get out there. Floats last two to three hours (unless

Around Austin

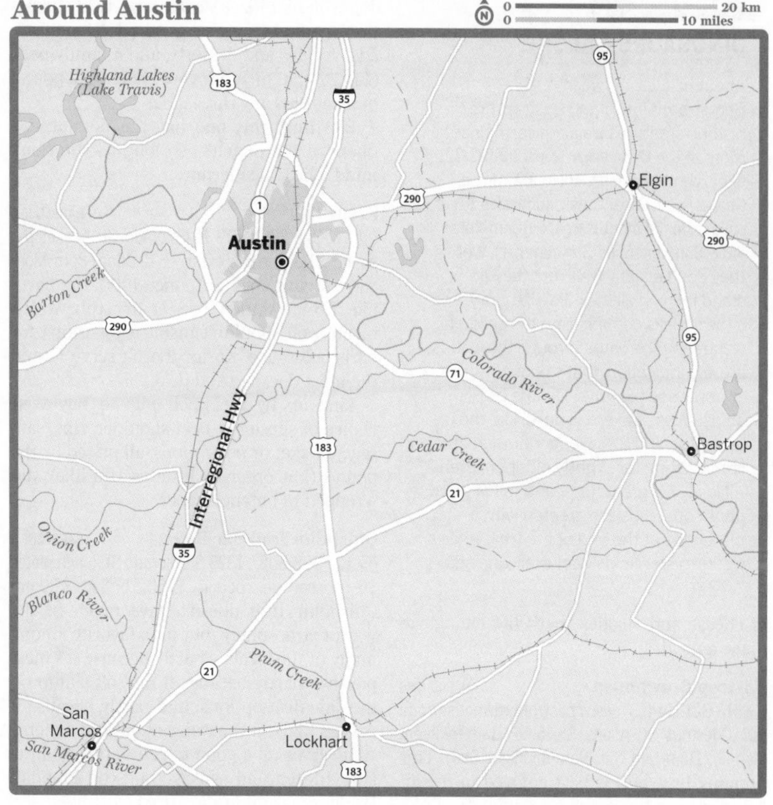

you're feeling ambitious and take the eight- to nine-hour route) and shuttle service back to downtown is included.

Sleeping

Pecan Street Inn B&B **$$**
(☎512-321-3315; www.pecanstreetinn.com; 1010 Pecan St; d $99-109, ste $119-125) Just a few blocks from downtown, this gracious B&B listed on the National Register of Historic Places sits under sprawling pecan trees and is lovingly furnished with unfussy antiques. Breakfast is a fancy, sit-down affair – and don't be surprised if your pancakes have pecans in them.

Hyatt Lost Pines Resort RESORT **$$$**
(☎512-308-1234; http://lostpines.hyatt.com; 575 Lost Pines Rd; d $129-299) About halfway between Austin and Bastrop, Lost Pines Resort has all the hallmarks of a Texas farmhouse – weathered grey exterior, tin roof, expansive porches – even though it's a rambling new resort opened mid-2006. Hiking, rafting and riding are all part of the experience here.

Eating & Drinking

Maxine's CAFE **$**
(☎512-303-0919; www.maxinesonmain.com; 905 Main St; dishes $5-12; ⏰7am-3pm Sun-Tue, to 9pm Wed & Thu, to 10pm Fri & Sat) This cute-as-can-be cafe turns on the small-town charm with down-home cooking in the heart of historic Main St. Griddle cakes for breakfast, fried-green-tomato BLT for lunch, or chicken-fried steak for dinner are among the specialties that keep people lining up.

Olde World Bakery & Cafe CAFE **$**
(☎512-321-3676; 601d Chestnut St; mains $4-9) Located in The Crossing, this convivial little place is a great spot to refuel between adventures. Try the vegetable bread if it's available: a huge hunk of bread stuffed full

DON'T MISS

DINOSAURS GALORE

About halfway between Austin-Bergstrom Airport and Bastrop, prehistoric creatures walk the earth once more at the **Dinosaur Park** (☎512-321-6262; www.thedinopark.com; 893 Union Chapel Road, Cedar Creek; admission $7, child under 24 months free; ⏰10am-4pm Sat & Sun winter, Tue-Sun summer). Well, they don't exactly walk, but they do stand there in all their life-size glory. And if the shrieks coming from the children wandering the paths through the woods are any indication, that's enough.

You'll see big guys, like the brachiosaurus, and small ones, like the oviraptor, and a scavenger hunt keeps it interesting for slightly older children. All in all, it's great fun – and full of great photo ops. Kids are greeted with a playscape at the end of the trail, while a water mister helps cool everyone off.

of cheese and veggies that's big enough to make a meal.

Bastrop Brewhouse AMERICAN **$$**
(☎512-321-1144; www.bastropbrewhouse.com; 601 Chestnut St; mains $8-15; ⏰11am-midnight Mon-Fri, 11am-1am Sat, 9am-midnight Sun) This hopping brewpub is best enjoyed in the afternoon from the deck overlooking the Colorado River, but live music on the weekends is also lots of fun. Burgers, salads and other pub staples are fine, but the atmosphere is definitely the draw.

Lockhart

In 1999 the Texas Legislature adopted a resolution naming Lockhart the Barbecue Capital of Texas. Of course, that means it's the barbecue capital of the *world*. You can eat very well for around $10 or less at any of these places, all of which have been named as one of the top 10 barbecue restaurants in the state by *Texas Monthly* magazine.

Eating

Black's Barbecue BARBECUE **$**
(215 N Main St; sandwiches $4-6, brisket per pound $11; ⏰10am-8pm Sun-Thu, to 8:30pm Fri & Sat) This longtime Lockhart favorite has been around and owned by the same family since 1932. The sausage was so good Lyndon Johnson had Black's cater a party at the nation's capital. There's a good selection of salads, veggies and desserts, and a family pack ($19.75) that includes your choice of a pound of meat plus any three sides.

We think this one has the best atmosphere of the bunch – so long as you don't mind a little taxidermy.

Kreuz Market BARBECUE **$**
(☎512-398-2361; 619 N Colorado St; brisket per pound $11.90, sides extra; ⏰10:30am-8pm Mon-Sat) Serving Lockhart since 1900, the barn-like Kreuz Market uses a dry rub, which means you shouldn't insult it by asking for barbecue sauce. Kreuz doesn't serve it, and the meat doesn't need it.

Line up by the open pits to buy your choice of succulent beef shoulder, ribs, sausage, brisket or pork chops, all priced by the pound (but order as little as you like) and wrapped in butcher paper.

Chisholm Trail Bar-B-Q BARBECUE **$**
(☎512-398-6027; 1323 S Colorado St; lunch plates $6, brisket per pound $7.50; ⏰8am-8:30pm) Chisholm Trail doesn't have much in the way of atmosphere, but it's a favorite among many of the locals – partly because it's inexpensive, partly because it doesn't skimp on the side-dish options, and partly because it isn't as high on the radar of out-of-towners.

It serves up a good selection of ribs, brisket, chicken and sausage and (on Monday, Wednesday and Friday) fried catfish.

Smitty's Market BARBECUE **$**
(208 S Commerce St; lunch plates $6, brisket per pound $11.90; ⏰7am-6pm Mon-Fri, 7am-6:30pm Sat, 9am-3pm Sun) The blackened pit room and homely dining room are all original (knives used to be chained to the tables). Ask to have the fat trimmed off the brisket if you're particular about that.

Located a block from the courthouse, Smitty's imbues the entire town square with the nonstop aroma of smoked meat, so if you smell like barbecue before you've even had lunch, you have them to thank.

Highland Lakes

Northwest of Austin, a series of dams along the Colorado River has blessed the area with the **Highland Lakes** (www.thehighlandlakes.org), six lakes with a handsome network of lakeside greenbelts and parks to help you enjoy them. Though recent years have seen serious droughts, one of the most popular lakes for recreation – when there's water – is the 19,000-sq-acre **Lake Travis** (www.laketravis.com).

Rent boats and Jet Skis at the associated marina, hang out at Hippie Hollow, or overnight at the Lakeway Resort and Spa. Not into roughing it? Head for **Lake Austin Spa Resort** (512-372-7300; www.lakeaustin.com; 1705 S Quinlan Park Rd, off FM 2222; 3-night packages from $1600;), one of the premier places to be pampered in the state.

Activities

Hippie Hollow BEACH

(www.hippiehollow.com; 7000 Comanche Trail; day pass car/bicycle $12/5; 9am-dusk Sep-May, 8am-dusk Jun-Aug) Nude, nekkid, clothing optional – call it what you will, but this adults-only spot on Lake Travis (formerly known as McGregor Park) has been drawing people of the clothes-less persuasion since the '60s. It's not exactly a nude beach but more of a bit of shoreline defined by rocky outcroppings that are perfect for sunning your buns.

The good news (or bad, depending on how you look at it) is that the amount of scrambling required prevents all but the most dedicated from doing the 'stroll and stare.' Eighteen and over only, please. The park is extracrowded on Splash Days, a gay and lesbian event that occurs on the first Sunday of May and September.

From the intersection of RR 620 and FM 2222, take RR 620 south 1⅓ miles to Comanche Trail; turn right and the entrance is 2 miles ahead on the left.

Sleeping

Lakeway Resort & Spa RESORT $$

(512-261-6600; www.lakewayresortandspa.com; 101 Lakeway Dr; r from $189;) Families have been towing their boats from around Texas to Lakeway for more than 30 years. They still come to use the marina and boat on Lake Travis, but a 2005 expansion added dozens more rooms and upped the luxe factor considerably.

Though Lakeway's gone upscale, it hasn't forgotten the kids. Two new pools, one with a water slide, bring the total to three. There are kids programs and even a summer camp of sorts. Of course, you could always bring them along when you rent that pontoon boat or Jet Ski and head out for a day on the water. Rooms in the newer, main lodge are divine but approachable, with beds dressed in textured-silk duvets. The old one-story buildings overlooking the marina have a lot more character – huge spaces, dark wood, king-size beds, secluded balconies and functional fireplaces. Newer doesn't always mean better.

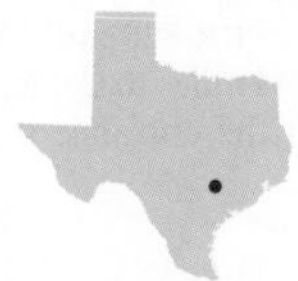

San Antonio & Hill Country

Includes ➡

Best Places to Eat

- Cove (p112)
- Pink Pig (p129)
- Il Sogno Osteria (p113)
- Grape Juice (p133)

Best Places to Stay

- Hotel Havana (p106)
- Hotel Faust (p133)
- Omni La Mansion del Rio (p107)

Why Go?

Tourism has been good to San Antonio and the sprawling city reciprocates with a wide variety of attractions to keep everyone entertained. In addition to its colorful European-style Riverwalk lined with cafes and bars, it rewards visitors with a well-rounded menu of museums, theme parks, outdoor activities and historical sites. The Alamo is a stalwart tourist favorite, and the scene of the most famous battle in the fight for Texas' independence from Mexico. You can find four other beautifully preserved Spanish Missions within the city limits.

San Antonio also puts you in close proximity to the Hill Country, a naturally beautiful region known for its wildflower-lined roadways, charming small towns and, yes, hills. Fredericksburg is the most touristy Hill Country town, but the area is more about winding roads and stopping along the way than any particular destination.

When to Go

San Antonio

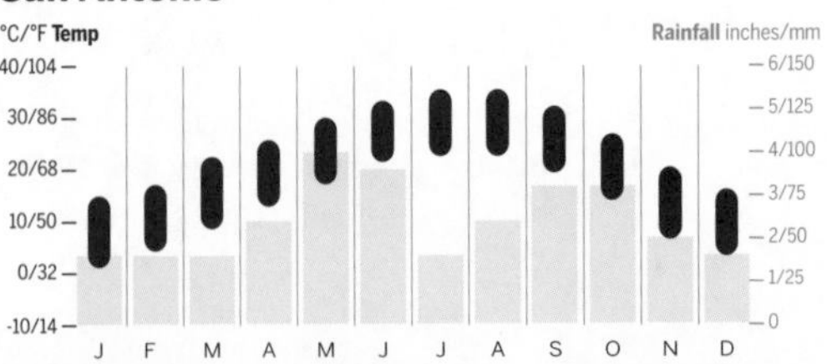

Mar & Apr Hill Country comes alive with bluebonnets, Indian paintbrushes and other wildflowers.

May & Jun The kids are out of school and temperatures are still bearable – mostly.

Dec & Jan Brush off cabin fever: it's warm enough to get outdoors, even if the trees are bare.

Getting Ready to Remember the Alamo

Seeing the Alamo for the first time? Many people are surprised to see that it's in the middle of downtown San Antonio, surrounded by tacky tourist attractions – but even more startling is its diminutive size. Whether it's because of the monument's sentimental stature or too many tightly cropped photographs that don't offer any indication of scale, the first thing many people say when they first see the Alamo is, 'Wow, it's a lot smaller than I thought it would be!'

EXPLORING THE HILL COUNTRY

With so many day-trip destinations so close to San Antonio, it's hard to choose between them. If you have some time to spare, the following route lets you cover a lot of ground. The entire loop can be driven in 4.5 hours, but how long you decide to linger is up to you.

From San Antonio, head northwest on I-10, stopping for a little antique shopping in Boerne and Comfort. Continue on to Kerrville and enjoy cowboy art or swimming in the Guadalupe River. From Kerrville, take Hwy 16 to Fredericksburg, the unofficial capital of the Hill Country, and listen to live music under the trees in tiny Luckenbach.

Next, continue west to the LBJ Ranch, and see JBJ's childhood home in Johnson City. Then head south at Dripping Springs, passing through Wimberley, and stop in San Marcos, land of the outlet mall. Don't miss Texas' oldest dance hall in Gruene – a short detour. Just south, New Braunfels invites you to float the Guadalupe River, then it's just 32 miles back to San Antonio.

Downtown Parking Tips

When visiting downtown, you'll definitely want to ditch your car, but street parking is hard to find. Here are some alternatives.

➡ Park on the street for free in the King William District, then take a VIA blue line streetcar into downtown.

➡ Park free at **VIA Ellis Alley Park & Ride** (btwn E Crockett & Center Sts) then pay $2.50 roundtrip to ride downtown.

➡ Park inexpensively at **Market Square** (2hr $3, flat rate $7) then walk 15 minutes to the Alamo.

➡ Park at **Riverbend Garage** (210 N Presa; 2hr $7, maximum $12; ⏲ 24hr), which is a little more expensive but puts you right in the heart of things.

RIVERWALK EXTENSION

Long a downtown tourist staple, San Antonio's Riverwalk now has 14 additional miles of paths that reach from the King William District south of downtown, all the way to the Pearl Brewery development to the north.

Hill Country for Kids

➡ Explore cool caves at Natural Bridge Caverns (p120)

➡ Activities abound at McKenna Children's Museum (p120)

➡ Take a wildlife tour at YO Ranch (p134)

➡ Visit the museum at the LBJ Ranch (p125)

➡ Burn off extra energy at Landa Park (p120)

Best Places to Cool Off

➡ Tubing on the Guadalupe (p120)

➡ Kerrville-Schreiner Park (p131)

➡ Splashtown (p105)

➡ Schlitterbahn Waterpark (p120)

➡ Blue Hole (p137)

Resources

➡ **Express-News** (www.mysanantonio.com)

➡ **San Antonio Current** (www.sacurrent.com)

➡ **Neighborhoods** (www.saculturaltours.com)

SAN ANTONIO

POP 1.3 MILLION

In most large cities, downtown is bustling with businesspeople dressed for office work hurrying to their meetings and luncheons. Not so in San Antonio. Instead, downtown is filled with tourists in shorts carrying cameras and consulting their maps. In fact, many people are surprised to find that two of the state's most popular destinations – the Riverwalk and the Alamo – are smack dab in the middle of downtown, surrounded by historical hotels, tourist attractions and souvenir shops. The rest of the city sprawls out around downtown, careful not to impinge on the tourist trade.

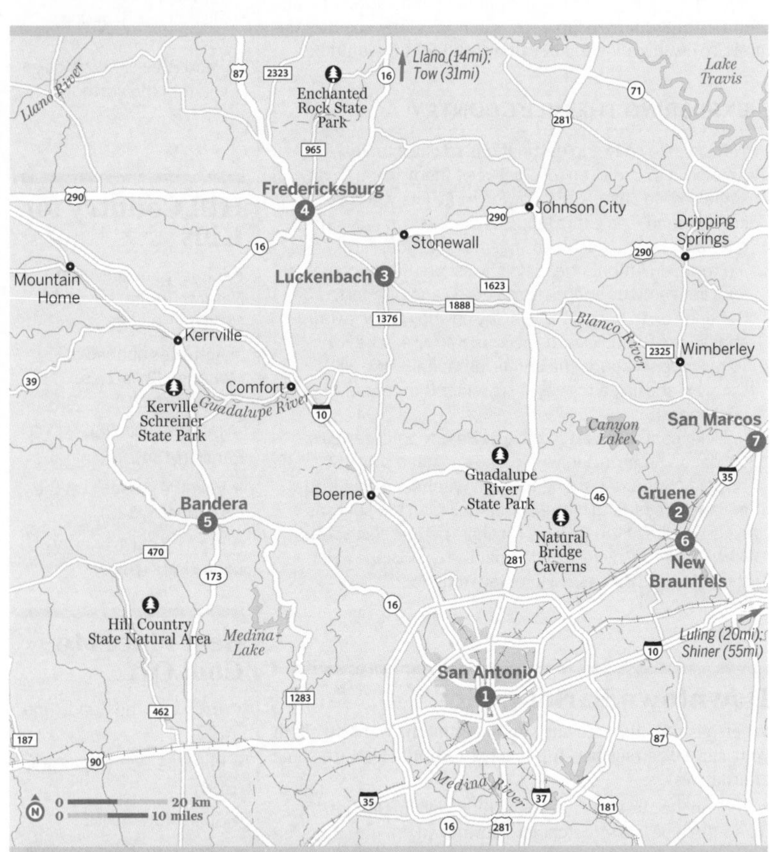

San Antonio & Hill Country Highlights

1. Pay your respects at the **Alamo** (p93), a historical shrine to the men who fought for Texas' independence.
2. Take a spin around the worn wooden floors at the oldest dance hall in Texas, **Gruene Hall** (p121).
3. **Luckenbach** (p130), population three, welcomes visitors with its cold beer and daily live music.
4. The unofficial capital of the Hill Country, **Fredericksburg** (p125) offers a hearty *wilkommen* to all.
5. Saddle up at a dude ranch in **Bandera** (p134), the Cowboy Capital of Texas.
6. Float along the Guadalupe River in **New Braunfels** (p120), a Texas summertime tradition.
7. Shopaholics should make haste to the **San Marcos Premium Outlets** (p124).

RIVERWALK

In 1921, floods destroyed downtown San Antonio when water 10ft deep gushed through the center of the city from the overflowing San Antonio River, obliterating homes and businesses and drowning as many as 50 people. As a result, the Olmos Dam was constructed to handle overflow and route the extra water around the downtown area through a canal called the Oxbow.

The fix was meant to be temporary, and was intended to be submerged and turned into an enormous storm drain beneath the city. Before this happened though, some locals formed the San Antonio Conservation Society and dedicated themselves to preserving and developing the canal into an attraction.

In 1938 the Works Progress Administration (WPA) assumed control of the canal's fate, and executed a plan to develop a central business district of shops and restaurants along a cobbled walk. More than 1000 jobs were created during the construction of the Riverwalk, and the project is one of the most beautiful results of the WPA effort.

History

Although the area around San Antonio was first populated by Native Americans, the city's official history begins in 1691, when Spanish explorers discovered the area on the feast day of St Anthony of Padua and declared it 'San Antonio.' In 1718 the Spanish established a military presidio there, as well as a mission called San Antonio de Valero – a mission that was meant to colonize and convert the native people and that would one day be known simply as 'the Alamo.'

At the time, Texas belonged to Mexico, which in turn belonged to Spain, and things stayed that way for nearly a hundred years after the Alamo was built. But after Mexico won its independence from Spain in 1821, it wasn't long before Texas followed suit and fought for its own independence from Mexico. One of the most important battles in the Texas Revolution was the Battle of the Alamo, where patriots fought to the death to defend the former mission. For more on the 13-day siege of the Alamo in 1836, see p344.

After Texas won its independence, San Antonio boomed as a cattle town. European settlers moved to the area, including vast numbers of Germans and Czechs, and the Germans built the city's King William area, named for Kaiser Wilhelm I of Prussia.

In 1879, Fort Sam Houston was established by the US Army. It was joined by Kelly Air Force Base in 1917 and then later by Lackland, Randolph and Brooks Air Force bases. Much of San Antonio's 20th-century growth was a result of the military's presence, although tourism will always be an important industry – thanks to the 300-year-old mission that sits right in the heart of downtown.

Sights

Downtown's major north–south arteries include Broadway St and Main Ave. East–west thoroughfares include Commerce St, Market St and Houston St. The intersection of Commerce and Losoya Sts is the very heart of downtown and below street level is the Riverwalk, a developed canal loop off the San Antonio River.

Downtown

★The Alamo HISTORIC BUILDING

(Map p96; ☎210-225-1391; www.thealamo.org; 300 Alamo Plaza; ⌚9am-5:30pm Mon-Sat, from 10am Sun) FREE Find out why the story of the Alamo can rouse a Texan's sense of state pride like few other things. For many, it's not so much a tourist attraction as a pilgrimage site and you might notice some of the visitors getting downright dewy-eyed at the description of how a few hundred revolutionaries died defending the fort against thousands of Mexican troops.

The main chapel building is now known as the **Shrine**. From here you can set off for a history talk in the Cavalry Courtyard, hearing one of many perspectives on the actual events, which are somewhat in dispute, or browse the museum in the **Long Barrack**, which served as a residence for the Spanish priests and later as a hospital for Mexican and Texan troops. There's also a 17-minute-long film, which not only gives you another perspective on the battle, but is an excellent place to escape the heat.

★Riverwalk WATERFRONT

(Map p96; www.thesanantonioriverwalk.com) A slice of Europe in the heart of San Antonio, the

San Antonio

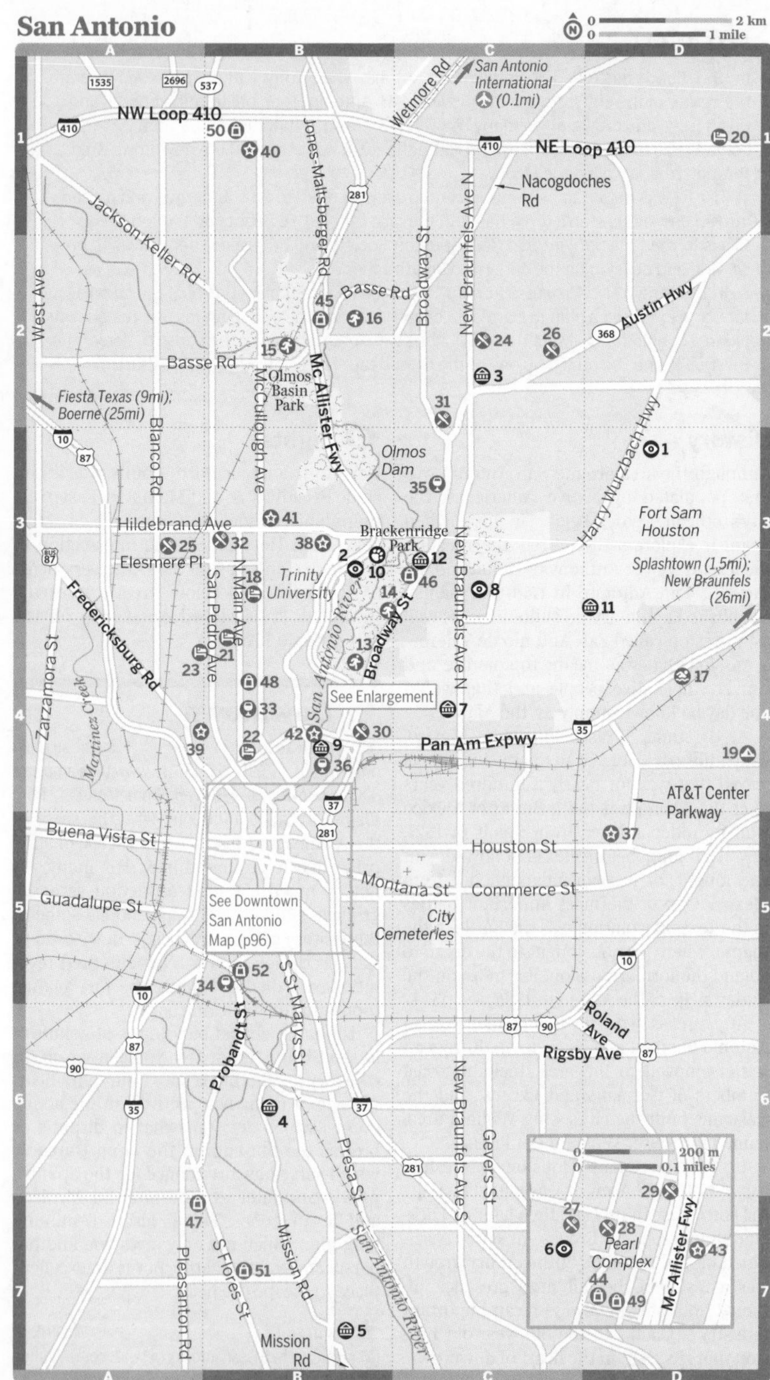

NW Loop 410
NE Loop 410
San Antonio International (0.1mi)
Wetmore Rd
Jones-Maltsberger Rd
Nacogdoches Rd
Jackson Keller Rd
Basse Rd
Broadway St
New Braunfels Ave N
Austin Hwy
West Ave
Olmos Basin Park
Mc Allister Fwy
McCullough Ave
Fiesta Texas (9mi); Boerne (25mi)
Blanco Rd
Olmos Dam
Harry Wurzbach Hwy
Fort Sam Houston
Hildebrand Ave
Brackenridge Park
Elesmere Pl
Trinity University
San Antonio River
Splashtown (1.5mi); New Braunfels (26mi)
Fredericksburg Rd
San Pedro Ave
N Main Ave
Zarzamora St
Martinez Creek
See Enlargement
Pan Am Expwy
AT&T Center Parkway
Buena Vista St
Houston St
Montana St
Commerce St
Guadalupe St
See Downtown San Antonio Map (p96)
City Cemeteries
Probandt St
S St Marys St
Roland Ave
Rigsby Ave
New Braunfels Ave S
Gevers St
Presa St
Mission Rd
S Flores St
Pleasanton Rd
Pearl Complex

San Antonio

Sights

1 Fort Sam Houston D3
2 Japanese Tea Garden B3
3 McNay Art Museum C2
4 Mission Concepción B6
5 Mission San José B7
6 Pearl Complex C7
7 Quadrangle C4
8 San Antonio Botanical Gardens C3
San Antonio Missions National Historical Park (see 4)
9 San Antonio Museum of Art B4
10 San Antonio Zoo B3
11 US Army Medical Department Museum D3
12 Witte Museum C3

Activities, Courses & Tours

13 Brackenridge Golf Course B4
14 Kiddie Amusement Park B3
15 Olmos Basin Golf Course B2
16 Quarry Golf Club B2
17 Splashtown D4

Sleeping

18 Bonner Garden B3
19 Dixie Campground D4
20 Hill Country Inn & Suites D1
21 Inn at Craig Place B4
22 Rodeway Inn Downtown B4
23 Ruckman Haus A4

Eating

24 Adelante Mexican Food C2
Amy's Ice Cream (see 45)
25 Chris Madrid's A3
Cove (see 39)
26 Earl Abel's C2
27 Green Vegetarian Cuisine C7
28 Il Sogno Osteria D7
29 Josephine Street Cafe D6
30 Mary Ann's Pig Stand B4
31 Paloma Blanca C2
32 Taco Cabana B3

Drinking & Nightlife

33 Heat B4
34 La Tuna Ice House B5
35 Mon Ami Lounge C3
36 VFW Post 76 B4

Entertainment

37 AT&T Center D5
38 AtticRep B3
39 Cove A4
Laurie Auditorium (see 38)
40 Martini Club B1
41 Olmos Bharmacy B3
42 Overtime Theater B4
43 Sam's Burger Joint D7

Shopping

44 Adelante Boutique D7
45 Alamo Quarry Market B2
46 CD Exchange C3
47 Dave Little's Boots A7
48 Hogwild Records B4
49 Melissa Guerra D7
50 North Star Mall B1
51 Papa Jim's Botanica B7
52 San Angel Folk Art Gallery B5

Riverwalk is an essential part of experiencing the city. This is no ordinary riverfront, but a charming canal and pedestrian street that is the main artery at the heart of San Antonio's tourism efforts. For the best view, hop on a Rio San Antonio river cruise (p105).

You can meander past landscaped hotel gardens and riverside cafes, and linger on the stone footbridges that stretch over the water. During summer it gets mighty crowded, but at peaceful times (and as you get away from downtown) it's a lovely place to stroll – especially during the holidays when it's bedecked with twinkling lights.

The Riverwalk used to be just a downtown thing, but a recent $259-million project expanded the Riverwalk to include 14 miles of paths. You can now walk south to the King William District, or north to the San Antonio Art Museum and even up to the Pearl Brewery complex.

Buckhorn Saloon & Museum MUSEUM
(Map p96; 210-247-4000; www.buckhornmuseum.com; 318 E Houston St; adult/3-11yr $19/15; 10am-5pm, to 8pm in summer) Waaaay back in 1881, when the original Buckhorn Saloon opened up, the owner promised patrons a free beer or whiskey shot for every pair of deer antlers they brought. Although the location has changed a couple of times, you can still see the collection – and the bar – at the Buckhorn Saloon & Museum

An overpriced beverage is enough to buy your admission to the Saloon, which has an impressive number of mounted animals watching over you, including a giraffe, a bear and all manner of horn-wielding mammals. If that doesn't quench your thirst for taxidermy, pony up for a kitsch adventure that includes wildlife from all over the world, as well as oddities like a two-headed cow and an eight-legged lamb.

Downtown San Antonio

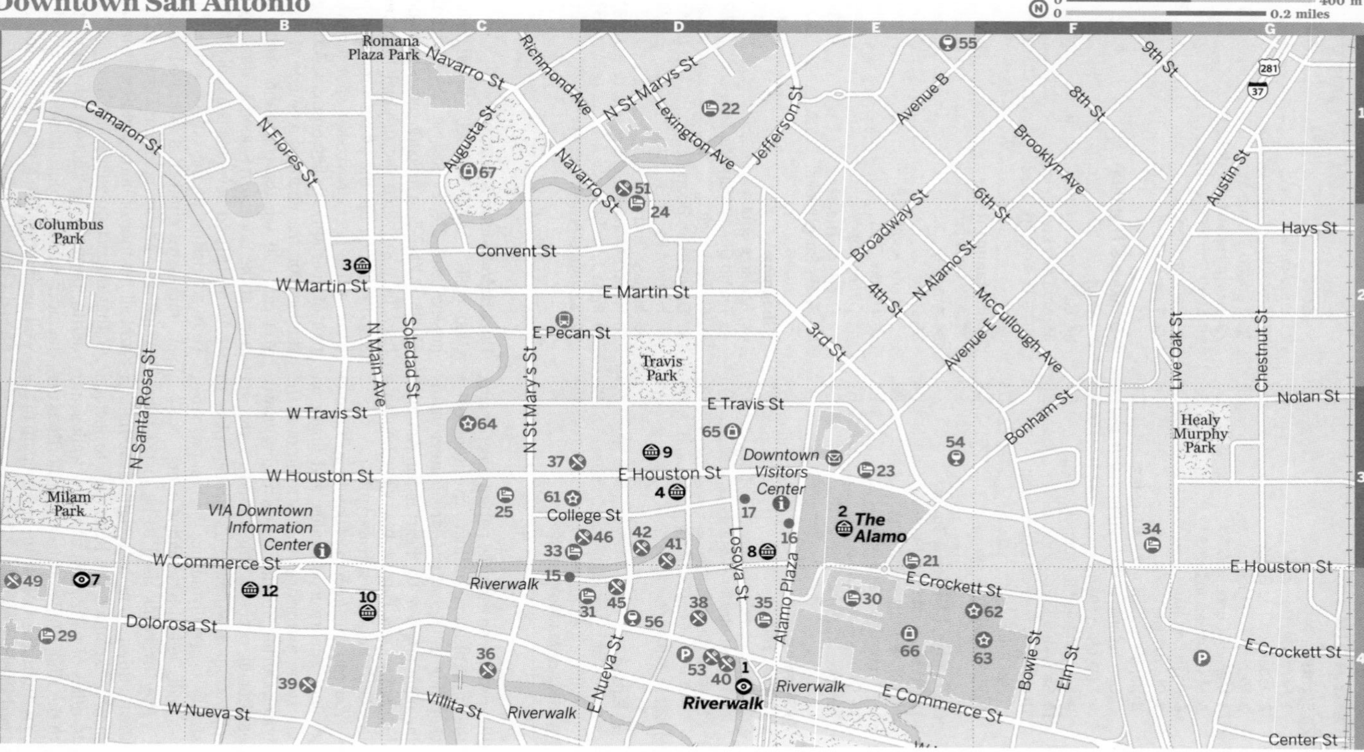

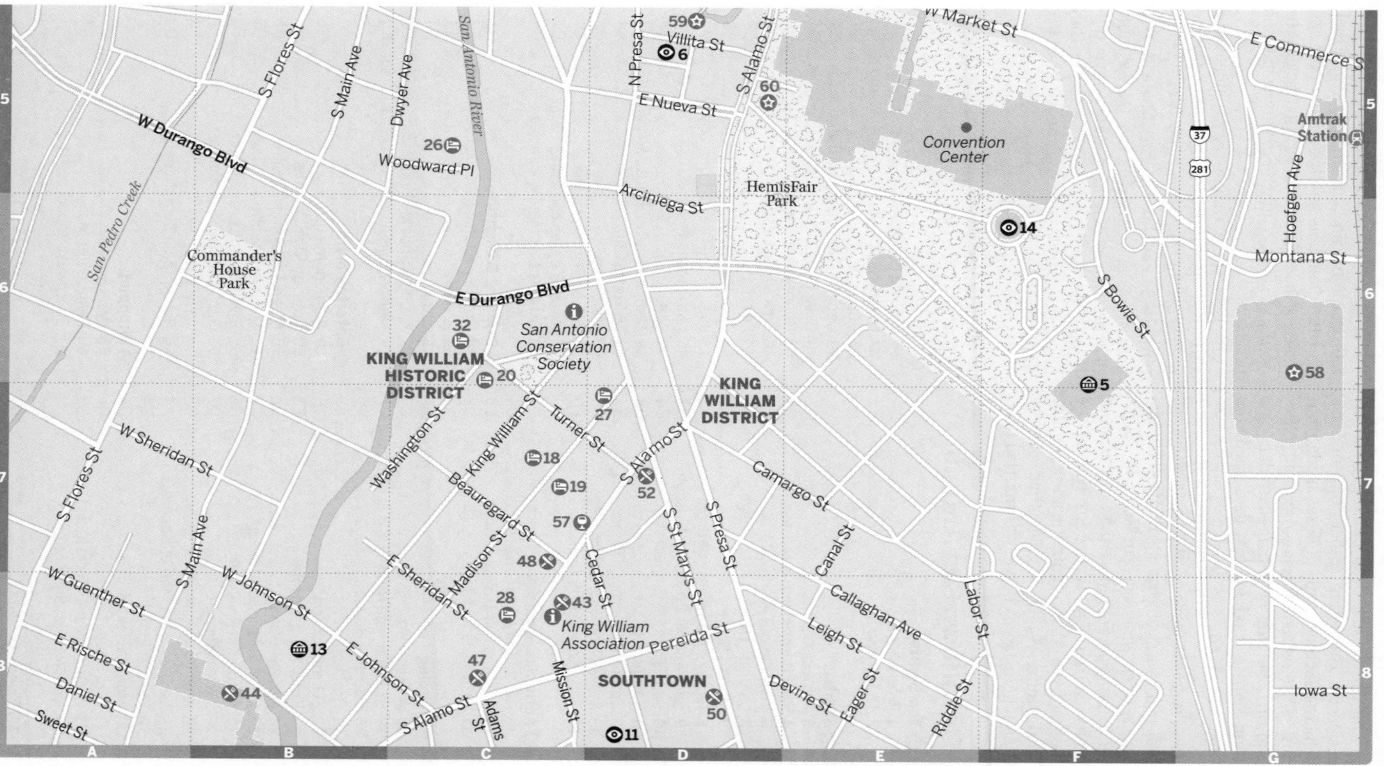

W Market St
E Commerce St
Amtrak Station
59
Villita St
6
N Presa St
S Alamo St
60
E Nueva St
Convention Center
37
281
Hoefgen Ave
W Durango Blvd
S Flores St
S Main Ave
Dwyer Ave
San Antonio River
26
Woodward Pl
Arciniega St
HemisFair Park
14
Montana St
San Pedro Creek
Commander's House Park
E Durango Blvd
S Bowie St
San Antonio Conservation Society
32
KING WILLIAM HISTORIC DISTRICT
20
27
KING WILLIAM DISTRICT
5
58
Washington St
King William St
Turner St
S Alamo St
18
W Sheridan St
19
52
Camargo St
S Flores St
Beauregard St
57
S St Marys St
S Presa St
Canal St
48
Madison St
Cedar St
S Main Ave
W Johnson St
E Sheridan St
28
43
W Guenther St
King William Association
Pereida St
Callaghan Ave
Labor St
Leigh St
13
E Rische St
E Johnson St
47
SOUTHTOWN
Devine St
Eager St
Riddle St
Iowa St
Daniel St
44
50
Sweet St
S Alamo St
Adams St
Mission St
11
A
B
C
D
E
F
G
5
6
7
8

And it's not just dead animals you'll experience. There are other only-in-Texas displays, such as maps of Texas made from rattlesnake rattles and a jaw-dropping collection of Lone Star Beer paraphernalia. Your admission is good for two days so there's time to see it all.

San Fernando Cathedral HISTORIC BUILDING
(Map p96; www.sfcathedral.org; 115 Main Plaza; donations welcome; ⏲9am-5pm Tue-Fri, to 6:30pm Sat, 8:30am-5pm Sun) More than just another pretty church, San Fernando's role in the Battle of the Alamo makes it an important local landmark. In happier times, future Alamo hero James Bowie was married here. But as Bowie defended the Alamo just across the river, Mexican general Santa Anna took over the church as an observation post and raised a flag of 'no quarter' that began the deadly siege – 'no quarter' meaning 'take no prisoners.'

In 1936 some remains were uncovered and, since they included charred bones and fragments of uniforms, they were wildly purported to be those of Davy Crockett, William Travis and James Bowie. (Never mind that the Alamo defenders didn't wear uniforms.) Pay your respects to whoever they are at the marble casket at the left entrance to the church.

Downtown San Antonio

Top Sights

1 Riverwalk ... D4
2 The Alamo ... E3

Sights

3 Artpace ... B2
4 Buckhorn Saloon & Museum ... D3
5 Institute of Texan Cultures ... F6
6 La Villita Historic Arts Village ... D5
7 Market Square ... A4
8 Ripley's Alamo Plaza Attractions ... D3
9 San Antonio Children's Museum ... D3
10 San Fernando Cathedral ... B4
11 Southtown ... D8
12 Spanish Governor's Palace ... B4
13 Steves Homestead Museum ... B8
14 Tower of the Americas ... F6

Activities, Courses & Tours

15 Rio San Antonio Cruises ... C4
16 San Antonio Trolley Tours ... E3
17 SegCity Ghost Tours ... D3

Sleeping

18 A Yellow Rose Inn ... C7
19 Brackenridge House B&B ... C7
20 Carriage House ... C6
21 Crockett Hotel ... E3
22 El Tropicano Hotel ... D1
23 Emily Morgan Hotel ... E3
24 Hotel Havana ... D2
25 Hotel Valencia ... C3
26 Inn on the Riverwalk ... C5
27 Jackson House ... D7
28 King William Manor ... C8
29 La Quinta Inn Market Square ... A4
30 Menger Hotel ... E4
31 Mokara Hotel & Spa ... D4
32 Ogé House ... C6
33 Omni La Mansion del Rio ... C3
34 Red Roof Inn San Antonio Downtown ... F3
35 Riverwalk Vista ... D4

Eating

36 Biga on the Banks ... C4
37 Bohanan's ... C3
38 Boudro's ... D4
39 Candy's Old Fashioned Burgers ... B4
40 Casa Rio ... D4
41 County Line Smokehouse ... D3
42 Dick's Last Resort ... D3
43 Feast ... C8
44 Guenther House ... B8
45 Justin's Ice Cream Company ... D4
46 Las Canarias ... D3
47 Liberty Bar ... C8
48 Madhatters Tea House & Café ... C7
49 Mi Tierra Cafe & Bakery ... A4
50 Monterey ... D8
51 Ocho at Hotel Havana ... D1
52 Rosario's Mexican Cafe ... D7
53 Schilo's German Delicatessen ... D4

Drinking & Nightlife

54 Bonham Exchange ... E3
55 Brooklynite ... E1
56 Drink Texas Bar ... D4
57 Friendly Spot Ice House ... C7
Menger Bar ... (see 30)

Entertainment

58 Alamodome ... G6
59 Arneson River Theater ... D5
60 Magik Children's Theatre ... D5
61 Majestic Theatre ... C3
62 Rivercenter Comedy Club ... F4
63 San Antonio IMAX Alamo Theatre ... F4
64 San Antonio Symphony ... C3

Shopping

65 Paris Hatters ... D3
66 Rivercenter Mall ... E4
67 Southwest School of Art & Craft ... C1

SAN ANTONIO IN...

Two Days

Start your day at the **Riverwalk**, then take some time to remember the **Alamo**. Check out whatever downtown sights you fancy, perhaps the **Buckhorn Museum** or **Market Square**. Later, explore the historic homes of the **King William District** and plan on dinner anywhere along Alamo St.

On your second day, head north to **Brackenridge Park**. Spend some time at the **San Antonio Botanical Gardens**, then visit the divine **McNay Art Museum** or the **San Antonio Museum of Art**.

Four Days

On your third day, explore the four missions along the Mission Trail or take your kids to **SeaWorld** or **Six Flags**, then head over to the new **Pearl development** at the old Pearl Brewery and stick around for dinner.

Finally, get out and explore any of the great small towns around San Antonio. Wildflowers in the **Hill Country** (p124)? Outlet malls in **San Marcos** (p122)? Tubing the **New Braunfels** (p120)? All are within an hour or two of the city.

Spanish Governor's Palace HISTORIC BUILDING
(Map p96; ☎210-224-0601; 105 Plaza de Armas; adult/7-13yr $4/2; ⏲9am-5pm Tue-Sat, 10am-5pm Sun) This low-profile adobe structure that was the seat of Texas' colonial government was already more than 150 years old when City Hall was built in 1889. But it was being occupied by commercial tenants back then, including a saloon, a clothing store and even a pawn shop – until the city realized its historical significance and bought the building back in 1928.

It's now been restored (approximately) to the way it looked back when it was first built and outfitted with period furnishings. Take a half hour out of your day to learn the building's fascinating history, and be glad San Antonio discovered what it had before the palace was torn down to build a parking lot.

Market Square MARKET
(Map p96; ☎210-207-8600; 514 W Commerce St; ⏲10am-6pm, to 8pm late May-early Sep) FREE A little bit of Mexico in downtown San Antonio, Market Square is a fair approximation of a trip south of the border, with Mexican food, mariachi bands and store after store filled with Mexican wares. A big chunk of the square is taken up by **El Mercado**, the largest Mexican marketplace outside of Mexico.

The market has historical roots – it goes back to the 1890s – but it can feel like a bit of a tourist trap at times. You can find some beautiful handicrafts if you take time to sort through the mass-produced sombreros and serapes. Wander the booths and stock up on Mexican doodads such as paper flowers, colorful pottery, maracas, *papel picado* (elaborate cut-paper designs), onyx figurines and the Virgin Mary in every conceivable medium.

Artpace MUSEUM
(Map p96; ☎210-212-4900; www.artpace.org; 445 N Main Ave; ⏲noon-5pm Wed-Sun) FREE This unique contemporary art museum hosts temporary exhibitions by its outstanding artists-in-residence, who are selected from a pool drawn from across Texas, the USA and abroad. Inside a 1920s automobile showroom, the renovated gallery space is inspiring and the works are often experimental. Artpace also schedules special community events, including lectures, films, artist conversations and more.

La Villita Historic Arts Village HISTORIC SITE
(Map p96; ☎210-207-8610; www.lavillita.com; 418 Villita St; ⏲most shops 10am-6pm) FREE History meets commerce at downtown's La Villita. San Antonio's first neighborhood, this 'little village' of stone and adobe houses dates back to the early 1800s and now contains a collection of touristy shops and galleries.

It doesn't exactly offer a portal into the past, but it's worth a stroll, especially if you pause for a walking tour that puts the village into the right historical context. (Maps are available all around the village.) La Villita occupies the space between Paseo de la Villita and Nueva St, and between Alamo and Presa Sts.

DRIVING DISTANCES

San Antonio to Kerrville 65 miles; 1 hour, 10 minutes

Kerrville to Fredericksburg 24 miles; 30 minutes

Fredericksburg to Johnson City 30 miles; 35 minutes

Johnson City to San Antonio 64 miles; 1 hour, 15 minutes

San Antonio to New Braunfels 33 miles; 40 minutes

Tower of the Americas LANDMARK
(Map p96; ☎210-223-3101; www.toweroftheamericas.com; 600 Hemisfair Plaza Way; adult/4-11yr $11/9; ⊙11am-10pm Sun-Thu, to 11pm Fri & Sat) San Antonio's 750ft-high Tower of the Americas is a skyline-defining landmark left over from the 1968 World's Fair. From the 579ft-high observation deck you'll mostly see the tops of buildings, but the sheer height alone might earn a few 'ooohs' and 'aaahs.' Your admission also includes **Skies over Texas**, a 3D film with special effects.

These observation towers always seem to have a revolving restaurant at the top, and this one's no exception. If you want the view to last all through dinner (or if you want to skip the admission price and the film), make a reservation to dine at the Chart House.

Institute of Texan Cultures MUSEUM
(Map p96; ☎210-458-2330; www.texancultures.com; 801 E Durango Blvd in HemisFair Park; adult/3-11yr $8/6; ⊙9am-5pm Mon-Sat, from noon Sun) Some thirty cultures have made Texas what it is; explore them at the museum of the Institute of Texan Cultures. This Smithsonian Affiliate explores the origins of Texas folk traditions and tells the stories of the state's earliest contributors. Behind the main exhibition, the Back 40 area has reconstructed living-history buildings such as a fort, schoolhouse, log cabin and a windmill.

The Latin American influence is fairly prominent in San Antonio, so this museum can be an eye-opener to visitors learning about Texas' diverse cultural background.

Ripley's Alamo Plaza Attractions MUSEUM
(Map p96; ☎210-226-2828; www.alamoplazaattractions.com; 329 Alamo Plaza; adult/4-12yr $26/16; ⊙10am-11pm Sun-Thu, to midnight Fri & Sat late May-early Sep, to 7pm Sun-Thu,to 10pm Fri & Sat early Sep-late May) Time to throw the kids a bone? After touring historical sites all day, you can reward them with a visit to this teen-friendly trio: **Ripley's Haunted Adventure**, **Guinness World Records Museum** and **Tomb Rider 3D**. It's a little cheesy, and definitely touristy, but a good antidote to slogging around the missions all day.

One admission price gets you into the haunted house, museum of oddities and theme-park-style ride, or you can pay a reduced admission if you only have time for one or two attractions.

King William District & Southtown

South of downtown on the banks of the San Antonio River, the charming King William District (once nicknamed 'Sauerkraut Bend') was built by wealthy German settlers at the end of the 19th century. The architecture here is mostly Victorian, though there are fine examples of Italianate, colonial-revival, beaux arts and even art-deco styles. Most of the district's houses have been renovated and are privately owned or run as B&Bs. Stop by the **King William Association** (Map p96; 1032 S Alamo St) or the **San Antonio Conservation Society** (Map p96; ☎210-224-6163; 107 King William St) for self-guided-walking-tour brochures; it's a very pleasant area for a stroll.

Southtown NEIGHBORHOOD
(Map p96; www.southtown.net) Southtown is a small arts district. On the first Friday of every month, galleries stay open late and restaurants host entertainment.

Steves Homestead Museum HISTORIC BUILDING
(Map p96; ☎210-225-5924; 509 King William St; adult/under 12yr $6/free; ⊙10am-4:15pm, last tour 3:30pm) Most of the mansions in the King William District can only be appreciated from the curbside, but one of them provides guided tours: the Steves Homestead. Volunteer docents from the San Antonio Conservation Society run guided tours through this Italianate villa and French Second Empire–style home that dates from 1876.

Built for Edward Steves, a wealthy lumber merchant, this stately house has been restored to demonstrate the life of the affluent at the end of the 19th century. Incidentally, San Antonio's first indoor swimming pool is on the property.

Brackenridge Park & Around

A couple of miles north of downtown, Brackenridge Park has been a favorite San Antonio getaway spot for more than a century, with boat rentals, playgrounds, rides and gardens. Its main attraction – other than a serene green setting – is that it's the headspring for the San Antonio River. Many of the park's sights are designed for children, but some such as the Witte Museum (p102), may be equally interesting for adults.

San Antonio Museum of Art MUSEUM

(SAMA; Map p94; www.samuseum.org; 200 W Jones Ave; adult/child $10/free, Tue free; 10am-9pm Tue, Fri & Sat, to 5pm Wed & Thur, to 6pm Sun) Housed in the original 1880s Lone Star Brewery, which is a piece of art in itself, the San Antonio Museum of Art is off Broadway St just north of downtown. San Antonio's strong Latino influence is reflected in an impressive trove of Latin American art, including Spanish colonial, Mexican and pre-Columbian – one of the most comprehensive collections in the US.

But more than just Latin America is represented here: the museum has a little of everything, from Egyptian antiquities to contemporary abstracts, and in 2005 a new Asian wing was opened to accommodate a growing collection of Chinese ceramics, paintings, decorative items and more.

San Antonio Botanical Gardens GARDENS

(Map p94; 210-207-3250; www.sabot.org; 555 Funston Pl; adult/3-13yr $8/5; 9am-5pm) This expertly tended, 33-acre garden complex showcases native Texas flora. There are also a fragrance garden and a wonderful conservatory, with a bit of everything from equatorial rainforest to alpine flowers and a tropical lagoon. Call or go online for a calendar of special events – from concerts under the stars and bonsai workshops to summer classes for children.

The strolling garden was designed and created by a 26th-generation gardener and one of Japan's living national treasures from the island of Kyūshū (specifically the city of Kumamoto), which is also home to one of Japan's most revered traditional gardens, Suizenji Park. A few of that famous garden's elements appear here.

Japanese Tea Garden GARDENS

(Map p94; 210-212-4814; www.japaneseteagarden.org; 3853 N St Mary's St; dawn-dusk) FREE Hard to believe that this lovely, tranquil place was just a clever way to hide a hole in the ground. What started out as an eyesore of a quarry nearly 100 years ago was transformed into a Japanese-style strolling garden, with stone bridges, floral displays and a 60ft waterfall.

The garden is meant to be enjoyed year-round, but it's especially pretty in spring when the flowers are in bloom.

Greater San Antonio

Leaving downtown yields a greater breadth of options, including theme parks and museums. With all the firepower in the area, the city is teeming with military museums. But note that access to the bases is restricted and you'll need to get visitor's passes (obtainable only through certain gates, and even then subject to change), so bring photo ID. Sometimes the bases may be closed entirely except to military personnel and their dependents, so always call ahead.

McNay Art Museum MUSEUM

(Map p94; 210-824-5368; www.mcnayart.org; 6000 N New Braunfels Ave; adult/12 and under $10/free, extra for special exhibits; 10am-4pm Tue, Wed & Fri, to 9pm Thu, to 5pm Sat, noon-5pm Sun, grounds 7am-6pm daily) Upon her death in 1950, Marion Koogler McNay left her impressive collection of European and American modern art to the city. It has since been supplemented with more works and the collection is now among the best in the Southwest.

In addition to seeing paintings by household names such as Van Gogh, Picasso, Matisse, Renoir, O'Keeffe and Cézanne, half the fun is wandering the spectacular Spanish Colonial revival-style mansion that was the private residence of Marion Koogler McNay.

The Stieren Center for Exhibitions was added in June 2008 and, while it doesn't integrate seamlessly with the original mansion (the center describes itself as a 'translucent, two-story box'), it does add 45,000 sq ft of exhibition space for temporary shows.

SeaWorld AMUSEMENT PARK

(800-700-7786, 210-523-3000; www.seaworld.com; 10500 SeaWorld Dr; adult/3-9yr $60/52; from 10am, closing hour from 5-10pm depending on date) A curious combination of marine mammals and roller coasters, SeaWorld San

SAN ANTONIO FOR CHILDREN

San Antonio is a very popular family destination, thanks to its theme parks and year-round mild climate.

San Antonio Children's Museum (Map p96; ☎210-212-4453; www.sakids.org; 305 E Houston St; adult/under 2yr $7/free; ⏱9am-5pm Mon-Fri, to 6pm Sat, noon-5pm Sun) Perfect for the 10-and-under set, even kids who are barely standing have a blast at this museum.

It has two floors of exhibits focusing on interactive play, including the Tot Spot, the Art Pavilion, the Bubble Ranch and Leonardo's Lab. There's plenty for kids to do: open an account and use an ATM at the Good Cents Bank; run an airport and fly an airplane; or learn about science in PowerBall Hall.

Community volunteers and local businesses come in for workshops and special events; check the website or call for a schedule. Parking is validated for one hour at MidCity Parking Garage at 240 E Houston St, and at St Mary's Garage at 400 N St Mary's St.

Witte Museum (Map p94; ☎210-357-1900; www.wittemuseum.org; 3801 Broadway St; adult/4-11yr $10/7; ⏱10am-5pm Mon & Wed-Sat, to 8pm Tue, noon-5pm Sun) If your kids are a little too grownup for the Children's Museum, they can graduate to this museum on the eastern edge of Brackenridge Park. The Witte (pronounced 'witty') is educational but engaging, with hands-on explorations of natural history, science and Texas history.

Don't miss the Science Treehouse, a high-tech activity center in back of the museum building. It's a hit with all ages, even the really big kids (aka parents). The museum is free on Tuesday from 3pm to 8pm.

Kiddie Amusement Park (Map p94; ☎210-824-4351; www.kiddiepark.com; 3015 Broadway St; 1 ticket $2.50, 6 tickets $11.25, day pass $13; ⏱10am-7pm Wed-Sun) This 1920s-vintage kiddie amusement park has a wonderful old carousel, a tiny roller coaster, a Ferris wheel, skee-ball alleys and more. It's a slice of carnival atmosphere year-round. Bargain discount days fall on Wednesday, which might save you a buck or two.

San Antonio Zoo (Map p94; ☎210-734-7184; www.sazoo-aq.org; 3903 N St Mary's St; adult/child 3-11yr $12/9.50; ⏱9am-5pm) The San Antonio Zoo is known for its conservation programs, which have given it one of the largest endangered-animal collections in the country. Overall, 750 species call this 9000-acre zoo home. At the time of writing, the zoo was gearing up for its 2014 Zoocentennial and big changes were afoot, including a new central plaza and carousel.

(Note: This isn't a good place to spend a hot summer afternoon; come early or late when the animals aren't inside complaining about the heat.)

Magik Children's Theatre (Map p96; ☎210-227-2751; www.magiktheatre.org; 420 S Alamo St; adult/child $10/8; ⏱box office 9am-5pm Mon-Fri, 10am-5pm Sat) This merry theater troupe stages adaptations of favorite children's books, hilarious original musicals and modern retellings of Texas legends and classic fairy tales, such as the witty (and bilingual!) *La Cinderella*. The theater's regular season runs from September to May, and includes a contemporary play series for adults, too.

Antonio is home to both Shamu the killer whale and Great White, an inverted 'heels-over-head' roller coaster. Animal feedings and shows take place at scheduled times, so plan your day to make sure you don't miss out.

Numerous opportunities arise to get wet – which is a welcome relief during the hot summer months – including the Shamu show, three different water rides and the Lost Lagoon Waterpark, all included in your admission.

Check the website for behind-the-scenes tours; parking is $17.

Six Flags Fiesta Texas AMUSEMENT PARK
(☎210-697-5050; www.sixflags.com/fiestatexas; 17000 IH-10 W, exit 555; adult/child under 48in tall $62/47; ⏱hours vary, daily Jun-Aug, Sat & Sun Sep-May) You don't have to be a kid to enjoy Fiesta Texas. This popular theme park has plenty of rides that you must be 'this tall' to ride. Of course, there are more than 25

kids' rides for the vertically challenged, as well as swimming pools and water rides over in the White Water Bay area (open May to September).

The setting – against a limestone quarry that looks similar to the Arizona desert – is dramatic, and there are plenty of shows and music. Parking is $17.

Fort Sam Houston HISTORIC SITE
(Map p94; ☎210-221-0213) 'Fort Sam' – as it's known 'round here – is ready to enlist you for a little military history. Its claims to fame? The Apache Chief Geronimo was held here for 40 days. It was also the site of the first military flight in US history in 1910. And it's home to several historic buildings with designated museums.

The oldest building at Fort Sam (and Geronimo's short-term residence) is the **Quadrangle** (Map p94; ☎210-221-1232; 1400 E Grayson St; ⊙8am-5pm Mon-Fri, noon-6pm Sat & Sun) FREE, built in 1876. Today the Quadrangle is open to the public, and it leads through to a sort of petting zoo: deer have been kept here for more than 100 years, and rabbits, ducks and chickens abound. At the time of writing, the **Fort Sam Houston Museum** was moving into the Quadrangle, and should be complete by the time you visit.

In the northeast section of the grounds, the **US Army Medical Department Museum** (Map p94; ☎210-221-6358; 2310 Stanley St; ⊙10am-4pm Tue-Sun) FREE has a display of army medical gear from the US and several other countries, including Germany, the former Soviet Union, Vietnam and China, and a cool collection of restored ambulances, helicopters and a hospital rail car. But what makes the AMEDD museum really worth the trip is the collection of Civil War surgical gear, notably the disturbing saws and portable amputation kits.

Texas Transportation Museum MUSEUM
(TTM; ☎210-490-3554; www.txtransportationmuseum.org; 11731 Wetmore Rd, off Wurzbach Pkwy; adult/under 13yr $6/4; ⊙9am-3pm Fri, 10am-5pm Sat & Sun) This modest volunteer-run museum just northeast of the airport boasts full-size, miniature and indoor scale-model railroads. On the weekends hourly train rides are included with the price of admission, and there are special holiday events for kids.

San Antonio Missions National Historical Park HISTORIC BUILDING
(Map p94; www.nps.gov/saan) Spain's missionary presence can best be felt at the ruins of the four missions south of town: **Missions Concepción** (1731), **San José** (1720), **San Juan** (1731) and **Espada** (1745–56). Religious services are still held in the mission churches of San José, San Juan and Espada, and the mariachi Mass at Mission San José at 12:30pm on Sunday is a San Antonio tradition.

From downtown, VIA transit bus 42 goes to San José. The Texas Trolley tours visit San José and Concepción. Otherwise, rent a bicycle or drive. From downtown, take St Mary's St south until it becomes Mission Rd, then follow the brown signs indicating pointing to the missions.

Mission Concepción HISTORIC BUILDING
(Map p94; 807 Mission Rd; ⊙9am-5pm) The first mission along the trail features a Spanish colonial church built in 1755. It's a passably interesting stop for history buffs, and essential for anyone who doesn't do things by half.

Mission San José HISTORIC BUILDING
(Map p94; 6701 San José Dr; ⊙9am-5pm) FREE Known in its time as the Queen of the Missions, it's certainly the largest and arguably the most beautiful of all on the Mission Trail. Because it's a little more remote and pastoral, surrounded by thick stone walls, you can really get a sense of what life was

MISSION TRAIL

The San Antonio missions were constructed in the early 18th century as part of an effort to provide way-stations and staging areas for Spanish colonial expansion to the north. The native Coahuiltecans, already under pressure from other nomadic Native American tribes pushing down from the north, showed a willingness to convert to Christianity, and labored for the colonial Spanish priests in order to receive food and protection at the missions.

Constructed in what is now downtown, the first and most impressive mission was what would come to be known as the Alamo (p93). With the destruction by war or disease of many east Texas missions, the Spanish quickly built four more missions south of the Alamo, which collectively are known as the 'Mission Trail.' (Not to be confused with the 8-mile hike-and-bike trail that connects them.)

WHAT THE...? F.I.S.H.

Fish gotta swim, birds gotta fly, right? Wait – or is it the other way around? Where I-35 passes over the San Antonio River near Camden St and the Museum of Art, a school of larger-than-life fish floats overhead – an art installment by Donald Lipski entitled *F.I.S.H.* The fiberglass fish are lit from within, turning the unlikeliest of spaces into an upside-down aquarium that is especially enchanting after dark.

like here in the 18th and 19th centuries. It's also the location of the main visitor center.

Ranger-led tours cover life in the mission and show up close the magnificent church and its famous rose window, a stunningly carved masterpiece attached to the sacristy. The best time to visit would absolutely be on Sundays at 12:30pm, when a mariachi Mass is held.

Mission San Juan HISTORIC BUILDING
(9102 Graf Rd; ⏲9am-5pm) The most somber of the missions, this is the next stop if you're on the let's-see-them-all plan. The surviving church is open, as is a small visitor center and a quarter-mile nature trail along the river.

Mission Espada HISTORIC BUILDING
(10040 Espada Rd; ⏲9am-5pm) Last but not least on the Mission Trail, Mission Espada is the oldest mission in the east Texas chain, and the best place to check out the historic *acequia* (aqueduct) – the missions' irrigation system that's still in use today and has been designated a Historic Civil Engineering Landmark.

Activities

Apart from Brackenridge Park and the Mission Trail, San Antonio is short on places to enjoy the great outdoors. You've usually got to head into the Hill Country or drive north on I-35 to the aquatic wonderlands of New Braunfels, Gruene and San Marcos, where you can go swimming and tubing to your heart's content on local rivers and at amusement parks. Golfers are in luck, however.

Golf

San Antonio is a favorite golf destination, thanks to the region's mild year-round climate. Rates vary from $35 to tote your own bag around a public course, to more than $150 to play at a private resort.

Brackenridge Golf Course GOLF
(Map p94; ☎210-226-5612; 2315 Ave B) A municipal golf course north of downtown in Brackenridge Park.

Olmos Basin Golf Course GOLF
(Map p94; ☎210-826-4041; 7022 N McCullough Ave) Even farther north is this municipal golf course in Olmos Basin Park.

Cedar Creek Golf Course GOLF
(☎210-695-5050; 8250 Vista Colina) The most remote municipal course is in far northwest San Antonio.

Canyon Springs Golf Club GOLF
(☎888-800-1511, 210-497-1770; 2440 Wilderness Oak Rd) This nationally renowned public golf course offers an 18-hole championship course.

Quarry Golf Club GOLF
(Map p94; ☎800-347-7759, 210-824-4500; 444 E Basse Rd) The back nine of this public course is located in a 100-year-old quarry pit.

La Cantera Golf Club GOLF
(☎800-446-5387, 210-558-4653; 16641 La Cantera Parkway) Attached to the Westin resort, this public golf club has two 18-hole courses.

Hiking & Cycling

Biking around Brackenridge Park or along the Mission Trail makes for a nice outing when the weather is mild.

Friedrich Wilderness Park HIKING
(☎210-372-9124; www.fofriedrichpark.org; 21395 Milsa Rd, north of Loop 1604; 7:30am-sunset) FREE This 230-acre park near Six Flags Fiesta Texas is just for hikers. It has 5.5 miles of walking trails, which are especially worth a detour to see wildflowers bloom in spring.

McAllister Park WALKING
(☎210-207-7275; 13102 Jones Maltsberger Rd; ⏲dawn-dusk) FREE For a taste of the Hill Country without venturing outside the city limits, head to this 850-acre park. It has about 7 miles of trails for walking and cycling; one of the trails is also wheelchair-accessible.

B-Cycle CYCLING
(☎210-281-0101; www.sanantonio.bcycle.com; day/week pass $10/24; ⏲4am-midnight) The B-Cycle racks you'll see all around downtown

make hopping on a bike convenient – not to mention tempting. It's great for sight-seeing; just dock your bike at a station while you're not using it and the meter stops. Come back when you're ready, hop on any bike and go.

The pricing structure is a little complicated, but it could end up saving you quite a bit of money over an all-day rental. First, you pay for your day pass, either online or at one of the stations. Then, you're charged only for the time you're actually on the bike ($2 per half hour).

Abel's Bicycle Repair & Rental CYCLING
(210-542-6272; www.abelsbicycleshop.com; 1119 Ada St; per day $30) If you want to rent a bike for the whole day, try Abel's. This company will deliver free of charge to the downtown area.

Swimming

Splashtown SWIMMING
(Map p94; 210-227-1400; www.splashtownsa.com; 3600 N IH-35; adult/child under 48in tall $30/$23, after 5pm $17; from 10:30am Jun-Aug) San Antonio can get awfully hot and sticky in summer, and one of the best remedies is putting on your swimsuit and heading to the water park. Splashtown is where you'll find Texas' biggest wave pool, a seven-story aquatic bobsled run, and inner tubing in total darkness. There are also gentler floating rides and a special 'Kids Kove' for preschoolers.

Call or check the website to find out the schedule before heading out. You can save between $3 and $6 per person by buying your tickets online.

Tours

The Downtown Visitors Center (p118) has information about these and other tours.

Rio San Antonio Cruises BOAT TOUR
(Map p96; 800-417-4139, 210-244-5700; www.riosanantonio.com; adult/child under 5yr $8.25/2; 9am-9pm) One of the best ways to experience the Riverwalk is with these 40-minute narrated cruises that give you a good visual overview of the river and a light history lesson. You can buy your tickets online, or get them on the waterfront at any of the stops. No reservations are necessary and tours leave every 15 to 20 minutes.

It's a nice way to pass a little time, especially if you've been walking around all morning.

San Antonio Trolley Tours TROLLEY TOUR
(Map p96; 210-492-4144; www.citytoursinc.com; ticket center 321 Alamo Plaza; 1hr tour adult/child $20/10, hopper pass $26/13; 9:30am-4:30pm) Get a quick overview of the town with a one-hour narrated tour, or spend a few dollars more for a two-day hopper pass that lets you get off and on at all the attractions. If you're looking to get out of town, there are also hill country tours and wine tours.

Alamo City Ghost Tours WALKING TOUR
(210-336-7831; www.alamocityghosttours.com; adult/5-17yr $16/11; tours 9pm) Two great options: The Alamo Ghost Hunt, where guides bring along enough EMF meters and dowsing rods for everyone; or the Haunted Pub Crawl, which is a fun, social tour just for grownups that combines ghosts and beer.

SegCity Ghost Tours SEGWAY TOUR
(Map p96; 210-224-0773; www.segcity.com; 124 Losoya St; tours $65) A fun twist on predictable ghost tours? Do it on a Segway. That means if you do see a ghost, it'll be easier to outrun it. This company also offers regular old nonhaunted tours of downtown and the King William District.

Festivals & Events

San Antonio is a city with a full calendar of festivals and events; visitors are bound to run into at least one, no matter when they arrive. For a complete list, check with the Downtown Visitors Center (p118). Advance tickets for many of the biggest events are sold through Ticketmaster (p114).

San Antonio Stock Show & Rodeo RODEO
(www.sarodeo.com; mid-Feb) Big-name concerts follow each night's rodeo; 16 days in mid-February.

Fiesta San Antonio CULTURAL
(www.fiesta-sa.org; mid-Apr) For over 10 days in mid-April there are river parades, carnivals, Tejano music, dancing and tons of food in a mammoth, citywide party.

Fiesta Noche del Rio PERFORMING ARTS
(www.fiestanochesa.com; late May-early Sep) All summer long, the Fiesta Noche del Rio brings Latin music to the Arneson River Theater in a series of concerts and dance performances.

Alamo Bowl SPORTS
(www.alamobowl.com; Dec) A college football championship of Big 10 vs Big 12 conference

FIESTA SAN ANTONIO

In late April, hundreds of thousands of partygoers throng the streets of San Antonio for Fiesta San Antonio (p105). A 10-day series of riotous events makes for the city's biggest celebration, with general mayhem, fairs, rodeos, races and a whole lot of music and dancing. Going strong after more than 120 years, the festival is the high point of the River City's year.

Fiesta San Antonio dates back to 1891, when local women paraded on horseback in front of the Alamo and threw flowers at each other, all meant to honor the heroes of the Alamo and the Battle of San Jacinto. Today's **Battle of the Flowers** (www.battleofflowers.org) is only a small piece of Fiesta, which has grown into an enormous party involving 75,000 volunteers, millions of spectators and more than 150 events.

At the beginning of Fiesta week, the **Texas Cavaliers' River Parade** kicks off with decorated floats drifting along the San Antonio River and a pilgrimage to the Alamo. On the final Saturday night, **Fiesta Flambeau** claims to be the largest lighted parade in the USA, with marchers carrying candles, sparklers, flashlights, torches and anything else handy.

But locals' top pick of Fiesta week is **A Night in Old San Antonio** (aka 'NIOSA') which runs for four nights, during which a small army of women volunteers transform La Villita into a multiethnic bazaar of food, music, dancing, arts and much, much more.

teams draws up to 65,000 spectators to the **Alamodome** (Map p96).

Sleeping

San Antonio has loads of places to stay that become booked solid – and much more expensive – during major National Collegiate Athletics Association (NCAA) games, city festivals and large conventions. Most motels and hotels raise their rates substantially during summer, too.

Even with so many hotel options, really cheap places downtown are few and far between. The downtown area does have a good selection of reasonably priced motels and there are a multitude of choices out by the airport and along the interstates.

San Antonio also has its fair share of B&Bs and generally speaking they are good value, ensconced in fine old homes in the more historic areas of the city, especially the King William District.

Downtown

For many large Riverwalk properties, you can often find special discounts when you book online.

★City View Inn & Suites Sunset Station MOTEL $
(☎210-222-2220; www.cityviewinnsa.com; 1306 E Commerce St; r $75-95; P ⊖ ❄ ☎) Just acriss I-37, less than a mile from the Alamo, sits a skinny little three-story building full of clean, new rooms. Amenities are few, but if you're just looking for a place to park your bags, this place is great. It's also just two blocks from the Amtrak station, if that's how you're arriving.

Rodeway Inn Downtown MOTEL $
(Map p94; ☎210-223-2951; www.rodewayinnsa.com; 900 N Main Ave; d $39-79; P ❄ ☎ ≋) You could walk to the Alamo and Riverwalk, which are just one mile away, but you don't even have to because the downtown trolley comes right to your door. Rooms are as basic as can be, but it'll save you some dollars, especially when you factor in free parking and continental breakfast.

Red Roof Inn San Antonio Downtown MOTEL $
(Map p96; ☎210-229-9973; www.redroof.com; 1011 E Houston St; d $68-149; P ⊖ ❄ ☎ ≋ 🐾) An easy walk to both the Alamo and Riverwalk, but the trade-off is the freeway location. Still, it's a good deal and the standard rooms are huge.

★Hotel Havana HOTEL $$
(Map p96; ☎210-222-2008; www.havanasanantonio.com; 1015 Navarro St; d $106-189; P ⊖ ❄ @ ☎ 🐾) Texas design guru and hotelier Liz Lambert could make a radish look cool. Luckily she's turned her sights to fixing up a few lucky properties such as this one, judiciously adding eclectic touches – a retro pink refrigerator, for example – to

her simple, clean designs. Check online for discounts for Texas residents or advance purchases.

El Tropicano Hotel HOTEL **$$**
(Map p96; ☎877-214-9768, 210-223-9461; www.eltropicanohotel.com; 110 Lexington Ave; d $99-129; P ⊖ ❄ ☜ ≋ 🐾; ⊡ blue line, car) The retro-tropical vibe is a little old-school Vegas, a little Miami Beach, but this breezy hotel comes about it honestly, having originally opened in 1962. A fresh, mid-century modern lobby and updated rooms make it feel fun instead of old. (The $18 parking, however, can dampen the fun.)

Inn on the Riverwalk B&B **$$**
(Map p96; ☎800-730-0019, 210-225-6333; www.innontheriverwalksa.com; 129 Woodward Pl; d $119-179; P ⊖ ❄ ☜) Presided over by a venerable pecan tree, this B&B is in a beautiful, peaceful setting by the river. Each cheery room has its own private bath, with the more expensive digs equipped with a Jacuzzi, private porch or balcony.

Riverwalk Vista B&B **$$**
(Map p96; ☎866-898-4782, 210-223-3200; www.riverwalkvista.com; 262 Losoya St; d incl breakfast $120-210, ste $180-270; ⊖ ❄ @) Soaring ceilings with enormous windows, exposed brick walls, crisp, white bedding – this is simplicity done right. And just because the decor is simple doesn't mean it doesn't pamper: there are still plenty of niceties like flat-screen TVs, leather chairs and feather blankets.

Menger Hotel HISTORIC HOTEL **$$**
(Map p96; ☎800-345-9285, 210-223-4361; www.mengerhotel.com; 204 Alamo Plaza; d from $125; P ⊖ ❄ ☜ ≋ 🐾) Historic? Definitely. This place was built in the shadow of the Alamo a scant 23 years after the famous battle. Oscar Wilde, Mae West, Teddy Roosevelt – the former guest list is impressive. Over the decades, new additions kept getting built on, so it's a bit rambling and confusing to get around.

The vaguely charming 'Antique Rooms' are the same price as the refurbished rooms, which are the same price as the unrefurbished rooms from the 1960s. Be clear about what you're reserving.

Crockett Hotel HOTEL **$$**
(Map p96; ☎800-292-1050, 210-225-6500; www.crocketthotel.com; 320 Bonham St; d $119-139; P ⊖ ❄ ☜ ≋ 🐾) No wonder pictures of the Alamo are always tightly cropped. Pull back and you can see the Crockett's sign hovering just behind the fort. (In Texas, they call that 'spittin' distance.') Rooms are basic but pleasant enough, and there's an outdoor pool, Jacuzzi and rooftop sundeck.

Emily Morgan Hotel BOUTIQUE HOTEL **$$**
(Map p96; ☎800-824-6674, 210-225-5100; www.emilymorganhotel.com; 705 E Houston St; d $159-199; P ⊖ ❄ ☜ ≋ 🐾) The name sounds as though this place should be awash in floral prints and lace runners, but this historic hotel right behind the Alamo is actually pretty stylish, and has been bought by Hilton. The boutique-style rooms are clean, large and enjoy all the luxury amenities, from Tazo teas and Aveda bath products to high-speed internet access.

La Quinta Inn Market Square HOTEL **$$**
(Map p96; ☎210-271-0001; www.laquinta.com; 900 Dolorosa St; d from $105; P ⊖ ❄ ≋ 🐾) The updated rooms have been tastefully redecorated (hooray for no more Southwestern motif!) and right accross the street is Mi Tierra Cafe & Bakery, which is ideal for 3am enchilada cravings. Prices vary widely depending on when you visit; shoot for the lower end of the spectrum to feel satisfied with your choice.

Omni La Mansion del Rio HISTORIC HOTEL **$$$**
(Map p96; ☎210-518-1000; www.lamansion.com; 112 College St; d $199-399; P ⊖ ❄ @ ≋ 🐾) This fabulous downtown property was born out of 19th-century religious school buildings in the Spanish-Mexican hacienda style. It's on a quiet stretch of the Riverwalk and its discreet oasis attracts stars and other notables. Enjoy in-room spa services, swim in the outdoor heated pool or unwind at the hotel's exceptional restaurant, **Las Canarias** (Map p96; ☎210-518-1000; 112 College St; breakfast $12-16, mains $31-50; ⏲6:30am-2pm & 5:30-10pm Mon-Sat, from 10am Sun).

Mokara Hotel & Spa HOTEL **$$$**
(Map p96; ☎866-605-1212; www.mokarahotels.com; 212 W Crockett St; d from $299; ⊖ ❄ @ ☜ ≋ 🐾) If you really want to go all out, this luxurious hotel (formerly the Watermark) is a good place to get pampered, with top-of-the-line amenities and an on-site spa. It's ultraserene, in stark contrast to the tourist scene waiting just downstairs, and ideally suited to people who want to just draw the blinds and enjoy some relaxation.

Hotel Valencia BOUTIQUE HOTEL $$$
(Map p96; ☎210-227-9700; www.hotelvalencia-riverwalk.com; 150 E Houston St; d $159-459; P⊖❄☜) Faux-mink throws, molded concrete, light shining through perforated metal – this place is all about texture. It could have been transported from New York City, both in its minimalist-chic style and in the size of some of the smaller rooms, but it's a hip option if you eschew chains and historic hotels.

King William District

This historic district is known for its beautiful homes, so it's no surprise that the majority of offerings here are B&Bs.

★**King William Manor** B&B $$
(Map p96; ☎800-405-0367, 210-222-0144; www.kingwilliammanor.com; 1037 S Alamo St; d incl breakfast $129-175; P⊖❄☜≋) In a neighborhood known for beautiful old houses and B&Bs, this grand, Greek Revival mansion occupying a large corner lot still manages to jump out at you and say, 'Hey, look at me!' Maybe it's the columns, maybe it's the sprawling lawn or perhaps it's the wraparound porches. The inside lives up to the exterior, with understatedly elegant rooms, some of which are enormous.

A Yellow Rose Inn B&B $$
(Map p96; ☎210-229-9903; www.ayellowrose.com; 229 Madison St; d incl breakfast $89-200; P⊖❄☜) True to its name, this butterscotch-colored house is a beauty. Spacious rooms are tastefully furnished, with well-thought-out amenities like fresh flowers, snacks, sodas and juice. We love the flexible breakfast policy, which allows you to take breakfast in your room or skip it all together and pay a little less.

Brackenridge House B&B B&B $$
(Map p96; ☎877-271-3442, 210-271-3442; www.brackenridgehouse.com; 230 Madison St; d $129-159; P⊖❄☜) This hospitable B&B likes to feed you, from the formal, three-course breakfast to sherry and chocolate treats later in the day. The rooms are of the frilly sort, with quilts, floral prints and lace, but they're also practical, with bar fridges and microwaves.

Noble Inns B&B $$
(☎800-242-2770, 210-223-2353; www.nobleinns.com; d incl breakfast from $139; P⊖❄☜≋) This collection of three inns has something for everyone – at least everyone who likes antiques and Victorian style. The **Ogé House** (Map p96; 209 Washington St; d $179-349; 🚌blue line) is the most elegant of the three, with lushly appointed rooms and a prime location on the residential end of the Riverwalk.

The **Jackson House** (Map p96; 107 Madison St; d $149-219; P⊖❄☜) is a little more traditional B&B style, plus it has a warm swim spa in a stained-glass conservatory. And the **Carriage House** (Map p96; 202 Washington St, check in at Ogé House; ste $159-259; P⊖❄☜≋) is the frilliest of all, but offers access to a pool and spa.

Brackenridge Park & Around

This neighborhood offers relief from downtown prices, but still keeps you close to the action.

Ruckman Haus B&B $$
(Map p94; ☎866-736-1468, 210-736-1468; www.ruckmanhaus.com; 629 W French St; d $115-145, ste $165; P⊖❄☜) Welcome home! It's hard to feel more at ease than you will at this homey, comfortable B&B, with lovely gardens, porches and common areas where you could hang out all day. We love the Sun Room because it has – surprise! – a sun room, as well as a private rooftop deck. The Highland Room is perfect for parties of three.

Bonner Garden B&B $$
(Map p94; ☎210-733-4222; www.bonnergarden.com; 145 E Agarita Ave; d $115-165; P⊖❄☜≋) This lovely Italianate villa dates from 1910 and was built for artist Mary Bonner. Original works by Texas artists hang on the walls and there's a fireplace with antique tiles. Our hands-down favorite is Mary Bonner's studio, a detached suite with whitewashed stone walls and Saltillo tile floors.

Inn at Craig Place B&B $$
(Map p94; ☎877-427-2447, 210-736-1017; www.craigplace.com; 117 W Craig Pl; d $155-195; P⊖❄☜) A quiet getaway in the historic Monte Vista neighborhood, this National Trust property is popular for weddings and honeymoons. Each of the romantic rooms has its own breakfast table, bath and telephone. Freshly baked cookies and chocolates appear in the evening, plus there's a three-course hot breakfast every morning. Peruse

the library or simply relax in the antique-furnished parlor.

Greater San Antonio

Rittiman Inn MOTEL $
(210-657-0808; 6364 IH-35 N; s/d $51/57;) This independently owned motel on the north side of town is a bit of a surprise. The outside has some quirky, faux Bavarian touches and the inside manages to pull off a look that, while it may not have been updated in ages, doesn't come off as shabby, like they just pulled the plastic slipcovers off right before you came.

It's, dare we say, kind of cute.

Hill Country Inn & Suites HOTEL $
(Map p94; 800-314-3424, 210-599-4204; www.stayhci.com; 2383 NE Loop 410; d incl breakfast $65-99;) Just north of downtown, this anachronistic place feels like it belongs in the Hill Country more than off an interstate, with cabin-style rooms, ranch-style porches and country-style furnishings. With its playground and picnic tables, it's great for families.

Dixie Campground CAMPGROUND $
(Map p94; 210-337-6501; 1011 Gembler Rd; tent sites with electricity $20, RV sites with hookups $27-35;) Dixie is northeast of downtown San Antonio near the SBC Center. It's about as flashy as your typical KOA campground and slightly cheaper, too.

Admiralty RV Resort CAMPGROUND $
(877-236-4715, 210-647-7878; www.admiraltyrvresort.com; 1485 N Ellison Dr; RV sites regular/luxury $40/60;) On the western edge of town, this top-notch RV park with a junior Olympic-size swimming pool and plenty of shade is convenient to **SeaWorld**, which runs a free shuttle service to the campground during summer. Discounts are available for weekly stays and association memberships (including AAA and AARP).

Super 8 Motel SeaWorld MOTEL $
(210-678-0888; www.super8.com; 2211 SW Loop 410; summer $68-100, winter $50-80;) All right, so you're not going for luxury. You're spending most of your time at SeaWorld (only 1.2 miles away) anyway. This Super 8 motel is slightly nicer than the norm, with an outdoor pool, making it a decent base of operations.

Hyatt Place Northwest MOTEL $$
(210-561-0099; www.sanantonionorthwest.place.hyatt.com; 4303 Hyatt Place Dr; d $109-149;) Almost everything out near Six Flags is a chain, but this awesome little Hyatt Place is one of the best. It's clean and fresh, with spacious rooms and a smartly modern decor, and it's just 6 miles from the park. Flat-screen TVs, continental breakfast and free computer access and printing make it a bargain.

Westin La Cantera Resort RESORT $$$
(800-937-8461, 210-558-6500; www.westinlacantera.com; 16641 La Cantera Pkwy; d from $199 plus resort fee per night $26;) Standard rooms are elegant but on the small side, so you'll enjoy this resort most if you're willing to get out and take advantage of the six pools, three hot tubs, golf course, tennis courts, health club and spa. Almost outside of town, the overwhelming offerings might upstage your other sightseeing activities.

This place must be trying to break the world record for most hospitality awards ever: *Condé Nast Traveler, Golf Digest* and *AAA Four Diamond* are among those that have recognized the destination property.

OCHO AT HOTEL HAVANA

You're never going to stumble across **Ocho** (Map p96; 210-222-2008; www.havanasanantonio.com; 1015 Navarro St; mains $10-20; 7am-10pm Sun-Thu, to midnight Fri & Sat) while roaming the Riverwalk or checking out the King William district, but this hidden-away lounge next to Hotel Havana is worth seeking out.

A glassed-in conservatory that looks onto the northern stretch of the Riverwalk has been fitted out with chandeliers and velvet furnishings for a eclectic-chic decor that's become hotelier Liz Lambert's trademark. The Cuban-inspired menu is not extensive, but it's excellent, serving everything from breakfast to late-night cocktails. Besides, you came for the ambience, right?

If it's a nice evening, you can get there by strolling along the Riverwalk about 20 minutes north of the main hub.

Eating

A location along the Riverwalk gives any restaurant instant atmosphere – especially when there's a patio involved. That makes it prime real estate, which means you're not going to find many bargains there.

Southtown has its share of hip eateries that are better value, and north of downtown around Brackenridge Park there are tons of inexpensive dining options.

Naturally, some of the best cooking is Tex-Mex and Mexican-style. Both the *San Antonio Current* and the *San Antonio Express-News'* 'Weekender' section regularly list their top pick of restaurants and are worth checking out.

Downtown

Schilo's German Delicatessen DELI **$**

(Map p96; ☎210-223-6692; www.schilos.com; 424 E Commerce St; meals $4-9; ⊙7am-8:30pm Mon-Sat) Schilo's has certainly earned its ambience: this German restaurant has been around since 1917 and looks the part, down to the wooden booths and the elaborate pattern of the hexagonal floor tiles. Specialties include wonderful split-pea soup, baked goods, fresh pumpernickel bread, German beer and homemade root beer.

Justin's Ice Cream Company ICE CREAM **$**

(Map p96; ☎210-222-2707; 245 E Commerce St, Riverwalk; ⊙11am-11pm) Ready to stop and rest for a bit? Cool off with a dish of home-made, Italian-style ice cream, gelato or sorbet at a table overlooking the river. Look for it across the river from the Omni Mansion del Rio hotel.

Candy's Old Fashioned Burgers BURGERS **$**

(Map p96; ☎210-222-9659; 115 S Flores St; mains $4-9; ⊙10am-7:30pm Mon-Fri) This little place across from the Bexar Co Courthouse has a tiny dining room with a nostalgic, small-town feel. If that sounds a bit quaint, wait till you see the whoppin' burgers and big fried catfish platters it serves up.

Mi Tierra Cafe & Bakery TEX-MEX **$$**

(Map p96; ☎210-225-1262; www.mitierracafe.com; 218 Produce Row; mains $12-16; ⊙24hr) Dishing out traditional Mexican food since 1941, this 500-seat behemoth in Market Square sprawls across several dining areas, giving the busy wait staff and strolling mariachis quite a workout. It's also open 24 hours, making it ideal for 3am enchilada cravings.

County Line Smokehouse BARBECUE **$$**

(Map p96; ☎210-229-1941; 111 W Crockett St, Riverwalk; sandwiches $10-13, platters $15-27; ⊙11am-10pm Sun-Thu, to 11pm Fri & Sat) San Antonio isn't known for its barbecues – it's clearly more of a Tex-Mex kind of town – but this outpost of the Austin minichain scratches the itch nicely with heaping dishes of brisket, ribs and sausages.

Portions are already big, but if you're feeling ambitious you can choose the all-you-can-eat Family Style ($29.99 per person) – which is often much more than you can or should eat.

Casa Rio MEXICAN **$$**

(Map p96; ☎210-225-6718; www.casa-rio.com; 430 E Commerce St, Riverwalk; mains $8-14; ⊙11am-9pm Sun-Thu, to 11pm Fri & Sat) Down on the Riverwalk, you can't help but notice the colorful array of umbrellas right on the water. One of San Antonio's oldest Mexican restaurants, Casa Rio has been around since 1946, and the building itself is a Spanish hacienda that dates back to the colonial period of Texas history. Overall, a cheerful (and affordable) place to soak in the ambience.

Dick's Last Resort AMERICAN **$$**

(Map p96; ☎210-224-0026; www.dickslastresort.com; 406 Navarro St, Riverwalk; lunch $8-10, dinner mains $13-23; ⊙11am-2am) Sure, this hopping chain restaurant serving standard pub grub is touristy but, well, so is the Riverwalk. The main reason to give in to Dick's is the purposefully and comically obnoxious service. (Let's just say its name is no coincidence.)

Boudro's TEX-MEX **$$$**

(Map p96; ☎210-224-8484; 421 E Commerce St, Riverwalk; lunch $8-12, dinner mains $20-32; ⊙11am-11pm Sun-Thu, to midnight Fri & Sat) This brightly colored restaurant is hugely popular with locals. Fresh guacamole is made right at your table. The upscale Tex-Mex menu reveals some gourmet surprises, such as black bean soup made with sherry and white cheddar, lobster tail fajitas drizzled with pineapple *pico de gallo* (salsa), and wines from Texas and California.

Biga on the Banks AMERICAN **$$$**

(Map p96; ☎210-225-0722; www.biga.com; 203 S St Mary's St, Riverwalk; mains $26-40; ⊙5:30-10pm Sun-Thu, to 11pm Fri & Sat) This is one of the most justifiably praised restaurants in town, run by chef Bruce Auden. The menu is a wonderful mix of European, Tex-Mex, American and Asian influences that prob-

BUILT ON BEER

Beer isn't the only good thing to come out of breweries. San Antonio was once a brewing town, home to two of Texas' largest breweries. The Lone Star Brewery and Pearl Brewery were both established by German settlers in the late 1800s, and while both of them eventually shut down, they left behind two remarkable buildings.

The Lone Star Brewery has provided an impressive setting for the San Antonio Museum of Art (p101), which opened in 1981. And the old Pearl Brewery has received a massive face-lift as part of the new **Pearl development** (Map p94; www.atpearl.com; 200 E Grayson St) north of downtown, including shops, cafes and restaurants. At the time of writing, a hotel was rumored to be moving into the gorgeous main building; by the time you hold this book in your hand, it may already be open.

ably don't cost as much as they should (certainly not what they could). It's stylish yet welcoming, and the wine list is impressive.

Bohanan's STEAKHOUSE **$$$**
(Map p96; ☎210-472-2277; www.bohanans.com; 219 E Houston St; most mains $25-60; ⏰5-10pm Mon-Thu, to 11pm Fri & Sat, to 9pm Sun) This place takes their steaks seriously and, at these prices, so should you. Lots of people can appreciate a great steak, but you'll treasure the experience even more if you're the type of person who throws around terms such as 'Akaushi beef.' These cows were raised in a humane and healthy fashion, and possibly given pedicures too, from the sound of it.

King William District & Southtown

Lots of fun new places are springing up just a few minutes south of downtown, especially along Alamo St.

Madhatters Tea House & Café CAFE **$**
(Map p96; ☎210-212-4832; www.madhatterstea.com; 320 Beauregard St; bakery items $1-5, meals $6-11; ⏰7am-9pm Mon-Fri, 8am-9pm Sat, 9am-3pm Sun; 📶🌱) A cute neighborhood cafe located in a former house, Madhatters is a pleasingly homey place to stop when you're feeling peckish. It has breakfast during the week, brunch on the weekends, and soups, sandwiches and great big salads to refuel during the day. Of course, you can always stop by for afternoon tea and there are more than 70 types to choose from.

Guenther House CAFE **$**
(Map p96; 205 E Guenther St; mains $7-9; ⏰7am-3pm) Located in the Pioneer Flour Mill complex, this is the kind of place you'd choose if you were meeting up with the gals or taking your mom out to lunch. Their speciality is the champagne chicken enchiladas, but they also serve yummy sandwiches and all-day breakfast.

★**Monterey** AMERICAN **$$**
(Map p96; ☎210-745-2581; www.themontereysa.com; 1127 S St Marys St; brunch $7-12, mains $10-17; ⏰5-11pm Tue-Thu, to midnight Fri & Sat, 10am-2pm Sun) Extra style points to this King William gastropub located in a former gas station with a big old patio. Despite the small number of options, the menu will please most foodies and you'll be dazzled by the choices available when it comes to the extensive selection of microbrews and wine. Generally a great place to hang out, day or night.

Liberty Bar AMERICAN **$$**
(Map p96; ☎210-227-1187; www.liberty-bar.com; 1111 S Alamo St; mains $10-18; ⏰7am-10pm Sun-Thu, to 11pm Fri & Sat, bar open later) The building itself is spectacular: an 1883 home that became a Benedictine convent in 1939 and has now been painted circus-peanut orange. Inside, soaring ceilings and big windows lend an airy vibe, and the menu includes a nice selection of salads, sandwiches and mains.

In the evening, you can finish your meal with a trip up to second-floor bar.

Rosario's Mexican Cafe TEX-MEX **$$**
(Map p96; ☎210-223-1806; www.rosariossa.com; 910 S Alamo St; mains $9-12; ⏰11am-10pm Mon-Thu, to 11pm Fri & Sat, to 9pm Sun) This lively restaurant is always hopping, with huge windows that let in natural light and wistful glances from hungry onlookers. The Tex-Mex style food is solid, and the complimentary basket of chips and salsa that show up at your table are better than most.

Feast TAPAS $$$
(Map p96; 210-354-1024; www.feastsa.com; 1024 S Alamo St; tapas $5-19, brunch $10-13; 5-10pm Tue-Thu, to 11pm Fri & Sat, 10:30am-2:30pm Sun) The eclectic tapas dishes are solid, but the atmosphere alone is worth the trip. Clear Lucite chairs, sparkly pendant lights and jauntily patterned faux taxidermy come together to provide a whimsically modern feel. Even the exterior is lit for effect, from the twinkle lights dripping from a big, shady tree to the circus-like sign out the front.

Brackenridge Park & Around

This area has some of the best-value eateries in the city. If you have a car, take advantage of the lower prices; most of these restaurants are just five to 10 minutes from downtown. The Pearl Complex (p111) has tons of great choices.

★**Cove** AMERICAN $
(Map p94; 210-227-2683; www.thecove.us; 606 W Cypress St; mains $8-12; 11am-10pm Tue-Thu, to 11pm Fri & Sat, noon-6pm Sun) This weird, wonderful place is a restaurant, bar, laundromat and car wash. As casual as the restaurant is, the food is top-notch, made from organic, sustainably grown meat and produce. Sure, it's just burgers, tacos and nachos, but they're made with love. There's even a playground for the kids so you can reward them for all their hard work in washing your car.

Green Vegetarian Cuisine VEGETARIAN $
(Map p94; 210-320-5865; www.greensanantonio.com; 200 E Grayson St; meals $6-10; 7am-9pm Mon-Thu, to 8pm Fri, 9am-9pm Sun;) Vegetarians rejoice: San Antonio's first vegetarian restaurant has a cool, new location in the Pearl Brewery complex. With dishes like enchiladas, eggplant parmesan and 'neatloaf,' it's the kind of place even a meat-eater can enjoy. Not only is it 100% vegetarian, it's 100% kosher and any meal can be made vegan.

Now, if we could just get them to open up on Saturday…

Chris Madrid's BURGERS $
(Map p94; 210-735-3552; www.chrismadrids.com; 1900 Blanco Rd; mains $5-8; 11am-10pm Mon-Sat) Two words: tostada burgers. Topping a burger with tortilla chips and refried beans sounds weird, but it works, combining two of our favorite meals into one deliciously unholy alliance. Throw some jalapeños on for a memorable meal.

Adelante Mexican Food MEXICAN $
(Map p94; 210-822-7681; 21 Brees Blvd; mains $8-10; 11am-9pm Tue-Sat;) This cute Mexican diner is a nice little secret. Located in a strip mall near the McNay Art Museum, it would be easy to overlook, but the inside has the feel of a Mexican *mercado*, with colorful handicrafts right down to the painted furniture. Plus, the food seems a little lighter than most and doesn't leave you wanting a siesta.

Taco Cabana TEX-MEX $
(Map p94; 210-733-9332; www.tacocabana.com; 3310 San Pedro Ave; tacos $1-3, plates $3-8; 24hr) This Texas chain is beloved across the state for its excellent (and cheap!) breakfast tacos, fajitas and burritos, and this is the location where it all began. It's a welcome sight when you're looking for food in the early hours of the morning.

Earl Abel's AMERICAN $
(Map p94; 210-822-3358; www.earlabelsa.com; 1201 Austin Hwy; breakfast $4-10, mains $8-18; 6:30am-10pm Sun-Thu, to 11pm Fri & Sat) Earl Abel's has been feeding San Antonians since 1933. This isn't the original location, but it keeps the tradition alive with photos and memorabilia from the original. More importantly, the homestyle meals (most less than $10) are deliciously satisfying, with breakfast staples served all day.

Mary Ann's Pig Stand AMERICAN $
(Map p94; 210-222-9923; 1508 Broadway St; mains $6-15; 6am-midnight Mon-Thu, 24hr Fri & Sat) The history, the ambience, the neon sign shaped like an enormous pig…it's hard to say what we love most about this place, which has been around since the 1920s. After the Pig Stand chain closed, Mary Ann, a long-term employee, brought this location back to life for San Antonians to enjoy in all its porcine glory.

Josephine Street Cafe AMERICAN $$
(Map p94; 210-224-6169; www.josephinestcafe.com; 400 E Josephine St; mains $7-15; 11am-10pm Mon-Thu, to 11pm Fri & Sat) The neon signs in the window advertise 'steak' and 'whisky.' There's a tree growing up through the floor and out the ceiling of the dining room. And the creaky hardwood floors slant more than a little. This isn't the place for fussy foodies. It is, however, the place for anyone who

wants good steak and seafood – hold the fine-dining ambience and matching prices.

Paloma Blanca MEXICAN $$
(Map p94; 210-822-6151; 5800 Broadway St; lunch $8-10, mains $10-18; 11am-9pm Mon-Wed, to 10pm Thu & Fri, 10am-10pm Sat, 10am-9pm Sun) There are oodles of great Mexican choices around, but this place sets itself apart with a sleek and stylish ambience – think dim lighting, exposed brick walls and oversized artwork – and food that definitely lives up to the decor.

Il Sogno Osteria ITALIAN $$$
(Map p94; 210-223-3900; 200 E Grayson St; mains $14-32; 11:30am-2pm & 6-9:30pm Tue-Sun) This stylish former warehouse space in the Pearl complex is frequently packed with people vying for a shot at the fresh, house-made pastas. Best for groups of four or less, since space is at a premium. If you can swing it, get a front-row seat facing the open kitchen and sitting at the bar.

Greater San Antonio

★**Amy's Ice Cream** ICE CREAM $
(Map p94; 210-832-8886; 255 E Basse Rd, the Quarry; 11am-11pm Sun-Thu, to midnight Fri & Sat) Choose your ice cream, pick a topping – then watch the staff pulverize the two into a blended little cup of heaven.

Drinking & Nightlife

A heavy concentration of the city's watering holes is downtown, but for more interesting choices, head to Southtown, which has a more independent-minded nightlife. Most bars stay open until 2am daily, while a few clubs stay hoppin' until 4am. San Antonio doesn't have a real club scene, but some of its dance clubs are big enough to pack in half the city. Club schedules vary. Check the local papers for schedules and drop-in classes for tango, salsa, folk and country two-step dancing.

Downtown

There's no shortage of beverages of the adult variety around the Riverwalk. But lest you end up at a chain such as Coyote Ugly, here are a few places to escape the madness.

★**VFW Post 76** BAR
(Map p94; 210-223-4581; 10 10th St; 9am-10pm Mon-Thu, to midnight Fri & Sat) We're giving this hidden-away joint near the Pearl development a medal for outstanding service in a dive bar. Don't get us wrong, it's one of the classiest dives you'll ever visit, where hipsters and old-timers chug longnecks side by side in a two-story Victorian that serves as the oldest Veterans of Foreign Wars post in Texas.

Brooklynite COCKTAIL BAR
(Map p96; 212-444-0707; www.thebrooklynitesa.com; 516 Brooklyn Ave; 5pm-2am) Beer and wine are easy to come by in San Antonio, but this is where you head for a creative, handcrafted cocktail. Vintage wallpaper and wingback chairs give the place a dark, Victorian-esque decor, where you can sip your Boulvardier or Widow's Kiss in a fittingly dignified atmosphere.

Menger Bar BAR
(Map p96; 210-223-4361; 204 Alamo Pl; 11am-midnight Mon-Fri, from noon Sat & Sun) More than 100 years ago, Teddy Roosevelt recruited Rough Riders from this bar that, incidentally, was a replica of the House of Lords Pub in London. To complete the image, picture a mounted moose head, scant lighting and lots of wood. There probably won't be a local in sight, but the history alone makes it a worthwhile stop.

Drink Texas Bar BAR
(Map p96; 210-224-1031; www.drinktexas.com; 200 Navarro St; 2pm-2am) This downtown bar is a nice alternative to the madness of the Riverwalk. Small and laid back with a lounge-style atmosphere, it's usually pretty chilled, and its generous happy hour goes from 2pm to 8pm.

Bonham Exchange CLUB
(Map p96; www.bonhamexchange.net; 411 Bonham St; 7pm-2am Wed-Sun) There's plenty of room for everyone at the Bonham. Although it's predominantly a gay bar, the sheer enormity of the place attracts a mixed crowd with drinking and dancing on its mind. Located in an imposing Victorian edifice built in 1892, it has huge dance floors and five bars spread over three floors.

King William District & Southtown

Refreshingly unpretentious is what you'll find the area just south of downtown. Several of the restaurants in this neighborhood double as bars, including the Monterey (p111), Liberty Bar (p111) and Rosario's (p111).

★ Friendly Spot Ice House BAR
(Map p96; ☎210-224-2337; 943 S Alamo St; ⏲3pm-midnight Mon-Fri, from 11am Sat & Sun; 👪🐾) What could be friendlier than a big, pecan tree–shaded yard filled with colorful metal lawn chairs? Friends (and their dogs) gather to knock back some longnecks while the kids amuse themselves in the playground area.

La Tuna Ice House BAR
(Map p94; ☎210-224-8862; 100 Probandt St; ⏲4pm-midnight Sun-Fri, to 1am Sat) When the sun starts to set over Southtown, scoot down by the railroad tracks to this beloved watering hole for a few cold beers and nostalgic school-size snacks. Locals, even families, crowd around outdoor tables until well after dark, especially on weekends when there's live music.

Blue Star Brewing Company BREWERY
(☎210-212-5506; 1414 S Alamo St; ⏲11am-11pm Tue-Thu, to midnight Fri & Sat; to 3pm Sun) See those great big brewing tanks behind the bar? That's your craft beer being made. The people watching, the relaxed vibe and the location inside the Blue Star Arts complex all invite you to linger.

Greater San Antonio

Mon Ami Lounge BAR
(Map p94; ☎210-822-3253; 4901 Broadway St; ⏲4pm-midnight) A cozy little lounge in Alamo Heights with a subtle French flavor and a sprinkling of *savoir faire*. The barkeeps are friendly and they know their way around a drink shaker. This isn't a place to see and be seen, but rather to enjoy an excellent cocktail with friends.

Flying Saucer Draught Emporium BAR
(☎210-696-5080; 11255 Huebner Rd; ⏲11am-1am Mon-Wed, to 2am Thu-Sat, noon-midnight Sun) More than 300 kinds of beer (from Abita Abbey Ale to Young's Double Chocolate Stout) make this place a beer-lover's paradise, as does the casual beer-garden vibe. It's a bit of a schlep from downtown – around a 15- to 20-minute drive – but it's a good place to unwind after a (child-free) visit to Fiesta Texas.

Cowboys Dance Hall DANCE
(☎210-646-9378; www.cowboysdancehall.com; 3030 NE Loop 410, east of I-35; cover from $5; ⏲8pm-2am Wed-Sat) This enormous dancehall packs in a mix of people – the proportion of actual cowboys is hard to say – ready to scoot their boots to country-and-western music. Check the website for drink specials, teen nights and ladies' nights festivities.

☆ Entertainment

Although the live music scene isn't as jumping as in Austin, there's still plenty of entertainment in San Antonio. Check the *San Antonio Current* or Jim Beal's 'Night Lights' column in the 'Weekender' section of the *San Antonio Express-News* for upcoming concerts. Both publications also have comprehensive listings of art exhibitions and openings, touring shows, theater, classical music and cinema.

Cover charges vary from $3 for local bands to $25 or more for big-name acts. Tickets for major sports and performing arts events can be purchased through **Ticketmaster** (☎210-525-1100; www.ticketmaster.

GAY & LESBIAN SAN ANTONIO

Despite its conservative outlook, there's definitely a vibrant LGBT community here. In addition to June's PrideFest San Antonio, one of the best times to visit is during Fiesta San Antonio.

➡ The River City's gay nightlife is concentrated along Main and San Pedro Aves, just north of downtown. Venues change, but the strips remain the same.

➡ San Antonio's **LGBT Chamber of Commerce** (www.sagaychamber.com) provides lists of gay-owned and gay-friendly bars, clubs, businesses and other services.

➡ There's nothing low-key about the Bonham Exchange (p113); this enormous dance club is dark, loud and packed on weekends.

➡ **Heat** (Map p94; ☎210-227-2600; 1500 N Main Ave; before 11pm free; ⏲4pm-2am Wed-Sat, to midnight Sun), an 18-and-up club, is frequently open after hours and caters to a late-night crowd that comes for the huge dancefloor, techno music, theme nights and drag shows.

com), which has more than a dozen city-wide ticket outlets.

Live Music

North of downtown along N St Mary's St, the **Strip** was once a very vibrant music and bar scene at the center of the university students' universe. Though not what it once was, it's still a good place to start your search for live local shows (and the occasional international act) in San Antonio. There are also a few places by the Riverwalk and on the city's outskirts.

There are lots of places to hear Tejano bands and conjunto music, but which place is hottest tends to shift; check the Spanish-language newspapers for listings.

Cove LIVE MUSIC
(Map p94; ☎ 210-227-2683; www.thecove.us; 606 W Cypress St; ⏲ 11am-11pm Tue-Thu, to midnight Fri & Sat, noon-6pm Sun; 🚸) Live music is just part of the reason to hang out at this chill beer hall. The Cove is a unique combo of food stand/cafe/laundromat/car wash. It even has a kiddie playground. (If you're not into the band, you can always escape to the patio. Or go wash your car.)

Olmos Bharmacy LIVE MUSIC
(Map p94; ☎ 210-822-1188; www.olmosbharmacy.com; 3902 McCullough Ave; ⏲ 7am-11pm Mon-Thu, to midnight Fri & Sun, to 1am Sat) This former pharmacy, built in 1938, will cure what ails you with wine, beer and live music seven nights a week. Grab a seat at the old-fashioned soda fountain and enjoy a little jazz, an open mike night or even a Celtic jam. Stop by during the day for a meal or a milkshake; it's also a restaurant.

Sam's Burger Joint LIVE MUSIC
(Map p94; ☎ 210-223-2830; www.samsburgerjoint.com; 330 E Grayson St; ⏲ shows Wed-Mon) More than just a burger joint, Sam's also has a hoppin' live-music venue with a full schedule of bands playing every night except Tuesday. Check online to see who's playing; Monday night brings Swing Nite, with a jazz band and dance lessons.

Martini Club LIVE MUSIC
(Martini's; Map p94; ☎ 210-344-4747; www.wayneharpersmartiniclub.com; 8507 McCullough Ave; ⏲ live music Fri & Sat, karaoke Wed & Thu) For a taste of Las Vegas in the heart of San Antonio, head to what can only be described as a kitsch lounge bar. On the weekends Wayne, the owner/singer/guitarist/trumpeter/saxophonist, fronts a three-piece band. On Wednesday and Thursday, the tables are turned as the audience takes the stage for karaoke night.

Located in a strip mall next to the Avon shop, the only indication of the bar's existence is a small brass plaque reading 'Martini's' screwed to the wall next to the entrance.

John T Floore Country Store DANCE
(☎ 210-695-8827; www.liveatfloores.com; 14492 Old Bandera Rd, Helotes; ⏲ live music Fri-Sun) Northwest of town in Helotes, this dancehall has been around since the 1940s and rivals Gruene Hall for authenticity. The hall hosts plenty of country-and-western concerts; Willie Nelson, Bob Wills, Patsy Cline and Elvis have all done shows here. Sunday is family night, with free admission and dancing after 6pm.

Comedy Clubs

Visiting headliners sometimes perform at the downtown Majestic Theatre (p116) and Trinity University's Laurie Auditorium; check the *Current* or the *Express-News'* 'Weekender' section for more information.

Rivercenter Comedy Club COMEDY
(Map p96; ☎ 210-229-1420; www.rivercentercomedyclub.com; 849 E Commerce St, 3rd level, Rivercenter Mall; most tickets $15; ⏲ 8:30pm Sun-Thu, 8:30pm & 10:30pm Fri & Sat) Check out up-and-coming comedians and local improv comics – as well as occasional major headliners – at this lively club in the Rivercenter. There's no cover for the open-mike show on Saturdays at 3:30pm and you usually get what you pay for (although you never know). There's also a free adults-only 'After Midnight Madness' show on Saturday night.

Three-hour parking at the Rivercenter Mall is available with validation.

Cinema

Check the *Current* or the *Express-News'* 'Weekender' section for cinemas and show times.

Alamo Drafthouse CINEMA
(☎ 210-677-8500; www.drafthouse.com; 1255 SW Loop 410; tickets $9.50) It's a bit of a drive from downtown, but you can catch both dinner and a movie at this theater, which surprisingly has nothing to do with the Alamo at all. (It actually started in Austin. Go figure.) It serves a full menu, including beer and wine that's brought right to your seat to enjoy during the first-run films.

Check the website for other locations around town.

San Antonio IMAX Alamo Theatre CINEMA
(Map p96; ☎800-354-4629, 210-247-4629; www.imax-sa.com; 849 E Commerce St, Rivercenter Mall; adult/child $11.50/9) Films shown here include the 45-minute award-winning film *Alamo: The Price of Freedom,* about... guess what? If you've never seen a film on a six-story-high screen in six-track surround sound, this theater plays several movies in the IMAX format – it's worth the admission price just for the experience.

Spectator Sports

San Antonio Spurs BASKETBALL
(www.nba.com/spurs) The hot ticket in town is the San Antonio Spurs, currently one of the top NBA teams in the country. The city is understandably proud, so you'll forgive locals if they indulge in a little Spurs mania for seven or eight months out of the year. Games held at the **AT&T Center** (Map p94; ☎tickets 800-745-3000; www.attcenter.com; 1 AT&T Center Pkwy) are exciting, action-packed spectacles.

Buy your tickets on the Spurs' website or through **Ticketmaster** (☎800-745-3000; www.ticketmaster.com).

San Antonio Missions BASEBALL
(☎210-675-7275; www.samissions.com; 5757 US 90 W; tickets $7-10; ⏲regular season Apr-Aug) Winners of the Texas League championships in 2003 and 2007, the San Antonio Missions play minor league baseball at Nelson Wolff Municipal Stadium, a short drive west of downtown.

Performing Arts

San Antonio's most historic downtown venue for the performing arts is the **Majestic Theatre** (Map p96; ☎210-226-3333; www.majesticempire.com; 226 E Houston St; ⏲box office 10am-5pm Mon-Fri, hours vary Sat), which hosts a variety of musical concerts, Broadway plays and other events year round. In La Villita, the **Arneson River Theater** (Map p96; ☎210-207-8610; 418 Villita St) is an outdoor venue for anything from Latin dance to plays to festival processions. Trinity University's **Laurie Auditorium** (Map p94; ☎210-999-8117; 1 Stadium Dr) also hosts a few musical concerts and dance and theater performances year round.

May is the month to celebrate dance in San Antonio, with recitals by local troupes, national touring companies and new choreographers' works at both indoor and outdoor venues around the city; contact **San Antonio Dance Umbrella** (☎210-212-6600; www.sadu.org) for details.

Visit www.satheatre.com for information on the following venues, as well as other theaters and dramatic companies performing year round.

Overtime Theater THEATER
(Map p94; ☎210-557-7562; www.theovertimetheater.org; 1203 Camden St) This upstart produces innovative shows and keeps ticket prices low. The names of some of its original shows gives you an idea of the vibe: *Sheer Bloody Lunacy!, Pirates vs Ninjas,* and *The Brain That Wouldn't Die: A New Musical.*

AtticRep THEATER
(Map p94; ☎210-999-8524; www.atticrep.org; 1 Trinity Pl) This cutting-edge theater company in residency at Trinity University knows how to pick a great script and produces shows that are edgy, compelling and current.

Classical Music

The Majestic Theatre and Laurie Auditorium are the main performance venues for both local and touring orchestras and chamber groups.

San Antonio Symphony PERFORMING ARTS
(Map p96; ☎210-554-1010; www.sasymphony.org; box office 5th fl, IBC Bank Bldg, 130 East Travis St, Suite 550; tickets from $16) The symphony performs a wide range of classical concerts, operas and ballets at different venues around town, including the spectacular Majestic Theatre. Tickets (which range wildly in price) can be bought from the symphony's box office or from Ticketmaster outlets.

Shopping

Don't overlook San Antonio's museum gift shops, especially those at the San Antonio Museum of Art and the McNay Art Museum; they can be exceptional. Popular attractions such as the Alamo, Buckhorn Saloon and Guenther House also make for unique souvenir shopping. If you forget to get gifts until the last minute, Texas-made goods are sold at stores in both terminals of San Antonio's airport.

For mall offerings such as Macys, Gap and Bath & Body Works, try **Ingram Park Mall** (☎210-684-9570; 6301 NW Loop 410, at Ingram Rd) or **North Star Mall** (Map p94; ☎210-340-6627; 7400 San Pedro Ave, Loop 410). Standard mall hours are 10am-9pm Monday to Saturday and noon to 6pm on Sunday.

Affordably priced Western-wear chains around town include **Sheplers** (☎210-681-8230; www.sheplers.com; 6201 NW Loop 410;

⌚9am-9pm Mon-Sat, 11am-6pm Sun), next to Ingram Park Mall, and **Cavender's Boot City** (☎210-520-2668; www.cavenders.com; 5075 NW Loop 410; ⌚9am-9pm Mon-Sat, noon-6pm Sun).

Southwest School of Art & Craft HANDICRAFTS
(Map p96; ☎210-224-1848; www.swschool.org; 300 Augusta St; ⌚10am-5pm Mon-Sat) The shop exhibits and sells works by the school's artists and visiting artists, representing an eclectic range of almost every medium imaginable.

Dave Little's Boots ACCESSORIES
(Map p94; ☎210-923-2221; www.davelittleboots.com; 110 Division Ave; ⌚9am-5pm Tue-Fri, 9am-1pm Sat) This high-quality bootmaker's shop, established in 1915, now caters to country music stars, actors and locals alike. Get your custom pair with a belt to match made from calf, crocodile, 'gator, lizard, eel, ostrich or even kangaroo skin. Allow a few months for delivery.

Melissa Guerra HOUSEWARES
(Map p94; ☎210-293-3983; 303 Pearl Pkwy; ⌚10am-6pm Mon-Fri, 9am-7pm Sat, noon-6pm Sun) San Antonio's answer to Williams Sonoma, Melissa Guerra has upscale kitchen implements and table settings with a Latin flavor, complemented by Mexican craft items such as *lotería* jewelry and painted pottery.

Rivercenter Mall MALL
(Map p96; ☎210-225-0000; 849 E Commerce St) It's the most accessible megamall in town, and its setting on the Riverwalk isn't bad at all. Because of the cinemas, IMAX theater, comedy club, restaurants and dozens of shops, you'll probably end up here at some point during your stay.

Paris Hatters ACCESSORIES
(Map p96; ☎210-223-3453; www.parishatters.com; 119 Broadway St; ⌚9:30am-6:30pm Mon-Sat, noon-5pm Sun) Despite the name, this is no Parisian millinery, but a purveyor of fine cowboy hats since 1917. You'll walk out looking like a real cowboy with headgear that's been shaped and fitted to your very own noggin. It's one of the best places in the state to get a Stetson (or whatever brand of hat is mutually agreed to suit you).

Alamo Quarry Market MALL
(Map p94; ☎210-824-8885; 255 E Basse Rd; ⌚10am-9pm Mon-Sat, noon-6pm Sun) Making fine use of an old 19th-century cement plant, this outdoor mall has plenty of top-brand stores, a multiplex cinema and restaurants. A few Austin-based chains here include Whole Foods Market for groceries, Amy's Ice Creams and the outdoors outfitter Whole Earth Provision Co. Cinema and restaurant hours vary.

San Angel Folk Art Gallery ARTS
(Map p94; ☎210-226-6688; www.sanangelfolkart.com; 110 Blue Star; ⌚11am-6pm) Located inside the Blue Star Arts Complex, this store has a fabulous collection of colorful and whimsical folk art, and is a good place to start when exploring the shops and galleries.

Adelante Boutique CLOTHING
(Map p94; ☎210-826-6770; www.adelantebou tique.com; 303 Pearl Pkwy, Suite 107; ⌚10am-5:30pm Mon-Sat) Like a romantic breath of fresh air, this shop has mix-and-match pieces in vibrant prints and fabrics you won't find anywhere else. It also sells designer jewelry imports in a new location over in the Pearl Complex.

Hogwild Records MUSIC
(Map p94; ☎210-733-5354; 1824 N Main Ave; ⌚10am-9pm Mon-Sat, noon-8pm Sun) With an expert selection of vinyl, Hogwild also vends tapes and CDs. If you're after alt-country, punk 'zines or rare drum'n'bass records, this independent music store is the place. Just look for the front door, plastered with band flyers and deep layers of stickers.

Ranch at the Rim CLOTHING
(☎210-319-3001; www.ranchattherim.com; 18007 IH-10 West; ⌚10am-8pm Mon-Sat, to 6pm Sun) It's a bit of a mosey from downtown, but if you want to get decked out in cowboy gear, including apparel, boots and hats, this is a great place to start.

CD Exchange MUSIC
(Map p94; ☎210-828-5525; 3703 Broadway; ⌚10am-9pm Mon-Sat, noon-7pm Sun) This reliable chain music store has lots of cheap secondhand CDs, DVDs and videotapes in all genres. Call for other locations around San Antonio; this one is near Brackenridge Park.

ℹ Information

DANGERS & ANNOYANCES

Downtown (which swarms with cops) is considered safe. East and west of downtown (basically, anywhere across the railway tracks) is not as well patrolled, so common sense is needed in these areas. North of downtown, Avenue B, which parallels Broadway beside Brackenridge

PAPA JIM'S BOTANICA

Embracing more than a few belief systems, **Papa Jim's Botanica** (Map p94; 210-922-6665; www.papajimsbotanica.com; 5630 S Flores St; 9am-6pm Mon-Fri, 10am-5:30pm Sat) offers help from above or help from the beyond for a wide variety of problems. It's basically a religious and Santeria superstore (mixed with a bit of voodoo), selling items to rid you of the problem of your choice: Get-Rich candles, Do-As-I-Say floor wash, Jinx Removal air-freshener, Run-Devil-Run and Get-out-of-Jail oil, and Stop-Gossip soap, all for a few dollars apiece.

Located in the southern part of the city, the store also has books, herbal teas, incense, good-luck charms and other items related to Santeria, a synthesis of Catholicism and the Nigerian Yoruba beliefs of slaves brought to the Caribbean. Papa Jim's motto is 'whatever works,' and obviously it works for some: the botanica has been around since 1980.

Park, may look handy for parking, but it's often deserted after dark and not well lit.

The San Antonio River is lovely, but there are several drownings a year. Be especially careful in areas near the Riverwalk that don't have fences.

Other hazards, especially during summer, are dehydration, heat exhaustion or even heat stroke. To avoid passing out in front of the Alamo (as a few tourists each year inevitably do), always maintain a good fluid intake.

EMERGENCY

Police (emergency 911, nonemergency 210-207-7273)

INTERNET ACCESS

San Antonio's public library system provides free internet access, but time online may be limited to 30 minutes. You must sign up in person (no phone reservations) for the next available terminal. Bring a library card or photo ID. The central **San Antonio Public Library** (www.mysapl.org; 600 Soledad St; 9am-9pm Mon-Thu, to 5pm Fri & Sat, 11am-5pm Sun) is a first-rate multimedia facility with children's programs and helpful staff. Validated parking at the library garage is free for one hour.

MEDIA

La Prensa (www.laprensa.com) A bilingual Spanish-language weekly.

San Antonio Current (www.sacurrent.com) The free alternative weekly is not nearly comprehensive enough, but it's still the best local what's-on guide.

San Antonio Express-News (www.mysanantonio.com) Daily news and travel info.

MEDICAL SERVICES

Baptist Medical Center (210-297-7690; 111 Dallas St) A central hospital, just east of Navarro and Soledad Sts.

Metropolitan Methodist Hospital (210-757-2200; 1310 McCullough Ave) Operates a 24-hour emergency room just north of downtown.

Walgreens (210-614-3590; 7802 Wurzbach Rd) A 24-hour pharmacy north of Loop 410, near the major hospitals and medical complexes. A downtown location at 300 E Houston St is more central, but only open 9am to 6pm Monday to Friday.

MONEY

ATMs accept most debit and credit cards and are located throughout the city, including in malls, major theme parks and the gift shop at the Alamo. You can change foreign currency and traveler's checks at **Frost Bank** (210-220-4011; 100 W Houston St; 9am-5pm Mon-Fri, ATM 24hr) or **Bank of America** (210-270-5540; 300 Convent St; 9am-4pm Mon-Thu, to 5pm Fri, ATM 24hr). There are also two foreign-exchange desks at the airport and one in Six Flags Fiesta Texas.

POST

Post office (USPS; Map p96; 210-212-8046; 615 E Houston St, enter off Alamo St; 9am-5pm Mon-Fri) Call 800-275-8777 to locate other branches.

TOURIST INFORMATION

Downtown Visitors Center (Map p96; 210-207-6875; www.visitsanantonio.com; 317 Alamo Plaza; 9am-5pm, to 6pm Jun-Aug) Stop by the well-stocked Convention & Visitors Bureau's visitor center, opposite the Alamo, for maps and brochures; the website also has loads of information useful for preplanning. The staff can answer any questions you have and can also sell you passes for tours or for VIA buses and streetcars.

Getting There & Away

AIR

San Antonio International Airport (SAT; 210-207-3433; www.sanantonio.gov/sat; 9800 Airport Blvd) San Antonio International Airport is about 9 miles north of downtown, just north of the intersection of Loop 410 and US 281. It's served by taxis, public transportation and shuttles.

The airport offers frequent flights to destinations in Texas and the rest of the USA, and there are also direct or connecting air services to Mexico. In Terminal A you'll find AeroMexico, AirTran Airways, Alaska Airlines, Delta, Interjet, Southwest, US Airways and VivaAerobus. Terminal B houses American and United Airlines.

Southwest Airlines (☎800-435-9792; www.southwestairlines.com) Southwest Airlines is the best airline for short-hop flights around Texas.

BUS

Greyhound (☎210-270-5824; www.greyhound.com) and **Kerrville Bus Co** (☎877-462-6342; www.iridekbc.com) share a **bus terminal** (Map p96; 500 N St Mary's St) right downtown. Kerrville Bus Co has direct services to the Hill Country.

CAR & MOTORCYCLE

Downtown San Antonio is bordered by I-35, I-10 and I-37, with concentric rings of highways around the center. I-35 connects Austin and San Antonio, and I-10 connects San Antonio with Houston to the east and El Paso to the west.

To get to the Hill Country, you can take I-10 north to Fredericksburg and Kerrville, or US 281, which is the northbound continuation of I-37, to Johnson City. All major rental-car agencies have outlets at San Antonio International Airport, and some have outlets downtown as well.

TRAIN

Squeezed between Sunset Station and the Alamodome, the **Amtrak station** (www.amtrak.com; 350 Hoefgen Ave) is served by *Sunset Limited* and *Texas Eagle* trains. It's a fully staffed Amtrak station, with an enclosed waiting area and free short-term parking. VIA streetcars ($1.20) on the yellow line connect Sunset Station with the downtown Riverwalk, where you can transfer to other streetcar and bus lines.

Getting Around

TO/FROM THE AIRPORT

VIA bus 5 runs at least hourly between the airport and downtown from around 6am (8am on weekends) until 9:30pm. The regular service costs $1.20, the express service $2.50; the journey takes between 45 minutes and an hour. Slower bus 550 (clockwise) and 551 (counterclockwise) circumnavigate the city on Loop 410, taking three hours and stopping at the airport on the way.

All of the major rental-car agencies have outlets at San Antonio International Airport. Major downtown hotels have free airport courtesy shuttles; be sure to ask. A taxi ride from the airport to downtown costs between $25 and $29 for up to four people. Or, if you're traveling solo, you can save a few bucks and take a shuttle with **Go Airport Shuttle** (☎210-281-9900; www.citytoursinc.com).

CAR & MOTORCYCLE

There are plenty of public parking lots downtown, including with most of the major hotels. The lots generally cost $3 per hour, or $5 to $8 for 24 hours. Otherwise you can park for free in the residential streets of the King William district and Southtown, then walk or ride VIA's blue line streetcars north into downtown.

PUBLIC TRANSPORT

VIA Metropolitan Transit (☎210-362-2020; www.viainfo.net) San Antonio's public-transport network, VIA Metropolitan Transit, operates more than 100 regular bus routes, plus four streetcar routes. VIA passes, bus schedules and streetcar route maps are available at VIA's downtown **information center** (Map p96; ☎210-362-2020; www.viainfo.net; 211 W Commerce St; ⏰7am-6pm Mon-Fri, 9am-2pm Sat).

Local VIA bus and streetcar fares are $1.20 (15¢ for a transfer), and exact change is required. VIA express buses, which use interstate highways and include buses to theme parks, cost $2.50. Discount fares are available for children, seniors and the mobility impaired. Otherwise, a $4 pass allows a full day of unlimited rides on all VIA buses and streetcars.

Note that the streetcars look more like trolleys, since there is no overhead cable. The streetcar routes are occasionally served by buses, too, although the fare remains the same in that case. VIA streetcars run to and from the Alamo, Market Square, HemisFair Park, the Alamodome, Sunset Station, Southtown and the King William district. There are stops throughout downtown and at several hotels. The main transfer station for all streetcar lines is near the Rivercenter Mall.

TAXI

Taxi stands are found at major downtown hotels, the Greyhound and Amtrak stations and the airport. Otherwise you'll probably need to telephone for one. Taxi rates are $2.50 at flag fall ($3.50 between 9pm and 5am), then $2.25 for each additional mile. Bigger companies include the following:

AAA Taxi (☎210-599-9999; www.aaataxi.com)

San Antonio Taxis (☎210-444-2222; www.sataxis.com)

Yellow Cab (☎210-222-2222; www.yellowcabsa.com)

AROUND SAN ANTONIO

The area directly north of San Antonio is known primarily as a haven for shoppers who stream by the hundreds of thousands into the factory-outlet malls in the cities of San Marcos and New Braunfels, off I-35. It's definitely something every bargain shopper should put on his or her itinerary. But these towns are also great destinations for outdoor recreation on local rivers, perfect for families or anyone else who needs to cool off on a hot summer's day.

Natural Bridge Caverns

About halfway between San Antonio and New Braunfels, the **Natural Bridge Caverns** (☎210-651-6101; www.naturalbridgecaverns.com; 26495 Natural Bridge Caverns Rd, Hwy 3009, west of I-35 exit 175; adult/3-11yr $20/12; ⏰9am-4pm, extended hours summer) is one of the state's largest underground formations. Its name comes from the 60ft natural limestone bridge that spans the entrance. Inside (where it's always 70°F/21°C) are simply phenomenal formations, including the Watchtower, a 50ft pedestal that looks like a crystallized flower.

You can only see the caverns as part of a guided tour, which includes the family-friendly Discovery Tour, the Hidden Passages Illuminations Tour, or the more challenging Adventure Tours. Attached is the Natural Caverns Wildlife Park, a small zoo with rare animals.

New Braunfels

The richly historic town of New Braunfels (named for its Prussian founder, Prince Carl of Solms Braunfels) was the first German settlement in Texas. Today residents from Austin and San Antonio flock to New Braunfels in summer for its main attraction: the cool and easy-flowing waters of the Guadalupe and Comal Rivers.

Sights & Activities

Floating down the Guadalupe in an inner tube is a Texas summer tradition. For the most part, the river is calm, with a few good rapids to make things exciting.

Dozens of local outfitters rent tubes, rafts, kayaks and canoes, then bus you upstream so you can float the three to four hours back to base. Put a plastic cooler full of snacks and beverages (no bottles) in a bottom-fortified tube next to you and make a day of it. Don't forget to bring sunscreen, a hat and drinking water. Wear shoes or sandals that you don't mind getting wet.

The bottom-fortified tubes cost $2 more than a regular old inner tube, but it's worth the splurge to keep your backside from scraping on the rocks that line the riverbed. Most outfitters offer coupons on their websites that will help defray the cost so you can treat yourself to a luxury ride. The waterway gets rockier the longer the region goes without rain, which can be for months during summer. The outfitters listed here all have current river conditions listed on their website so you'll know what to expect.

You can rent tubes from **Gruene River Company** (☎830-625-2800; www.grueneriver company.com; 1404 Gruene Rd; tubes $17), **Riverbank Outfitters** (☎830-625-4928; www.river bankoutfitters.com; 6000 River Rd; tubes $17) and **Rockin' 'R' River Rides** (☎830-629-9999; www.rockinr.com; 1405 Gruene Rd; tubes $17). Their rental prices include shuttle service, and for an additional fee they can also hook you up with an ice chest and a tube to float it on.

McKenna Children's Museum MUSEUM
(☎830-606-9525; www.mckennakids.org; 801 W San Antonio St; late May-early Sep $7.50, early Sep-late May $5.50; ⏰10am-5pm Mon-Sat) Looking for family fun on dry land? Kids can explore everything from outer space to dude ranches at the McKenna Children's Museum. The Shadow Room is particularly mesmerizing, with interactive graphics that respond to kids' movements.

Schlitterbahn Waterpark Resort SWIMMING
(☎830-625-2351; www.schlitterbahn.com; 400 Liberty Ave; all-day pass adult/child $48/38; ⏰10am-6pm or later daily May-Sep, Sat & Sun early May & late Sep) For an exhilarating experience, try Texas' largest water park, featuring about 30 different slides and water pools all using water from the Comal River. It's one of the best places to be with kids on a hot day.

Landa Park PARK
(☎830-221-4350; 110 Golf Course Dr; park admission free) If you don't have a full day but still want to splash around a little, head to this scenic community park just west of Schlitterbahn. The park has an Olympic-size swimming pool (350 Aquatic Circle, summer only, adult/child $4/3), an 18-hole golf course ($2), a miniature railroad ($2.50),

paddleboats ($3) and shady picnic facilities. All have different opening hours, so call first.

City Tube Chute WATER SPORTS
(☎830-608-2165; 100 Leibscher Dr; admission $5, tube rental $7; ⏲10am-7pm daily Jun-Aug, Sat & Sun May) In Price Solms Park, the City Tube Chute is like a water slide for your inner tube that shoots you around a dam on the Comal River. Parking costs $5 on weekends.

Sleeping & Eating

Faust Hotel HISTORIC HOTEL $$
(☎830-625-7791; www.fausthotel.com; 240 S Seguin Ave; d $79-149, ste $169-189) Built in the 1920s as a travelers' hotel, the Faust retains its old-fashioned charm – while the rooms have been updated, there's still plenty of evidence of the hotel's historic roots. The cheapest rooms are rather small, but they're a great deal, all things considered.

Prince Solms' Inn B&B $$
(☎800-625-9169, 830-625-9169; www.princesolmsinn.com; 295 E San Antonio St; d $125, ste $150) With a convenient downtown location, the popular Prince Solms' Inn is one of the oldest still-operating inns in Texas. Its floral Victorian and rustic Western-themed rooms offer authentic furnishings, and there is a variety of accommodations for groups of up to six people ($175 to $195). The romantic cabin out back has a full kitchen.

Naegelin's Bakery BAKERY $
(☎830-625-5722; www.naegelins.com; 129 S Seguin Ave; ⏲6:30am-5:30pm Mon-Fri, to 5pm Sat) More than just a great place to pick up German strudels and Czech kolaches, Naegelin's is also the oldest bakery in Texas, with nearly 150 years under its belt, having opened in 1868.

Faust Brewing Co PUB $$
(☎830-625-7791; www.faustbrewing.com; 240 S Seguin Ave; mains $8-14; ⏲4pm-midnight Mon-Thu, noon-midnight Fri-Sun) Located in the Faust Hotel, this convivial pub complements its microbrews with bar food with a German twist – perfectly befitting its setting in this oh-so-German town. It's known for its German nachos: house-made potato chips topped with brats, sauerkraut and beer cheese sauce.

Huisache Grill & Wine Bar AMERICAN $$
(☎830-620-9001; www.huisache.com; 303 W San Antonio St; mains $9-19; ⏲11am-10pm) Located in a converted home, this cozy, stylish eatery breaks with local tradition by not being even remotely German. An impressively lengthy wine list is one of the draws, as is the variety of the menu, everything from sandwiches to seafood and steaks.

Friesenhaus GERMAN $$
(☎830-625-1040; www.friesenhausnb.com; 148 South Castell Ave; lunch $9, mains $11-18; ⏲11am-10pm Mon-Sat, 11am-9pm Sun; 👪🐾) Schnitzel, *leberkäse* and *sauerbraten* are among the specialties you can expect at this German restaurant and bakery. (It also serves several fish dishes if you're not into meat.) On Friday and Saturday nights, you can enjoy your meal to the tune of German accordion music, and dogs are welcome in the lively *biergarten*.

Myron's Prime Steakhouse STEAKHOUSE $$$
(☎830-624-1024; www.myronsprime.com; 136 N Castell Ave; mains $23-43; ⏲4-10pm Mon-Thu, 4-11pm Fri & Sat) Despite its location in the old Palace Movie Theatre, Myron's isn't the place to go for kitsch. The atmosphere – and the steaks – are serious.

Information

Visit the Greater New Braunfels **Chamber of Commerce** (☎800-572-2626; www.nbcham.org; 390 S Seguin Ave; ⏲8am-5pm Mon-Fri) or the highway **visitors center** (☎830-625-7973; 237 IH-35 N; ⏲9am-5pm) to pick up maps, historic downtown walking tour brochures and loads more information on local attractions.

Gruene

The charming and historic town of Gruene (pronounced 'green') is just 4 miles northeast of New Braunfels. It's close to the Guadalupe River tubing outfitters and loaded with antiques and crafts shops. **Old Gruene Market Days** are held on the third weekend of the month from February through November.

The town is best known for **Gruene Hall** (www.gruenehall.com; 1280 Gruene Rd; ⏲11am-midnight Mon-Fri, 10am-1am Sat, 10am-9pm Sun). Folks have been congregating here since 1878, making it one of Texas' oldest dancehalls and the oldest continually operating one. Toss back a longneck, two-step to live music on the well-worn wooden dance floor or play horseshoes out in the yard. There's no air-conditioning, but it's got cold beer and great bands. It seems that anyone who's anyone has played here, from Jerry Lee Lewis to Willie Nelson, and on Friday and Saturday nights it's always packed. There's

WORTH A TRIP

SHINER

For some it's a detour, for others a pilgrimage, but a trip to Shiner to visit the **Spoetzl Brewery** (www.shiner.com; 603 E Brewery St; tours free; ⊙tours 11am & 1:30pm Mon-Fri year round, plus 10am & 2:30pm Jun-Aug) FREE is a must-do for any self-respecting lover of Texas' favorite microbrew: Shiner Bock.

Longing for a taste of the old country, Czech and German settlers founded the brewery over 100 years ago and hired brewmaster Kosmos Spoetzl (pronounced '*shpet*-zul') to create a traditional German-style bock. Today the brewery still produces the beloved Shiner Bock, as well as honey wheat, blonde and winter ales – all of which you can sample for free right after the tour.

By car from San Antonio, take I-10 past Luling to US 95 and go south to get to Spoetzl Brewery. From Austin, take US 183 south through Luling to Gonzales, then turn east and follow US 90A, which brings you right into the center of town; cross the railroad tracks and make a left turn on US 95.

only a cover on weekend nights and when big acts are playing, so at least stroll through and soak up the vibe.

For a rural escape from the big city, you can't beat **Gruene Mansion Inn** (☎830-629-2641; www.gruenemansioninn.com; 1275 Gruene Rd; d $195-250). This cluster of buildings is practically a village on its own, with rooms in the mansion, the former carriage house and the old barns. Richly decorated in a style the owners call 'rustic Victorian elegance,' the rooms feature lots of wood, floral prints and pressed-tin ceiling tiles. Each room is different, but you can get a sneak peek on the website and pick your favorite.

Another accommodations option is just down the road at the **Gruene River Inn** (☎830-627-1600; www.grueneriverinn.com; 1111 Gruene Rd; d $145-185; 📶). It's more of a traditional-style B&B with quilts and antiques - think Grandma's house - but the real draw is the private decks overlooking the Guadalupe River.

Gruene has a couple of restaurants, but the one you should definitely not miss is the **Gristmill River Restaurant & Bar** (www.gristmillrestaurant.com; 1287 Gruene Rd; mains $7-20; ⊙11am-9pm Sun-Thu, to 10pm Fri & Sat). Situated inside the brick remnants of an 80-year-old cotton gin behind Gruene Hall, it's got oodles of ambience, and outdoor tables get a view of the river. The extensive menu has lots of Texas favorites like chicken-fried steak, as well as lots of salads and sandwiches.

San Marcos

Around central Texas, San Marcos is practically synonymous with outlet malls. But the town is also home to Southwest Texas State University, as well as both natural and tourist attractions.

Sights & Activities

Witliff Collections ARTS CENTER
(☎512-245-2313; www.thewittliffcollections.txstate.edu; Alkek Library, TSU; ⊙8am-5pm Mon-Fri, from 11am Sat, 2-6pm Sun) FREE Screenwriter/photographer Bill Witliff founded this repository of literary and photographic archives on the campus of Texas State University. Check out the excellent (and free!) photography exhibits. The 6600 sq ft of gallery space is room enough for several exhibitions, which always includes the Lonesome Dove Collection.

The Witliff Collections is located on the 7th floor of the Alkek Library. Look online for directions on how to get there.

Aquarena Center OUTDOORS
(Aquarena Springs; ☎512-245-7570; www.aquarena.txstate.edu; 167 Spring Lake; tours adult/4-15yr $9/6; ⊙10am-5pm, later in summer) FREE Famed for its glass-bottom boat tours, this enjoyable place is home to family-oriented exhibitions on ecology, history and archaeology. It also includes the ruins of a Spanish mission founded here on the Feast of San Marcos.

Boat tours last an hour and let visitors peep beneath the surface of the lake formed by the town's namesake springs, which gush forth 1½ million gallons of artesian water every day.

San Marcos Lions Club Tube Rental RIVER TUBING
(☎512-396-5466; www.tubesanmarcos.com; tubes $8-10; ⊙10am-7pm daily Jun-Aug, Sat & Sun May & Sep) Just south of the Aquarena Center, the

Lions Club rents tubes in City Park (next to the Texas National Guard Armory) to tackle a usually docile stretch of the San Marcos River. The last tube is rented at 5:30pm and the last shuttle pickup from Rio Vista Dam is at 6:45pm sharp.

Wonder World CAVE
(☎512-392-3760; www.wonderworldpark.com; 1000 Prospect St; combination tickets adult/child 3-5yr $20/8.50; ⏲8am-8pm daily Jun-Aug, 9am-5pm Mon-Fri & to 6pm Sat & Sun Sep-May) A mini-theme park has been built around this earthquake-created cave – the most visited cave in Texas. Take a one-hour tour through the Balcones Fault Line Cave, where you can look at the Edwards Aquifer up close; tours leave every 15 to 30 minutes year round. Outside, in the 110ft Tejas Observation Tower, you can make out the fault line itself.

Other attractions include a petting park filled with Texas animals, a train ride around the park and the quaint 'Anti-Gravity House,' a holdover from family vacations of yesteryear. There's a picnic area on the grounds.

Sleeping & Eating

Chains abound 'round these parts, both for sleeping and eating, especially along I-35.

Viola Street Inn B&B $$
(☎512-392-6242; www.violastreetinn.com; 714 Viola St; d $95-160; P ⊖ ❄ ᯤ) Awash in antiques, floral prints and Victorian charm, this inn takes traditional bed-and-breakfast style to the max. Relax in one of several lavish common areas or sit a spell on the sprawling front porch. Two of the four rooms have big ol' Jacuzzi tubs in the oversized bathrooms.

Railyard Bar & Grill AMERICAN $
(☎512-392-7555; www.railyardbarandgrill.com; 116 S Edward Gary St; dishes $4-8; ⏲11am-2am Tue-Sat, to minight Sun & Mon) Grab some fried pickles and play a game of ping pong, or enjoy a burger and beer while watching a game of horseshoes out on the patio. No surprise that the Railyard is a popular hangout for college students; the vibe is easy and casual and there's plenty to keep you entertained.

Root Cellar Cafe CAFE $$
(☎512-392-5158; www.rootcellarcafe.com; 215 N LBJ Dr; mains breakfast & lunch $4-10, dinner $9-25; ⏲7am-10pm Tue-Sun) This intimate little cafe sits a few steps below street level and has rock walls, but that's where the similarity to an actual root cellar ends. The atmosphere is on the cozy side of upscale, with local art adorning the walls of the small dining rooms. Lots of tempting menu choices make it a no-brainer when you're looking for a more grown-up lunch or dinner.

Drinking & Nightlife

Cheatham St Warehouse LIVE MUSIC
(☎512-353-3777; www.cheathamstreet.com; 119 Cheatham St; ⏲3pm-2am Mon-Fri, from 4pm Sat, 4-8pm Sun) Down by the railroad tracks in an old warehouse covered in corrugated tin, sits this 1970s-era honky-tonk that has helped launch many a career, including George Strait and Stevie Ray Vaughn, who both had regular gigs there in the early days.

WORTH A TRIP

LULING

Luling trumpets that it's the 'crossroads to everywhere.' But the main reason to stop here these days as you whiz through on the way to Shiner is to see the annual **Luling Watermelon Thump** (www.watermelonthump.com), which has been covered in *People* magazine and the *New York Times*. The famous fruit-growing contest, complete with a crowned queen, takes place the last full weekend of June. (Incidentally, Luling is also the two-time holder of the world watermelon-seed-spitting championship, as documented in the *Guinness Book of World Records*.)

Luling was founded as the western end of the Sunset branch of the Southern Pacific Railroad in 1874, and in 1922 oil was discovered beneath it. The downtown **Central Texas Oil Patch Museum** (☎830-875-1922; www.oilmuseum.org; 421 E Davis St; admission by donation; ⏲9am-5pm Mon-Fri) is dedicated to Luling's history and heritage. In the same building, the Luling **Chamber of Commerce** (☎830-875-3214; www.lulingcc.org) has more information on the area, including its antiques shops.

Luling is on US 183 where it meets Hwys 80 and 90, just north of I-10; it's about an hour's drive from San Antonio or Austin, and is served by Greyhound.

Their signature event is the Wednesday night Songwriters Circle.

You can catch free shows during happy hour every weekday between 5:30 and 7pm. San Marcos hasn't banned smoking, so don't be surprised to find some enthusiastic smokers sitting next to you.

Shopping

San Marcos Premium Outlets MALL
(☎512-396-2200; www.premiumoutlets.com; 3939 S IH-35, exit 200; ⏲10am-9pm Mon-Sat, to 7pm Sun) There are 140 name-brand factory-outlet stores at this enormous – and enormously popular – shopping complex. Outlet shops at the mall offer at least a 30% discount on regular retail prices and sometimes as much as 75% off brands. Stores include Last Call by Neiman Marcus, Tory Burch, Calvin Klein, J.Crew and Coach, just to name a few.

Tanger Outlets MALL
(☎512-396-7446; www.tangeroutlet.com/sanmarcos; 4015 S IH-35; ⏲9am-9pm Mon-Sat, 10am-7pm Sun) What? You're not exhausted yet? You still have money left to spend? Just south of the Premium Outlets is the Tanger Outlet center – if you weren't paying attention, you might not even notice it's a separate mall.

Stores include a few big names, but for the most part they're not as high end as they are across the street. Think Old Navy, Van Heusen, Reebok and such.

Information

The **San Marcos Tourist Information Center** (☎512-393-5930; www.toursanmarcos.com; 617 N IH-35, exit 204B/205; ⏲9am-5pm Mon-Sat, 10am-4pm Sun) has maps, brochures and information on trolley tours of the town's historic districts. Since San Marcos is so close to San Antonio, visitors rarely need to avail themselves of overnight accommodations.

HILL COUNTRY

New York has the Hamptons, San Francisco has the wine country, and Texas has the Hill Country. Just an hour or two's drive from both Austin and San Antonio, the area is an easy day trip or weekend getaway, and its natural beauty paired with the locals' easy-going nature has inspired more than a few early retirements.

Thanks to former First Lady Claudia Taylor Johnson – 'round here everyone calls her Lady Bird – each spring the highways are lined with eye-popping wildflowers that stretch for miles and miles, planted as part of her Highway Beautification Act.

In addition to the bluebonnets, Indian paintbrushes and black-eyed Susans that blanket the roads, the Hill Country contests Texas' reputation as being dry and flat, with its rolling hills, giant oak trees, spring-fed creeks and flowing rivers.

Orientation

Ask 10 people the boundaries of the Hill Country and you'll get 11 different answers but, generally speaking, the Hill Country is an area west of the I-35 corridor between Austin and San Antonio, with Fredericksburg and Kerrville being the westernmost points and largest towns. Some people consider San Marcos, New Braunfels and Gruene to be part of the Hill Country, but you really have to leave the interstate to get the effect.

Information

You can spend an entire vacation in the Hill Country and not see it all. The best time to visit is spring when temperatures are mild and the wildflowers are in full bloom, but many people also enjoy visiting in December when the towns light up for the holiday season. Visit www.hill-country-visitor.com for information on special events, accommodations, outdoor recreation and other Hill Country destinations.

Johnson City & Stonewall

POP 1660

You might assume Johnson City was named after President Lyndon Baines Johnson, who lived here as a child and spent most of his life at a ranch nearby. But the bragging rights go to James Polk Johnson, a town settler back in the late 1800s. The fact that James Johnson's grandson went on to become the 36th president of the United States was just pure luck.

Sights

Johnson's Boyhood Home HISTORIC BUILDING
(100 E Ladybird Lane; ⏲tours every half hour 9am-11:30 & 1:00-4:30pm) FREE Lyndon B Johnson himself had this house restored for posterity. Park rangers from the **Visitor Center** (8:45am-5pm daily; Ladybird Lane & Ave G), where you can also find local information and exhibits on the former President and First Lady, offer free guided tours every half hour that meet on the front porch. On the surface, it's just an old Texas house, but it's fascinat-

DON'T MISS

PIECES OF THE PAST

Salvaged doors, metal sign letters, movie theater lights...you never know what you'll find wandering around the yard at **Pieces of the Past** (☎830-868-2890; www.pieces-of-the-past.com; 104 Hwy 281 S, Johnson City; ⏲10am-5pm Fri & Sat, from noon on Sun) but it sure is fun to hunt.

ing when you think about the boy who grew up there.

LBJ Ranch HISTORIC SITE
(www.nps.gov/lyjo; Hwy 290; house tour $3; ⏲9am-5:30pm, house tours 10am-4:30pm) Fourteen miles to the west is the LBJ Ranch, now part of the Lyndon B Johnson National Historical Park. Stop by the Visitor Center to get your free park permit, map and CD audio tour; admission is only charged if you opt to take the half-hour tour of the Johnson home.

The park is a beautiful piece of Texas land where LBJ was born, lived and died. It includes the Johnson birthplace, the one-room schoolhouse he briefly attended and a neighboring farm that now serves as a living history museum. The centerpiece of the park is the ranch house where LBJ and Lady Bird lived and where he spent so much time during his presidency that it became known as the 'Texas White House.'

You can also see the airfield that he and other foreign dignitaries flew into, the private jet he used as president and the Johnson family cemetery, where LBJ and Lady Bird are both buried under sprawling oak trees.

Sleeping & Eating

There aren't many hotels or motels in the area although a few B&Bs do a solid business.

Chantilly Lace Country Inn B&B $$
(☎830-660-2621; www.chantillylacesoaps.com; 625 Nugent Ave, Johnson City; ste incl breakfast $125-149; ⊖❄) The Chantilly Lace Country Inn in Johnson City offers Texas-style rooms that aren't as lacy and countrified as its name would imply.

Rose Hill Manor B&B $$$
(☎830-644-2247; www.rose-hill.com; 2614 Upper Albert Rd, Stonewall; ste incl breakfast $199-259; ⊖❄@) This exquisite B&B in Stonewall offers top-notch accommodation, with beautifully appointed suites and cottages.

Pecan Street Brewing PUB $
(☎830-868-2500; www.pecanstreetbrewing.com; 106 E Pecan Dr, Johnson City; mains $7-15; ⏲11am-9pm Tue-Thu, 8am-10pm Fri & Sat, 8am-10pm Sun) A friendly neighborhood brew pub that serves up a variety of dishes alongside its own microbrews in a casual, friendly environment. It usually has live music on Saturday nights, which means it doubles as nightlife.

Fredericksburg

POP 10,530

Although we highly recommend meandering through the Hill Country, if you're only going to see one town, make it this one. The 19th-century German settlement packs a lot of charm into a relatively small amount. There is a boggling array of welcoming inns and B&Bs, and a main street lined with historic buildings that house German restaurants, beer gardens, antique stores and shops.

Many of the shops are typical tourist-town offerings (think T-shirts, fudge and faux-quaint painted signs), but there are enough interesting stores to make it fun to wander. Plus, the town is a great base for checking out the surrounding peach orchards, vineyards and natural getaways, such as Enchanted Rock and Johnson City, as well as little Luckenbach, just 10 miles away.

Sights

National Museum of the Pacific War MUSEUM
(www.pacificwarmuseum.org; 340 E Main St; adult/child $14/7, children 5 & under free; ⏲9am-5pm) This museum complex consists of three

URBAN PLANNING

Street names in Fredericksburg appear to be a mishmash of trees, Texas towns and former US presidents. But they were actually named so their initials spell out secret codes. The streets crossing Main St to the east of Courthouse Sq are Adams, Llano, Lincoln, Washington, Elk, Lee, Columbus, Olive, Mesquite and Eagle. And the streets to the west are Crockett, Orange, Milam, Edison, Bowie, Acorn, Cherry and Kay.

war-centric galleries: the **Admiral Nimitz Museum**, chronicling the life and career of Fredericksburg's most famous son; the **George Bush Gallery of the Pacific War**, a large, impressive building housing big planes, big boats and big artillery; and the **Pacific Combat Zone**, a 3-acre site that's been transformed into a South Pacific battleground.

History buffs can learn about (or refresh their memories on) the battles and campaigns, and kids will be awed by the enormous vehicles. Admission is free for WWII veterans.

Pioneer Museum HISTORICAL BUILDINGS
(☎830-990-8441; www.pioneermuseum.net; 325 W Main St; adult/6-17yr $5/3; ⏰10am-5pm Tue-Sat, plus Mon in summer) Find out what life was like for the town's early inhabitants as you wander the 3 acres of the Gillespie County Historical Pioneer Museum. If nothing else, this collection of restored homes and businesses from the late 1800s will help you appreciate the modern conveniences awaiting you at your guesthouse.

Vereins Kirche HISTORICAL BUILDING
(100 W Main St; ⏰10am-4:30pm Tue-Sat, plus Mon in summer) Your admission to the Pioneer Museum includes a visit to the city's Vereins Kirche, which was the original town church, meeting hall and school. The tiny building contains archival photos and historical artifacts that can be interesting for history buffs and, if you're lucky, you'll get a great docent who will really bring the stories to life.

Activities

Peach Picking OUTDOORS
Fredericksburg is known throughout the state for its peaches, and for good reason. They're fat, juicy and nothing like the fruit you'll find in your local produce department. Mid-May through June is peach-picking season around town. You can get peaches straight from the area's farms; some farms will let you pick your own. For a list of more than 20 local peach farms, visit www.texaspeaches.com.

Old Tunnel Wildlife Management Area WILDLIFE WATCHING
(☎866-978-2287; www.tpwd.state.tx.us; 10619 Old San Antonio Rd; ⏰sunrise-sunset) Right around dusk from May to October, you can watch a colony of bats emerging from an abandoned railroad tunnel for their nightly meal. Over three million Mexican free-tailed bats make their home here.

The upper-deck viewing area is open daily and it's free, but the **lower viewing area** (per person $5), which is open Thursday to Sunday, affords an up-close view that is decidedly more impactful.

Tours

Despite having more than its share of touristy shops, Fredericksburg's historic district has retained the look (if not the feel) of 125 years ago. Beautiful limestone-clad buildings with gingerbread-style storefronts, hand-hewn ceiling joists and longleaf pine floors line Main St from end to end. A free self-guided walking tour map of the district is available at the visitor center (p129).

Stardust Carriage Service TOUR
(☎830-992-0700; whole carriage per 15min $25) Fredericksburg is a horse-and-carriage kind of town, and you can clip-clop your way down Main St with this carriage service. Look for it in front of Silver Creek Restaurant (310 E Main St) or call for a reservation.

SCENIC DRIVE: WILDFLOWER TRAILS

You know spring has arrived in Texas when you see cars pulling up roadside and families climbing out to take the requisite picture of their kids surrounded by bluebonnets – Texas' state flower. From March to April in Hill Country, orange Indian paintbrushes, deep-purple wine-cups and white-to-blue bluebonnets are at their peak.

To see vast cultivated fields of color, there's **Wildseed Farms** (www.wildseedfarms.com; 100 Legacy Dr; ⏰9:30am-6:30pm) FREE, which is 7 miles east of Fredericksburg on US 290.

For a more do-it-yourself experience, check with TXDOT's **Wildflower Hotline** (☎800-452-9292) to find out what's blooming where. Taking Rte 16 and FM 1323, north from Fredericksburg and east to Willow City, is usually a good route. Then again you might just set to wandering – most back roads host their own shows daily.

HILL COUNTRY WINERIES

When most people think of Texas, they think of cowboys, cactus and Cadillacs – not grapes. But the Lone Star State has become the fifth-largest wine-producing state in the country (behind California, Washington, New York and Oregon). The Hill Country, with its robust Provence-like limestone and hot South African–style climate, has become the most productive wine-making region in the state, and these rolling hills are home to more than a dozen wineries. The largest concentration of vineyards is around Fredericksburg.

Most wineries are open daily for tastings and tours. Many also host special events, such as grape stompings and annual wine and food feasts. Local visitors bureaus stock the handy *Texas Hill Country Wine Trail* leaflet, which details the wineries and schedules of wine-trail weekends (or visit www.texaswinetrail.com). You could leave the driving to someone else with **Texas Wine Tours** (☎830-997-8687; www.texas-wine-tours.com; tours per person $109-219), which run tours in a limousine-style bus, or **Fredericksburg Limo & Wine Tours** (limo tours $99-149, shuttle bus tours $89-139), which offer limo tours or more affordable shuttle van tours. Some Hill Country wineries to check out include the following.

Becker Vineyards (☎830-644-2681; www.beckervineyards.com; Jenscheke Lane; ⏰10am-5pm Mon-Thu, to 6pm Fri-Sat, noon-5pm Sun) Located 10 miles east of Fredericksburg, just off US 290, this is one of the state's most decorated wine producers. Its vineyard has 36 acres of vines and allegedly Texas' largest underground wine cellar. Its tasting room is housed in a beautiful old stone barn.

Fall Creek Vineyards (☎915-379-5361; www.fcv.com; 1820 CR 222; ⏰11am-4pm Mon-Fri, to 5pm Sat, noon-4pm Sun) This well-known vineyard is located just over 2 miles north of the post office in the town of Tow, close to Llano, and perched beautifully on the shores of Lake Buchanan. Fall Creek churns out several different French- and German-style varietals, including a popular chenin blanc and a tasty Riesling. The winery offers a colorful, modern tasting room as well.

Dry Comal Creek Winery & Vineyards (☎830-885-4076; www.drycomalcreek.com; 1741 Herbelin Rd, off Hwy 46; ⏰noon-5pm daily) A smaller vineyard with wines that have begun to turn heads is the unique Dry Comal Creek Winery & Vineyards, located about 7 miles west of New Braunfels. Proprietor Franklin Houser gives his own tours around the tiny winery, which is constructed of stone and cedar wood.

Festivals & Events

Oktoberfest FESTIVAL
(☎830-997-4810; www.oktoberfestinfbg.com; adult/6-12yr $6/$1) Every October, Fredericksburg celebrates its German heritage in a big way with Texas' largest Oktoberfest. Families crowd around the Vereins Kirche for oompah bands, endless kegs of German beer, and schnitzels and pretzels galore.

Fredericksburg Food & Wine Fest FESTIVAL
(☎830-997-8515; www.fbgfoodandwinefest.com; admission $20) Toward the end of October, the festivities continue with this amer version of Oktoberfest.

Sleeping

Fredericksburg is a popular weekend getaway, especially during the spring, which means room rates are at their highest then. It's easier to find rooms during the week if you have that sort of flexibility and, depending on the hotel, you might save a bucket of money on room rates.

Guesthouses and B&Bs are a popular choice in Fredericksburg – there are hundreds. Local reservations services, including **Gastehaus Schmidt** (☎830-997-5612, 866-427-8374; www.fbglodging.com; 231 W Main St), **Main Street B&B Reservation Service** (☎830-997-0153, 888-559-8555; www.travelmainstreet.com; 337 E Main St) and **Absolute Charm Luxury B&B Reservation Service** (☎866-244-7897; www.absolutecharm.com; 709 W Main St), can help you find anything from a flowery guestroom in a B&B to your own 19th-century limestone cottage.

Dietzel Motel MOTEL $
(☎830-997-3330; www.dietzelmotel.com; 1141 W US 290; d $60-96;) This family-run motel is a great budget option located at the west end of town, away from the hustle and bustle. Rates are higher during special events, lower in winter; all in all, it's a good deal.

Lady Bird Johnson Municipal Park CAMPGROUND $
(☎830-997-4202; 432 Lady Bird Drive off Hwy 16; campsites/RV sites $10/30;) This pretty country park sits 3 miles south of town on the Pedernales River. There are plenty of RV hookups but no tent sites per se, just a big field behind the park's headquarters.

Cotton Gin Village CABINS $$
(☎830-990-8381; www.cottonginlodging.com; 2805 S Hwy 16; cabins $159-189) Just south of town, this cluster of rustic cabins made from stone and timber offers guests a supremely private stay away from both the crowds and the other guests. Romantic getaway? Start packing.

Fredericksburg Inn & Suites MOTEL $$
(☎830-997-0202; www.fredericksburg-inn.com; 201 S Washington St; d $109-179 ste $139-209;) Tops in the midpriced-motel category, this place was built to look like the historic house it sits behind, and it succeeds. A fabulously inviting pool with a waterslide, all-day complimentary beverages and clean, modernised rooms make it good value for the price.

Hangar Hotel $$
(☎830-997-9990; www.hangarhotel.com; 155 Airport Rd; d $109-179) If you didn't know better, you'd think this rounded, barnlike structure right on the tarmac of the Gillespie County Airport was a converted hangar from the 1940s, but it's actually a new building with a fun aviation shtick. The Observation Deck is a great place to watch the small aircraft buzz in and out, or you can just throw open your windows for a similar effect.

Roadrunner Inn INN $$
(www.theroadrunnerinn.com; 306-B E Main St; d $129-189;) If you want to ensure your lodging is doily-free, check out one of the three smartly retro rooms that feature kitchenettes, Jacuzzi tubs and flat-screen TVs. Make bookings through Main Street B&B Reservation Service (p127).

Bed & Brew HOTEL $$
(☎830-997-9900; www.yourbrewery.com; 245 E Main St; d $99-129) Here's an amenity you don't find just anywhere: beer. The 12 rooms owned by the Fredericksburg Brewing Company are right upstairs from the brewery, and each day you get a free sample of suds (which helps explain its no-kids policy). Some of the eclectic rooms have themes and some don't; the crazy Red Stallion room has a mural of big red mustangs stampeding toward the bed.

Eating & Drinking

Mahaley's Cafe CAFE $
(☎830-997-4400; 341 E Main St; menu items $2-8; 6:30am-3pm Mon-Sat, from 7:30 Sun;) Breakfast tacos are the big draw at this little cafe in a former gas station, but the cupcakes and coffee drinks are pretty tasty, too. It's also mighty generous with the wifi.

Hondo's on Main AMERICAN $$
(☎830-997-1633; www.hondosonmain.com; 312 W Main St; mains $7-11; 11am-10:30pm Wed, Thu & Sun, to midnight Fri & Sat) Named after local legend Hondo Crouch, this hoppin' place caters to your need for both food and fun, with live music on the patio five nights a week. It's famous for its 'donut burger', which has more to do with the way the patty is formed than the actual ingredients.

Silver Creek Restaurant AMERICAN $$
(☎830-990-4949; www.silvercreekfbg.com; 310 E Main St; mains $7-28; 11am-4pm & 5-9pm Wed-Mon) A great compromise when only some of you want schnitzel, this place serves both American and German dishes, mostly under $20, though the steaks can get a little spendy. Its shady patio is a great place to hang out – and one of the *only* places to go on a Monday night.

Altdorf Restaurant & Biergarten GERMAN $$
(☎830-997-7865; www.altdorfbiergarten-fbg.com; 301 W Main St; mains $7-16; 11am-9pm Wed-Sat & Mon, to 4pm Sun) German food is a Fredericksburg staple, and while no single restaurant knocks it out of the park, this place is as good as any for Bavarian-style specialties, with a traditional beer garden where you can get your oompah on.

Hill Top Café AMERICAN $$
(☎830-997-8922; mains $12-25; 11am-2pm & 5-9pm Tue-Sun) Ten miles north of town inside a renovated 1950s gas station, this cozy roadhouse serves up satisfying meals and

DON'T MISS

THE PINK PIG

Fredricksburg's Main Street suffered a loss when Rather Sweet Bakery & Cafe closed down. ('But, but... the cupcakes!?!?') But we're happy there was a really, really good reason for it: the owner, Rebecca Rather, was hard at work opening a new restaurant: **The Pink Pig** (☎830-990-8800; www.pinkpigtexas.com; 6266 E US Hwy 290; lunch $9-12, dinner $18-28; ⏲11am-2:30pm Tue & Wed, 11am-2:30pm & 5:30-9pm Thu-Sat, from 10am Sun).

It'd be easy enough to miss, since it's about 10 minutes southeast of town on Hwy 290, but it's worth the trip. Pick up baked goods or a boxed lunch from the bakery counter, or stay and enjoy a meal inside the historic log building, where Southern-inspired dishes like shrimp and grits or pulled pork are imaginatively prepared.

Of course, it should go without saying that when you dine at a restaurant opened by a woman with the title of The Pastry Queen, you definitely have to save room for dessert.

Hill Country ambience at its best. Reservations recommended. On weekends the owner, Johnny Nicholas, a former member of the West Coast swing band Asleep at the Wheel, plays the blues. Reservations are recommended.

Navajo Grill AMERICAN **$$$**
(☎830-990-8289; 803 E Main St; mains $18-33; ⏲5:30-9pm Sun-Thu, to 10pm Fri & Sat) For something more upmarket, head straight to the Navajo Grill, which boasts a lovely patio, creative Southern cuisine and a list of about 40 different wines. Reservations recommended on weekends, especially in the spring.

ℹ Orientation

Most of the action on Main St happens between Washington and Adams St (the latter divides Fredericksburg addresses into east and west). Most shops and restaurants are on (or a block off) Main St, starting near the prow-like facade of the former Nimitz Hotel (now the Museum of the Pacific War) and continuing to Friedhelms Bavarian Inn, where US 290 and US 87 split.

ℹ Information

Fredericksburg Visitor Information Center (☎888-997-3600, 830-997-6523; www.visitfredericksburgtx.com; 302 E Austin St; ⏲8:30am-5pm Mon-Fri, from 9am Sat, 11am-3pm Sun) has a friendly staff and a nice new building a block off Main St.

You'll find a 24-hour ATM at **Broadway National Bank** (☎830-997-7691; 204 W Main St). Internet access is free at the **Pioneer Public Library** (☎830-997-6513; 115 W Main St; ⏲9am-6pm Mon-Thu, to 2pm Fri & Sat), although service can be weak (you might be better off at Mahaley's Cafe). The library itself is a beautiful building. If you do go, check out the enormous tapestry on the 2nd floor that highlights many of Fredericksburg's landmarks.

The **Hill Country Memorial Hospital** (☎830-997-4353; 1020 Hwy 16 via S Adams St) has 24-hour emergency services.

ℹ Getting There & Around

Heading west from Austin, US 290 becomes Fredericksburg's Main St. Hwy 16, which runs between Fredericksburg and Kerrville, is S Adams St in town. It isn't easy to get to Fredericksburg without a car; the closest bus service is into Kerrville.

You can get shuttle service from the San Antonio Airport through **Stagecoach Taxi and Shuttle** (☎830-385-7722; www.stagecoachtaxiandshuttle.com); the cost is $95 each way for up to four people. However, since driving around the Hill Country is half the fun, your best bet is to drive yourself.

When in town, you can rent bicycles at **Hill Country Bicycle Works** (☎830-990-2609; 702 E Main St; ⏲10am-6pm Mon, Tue, Thu & Fri, to 4pm Sat) for $28 per day.

Enchanted Rock State Natural Area

What's so enchanting about a rock, you might ask? Well, when you see the dome of pink granite dating from the Proterozoic era rising 425ft above ground – one of the largest batholiths in the US – you certainly know you're not looking at just any old rock. (And remember, that's just the part you can see; most of the rock formation is underground.) The dome heats up during the day and cools off at night, making a crackling noise that the Tonkawa people believed were ghost fires.

Two of the most popular activities at this popular park are hiking and rock climbing. **Enchanted Rock** (☎830-685-3636; www.tpwd.

state.tx.us; 16710 Ranch Rd 965; adult/child 12 and under $7/free; ⌚8am-10pm) is 18 miles north of Fredericksburg off RR 965 and just south of Llano. It gets crowded on weekends, spring break and holidays, so get there early during peak times (by 11am at the latest) or risk finding the gates closed.

Luckenbach

POP 3

As small as Luckenbach is – there are only three permanent residents, not counting the cat – it's big on Texas charm. You won't find a more laid-back place. The main activity is sitting at a picnic table under an old oak tree with a cold bottle of Shiner Bock and listening to guitar pickers, who are often accompanied by roosters. Come prepared to relax, get to know some folks, and bask in the small-town atmosphere.

Actually, 'small town' doesn't describe it just right: Luckenbach is more like a cluster of buildings than a town, and its permanent structures are outnumbered by the port-a-potties brought in to facilitate weekend visitors. The heart of the, er, action is the old trading post established back in 1849 – now the **Luckenbach General Store** (⌚10am-9pm Mon-Sat, from noon Sun), which also serves as the local post office, saloon and community center.

Despite the lack of amenities, there is a website where you can find the **music schedule** (www.luckenbachtexas.com). Sometimes the picking circle starts at 1pm, sometimes at 5pm. There are usually live-music events on the weekends in the old **dancehall** – a Texas classic. The 4th of July and Labor Day weekends see a deluge of visitors for concerts.

We'd be remiss if we didn't mention that Luckenbach was made famous in a country song by Waylon Jennings. But we figured you either already knew that or wouldn't really care.

To get there from Fredericksburg, take US 290 east, then take FM 1376 south for about 3 miles.

Kerrville

POP 22,373

If Fredericksburg feels too fussy for you, Kerrville also makes a good base for exploring the Hill Country. What it might lack in historic charm, it makes up for in size, offering plenty of services for travelers as well as easy access to kayaking, canoeing and swimming the Guadalupe River. It's also home to one of the world's best museums of cowboy life and a jam-packed springtime folk festival. It may not turn on the charm, but it's also a welcome relief for anyone suffering quaintness overload.

Sights

Kerr Arts & Cultural Center ARTS CENTER
(☎830-895-2911; www.kacckerrville.com; 228 Earl Garrett St; ⌚10am-4pm Tue-Sat, from 1pm Sun) FREE Catch the pulse of the Hill Country art scene here. Located in the old post office, it frequently changes exhibits, which could

THE STORY BEHIND THE SONG

A famous saying in Luckenbach goes something like this: 'We have discovered that, on the globe, Luckenbach is at the center of the world.' And while today's casual visitor may question that logic over a cold beer and a lazy afternoon, not so in 1977, when the town was at the center of the world – or at least the country-music world. Waylon Jennings and Willie Nelson's hit song 'Luckenbach, Texas (Back to the Basics of Love)' stayed at number one on the country-music charts for nearly the entire summer.

What's odd about one of the most catchy country tunes ever recorded is that it was written by Bobby Emmons and Chips Moman, two Nashville producers who'd never been to Luckenbach. Even Jennings couldn't say he'd actually set foot in any one of the three buildings in town until the first and only time he made the trip, in 1997, 20 years after the song's original release. Still, 'Luckenbach, Texas' was and remains a well-loved tribute to the Hill Country hamlet, partly because Nelson is a Texas fixture and has held his famous 4th of July Picnic here off and on for years. Also, since Jennings' death in 2002, Luckenbach has thrown an annual mid-July tribute party to the musician, giving the town's regulars (and its three permanent residents) one more reason to call Luckenbach the center of the world.

WHAT THE...? STONEHENGE II

So Stonehenge II isn't the real Stonehenge. We're not real druids, so there you go. This second-string henge has much less mysterious origins than the ancient megalithic structure near Salisbury, England. Two locals built the 60% scale model out of concrete and threw in some Easter Island statues for good measure.

Just a few years back you could find it out in a field on a country road, but alas, the property changed hands and the new owners weren't interested in maintaining the henge's important cultural legacy. Luckily, the installation has been saved by the **Hill Country Arts Foundation** (120 Point Theatre Road S, Ingram), whose lawn it now graces.

include anything from quilts to watercolors to gourd art.

Schreiner Mansion HISTORIC BUILDING
(☎830-896-8633; 226 Earl Garrett St; ⊙11am-4pm Tue-Sat) FREE Check out the opulent former residence of Charles Schreiner (the man who built half the town). The exterior stonework is impressive, and if you like historic homes, head inside to see more.

Museum of Western Art MUSEUM
(☎830-896-2553; www.museumofwesternart.com; 1550 Bandera Hwy; adult/student/under 8yr $7/5/free; ⊙10am-4pm Tue-Sat) This is a nonprofit showcase of Western Americana. The quality and detail of the work, mostly paintings and bronze sculptures, is astounding; all depict scenes of cowboy life, the Western landscape or vignettes of Native American life.

The museum has permanent displays of two artists' studios, the equipment of cowboy life (where kids can climb on saddles, feel a lasso and play with spurs) and a research library available to anyone interested in learning more about the frontier. The building itself is beautiful, with handmade mesquite parquet and unique vaulted domes overhead.

Activities

The Guadalupe River runs through Kerrville, and there are lots of different ways to enjoy it.

Kerrville-Schreiner Park PARK
(2385 Bandera Hwy; day-use adult/child/senior $4/1/2; ⊙8am-10pm) Three miles southeast of town, this is a beautiful place for cycling, hiking, canoeing, tubing and camping. The park's concession stand rents inner tubes (per day $4) and four-person canoes (per hour from $7) for lazy floats along the Guadalupe River.

Louise Hays City Park PARK
(202 Thompson Dr; ⊙dawn-11pm) At 60 acres it's smaller than Kerrville-Schreiner but, on the plus side, it's free. Enjoy river access, shaded picnic tables, sports courts and barbecue pits.

Guadalupe Street City Park PARK
(1001 Junction Hwy; ⊙7:30am-11pm) Take a refreshing swim in the river at this spot, behind the Inn of the Hills Resort. The water here is deep and not recommended for children.

Riverside Nature Center PARK
(☎830-257-4837; 150 Francisco Lemos St; ⊙dawn-dusk) Near the river, at the south end of downtown, the center has walking trails, a wildflower meadow and Guadalupe River access.

Kerrville Kayak & Canoe Rentals KAYAKING
(☎830-895-4348; www.paddlekerrville.com; 130 W Main St; per hr $10-15) Rents watercraft by the hour from Kerrville-Schreiner Park. You can save money with half-day or full-day rentals, and also by picking up your craft from the shop.

Festivals & Events

Kerrville Folk Festival MUSIC
(☎830-257-3600; www.kerrville-music.com; 3876 Medina Hwy) The Quiet Valley Ranch turns up the volume each spring. This 18-day musical extravaganza starts right around Memorial Day and features music by national touring acts and local musicians. One-day tickets cost $25 to $40; check the website for information about camping at the ranch.

Kerrville Wine & Music Festival MUSIC
(⊙Labor Day weekend) A four-day miniversion of the folk festival.

Sleeping

If you're planning on heading to Kerrville during any of the festivals, book months in advance. Kerrville doesn't have the glut of charming B&Bs you'll find in Fredericksburg; the lodging here caters to practical

WORTH A TRIP

LOST MAPLES STATE NATURAL AREA

The foliage spectacle in October and November at **Lost Maples State Natural Area** (830-966-3413, reservations 512-389-8900; www.tpwd.state.tx.us; 37221 RR 187, 5 miles north of Vanderpool; day use $3-6, primitive camping $10, tent sites $20) is as colorful as any you'd see in New England. In autumn, big-tooth maple trees turn shocking golds, reds, yellows and oranges. In the summertime there's good swimming in the Sabinal River. At any time of the year, campers will find back-country primitive areas where they can pitch a tent, as well as more convenient sites supplied with water, electricity and nearby showers. Hiking trails will take visitors into rugged limestone canyons and prairie-like grasslands populated by bobcats, javelinas and gray foxes. Bird-watching is another popular attraction at Lost Maples because of the green kingfishers, who take up residence in the park year round.

travelers. There are several chains right off the highway on Sidney Baker St. They're interchangeable, but they're there if you need them.

★Inn of the Hills Resort & Conference Center MOTEL $
(830-895-5000, 800-292-5690; www.innofthehills.com; 1001 Junction Hwy; d $77-104;) The renovated rooms that open onto the pool were a lovely surprise; they were among the nicest we saw in town. However, the unrenovated rooms have a lot of catching up to do, so make sure you know what you're getting when you book.

The common areas are nice enough, although the restaurant is a little countrified. The best feature of all is the beautiful Olympic-style pool surrounded by shade trees.

Kerrville-Schreiner Park CAMPGROUND $
(830-257-5392; 2385 Bandera Hwy; day-use per person $4, campsites $10-20, RV sites $23-28;) This is a beautiful park set right on the river. Pitch a tent or hook up your RV in one of the well-tended campsites, then go enjoy the 500 acres.

YO Ranch Resort Hotel HOTEL $$
(830-257-4440, 877-967-3767; www.yoresort.com; 2033 Sidney Baker St; r from $79, ste from $185;) If you're one of those folks who's freaked out by taxidermy, you might want to mosey on past. If you're not, this is one of the more interesting hotel lobbies you'll see, lined with trophy mounts of elk, moose and longhorns, plus a large, stuffed grizzly bear.

Oh, you wanted to know about the rooms as well? They're on the bland side, but who needs 'em: the resort also has court facilities for tennis, basketball and volleyball, a walking track and a playground.

Trail's End Guesthouse B&B $$
(830-377-1725; www.trailsendguesthouse.com; 180 Gay Dr N; d $99-139;) East of town, this guesthouse has a rustic charm that fits right into the surrounding hills, with exposed beams and plank walls in every room and cabin. Did we mention a hearty breakfast is delivered right to your door?

Eating

★Taco To Go MEXICAN $
(830-896-8226; 428 Sidney Baker St; most tacos $2; 6am-9pm Mon-Sat, 7am-2pm Sun) You can take your tacos to go or eat inside, but don't miss out on the excellent soft tacos – including breakfast tacos served all day – made with homemade tortillas and salsa.

Hill Country Cafe CAFE $
(830-257-6665; www.hill-country-cafe.com; 806 Main St; menu items $2-10; 6am-2pm Mon-Fri, 6-11am Sat) This tiny hole-in-the-wall diner near the historic district serves up hearty home cooking in heaping portions, including just about everything you could want for breakfast as well as sandwiches and lunch plates.

Conchita's Mexican Cafe MEXICAN $
(830-895-7708; 810 Main St; mains $8-11; 11am-3pm Mon-Fri, from 10am Sat & Sun) Located in an unassuming storefront on Main St, Conchita's doesn't look like much, but the inventive dishes such as Mexican eggrolls really stand out from typical Mexican fare.

Classics Burgers & 'Moore' BURGERS $
(830-257-8866; 448 Sidney Baker St; mains $7-11; 11am-3pm & 5-8pm Mon-Fri, 11am-3pm Sat) This burger joint does have sort of a classic quality to it, and its burgers and fries

blow the fast-food-chain burgers out of the water.

★**Grape Juice** AMERICAN $$
(☎830-792-9463; www.grapejuiceonline.com; 623 Water St; mains $10-15; ⏲11am-11pm Tue-Sat) For us, it was love at first sight – the sight being a little menu item called the Honey Badger that's a ridiculously wonderful combination of 'crack'-aroni and cheese surrounded by a moat of chili with Fritos on top. It's a somewhat undiginified dish considering the lovely wine-bar atmosphere, which is exactly what we love about it.

La Four's Seafood Restaurant SEAFOOD $$
(☎830-896-1449; 1705 Junction Hwy; mains $12-22; ⏲11am-2pm & 4-9pm Tue-Sat, 11am-2:30pm Sun) Head to this riverside spot that looks like a big tin shed for excellent fried shrimp and Cajun-influenced fare such as frogs legs and spicy jalapeño hush puppies.

Rails Cafe at the Depot AMERICAN $$
(☎830-257-3877; www.railscafe.com; 615 E Schreiner; meals $9-19; ⏲11am-9pm Mon-Sat) This cute cafe in the old train depot is awfully pleasant. Make a lunch of panini or salad, or splurge a bit with the osso bucco or beef tenderloin.

Francisco's AMERICAN $$
(☎830-257-2995; www.franciscos-restaurant.com; 201 Earl Garrett St; lunch $7-10, dinner $13-38; ⏲11am-3pm Mon-Wed, 11am-3pm & 5:30-9pm Thu-Sat) Colorful, bright and airy, this bistro and sidewalk cafe is housed in an old limestone building in the historic district. It's packed at lunch, and is one of the swankiest places in town for a weekend dinner.

ℹ Information

Kerrville's excellent **visitor center** (☎830-792-3535, 800-221-7958; www.kerrvilletexascvb.com; 2108 Sidney Baker St; ⏲8:30am-5pm Mon-Fri, 9am-3pm Sat, 10am-3pm Sun) has everything you'll need to get out and about in the Hill Country, including heaps of brochures and coupon books for accommodations.

The **Butt-Holdsworth Memorial Library** (☎830-257-8422; 505 Water St; ⏲10am-6pm Mon-Sat, to 8pm Tue & Thu, 1-5pm Sun) provides free internet access. You can change money at **Bank of America** (☎830-792-0430; 601 Main St; ⏲9am-4pm Mon-Thu, to 5pm Fri, 9am-noon Sat), which has an ATM. **Peterson Regional Medical Center** (☎830-896-4200; www.petersonrmc.com; 551 Hill Country Dr) has a new facility and 24-hour emergency services.

ℹ Getting There & Around

Kerrville is half an hour south of Fredericksburg on Hwy 16, or just over an hour northwest from San Antonio on I-10. In town, Hwy 16 becomes Sidney Baker St, and Hwy 27 (aka Junction Hwy) becomes Main St.

By car from Austin, take US 290 west to Fredericksburg, then turn south onto Hwy 16, which meets Kerrville south of I-10. From San Antonio, take I-10 north to Hwy 16, then head south. **Greyhound** (☎800-231-2222; www.greyhound.com; San Antonio $28, Austin $43) has service to and from both cities.

In town, **Bicycle Works** (☎830-896-6864; www.hillcountrybicycle.com; 141 W Water St; full-day rental $28; ⏲10am-6pm Mon-Fri, to 4pm Sat) rents bikes.

Comfort

POP 2363

Another 19th-century German settlement tucked into the hills, Comfort is perhaps the most idyllic of the Hill Country bunch, with rough-hewn limestone homes from the late 1800s and a beautifully restored historic center in the area around High St and 8th or 9th Sts.

Shopping for antiques is Comfort's number-one activity, but you'll also find a few good restaurants, a winery and, as the town's name suggests, an easy way of life. Start at the **Comfort Antique Mall** (☎830-995-4678; 734 High St; ⏲10am-5pm Sun-Fri, to 6pm Sat) where you can pick up a map of antique stores, or go to www.comfort-texas.com to discover all your options.

For some true historic charm, spend the night at **Hotel Faust** (☎830-995-3030; www.hotelfaust.com; 717 High St; d $110-160, 2-bedroom cottage $175-195; ⊖❄). The limestone building dates from the late 1800s, but the rooms have all been gutted and beautifully restored. For a special treat, stay in their **Ingenhuett Log Cabin**, built in the 1820s and moved to its present location from Kentucky.

The nicest restaurant in town is **814: A Texas Bistro** (☎830-995-4990; www.814atexasbistro.com; 713 High St; dinner $23-30; ⏲6-9pm Thu & Fri, 11:30am-2pm & 6-9pm Sat, 11:30am-2pm Sun). Located in the former Comfort post office and sporting a rustic decor, this place is pure Hill Country. There's not a huge array of choices: dinner has three mains options that change weekly, so the focus is on doing just a couple of things but doing them really well.

WORTH A TRIP

YO RANCH

Texas is full of ranches, but not many of those ranches are full of exotic game. Established in 1880 by Kerrville merchant Charles Schreiner, the **YO Ranch** (☎830-640-3222; www.yoranch.com; 1736 YO Ranch Road, Mountain Home) once encompassed 600,000 acres. It was Charles Schreiner III who started a wildlife conservation program in the 1960s, and these days you can find up to 55 species of exotic animals roaming the ranch, from gazelles to wildebeests to the beautiful scimitar-horned oryx.

The best way to experience it is on a wildlife tour, where you'll be loaded on a bus and taken up close enough to get some pretty great pictures. And not to spoil any surprises, but at the end you might just get to feed a giraffe (bring wet wipes; they're slobbery). The regular two-hour tour ($35) is offered Thursday through Sunday and includes a chuck-wagon lunch. If that's just not enough time, you can go all out and book a five-hour photo safari ($250).

The ranch also offers horseback rides (per first hour $45, per each additional hour $35) and overnight visits. There are also hunting tours (which do take place away from the above tours).

For something more casual, you can't beat **Comfort Pizza** (☎830-995-5959; 802 High St; whole pizza $15-20; ⏲11am-10pm Mon-Sun). Creative ingredient combos make choosing your pizza fun: the prosciutto, pineapple and serrano chile pizza, for example, is known as the Angry Samoan. Enjoy a glass of wine or a prickly pear cactus drink on the colorful patio, filled with big metal lawn chairs.

Comfort is about halfway between Kerrville and Boerne on TX 27, just 2 miles west of I-10.

Bandera

POP 859

It's not always easy to find real, live cowboys in Texas, but the pickin's are easy in Bandera, which has branded itself the Cowboy Capital of Texas. There are certainly lots of dude ranches around, and rodeos and horseback riding are easy to come by. Another great reason to come to Bandera? Drinking beer and dancing in one of the many hole-in-the-wall cowboy bars and honky-tonks, where you'll find friendly locals, good live music and a rich atmosphere. Giddy up!

Sights

The **Bandera County Convention & Visitors Bureau** (CVB; ☎800-364-3833; www.banderacowboycapital.com; 126 Hwy 16; ⏲9am-5pm Mon-Fri, 10am-3pm Sat) stocks a handy historical walking tour brochure covering many of the old buildings scattered around town. You'll spot the St Stanislaus Catholic Church, the adjacent convent cemetery and the historic Bandera jail.

Frontier Times Museum MUSEUM
(☎830-796-3864; www.frontiertimesmuseum.org; 510 13th St; adult/6-17yr/senior $5/2/3; ⏲10am-4:30pm Mon-Sat) To get some historical perspective, stop by this museum displaying Western art, cowboy tchotchkes such as guns, branding irons and cowboy gear. There are also 'curiosities' collected by the museum's founder, J Marvin Hunter – including the famous two-headed goat.

Rodeo RODEO
The real reason you'll want to visit Bandera is to get a taste of cowboy life, and one of the best ways to do that is to attend a rodeo. During the summer, there are usually rodeos every weekend, and on Saturday afternoons, gunslingers and cowboys roam the streets and entertain the crowds during Cowboys on Main. Check the CVB website for the exact schedules and locations.

Activities

If you're feeling inspired to saddle up, the CVB can provide you with a list of a dozen or so dude ranches in and around town where you can go horseback riding for $35 to $55 an hour. (Please note that according to Texas law, riders must not weigh more than 240 lbs.) Some offer packages that include meals, and some even host overnight rides; many of them take advantage of the Hill Country State Natural Area, a park covering over 5000 acres.

If you'd like to stay longer, these dude ranches offer all-inclusive experiences with horseback riding, meals and a place to hang up your hat for the night. Overnight stays all cost about the same; plan on spending about $130 to$160 per adult per night and $45-90 for the young'uns, and don't be surprised if there's a two-night minimum stay.

Some ranches offer unique features to set themselves apart, but you can generally expect enormous ranch houses set on hundreds of acres, with horseback riding included in the price of your stay. Other amenities might include hayrides, campfires and barbecues.

Dixie Dude Ranch DUDE RANCH
(☎800-375-9255, 830-796-7771; www.dixiedude ranch.com; 833 Dixie Dude Ranch Rd) This working stock ranch founded in 1901 has an authentic Western feel and 725 acres.

Twin Elm Guest Ranch DUDE RANCH
(www.twinelmranch.com; cnr Rte 470 & Hwy 16; rodeos adult/under 6 $6/free; ⊙rodeos 8pm Fri May-Aug) Provides lots of family friendly activities, including river tubing, and hosts open-to-the-public rodeos on Fridays in season.

Mayan Ranch DUDE RANCH
(☎830-460-3036; www.mayanranch.com; 350 Mayan Ranch Rd) From tubing on the river to tennis to nightly programs, the Mayan has tons to do for both the adults and the kids.

Flying L Guest Ranch DUDE RANCH
(☎830-796-9025; www.flyingl.com; 566 Flying L Dr) As much a resort as a dude ranch, the Flying L includes a water park and golf course.

Silver Spur Guest Ranch DUDE RANCH
(☎830-796-3037; www.ssranch.com; 9266 Bandera Creek Rd) A junior Olympic pool provides good way to cool off after a long day on the dusty trails.

Sleeping & Eating

River Front Motel CABINS $
(☎830-460-3690, 800-870-5671; www.theriver frontmotel.com; 1003 Maple St; cabins $69-79; P) This friendly, family-run motel on the south end of town offers 11 cabins on the river, each with a fridge, coffeemaker and cable TV. It's your best bet for the money.

River Oak Inn INN $$
(☎830-796-7751; 1203 Main St; d $69-119; P ❄ ☜) A good choice, where all of the clean rooms have a fridge and microwave.

OST Restaurant AMERICAN $
(☎830-796-3836; 311 Main St; mains $6-14; ⊙6am-9pm Mon-Sat, from 7am Sun) It should come as no surprise that cowboy cuisine is the dominant theme 'round these parts. The OST (which stands for 'Old Spanish Trail') serves up hearty chuck-wagon-style breakfasts, along with Tex-Mex and the ubiquitous chicken-fried steaks at dinner. The decor includes wagonwheel chandeliers, saddle seats at the bar, and an entire wall devoted to John Wayne.

Sid's Main Street BBQ BARBECUE $
(☎830-796-4227; www.sidsmainstreetbbq.com; 702 Main St; $7-12; ⊙11am-8pm Mon-Sat) Head here for your barbecue fix. It serves smoky, succulent meat dishes in a former gas station.

Entertainment

If it's honky-tonkin' and beer drinkin' you're looking for, you've come to the right place.

11th Street Cowboy Bar BAR
(www.11thstreetcowboybar.com; 307 11th St; ⊙10am-2am Tue-Fri, Sat from 9am, Sun from noon) This not-to-be-missed spot just north of Cypress St is the 'Biggest Little Bar in Texas' The quirky main room features dozens of liberated ladies' undergarments and is a great place to go for some local color. The huge outdoor space in back hosts big-name acts as well as special events such as grill-your-own-steak night. Check the website for a schedule of events.

Arkey Blue's Silver Dollar Saloon DANCE HALL
(308 Main St; ⊙10am-2am) At this small but atmospheric dance hall, you can cotton-eyed-Joe with the best of them. Look for Hank Williams Sr's carved signature in one of the wooden tables.

Getting There & Away

Main St runs roughly north–south through the center of town. At the southern edge of downtown, Cypress St heads east–west, continuing as Hwy 16 at the eastern end of town. From Kerrville, the most direct route is Hwy 173 (Bandera Hwy). The more pleasant and scenic way – through hill and dale and past Medina – is to take Hwy 16 south.

Boerne

POP 10,884

Twenty-three miles east of Bandera on Hwy 46 is the bustling little center of Boerne (pronounced 'Bernie'), settled by German immigrants in 1849. The town, which clings

WORTH A TRIP

GUADALUPE RIVER STATE PARK

Thirty miles north of San Antonio, this exceptionally beautiful **park** (830-438-2656; www.tpwd.state.tx.us; 3350 Park Rd 31, Spring Branch; adult/under 12yr $7/free, campsites $14-20; dawn-dusk) straddles a 9-mile stretch of the sparklingly clear, bald-cypress-lined Guadalupe River, and it's great for canoeing and tubing. There are also 3 miles of hiking trails through the park's almost 2000 acres. Two-hour guided tours of the nearby Honey Creek State Natural Area are included in the price of admission. The tours leave at 9am on Saturday morning from the Guadalupe ranger station.

strongly to its German roots, is less overrun with tourists than Fredericksburg and is a pleasant place to spend a few hours.

The **Boerne Convention & Visitors Bureau** (830-249-7277; www.visitboerne.org; 1407 S Main St; 9am-5pm Mon-Fri, to noon Sat) has tons of information about the town and surrounding area. Main St seems to focus on antique stores; most stock a handy leaflet that will help you navigate the plethora of shops.

Sights & Activities

Cibolo Nature Center OUTDOORS
(830-249-4616; www.cibolo.org; 140 City Park Rd, off Hwy 46; 8am-dusk) East of Main St, this small park has rewarding nature trails that wind through native Texan woods, marshland and along Cibolo Creek. Call the park visitor center to ask about the series of live-music concerts and events held here during summer.

Cascade Caverns CAVE
(830-755-8080; www.cascadecaverns.com; 226 Cascade Caverns Rd, off I-10 exit 543; adult/child 4-11yr $15/9.50) Natural attractions outside town include popular Cascade Caverns, about 3 miles south of Boerne. The caverns include a 140ft-deep cave that features giant stalagmites and stalactites and a 100ft waterfall, which you can see by taking the one-hour tour. Opening hours vary, so check the website for details.

Sleeping & Eating

Ye Kendall Inn HISTORIC HOTEL $$
(800-364-2138; www.yekendallinn.com; 128 W Blanco Rd; d $100-200, cabins $109-249; P) A national-landmark hotel dating from 1859, this is the nicest place to stay in Boerne. The creekside main house is made of hand-cut limestone and features a two-story, 200ft-long front porch. The hotel also has three cabins and a small church, all of which date from the 1800s and were relocated to the property from various sites around the state (the stunning Enchanted Cabin was built near Enchanted Rock).

Bear Moon Bakery & Cafe CAFE $
(830-816-2327; 401 S Main St; mains $4-11; 6am-5pm Tue-Sat, 8am-4pm Sun) For a fresh, delicious breakfast buffet, don't look any further than Bear Moon Bakery & Cafe. On weekends, be sure to arrive early – it's always packed. There are plenty of home-baked goodies to tempt you, along with fresh soups, salads and sandwiches for lunch.

Daily Grind CAFE $
(830-249-4677; 143 S Main St; 7am-6pm Mon-Fri, 8am-6pm Sat, 9am-5pm Sun) A prime choice for early-morning coffee and tea is this cute little spot right on the main strip.

Dodging Duck Brewhaus BREW PUB $$
(830-248-3825; 402 River Rd; mains $9-17; 11am-9pm Mon-Thu, to 10pm Sat & Sun) Offers a tasty mix of Mexican and German fare and homemade beers in an eclectic atmosphere. In addition to lunch and dinner, it also has plenty of shareable bar snacks.

Po Po Family Restaurant AMERICAN $$
(830-537-4194; 829 FM 289; mains $10-40; 11am-8:30pm Sun-Thu, to 9:30pm Fri & Sat) Out on the edge of town, this restaurant serves steaks and seafood – including hard-to-find frog legs – but the main reason to come here is to see the absolutely astounding collection of souvenir plates: more than 2000 of them cover almost every inch of wall space.

Wimberley

POP 2626

It's not really on the way to or from anywhere else, so, as the locals like to say, 'You have to mean to visit Wimberley.' A popular weekend spot for Austinites, this artists' community gets absolutely jam-packed during summer weekends – especially on the first Saturday of each month from April to December, when local art galleries, shops and artisans set up booths for **Wimberley Market Days** (www.shopmarketdays.com; 601 FM 2325; parking $5; 7am-4pm first Sat of month), FREE a bustling collection of live music, food and more than 400 vendors at Lion's Field.

Even on weekends when there's no market, there are plenty of shops to visit, stocked with antiques, gifts, and local arts and crafts. You can also taste olive oil in one of the state's only commercial olive orchards, eat expertly baked homemade pies or simply kick back at one of the many B&Bs along the creek.

For more information on market days and other happenings around town, contact the **Wimberley Convention & Visitors Bureau** (CVB; 512-847-2201; www.visitwimberley.com; 14001 RR 12; 9am-4pm Mon-Sat, noon-4pm Sun) near Brookshires grocery store.

Sights & Activities

Bella Vista Ranch OLIVE ORCHARD
(512-847-6514; www.bvranch.com; 3101 Mt Sharp Rd, off CR 182; 10am-5pm Thu-Sat, noon-4pm Sun) An unusual sight in Wimberley (and the rest of Texas, for that matter) is the only producing olive orchard in the Hill Country, found at Bella Vista Ranch. It has a gift shop with free tastings as well as tours of the orchard and the olive press, one of only two in Texas.

Devil's Backbone DRIVING
For excellent scenic views of the limestone hills surrounding Wimberley, take a drive on FM 32, otherwise known as the Devil's Backbone. From Wimberley, head south on RR 12 to FM 32, then turn right toward Fischer and Canyon Lake. The road gets steeper, then winds out onto a craggy ridge (the 'backbone') with a 360-degree vista.

About the only establishment on this stretch of road, **Devil's Backbone Tavern** (830-964-2544; 4041 FM 32, Fischer; noon-midnight, to 1am Sat) is a perfectly tattered and dusty beer joint with a country-music jukebox and live acoustic music some nights.

Blue Hole SWIMMING
(512-847-9127; www.friendsofbluehole.org; 100 Blue Hole Lane, off CR 173; admission adult/child/under 3yr $8/4/free; 10am-6pm Mon-Fri, to 8pm Sat, 11am-6pm Sun) One of the Hill Country's best swimming holes, this is a privately owned spot in the calm, shady and crystal-clear waters of Cypress Creek. To get here from Wimberley, head down Hwy 12 south of the square, turn left on County Rd 173, and then after another half-mile, turn onto the access road between a church and cemetery.

Sleeping & Eating

There are dozens of B&Bs and cottages in Wimberley; call the CVB or visit its website for more information.

Wimberley Inn MOTEL $$
(512-847-3750; www.wimberleyinn.com; 200 RR 3237; d $89-149) Close to the action and just a quarter-mile east of the square, this motel has large rooms at a fair price. Standard rooms are inexpensive and simple, deluxe rooms step it up a notch. Either way, the grounds are lovely.

Blair House Inn B&B $$
(512-847-1111, 877-549-5450; www.blairhouseinn.com; 100 Spoke Hill Rd; d $152-173, ste $220-240, cottages $275-300;) Two miles south of town, this quiet, lovely B&B has eight rooms and two cabins. Some of the suites are knockouts, with big windows and stone fireplaces. There's also a cooking school, restaurant and spa on site, so you can really hole up here for a while.

Leaning Pear AMERICAN $
(512-847-7327; www.leaningpear.com; 111 River Rd; mains $7-9; 11am-3pm Sun, Mon, Wed & Thu, 11am-8pm Fri & Sat) Get out of the crowded downtown area for a relaxed lunch. This cafe exudes Hill Country charm like a cool glass of iced tea, with salads and sandwiches served in a restored stone house.

Wimberley Pie Company DESSERTS $
(512-847-9462; www.wimberleypie.com; 13619 RR 12; 9:30am-5:30pm Tue-Fri, 10am-5pm Sat, noon-4pm Sun) You haven't eaten until you've wrapped your mouth around a pie from this small but popular bakery that supplies many of the area's restaurants (and a few in Austin) with every kind of pie and cheesecake you can imagine, and then some. It's about a quarter-mile east of the square.

Shopping

Art galleries, antique shops and craft stores surround Wimberley Square, located where Ranch Rd 12 crosses Cypress Creek and bends into an 'S.' The best browsing is 1½ miles north of the square on Ranch Rd 12 at **Poco Rio** (15406 RR 12), a shopping center with boutique clothing stores, artists' galleries, eateries, a health spa for acupuncture and massage, and an 18-hole putt-putt golf course, all set among lush gardens and tree-shaded pathways.

Getting There & Away

There is no public transportation to Wimberley. To make the 1½-hour drive from Austin, take US 290 west to Dripping Springs, then turn left onto Ranch Rd 12. From San Antonio, take I-35 north to San Marcos, where you can pick up Ranch Rd 12 headed west and then north into town.

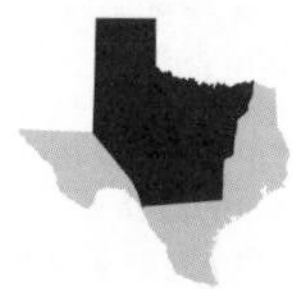

Dallas & the Panhandle Plains

Includes ➡

Best Places to Eat

- Javier's (p155)
- Lonesome Dove Western Bistro (p169)
- Patina Green (p173)

Best Small Towns

- Grapevine (p171)
- McKinney (p172)
- Denton (p173)
- Waxahachie (p175)

Why Go?

Dallas and Fort Worth may be next-door neighbors, but they're hardly twins – or even kissing cousins. Long regarded as being divergent as a Beemer-driving sophisticate and a rancher in a Ford pickup truck, these two cities have starkly different facades. Beyond appearances, however, they share a love of high (and low) culture and good old-fashioned Texan fun. In the surrounding area is a plethora of fabulous small towns worthy of a road trip, including Waxahachie and McKinney.

Leave the big smoke behind and you'll find that the Panhandle and Central Plains may be the part of Texas that most typifies the state to outsiders. This is a land of sprawling cattle ranches, where people can still make a living on horseback. The landscape appears endlessly flat, punctuated only by utility poles and windmills, until a vast canyon materializes and seems to plunge into another world.

When to Go

Dallas

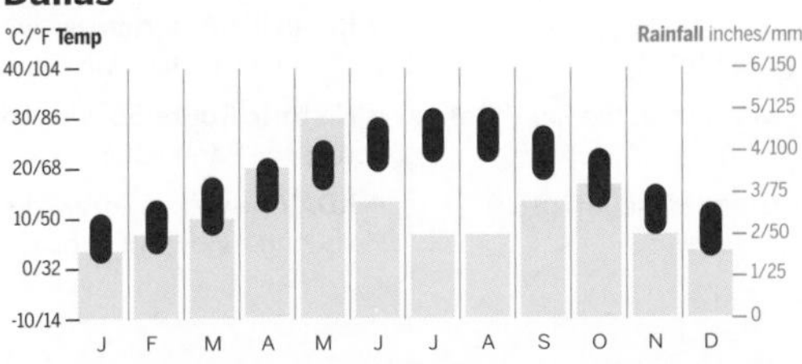

Mar–May Spring comes early to Texas and the wildflowers stage a grand show.

Jun–Aug It's hot! But air-con and swimming in water holes will cool you down.

Sep–Oct Forget winter – balmy fall days are the best.

BACKROAD BBQ

The rule of thumb for back-road Texas barbecue is simple: if you see lots of smoke and pickups, stop and eat.

Biggest to Smallest

➡ **Dallas population** 1,250,000

➡ **Turkey population** 380

Top Sights for Kids

➡ Perot Museum of Nature & Science (p150)

➡ George W. Bush Presidential Library & Museum (p153)

➡ Kimbell Art Museum (p165)

➡ Grapevine Historical Society (p171)

➡ Hotel Settles (p182)

Best Museums

➡ Perot Museum of Nature & Science (p150)

➡ Six Flags Over Texas (p174)

➡ Six Flags Hurricane Harbor (p174)

➡ Museum of the Southwest (p180)

➡ Grace Museum (p187)

Planning Ahead

Sports are the big consideration if you're making advance plans to visit Dallas or Fort Worth and the Plains. Dallas Cowboys games will be sold out so you'll have to find a source for tickets. The same goes for the many college football and basketball tournaments. Otherwise this is a pretty easy place to visit at the drop of a (cowboy) hat.

You'll rarely encounter times (outside of the sporting events above) when rooms are booked solid. A few tours and activities, such as guided hikes, may require advance booking but these are an exception.

TRANSPORTATION

Transportation in this part of Texas is almost entirely limited to two modes: cars and trucks. If you're fiying in, shop around for the best rental-car deal you can find and make sure the car comes with unlimited mileage – in order to fully enjoy the wide open spaces, you'll be doing a fair bit of driving. You'll also soon realize that Texas is in the midst of the greatest open-air sculpture construction in history. Enormous freeway overpasses and cloverleafs that dwarf anything found in California are rising around major cities as part of an unprecedented highway-building boom.

Note that on many back roads, which are often by far the most scenic, there is a paucity of gas stations. Even some rural county seats have lost their last place to fill up. So when the tank gets below a half, fill up.

Resources

➡ **D Magazine** (www.dmagazine.com) Dallas' glossy magazine has regional dining, culture and shopping news.

➡ **Eats Blog** (http://eatsblog.dallasnews.com) The food blog of the *Dallas Morning News* is the place to find out what's new in dining.

➡ **Roadside America** (www.roadsideamerica.com) Strange and wonderful things in Texas towns large and small.

➡ **Historic Route 66** (www.historic66.com) The historic way across the Panhandle.

➡ **KDAV** (www.kdav.org/kdav) This radio station in Buddy Holly's hometown of Lubbock streams his music.

DALLAS

POP 1,250,000

Dallas is Texas' most mythical city, with a past and present rich in the stuff that American legends are made of. The 'Big D' is famous for its contributions to popular culture – notably the Cowboys and their cheerleaders, and *Dallas,* the TV series that for a time was a worldwide symbol of the USA. An upscale ethos makes for an amazing dining scene (you can tell which place is hot by the caliber of cars the valet leaves out front) and the nightlife's not too shabby either.

The museums are not only excellent, but unique – history buffs should not miss the memorials to President John F Kennedy's assassination. The most impressive addition to Dallas' cultural landscape in recent years is the massive 68-acre Arts District, now the largest in the country.

Don't worry, though: despite all this culture Dallas is still a paragon of conspicuous consumption. With more malls per capita than anywhere else in the US, shopping is definitely this city's guiltiest pleasure. So if you feel the urge to take out your credit card, throw frugality to the winds and say 'When in Dallas...,' you definitely won't be alone.

History

In 1839 John Neely Bryan, a Tennessee lawyer and Indian trader, stumbled onto the three forks of the Trinity River, a site he thought had the makings of a good trading post. Dallas County was created in 1846, and both county and town were probably named for George Mifflin Dallas, US vice president under James K Polk; the two were elected on a platform favoring Texas statehood.

Dallas grew slowly for 30 years, though from the start the city had a flair for self-promotion: Bryan saw to it that Dallas was placed on maps even before there was much of a town. In the 1870s the state decided Dallas would be the junction of the north–south Missouri, Kansas and Texas Railroad and the east–west Texas and Pacific Railroad. It worked like magic: merchants from New York, Chicago, Boston and St Louis invested heavily in the city.

Cotton created another boom. In 1885 farmland sold for $15 an acre. By 1920, with cotton prices soaring, land values had risen to $300 an acre. And when the East Texas Oil Field was struck 100 miles east of town in 1930, Dallas became the financial center of the oil industry.

Post-WWII Dallas continued to build on its reputation as a citadel of commerce. But its image took a dive when President John F Kennedy was assassinated during a November 1963 visit to the city. This tragic incident, coupled with the ensuing turmoil of the 1960s, badly battered Dallas' self-esteem. Gradually, however, the city reclaimed its Texas swagger with help from a few new chest-thumping sources of civic pride: the Dallas Cowboys won the first of five Super Bowl titles in 1972. And then there was that little ol' TV show, the top-rated series in the US from 1980 to '82. Dallas was back, louder and prouder than ever – a roll it's been on with hardly a bump in the road since.

DRIVING DISTANCES

Abilene to Austin 213 miles, 3½ hours

Amarillo to Odessa 268 miles, four hours

Amarillo to San Angelo 293 miles, 4½ hours

Dallas to Houston 242 miles, four hours

Dallas to Waco 100 miles, two hours

Fort Worth to Austin 187 miles, three hours

Fort Worth to San Antonio 265 miles, 4½ hours

Lubbock to Fort Worth 292 miles, 4½ hours

Odessa to El Paso 274 miles, 4¼ hours

Sights

Most of Dallas' major sights are blissfully compact, which you'll appreciate all the more on hot days. Downtown museums and Arts District attractions are in areas easily traversed by either walking or taking the McKinney Ave trolley – in fact, there's no reason to drive between them. Outside of these areas, the major cultural attractions lie in Fair Park, 3 miles east of downtown.

Downtown

Downtown is the epicenter of Dallas' interesting – and tragic – history, with museums that both commemorate and celebrate. It's also growing into a live-work community, with scores of condos popping up and

Dallas & the Panhandle Plains Highlights

❶ Bull-riding and two-steppin' at the biggest honky-tonk on earth, the Stockyards' **Billy Bob's Texas** (p170), in Fort Worth.

❷ Reliving the tragic day of JFK's assassination at the **Sixth Floor Museum** (p146), in Dallas.

❸ Being inspired by the **Dallas Arts District** (p150) with its top-notch museums, music, theater and stunning modern architecture.

❹ Wandering the beautifully preserved town of **Waxahachie** (p175)

❺ Following **Texas Hwy 70** (p195) as it wanders through forgotten small towns, lush ranches and evocative wide open spaces.

❻ Daring to take the challenge at Amarillo's **Big Texan Steak Ranch** (p203): eat a huge steak and sides in under an hour and it's free; don't and pay.

❼ Wandering the old streets and beautiful river trails of **San Angelo** (p183), then getting outfitted in Texas style in a Western gear store.

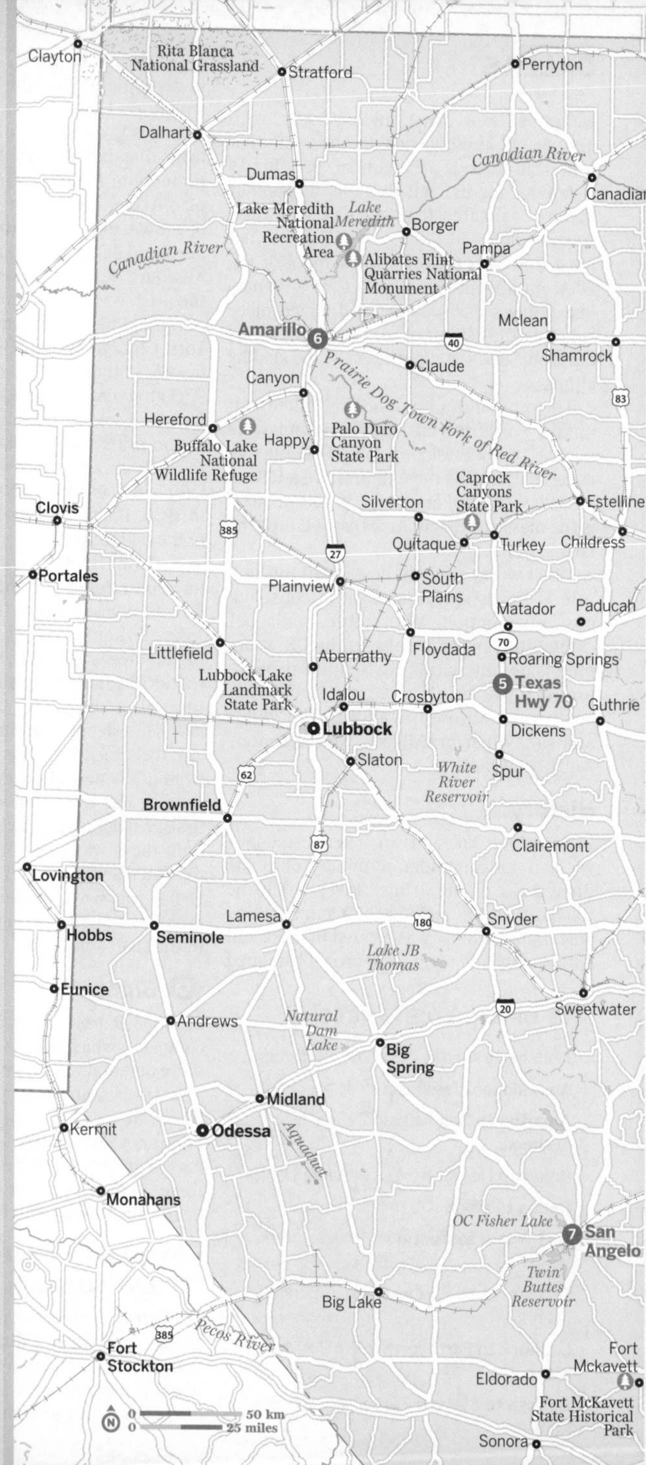

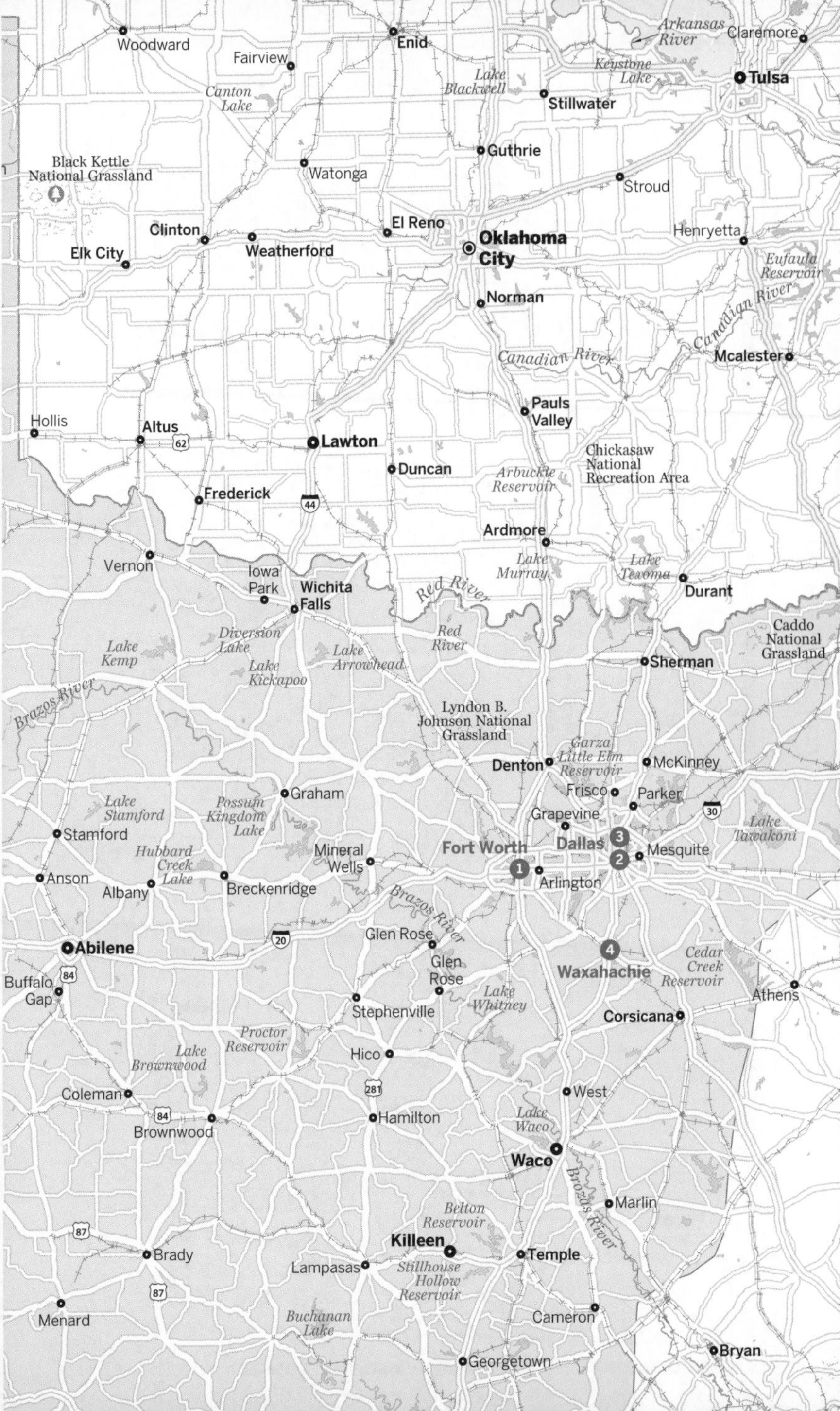

Woodward
Enid
Fairview
Arkansas River
Claremore
Keystone Lake
Tulsa
Lake Blackwell
Stillwater
Canton Lake
Guthrie
Black Kettle National Grassland
Watonga
Stroud
El Reno
Clinton
Oklahoma City
Henryetta
Weatherford
Elk City
Eufaula Reservoir
Canadian River
Norman
Canadian River
Mcalester
Pauls Valley
Hollis
Altus
62
Lawton
Duncan
Chickasaw National Recreation Area
Arbuckle Reservoir
Frederick
44
Ardmore
Vernon
Lake Murray
Lake Texoma
Iowa Park
Wichita Falls
Red River
Durant
Diversion Lake
Red River
Caddo National Grassland
Lake Kemp
Lake Arrowhead
Lake Kickapoo
Sherman
Brazos River
Lyndon B. Johnson National Grassland
Garza Little Elm Reservoir
Denton
McKinney
Frisco
Parker
Graham
Lake Stamford
Possum Kingdom Lake
Grapevine
30
Lake Tawakoni
Stamford
3
Dallas
Fort Worth
Mineral Wells
Mesquite
Hubbard Creek Lake
2
1
Anson
Albany
Breckenridge
Arlington
Brazos River
Glen Rose
20
Abilene
4
Waxahachie
Cedar Creek Reservoir
Glen Rose
84
Buffalo Gap
Lake Whitney
Athens
Stephenville
Corsicana
Proctor Reservoir
Lake Brownwood
Hico
281
Coleman
West
84
Hamilton
Brownwood
Lake Waco
Waco
Brazos River
Marlin
Belton Reservoir
87
Killeen
Brady
Temple
Lampasas
Stillhouse Hollow Reservoir
87
Menard
Cameron
Buchanan Lake
Bryan
Georgetown

Greater Dallas

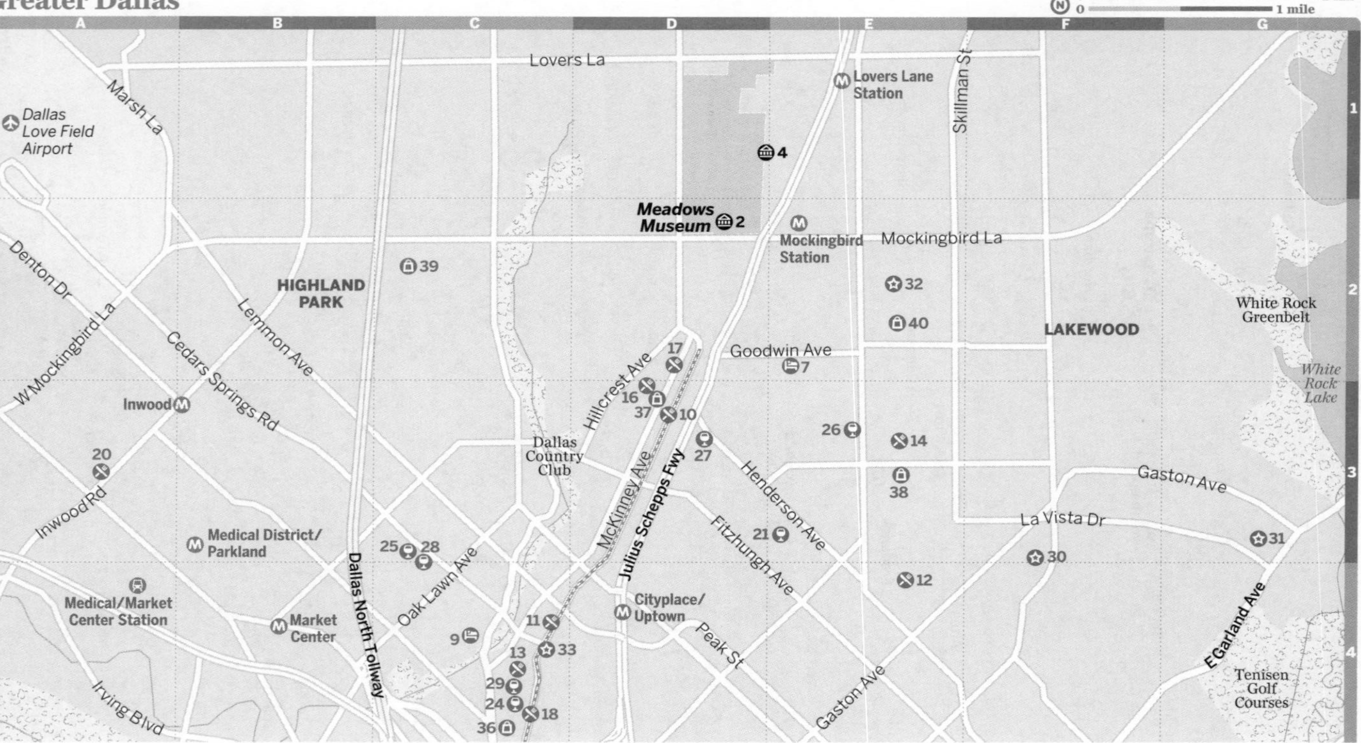

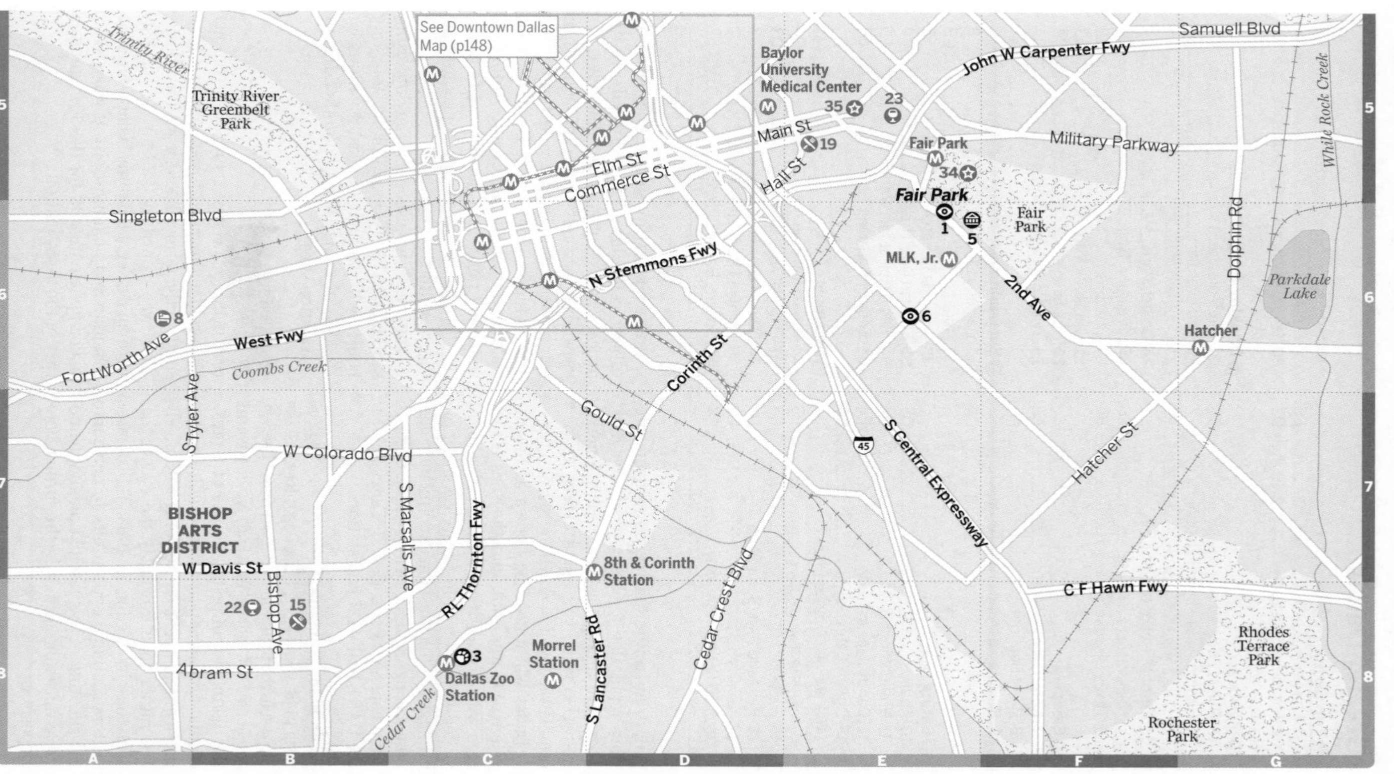

See Downtown Dallas Map (p148)
Samuell Blvd
John W Carpenter Fwy
White Rock Creek
Baylor University Medical Center
35
23
Main St
19
Hall St
Military Parkway
Fair Park
34
Fair Park
1
5
Fair Park
MLK, Jr.
2nd Ave
6
Dolphin Rd
Parkdale Lake
Hatcher
Trinity River
Trinity River Greenbelt Park
Elm St
Commerce St
Singleton Blvd
N Stemmons Fwy
8
West Fwy
Fort Worth Ave
Coombs Creek
Corinth St
Gould St
S Tyler Ave
W Colorado Blvd
45
S Central Expressway
Hatcher St
BISHOP ARTS DISTRICT
W Davis St
S Marsalis Ave
RL Thornton Fwy
8th & Corinth Station
Cedar Crest Blvd
C F Hawn Fwy
22
15
Bishop Ave
3
Morrel Station
Abram St
Dallas Zoo Station
Cedar Creek
S Lancaster Rd
Rhodes Terrace Park
Rochester Park

Greater Dallas

Top Sights
1 Fair Park E6
2 Meadows Museum D2

Sights
3 Dallas Zoo C8
4 George W. Bush Presidential Library & Museum D1
5 Perot Museum of Nature & Science at Fair Park E6
6 Texas Discovery Gardens E6

Sleeping
7 Abby Guest House E2
8 Hotel Belmont A6
9 Rosewood Mansion on Turtle Creek C4

Eating
10 Abacus D3
11 Bread Winners C4
12 Daddy Jack's E4
13 Dream Cafe C4
14 Greenville Avenue Pizza Company E3
15 Hattie's B8
16 Highland Park Soda Shop D3
17 Javier's D2
18 S&D Oyster Company C4
19 Santiago's Taco Loco Express E5
Smoke .... (see 8)
20 Sonny Bryan's Smokehouse A3

Drinking & Nightlife
21 Barcadia E3
22 Boulevardier B8
23 Double Wide E5
24 Ginger Man C4
25 JR's Bar & Grill C3
26 Libertine E3
27 Old Monk Pub D3
28 Sue Ellen's C4
29 Two Corks and a Bottle C4

Entertainment
30 Balcony Club F3
31 Goat G3
32 Granada Theater E2
33 Kitchen Dog Theater C4
34 Music Hall at Fair Park E5
35 Sons of Hermann Hall E5

Shopping
36 David Dike Fine Art C4
37 Froggie's 5 & 10 .... D3
38 Good Records E3
39 Highland Park Village C2
40 Society Bakery E2

pedestrian traffic defying downtown's previous reputation for being dead after dark. There are times, however, even at midday, midweek, when you might expect to see a tumbleweed rolling down the street.

Dallas will forever be known as the city where JFK was shot, and the sites associated with his death are among Dallas' most visited attractions. Most travelers make pilgrimages to the museums and monuments; others congregate at Dealey Plaza, eager to swap conspiracy theories. JFK sites lie near the DART Rail West End station.

Sixth Floor Museum MUSEUM

(Map p148; www.jfk.org; Book Depository, 411 Elm St; adult/child $16/13; ⏲10am-6pm Tue-Sun, noon-6pm Mon; light rail West End) No city wants the distinction of being the site of a presidential assassination – especially if that president happens to be John F Kennedy. But rather than downplay the events that sent the city reeling in 1963, Dallas gives visitors a unique opportunity to delve into the shooting in this fascinating and memorable museum, located in the former Book Depository.

And while any museum dedicated to the subject could have reconstructed the historical event using footage, audio clips and eyewitness accounts, this museum offers you a goosebump-raising view through the exact window from which Lee Harvey Oswald fired upon the motorcade. (If that last statement raises your hackles, not to worry: the displays don't shy away from conspiracy theories either.)

The museum also offers an interesting self-guided Cell Phone Walking Tour (one hour; with/without museum admission $2.50/5) of Dealey Plaza and other JFK assassination sites.

Dealey Plaza & the Grassy Knoll PARK

(Map p148; light rail West End) Now a National Historic Landmark, this rectangular park is south of the former Book Depository. Dealey Plaza was named in 1935 for George Bannerman Dealey, a longtime Dallas journalist, historian and philanthropist. It was given a major update in 2013 for the 50th anniversary of the assassination.

The grassy knoll is the hillock that rises from the north side of Elm St to the edge of the picket fence separating Dealey Plaza from the railroad yards. While some witnesses to the assassination claim shots came from this area, investigators found only cigarette butts and footprints on the knoll after the shooting. The House Select Committee on Assassinations, investigating from 1976 to 1978, concluded via acoustical analysis that a sniper did fire from behind the picket fence but missed. That bolstered the belief that Kennedy's assassination was part of a conspiracy. We may never know the truth.

Kennedy Memorial MONUMENT

(Map p148; 646 Market St) You can pay your respects here to the fallen ex-president. Designed by architect Philip Johnson, the roofless room with a view of the sky and the carved words 'John Fitzgerald Kennedy' is a cenotaph, or open tomb, meant to evoke a sense of the freedom that JFK epitomized.

Old Red Museum MUSEUM

(Map p148; ☎214-745-1100; www.oldred.org; 100 S Houston St; adult/child $8/5; ⏲9am-5pm) The 1892 Old Red Courthouse that houses this museum is almost as interesting as the museum's interactive exhibits on Dallas county history. Entry includes a building tour (daily, call for times).

Thanks-Giving Square SQUARE

(Map p148; ☎214-969-1977; www.thanksgiving.org; bounded by Bryan St, Pacific Ave & Ervay St; ⏲buildings 9am-5pm Mon-Fri, from 10am Sat & Sun) FREE For all its din, drive and shopping malls, Dallas has a surprisingly quiet side – a triangular piece of prime downtown real estate set aside for spiritual renewal and reflection. Thanks-Giving Square was established by the Thanks-Giving Foundation as a 'place where people can use gratitude as a basis for dialogue, mutual understanding and healing.'

Designed by Philip Johnson, the tranquil center includes a meditation garden, a Wall of Praise, an interdenominational Chapel of Thanksgiving and a museum of gratitude.

DALLAS & FORT WORTH IN...

Two Days

It's time to get your history on (yep, Dallas has a serious side). Relive the epic events of the early 1960s by taking a stroll through **Dealey Plaza**, the site where JFK was shot in 1963. After chatting with various conspiracy theorists on the **Grassy Knoll**, take a deep breath and head up to the moving **Sixth Floor Museum**. After a stop in the **Old Red Museum** for a peek into Dallas' past, head over to the **Kennedy Memorial** to pay your respects. Lunch at the **Zodiac** will give you a vivid window into a classic Dallas tradition (and feel free to shop at the original **Neiman Marcus** while you're at it). You're probably in a reflective mood, so wander over to **Thanks-Giving Square**. (Shoppers, skip the reflection and go to the **West Village**.) Evening, chill out in **Deep Ellum** and immerse yourself in Dallas' old-school musical roots at one of the many nightclubs.

Spend the next morning in the **Arts District** and check out either the **Nasher Sculpture Center** or the **Trammell & Margaret Crow Center for Asian Art** before dashing off to Fort Worth's **Stockyards**. Grab a burger and a shake at the **Love Shack** and check out the 4pm **cattle drive**. Walk around and soak up the cowboy action before heading to the cafes and bars of Magnolia Ave.

Four Days

Rest your head in Fort Worth so that come morning, y'all can gallop over to the **National Cowgirl Museum**, and then explore the fabulous **Kimbell Art Museum**. Stroll around the **Cultural District** before heading back to Dallas, stopping for some thrills at **Six Flags Over Texas**.

Day four, spend the morning visiting anything you missed in the **Arts District** and then head north for lunch in the charming little town of **McKinney**. Back in Dallas, hit the funky **Bishop Arts District** to poke around the shops. Dinner and drinks are your call. What's left that grabs your fancy?

Downtown Dallas

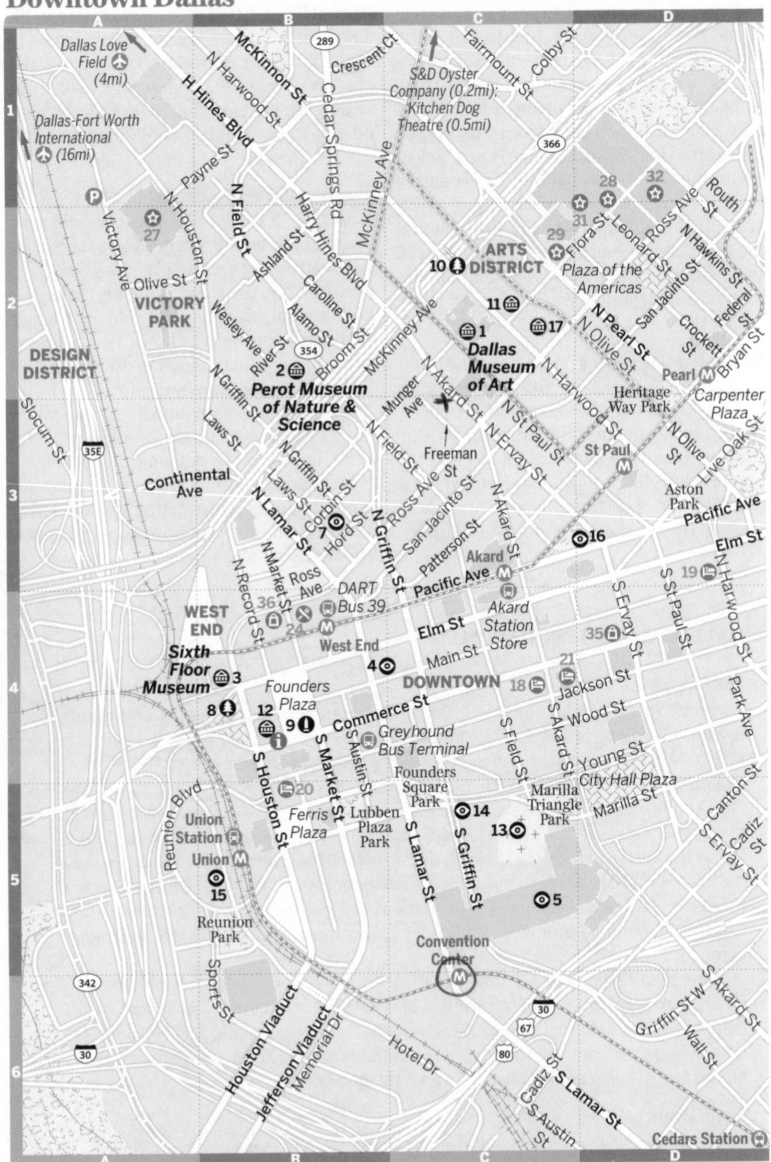

Dallas Heritage Village HISTORIC SITE

(Map p148; ☎214-421-5141; www.dallasheritagevillage.org; 1515 S Harwood St; adult/child $9/5; ⏰10am-4pm Tue-Sat, noon-4pm Sun) This 13-acre museum of history and architecture, set on a wooded property south of downtown, shows what it was like to live in north Texas from about 1840 to 1910. The modern skyline makes for a striking backdrop for the living-history exhibits, comprised of 38

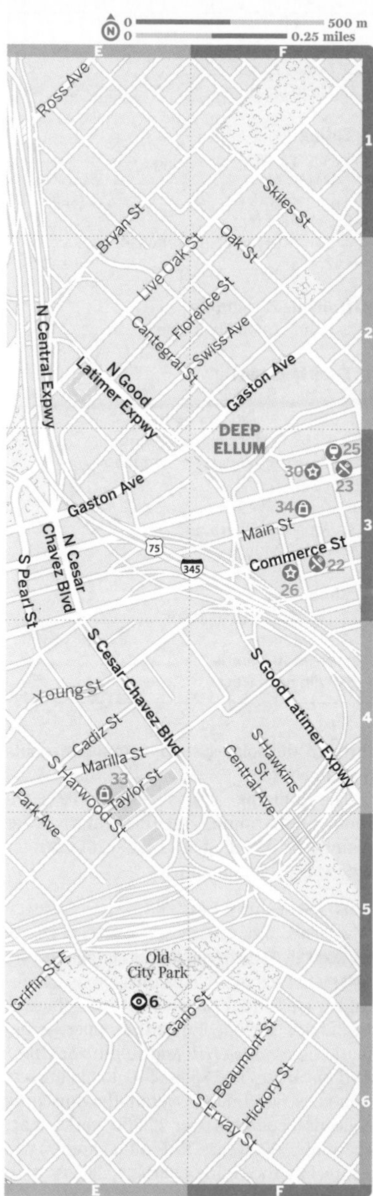

historic structures including a tepee and a Civil War–era farm.

Pioneer Plaza SQUARE

(Map p148; cnr S Griffin & Young Sts) For a Texas-sized photo op or just a sight of the largest bronze monument on earth, head to Pioneer Plaza. Its showpiece is a collection of 40 bronze larger-than-life longhorns, amassed as if they were on a cattle drive.

Pioneer Cemetery CEMETERY

(Map p148) This is the resting place of many early Dallas settlers, with gravestones from the 1850s through the 1920s.

Convention Center & Reunion Area

If it seems like downtown Dallas come evening is full of roaming businesspeople looking to burn off the stress of their workday but not entirely sure where to go, you're right. Everything's a short walk from either DART Rail's Convention Center Station or Union Station.

Convention Center BUILDING

(Map p148; www.dallasconventioncenter.com; 650 S Griffin St) Dallas is one of the world's biggest convention cities, and its convention center boasts more than a million square feet of exhibit space.

Reunion Tower LANDMARK

(Map p148; ☎214-571-5744; www.reuniontower.com; 300 Reunion Blvd E) What's 50 stories high and has a three-level spherical dome with 260 flashing lights? No, it's not a spaceship, it's Reunion Tower, the unofficial symbol of Dallas. Get a workout by taking the steps up to the observation deck, or enjoy the sky-high panoramic view from the stunning celebrity-chef restaurant and lounge **Five Sixty by Wolfgang Puck** (☎214-741-5560; www.wolfgangpuck.com; Reunion Tower; mains from $15; ⏱restaurant 5-10pm Mon-Sat, 11am-5pm Sun, bar 5-11pm Mon-Sat). An underground pedestrian tunnel connects Reunion Tower with Union Station.

West End

The convention trade and top-end corporate hotels give West End a permanent 'smart-casual' air. The several blocks of rehabbed brick warehouses host an array of chain restaurants and bars; good for people staying nearby who want to avoid a cab ride. Otherwise, between trade shows the area can be pretty quiet.

Dallas World Aquarium AQUARIUM

(Map p148; www.dwazoo.com; 1801 N Griffin St; adult/child $21/13; ⏱9am-5pm; 👪) The flora

Downtown Dallas

Top Sights
1 Dallas Museum of Art C2
2 Perot Museum of Nature & Science B2
3 Sixth Floor Museum B4

Sights
4 Bank of America Plaza B4
5 Convention Center C5
6 Dallas Heritage Village E5
7 Dallas World Aquarium B3
8 Dealey Plaza & the Grassy Knoll B4
9 Kennedy Memorial B4
10 Klyde Warren Park C2
Magnolia Petroleum Company Building .... (see 21)
11 Nasher Sculpture Center C2
12 Old Red Museum B4
13 Pioneer Cemetery C5
14 Pioneer Plaza C5
15 Reunion Tower B5
16 Thanks-Giving Square D3
17 Trammell & Margaret Crow Center for Asian Art C2

Sleeping
18 Adolphus C4
19 Hotel Indigo D3
20 Hotel Lawrence B5
21 Magnolia Hotel C4

Eating
22 Angry Dog F3
DMA Cafe .... (see 1)
Pecan Lodge .... (see 33)
23 Serious Pizza F3
24 Sonny Bryan's Smokehouse B4
Zodiac .... (see 35)

Drinking & Nightlife
25 Reno's Chop Shop Saloon F3

Entertainment
26 Adair's Saloon F3
27 American Airlines Center A2
28 AT&T Performing Arts Center D1
29 Morton H Meyerson Symphony Center C2
30 Trees Dallas F3
31 Winspear Opera House D2
32 Wyly Theatre D1

Shopping
33 Dallas Farmers Market E4
34 Millennium F3
35 Neiman Marcus D4
36 Wild Bill's Western Store B4

and fauna of 14 countries (think the watery Mayan cenote swimming with sharks and rays) come alive here.

Arts District

In one word: wow. This is the largest arts district in the nation, with 68 acres of arts, entertainment and culture. Whether you're an opera fanatic or go gaga for abstract sculpture, this urban oasis has something for you. And there's more here all the time; check online for more details at www.thedallasartsdistrict.org.

Perot Museum of Nature & Science MUSEUM

(Map p148; ☎214-428-5555; www.perotmuseum.org; 2201 N Field St; adult/child from $15/10; ⏰10am-6pm Mon-Sat, noon-6pm Sun; 👪; light rail St Paul) The biggest addition yet to the Arts District, this striking museum opened in 2012. It wows both on the outside (thanks to award-winning architect Thom Mayne) and on the inside (there are six floors of wonder). Most of the exhibits are interactive – visitors can design their own bird, journey through the solar system, command robots and much more.

The building is designed to be environmentally sound, and this feature is explained in detail. It also has a 3D theater with ever-changing movies.

Dallas Museum of Art MUSEUM

(Map p148; www.dallasmuseumofart.org; 1717 N Harwood St; ⏰11am-5pm Tue-Sun, to 9pm Thu; 👪; light rail St Paul) FREE This museum is a high-caliber world tour of decorative and fine art. Highlights include Edward Hopper's enigmatic *Lighthouse Hill* and Rodin's *Sculptor and his Muse*. The Spanish Colonial art section is extraordinary. Overall, the museum's collection contains over 22,000 works of art spanning 5000 years. Kids (and parents) will appreciate the Young Learners Gallery, with fun projects for kids.

Trammell & Margaret Crow Center for Asian Art MUSEUM

(Map p148; ☎214 -979-6430; www.crowcollection.com; 2010 Flora St; ⏰10am-9pm Tue-Thu, 10am-6pm Fri & Sat, noon-6pm Sun; light rail St Paul) FREE Enter another world in this calm, pagoda-like oasis of a museum that's nearly as remarkable for its ambience as for its rich collection of artworks from China, Japan, India and Southeast Asia, dating from 3500 BC to the early 20th century. Don't miss the gorgeous sandstone facade from North India. There are free guided tours at 1pm on Saturdays.

A DARK DAY IN NOVEMBER: THE JFK ASSASSINATION

In the early 1960s the USA was fascinated with its young president, his little children at play in the Oval Office and his regal wife. They seemed the perfect family, and the USA – still awash in postwar prosperity – considered itself a place where justice and amity prevailed.

But beneath the glossy surface, the USA was heading into its most divisive decade since the Civil War. By no means universally popular, Kennedy had won the election over Richard Nixon by fewer than 120,000 votes from among 69 million cast. His 1961 Bay of Pigs invasion of Cuba was a foreign-policy disaster.

In the eyes of many, Kennedy redeemed his presidency in the fall of 1962, when he stood up to Soviet premier Nikita Khrushchev after US intelligence services discovered Soviet offensive missile sites in Cuba. Yet in the nine months prior to his Dallas appearance, Kennedy had received more than 400 death threats, from critics on both the left, who felt him guilty of warmongering during the Cuban missile crisis, and the right, who felt him soft on communism. The president's advisers were seriously concerned about the trip to Dallas, where right-wing groups, including the John Birch Society and the Indignant White Citizens Council, held powerful sway. Yet nearly a quarter-million people lined the streets on November 23, 1963, to greet him.

Shots Ring Out

What happened next has been endlessly debated and dissected by conspiracy theorists, but the events as officially recorded took place like this: Kennedy, his wife Jacqueline, Texas governor John Connally and the rest of the motorcade left Love Field at 11:50am and arrived downtown under sunny skies. Kennedy's open-air limousine made its way down Main St to Dealey Plaza, where three streets – Main in the middle, Commerce to the south and Elm to the north – converged under a railroad bridge known as the triple underpass.

The limo made a one-block jog on Houston St, turning onto Elm St beneath the Texas School Book Depository building. Just as the limousine completed its turn at 12:30pm, one shot rang out, then another. Both Kennedy and Connally appeared wounded, and then a third shot was heard, and part of the president's head exploded. Jacqueline Kennedy cradled her husband's body as the limo raced up the Stemmons Fwy toward Parkland Memorial Hospital. They arrived at 12:36pm, but doctors could not save Kennedy, who had a bullet wound in his neck in addition to the massive head wound. He was pronounced dead at 1pm.

Manhunt & Murder

Even before the announcement, Dallas and the nation were thrown into turmoil. Dallas police officer Marrion Baker, who had seen pigeons fly off the Book Depository roof as the shots were fired, entered the building and found a man in the employee lunchroom at 12:32pm. Depository superintendent Roy Truly identified the suspect as Lee Harvey Oswald – an employee hired five weeks earlier – so Baker let him go. Soon after, police found the sniper's perch on the 6th floor, together with spent cartridges, and finger- and palm prints later identified as Oswald's. Meanwhile, Oswald was arrested at 1:50pm in the Oak Cliff section of town as a suspect in the shooting of Dallas police officer JD Tippit. He was later charged with the murder of Kennedy, but denied both murders. The next morning, as Oswald was being transferred to the county jail pending trial, Dallas nightclub owner Jack Ruby shot him in the basement of Dallas police headquarters. Kennedy was buried the following day at Arlington National Cemetery, outside Washington, DC.

Amid a country in mourning, the phrase 'Where were you the moment you found out that JFK had been shot?' became a touchstone question for an entire generation. And debate over what may have really happened that day has never stopped.

Nasher Sculpture Center MUSEUM

(Map p148; www.nashersculpturecenter.org; 2001 Flora St; adult/child $10/free; ⏲11am-5pm Tue-Sun; light rail St Paul) Modern-art installations shine at the fabulous glass-and-steel Nasher Sculpture Center. The Nashers accumulated what might be one of the greatest privately held sculpture collections in the world, with works by Calder, de Kooning, Rodin, Serra and Miró, and the divine sculpture garden is one of the best in the country.

Klyde Warren Park PARK

(Map p148; www.klydewarrenpark.org; btwn Pearl & St Paul Sts) FREE New in 2013, this innovative 5.2-acre park is an urban green space built over the recessed Woodall Rodgers Freeway. It has its own programming and, besides outdoor areas for chess, yoga and other activities, it offers performances, book signings and more.

Fair Park

Created for the Texas Independence–themed 1936 Centennial Exposition, the art-deco buildings of **Fair Park** (Map p144; www.fairpark.org; 1300 Robert B Cullum Blvd; light rail Fair Park) today contain several interesting museums. While the grounds themselves are safe, the surrounding area – particularly to the east and south – can have safety issues. Outside of the State Fair, on-site parking is plentiful and free. DART light rail also stops right at the main entrance. Parking costs $10.

In 2012 tragedy struck the park when **Big Tex**, the 52-ft-tall icon of the fair burst into flames and was destroyed. The loss of his unctuous mug was widely mourned and there is a campaign to get him rebuilt.

Fair Park is at its busiest during the annual three-week State Fair of Texas (p153).

Hall of State MONUMENT

(3939 Grand Ave; ⏲9am-5pm Tue-Sat, 1-5pm Sun) Fair Park is full of superb 1930s art-deco architecture, none of it quite as inspired as this tribute to all things Texan. The **Hall of Heroes** pays homage to such luminaries as Stephen F Austin and Samuel Houston; the **Great Hall of Texas** features huge murals depicting episodes in Texas history from the 16th century on.

As you leave the Hall of State, stop by the reflecting pool outside of the entrance: the golden Greek-inspired statues will thrill art-deco buffs.

Texas Discovery Gardens GARDENS

(Map p144; ☎214-428-7476; www.texasdiscoverygardens.org; 3601 Martin Luther King Jr Blvd; butterfly house & garden adult/child $8/4; ⏲outdoor gardens always open, indoor gardens 10am-5pm) These pretty indoor-outdoor gardens include a tropical conservatory, a fragrance garden and a butterfly garden. Don't miss the native Texas plants.

Perot Museum of Nature & Science at Fair Park MUSEUM

(Map p144; ☎214-428-5555; www.perotmuseum.org; 3535 Grand Ave; admission $1; ⏲noon-5pm Fri-Sun) Largely replaced by the huge new Perot Museum of Nature and Science in the Arts District, the old facility remains open for people nostalgic for its historic dioramas of nature and science.

African American Museum MUSEUM

(☎214-565-9026; www.aamdallas.org; 3536 Grand Ave; admission free, tours $5; ⏲11am-5pm Tue-Sat, 1-5pm Sun) FREE This museum has exhibits of more than 1000 objects that richly detail the art and history of African American people from precolonial Africa through the present. Its folk-art collection is one of the best nationwide.

DALLAS ARCHITECTURE

The Dallas skyline has long been one of the most vibrant in the USA, and it's getting more interesting all the time. Sleek contemporary designs mix with buildings inspired by French neoclassicism. Some buildings to look out for include the following:

Magnolia Petroleum Company Building (Map p148; 1401 Commerce St) The red neon pegasus became a symbol of Dallas when it first flew atop this building in 1934. It disappeared for decades before re-emerging atop the newly renovated building, now a hotel, in 1999.

Bank of America Plaza (Map p148; 901 Main St) One of the tallest buildings in Texas, this modernist skyscraper is outlined each night in cool green argon tubing which plays well with all the other colored-by-night buildings downtown.

Elsewhere in Dallas

George W. Bush Presidential Library & Museum MUSEUM

(Map p144; ☎214-346-1557; www.georgewbushlibrary.smu.edu; 2943 SMU Blvd; adult/child $16/10; ⏲9am-5pm Mon-Sat, noon-5pm Sun; light rail Mockingbird station) Opened on the campus of Southern Methodist University (SMU) in 2013 at a cost of over $300 million, this vast facility documents the presidency of George W Bush. Like other presidential libraries it has two missions: to allow research and to present a record of the president to the public. Exhibits include all manner of gifts Bush received while president.

Its most interactive feature is the Decision Points Theater, which allows you to see how Bush made decisions around events such as 9/11 and the invasion of Iraq. The approach is genial throughout. Although Bush had no connection to SMU, the university outbid others to host the facility. (Bush's father George HW Bush went through the same process when he located his presidential library at Texas A&M, a school where he had no previous connection.)

It's close to the DART Mockingbird station.

Meadows Museum MUSEUM

(Map p144; ☎214-768-2516; www.meadowsmuseumdallas.org; 5900 Bishop Blvd; adult/child $10/4; ⏲10am-5pm Tue-Sat, to 9pm Thu, noon-5pm Sun; light rail Mockingbird Station) Located on the Southern Methodist University campus, this museum exhibits perhaps the best and most comprehensive collection of Spanish art outside of Spain, including masterpieces by Velázquez, El Greco, Goya, Picasso and Miró.

Dallas Zoo ZOO

(Map p144; ☎469-554-7500; www.dallaszoo.com; 650 S RL Thornton Fwy (I-35E); adult/child $15/12; ⏲9am-5pm; 👪) Africa is the focus of this urban zoo, which is just 3 miles south of downtown. It has gorilla and chimpanzee habitats and an entire exhibit called Giants of the Savanna. Kids like the Children's Zoo with its winsome, furry critters.

Activities

★Katy Trail WALKING

(www.katytraildallas.org) For see-and-be-seen running and cycling, hit the tree-lined Katy Trail that runs 3.5 miles from the American Airlines center downtown almost all the way to SMU, passing through interesting neighborhoods along the way. The old railway route is tree-lined and at times feels like the country.

Festivals & Events

★State Fair of Texas Fair FAIR

(www.bigtex.com; Fair Park, 1300 Cullum Blvd; adult/child $17/13; ⏲late-Sep-Oct) This massive fair is the fall highlight for many a Texan. Come ride one of the tallest Ferris wheels in North America, eat corn dogs (it's claimed that this is where they were invented), and browse among the prize-winning cows, sheep and quilts.

Deep Ellum Arts Festival FESTIVAL

(☎214-855-1881; www.deepellumartsfestival.com; ⏲early April) To experience Dallas at its most bohemian, diverse and relaxed, head down to the live-music stages and eclectic arts booths.

Sleeping

Staying uptown is pricey, but you're closest to restaurants and nightlife. Otherwise you'll find all manner of chains for all manner of budgets along the highways, especially US 75 and to the west and north of the center.

Abby Guest House COTTAGE $

(Map p144; ☎214-264-4804; www.abbyguesthouse.com; 5417 Goodwin Ave; cottage from $65; P❄@📶) This bright and cheerful garden cottage is within walking distance of great cafes and bars on Upper Greenville Ave. With a full kitchen and sunny private patio, it's a great deal although often booked. Two night minimum.

Hotel Lawrence HOTEL $$

(Map p148; ☎214-761-9090; www.hotellawrencedallas.com; 302 S Houston St; r $90-180; ❄@📶) One of the better deals among the midrange indie hotels, Hotel Lawrence has a convenient downtown location in a 1925 building. Rooms include a great buffet breakfast.

Hotel Indigo HOTEL $$

(Map p148; ☎214-741-7700; www.hotelindigo.com; 1933 Main St; r from $80-170; ❄📶🐾) After a hot day of sightseeing, this downtown hotel offers good respite. Part of a small chain, it offers rooms with sprightly decor, hardwood floors and extras such as gourmet coffeemakers. The 170 rooms are in a restored vintage building.

Hotel Belmont BOUTIQUE HOTEL $$
(Map p144; ☎866-870-8010; www.belmontdallas.com; 901 Fort Worth Ave; r $100-200; ❄@🛜≋) Just 2 miles west of downtown, this stylish 1940s bungalow hotel is a fabulously low-key antidote to Dallas' flashier digs, with a touch of mid-century modern design and more than its share of soul. The garden rooms – with soaking tubs, Moroccan-blue tile work, kilim rugs and some city views – are tops.

Magnolia Hotel BOUTIQUE HOTEL $$
(Map p148; ☎214-915-6500; www.magnoliahotels.com; 1401 Commerce St; r $120-250; ❄@🛜≋) Housed in the 1922, 29-story Magnolia Petroleum Company Building, this gracious hotel offers a sumptuous stay. Rooms have period details including wooden blinds and retro furniture. The commodious rooms have fridges, while the suites have kitchenettes.

Adolphus HISTORIC HOTEL $$$
(Map p148; ☎214-742-8200; www.hoteladolphus.com; 1321 Commerce St; r from $140-300; ❄@🛜🐾; light rail Akard) Feel like royalty (yes, Queen Elizabeth has stayed here) the old-fashioned way. The 422-room Adolphus takes us back to the days when gentlemen wore ties and hotels were truly grand, not bastions of ascetic minimalism. Just exploring the 22 floors is an adventure. Note that room sizes vary widely.

Rosewood Mansion on Turtle Creek LUXURY HOTEL $$$
(Map p144; ☎214-559-2100; www.rosewoodhotels.com; 2821 Turtle Creek Blvd; r $275-600; ❄@🛜≋🐾) Step into a life of ease, where for every two guests there's one staff member attending. This is the definitive five-star Dallas hotel, and a worthy splurge. Rooms have fresh flowers and hand-carved European furnishings, and dinner is served in the original, marble-clad, 1925 Italianate villa.

Eating

Deep Ellum, just east of downtown, is your choice for eclectic eats. This area, 'deep' up Elm St, gets its name from the Southern-drawl pronunciation of 'Elm.' Otherwise head to uptown for myriad choices. Bishop Ave, dotted with interesting places to eat and drink, merges hipster and funky – walk off your vittles by window-shopping the idiosyncratic boutiques.

★ **Santiago's Taco Loco Express** MEXICAN $
(Map p144; 3014 Main St; mains $3-8; ⏲6am-10pm Mon-Thu, to 3am Fri & Sat) The breakfast tacos and tamales are addictive and draw locals who know how to start their day. At any time the fine range of tacos includes massive combos that make for an all-day meal. Service is from a window, with tables outside.

Greenville Avenue Pizza Company PIZZA $
(Map p144; ☎214-826-5404; 1923 Greenville Ave; mains from $4; ⏲5pm-midnight Sun-Thu, noon-4am Fri & Sat) Fresh, hot and wonderfully thin slices to keep you fueled late into the night.

Serious Pizza PIZZA $
(Map p148; www.seriouspizza.net; 2807 Elm St; mains from $6; ⏲noon-midnight Sun-Thu, till 3am Fri & Sat) Despite the name, the pizza was so good we were forced to smile. Pizza slices are huge but for real pleasure, eat in and customize your pizza from the multitude of toppings. Cooks toss the seasoned dough in the air.

Angry Dog AMERICAN $
(Map p148; 2726 Commerce St; mains $5-9; ⏲11am-midnight Mon-Thu, to 2am Fri & Sat, noon-10pm Sun) Nice, greasy, old-style burgers lure folks into this saloon at all hours. Other bar stalwarts, including wings, are good. The beer selection is tops.

Highland Park Soda Shop AMERICAN $
(Map p144; ☎214-521-2126; 3229 Knox St; mains $4-8; ⏲7am-6pm Mon-Sat, 10am-5pm Sun; 👪) Since 1912 this classic soda fountain has been serving up malts and comfort fare such as grilled-cheese sandwiches to generations of diners. When in doubt, get the root-beer float.

★ **Zodiac** AMERICAN $$
(Map p148; ☎214-573-5800; Neiman Marcus, 1618 Main St; mains $14-24; ⏲11am-3pm Mon-Sat; 👪) This classic downtown lunch spot, which has been tucked into Neiman Marcus for more than 50 years, evokes old-school Dallas. Attentive waiters bustle about, soothing and pampering diners with hot chicken consommé, popovers with strawberry butter, and elegant salads.

DMA Cafe AMERICAN $$
(Map p148; Dallas Museum of Art, 1717 N Harwood St; mains $7-10; ⏲11am-4pm Tue-Sun; 👪; light rail St Paul) Great and creative cafe fare in the

museum. The burgers, chicken sandwiches, soups and more are made with flair. Look for seasonal specials and a kids' menu that doesn't just feature frozen chicken nuggets. Your best lunch choice in the Arts District.

Hattie's SOUTHERN **$$**

(Map p144; ☎ 214-942-7400; www.hatties.com; 418 N Bishop Ave; mains $8-30; ⏰ 11:30am-2:30pm & 5:30-10:00pm Mon-Sat, 11am-2:30pm & 5:30-10:00 Sun) Upscale Southern comfort food with a modern twist keeps this fave packed with locals. Dig into fried green tomatoes, low-country shrimp and grits, and pecan-crusted catfish. Amid butter-colored walls, savor classic cocktails including brandy alexanders and juleps.

Sonny Bryan's Smokehouse BARBECUE **$$**

(Map p148; ☎ 214-744-1610; www.sonnybryans.com; 302 N Market St; mains $6-15; ⏰ 11am-10pm; 👪) Sonny Bryan's barbecue has been around in one form or another since 1910. Although the **main location** (Map p144; 2202 Inwood Rd) is obscurely located, this branch holds up the tradition well and is easily the best dining option in the West End.

Dream Cafe CAFE **$$**

(Map p144; www.thedreamcafe.com; 2800 Routh St; mains $8-20; ⏰ 7am-9pm Sun & Tue-Thu, to 10pm Fri & Sat, to 3pm Mon; 🌿👪) Start your day early with a fabulous breakfast, or chill on the shady patio at lunchtime with some healthy, hearty fare. It has a playground plus on some nights it also has live jazz.

Bread Winners AMERICAN **$$**

(Map p144; www.breadwinnerscafe.com; 3301 McKinney Ave; mains $9-20; ⏰ 7am-10pm; 🌿👪) If sipping a peach Bellini in a lush courtyard atrium is the reward for the agony of choosing what to order for brunch, then bring on the pain. Lunch and dinner offer similar, though less tortuous, conundrums. In a pinch, at least stop in for something decadent from the bakery.

Daddy Jack's SEAFOOD **$$**

(Map p144; ☎ 214-826-4910; www.daddyjacks.org; 1916 Greenville Ave; mains from $12; ⏰ 5-10pm) Excellent seafood in relaxed neighborhood surrounds. This restaurant not only does briney denizens well, it does so with praiseworthy service. Casual yet attentive is a quality that never goes out of style. Expect lots of lobster dishes.

S&D Oyster Company SEAFOOD **$$**

(Map p144; www.sdoyster.com; 2701 McKinney Ave; mains $12-20; ⏰ 11am-10pm Mon-Sat) An uptown staple for years (gents of a certain age wearing bow ties are not uncommon), the simple Gulf Coast decor and great fried seafood keep 'em coming back. Try the BBQ shrimp. Try to finish with the bread pudding.

★ **Javier's** MEXICAN **$$$**

(Map p144; ☎ 214-521-4211; www.javiers.net; 4912 Cole Ave; mains $20-30; ⏰ 5:30-10:30pm Mon-Sat) Discard any ideas you have about Tex-Mex at this deeply cultured restaurant which takes the gentrified food of old Mexico City to new levels. The setting is dark, leathery and quiet. The food meaty and piquant. Steaks come with a range of Mexican flavors that bring out the best in beef. Get a table under the stars.

Abacus AMERICAN **$$$**

(Map p144; ☎ 214-559-3111; www.kentrathbun.com; 4511 McKinney Ave; mains $35-60, tasting menus from $65; ⏰ 6-10pm Mon-Sat) Too many steakhouses in Dallas are part of chains. For the real deal with a contemporary twist, Abacus delivers the beef. Start with sushi or the wildly popular lobster shooters and then make your way through a menu of small, seasonal plates. Then feast on simply superb steaks. The bar is excellent.

Drinking

Those seeking a mix of high and low culture will dig the numerous pubs (usually with outdoor patios) that line Greenville Ave and Knox-Henderson. Deep Ellum is dive-bar central, but it's also the edgiest neighborhood and prime territory for hitting the streets and making your own discoveries.

★ **Ginger Man** PUB

(Map p144; ☎ 214-754-8771; www.dallas.gingermanpub.com; 2718 Boll St; ⏰ noon-2am) An appropriately spice-colored house is home to this always-busy neighborhood pub. It has multilevel patios and porches, out front and back. And dartboards.

Double Wide BAR

(Map p144; ☎ 214-887-6510; www.double-wide.com; 3510 Commerce St; ⏰ 6pm-2am) Are these rednecks pretending to be hipsters or hipsters pretending to be rednecks? Live music keeps the irony from killing the fun. The two sides of the bar explain the name, with a fine patio in between.

Reno's Chop Shop Saloon BAR
(Map p148; 214-742-7366; www.renoschopshop.com; 2210 N Crowdus St; 6pm-2am Mon-Fri, 2pm-2am Sat & Sun) Slightly off Deep Ellum's Elm St artery, this is where you'll find Dallas' friendliest bikers. Higs line the front while a delightfully jovial crowd parties inside. The rear patio has great tables with umbrellas and on Sunday, bands.

Barcadia BAR
(Map p144; 214-821-7300; www.barcadiadallas.com; 1917 N Henderson Ave; 4pm-2am Mon-Thu, from 3pm Fri & Sat, from 11am Sun) Come for the games, stay for the drinks. Value-conscious imbibers will like the specials that include carafes of mimosas at Sunday brunch. The food's good and the vibe is nice and easy.

Two Corks and a Bottle LOUNGE
(Map p144; 214-871-9463; www.twocorksandabottle.com; 2800 Routh St; noon-7pm Sun & Tue, to 10pm Wed-Thu, to 11pm Fri & Sat) Creative owners make all the difference and the pair behind this cork-sized little wine bar prove it. Besides a fine selection of vino, they have frequent diversions such as acoustic, blues or jazz. That it's romantic is a bonus.

Old Monk Pub PUB
(Map p144; 214-821-1880; www.oldmonkdallas.com; 2847 N Henderson Ave; 4pm-2am Mon-Fri, 11am-2am Sat & Sun) The dimly lit patio on a starry night! The perfect cheese plate! The Belgian beers! Add in the upscale pub food and outdoor seating and you may not leave!

Libertine BAR
(Map p144; 214-824-7900; www.libertinebar.com; 2101 Greenville Ave; 4pm-2am Mon-Fri, from 11am Sat & Sun;) Hipsters happily toss back fine beers and munch sophisticated pub food here. The place has a convivial neighborhood vibe, all wrapped up in a sultry retro setting. Nice back bar.

Boulevardier WINE BAR
(Map p144; 214-942-1828; www.dallasboulevardier.com; 408 N Bishop Ave; 4-10pm Tue & Wed, to 11pm Thu-Sat, 11am-10pm Sun) A fine French bistro, this local hangout for the arts crowd has a vast selection of wines by the glass. Enjoy top global vintages, possibly with a plate of house-made charcuterie.

☆ Entertainment

High culture, low culture, country culture... Dallas has it in spades.

Live Music

Check the blog at www.popcultureblog.dallasnews.com for the scoop on local music happenings. Though it's been through several cycles of downturns and upswings, Deep Ellum is Dallas' unofficial headquarters for live music.

★Granada Theater LIVE MUSIC
(Map p144; 214-824-9933; www.granadatheater.com; 3524 Greenville Ave) This converted movie theater, often praised as the best live music venue in town, books popular rock and country bands. It's the anchor of Lower Greenwood. Check the website for what's on.

Adair's Saloon LIVE MUSIC
(Map p148; 214-939-9900; www.adairssaloon.com; 2624 Commerce St; 11am-2am) The regulars call it 'Aayy-dares.' Down-to-earth patrons and infectious country and redneck rock bands go down well with cheap beer and shuffleboard.

Sons of Hermann Hall LIVE MUSIC
(Map p144; 214-747-4422; www.sonsofhermann.com; 3414 Elm St; 7pm-midnight Wed & Thu, to 2am Fri & Sat) For 95 years, this classic Texas dance hall has been a chameleon: equal parts pickup bar, live-music venue, honky-tonk and swing-dancing club. A Deep Ellum stalwart. The opening hours can vary, so call to find out what's on.

Balcony Club JAZZ
(Map p144; 214-826-8104; www.balconyclubdallas.com; 1825 Abrams at La Vista; 5pm-2am) This mysterious upstairs hideaway feels like

GAY & LESBIAN DALLAS

You've got to love that the top gay and lesbian bars in Dallas are named JR's and Sue Ellen's, respectively, after the two lead characters in *Dallas*.

JR's Bar & Grill (Map p144; www.jrsdallas.com; 3923 Cedar Springs Rd; 11am-2pm) One of the busiest bars in Texas, JR's serves lunch daily and boasts a variety of fun entertainment at night. From the patio you can cheer on Dallas' modest cruising scene.

Sue Ellen's (Map p144; www.sueellensdallas.com; 3014 Throckmorton St; 4pm-2am) Chill out in the 'lipstick lounge' or on the dancefloor at Dallas' favorite lesbian bar. Good back garden.

a secret even though it's not. With emerald walls, a tiny stage and a cozy patio nook above the Landmark Theater, this spot draws all ages for nightly live music – mostly jazz – and sassy drinks such as moonlight martinis and three-way tropical punch.

Goat BLUES
(Map p144; ☎214-317-8119; www.thegoatdallas.com; 7248 Gaston Ave, Lakewood; ⏲7am-2am Mon-Sat, noon-2am Sun) Open at the crack of dawn for those impromptu morning pub crawls, the Goat's a divey neighborhood bar with live blues four nights a week.

Trees Dallas LIVE MUSIC
(Map p148; ☎214-741-1122; http://treesdallas.com; 2709 Elm St, Deep Ellum) Large and loud, this famous Deep Ellum club is back after a major 2012 renovation. Check the website for events.

Sports

The Dallas Cowboys play in Arlington (p175).

American Airlines Center STADIUM
(Map p148; www.americanairlinescenter.com; 2500 Victory Ave) Located in Victory Park this stadium hosts megaconcerts and is home to the Dallas Stars ice-hockey team and the Dallas Mavericks pro-basketball team.

Classical Music & Dance

AT&T Performing Arts Center THEATER
(Map p148; www.attpac.org; 2403 Flora St) Four architecturally noteworthy performance venues are here, including the 2000-seat **Winspear Opera House** (Map p148; 2403 Flora St), home to the **Dallas Opera** (☎214-443-1000; www.dallasopera.org); the 1500-seat **Wyly Theatre** (Map p148; 2400 Flora St); and Strauss Sq, an open-air stage.

Morton H Meyerson Symphony Center CONCERT HALL
(Map p148; ☎214-670-3600; www.dallasculture.org/meyersonsymphonycenter/; 2301 Flora St) Renowned architect IM Pei designed the Morton H Meyerson Symphony Center where the **Dallas Symphony Orchestra** (☎214-692-0203; www.dallassymphony.com) performs.

Theater & Comedy

Music Hall at Fair Park THEATER
(Map p144; ☎214-565-1116; www.liveatthemusichall.com; 909 1st Ave, Fair Park) Hosts summer performances of the Broadway blockbuster-style Dallas Summer Musicals (see www.dallassummermusicals.org).

Kitchen Dog Theater THEATER
(Map p144; ☎214-953-1055; www.kitchendogtheater.org; 3120 McKinney Ave) You'll get professional theater with attitude from Kitchen Dog, in Uptown.

Shopping

Have we mentioned that Dallas is a shopper's nirvana? That being said, it's easy to get lost in the merchandise.

For quirky and one-of-a-kind items, such as vintage Fiestaware plates, funky chandeliers and DIY crafts, head to the Bishop Arts District. Check the internet for periodic festivals where local artists showcase their wares, including the **Oak Cliff Art Crawl** held in April. Other good places to browse for those seeking all things arty and antique-y include uptown and Henderson St west of Greenville Ave, while Deep Ellum sports tattoo shops and Vespa stores alongside design stores.

On the northern end of uptown (at Lemmon and McKinney Aves), the West Village neighborhood has a distinctly So-Cal outdoor-mall vibe with a vast collection of pricey chains and one-off boutiques.

Dallas is also home to two famous megamalls, NorthPark Center and the Galleria, that are larger than many small towns and draw hordes of shoppers.

Froggie's 5 & 10 TOYS
(Map p144; ☎214-522-5867; www.froggies5and10.com; 3211 Knox St; ⏲10am-9pm Mon-Sat, noon-6pm Sun; 👪) Kids will adore this old-fashioned toy store with a smart-alecky edge: wash-off tattoos, retro candy, books and silly stuff.

Highland Park Village SHOPPING CENTER
(Map p144; ☎214-528-9401; www.hpvillage.com; Douglas Ave & Mockingbird Lane; ⏲varies by store) For an eye-rolling, gasp-inducing and credit-card-maxing experience, head to Spanish Mission–style Highland Park Village in upper-crust Highland Park, which claims to be the oldest suburban shopping center in the world. If Jimmy Choo and Harry Winston are among your intimate acquaintances, you'll feel at home.

If they're not, it's still worth a look around to see Dallas money in action (or just to see who wins when an Escalade and a Jaguar face off for a prime parking spot).

David Dike Fine Art GALLERY
(Map p144; ☎214-720-4044; www.daviddikefineart.com; 2613 Fairmount St; ⏲10am-5pm Mon-Fri, 11am-

4pm Sat) A long-established gallery that reps some of the best Texas painters of the last 100 years. An anchor of the uptown arts scene.

Good Records MUSIC
(Map p144; ☎214-752-4663; www.goodrecords.com; 1808 Lower Greenville Ave; ⊙10am-11pm Mon-Thu, to midnight Fri & Sat, 11am-9pm Sun) Greenville Ave is home to one of Dallas' only indie record stores. According to the store philosophy, it carries whatever's 'good.'

Millennium VINTAGE
(Map p148; ☎214-613-5453; 2707 Main St; ⊙noon-7pm Mon-Fri, 11am-9pm Sat, noon-6pm Sun) Amid all the funk of Deep Ellum, this store stands out for the slack-jawed people outside looking in the window. Dedicated to 'the best of the last millennium' it sells the kind of old toys, lunch boxes and memorabilia that make people weak-kneed with nostalgia.

Neiman Marcus DEPARTMENT STORE
(Map p148; ☎214-741-6911; www.neimanmarcus.com; 1618 Main St; ⊙10am-6pm Mon-Sat, to 8pm Thu) A downtown landmark, this six-story veteran was the first Neiman Marcus store. Today it's still a wonderful place to enjoy a timeless shopping experience.

Wild Bill's Western Store WESTERN WEAR
(Map p148; ☎214-954-1050; www.wildbillswestern.com; 311 N Market, West End; ⊙10am-6pm Mon-Sat) Bill's motto is 'from the affordable to the extravagant,' and we like that you can grab a $15 T-shirt or blow your bonus on a pair of handmade and measured snakeskin boots just like Eric Clapton's – he is but one of the many celebrities who've made their feet happy here. Enjoy a cold beer while you shop.

Dallas Farmers Market MARKET
(Map p148; ☎214-670-5880; www.dallasfarmersmarket.org; cnr Marilla Blvd & S Harwood St; ⊙7am-6pm) Buy produce directly from the growers, or shop for flowers and antiques at this multibarn market. It's at its best Thursday to Saturday. After the Food Network gave it some hype, the **Pecan Lodge** (Map p148; ☎214-748-8900; www.pecanlodge.com; Dallas Farmers Market, 1010 S Pearl Expy; mains from $5; ⊙11am-3pm Thu-Sun), an outlet for beef brisket, has been mobbed.

Society Bakery BAKERY
(Map p144; ☎214-827-1411; www.societybakery.com; 3426 Greenville Ave; treats $3; ⊙8am-6pm Mon-Fri, to 5pm Sat) Dallas' version of bakery heaven features from-scratch, all-butter cupcakes in banana chocolate chip, Italian cream and red velvet, among others.

Malls

★NorthPark Center MALL
(☎214-363-7441; www.northparkcenter.com; 8687 N Central Expressway; ⊙10am-9pm Mon-Sat noon-6pm Sun) Almost 2 million sq ft of retail space, NorthPark's major stores include Neiman Marcus, Nordstrom and Macy's. It has hundreds of other retailers, including most upscale brands. Despite its size, it gets jammed and parking on a Saturday afternoon can be a pain.

Galleria MALL
(☎972-702-7100; www.galleriadallas.com; 13355 Noel Rd at I-635; ⊙10am-9pm Mon-Sat, noon-6pm Sun) The Galleria defined Dallas and conspicuous consumption in the 1980s and 1990s. Its main anchors include Nordstrom, Saks Fifth Ave and Macy's, as well as an iconic ice-skating rink. But the last time we were there, we couldn't wonder if hadn't, well, peaked.

ℹ Information

MEDIA

D Magazine (www.dmagazine.com) The glossy city monthly: good restaurant reviews and a window into all things elite and upscale in Dallas society.

Dallas Morning News (www.dallasnews.com) The city's daily newspaper.

Dallas Observer (www.dallasobserver.com) Culture, dining, entertainment, reviews and news.

KERA 90.1 FM The local NPR affiliate, with local and national programming.

KXT 91.7 FM That rare indie station that plays great music and has local bands on live.

MONEY

Travelex (☎214-559-3564; www.travelex.com; 2911 Turtle Creek Blvd; ⊙9am-5pm Mon-Fri) Foreign-currency exchange.

TOURIST INFORMATION

Dallas CVB Visitor Center (Map p148; ☎214-571-1000; www.visitdallas.com; Old Red Courthouse, 100 S Houston St; ⊙9am-5pm) Vast amounts of material.

ℹ Getting There & Away

American Airlines' main hub is **Dallas-Fort Worth International Airport** (DFW; www.dfwairport.com), 16 miles northwest of the city via I-35 E.

Dallas–Fort Worth Metroplex

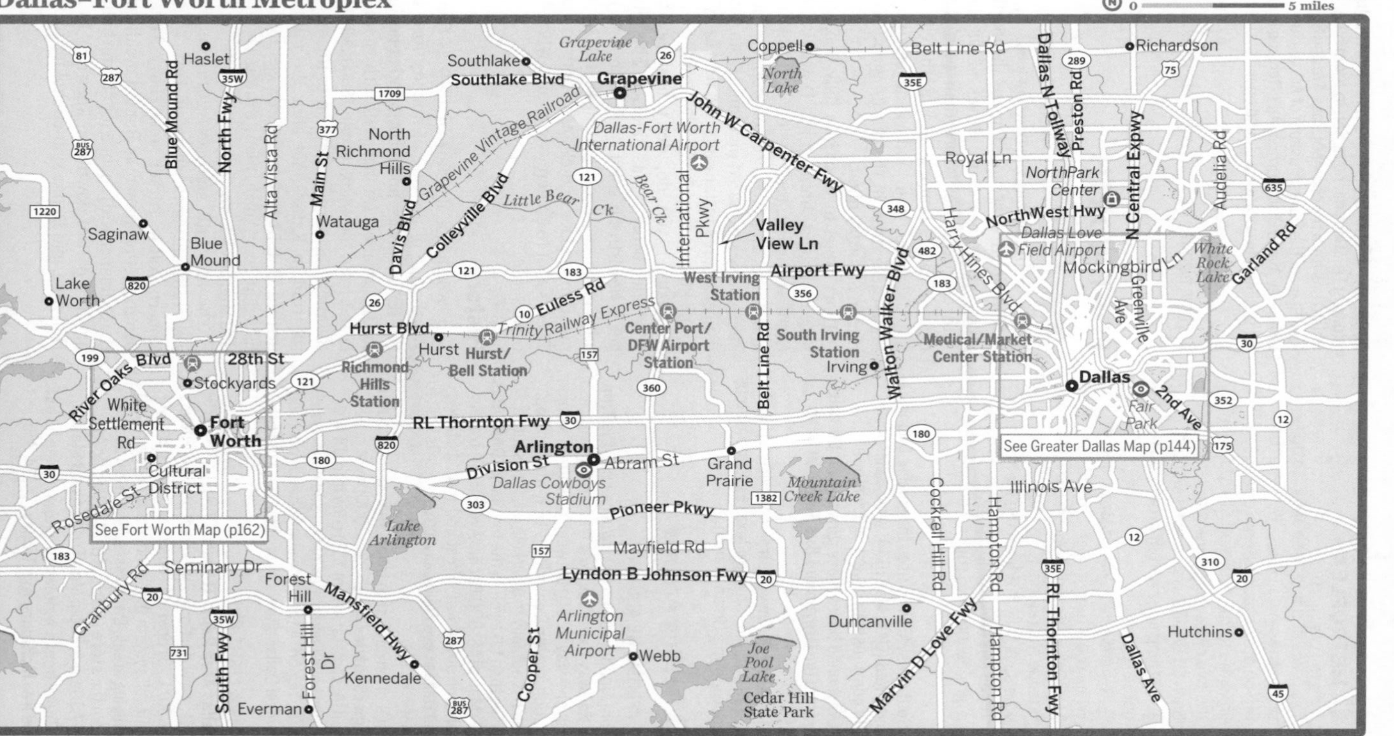

METROPLEX

The roots of using 'Metroplex' to describe the whole Dallas–Fort Worth region are obscure. Some evidence links the term to the early 1970s when the two cities were joining together to build DFW airport. Boosters wanted something snazzy that promoted the entire region.

Regardless, the word stuck, sort of. While you'll hear it used around the Metroplex, it's not a word locals use outside the region. Rare is the local who says they are from the Metroplex. *Texas Monthly* summed up the term as a 'grotesque word that means nothing.'

Southwest Airlines uses the smaller **Dallas Love Field** (DAL; Map p144; www.dallas-lovefield.com), just northwest of downtown.

Greyhound buses make runs all over the country from the **Greyhound Bus Terminal** (Map p148; 205 S Lamar St).

The **Amtrak** (www.amtrak.com; 401 S Houston St) San Antonio–Chicago *Texas Eagle* train stops at downtown's Union Station.

Getting Around

TO/FROM THE AIRPORT

From Monday to Saturday you can ride the **Trinity Railway Express** (www.trinityrailwayexpress.org; one-way $2.50) between downtown's Union Station and the CenterPort/DFW Airport stop, which is actually in a parking lot; free shuttle buses then take you to the terminals. **DART Bus 39** (Map p148; 800 Pacific Ave; $2.50) travels between downtown's West End Transit Station and Dallas Love Field daily, but service is limited on weekends.

It's often easiest to take a shared-ride shuttle: **SuperShuttle** (☎817-329-2000; www.supershuttle.com; fare from $17) runs from DFW or Dallas Love Field to downtown and major hotels in the region. A taxi between either airport and central Dallas should cost about $40 to $60.

BUS & LIGHT RAIL

Dallas Area Rapid Transit (DART; ☎214-979-1111; www.dart.org; 2-hr ticket peak/off-peak $2.50/1.75) operates buses and an extensive light-rail system that connects downtown with outlying areas. Day passes ($5) are available from the **store** (Map p148; 1401 Pacific Ave; ⊙7:30am-5:30pm Mon-Fri) at Akard Station.

Travel from downtown to uptown on the historic and free **McKinney Ave Trolley** (☎214-855-0006; www.mata.org; ⊙7am-10pm Mon-Thu, to midnight Fri, 10am-midnight Sat, to 10pm Sun), which runs from the corner of Ross Ave and St Paul St, near the Dallas Museum of Art, and up McKinney Ave to Blackburn St. An extension bringing the line into downtown should open.

CAR & MOTORCYCLE

Daytime highway traffic is bad. Enough said.

FORT WORTH

POP 653,000

Oft-called 'Where the West Begins,' Fort Worth definitely has the cowboy feel.

The city first became famous during the great open-range cattle drives of the late 19th century, when more than 10 million head of cattle tramped through the city on the Chisholm Trail. Today you can see a mini–cattle drive in the morning and a rodeo on Saturday night.

Don't forget to scoot into Billy Bob's, the world's biggest honky-tonk. Down in the Cultural District, tour the Cowgirl Museum and three amazing art collections. Then, after you've meditated on minimalism, Sundance Square's restaurants and bars call you to the kick-up-your-heels downtown.

Whatever you do, don't mistake Fort Worth for being Dallas' sidekick. This city's got a headstrong spirit of its own, and it's a lot more user-friendly than Dallas (not to mention greener and cleaner). Bottom line? There's a lot to do here – without a whole lot of pretense.

History

Fort Worth got its start in 1849 as Camp Worth, one of a string of military forts on the Texas frontier, and later found fame during the great open-range cattle drives, which lasted from the 1860s to the 1880s. Most of the time, the herds moved on to the end of the trail in Kansas. Yet after the railroad arrived in 1873 and stockyards were established at Fort Worth, many drovers chose to end their trek here.

The late 19th and early 20th centuries saw rampant lawlessness in Fort Worth. Robert LeRoy Parker and Harry Longabaugh (better known as Butch Cassidy and the Sundance Kid) spent a lot of time hiding out in a part of downtown known as Hell's Half Acre, and Depression-era holdup artists

Bonnie Parker and Clyde Barrow also kicked around the city.

Yet most of the mayhem in Fort Worth came not from celebrity ne'er-do-wells but from rank-and-file cowboys with too much pent-up energy from the trail. They were the ones who boozed and brawled their way down Exchange Ave, giving Fort Worth a far different image than that of Dallas.

Museums put the city on the high-culture map back in 1892 when the Kimbell became the first museum in Texas. Since then, the nationally renowned Cultural District has continued to expand, and Sundance Square has became one of the most successful downtown-revitalization projects in the US. All this pretty much solidifies Fort Worth's claim to the somewhat paradoxical title, 'City of Cowboys and Culture.'

Sights

The Stockyards are cowboy central, while most of the area's museums call the leafy Cultural District home. Between these two areas and downtown, you can easily spend a couple of days savoring Fort Worth.

Stockyards National Historic District

Sure, you'll spot cowboys on horseback roaming around, but wander the dusty streets of the Stockyards and you'll be soon mingling with a mix of families, curious international tourists and the odd freelance guitar player. This place puts fun first, with equal parts authentic history and camera-ready tourism, but it never crosses the line and becomes hokey, despite petting zoos and other gimcrackery.

Most parking lots offer $5 all-day parking, otherwise park on E Exchange Ave, or in the free lot to the northeast of Stockyards Station.

Stockyards HISTORIC SITE
(www.fortworthstockyards.org; Exchange Ave) Western-wear stores and knickknack shops, saloons and steakhouses occupy the Old West–era buildings of the Stockyards. City-paid cowboys on horseback roam the district, answering questions and posing for photos.

Stop into the **Visitor Center** (Map p164; 817-625-9715; www.stockyardsstation.com/information; 130 E Exchange Ave; 8.30am-6pm Mon-Fri, 9am-6pm Sat, 11am-5pm Sun) for info; it offers a **self-guided audio walking tour** ($12). Or you can opt for a 90-minute **guided walking tour** (Map p164; 817-625-9715; www.stockyardsstation.com/attractions/historic-walking-tour; Stockyards Station; adult/child from $8/6; tours 10am, noon, 2pm & 4pm Mon-Sat, noon, 2pm & 4pm Sun) that leaves from Stockyards Station.

Stockyards Cattle Drive SPECTACLE
(drives 11:30am & 4pm daily;) FREE Don't miss the cattle drive down Exchange Ave. While it's more surreal than spectacular, it's still interesting to watch a cowboy drive a small herd of Texas longhorns down the block in front of the Visitor Center. It's a gol-dang Kodak moment, pardner.

Cowtown Coliseum RODEO
(Map p164; 817-625-1025; www.stockyardsrodeo.com; 121 E Exchange Ave, Fort Worth; adult/child $15/10; 8pm Fri & Sat;) For intense rootin'-tootin' action, catch a real live rodeo.

Texas Cowboy Hall of Fame MUSEUM
(Map p164; 817-626-7131; www.texascowboyhalloffame.org; 128 E Exchange Ave; adult/child $5/3; 10am-6pm Mon-Thu, to 7pm Fri & Sat, 11am-5pm Sun) Do you know your rodeo clowns from your cowboys? Learn this important distinction at the Texas Cowboy Hall of Fame, which features booths of medals and video footage of each cowboy inductee.

RODEO CLOWNS

While it sounds like a particularly cruel cowboy insult, it's an actual profession, and one of the most notoriously dangerous in the rodeo industry. As a performer who works in bull-riding events, a rodeo clown's function is to protect a rider from being gored by the bull should they fall off the horse. But how? By distracting the bull, of course, which accounts for their colorful clothes. Sometimes the clowns jump in and out of a barrel, which offers minimal protection but requires even more agility, and sometimes the clowns entertain the crowd between events. Through it all, this remains a job for the wily and fleet-footed: the bulls never laugh.

Fort Worth

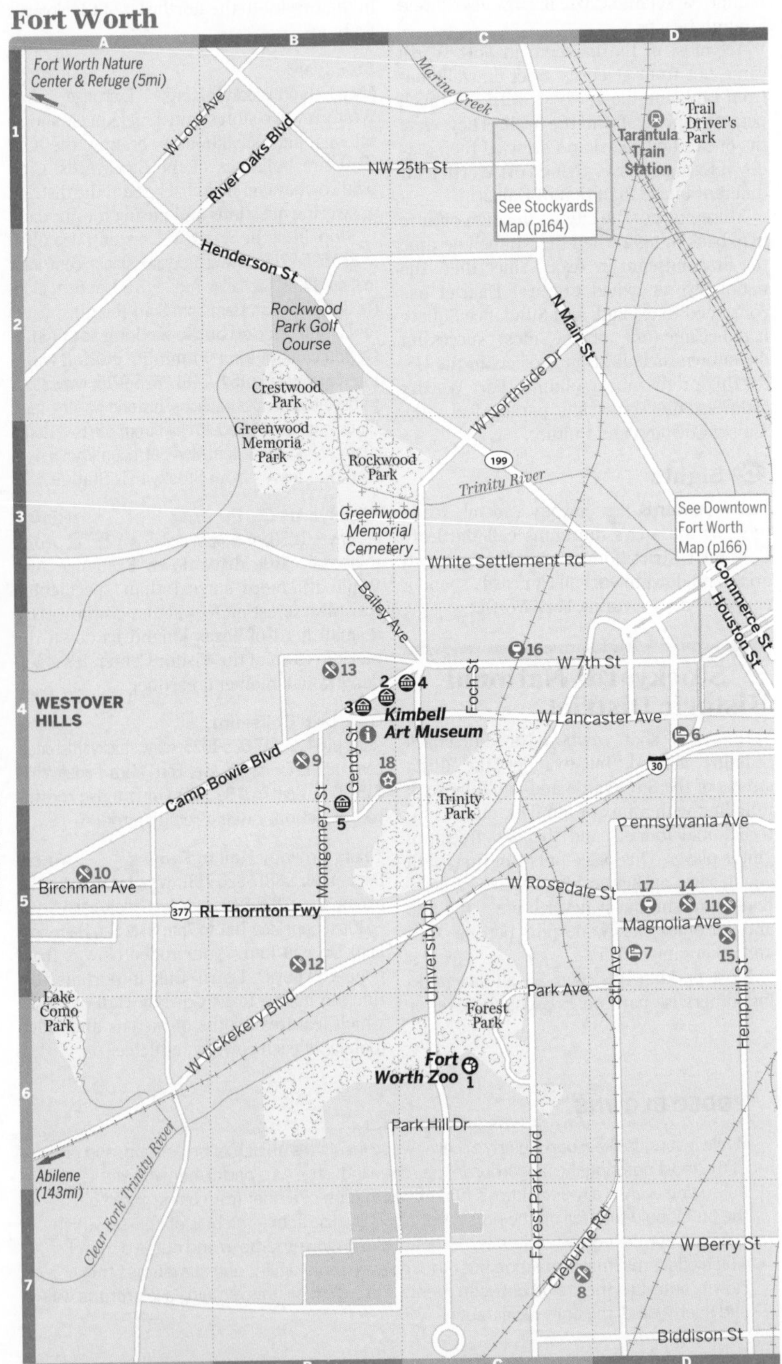

Fort Worth Nature Center & Refuge (5mi)
W Long Ave
River Oaks Blvd
Marine Creek
NW 25th St
Tarantula Train Station
Trail Driver's Park
See Stockyards Map (p164)
Henderson St
Rockwood Park Golf Course
N Main St
Crestwood Park
Greenwood Memoria Park
W Northside Dr
Rockwood Park
199
Trinity River
See Downtown Fort Worth Map (p166)
Greenwood Memorial Cemetery
White Settlement Rd
Bailey Ave
Commerce St
Houston St
16
W 7th St
13
2
4
Foch St
WESTOVER HILLS
3
Kimbell Art Museum
W Lancaster Ave
6
Gendy St
Camp Bowie Blvd
9
18
30
Montgomery St
5
Trinity Park
Pennsylvania Ave
10
Birchman Ave
W Rosedale St
17
14
11
377
RL Thornton Fwy
Magnolia Ave
7
15
12
University Dr
8th Ave
Hemphill St
Park Ave
Lake Como Park
W Vickekery Blvd
Forest Park
Fort Worth Zoo
1
Park Hill Dr
Abilene (143mi)
Clear Fork Trinity River
Forest Park Blvd
Cleburne Rd
W Berry St
8
Biddison St

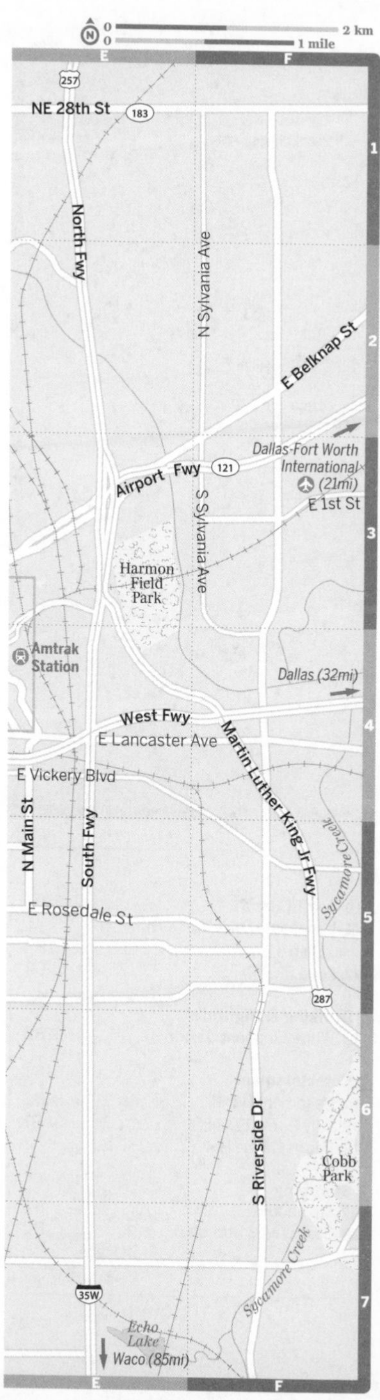

Cattle Auction

SPECTACLE

(Map p164; ☎800-422-2117; www.superiorlivestock.com; 131 E Exchange Ave; ⏰from 8am) The truly curious will want to venture into this live cattle auction, held every other Friday in a totally high-tech atmosphere inside the 1903 **Fort Worth Livestock Exchange** building. The heifers strut their stuff on flat-screen TVs and cowboy-hat-wearing ranchers make phone bids on the spot. Don't be intimidated by the fast-talkin' auctioneer: visitors are welcome to observe.

Fort Worth Herd

COWS

(Map p164; 👪) See the cows for real out behind the Livestock Exchange Building: the Fort Worth Herd are the longhorns that parade daily. You can see them in their corral from a viewing area which comes complete with picture-portraits of each – see if you can match names to critter.

Stockyards Museum

MUSEUM

(Map p164; ☎817-625-5082; 131 E Exchange Ave; $2 donation requested; ⏰10am-5pm Mon-Sat year-round, noon-5pm Sun Jun-Aug) For

Fort Worth

Top Sights

1 Fort Worth Zoo.......C6
2 Kimbell Art Museum.......B4

Sights

3 Amon Carter Museum of American Art.......B4
4 Modern Art Museum of Fort Worth.......C4
5 National Cowgirl Museum.......B5

Sleeping

6 Holiday Inn Express.......D4
7 Texas White House.......D5

Eating

8 Carshon's Deli.......C7
9 Curly's Frozen Custard.......B4
10 Kincaid's.......A5
11 Paris Coffee Shop.......D5
12 Railhead Smokehouse.......B5
13 Saint-Emilion.......B4
14 Spiral Diner & Bakery.......D5
15 Zio Carlo Magnolia Brew Pub.......D5

Drinking & Nightlife

Chat Room.......(see 14)
16 Lola's Saloon.......C4
17 Usual Bar.......D5

Entertainment

18 Will Rogers Memorial Center.......B4

Stockyards

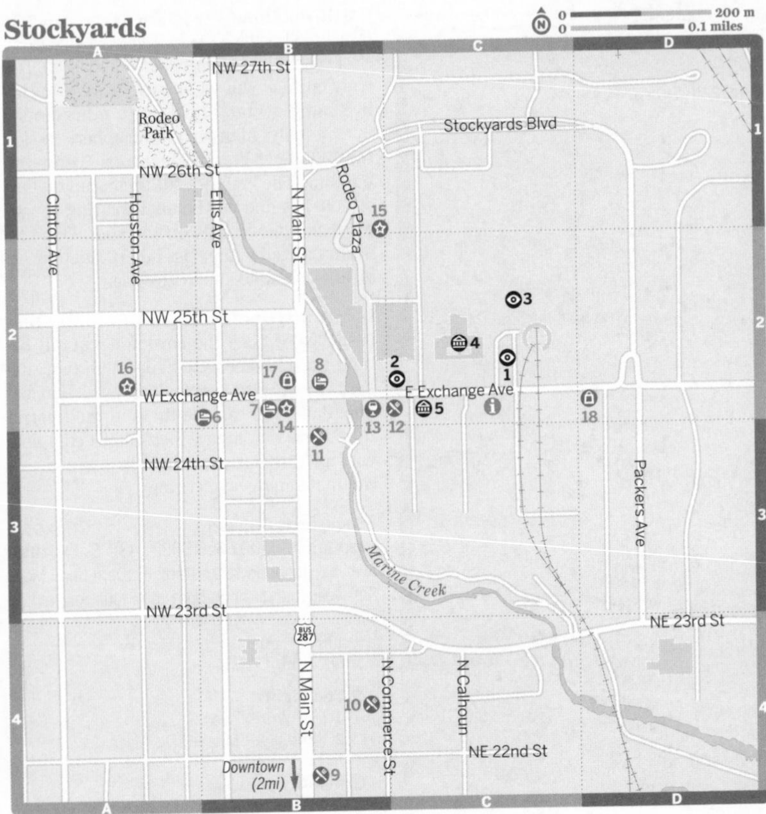

Stockyards

Sights

1 Cattle Auction C2
2 Cowtown Coliseum C2
3 Fort Worth Herd C2
4 Stockyards Museum C2
5 Texas Cowboy Hall of Fame C2

Activities, Courses & Tours

Stockyards Guided Walking Tour .... (see 18)

Sleeping

6 Hotel Texas B2
7 Miss Molly's Hotel B2
8 Stockyards Hotel B2

Eating

9 Esperanza's Bakery & Cafe B4
10 Joe T Garcia's B4
11 Lonesome Dove Western Bistro B3
12 Love Shack C2

Drinking & Nightlife

13 White Elephant Saloon B2

Entertainment

14 Basement Bar B2
15 Billy Bob's Texas B1
16 Pearls Dance Hall A2

Shopping

17 ML Leddy's B2
18 Stockyards Station D2

an eye-opening glimpse into cow culture, check out the unique historic artifacts in this museum.

Cultural District

Fort Worth has some of the best museums of any city in Texas. Plus, it's easy to museum-hop around the parklike Cultural District on Camp Bowie Blvd, west of Downtown.

★Kimbell Art Museum MUSEUM
(Map p162; 817-332-8451; www.kimbellart.org; 3333 Camp Bowie Blvd; 10am-5pm Tue-Thu & Sat, noon-8pm Fri, to 5pm Sun) FREE Some art aficionados say this is the country's best 'small' art museum, while others say it's one of the unqualified best. Take your time perusing: the stunning architecture lets in natural light that allows visitors to see paintings from antiquity to the 20th century the way the artists originally intended.

European masterpieces include works by Caravaggio, El Greco and Cézanne, as well as Michelangelo's first painting, *The Torment of St Anthony*.

And the museum's days of being 'small' are over. The original building, an award-winning stunner designed by Louis I Kahn, was joined by a large new edition in 2013, designed by celebrity architect Renzo Piano.

Modern Art Museum of Fort Worth MUSEUM
(Map p162; www.themodern.org; 3200 Darnell St; adult/child $10/free; 10am-5pm Tue-Sun, to 8pm Thu) In a stunning, soaring space, this museum houses an incredible number of provocative and mind-expanding works by luminaries such as Mark Rothko and Picasso.

Can't-miss pieces include Anselm Kiefer's *Book with Wings*, Martin Puryear's *Ladder for Booker T Washington* and Andy Warhol's *Twenty-Five Colored Marilyns*. The museum restaurant, Café Modern, is drop-dead gorgeous, seeming to float on the water of the surrounding reflective pools.

Amon Carter Museum of American Art MUSEUM
(Map p162; www.cartermuseum.org; 3501 Camp Bowie Blvd; 10am-5pm Tue-Sat, to 8pm Thu, noon-5pm Sun) FREE Pre-1945 American art shines at this museum, including iconic works by John Singer Sargent, Winslow Homer and Alexander Calder, as well as an impressive collection of works depicting the American West by artists Frederic Remington and Charles M Russell.

There's also an extensive photography collection. Walking through the exhibits is like taking a visual tour of the US – from Yosemite National Park with Albert Bierstadt to New Mexico with Georgia O'Keeffe.

National Cowgirl Museum MUSEUM
(Map p162; 817-336-4475; www.cowgirl.net; 1721 Gendy St; adult/child $10/8; 10am-5pm Tue-Sat, noon-5pm Sun) This airy, impressive museum explores the myth and the reality of cowgirls in American culture. From rhinestone costumes to rare film footage, this is a fun and educational ride: by the time you walk out, you'll have a whole new appreciation for these tough workers.

Downtown & Around

Sundance Square NEIGHBORHOOD
(www.sundancesquare.com) You can stroll yourself happy in the 14-block Sundance Square, near Main and 3rd Sts. Colorful architecture, art galleries and a host of bars and restaurants make this one 'hood not to miss. New in 2013 was a big, spurting fountain and lots of surrounding condos.

Sid Richardson Collection of Western Art MUSEUM
(Map p166; www.sidrichardsonmuseum.org; 309 Main St; 9am-5pm Mon-Thu, to 8pm Fri & Sat, noon-5pm Sun) FREE If the Stockyards didn't sate your hunger for all things Western, pop in here for some art. It's known for its Frederic Remington paintings and bronzes.

★Fort Worth Zoo ZOO
(Map p162; 817-759-7555; www.fortworthzoo.com; Forest Park off S University Dr; adult/child $12/9, parking $5; 10am-5pm;) A highly regarded American zoo (and the second most popular attraction in the state), it's home to about 5000 inhabitants representing 650 species, including many endangered species. Check out the Komodo dragons and the Great Barrier Reef exhibit. From March to September the zoo is open until 6pm on weekends; from late October to February it closes daily at 4pm.

Activities

Trinity Trails HIKING
(www.trinitytrails.org) This network of hiking, biking and equestrian trails covers 35 miles along the Trinity River, by some of Fort Worth's major parks.

Fort Worth Nature Center and Refuge NATURE RESERVE
(☎817-237-1111; www.fwnc.org; Hwy 199; adult/child $5/2; ⏰8am-5pm) 25 miles of hiking and nature trails and an interpretive center.

Festivals & Events

Fort Worth Stock Show & Rodeo RODEO
(www.fwssr.com; ⏰Jan) Catch the rodeo craze with nearly a million other people. Held in January for several weeks each year at **Will**

Downtown Fort Worth

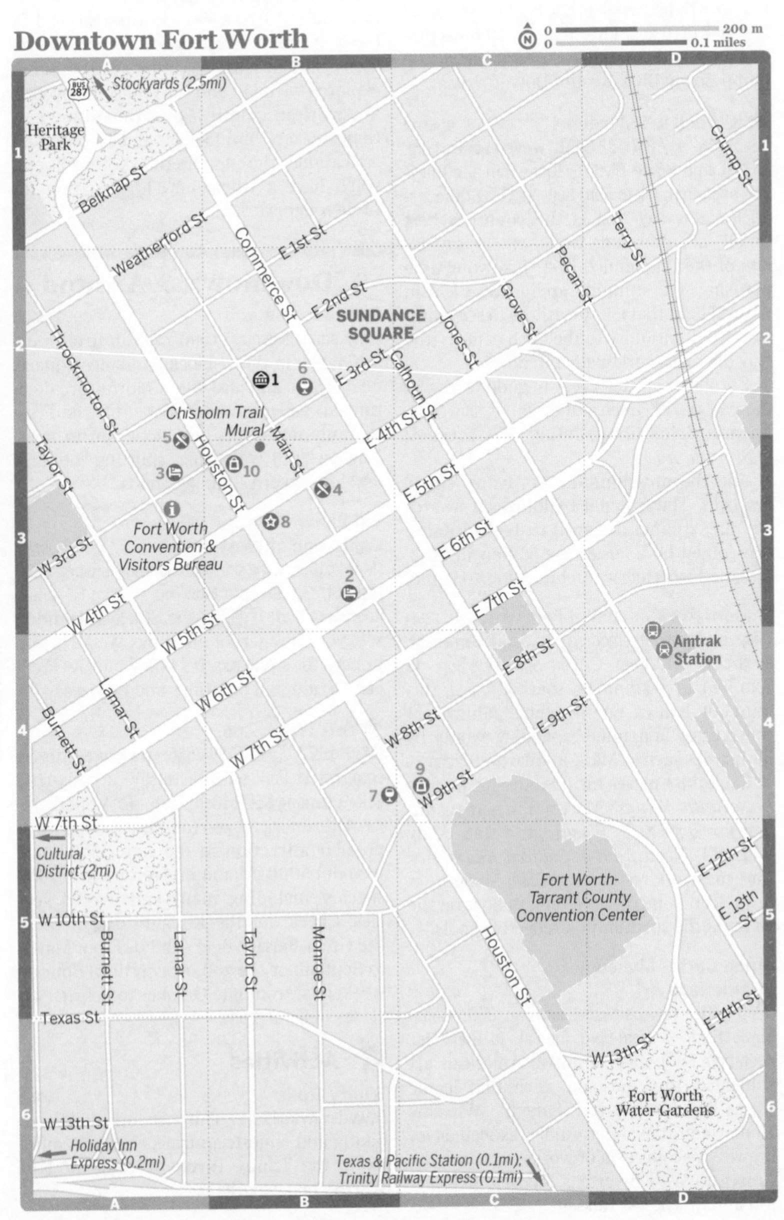

Rogers Memorial Center (Map p162; 1 Amon Carter Sq) in the Cultural District.

Main Street Arts Festival FESTIVAL
(www.mainstreetartsfest.org; ⏲ Apr) One of the Southwest's biggest arts festivals, this April event turns Sundance Square into a festive epicenter of live music, art shows and food booths.

Sleeping

Budget motels cluster near highway interchanges and along the Jacksboro Hwy (Hwy 199), northwest of downtown. You'll find decent chains along S University Dr, near the Cultural District. Staying near the Stockyards puts you close to the fun night and day.

★Hotel Texas INN $
(Map p164; ☎817-624-2224; 2415 Ellis Ave; r $90-100; ❄ 📶) This 1939 'cattleman's home away from home' is a good deal, smack in the center of the Stockyards action. It's a real find, with simple, clean rooms decorated with framed Western art.

Holiday Inn Express HOTEL $$
(Map p162; ☎817-698-9595; www.hiexpress.com; 1111 W Lancaster Ave; r $110-160; ❄ @ 📶 🏊 🐾) A retro vibe pervades this surprisingly stylish hotel, 1 mile southwest of downtown. The 132 rooms are spread across three floors. Guests receive a full breakfast and there's a shuttle to nearby attractions.

Miss Molly's Hotel B&B $
(Map p164; ☎817-626-1522; www.missmollyshotel.com; 109 W Exchange Ave; r incl breakfast $100-175; ❄ 📶) Set in the heart of the Stockyards, eight-room Miss Molly's occupies a former bordello. Its heavily atmospheric vibe will feel authentic to some (Miss Josie's room still looks like a bordello), eerie to others (they say it's haunted...), but probably at least a little charming either way. Look for cheap deals during the week – as low as $50.

Texas White House B&B $$
(Map p162; ☎817-923-3597; www.texaswhitehouse.com; 1417 Eighth Ave; r $150-250; ❄ 📶) A large historic home with contemporary Texas style near downtown. The five rooms are well equipped; larger suites have fridges and microwaves.

Etta's Place INN $$
(Map p166; ☎817-255-5760; www.ettas-place.com; 200 W 3rd St; r $150-240; ❄ 📶) A grand piano, a comfy library and quilts galore are among the cozy pleasures at this Sundance Square inn. Breakfast can be taken on the airy patio. The 10 rooms are large; suites have kitchenettes.

Stockyards Hotel HISTORIC HOTEL $$$
(Map p164; ☎817-625-6427; www.stockyardshotel.com; 109 E Exchange Ave; r $140-350; ❄ 📶) First opened in 1907, this 52-room place clings to its cowboy past with Western-themed art, cowboy-inspired rooms and a grand Old West lobby with lots of leather. Hide out in the Bonnie and Clyde room, actually occupied by Clyde Barrow during his 1932 Fort Worth stay (the faux bullet holes and boot jacks only add to the mystique).

Ashton Hotel BOUTIQUE HOTEL $$$
(Map p166; ☎866-327-4866; www.theashtonhotel.com; 610 Main St; r $208-290; ❄ 📶 🐾) This 39-room six-story boutique hotel in a turn-of-the-century building off Sundance Square offers hush-hush elegance without an ounce of snootiness. Parking is valet-only.

Eating

Put on the feed bag and grab some Texas-style fixins' in Sundance Square and in the Stockyards. Head to West 7th for new-fangled additions to the dining scene, or just walk down Magnolia and breathe in the foodie revolution. Many of the museums,

Downtown Fort Worth

Sights
1 Sid Richardson Collection of Western Art B2

Sleeping
2 Ashton Hotel B3
3 Etta's Place A3

Eating
4 Grace B3
5 Reata A2

Drinking & Nightlife
6 Flying Saucer Draught Emporium B2
7 Zambrano Wine Cellar & Bistro B4

Entertainment
8 Scat Jazz Lounge B3

Shopping
9 Peters Bros Hats C4
10 Retro Cowboy B3

such as the Kimbell, also have excellent cafes. PS: you're in Fort Worth – have a steak.

★Curly's Frozen Custard ICE CREAM $
(Map p162; ☎817-763-8700; www.curlysfrozencustard.com; 4017 Camp Bowie Blvd; treats from $2; ⊙11am-9pm) Creamy frozen custard which you can customize with all sorts of mix-ins to make a 'concrete'. Good any day the temp is above freezing.

Carshon's Deli DELI $
(Map p162; ☎817-923-1907; www.carshonsdeli.com; 3133 Cleburne Rd; mains $5-9; ⊙9am-3pm Mon-Sat) Since 1928 Fort Worth's only kosher deli has served up classic New York sandwiches. Half the fun's in watching local movers and shakers make and break deals in between bites of corned beef on rye.

Paris Coffee Shop CAFE $
(Map p162; ☎817-335-2041; www.pariscoffeeshop.net; 700 W Magnolia Ave; mains $4-8; ⊙6am-3pm Mon-Fri, to 11am Sat) The venerable, Depression-era Paris is an old-school 'coffee shop,' which means it's really a diner: cheap prices, reliable classics, homemade pie and salty-tongued regulars at the counter.

Spiral Diner & Bakery CAFE $
(Map p162; ☎817-332-8633; 1314 W Magnolia Ave; mains $7-10; ⊙11am-10pm Tue-Sat, to 5pm Sun; 🌿👪) One of the most inventive organic vegan restaurants in the South, this retro-feel diner serves up fresh juices, smoothies, salads and a whole bevy of healthy dishes.

DON'T MISS

SHOW ME THE MONEY

Watch millions roll off the presses at one of two places in the nation where 'In God We Trust' and Ben Franklin's face are legally printed on oh-so-hard-to-find paper: Fort Worth's **Bureau of Engraving and Printing** (☎817-231-4000; www.moneyfactory.gov; 9000 Blue Mound Rd; ⊙8:30am-5:30pm Tue-Fri) FREE. This US Treasury facility produces currency not just for the US but for the scores of other nations around the world, such as Panama, which use US dollars. Learn how the money's design is ever-shifting in an effort to stay ahead of high-tech counterfeiters. It's 7 miles north of the Stockyards.

Breakfast is served all day. The beer list is great, as are the tables outside.

★Kincaid's BURGERS $
(Map p162; ☎817-732-2881; www.kincaidshamburgers.com; 4901 Camp Bowie Blvd; mains $4-7; ⊙11am-8pm Mon-Sat, to 3pm Sun) Sit on picnic tables amid disused grocery shelves at this local institution (which unfortunately has an institutional shade of green on the walls) and wolf down some of the best burgers in the region. They are thick, juicy and come covered in condiments.

Railhead Smokehouse BARBECUE $
(Map p162; ☎817-738-9808; www.railheadsmokehouse.com; 2900 Montgomery St; mains $4-11; ⊙11am-9pm Mon-Sat) Railroad is, to some, *the* legendary barbecue of Fort Worth. It's a no-frills rustic place, where you holler your order and in return get a big ol' mess of brisket or ribs. Add on a pile of fries and goblet of frosty beer.

Love Shack BURGERS $
(Map p164; 110 E Exchange Ave; mains from $6; ⊙11am-10pm Sun-Thu, to 1am Fri & Sat) Enjoy a gourmet burger (the spicy Amore Caliente, yum!) at this joint owned by Texas-born TV chef Tim Love. Don't miss the home-cut fries or Parmesan chips. There's live local music many nights.

★Zio Carlo Magnolia Brew Pub PIZZA $$
(Map p162; ☎817-923-8000; www.gr8ale.com; 1001 Magnolia Ave; mains $12-16; ⊙11:30am-midnight Mon-Fri, 1:30am-1am Sat, 10:30am-midnight Sun; 📶) Pizza and beer. The perfect combo and here both are superb. The pizza is thin-crust Italian and comes in 17 varieties. The beers are also fine and diverse. Enjoy some of both in the exposed-brick dining area or outside on the patio.

Esperanza's Bakery & Cafe MEXICAN $$
(Map p164; ☎817-626-5770; 2122 N Main St; mains $7-15; ⊙6:30am-5:30pm) Breakfasts are spicy, plentiful and awfully tasty at this always-busy local fave. It even has a full bar so you can get a leg up on the day. Lunch items include Tex-Mex in fine form. Get *campanchanas* (crunchy sweet bread) from the bakery to go, or let the sun warm you on the terrace.

Joe T Garcia's MEXICAN $$
(Map p164; www.joets.com; 2201 N Commerce St; mains $8-14; ⊙11am-2:30pm & 5-10pm Mon-Thu, 11am-11pm Fri & Sat, to 10pm Sun) The

most famous restaurant in Fort Worth, this fourth-generation place takes up a city block. Dinners in the candlelit walled courtyard are magical, as Mexican-tile fountains bubble among the acres of tropical foliage. On weekends the line (no reservations!) often stretches around the block.

★Lonesome Dove Western Bistro SOUTHERN $$$
(Map p164; ☎817-740-8810; www.lonesomedovebistro.com; 2406 N Main St; mains $20-40; ⏲11:30am-2:30pm & 5-10pm Tue-Sat, 5-10pm Mon) At Tim Love's mod-Western dining experience, even the chefs wear cowboy hats. It's Southern fusion, with the traditional flavors of the region enlivened by all manner of influences. The wine list is superb and the $9 lunch special is truly the best deal in town.

Reata AMERICAN $$$
(Map p166; ☎817-336-1009; www.reata.net; 310 Houston St; mains lunch $9-15, dinner $16-45; ⏲11am-2pm & 5-10pm) The proprietors also own their own cattle ranch, so the sizable steaks are worth their weight. But you might also try the Texas specialties such as tenderloin tamales and jalapeño-cheddar grits. The rooftop has fab views over downtown.

Grace AMERICAN $$$
(Map p166; ☎817-877-3388; 777 Main St; mains from $20; ⏲5:30-9:30pm Mon-Thu, to 10:30pm Fri & Sat, bar to late) At Grace, local luminaries hold court (and martinis) on the couch-strewn outdoor patio. In the stunning dining room, a seasonal menu features fresh and inventive fare.

Saint-Emilion FRENCH $$$
(Map p162; ☎817-737-2781; www.saint-emilionrestaurant.com; 3617 W 7th St; mains $30-40; ⏲6-9pm Tue-Sat) Perfect for capping off a day at the museums, this quaint Cultural District charmer serves rustic French food. You can order off the menu or go for a prix fix meal. There's a great $25 deal on Tuesday and Wednesday. You can almost smell the lavender of Provence out on the terrace.

Drinking

Usual Bar COCKTAIL BAR
(Map p162; ☎817-810-0114; www.theusualbar.com; 1408 W Magnolia Ave; ⏲4pm-2am) Craft-cocktail lust packs hipsters in nightly at this bar that serves up debonair drinks such as 'Jimador's Revenge' and 'Taxation & Representation.' Of course you can be ironic and just have a well-poured Old Fashioned. Great terrace.

Chat Room BAR
(Map p162; ☎817-922-8319; 1263 W Magnolia Ave; ⏲4pm-2am; 🛜) The Usual Bar's low-key sibling has cheap drinks, a great jukebox and a pool table.

Flying Saucer Draught Emporium BAR
(Map p166; ☎817-336-7470; 111 E 3rd St; ⏲11am-1am Mon-Thu, to 2am Fri & Sat, noon-midnight Sun) You definitely won't go thirsty: with 80 beers on tap, this downtown joint is made for craft-beer lovers. How can you not love a bar with a jam-packed patio called 'Half-Acre Hell?'

Lola's Saloon BAR
(Map p162; ☎817-877-0666; www.lolasfortworth.com; 2736 W 6th St; ⏲noon-2am) Dive into this dive bar for a fairly intimate music experience. Good bands many nights, otherwise a good local crowd more than happy to tell you where to go – in a nice, helpful way.

Zambrano Wine Cellar & Bistro WINE BAR
(Map p166; ☎817-850-9463; 910 Houston St; ⏲4pm-midnight Mon-Thu, to 2am Fri & Sat) With 50 wines available by the glass that change bimonthly, this modern wine bar – all velvet curtains, amethyst colors and candlelight – is an appealing option downtown.

White Elephant Saloon BAR
(Map p164; www.whiteelephantsaloon.com; 106 E Exchange Ave; ⏲noon-midnight Sun-Thu, to 2am Fri & Sat) Stockyards cowboys have been bellying up to this bar since 1887 (now owned by Tim Love). Local singers and songwriters are regularly showcased.

☆ Entertainment

Toward the weekend, you'll hear live country music wafting from the Stockyards District. Sundance Square kicks a more diverse beat.

★Pearls Dance Hall MUSIC
(Map p164; www.pearlsdancehall.com; 302 W Exchange Ave; ⏲7pm-2am) On the edge of the stockyards, this raucous old brothel once owned by Buffalo Bill Cody is an atmospheric place to hear traditional country music with an edge. Texas luminaries like Dale Watson are known to rock out here.

Basement Bar LIVE MUSIC
(Map p164; ☎817-458-1803; 105 W Exchange St; ⏲3pm-2am) This dark, intimate bar tucked underneath the Stockyards hosts eclectic local music.

BILLY BOB'S TEXAS

The 100,000-sq-ft building that is now the world's largest honky-tonk, called **Billy Bob's Texas** (Map p164; ☎817-624-7117; www.billybobstexas.com; 2520 Rodeo Plaza; cover $2-5 Sun-Thu, varies Fri & Sat; ⏰11am-2am Mon-Sat, noon-2am Sun), was once a barn that housed prize cattle during the Fort Worth Stock Show. After the stock show moved to the Will Rogers Memorial Center, the barn became a department store so big that the stock keepers wore roller skates.

Now Billy Bob's can hold more than 6000 people and has 40 bars to serve the thirsty masses. The most bottled beer sold in one night was 16,000 bottles, during a 1985 Hank Williams Jr concert. Top country-and-western stars, house bands and country DJs play on two stages. On Friday and Saturday nights a live bull-riding competition takes place at an indoor arena. Pool tables and games help make this a family place; under 18s are welcome with a parent.

Scat Jazz Lounge JAZZ
(Map p166; ☎817-870-9100; www.scatjazzlounge.com; 111 W 4th; ⏰5pm-2am Tue-Fri, from 6pm Sat, 7pm-1am Sun) Tucked into a downtown alley, this subterranean jazz spot is low-key, with just a touch of smoky glamor.

Texas Motor Speedway SPECTATOR SPORTS
(☎817-215-8500; www.texasmotorspeedway.com; cnr Hwy 114 & I-35; tours adult/child $8/6; ⏰9am-5pm Mon-Fri, 10am-5pm Sat & Sun) Have yourself a full-on Nascar experience. The annual stock-car race is in November, but there are races through the year. You can go for a ride with a racer (from $125). The speedway is 20 miles north of downtown, on I-35 W.

Shopping

As you drive down Camp Bowie Blvd toward the Cultural District, don't be put off by the endless strip malls – behind their nondescript facades you'll find good local boutiques. Head to the Stockyards for Western gear and the most over-the-top Texas kitsch.

★**Peters Bros Hats** ACCESSORIES
(Map p166; ☎817-335-1715; www.pbhats.com; 909 Houston St; ⏰10am-5pm Mon-Sat) Get your Stetson on at this downtown hat shop, in business since 1911.

ML Leddy's WESTERN WEAR
(Map p164; ☎888-565-2668; www.leddys.com; 2455 N Main St, Stockyards; ⏰10am-6pm Mon-Sat) Ah, the smell of leather that unmistakably says 'new boots.' Check out the bank ledgers, which contain the foot measurements of rock stars and presidents. If you still don't feel like kicking up your heels, the selection of hats, buckles and clothes might fit the bill.

Retro Cowboy WESTERN WEAR
(Map p166; ☎817-338-1194; 406 Houston St; ⏰10am-7pm Mon-Sat, noon-5pm Sun) Cool cowboy-themed stuff that screams 'perfect Fort Worth souvenir!'

Stockyards Station SOUVENIRS
(Map p164; www.stockyardsstation.com; 140 E Exchange Ave; ⏰9am-6pm) The former sheep and hog pens of Stockyards Station house a (mostly mediocre) mall of sorts. More authentic Western-themed antique shops line Main St.

Information

MEDIA

FW Weekly (www.fwweekly.com) The free, local alternative paper: good listings for dining and the arts.

KFWR The Ranch plays 'The Sound of Texas' at 95.9 FM.

KTFW Country Legends at 92.1 FM.

TOURIST INFORMATION

Fort Worth Convention & Visitors Bureau (www.fortworth.com) The most together tourist board in the state, with three branches: Cultural District (Map p162; ☎817-882-8588; 3401 W Lancaster Ave; ⏰9am-5pm Mon-Sat); downtown (Map p166; ☎800-433-5747; 415 Throckmorton St; ⏰8:30am-5pm Mon-Fri, 10am-4pm Sat); Stockyards (p161). Ask for the spiffy free 3D maps.

Getting There & Away

Dallas-Fort Worth International Airport (p158), is 17 miles east of Fort Worth.

Several **Greyhound** (Map p166; www.greyhound.com; 1001 Jones St) buses a day make the one-hour trip from the downtown Fort Worth to Dallas ($9). There's also service to other major Texas cities. Trains and buses in Fort Worth share the **Intermodal Transportation Center** (1001 Jones St), easing transfers.

The **Amtrak** (www.amtrak.com; 1001 Jones St) *Texas Eagle* stops in Fort Worth en route to San Antonio and Chicago. The *Heartland Flyer* serves Oklahoma City.

Monday to Saturday the **Trinity Railway Express** (TRE; ☎ 817-215-8600; www.trinityrailwayexpress.org; 1001 Jones St) connects downtown Fort Worth with downtown Dallas ($5, 1¼ hours).

Getting Around

Fort Worth is fairly compact and easy to drive around: I-30 runs east–west through downtown, and I-35 W runs to the south.

The **Fort Worth Transit Authority** (The T; ☎ 817 215 8600; www.the-t.com; single ride/day pass $1.75/3.50) runs bus 1N to the Stockyards and bus 2 to the Cultural District. Stops include the Intermodal Transportation Center. Both of these lines run well into the evening.

A useful and free bus route, deceptively called **Molly the Trolley** (☎ 817-215-8600; www.mollythetrolley.com; free; ⏰ 10am-10pm), shuttles around downtown.

NORTH OF DALLAS & FORT WORTH

Much of region's phenomenal growth is in the north. Quaint little towns such as McKinney are now enveloped by the Metroplex. Towns such as Grapevine, however, have their own inherent charms and you can go far enough north that you leave all the urban hubbub far behind.

Grapevine

POP 47,400

Although it's right next to DFW International Airport, Grapevine is as quaint a town as you'll find in the Metroplex. Its classic Main St oozes history and appeal, and begs a stroll. Thanks to the airport fees, its myriad civic attractions are well funded.

Sights

With the exception of the Grapevine Mills mall, everything listed here is in the walkably compact historic downtown.

★ **Grapevine Vintage Railroad** RAILROAD
(☎ 817-410-3123; www.gvrr.com; 636 S Main St; adult/child from $20/10; ⏰ departs 12:30pm Fri-Sun Jun-Aug, Sat & Sun only Feb-May & Sep-Nov) Grapevine's own historic railroad runs tourist trains to and from Fort Worth. The ride takes 90 minutes one way and you have about 90 minutes in Fort Worth. Extra cash gets you air-con in first class or a ride in the caboose. Some runs have a steam engine. Trains leave from the restored Cotton Belt depot.

Grapevine Historical Society MUSEUM
(☎ 817-488-0235; www.grapevinehistory.org; W Hudgins St; ⏰ 10am-5pm Tue-Sat) FREE This well-funded museum moved to new quarters in 2013, next to the Visitor Information Center. It has excellent displays covering just who settled in Grapevine and why.

Blacksmith Shop HISTORIC SITE
(☎ 940-435-1684; 707 S Main St; ⏰ 11am-5pm Thu-Sun) FREE Just east of the train station, this is a fascinating place to watch genial smithies demonstrate their craft.

Eating & Drinking

Weinberger's Delicatessen DELI $
(☎ 817-416-5577; www.weinbergersdeli.com; 601 S Main St; mains from $7; ⏰ 10am-7pm Mon-Sat, 11am-5pm Sun) This Chicago-style deli is a transplant from the Windy City and has a bevy of local fans. Thick-cut sandwiches and dripping Italian beefs are among the 100 items on the menu. Daily specials can be excellent.

Su Vino Winery WINE BAR
(☎ 817-416-9333; www.suvinowinery.com; 120 S Main St; ⏰ noon-7pm Tue-Sat, 1-5pm Sun) Look out your window at the right moment as you fly into DFW and you might spot the vineyards of one of Grapevine's eight wineries. Su Vino is one of the best. Right downtown, you can sample its range of wine and enjoy light snacks.

Shopping

Grapevine Mills Shopping Center MALL
(☎ 972-724-4900; www.simon.com/mall/grapevine-mills; 3000 Grapevine Mills Pkwy at I-635 & TX 121; ⏰ 10am-9:30pm Mon-Sat, 11am-7pm Sun) Almost as big as Minnesota's Mall of America, the Grapevine Mills Shopping Center is an outlet mall with over 200 stores selling off-price goods by famous brands and labels. Bored? It has a 30-screen movie theater.

Information

Visitor Information Center (☎ 817-410-3185; www.grapevinetexasusa.com; 636 South Main St; ⏰ 8am-6pm Mon-Fri, 10am-6pm Sat, noon-

5pm Sun) Housed in a lavish brick edifice downtown, this center brims with useful information and helpful staff. It also has a free gallery with rotating exhibits.

Getting There & Away

Unlike many other Metroplex cities (we're looking at you Arlington!), Grapevine has a **Visitor Shuttle** (817-410-8136; www.grapevinetexasusa.com/shuttle; day pass individual/family $5/10; 11am-10pm Mon-Sat, to 6pm Sun) that links the airport, Grapevine Mills and the historic downtown.

Frisco

POP 132,500

Frisco has arrived! Regularly named America's fastest growing city, its population was a mere 33,000 as recently as 2000. This means that the city is trying to define itself even as new multilane roads are plowed through in all directions.

There's much excitement around the construction of the **Museum of the American Railroad** (214-428-0101; www.museumoftheamericanrailroad.org; temporary location 6455 Page St; 10am-5pm Wed-Sat, 1-5pm Sun). One of the best collections of historic railroad locomotives and cars in the country was hosted for years at the state fairgrounds. But Frisco has offered a lot more space for what's literally a huge collection and beginning in 2013 the museum is moving north. The new location will open in stages starting with temporary exhibits. The vast permanent facility is two blocks south, bordering Cotton Gin Rd.

McKinney

POP 137,800

Visitors to McKinney will find no shortage of reminders that the historic town finished second in *Money* magazine's 2012 list of the best places to live in the US (FYI: Carmel, Indiana finished first). Laminated copies of the article are posted everywhere. But once you look past the hype you might well decide that the editors were on to something.

Even as the Metroplex edies around its edges, McKinney has lovely small-town streets lined with restored Queen Anne and Victorian houses that exude charm. And the town's center is easily the most vibrant downtown of any historic town in north Texas. All manner of shops, boutiques, cafes and bistros buzz with action. The main square is bounded by Kentucky, Louisiana, Tennessee and Virginia Sts. You can easily spend a half day or more enjoying the charms of McKinney.

Sleeping & Eating

Excellent dining and drinking options abound.

Farmers Market MARKET
(www.chestnutsquare.org; 315 S Chestnut St at Anthony St; 8am-noon Sat Apr-Oct;) Features the best organic vendors and food producers in the region.

Grand Hotel HISTORIC HOTEL **$$**
(214-726-9250; www.grandhotelmckinney.com; 107 N Kentucky St; r from $160;) In an 1880 building that once was McKinney's opera house, this inn has 45 plush, modern rooms

SOUTHFORK RANCH

Seen by billions of glossy TV soap fans worldwide, **Southfork Ranch** (972-442-7800; www.southfork.com; 3700 Hogge Rd/FM 2551; adult/child $13.50/9.50; 9am-5pm) is the real-world mansion that posed as the home of JR Ewing and company on *Dallas*. Built as a rich family's home in 1970, the ranch was chosen to be the Ewing Ranch when *Dallas* hit the airwaves in 1978. From then on it was used for certain exterior shots for the series until 1989.

The ranch was called back to duty for reunion movies over the years and then for the return of the series in 2012. In the meantime, fans kept coming by to see the mansion and by the 1990s it had been converted into a conference center hosting corporate events, Tea Party rallies and a memorial for actor Larry Hagman (who played JR in *Dallas*) after his death in 2012.

Southfork is still popular with *Dallas* fans. While it does have some old props from the show (like the gun that shot JR), don't expect to see Miss Ellie's kitchen or JR's bedroom, as interior shots of the ranch were filmed on a Hollywood set. It's 20 miles northwest of Dallas, near Parker.

set amid exposed bricks and other small luxurious details. It's right on the main square.

★ **Patina Green** CAFE $$

(☎972-548-9141; www.patinagreenhomeandmarket.com; 116 N Tennessee St; mains from $12; ⏲store 10am-6pm Mon-Sat, 11am-4pm Sun, lunch served 11am-2pm Tue-Sat) For most of the day, Patina Green is an attractive shop with creative and tasteful housewares plus a deli section with some of the best local prepared foods and cheeses. But at lunchtime five days a week, a line forms and happy diners enjoy whatever the chef has decided to make for the day. The emphasis is on sustainability and seasonality.

Denton

POP 118,700

A bastion of college cool and indie cred, Denton has a great music scene. Home to the University of North Texas and its renowned arts programs, the fast-growing city rightfully claims the title as the most musical city in the region. The downtown, centered on **Courthouse Square**, boasts a plethora of music venues, music shops and instrument stores.

By day, pop into the **Courthouse on the Square Museum** (☎940-349-2850; 110 W Hickory St; admission free; ⏲10am-4:40pm Mon-Fri, 11am-3pm Sat) for local lore and an amazing display of art created with pecans. It's nuts! Outside check out the 1918 **Confederate War Memorial** which has been modified with apologetic disclaimers. Nearby, **Recycled Books Records CDs** (☎940-566-5688; www.recycledbooks.com; 200 N Locust St; ⏲9am-9pm) has hard-to-find tunes.

For music, the top venue is **Dan's Silver Leaf** (☎940-320-2000; www.danssilverleaf.com; 103 Industrial St; ⏲7pm-2am), with a revered owner who books top bands but doesn't gouge on drink prices. Other clubs and bars are nearby.

Every March the city hosts **35 Denton** (www.35denton.com; ⏲Mar), a music festival featuring everything from rock to blues to jazz.

Decatur

POP 6200

For 20 years beginning in the late 1860s, Decatur was an important waypoint on the Chisholm Trail, the legendary cowboy route along which millions of head of Texas cattle were driven north to markets. As the beef went one way, the state's first fortunes came south with the the first cattle barons. Today you'll most likely stop in Decatur on your way to the Panhandle.

Decatur's 1895 **Wise County Courthouse** (101 N Trinity St) is a marvel in pink granite. Surrounding the square where State and Main Sts meet are lively shops and cafes. **Sweetie Pie's Ribeyes** (☎940-626-4555; 201 W Main St; mains $12-25; ⏲11am-8pm Mon-Sat; 📶) serves up Texas menu stalwarts with flair while nearby **Cakes by Leisha** (☎940-626-4783; 103 S Trinity St; treats from $2; ⏲8am-5pm Mon-Sat) has irresistable bakery treats for the onward journey.

As you head northwest from Decatur on US 287 you'll pass through grasslands little changed since the days of cattle drives.

> **DON'T MISS**
>
> **MESQUITE RODEO**
>
> The very best cowboys compete in the vaunted Mesquite Rodeo, otherwise known as the **Mesquite ProRodeo** (☎972-285-8777; www.mesquiterodeo.com; 1818 Rodeo Dr, Mesquite; ⏲7:30pm Fri & Sat, Jun–late-Aug). For almost three months, the competition is fierce in classic rodeo events including bareback, steer wrestling and bull riding. The prize money attracts top talent to this series. Outside of the main season there are smaller events in April and December. Mesquite is 14 miles straight east of Dallas.

SOUTH OF DALLAS & FORT WORTH

From the big attractions in Arlington to the prehistoric sights in Glen Rose, the lands south of Dallas and Fort Worth are diverse. Enjoy Waxahachie, one of the state's best small towns, and feel the bliss of wide open spaces as you head southwest.

Arlington

POP 367,500

For once the hype is real: Arlington really is the home of sports and thrills. Blockbuster attractions draw people from far and wide to icons of today's Texas.

Sights & Activities

★Six Flags Over Texas AMUSEMENT PARK
(☎817-530-6000; www.sixflags.com; I-30 & Hwy 360; admission $42-60, parking from $20;) The most popular attraction in the state and only 20 minutes' drive from the downtowns of Dallas and Fort Worth, this amusement park can be a blast – plan ahead to avoid the worst crowds (weekends, midday in summer). Roller coasters rule: there are 13 of them, including two of the old-fashioned (wooden) kind.

Plan to hit the most popular rides either first thing in the morning or in the evening, when lines are shortest. Aside from the mighty, scream-inducing roller coasters such as Batman the Ride, Mr Freeze, and Shock Wave (once the world's tallest coaster), other reliable thrills include the adrenaline-charged Superman: Tower of Power, which shoots brave souls up into the sky at 45mph (cape not included) and La Vibora, a bobsled ride that gives riders a fun taste of the Olympic sport.

New in 2013, the Texas SkyScreamer whisks you around 400 feet from the ground. Other highlights are the legendary Texas Giant, which has the steepest drop (79 degrees) of any wooden coaster in the world.

To ease your visit, stow valuables and bags in lockers at the entry mall just inside the park gate, where you can also rent strollers and wheelchairs, or board your pets ($10). Remember that height restrictions vary per ride and range from 42in to 54in; to avoid disappointment, check before you get in line.

Purchase tickets online for discounts. Unfortunately there is no public transportation to Six Flags; however, some local hotels offer shuttles. The hours vary, but in June and July the park is open daily. Opening hours and days vary from March to May and August to December. It's best to check the online calendar.

Six Flags Hurricane Harbor WATER PARK
(☎817-265-3356; www.sixflags.com; 1800 E Lamar Blvd, off I-30; admission $25-30, parking from $15) Across I-30 from Six Flags Over Texas you can get soaked at Six Flags Hurricane Harbor, an over-the-top water park with a good mix of thrills, chills and family-friendly rides. The adventurous can surf at the Surf Rider, free-fall six stories on the Geronimo, or brave the dubiously named Mega Wedgie (no explanation needed).

Of course, nothing beats just chilling out in the Surf Lagoon (a pool with 4ft-high waves) or gliding on an inner tube down the Lazy River. For kids, the Hook's Lagoon Treehouse is loads of fun. Hours vary, but the park is open daily in June and July. Days and opening hours vary in May, August and September – check the online calendar for more details.

Sleeping & Eating

At first Arlington may seem like a showplace for every sleeping and eating chain in America – and it is (especially with hotels and motels). But you can find some excellent indie restaurants and it has a surprising number of top-notch Vietnamese places.

Wingate by Wyndham HOTEL $$
(☎817-640-8686; www.wingateinnarlington.com; 1024 Brookhollow Plaza Dr; r $80-180;) This tidy hotel has 92 large, well-appointed rooms (fridges, microwaves and large work areas) spread over four floors. Bonuses include an indoor Jacuzzi and an outdoor pool. It's on the trolley-bus system linking area hotels with Arlington's major attractions.

★Pho Pasteur Restaurant VIETNAMESE $
(☎817-274-6232; 100 W Pioneer Pkwy; mains $5-10; 9am-9:30pm) A real find southwest of the stadiums and parks, this Vietnamese restaurant specializes in pho, the iconic beef soup. Steaming bowls are served from pots that have been simmering for 12 hours or more. The menu also includes spring rolls and noodle dishes.

Damian's Cajun Soul Cafe CAJUN $$
(☎817-649-7770; 185 S Watson Rd at TX 360 & E Abram St; mains from $10; 11am-4pm) It's not much to look at from the outside, but at Damian's it's what's inside that counts. The Cajun fare is good and spicy. Many drive miles just for the pork chops and macaroni and cheese. It pays to visit early as popular items sell out.

Entertainment

★Rangers Ballpark in Arlington BASEBALL
(☎817-273-5222; http://texas.rangers.mlb.com; 1000 Ballpark Way, at I-30 exits 28 or 30; tickets $11-80) From April to October the Texas Rangers play at this vintage-ballpark-inspired stadium, which features replicas of the Fenway Park scoreboard and the right-field home-run porch from Tiger Stadium. **Guided tours**

INTERNATIONAL BOWLING MUSEUM

It's not just the strikes at Rangers Ballpark that are celebrated in Arlington, the strikes of bowling get their due as well at the **International Bowling Museum** (☎817-385-8215; www.bowlingmuseum.com; 621 Six Flags Dr; adult/child $9.50/7.50; ⊙9:30am-5pm). All facets of the game of big balls, garish shoes and pitchers of beer are celebrated. You might just want to spare a moment for a visit.

(☎817-273-5098; adult/children $12/6; ⊙off-season 10am-4pm Tue-Sat, on-season 9am-4pm Mon-Sat, from 11am Sun) are better off-season: they include a peek into the ballplayers' inner sanctum. With over 49,000 seats, you can usually get tickets to weekday games on short notice.

Dallas Cowboys Stadium FOOTBALL
(☎817-892-4467; http://stadium.dallascowboys.com; 1 Legends Way, off I-30 exits 28 & 29) The Dallas Cowboys gave themselves the nickname 'America's Team' after they had great success (with cheerleaders and otherwise) in the 1970s. Although the team's fortunes have been modest of late, they still have swagger, as shown in their enormous, retractable-roof home, which opened in 2009.

Tours ($15-28; ⊙10am-4:30pm Sat, 11:30am-3:30pm Sun) last 90 minutes and leave from Entry A. If you want to see the spectacle that is a Dallas Cowboys home game, you'll need to find tickets on the secondary market as the games are always sold out. There are many other events in the stadium during the year, including college football bowl games, high school football championships, truck exhibitions and concerts.

Waxahachie

POP 30,300

With sensational Victorian, Greek Revival and Queen Anne architecture lining its main square, Waxahachie is easily one of the most beautiful small towns in Texas. That it has a real vibrancy only adds to its appeal. And it's just 30 miles south of Dallas.

Sights

You can easily spend a half day or more touring Waxahachie. Be sure to pick up the walking- and driving-tour maps and brochures at the Ellis County Museum. On foot you can explore the beautiful downtown in a just a couple hours, while by car you can appreciate some of the area's mansions.

★**Ellis County Courthouse** HISTORIC BUILDING
(Courthouse Square; ⊙9am-5pm Mon-Fri) This stunner of a courthouse uses every Romanesque trick in the book to awe you. The pink granite and red limestone are magnificent and a recent restoration has only added sheen to the splendor. On weekdays you can wander the compact interior and look into the wood-trimmed courtroom.

Ellis County Museum MUSEUM
(☎972-937-0681; 201 S College St; ⊙10am-5pm Mon-Sat, 1-4pm Sun) FREE Housed in the 1893 Masonic Lodge, this well-curated museum gives a good sense of the history of the area. Don't miss the details on all the shenanigans behind the construction of the courthouse.

Webb Gallery GALLERY
(☎972-938-8085; www.webbartgallery.com; 209-211 W. Franklin St; ⊙1-5pm Sat & Sun) Inside this ornate brick building (1902) is an eclectic and intriguing gallery which showcases works by numerous local artists. You'll need to hang onto your jaw when see the works of Venzil Zastoupil in the window. Over many years the late artist used hundreds of thousands of toothpicks to create all manner of large objects, from working Ferris wheels to airplanes.

Eating & Drinking

College Street Pub BAR
(☎972-938-2062; 210 N College St; mains from $8; ⊙11am-late) Take a pause in your downtown rambling at this old corner tavern. Seek out the secret terrace and choose from the splendid beer selection and a menu that includes fried green tomatoes, a French burger and fish and chips.

Glen Rose

POP 2500

Some 100 million years ago dinosaurs wandered this part of Texas, feasting on the lush primeval vegetation (not knowing that someday they'd be part of the oil that would make a not-yet-existing species rich – and dependent).

Evidence of these dinosaurs has survived in fossil form and today fuels a thriving tourism industry. Least commercial is **Dinosaur Valley State Park** (☎254-897-4588; www.tpwd.state.tx.us; 1629 Park Rd 59, off FM 205; adult/child $7/free; ⏲8am-10pm), where you can see actual tracks left by a Tyrannosaurus ex.

Elsewhere the ancient visitors are more hyped. **Dinosaur World** (☎254-898-1526; www.dinosaurworld.com; FM 205 at Park Rd 59; adult/child $13/10; ⏲9am-5pm) has huge statues of dinosaurs set on 22 acres. In comparison to the animated dinosaurs in films such as *Jurassic Park*, those here seem all the more, well, static. Over at **Fossil Rim Wildlife Center** (☎254-897-2960; www.fossilrim.org; off US 67; admission $15-24; ⏲8:30am-5:30pm daily, Mar-Sep), you can drive a nearly 10-mile course through an open-air zoo that's home to 52 animal species, including cheetahs and giraffes.

Meanwhile, for an alternative view on all this evolution stuff, the **Creation Evidence Museum** (www.creationevidence.org; 3102 FM 205; adult/child $5/free; ⏲10am-4pm Thu-Sat) aims to dispel evolutionary theories and promote the many unique theories of its founder.

Glen Rose is 76 miles southwest of Dallas.

West

POP 2900

A modest farm town with an unusually strong ethnic heritage, West suffered great tragedy in 2013 when a fertilizer plant exploded, killing 15, injuring over 160 and destroying several square blocks. It was a low moment for a town that wears its Czech roots for every one to see – and taste.

West is home to several Czech bakeries and cafes (and even gas stations) that specialize in *kolaches* (large soft buns filled with all manner of savoury and sweet fillings). The best outlet is easily **Village Bakery** (☎254-826-5151; 113 E Oak St; snacks from $2; ⏲6:30am-5pm Mon-Sat), which exudes fresh-from-the-oven goodness the moment you get your first whiff of its baked treats. You can have *kolaches* (most people have at least two) filled with sausage, ham and cheese, apricots, prunes and many more fillings. And if you want further variety, the fresh cinamon rolls are sublime.

Waco

POP 126,700

Don't feel bad if you associate this unassuming town with its unlucky past: it's probably best known for the infamous 1993 'Waco Siege' that took place nearby. While lacking any major thrills, this is a pleasant little city with a few fun museums (Dr Pepper, anyone?).

Waco is home to the largest Baptist university on earth (Baylor University) and college legend claims that students can ostensibly attend a different-area Baptist church every weekend during their four years. (It's true – there are a whopping 97 of them.) Churchgoing aside, you'll find some diversions in this town that is a gateway to the Plains beyond.

Sights & Activities

Spend the morning checking out Waco's unique museums, then take a leisurely stroll through Cameron Park.

Make sure to visit the stately 475ft pedestrian-only **Waco Suspension Bridge**, built from 1868 to 1870 and the first to cross the Brazos.

Armstrong Browning Library MUSEUM
(☎254-710-3566; www.browninglibrary.org; 710 Speight Ave; ⏲9am-5pm Mon-Fri, 10am-2pm Sat) FREE On the Baylor campus, this peaceful refuge of a museum houses a beautiful collection of stained glass, as well as the world's largest collection of original manuscripts and personal effects of the Romantic English poets Robert and Elizabeth Barrett Browning. Don't miss the 'sunrise-sunset' windows in the gorgeous Foyer of Meditation.

Dr Pepper Museum MUSEUM
(☎254-757-1024; www.drpeppermuseum.com; 300 S 5th St; adult/child $8/5; ⏲10am-5pm Mon-Sat, noon-4pm Sun; 👪) The Dr Pepper soft drink was invented by Waco pharmacist Charles C Alderton in 1885. This museum celebrates his

WHAT THE...? SKYSCRAPER

No, that's not the set of a post-apocalyptic sci-fi film: that's Waco's skyline. The view of Waco from I-35 has long puzzled many freeway passersby unfamiliar with Waco. The historic 22-story **Alico Building** towers above the rest of the flat downtown grid and can be seen from miles away. After a 1954 tornado wiped out most of the other buildings in downtown, this one was left standing all by its lonesome.

WORTH A TRIP

HICO & US 281

Famed outlaw Billy the Kid was gunned down in New Mexico at age 21 in 1881, unless of course, he wasn't. The model-on-a-mantel cute village of Hico, 100 miles southwest of Dallas, would just as soon hope that you'll believe otherwise – or at least be curious enough to pay the town a visit.

Their story – and they're sticking to it – is that Billy survived and lived to a ripe old age *right here in Hico!* You can learn about the whole far-fetched notion at the **Billy the Kid Museum** (☎254-796-2523; www.billythekidmuseum.com; 114 N Pecan St; ⏱10am-5pm Mon-Sat, 1-5pm Sun) FREE, right in the center of town. The surrounding blocks have an appealing mix of restored and gently decaying 19th-century buildings.

Stay the night at the **Old Rock House** (☎214-538-1201; www.oldrockhousehico.com; 302 E 3rd St; r $90-125), a fine little B&B set in a grove of oaks right downtown. Feast on hearty Texas fare at the **Koffee Kup** (☎254-796-4839; 300 W 2nd St; mains from $6; ⏱6:30am-9pm) and finish with banana cream pie.

Cruise south along US 281 and you'll pass through lovely, gently rolling land that could be the Hill Country. As you near Hamilton, watch for the **Dutchman's Hidden Valley Country Store** (☎254-386-3018; www.dutchmans-hiddenvalley.com; Hwy 281 N; ⏱9am-6pm Thu-Tue). The selection is eclectic: have a sandwich, buy some bison meat, sniff some popourri, go rocking on a rocker, and sample the locally grown pecan treats. Be sure, however, to buy some of the lovely housemade chocolates.

creation and is housed in a stately brick building that was one of company's first facilities.

The collection is vast and offers a fascinating look at one of the few companies (including Coca-Cola!) to survive from the days when pharmacists created hundreds of soft drinks nationwide. There is a small, old-style soda fountain (admission not required) where you can get sodas and other treats.

Cameron Park & Zoo ZOO
(☎254-750-8400; 1701 N 4th St; adult/child $9/6; ⏱9am-5pm Mon-Sat, 11am-5pm Sun; 👪) Hills, limestone cliffs and 20 miles of trails make this park a great place for hiking and mountain biking.

At the eastern end of the park, the Cameron Park Zoo features 52 acres of natural habitat. A Texas section with about 30 native species balances an impressive range of African animals, including elephants, white rhinos and giraffes.

Waco Mammoth Site HISTORIC SITE
(☎254-750-7946; www.wacomammoth.com; 6220 Steinbeck Bend Rd; adult/child $7/6; ⏱11am-5pm Tue-Fri, 9am-5pm Sat) In 1978 two Waco arrowhead hunters found a bone in a ravine. It turned out to belong to a Columbian mammoth that had perished there about 68,000 years ago. Now open to the public after 30 years of excavation, the Waco Mammoth Site features the nation's only recorded discovery of a herd of Pleistocene mammoths.

Texas Sports Hall of Fame MUSEUM
(☎254-756-1633; www.tshof.org; 1108 S University Parks Dr; adult/child $7/3; ⏱9am-5pm Mon-Sat, noon-5pm Sun) All manner of Texas sports legends, including golfer Byron Nelson, boxer and pitchman George Foreman and pitcher Nolan Ryan, are saluted here.

Texas Ranger Hall of Fame & Museum MUSEUM
(☎254-750-8631; www.texasranger.org; Fort Fisher Park; adult/child $7/3; ⏱9am-5pm) It's an NRA member's fantasy come true! Ponder hundreds of guns while you explore the history of the famous Rangers, from their early-19th-century origins through their days fighting cattle rustlers, Indians and Mexicans, to their present-day role as Texas' most elite state-police unit.

Sleeping

Rooms get scarce during Baylor University events such as fall football weekends. You'll find plenty of chain motels and hotels along I-35.

Super 8 Waco MOTEL $
(☎254-754-1023; 1320 Jack Kultgen Frwy, just north of I-35 exit 334 on E frontage road.; r $50-140; ❄📶🐾) A standard Super 8 (three stories, 78 rooms with inside corridors), this well-located motel is close to downtown and Baylor. Most rooms have fridges and microwaves.

BRANCH DAVIDIANS & THE WACO SIEGE

For the last two decades Waco has been associated with the Branch Davidians and the standoff that ended in the fiery deaths of dozens on live television. The aftereffects of this event are still felt locally.

The Branch Davidians were an offshoot of a radical sect of Seventh Day Adventists. The original group, the Davidians, set up shop in Waco in 1935 but moved outside the city in 1959 to establish a compound called New Mt Carmel, near the town of Elk. Fighting between internal factions led to splits and drama, and in 1987 Vernon Howell, who had joined the group in 1981, took control and changed his name to David Koresh.

Koresh's platform involved, among other things, arming the compound to defend it against the apocalyptic nightmare the world would become after the second coming of Christ. Believing that Koresh was buying, selling and storing illegal weapons, the federal Bureau of Alcohol, Tobacco and Firearms (ATF) staged a disastrous raid that a 1993 US Treasury report deemed 'tragically wrong.' The agents were fired on; four ATF agents and five cult members were killed in the ensuing firefight. The resulting standoff lasted 51 days.

As local authorities and FBI hostage negotiators surrounded the compound with hundreds of police cars and even a tank, the standoff became a media sensation; viewers around the world were treated to deadly scenes from the original raid plus the day-to-day drama of the situation.

The standoff ended on April 19, 1993, when federal agents fired tear-gas bombs into the compound. Within hours, the buildings were completely engulfed in flames fueled by the ignition of the tear-gas canisters. Some 76 Branch Dividians died, including Koresh and many children. Nine cult members survived. The government's handling of the incident is still the subject of controversy and conspiracy theories. (Timothy McVeigh said the Waco seige was his primary motivation for bombing the federal building in Oklahoma City in 1995.)

For more information on the siege, including interviews and photos, PBS has an excellent website: www.pbs.org/wgbh/pages/frontline/waco.

Visiting the Site

You can easily visit the site of the Branch Davidian compound. Take Elk Rd (FM 2491) east from TX 340 for 5 miles. At a fork in the road, take the gravel Double EE Ranch Rd to the left and you'll see the site on your right.

The site today is occupied by an offshoot sect of the Branch Davidians (who number less than 10). There has been a struggle for control of the site among various survivors.

At present there is a small **church**, which uses the double doors from the ill-fated original compound. There is usually a rack of brochures that have a useful map of the site along with the current sect's version of events. A $1 donation is asked. Nearby are **memorials** to the Branch Davidians killed in 1993, the federal agents who died during the initial raid and the Oklahoma City bombing victims.

Often one of the present – and friendly – occupants will show up to offer their own take on the events of 20 years ago as well as the political scene today.

The site itself is peaceful, with views across the surrounding plains. The water-filled foundations where so many died, however, are truly haunting.

Best Western Old Main Lodge HOTEL **$$**
(☎254-753-0316; I-35 & S 4th St; r $80-130; ❄📶🏊🐾) Adjacent to the Baylor campus, on the Baylor side of I-35, this hotel has 84 rooms in a two-story building with exterior corridors. Enjoy the English hunting-lodge decor, the courtyard pool and the free breakfast.

Cotton Palace Bed & Breakfast B&B **$$**
(☎254-753-7294; www.thecottonpalace.com; 1910 Austin Ave; r incl breakfast $120-160; ❄📶) Find big breakfasts and a lovely sun porch at this grand old arts-and-crafts style house. The six rooms have a luxurious, frilly and plush decor.

Eating & Drinking

Waco may be a heavily Baptist town but it has some good bars where you'll even find some Baylor students.

★Lolita's Tortilleria & Restaurant MEXICAN $

(☎254-755-7301; 1911 Franklin Ave; mains $4-10; 7am-3pm Tue-Sun) Lolita's exudes that family-run, small-town spirit that can't be manufactured. The hugely popular all-day breakfast menu includes tacos, huevos rancheros, *migas* (a signature Texas dish: think eggs scrambled with corn tortillas, onions, tomatoes, peppers and often cheese) and the 'elephante', a massive breakfast burrito with six fillings. Locals swear by the fresh salsa and queso.

Dubl-R Old Fashioned Hamburgers BURGERS $

(☎254-753-1603; www.dubl-r.com; 1810 Herring Ave; mains $3-6; 10am-6:30pm Mon-Fri, to 2pm Sat) Char-grilled burgers with grilled onions and all the usual toppings are the thing at this near-shack local legend. Have a shake, maybe some tots and scarf down pure Americana.

Vitek's BBQ BARBECUE $$

(☎254-752-7591; www.viteksbbq.com; 1600 Speight Ave; mains $6-12; 10:30am-3pm Mon, to 6pm Tue & Wed, to 9pm Thu-Sat) Since 1915 Vitek's has drawn the hungry crowds. Whatever your carnivorous pleasure, it's all homemade and excellent. Big appetite? Order the legendary Gut Pak, a monster of a sandwich with Fritos, cheese, chopped beef, beans, sausage, pickles, onions and jalapeños. Great beer selection.

★Dancing Bear BAR

(☎254-753-0025; 1117 Speight Ave; 4pm-midnight Sun-Fri, noon-1am Sat) A few blocks from the Baylor campus, you'll find 16 microbrews on tap, along with helpful advice and beer samples for neophytes and connoisseurs alike. Over 100 bottles of craft beers round out the superlative selection. Enjoy a frosty one on the back terrace.

Common Grounds CAFE

(☎254-757-2957; www.cgwaco.com; 1123 S 8th St; snacks from $3; 7am-midnight, from 1pm Sun;) Tucked across from the Baylor University campus, this feel-good coffeehouse packs in students, professors and everyone else with live music and a killer outdoor patio. We dig the rustic-cabin feel and the 'sleep is overrated' espresso drinks. The baked goods and breakfast burritos are tasty.

Cricket's Grill BAR

(☎254-754-4677; 221 Mary Ave; mains $6-12; 11am-2am) A cavernous beer hall with fine pizzas, lots of beers on tap and tons of games, including darts, pool and shuffleboard.

Information

Waco Tourist Information Center (☎254-750-8696, 800-922-6386; www.wacocvb.com; University Parks Dr, off I-35, exit 335B; 8am-5pm Mon-Sat, 10am-5pm Sun) At the western end of Fort Fisher Park. It has free coffee and friendly staff who will help with hotel reservations and offer advice.

Getting There & Around

Waco is easy to reach by car: it's right on I-35, halfway between Dallas–Fort Worth and Austin, about two hours from either.

Greyhound buses (☎254-753-4534; www.greyhound.com; 301 S 8th St) run between Waco and Dallas ($27, 2½-3 hours, six daily) and Waco and Austin ($24, 1¾ hours, six daily).

Local buses are run by **Waco Transit** (☎254-753-0113; www.waco-texas.com/transit/; single ride $1.50).

PANHANDLE & PLAINS

The vast open stretch of the Texas Panhandle and Plains is a region of long drives on lonely two-laners. Its cities are few and small. The scope and scale make this a place where people tend to think big, but some of the area's purest pleasures are in its details: the scent of sage after rainfall, a flint quarry plied by Texas' first inhabitants thousands of years ago, or the wistful love songs written by young troubadours whose legacies ultimately reached far beyond the Plains.

And it's not all tumbleweeds. Midland is at the heart of the Texas energy boom, Lubbock embodies the region's rich music heritage with its favorite son, Buddy Holly, and Amarillo keeps cattle king of the Panhandle. Natural wonders include America's second-largest canyon, Palo Duro, where the Comanche fought on long after other tribes gave in. But the region's greatest assets are the tiny towns seemingly lost in the past. Slumbering in the sun are forgotten architectural gems and small-town cafes that have you itching for the next mealtime.

Permian Basin

The Permian Basin is a flat, physically charmless region of Texas with a lack of vegetation so pronounced that early settlers named one small town Notrees. Instead, you'll see (and smell) forests of oil rigs, pump jacks and petroleum tanks, which have ruled the boom-and-bust economy here since the late 1920s. This is a place where all those testosterone-fueled pickup ads could be filmed.

Although it will never make a top destinations list, the basin's twin towns of Midland and Odessa are excellent places to learn about the oil industry and the roots of an American political dynasty, the Bush family. The growing towns are edging towards each other across the 15 miles that separate them along busy I-20.

Midland

POP 114,200

'Experienced Gang Pusher Wanted' read the signs on the way into Midland. They're not talking about a new vendor for the Crips and the Bloods; it's just another of the countless pleas for workers in the booming local energy industry.

Midland is the more dudelike of the twin cities, a sprawling series of middle class, white-collar subdivisions, with mirrored high-rises towering above a nearly lifeless downtown. The oil industry is conservative, and Midland County has one of the most conservative voting records in the country: in 2012 80% of voters chose Mitt Romney.

Sights

★CAF Airpower Museum MUSEUM

(☎432-563-1000; www.airpowermuseum.org; 9600 Wright Dr; adult/child $10/7; ⏲9am-5pm Tue-Sat) Historic warplanes are the stars at this impressive museum at Midland International Airport. The home of the Commemorative Air Force (formerly the politically incorrectly named Confederate Air Force), this sizable museum has a large collection of planes, mostly from WWII. It has an excellent section devoted to that war, which doesn't flinch from tough subjects such as the atom bomb.

Most moving is the nose-art collection: the bawdy images painted on aircraft by men far from home tasked with unspeakable duties.

George W Bush Childhood Home HISTORIC SITE

(☎432-685-1112; www.bushchildhoodhome.com; 1412 W Ohio St; adult/child $5/3; ⏲10am-5pm Tue-Sat, 2-5pm Sun) George and Barbara Bush moved to west Texas from patrician New England in 1948. A growing family, the Bushes lived in this house from 1952 to 1956, when their son George W was aged five to nine.

What's most surprising about this modest house is that even a rising oil exec like George HW didn't live in the 1950s equivalent of a McMansion. There's plenty of material on the life of W that may delight fans and irritate others, but all will find this well-curated museum within a perfectly restored house to be a fascinating look at life in a simpler era.

The museum gift shop has pretty much every book about W by aids and acolytes you can imagine, plus material on W's wife, Laura, who writes about growing up in Midland in *Spoken from the Heart*. There's also an earlier Bush house in Odessa.

Permian Basin Petroleum Museum MUSEUM

(☎432-683-4403; www.petroleummuseum.org; 1500 I-20 W exit 136, north side; adult/child $8/5; ⏲10am-5pm Mon-Sat, 2-5pm Sun) This museum is worth a stop even if you're not utterly fascinated with the oil business, for it's as much a history and geology museum as a shrine to the prominent local industry (it has a hall of fame and an ironically entertaining 1970s sensibility).

Outside is a big collection of antique oil-drilling equipment. Inside, interactive exhibits include one in which players can drill their own wells and another that simulates the roar of a blowout, an oil well gone wild.

Museum of the Southwest MUSEUM

(☎432-683-2882; www.museumsw.org; 1705 W Missouri Ave; ⏲10am-5pm Tue-Sat, 2-5pm Sun; 👪) Housed in the 1937 Turner Mansion, itself a work of art, this museum has an art gallery (admission free), planetarium (shows adult/child $6/4) and a children's museum (admission $3). Larger-than-life sculptures from the permanent collection dot the tree-shaded grounds, which were built by oil baron Fred Turner.

Sleeping

Midland offers more options than Odessa, even if they're all chains. Budget choices are north of I-20 exit 134; more upscale brands can be found on the TX 250 Loop where it meets TX 158 west of the center. Note that the energy boom means that prices are high, selection is low and many places have reduced services due to employee shortages.

Super 8 MOTEL $

(☎432-689-6822; 3828 W Wall Ave; r $60-120; ❄📶🏊) A tidy two-story version of the ubiquitous budget chain. The neighborhood is charmless except for other cheap motels – and industry. It's north of I-20 exit 134, off Midkiff Rd.

Residence Inn HOTEL $$$

(☎432-689-3511; www.residenceinn.com; 5509 Deauville Blvd; r $150-300; ❄@📶🏊🐾) Amid a plethora of brightly lit franchise restaurants, this extended-stay hotel has 131 units in an attractive, if generic, complex. All come with kitchen facilities and are ideal for families.

Eating

★KD's Bar-B-Q BARBECUE $$

(☎432-683-4013; 3109 Garden City Hwy/TX 158; mains from $9; ⏱11am-9pm Tue-Sat) If you had to go to one Texas 'cue joint, this would do. Line your platter with wax paper and tell the cook what to pile on (the brisket is divine). Add sides such as potato salad, then head to the amazing bar where you can get beans, pickles and an ocean of sauces. And the peach cobbler? Dang! This rambling place is east of town, just off I-20 at exit 138.

Basin Burger BURGERS $$

(☎432-687-5696; 607 N Colorado St; mains from $10; ⏱11am-10pm) It looks so sprightly from the outside that this upscale burger joint, all retro chrome inside, could be a chain, but it's not. The burgers are excellent and come in myriad forms (including a great salmon burger). Zippy touches abound, such as serving aioli with the onion rings.

Garlic Press MEDITERRANEAN $$$

(☎432-570-4020; www.thegarlicpress.net; 2200 W Wadley Ave; mains $15-35; ⏱11am-2pm & 5-9:30pm Tue-Fri, 5-9:30pm Sat) In an upscale little shopping plaza north of town, the Garlic Press is one of the more stylish places in town. Med-style fare is best enjoyed outside under the shady trees. There's an array of steaks with a variety of preparations and, yes, there's warm bread served with roasted garlic.

Information

Midland Visitors Center (☎432-683-3381, 800-624-6435; www.visitmidlandtexas.com; 1406 W I-20, northside frontage road; ⏱9am-5pm Mon-Sat) Near the Permian Basin Petroleum Museum and I-20 exit 136, this large facility is filled with genial volunteers.

Getting There & Around

Fittingly for oil towns, Midland and Odessa are nearly impossible to navigate without a car.

Midland International Airport (MAF; ☎432-560-2200; www.flymaf.com) sits midway between Midland and Odessa near exit 126 on I-20 and TX 191. The airport is served by American Eagle (Dallas–Fort Worth), Southwest (Dallas, Houston and Las Vegas) and United Express (Denver and Houston).

For a long-distance bus service, you'll need to use Greyhound in Odessa.

Odessa

POP 99,300

In contrast to somewhat prim Midland, hardscrabble Odessa has a downbeat feel. It's the classic split between management and workers, with the latter making their homes here. The low-rise downtown has some barely perceptible glories left over from the original boom; most notably, however, it has a very big rabbit.

Sights

White-Pool House HISTORIC SITE

(☎432-333-4072; 112 E Murphy St; ⏱10am-3pm Wed-Sat) FREE Built in 1887, this is the oldest existing house in Ector County. It had just two owners for nearly a century when in 1973 the Pool family deeded it to the county for preservation. It shows the change in local fortunes from ranching in the 1880s to the oil boom of the 1920s.

Presidential Archives & Leadership Library MUSEUM

(☎432-363-7737; www.utpb.edu/presidential-archives; 4919 E University Ave; ⏱10am-5pm Tue-

WHAT THE...? JACKRABBIT

Odessa claims to have the world's largest **jackrabbit statue**. The 10ft-tall photo op is at 802 N Sam Houston Ave and was built in honor of the first Championship Jackrabbit Rodeo in 1932.

FRIDAY NIGHT LIGHTS

In 1990 the book *Friday Night Lights*, written by journalist HG 'Buzz' Bissinger, was published to much critical acclaim. It follows the Panthers football team of **Permian High School** (1800 W 42nd St) during the team's 1988 season. No fawning bit of fluff, the book delves deeply into the lives of the young players and their coaches. It displays teenage angst and portrays a community where academic excellence is ridiculed in favor of success on the playing field. Many locals were horrified at its exposure of racism and other social ills in Odessa. The book was adapted into a 2004 movie and used as the basis for the popular TV series that ran from 2006 to 2011.

The huge Ratliff Stadium, which seats nearly 20,000, is next to the school. Signs, emblazoned with the nickname 'Mojo,' show the team's long history of victory, which coincidentally went into decline when the book was published. (Archrival Midland Lee High School has been doing much better.) But fall Friday nights here under the lights are still *the* place in Texas to watch high school football. See www.mojoland.net for more info.

Sat) FREE This much-lauded museum has had fiscal problems and periodically shuts down. However, when open it has an interesting collection of items and info on all the presidents. Out back is the very modest 1948 home of the Bush family, which was moved here and restored.

Eating

Ben's Little Mexico MEXICAN $
(432-333-4529; 620 N Grandview Ave; mains from $6; 11am-8pm Mon-Sat) Like the rest of Odessa, Ben's doesn't look like much (even in its new location). But from this humble eatery comes some of the region's best *chile verde* (succulent chunks of marinated pork in a piquant green sauce.) Yum!

Whitehouse Meat Market BURGERS $
(432-367-9531; 200 E 52nd St; meals from $7; 6am-6pm Tue-Sat) Hidden among some industrial buildings north of the center, this is the place to get a great burger, cooked or uncooked. Besides fine Texas beef in deli cases, it serves up fab burgers in simple surrounds. Get a double.

Information

Odessa Convention & Visitors Bureau (432-333-7871, 800-780-4678; www.odessacvb.com; 700 N Grant Ave, Suite 200; 9am-5pm Mon-Fri) In the Bank of America building.

Getting There & Away

Odessa is about 12 miles west of Midland International Airport. The **Greyhound bus terminal** (432-332-5711; www.greyhound.com; 2624 E 8th St) is served by regular buses along the I-20 corridor between El Paso ($74, five hours) and Fort Worth ($83, six hours).

Big Spring

POP 27,300

The relentlessly flat Permian Basin landscape starts to show signs of a change 40 miles east of Midland. Big Spring is on the edge of the Edwards Plateau Caprock Escarpment, the defining topographical feature of the Texas Panhandle. The spring for which the town is named sits in **Comanche Trail Park**.

Nearby, 380-acre **Big Spring State Park** (432-263-4931; www.tpwd.state.tx.us; 1 Scenic Dr; admission free; dawn to dusk) has a fine nature trail with labels describing the hearty plants, such as the spiky argarita bush. A short drive around the top of the park has sweeping views out across the basin and plateau.

The 15-story **Hotel Settles** (432-267-7500; www.hotelsettles.com; 200 E Third St; r $150-300;) is a classic Texas story: born during a 1930s boom, it eventually closed, leaving a humungous corpse looming over an otherwise tiny town. Enter Brint Ryan, a local boy who made zillions helping corporations avoid taxes. He bought the Settles' remains and millions of dollars later it reopened in 2013 as a lavish hotel.

The Settles definitely looms large locally and although public areas have been restored to period glory, the suites and smaller guest rooms are modern and lavish. There's a top-end restaurant and a sumptuous bar, perfect for sipping bourbon and telling lies.

There are few west Texas dance-halls more authentic than the **Stampede** (432-267-2060; 1610 E TX 350), a bare-bones, early-1950s affair 1.5 miles northeast of Big Spring. If you're real lucky you'll catch Jody Nix and the Texas Cowboys (www.jodynix.com), a legendary family band that has been fueling two-steppers for years. Stampede schedules, however, are sporadic.

San Angelo

POP 93,200

Situated on the fringes of the Hill Country, San Angelo is the kind of place where non-poser men in suits ride motorcycles, while women in pickups look like they could wrestle a bull and then hit the catwalk. It's a purely Western town with an appealing overlay of gentility. The Concho River, which scenically runs through the town, offers numerous walks along its wild, lush banks. It's worth a detour just to enjoy time here.

Sights & Activities

★Fort Concho National Historic Landmark HISTORIC SITE
(☎325-481-2646; www.fortconcho.com; 630 S Oakes St; adult/child $3/1.50; ⊙9am-5pm Mon-Sat, 1-5pm Sun) No matter how many forts you've seen in your Texas travels, this one is likely to be a highlight. Many folks claim it's the best-preserved Western frontier fort in the US, and much of it has been restored by the city over the decades.

Designed to protect settlers and people moving west on the overland trails, the fort went up in 1867 on the fringes of the Texas frontier and saw service until 1889. Among its highlights are the Headquarters Building, which includes the Fort Concho Museum, and the Post Hospital.

San Angelo Museum of Fine Arts MUSEUM
(SAMFA; ☎325-653-3333; www.samfa.org; 1 Love St; adult/child $2/1; ⊙10am-4pm Tue-Wed & Sat, to 6pm Thu, to 9pm Fri, 1-4pm Sun) This impressive saddle-shaped musuem is best known for its ceramics collection. Run in partnership with Angelo State University, SAMFA often has compelling special exhibits.

Concho Avenue Historic District HISTORIC SITE
At the heart of downtown, the Concho Avenue Historic District is a good place to stroll – be sure to pick up a historic walking tour brochure at the Visitor Center. The most interesting section, known as Historic Block One, is between Chadbourne and Oakes Sts. Don't miss the elegant and restored lobby of the 14-story 1929 **Cactus Hotel** (36 E Twohig Ave).

Miss Hattie's Bordello Museum MUSEUM
(☎325-653-0112; 18 E Concho Ave; admission free, tours $5; ⊙10am-4pm Tue-Sat, tours 1-4pm Thu-Sat) Few can resist the come-on of Miss Hattie's Bordello Museum, which operated as a downtown house of pleasure from 1896 until the Texas Rangers shut it down in 1946. Rooms re-create the plush velvet look considered essential back in the day, but the best feature is the stories of the women and their clients. Opening hours can be erratic.

Railway Museum of San Angelo MUSEUM
(☎325-486-2140; www.railwaymuseumsanangelo.homestead.com; 703 S Chadbourne St; adult/child $2/1; ⊙10am-4pm Sat) The beautifully renovated Santa Fe Depot is home to much railroad nostalgia. The station, on the El Paseo, is the main attraction. Inside, the museum has models of 1920s San Angelo and old rail cars.

San Angelo State Park PARK
(☎325-949-4757; www.tpwd.state.tx.us; adult/child $4/free; ⊙dawn to dusk) This state park is on the western outskirts of town, accessible via FM 2288 (Loop 2288) off W Ave N (which becomes Arden Rd west of downtown), US 87 or US 67. The 7600-acre park surrounds the 1950s reservoir, OC Fisher Lake. More than 50 miles of trails are popular with animal- and bird-watchers.

Producer's Livestock Auction SPECTACLE
(☎325-653-3371; www.producersandcargile.com; 1131 N Bell St; ⊙9am Tue & Thu) FREE No one has a baaad time at the largest sheep auction in the USA, the Producer's Livestock Auction. Sheep are sold on Tuesday and cattle on Thursday. The auctioneers' banter is the most fascinating aspect of the whole deal – it's totally incomprehensible.

El Paseo de Santa Angela WALKING TOUR
The El Paseo is a family-friendly, pleasure-filled stroll that is part of the 4-mile-long river walk that follows the Concho, from just west of downtown heading east to Bell St. Celebration Bridge links San Angelo's main street, Concho Ave, to the main attractions south of the river, which include a collection of historic buildings along Orient St.

Santa Angela was San Angelo's original name, and the El Paseo de Santa Angela marks the route that soldiers stationed at Fort Concho once used to visit the wanton town in its heyday. In 1870 the post surgeon at the fort wrote that 'the village across the Concho…is attaining an unenviable distinction from the numerous murders committed there… Over 100 murders have taken place in the radius of 10 miles.' And then there were the 35 bordellos and saloons that lined Santa Angela's sidewalks.

Festivals & Events

The big annual **San Angelo Stock Show & Rodeo Cowboys Association Rodeo** (www.sanangelorodeo.com) runs over two weeks in February. It is one of the largest in the Southwest.

Sleeping

Most motels are situated on the major highways on the periphery of town. Check with the tourist office for a list of the many good B&Bs.

San Angelo State Park CAMPGROUND $
(325-949-4757; www.tpwd.state.tx.us; campsites $10-22) San Angelo State Park has beautifully located backpacker's tent sites; the sites with hookups have some shade.

Inn of the Conchos MOTEL $
(325-658-2811, 800-621-6041; www.inn-of-the-conchos.com; 2021 N Bryant Blvd; r $50-100;) On the northwest edge of downtown US 87, this is an older, modest 125-room motel that is valiantly hanging on in the face of the chains. Free hot breakfast buffet plus microwaves and fridges in the rooms are its ammo.

Inn at the Art Center B&B $$
(325-658-3333; www.innattheartcenter.com; 2503 Martin Luther King; r $85-135;) Funky is an understatement for this three-room B&B at the back of the bohemian Chicken Farm Art Center. Rooms are as artful as you'd expect at a 1970s chicken farm turned artists' co-op.

★ **Sealy Flats Blues Inn** INN $$
(325-653-0437; www.sealyflats.com; 204 S Oakes St; r $120-200;) Part of the excellent downtown blues club and diner, this inn is housed in a much-restored historic hotel. The three suites have names like T-Bone Walker, and blues memorabilia is everywhere. It's very comfortable and guests enjoy a private terrace for live music at the club on weekends.

Eating & Drinking

San Angelo has several excellent pubs right downtown.

Concho Valley Farmers Market MARKET $
(325-658-6901; El Paseo de Santa Angela; 7am-1pm Tue-Sat late May-Oct) Choose from top west-Texas produce until it's all gone. The market is held near the fort.

Charcoal House BURGERS $
(325-657-2931; 1205 N Chadbourne St; mains from $4; 7am-9pm) The name raises great hopes for the burgers, and they deliver. Options abound at this traditional drive-in with in-car (or truck) service. Details such as the thick bacon win raves, as do the breakfasts.

Packsaddle Bar-B-Que BARBECUE $
(325-949-0616; 6007 Knickerbocker Rd; mains $6-8; 11am-8pm Wed-Mon) Don't let the downmarket location in a strip mall six miles southwest of the center put you off – the brisket here is among the finest you'll find anywhere in these parts (and beyond). It's bone-simple here but it has diverting Nascar displays.

★ **Peasant Village Restaurant** DELI/BISTRO $$
(325-655-4811; 23 S Park St; lunch mains from $8, dinner mains $17-27; 11am-1:30pm Mon, 11am-1:30pm & 5-9pm Tue-Fri, 5-9pm Sat) Located in a beautiful 1920s house near downtown, this refined restaurant is just the place if you'd like some fine wine to go with a meal from a menu that changes with the seasons. Creative mains of steak and seafood are always listed and there's a touch of the Mediterranean throughout. The desserts are simply fab.

Jason Helfer, the talented chef, also assembles the best deli sandwiches and salads in town at lunch. With the lavish desserts (including bread pudding and key lime pie), you can have a picnic across the street in beautiful rose gardens.

Miss Hattie's Café & Saloon SOUTHERN $$
(325-653-0570; 26 E Concho Ave; mains from $8; 11am-8pm Mon-Sat, but hours can vary) This place tips its hat to the bordello museum up the block, with early-20th-century decor featuring tapestries and gilt-edged picture frames. However, the tasty meat is the main attraction, especially the hunk of seasoned beef grilled into a hamburger and finished with an array of yummy toppings.

Sealy Flats MUSIC BAR
(☎325-653-1400; www.sealyflats.com; 208 S Oakes St; ⏲11am-late) A real find if you want to hear live blues. There's open-mike night on Monday, local acts the rest of the week and usually well-known blues musicians on weekends. The back terrace is where it's at. Get a brew and enjoy the jammin'.

Shopping

San Angelo is well known for the pearls that form in the Concho River. These precious orbs occur naturally – and they're not just any pearls. They come in shades of pink and purple, usually in pastels but occasionally in vivid shades.

Historic Concho Ave has antique shops and vintage-clothing stores.

Eggemeyer's General Store GIFTS
(☎325-655-1166; 35 E Concho Ave) This old-style place has penny candy and lots of gift-item nonsense. (OK we like the fudge.)

Legend Jewelers JEWELRY
(☎325-653-0112; 18 E Concho Ave; ⏲10am-5pm Mon-Sat) The best place to shop for Concho River pearls.

JL Mercer & Son WESTERN WEAR
(☎325-658-7634; www.jlmercerboots.com; 224 S Chadbourne St; ⏲10am-5pm Mon-Sat) Noted for its custom boots, spurs and other Western gear. Texas legends such as Lyndon Johnson got their boots here (as did on-screen-cowboy John Wayne). Custom boots start at $600, but with options (there are many!) you can scoot past $2000 without breaking stride.

Chicken Farm Art Center ARTS & CRAFTS
(☎325-653-4936; www.chickenfarmartcenter.com; 2502 Martin Luther King Blvd; ⏲10am-5pm Tue-Sat) More than 20 artists create and display their works in studios in this old chicken farm. Many feather their nest further by also living here.

Cactus Book Shop BOOKS
(☎325-659-3788; 6 E Concho Ave; ⏲10am-5pm Tue-Sat) Right downtown, it carries new and used books plus a good selection of Texana titles.

Information

San Angelo Convention and Visitors Bureau (☎325-655-4136, 800-375-1206; www.visitsanangelo.org; 418 W Ave B; ⏲9am-5pm Mon-Sat, noon-4pm Sun) This helpful center has a stunning location on the Concho River, near downtown. A pedestrian bridge links to a groovy kids' playground.

Getting There & Around

Located just a bit west of Texas' geographical center, San Angelo is at the intersection of US 67, US 87 and US 277. Within town, US 87 becomes Bryant Blvd, which – along with Chadbourne St – is the city's main north–south road.

FUNDAMENTALIST WORRIES

The Mormon Church has spawned many offshoot sects which have broken with the main church over its disavowal of polygamy. In recent years none has been more notorious than the Fundamentalist Church of Jesus Christ of Latter Day Saints (FLDS).

Under the auspices of imprisoned sex offender, Warren Jeffs the FLDS has secretive communities across North America, including Arizona, Utah and British Columbia. In 2003 the sect purchased a ranch 4 miles northeast of Eldorado, in a spot as isolated as any in Texas (San Angelo, the nearest city, is 40 miles north).

Named the Yearning for Zion Ranch (YFZ Ranch), the property has housed 700 or more people at various times and is rumored to be the current headquarters of the church. In 2008 the ranch made headlines when the Texas Department of Child Protective Services, acting on a phone tip claiming that children had been sexually abused at the ranch, removed more than 400 children and placed them in protective custody in San Angelo. A legal (and media) circus ensued, during which it was established that the original phone call had been a hoax.

Eventually, most of the children were returned to their mothers, but a number of men at the YFZ Ranch have been indicted and convicted of a variety of sex offences with underage girls.

Visitors to Eldorado, the namesake of the John Wayne movie, are unlikely to see any of the very plainly dressed and reclusive FLDS members. However, locals are quick to assert that they wish the sect would pack up and move on.

Around San Angelo

Sights & Activities

Fort McKavett State Historical Park HISTORIC SITE
(325-396-2358; www.visitfortmckavett.com; FM 864; adult/child $4/3; 8am-5pm) General William Tecumseh Sherman once called this fort along the San Saba River 'the prettiest post in Texas.' Today, Fort McKavett State Historical Park, about 75 miles southeast of San Angelo, preserves the striking ruins of a once-important fort.

Fort McKavett was established by the Eighth Infantry of the US Army in 1852 as a bulwark against Comanche and Apache raids. The fort saw its peak in the mid-1870s, when it housed more than 400 troops and many civilians. Some of the 25 buildings have been restored; the grounds are alive with wildflowers for much of the year. Check out the boiled turnips recipe in the excellent museum.

Presidio de San Sabá HISTORIC SITE
(www.presidiodesansaba.com; off US 190; 8am-5pm) FREE What was once the largest Spanish fort in Texas has been beautifully restored. Presidio de San Sabá dates to 1757 and is close to the town of Menard, some 21 miles northeast of Fort McKavett. The site is great for wandering, especially when it's just you, bird calls and the buzz of cicadas.

X Bar Ranch RANCH
(888-853-2688, 325-853-2688; www.xbarranch.com; 5 N Divide, Eldorado; day use $10) Near Eldorado, a town best known for its wool mills, this 7100-acre ranch may be just what you're looking for if you're hankering for a real Western holiday. There's horseback riding, of course, plus stargazing, hikes to view Indian mounds, bird-watching and ranch activities. Accommodation at the ranch includes campsites (from $10) and comfortable cabins (from $100). The ranch is 40 miles south of San Angelo, off US 277.

Sonora

POP 3100

Go underground in the famous local caverns and then squint your eyes in the bright light of day in the compact and well-preserved center of diminutive Sonora, a worthy stop on either I-10 or US 277.

Marvel at the geological splendor of the **Caverns of Sonora** (325-387-3105; www.cavernsofsonora.com; RM 1989; adult/child from $20/16; tours 8am-6pm Mar-Aug, 9am-5pm Sep-Feb) on a two-hour tour that covers 2 miles underground. Oddities include sound-absorbing cave sponges and tubular 'soda straw' stalactites. The caverns are located 7 miles south of I-10 exit 392, which is 8 miles west of Sonora. The temperature inside the caverns is always about 70°F, with 98% humidity. Tours include about 360 steps.

Stop by the **Sonora Chamber of Commerce** (325-387-2880; 205 Hwy 277 N; 9am-5pm Mon-Fri) for a free **walking tour** brochure. Highlights include the handsome Sutton County Courthouse and the site where Will Carver, a member of Butch Cassidy's Hole in the Wall Gang, was shot to death in 1901.

The perfect antidote to chain restaurants, the **Sutton County Steakhouse** (325-387-3833; 1306 N Service Rd; mains from $7; 7am-9pm) is close to the I-10 and US 277. Like many places across west Texas, it excels at chicken-fried steak as well as other comfy faves such as cheeseburgers and catfish.

Junction

POP 2600

Winding through the lush and beautiful South Llano River valley, US 377 is light on traffic but big on vistas on its 100-mile route southwest from the pretty little town of Junction toward the border and Del Rio.

Junction proper has a few places where you can get organized for a rafting trip on the river. Or you can go hiking and spot deer, squirrels and the iconic Rio Grande turkey in **South Llano River State Park** (325-

WORTH A TRIP

FRIO CANYON

Since prehistoric times, humans have been enjoying the beauty of the Frio River and its lovely canyon and valley. The region is lush with trees that provide their own harmonious color in the fall. The tiny town of **Leakey** is little more than a crossroads, but what a crossroads! US 83 follows the river north and south, while FM 337 runs east and west through wooded hills and secluded little valleys.

446-3994; www.tpwd.state.tx.us; off US 377; adult/child $4/free; 24hr). It's also ideal for a picnic, a swim or a stroll.

An old gas station is home to one of the region's best barbecue joints. **Lum's** (325-446-3541; 2031 Main St; mains from $8; 8am-11pm Mon-Sat) has the requisite dining area cluttered with high school team pennants and Bud signs. Amid a classic menu, the ribs, brisket, jalapeno sausage and potato salad earn raves.

Abilene

POP 119,700

Abilene is frequently called the 'buckle of the Bible Belt,' and not without reason (it has three bible colleges, for one). This is a buttoned-down town where nonconformists can feel seriously out of place. About 150 miles from either Midland or Fort Worth, the cow-dotted plains barely seem to yield to the city. However, Abilene makes for a good stop owing to one mighty fine museum and some traditional places to eat that will have you happy that modernity seems in short supply.

Sights

All the following sights, except for the zoo, are within a few blocks of each other downtown. Treadway Blvd (Business Route 83D) is the main north–south street running through downtown; it is marked by little of architectural interest.

★Frontier Texas! MUSEUM
(325-437-2800; www.frontiertexas.com; 625 N First St; adult/child $8/4; 9am-6pm Mon-Sat, 1-5pm Sun;) Reason enough to stop if you're anyplace near Abilene, Frontier Texas! makes 100 years of frontier history (1780–1880) possibly more interesting than the real thing. The museum also serves as the main visitor information center for the region.

Life-size holograms and other special effects take you inside a buffalo stampede, next to a conniving card shark and at home on a firefly-filled range. Hairs will raise on your arms at the appearance of Comanche chief Esihabitu.

Abilene Zoo ZOO
(325-676-6085; www.abilenezoo.org; 2070 Zoo Lane; adult/child $5/2.50; 9am-5pm;) Jaguars, ocelots, elephants and giraffes are among the more than 160 species making their home at the Abilene Zoo, located in Nelson Park in southeast Abilene near the junction of Loop 322 and Highway 36.

Highlights include the Creepy Crawly Center and the Discovery Center, which compares plants and animals of the Southwest USA and Central America to similar areas in Africa and Madagascar.

Grace Museum MUSEUM
(325-673-4587; www.thegracemuseum.org; 102 Cypress St; adult/child $8/4; 10am-5pm Tue-Sat, to 8pm Thu) This fine museum complex includes three distinct museums housed in the former Grace Hotel, once the grandest in Abilene. The art museum features periodically changing exhibitions. The historical museum focuses on Abilene's history from 1900 through 1950.

It's heavy on railroad and military memorabilia plus what home life was like in a simpler time. The children's museum has fun science experiments, including one where you can ponder gravity.

National Center for Children's Illustrated Literature MUSEUM
(325-673-4586; www.nccil.org; 102 Cedar St; 10am-4pm Tue-Sat;) FREE This small museum has a permanent exhibition of works by William Joyce and other well-known children's book illustrators. The real attractions are the constant special exhibits, which highlight the works of individual artists.

Center for Contemporary Arts GALLERY
(325-677-8389; Grissom Bldg, 220 Cypress St; 11am-5pm Tue-Sat) FREE This gallery features exhibits by noted artists and is home to 10 working studios.

Paramount Theatre HISTORIC BUILDING
(325-676-9620; www.paramount-abilene.org; 352 Cypress St; admission free for self-guided tours; noon-5pm Mon-Fri) Stars twinkle and clouds drift across the velvet blue ceiling of this magical movie and performing-arts palace. You can tour the beautifully restored Paramount or take in a movie, concert or other performance many nights.

Festivals & Events

Western Heritage Classic RODEO
(www.westernheritageclassic.com; 2nd weekend in May) A big rodeo featuring working cowboys from ranches across the USA, complete with campfire cook-offs, a Western art show and dances.

Sleeping

It's chain city in Abilene. Exits 285, 286 and 288 off I-20 are dotted with motels. Older indie operations south of the center on South 1st St are mostly dubious.

For camping, Abilene State Park is the best choice.

Antilley Inn MOTEL $
(325-695-3330; www.antilleyinn.com; 6550 US 83/84; r $40-80;) The Antilley offers great value. It's an updated motel, with stories of rooms and outside walkways. The rooms have fridges and microwaves and a modest continental breakfast is set out each morning.

Whitten Inn Expo MOTEL $
(325-677-8100; www.whitteninn.com; 840 E US 80; r $65-90;) Part of a tiny local chain, this well-managed motel has a pool area that goes beyond the puddle-in-a-parking-lot standard elsewhere: it's big and even has shade from a large tree. Rooms have a fridge and microwave, and a better-than-average breakfast is included.

Courtyard by Marriott MOTEL $$
(325-695-9600; www.marriott.com; 4350 Ridgemont Dr; r $100-200;) Within sight of the Mall of Abilene, this corporate hotel is one of many slathered across these flatlands of national franchises. The three-story building has 100 sizable units, some with slivers of balcony-like diversion.

Eating

Abilene has some excellent restaurants that are as casual and timeless as a big-sky sunset on the wide open plains.

Larry's Better Burger Drive-in BURGERS $
(325-677-6801; 1233 N Treadway Blvd/US 83 Business; meals from $4; 10am-9pm) The turquoise neon sign could use a spruce up, as could the view (a tombstone dealer and a busy road), but there's nothing tired about the food, which is top-notch, from the drippy cheeseburger to the tasty steak sandwich.

Belle's Chicken Dinner House SOUTHERN $
(325-677-7100; 2002 N Clack St, off US 83/277; mains $7-12; 11am-2pm & 5-9pm Mon-Sat, 10:30am-2pm Sun) Part shack, part steakhouse, this locally loved institution spares you choices. It offers chicken in various forms or chicken-fried steaks and that's it. Unlimited sides of mashed potatoes, cream corn, greens beans and a basket of rolls are trundled out – just as you'll need to be at the end of the meal. Should dessert happen, have the banana cream pie.

Al's Mesquite Grill BARBECUE $$
(325-692-4797; www.alsmesquitegrill.com; 4801 Buffalo Gap Rd; mains $7-18; 11am-9pm Mon-Sat, 10:30am-2pm Sun) Order up some barbecue or a burger, chicken sandwhich or even a steak, then stroll down the cafeteria line and sample the sides on offer, including cheesy broccoli and some very good squash. The peach cobbler dessert tops everything else. It's south of the town center.

Beehive STEAKHOUSE $$
(325-675-0600; www.beehivesaloon.com; 442 Cedar St; mains from $10; 11am-1:30pm Tue-Fri, 5-9:30pm Tue-Sat) This is the place for a tasty lunch or dinner after the high culture of the sights downtown. The menu takes supper-house standards such as shrimp cocktail and steaks and does them up just right (the lunchtime burgers are also good). The cocktails are renowned in teetotaling Abilene for not only having alcohol but being made just right.

Entertainment

Check to see what's on at the beautiful Paramount Theatre.

Big Country Raceway SPECTATOR SPORT
(325-673-7223; www.bigcountryraceway.com; 5601 W Stamford St; admission from $10) Racing cars is a Texas tradition and Abilene's drag strip is open to everyone. Watch dudes in their pickups challenge each other or go nuts and trash your minivan. The track is generally open Friday nights and all day weekends from spring to fall. It's just off I-20 exit 281, Shirley Rd.

Shopping

Hickory St, between 5th and 8th Streets near downtown Abilene, has a good selection of antique and gift shops selling everything from fudge to stained glass to vintage clothing.

Abilene has several noted small manufacturers of custom-made Western gear.

James Leddy Boots WESTERN WEAR
(325-677-7811; www.jamesleddyabilene.com; 1602 N Treadway Blvd; 8:30am-5pm Mon-Fri) A legendary maker of custom boots, this family-run store has prices ranging from $500 to five figures. You can usually get a tour of the shop and work area. Breath deep.

WORTH A TRIP

FORT PHANTOM HILL

Boredom rather than combat doomed this 1851 fort along the clear fork of the Brazos River. **Fort Phantom Hill** (FM 600; dawn-dusk) was among the outposts constructed to protect settlers on the Texas frontier; it was abandoned just three years later after droves of bored soldiers left it (and the service). Time and fires have taken their toll on the fort and the nearby ghost town – by 1880, 546 people had moved to the settlement, but a letter written to the *San Antonio Daily Express* in 1892 indicated the town had dwindled to 'one hotel, one saloon, one general store, one blacksmith shop and 10,000 prairie dogs.' Today, visitors find only a handful of buildings and about a dozen chimneys among the windy, lonely ruins.

Fort Phantom Hill is on private land but the site is open during daylight hours. The grounds are 11 miles north of I-20 on FM 600. Nearby Lake Fort Phantom is popular for fishing, boating, picnicking and camping.

Art Reed Leather WESTERN WEAR
(325-677-4572; www.artreedchaps.com; 361 East S 11th St; 9am-5pm Mon-Fri) Art Reed has a month-long waiting list for saddles that start at about $2000. Chaps can also be had, perfect for a starring role as a cowpoke on the range or in some urban leather bar.

Information

Tourist info is available at Frontier Texas!.

Getting There & Away

Abilene is circled by US 83 on the west side of town, by Loop 322 on the southeast side and I-20 on the northeast.

Greyhound (325-677-8127; www.greyhound.com; 1657 TX 351, off I-20) is on the northwest side. Abilene is on the I-20 line running west from Fort Worth ($42, 2½ hours).

Buffalo Gap

POP 490

Bison used this natural pass in the Callahan Divide for many centuries; later on, it became an outpost on the Dodge Cattle Trail. Today's Buffalo Gap seems to have stolen any charm not claimed by Abilene (which is quite a bit actually). It's a fine detour from Abilene and I-20, just 14 miles southwest via FM 89. Besides the historic village, antique shops abound on the old main drag.

Step back to a time long before the invention of air-conditioning made the plains safe for city slickers at **Buffalo Gap Historic Village** (325-572-3365; www.tfhcc.com; 133 William St; adult/child $7/4; 10am-5pm Mon-Sat, noon-5pm Sun). This living-history museum has almost two dozen buildings, themed for the 1880s, 1905 and 1925. Volunteers bring the past to life, although everybody smells too fresh. Check out the old courthouse, the log cabin that's the oldest structure in the area, a train station, church, doctor's office and filling station.

Perini Ranch Steak House (325-572-3339; www.periniranch.com; FM 89 W; mains $15-30; 5-10pm Tue-Thu, 11:30am-10pm Fri-Sun) is frequently named among Texas' best steakhouses. Enter under the trees and through the screen door. Try an amazing rib eye at a picnic table outside or sample specialties such as one of the state's best cheeseburgers (get it with chilies). The Sunday brunch draws folks from miles around. It has a full bar.

Play Wile E Coyote and go looking for road runners at 529-acre **Abilene State Park** (325-572-3204; www.tpwd.state.tx.us; 150 Park Rd 32, Tuscola, off FM 89; adult/child $5/free; 24hr), which is 4 miles southwest of Buffalo Gap. Attractions include hiking, bird-watching and wildlife-viewing (species include armadillos, white-tailed deer, Mississippi kites and hummingbirds).

The **campground** has 102 campsites ($12 to $22 per night) including the 12 atmospheric tent-only sites. Reserve in advance.

Albany

POP 2000

Albany ranks among the most interesting small towns in Texas. Sitting 35 miles northeast of Abilene, the Shackleford County seat of about 2000 people is a bit off the beaten path on TX 180. It's a worthy 25-mile detour off I-20 or a highlight of one of the loneliest roads in Texas, US 283.

A remarkable facility, the 1877 **Old Jail Art Center** (325-762-2269; www.theoldjailartcenter.org; 201 S 2nd St; 10am-5pm Tue-Sat,

DON'T MISS

FORTS TRAIL

The Texas plains west of the Hill Country are only somewhat less sparsely populated than they were a century and more ago. In the 18th century this region marked the high-water mark of Spain's expansion north. A century later it was the scene of the frontier wars as settlers and ranchers fought for control of the land against the tribes who had called it home for eons.

Forts for militia and troops were built at regular intervals during the 1850s. Many are now historic sites and the Forts Trail links many across this vast region. Contrary to stereotype, a lot of the country here is fairly lush, with rolling hills and winding streams. You can still get a sense of what it must have been like to be a young soldier on the edge of wilderness in the often-lonely sites below.

- Fort Concho (p183)
- Fort Griffin (p190)
- Fort McKavett (p186)
- Fort Phantom Hill (p189)
- Presidio de San Sabá (p186)

2-5pm Sun) FREE houses a surprising collection that includes ancient terra-cotta Chinese tomb figures and art by such masters as Pablo Picasso, Amedeo Modigliani, Henry Moore and Grant Wood.

Each June, several hundred Albany townspeople get together and put on a show, **Fort Griffin Fandangle** (☎325-762-3838; www.fortgriffinfandangle.org; Prairie Theater, 1490 CR 1084, 1 mile west of town; admission $10-20; ⏰Thu-Sat, last 2 weeks of Jun). This energetic musical tells the story of the area's pioneer days, complete with a cattle drive, stagecoach chase and plenty of Old West tomfoolery. Meals are available before the shows.

Some 15 miles north of Albany, the **Fort Griffin State Historic Site** (☎325-762-3592; www.visitfortgriffin.com; 1701 N US 283; adult/child $4/free; ⏰8am-5pm) showcases a handful of somewhat restored buildings and the ruins of a fort that served the frontier during the Comanche wars from 1867 through 1881. Today, the park is probably best known as a principal home of the official Texas longhorn herd.

Lubbock

POP 229,500

'Lubbock or leave it' sing the Dixie Chicks, but this seemingly characteristic bit of Texas bravado isn't what it seems, as the song includes sardonic lines such as 'Got more churches than trees.' And while you'll see plenty of steeples on the horizon, what will really strike you about west Texas' liveliest city is its celebration of life beyond cotton and cows.

Buddy Holly grew up in Lubbock and the town celebrates his legacy in both attractions and an entire entertainment district. It's possible to still find the rockabilly sound that Holly made famous. The other big sound happens on fall weekends when the roar of fans at sport-mad Texas Tech football games can stop a tumbleweed in its tracks.

Lubbock is known as 'Hub City' because so many major highways meet here.

Sights

Buddy Holly's roots in Lubbock are reason enough to visit.

The Texas Tech campus sprawls all over the city's near-northwest side, but is mainly centered between 4th and 19th Sts north and south and University and Quaker Aves east and west. The Depot District, Lubbock's liveliest dining and nightlife area, is centered on Buddy Holly Ave (formerly known as Ave H) and 19th St.

★**Buddy Holly Center** MUSEUM
(☎806-767-2686; www.buddyhollycenter.org; 1801 Crickets Ave; adult/child $5/2; ⏰10am-5pm Tue-Sat, from 1pm Sun) A huge version of Holly's trademark horn-rims mark the Buddy Holly Center. The center is home to the Buddy Holly Gallery; a room devoted to the man with those glasses and pristine teeth. The gallery includes some of his schoolbooks, shoes and records, but best of all are Holly's Fender Stratocaster and hallmark glasses.

The collection delves into Holly's life and gives a good idea of all the rock musicians he inspired, including Bob Dylan, the Beatles and the Rolling Stones.

The center also houses a fine arts gallery, a gift shop, and the Texas Musicians Hall of Fame, which features ever-changing exhibitions on the music and musicians of Texas.

Buddy Holly Statue & Walk of Fame MONUMENT

(8th St at Ave Q) In front of the Civic Center, a larger-than-life-size statue of Holly is surrounded by plaques honoring him and other west Texans who made it big in arts and entertainment. Honorees include musicians Joe Ely, Roy Orbison, Bob Wills, Tanya Tucker and Mac Davis.

Buddy Holly's Grave CEMETERY

(2011 E 31st St, east of Martin Luther King Jr Blvd; dawn-dusk) The headstone in the Lubbock City Cemetery reads 'In Loving Memory of Our Own Buddy Holley. September 7, 1936 to February 3, 1959.' Musical notes and an electric guitar are engraved on the marker too. Some visitors leave guitar picks, coins and other tokens. The cemetery is located on the eastern edge of town. Once inside the gate, turn down the lane to your right.

Texas Tech University UNIVERSITY

(806-742-1299; www.ttu.edu; University Ave) About 30,000 students attend Texas Tech University. Established in 1925, this is not the place to see Gothic treasures of academic architecture, but it is a big and busy place during school terms.

★National Ranching Heritage Center MUSEUM

(806-742-0498; www.nrhc.ttu.edu; 3121 4th St; 10am-5pm Mon-Sat, 1-5pm Sun) FREE A real Lubbock gem, this open-air museum, part of the Texas Tech museum complex, tells a detailed story of what life was like on the Texas High Plains from the late 1700s until the Dust Bowl era of the 1930s. Nearly 50 preserved ranch structures are arrayed on 16 acres.

Among the highlights are the gun ports on the 1780 Los Corralitos house, the second-story stronghold on the 1872 Jowell House and the grand 1909 Barton House.

Museum of Texas Tech University MUSEUM

(806-742-2490; www.depts.ttu.edu/museumttu; 3301 4th St & Indiana Ave; 10am-5pm Tue-Sat, to 8:30pm Thu, 1-5pm Sun) FREE Art, natural history and science are showcased at this campus museum, which has more than five

BUDDY HOLLY, A REAL LEGEND

Lubbock native Charles Hardin 'Buddy' Holley was just five years old when he won a local talent contest playing a toy violin. By the time he was a teen, Buddy became a regular performer on local radio in a band that blended country and western with rhythm and blues. But Holly (the 'e' was dropped by an early concert promoter) soon became a leading pioneer of a new kind of music – rock and roll. Together with his backup band, the Crickets, Holly drove to Clovis, New Mexico, in early 1957 to record a demo of a song called 'That'll Be the Day.' Within months, Holly had a Top 10 record to his credit, with many more hits to follow, including 'Peggy Sue,' 'Not Fade Away,' 'Maybe Baby,' 'It's So Easy,' 'Rave On,' 'Fool's Paradise' and 'Oh, Boy!'.

Buddy Holly was among the first rock performers to write his own material, and he was among the first to experiment with multitrack overdubbing and echo in the studio. An accomplished guitarist and pianist, Holly also used his voice as an instrument, employing a hiccup here and falsetto there to distinctive effect. He and the Crickets were the real deal. In Texas, they often served as a warm-up act to visiting stars (including a young Elvis Presley), and when they hit it big they were among the first white performers to perform at the legendary Apollo Theater in Harlem, New York City.

If his talents weren't enough, Holly was guaranteed immortality by dying young – he was killed in a plane crash on February 3, 1959, near Clear Lake, Iowa. (Fellow rockers JP 'The Big Bopper' Richardson and Ritchie 'La Bamba' Valens were also on board.) His legend continues to grow and his songs and style are emulated endlessly.

The Buddy Holly Story, a 1978 film that starred Gary Busey and which won an Oscar for its music, is a highly fictionalized account of his life. In a classic bit of melodrama, Holly's parents are falsely shown opposing his music career, while the mountains behind the 'Lubbock' bus station are pure Hollywood, literally.

million items in its rather eclectic collection. Special exhibits are usually the highlights.

Lubbock Lake Landmark HISTORIC SITE
(806-742-1116; www.museum.ttu.edu/lll; 2401 Landmark Dr; 9am-5pm Tue-Sat, 1-5pm Sun) FREE Another Tech-run attraction, this site is a sort of time capsule for all the cultures that have inhabited the South Plains for the last 12,000 years. Bones of critters such as wooly mammoths were first unearthed here when agricultural irrigation caused Lubbock Lake's water table to decline in the 1930s, and excavations have gone on here since 1939.

Four miles of trails now wend through the site, where digs are ongoing. A visitor center provides information on long-gone species such as the giant short-faced bear.

To get there, follow Loop 289 to Clovis Rd west of I-27 on the northwest side of town.

Mackenzie Park PARK
(at US 87 & 4th St; dawn-dusk) Located off I-27 at Broadway St and Ave A, 248-acre Mackenzie Park has two dynamite highlights amid what's otherwise a mundane urban park.

Prairie dogs are the stars of **Prairie Dog Town**, a hugely popular 7-acre habitat for the winsome rodents who keep busy excavating their 'town' and watching for groundskeepers.

The irresistibly named **Joyland** (806-763-2719; www.joylandpark.com; admission $6-19; varies mid-Mar–Oct, until 10pm Jun-Aug) has three roller coasters, 30 other rides and an array of carnival arcades and games that are little changed from Holly's time.

American Wind Power Center MUSEUM
(806-747-8734; www.windmill.com; 1701 Canyon Lake Dr; admission $5; 10am-5pm Tue-Sat year-round, 2-5pm Sun summer) A squeaky windmill is part of the iconic opening to *Once Upon a Time in the West,* and you can see more than 90 examples of these Western icons at the American Wind Power Center, located on a 28-acre site at E Broadway St south of MacKenzie Park. Seen together, the windmills form their own compelling sculpture garden.

Festivals & Events

National Cowboy Symposium and Celebration FESTIVAL
(806-798-7825; www.cowboy.org) September is a big time in Lubbock, with returning Tech students and this huge gathering of cowboys, cowboy wannabes, cowboy scholars, cowboy musicians and cowboy cooks. Yee-haw!

Sleeping

There are several motels on Ave Q just south of US 82. They are close to downtown and a reasonable 1.3-mile walk southeast to the Depot District. There's another cluster of chains south of the center at exit 1 off I-27 and still more scattered along TX 289, the ring road southwest of town.

Buffalo Springs Lake CAMPGROUND $
(806-747-3353; www.buffalospringslake.net; FM 835 & E 50th St; tent sites $15-35;) The lake is 5 miles southeast of Lubbock and is big on fun (think ATV trails) as opposed to natural splendor. Sites vary from basic tent-only ones to those with full hookups.

KoKo Inn MOTEL $
(800-782-3254, 806-747-2591; 5201 Ave Q; r $50-100;) This locally owned nonchain motel has character. You can lounge around on a large redwood deck surrounding the indoor pool – perfect during a winter blast. Rooms have fridges and microwaves. There's a lively nightclub; this southside neighborhood is a bit frayed.

Super 8 Civic Center MOTEL $
(806-762-8726; www.super8.com; 501 Ave Q; r $55-110;) Across from a Super Wal-Mart, so you have quick access to cheap pizza (which you can heat up in the rooms with microwaves), the 35 basic rooms are arranged over two floors, with outside walkways. Wi-fi reception is best near the office.

Woodrow House B&B $$
(806-793-3330; www.woodrowhouse.com; 2629 19Th St; r $100-180;) Right across from Texas Tech, this professionally run B&B offers a range of themed rooms. Up-and-comers may enjoy the sumptious charms of the Honeymoon Suite while those who prefer to bring up the rear may enjoy the suite in an actual caboose in the garden. All 10 rooms have bathrooms.

Overton Hotel HOTEL $$$
(806-776-7000; www.overtonhotel.com; 2322 Mac Davis Lane; r $120-350; @) The best place to stay in town, the 15-story independently owned Overton is close to the Tech campus. From the valets to the turn-down service this is a luxurious hotel. Percolate your cares away in the Jacuzzi then unwind in your boldly decorated room.

Eating

Good restaurants are scattered around town, although you won't go wrong basing yourself in the Depot District and browsing. An organic **farmers market** (cnr Ave A & 19th St; 9am-5:30pm Mon-Sat Jun-Nov) sells the best produce from the region.

Ranch House Restaurant AMERICAN $
(806-762-3472; 1520 Buddy Holly Ave; mains from $5; 6am-4pm Mon-Sat) Formica tables and waiters who know what you want before your morning mouth can form the words help make this huge old diner a classic. Eggs fuel the breakfast hordes, while lunchers vie for pot roast and Red Top stew (beef, carrots and chiles).

Tom & Bingos Bar-B-Que BARBECUE $
(806-799-1514; 3006 34th St; mains from $6; 10:30am-4pm Mon-Sat) Calling this place a shack is an insult to decrepit buildings everywhere, but appearances are forgotten when you taste the smoked ham and brisket sandwiches (have the latter chopped). Sides are few: use the fries to mop up the tangy, sweet sauce. Open since 1952.

Picantes MEXICAN $$
(806-793-8304; 3814 34th St; mains $6-12; 9am-10pm) In an otherwise nondescript old coffee shop, this hugely popular Tex-Mex stalwart turns out excellent *chile rellenos* (pepper stuffed with ground beef) and other standards. On weekends folks settle into the booths for all-you-can-eat menudo, the suitably picante beef soup.

★**Crafthouse Gastropub** BISTRO $$
(806-687-1466; www.crafthousepub.com; 3131 34th St; mains $9-22; 11am-10pm Mon-Thu, 11am-midnight Fri & Sat;) Lubbock's most creative restaurant is the work of Jason and Kate Diehl. From the pickled seasonal vegetables on the starter list to inventive seasonal fare, it has something to catch your eye. Mindful of local budgets, it serves cheeseburgers, but what burgers they are. The twice-fried fries are sublime. The beer and wine list is superb.

★**La Diosa Cellars** TAPAS $$
(806-744-3600; 901 17th St; mains $5-20; 11am-10pm Tue-Thu, to midnight Fri & Sat) One of several local wineries, La Diosa uncorks a range of Texas wines beyond its own label. There's inventive Mediterranean-style snacks and meals as well as a coffee bar. On many nights there's live entertainment. Come for a glass of wine, a snack, a meal or just to get down. A Depot District fave.

Triple J Chop House & Brewery STEAKHOUSE $$
(806-771-6555; 1807 Buddy Holly Ave; mains from $12; 11am-10pm Mon-Thu, to midnight Fri & Sat) The airy, exposed-brick dining room has a glass wall looking into a microbrewery. The White Gold Cream and Sip-O-Whit outclass any of the domestic swills favored by locals. Steaks live up to west Texas standards and there are also tasty alternatives with a Southwestern flair.

Drinking & Nightlife

Go!, a free weekly by the town's wonderfully named newspaper, the *Lubbock Avalanche-Journal*, has full listings of what's on.

The Depot District is Lubbock's nightlife HQ (fittingly, the namesake building at the Buddy Holly Center looks hungover), and covers a few blocks adjoining Buddy Holly Ave between 17th and 19th Sts. Otherwise, raucous bars, cheap burrito joints and plasma dealers mark the classic college neighborhood where Broadway crosses University Ave into the campus.

★**Blue Light** LIVE MUSIC
(806-762-3688; www.thebluelightlive.com; 1806 Buddy Holly Ave; noon-late) This legendary club has plenty of live Texas country and rock. Watch for hall-of-famer Gary P Nunn.

Cactus Courtyard BAR
(806-535-5610; www.cactuscourtyard.com; 1801 Buddy Holly Ave; 3pm-late Apr-Oct) Huge open-air venue with west Texas music and all the domestic beers you can quaff.

Bash Riprock's BAR
(806-762-2274; 2491 Main St; 11am-2pm) Dark and grungy, and the huge beer selection gets a workout during the 4 to 7pm happy hour.

Cricket's Grill & Draft House BAR
(806-744-4677; 2412 Broadway St; 11am-2am) A slightly more upscale college joint with a huge selection of draft beer and all sorts of fried treats.

Entertainment

Cactus Theater THEATER
(806-747-7047; www.cactustheater.com; 1812 Buddy Holly Ave) This handsome 1938 theater mostly presents variety shows, including the *Buddy Holly Story, Always...Patsy Cline* and *Honky Tonk Angels.*

END OF THE COMANCHE TRAIL

Until 1871, the Comanches were the most feared of the Plains Indian tribes. While others had been beaten by the US Army and forced into camps and reservations, the Comanches were undefeated and had actually expanded their territory, Comancheria, which encompassed what is today everything in Texas and Oklahoma north and west of Austin. Beginning that September, cavalry led by Colonel Ranald S Mackenzie fought a series of running skirmishes with bands of Comanches in and around the Blanco Canyon (other battles had taken place in Caprock and Palo Duro Canyons). The conflict proved to be the beginning of the end for the Comanches, who lost much of their goods and wealth in addition to having the heart of their territory invaded by the army for the first time. By 1875 the last free band of Comanches had surrendered.

The pivotal battles were fought in the Blanco Canyon, which can be easily seen just 3 miles east of Crosbyton on US 82, itself 38 miles east of Lubbock. Various paved farm roads running north of here penetrate into the canyon, which remains windy and largely desolate today. As you follow the White River, try to imagine Comanches and cavalry troops eyeing each other from the valley and escarpments.

Texas Tech Sports SPECTATOR SPORTS
(www.texastech.com/tickets) For alumni and most locals, Texas Tech's sports teams, the Red Raiders, are a huge deal. Both the football team and the men's basketball team had great success in the last decade, before controversies caused high-profile coaches Mike Keach and Bobby Knight to move on.

The last seasons have been notably less succesful although that hasn't stopped the school from constantly expanding the football venue, **Jones AT&T Stadium** (current capacity about 61,000).

Football tickets are mostly sold for the entire season although if the team is faring poorly you may find individual tickets. Basketball games are much easier to buy on the same day.

Shopping

Dollar Western Wear WESTERN WEAR
(☎806-793-2818; 5011 Slide Rd; ⏰10am-6pm Mon-Sat) This place is among the biggest of Lubbock's many Western-gear shops.

Information

Buddy Holly had a live show on KDAV AM 1590 in the 1950s. It still plays music from the era. **Visit Lubbock** (☎800-692-4035, 806-747-5232; www.visitlubbock.org; 1500 Broadway St, 6th fl; ⏰9am-5pm Mon-Fri) has a small selection of brochures, but isn't a vital stop.

Getting There & Around

Lubbock International Airport (LIA; ☎806-775-3126; www.flylia.com) is situated 7 miles north of town, at exit 8 off of I-27. Airlines include American Eagle (Dallas–Fort Worth), Southwest (Dallas, Houston and Las Vegas) and United Express (Houston).

Lubbock is a hub for **Greyhound** (☎806-687-4501; www.greyhound.com; 801 Broadway), with buses serving most major Texas cities including Dallas ($84, 6½ hours).

Citibus (☎806-762-0111; www.citibus.com; adult/child $1.75/1.25) provides basic public transportation. Most routes originate from the Downtown Plaza at Broadway St and Buddy Holly Ave downtown.

Around Lubbock

Down in the Texas Hill Country, wine seems to make sense. Up here on the boot-scootin,' teetotalin' High Plains, it sounds like a joke. But hold those 'yucks,' as the Lubbock region has near-ideal wine-grape-growing conditions: sandy soil, hot days and cool nights.

Cabernets are the local specialty and more than 20 vineyards are now producing bold reds. You can try many of these while in Lubbock at La Diosa Cellars, a welcoming wine bar run by its namesake winery. Several others are good for a visit, and tours are generally free.

Sights & Activities

Llano Estacado Winery WINERY
(☎806-863-2704; www.llanowine.com; 3426 E FM 1585 east of US 87; ⏰10am-5pm Mon-Sat, noon-5pm Sun) This winery was founded in 1976, making it not only the largest but also the oldest of the modern Texas wineries. Among

the two dozen wines produced, the Chardonnays have won plaudits.

Llano's (yah-no's) shop features its wines (most $10 to $20, although a gulpable blush is $8) and myriad gourmet items, such as jalapeño mustard, that find their way to the back of the fridge.

CapRock Winery WINERY
(☎806-686-4452; www.caprockwinery.com; 408 E Woodrow Rd south of FM 1585, half a mile east of US 87; ⏰10am-5pm Mon-Sat, 12:30-5pm Sun) About 4 miles southwest of Llano Estacado, CapRock Winery is worth a visit for its beautiful mission-style headquarters, a showplace both inside and out. CapRock makes about a dozen wines.

Pheasant Ridge Winery WINERY
(☎806-746-6033; www.pheasantridgewinery.com; 3507 E County Rd 5700; ⏰noon-6pm Fri & Sat, 1-5pm Sun) Located 14 miles north of Lubbock near the town of New Deal, this winery is known for its range of wines, including the expected cabs but also a zesty chenin blanc.

Apple Country Hi-Plains Orchards OUTDOORS
(☎806-892-2961; www.applecountryorchards.com; 12206 E US 62/82; ⏰9am-6pm Mon-Sat, to 4pm Sun) The sweet smell of apple blossoms in spring perfumes the air as you head east of Lubbock on US 62/82. Some 16 miles east of the city is this spot with pick-your-own apple orchards, a popular lunch cafe and a shop that sells produce, including wild honey.

Along Texas Hwy 70

Evocative small towns – some thriving, others nearly gone – are found throughout west Texas. One little burg after another seems ripped from the pages of a Larry McMurty novel. Texas Hwy 70 manages to link a string of these nearly forgotten places: a drive along this road puts you further than simple geography from the 21st century.

Begin in the south in **Sweetwater**, along I-20, some 40 miles west of Abilene. Long and lonely vistas of lush ranch land await as you drive north on Hwy 70. About 55 miles north, turn west at the T-junction with US 380 and drive 5 miles to the nearly evaporated ghost town of **Claremont**. About all that remains is a red stone jail, which could be a movie set.

Return east and rejoin Hwy 70. Some 40 miles of occasional rivers, scattered annuities (oil wells) and countless cattle later, you're in the modestly named hamlet of **Spur**. Most of the once-proud brick structures downtown are barely hanging on, like a chimney with bad grout. Stop into **Dixie Dog Drive-In** (216 W Hill St; mains from $3; ⏰8am-8pm) for a timeless small-town fast-food experience. The chili cheeseburger is the bomb.

Just another 11 miles north brings you to the seat of Dickens County: **Dickens**. Another fading burg, here you can still sense the pride of the original settlers in the massive courthouse built from carved limestone. Catch up on all the gossip at **TC's Ponderosa** (☎806-623-5260; 136 US 82; mains from $5; ⏰7am-8pm), which is inside the a gas station. Great barbecue is served up simply on Formica tables. Try the hot links and get a pickled egg and a pineapple pudding for the road.

From here it is nearly 57 miles almost due north through verdant cattle and cotton country to your ultimate destination, **Turkey**. Pause in towns such as **Roaring Springs** in Motley County for smatterings of tiny shops that will never attract the attention of Wal-Mart.

Turkey

POP 380

The lovely lady in city hall told us that 'people are dying too quick.' And indeed, like the flight path of its namesake bird, Turkey has been descending for decades. But amid the grizzled streets is a not-to-be-missed cultural attraction.

'As heaven would miss the stars above. With every heartbeat I still think of you,' sang Bob Wills in his iconic song 'Faded Love.' One of the most important Texas musicians, his life is recalled at the **Bob Wills Museum** (☎806-423-1146; www.turkeytexas.net; ⏰9-11:30am & 1-4:30pm Mon-Fri, 9am-noon Sat) FREE. Located in the old elementary school (which also has the tiny city hall and library), the recently redone displays cover much of Wills' adventurous life, which included a string of B-movie Westerns. But it's the music that survives. Wills was a major creator of a genre of music known as Western Swing, described by David Vinopal in the *All-Music Guide* like this:

Take fiddle-based old-time string-band music from the '20s and '30s, move it to a city such as Tulsa or Fort Worth, add jazz and blues and pop and sacred music, back it with strings and horns played by a dozen or so musicians, add an electric steel guitar along the way, and you have Western swing; and when you talk Western swing, you start with Bob Wills.

Wills reached his greatest fame in the 1940s with his band the Texas Playboys, with whom he recorded such hits as 'San Antonio Rose' and 'Faded Love.'

The museum includes lots of artifacts from the musician's life, including his fiddles, scrapbooks, movie posters and a gazillion photos. In the halls outside are haunting class photos from the adjoining high school, which closed in 1972. They tell stories of a time when the future of Turkey looked much different.

Turkey celebrates Wills' legacy with **Bob Wills Days** (www.bobwillsday.com; late April), when 10,000 or more people stuff themselves into Turkey for a weekend of pickin' and grinnin', with jam sessions galore. Many well-known musicians appear and jam.

Quitaque

POP 410

Quitaque has been a rival of Turkey's for decades; the latter never forgave the former for getting the town's combined schools in the 1970s. But this small town isn't doing much better than Turkey, although the beauty of Caprock Canyons brings a steady stream of travelers.

Quitaque's website (www.quitaque.org) lists guesthouses in the area, but many people choose to camp in the Caprock Canyons State Park.

It doesn't look like much, but then again you don't have much choice, so fortunately the **Caprock Cafe** (806-455-1429; 201 Main; mains $6-12; 6am-8pm Mon-Wed, to 9pm Thu-Sat) scores with excellent small-town fare. Lunch buffets are big, with a different special each day (chicken one day, catfish the next). Otherwise it also offers breakfasts and burgers. It's very popular with Caprock Canyons campers fed up with campfire meals.

Caprock Canyons State Park

Although it's not as well known as Palo Duro Canyon State Park, **Caprock Canyons** (806-455-1492; www.tpwd.state.tx.us; Quitaque; adult/child $4/free, campsites $10-20) shares the same kind of stunning topography and abundant wildlife. Even the casual visitor is likely to see mule deer, roadrunners and aoudad, the North African barbary sheep transplanted to the Panhandle in the 1950s. The sunsets are stupendous, but the trail system here is what makes Caprock Canyons one of Texas' best state parks: 90 miles of outstanding and diverse hiking, mountain biking and horseback riding, including 26 miles in the park proper and another 64 miles on the Trailways System, a rails-to-trails project. Many visitors are just content to drop a line in the serene waters of little Lake Theo.

The park is home to a donated bison herd from the JA Ranch – the very herd started by pioneer rancher Charles Goodnight in 1876.

Sights & Activities

Caprock Canyons Trailways HIKING

Running through three counties from Estelline to the northeast to South Plains to the southwest, the 64-mile abandoned-railroad-bed Trailways opened in 1993. Highlights include some 50 bridges and the 742ft Clarity Tunnel, a historic railroad passage. It's popular with hikers, bikers and riders. The route runs across the fertile plains and drops into the appropriately named Red River Valley.

Trail access points and parking lots can be found along TX 86 at Estelline, Parnell, Tampico Siding, Turkey and Quitaque. On this section, the trail runs parallel to, but a good distance from, the highway. At Quitaque, the trail swings south then west for the final 23 miles to South Plains – the portion that includes the tunnel. Access points on this part of the trail are at Monk's Crossing and South Plains.

Caprock Canyons State Park Trails HIKING

The state park has some outstanding trails. Stop at the park visitor center for a map showing trailheads and distances. For an easy trail of about 2.5 miles round-trip, follow the hikers-only Upper Canyon Trail from the South Prong tent camping area trailhead to the South Prong primitive camping area and back. Beyond the primitive camping area, the Upper Canyon Trail becomes increasingly steep and rugged; the cliffs and bluffs are not for the foolhardy. It won't be hard to imagine what it was like for the Comanche people in their final days on the run from the US Army here in the early 1870s.

Sleeping

Primitive campsites ($10) are available along the Trailways and in the more remote reaches of the park; get a permit from the state park before setting out. The park also has more developed campgrounds. **Walk-in campsites** ($12) are the most atmospheric.

Honey Flat (per site $15-20) is the park's most developed camping area, with 35 sites with water and electricity. It's an easy walk to Lake Theo.

Other options are few: most motels are along I-27 in Tulia, Canyon and Amarillo.

Information

Day users can pay their fees at the self-pay station at each trailhead. Trail users should carry drinking water; in summer it gets hot as blazes and unwise hikers regularly get ill from dehydration.

At the park's **Visitor Center** (9am-5pm) you can rent an audio tour for use with a vehicle or possibly arrange for a trail bike.

Getting There & Away

To get here, take well-marked FM 1065 from Quitaque 3 miles to the Visitor Center.

Cyclists and hikers can use the services of **Caprock Home Center** (806-455-1193; www.caprockhomecenter.com; 126 W Main St, Quitaque; 8am-5pm Mon-Fri, to noon Sat), where the owner, Roland Hamilton, can arrange shuttles to/from various parts of the Trailways as well as provide supplies.

Palo Duro Canyon

The pancake-flat Texas plains have some real texture at Palo Duro Canyon, it's just that all the drama is below the horizon rather than above it. The meandering gorge is a place of brilliant colors and vibrant life (the name means 'hard wood', for the groves of mesquite). The nearby town of Canyon, 20 miles south of Amarillo, makes for a comfy base.

Getting to Canyon (and the actual canyon) is easiest by car.

Canyon

POP 13,600

Small yet cultured, Canyon is in many ways more interesting than Amarillo to the north. Georgia O'Keeffe once taught art at what is now west Texas A&M University, and today's campus is home to what many people figure is the best history museum in Texas – the Panhandle-Plains Historical Museum. Moreover, this is an ideal starting spot for Palo Duro Canyon State Park, one of the state's natural showpieces.

Sights

★Panhandle-Plains Historical Museum MUSEUM
(806-651-2244; www.panhandleplains.org; 2401 4th Ave; adult/child $10/5; 9am-6pm Mon-Sat Jun-Aug, to 5pm Sep-May) The many ways to skin a buffalo is but one of the myriad highlights of this magnificent museum, a Texas plains must-see. You can hit the highlights in an hour or easily lose a day.

Collections and displays include the Panhandle's oil heyday as seen through the prism of the boomtown of Borger and an old-time filling station; life-size casts of dinosaurs; the oldest assembly-line auto in the world (a 1903 Ford); world-class art from Texas painters and photographers; and the role of the buffalo in the rich cultures of Native Americans.

Sleeping

The drive south from Amarillo can be a chore at busy times, so it's better to stay in Canyon for a visit to the park. Campers should head straight to the park.

Buffalo Inn MOTEL $
(806-655-2124, 800-526-9968; www.buffaloinncanyontx.com; 300 23rd St/US 87; r $40-75;) This classic 1950s single-story motor court is centrally located by the west Texas A&M campus. It's snappily maintained and has the charm lacking in new chains.

Best Western Palo Duro Canyon MOTEL $$
(806-655-1132; www.bestwestern.com; 2801 4th Ave; r $70-180;) As tidy inside as the white paint is outside, this recently built 51-unit motel lacks any regional charm but is convenient to the canyon and I-27. The pool, alas, is indoors away from the balmy Texas air.

Eating

Canyon has good eats, but choices in the canyon itself are basic.

Ranch House Cafe AMERICAN $
(806-655-8785; 810 23rd St; mains from $6; 7am-9pm) Look for the classic trapezoidal red sign along the old US 87 strip. Chicken-fried steak and chicken-fried chicken(!) lead the long list of diner specials. Ponder the posies on the spare yellow exterior and then enter a kingdom of fresh north Texas chow.

SCENIC DRIVE: TEXAS 207 HIGHWAY

Many Panhandle locals say the best views of Palo Duro Canyon aren't in the park but along TX 207 between Claude and Silverton in the south. This quiet 48-mile stretch enters the canyon lands about 13 miles south of Claude (where the 1963 Paul Newman classic *Hud* was filmed). Some of the most dramatic scenery is at the crossings of the Prairie Dog Town Fork of the Red River and Tule Creek. From Silverton both Turkey and Caprock Canyons are short drives.

Feldman's Wrong Way Diner AMERICAN $
(☎806-655-2700; www.feldmansdiner.com; 1701 5th Ave; mains from $7; ⏲11am-9pm; 👪) As the menu says, this classy diner is dedicated to anyone who has made a wrong turn, wrong decision or wandered off the beaten path. Here, at least, you'll know you've done the right thing. Steaks, chicken and burgers star and are supported by a cast of sides including perfect okra and lovely broccoli. Lots of salads too.

Look for the windsock on the roof.

Palo Duro Canyon State Park

At 120 miles long and about 5 miles wide, Palo Duro Canyon is second in size in the USA only to the Grand Canyon. The cliffs striated in yellows, reds and oranges, rock towers and other geologic oddities are a refreshing surprise among the seemingly endless flatness of the plains, and are worth at least a gander.

The multihued canyon was created by the Prairie Dog Town Fork of the Red River, a long name for a little river. The great gorge has sheltered and inspired people for a long time. Prehistoric Indians lived in the canyon 12,000 years ago, and Coronado may have stopped by in 1541. Palo Duro was the site of an 1874 battle between Comanche and Kiowa warriors and the US Army. The over 26,000 acres that make up the **park** (☎806-488-2227; www.tpwd.state.tx.us; 11450 Park Road 5; adult/child $5/free; ⏲main gate 6am-8pm Mon-Thu, to 10pm Fri & Sat, shorter hours in winter) attract hikers, horseback riders and mountain bikers eager for recreation, and artists and photographers drawn by the magnificent blend of color and desert light.

Activities

There are plenty of great mountain-biking trails throughout the canyon, but nowhere to rent bikes.

Lighthouse Trail HIKING
Palo Duro's most popular hiking trail leads to the Lighthouse, a hoodoo-style formation that's nearly 300ft tall. Almost all of the nearly 6-mile round-trip is flat and easily traversed. The floodplain to the southwest of the trail has perhaps the park's greatest concentration of wildlife, including aoudad sheep, white-tailed mule deer and wild turkeys.

Old West Stables HORSEBACK RIDING
(☎806-488-2180; www.oldweststables.com; 11450 Park Road 5; rides from $35; ⏲Mar-Nov) Offers a variety of trips in Palo Duro Canyon.

Sleeping & Eating

For motels and restaurants, you'll need to be in Canyon or Amarillo.

Campsites CAMPING $
(sites $12-24) Range from attractive and remote campsites aimed at backpackers, to regular sites with full hookups.

Cabins CABINS $
(☎512-389-8900; per night $60-125) These are a treat but there are only seven, so reserve ahead.

Trading Post MARKET, CAFE $
(☎806-488-2821; www.palodurotradingpost.us; 11450 Park Road 5; mains from $7; ⏲8:30am-7:30pm Mon-Sat, 11am-7pm Sun Mar-Nov) Has supplies and burgers.

Entertainment

Texas THEATER
(☎806-655-2181; www.texas-show.com; 11450 Park Road 5; tickets $12-30, meal adult/child $14/7; ⏲8:30pm Tue-Sun early Jun–mid-Aug) Hokey, jingoistic, over-the-top, effervescent and loud are just some of the adjectives for this open-air musical show in the natural beauty of the park's Pioneer Amphitheatre. From 6pm on show nights, it offers an extra-cost dinner catered by Amarillo's Big Texan Steak Ranch.

Information

A small but pretty 1934 Visitors Center overlooks the canyon, has interpretive exhibits on the area's geology and history, the region's best bookstore and good tourist info.

The best time to visit is in the fall or winter because it gets dang hot here in the summertime (carry lots of water!).

Getting There & Away

The park is at the end of TX 217, 12 miles east of Canyon and 24 miles southeast of Amarillo.

Amarillo

POP 193,700

Long an unavoidable stop, roughly halfway between Chicago and LA on old Route 66, Amarillo continues to figure in travel plans, simply by being the brightest light on the 543-mile stretch of I-40 between Oklahoma City, OK, and Albuquerque, NM.

And though the town may seem as featureless as the surrounding landscape, there's plenty here to sate even the most attention-challenged during a road respite. Beef, the big local industry, is at the heart of Amarillo and it features in many of its attractions, including a starring role at the Big Texan Steak Ranch.

Like a good steak, Amarillo is marbled – with railroad tracks. Running south of town, I-40 is especially charmless. Instead, follow SE 3rd Ave from the east through the comatose center and decaying west side to SW 6th Ave. Locally dubbed the San Jacinto District, the strip between Georgia St and Western St was once part of Route 66 and is Amarillo's best shopping, dining and entertainment district.

Sights

Cadillac Ranch MONUMENT

(I-40, btwn exits 60 & 62) To millions of people whizzing across the Texas Panhandle each year, the Cadillac Ranch, also known as Amarillo's 'Bumper Crop,' is the ultimate symbol of the US love affair with wheels. A salute to Route 66 and the spirit of the American road, it was created by burying, hood first, 10 west-facing Cadillacs in a wheat field outside town.

In 1974 controversial Amarillo businessperson and arts patron Stanley Marsh funded the San Francisco–based Ant Farm collective's 'monument to the rise and fall of the Cadillac tail fin.' The cars date from 1948 to 1959 – a period in which tail fins just kept getting bigger and bigger – on to 1963, when the fin vanished. Marsh relocated the cars in 1997 to a field 2 miles west of its original location due to suburban sprawl (which is again encroaching on this location).

The cars are easily spotted off the access road on the south side of I-40. The accepted practice today is to leave your own mark on the art by drawing on the disintegrating cars, which gives them an ever-changing patina. Bring spray paint in case other visitors haven't left any around.

Wonderland Amusement Park AMUSEMENT PARK

(☎806-383-3344; www.wonderlandpark.com; 2601 Dumas Dr, off US 87 north of the centre; admission $14-25; ⏲Apr-Aug; 👪) If plowing along sedately for hours on the bland interstate has you ready for a little more excitement, then careening through the double loops of this park's Texas Tornado roller coaster should shake you out of your lethargy. A fun local amusement park (ignoring the hideous garden gnome mascot), Wonderland has thrill rides, family rides and a water park. Check the online calendar for opening days and hours.

★ **Amarillo Livestock Auction** SPECTACLE

(☎806-373-7464; www.amarillolivestockauction.com; 100 S Manhattan St; ⏲10am Mon) A slice of the real West is on display every Tuesday morning at the Amarillo Livestock Auction, just north of SE 3rd Ave on the city's east side. The auction is still one of the state's largest, moving more than 100,000 animals annually (down from its 1970s peak of 715,000).

Once the auction starts up things happen very quickly: cattle are herded in through one pneumatic gate and out through another, and most animals sell within about 30 seconds. The auctions draw few tourists,

RV MUSEUM

Long before today's posh gas guzzling Recreational Vehicles (RVs) hit the road, laden with every convenience right down to the satellite dish, intrepid Americans looking for adventure had much simpler vehicles. This **museum** (☎806-358-4891; www.rvmuseum.net; 4341 Canyon Dr, off I-27 south of town; admission free; ⏲9am-5pm Mon-Sat) has trailers and RVs from the 1930s to the 1970s, a time when entertainment meant watching Dad hit his head on the pint-sized door frame.

Amarillo

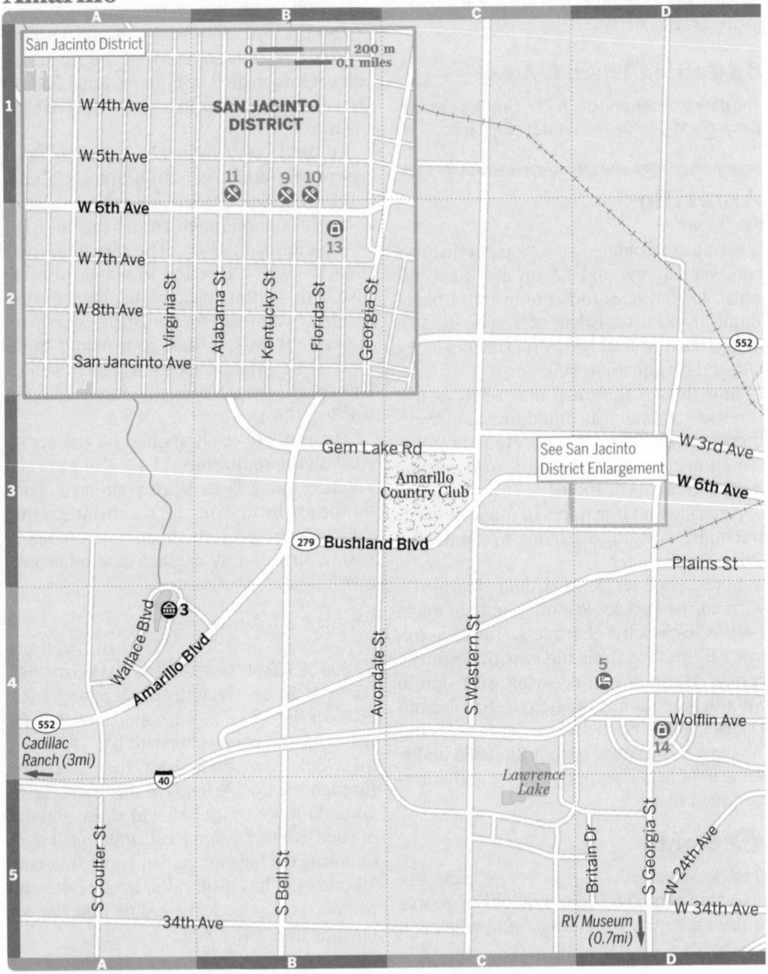

Amarillo

Top Sights

1 Amarillo Livestock Auction G3
2 American Quarter Horse Hall of Fame & Museum G4

Sights

3 Don Harrington Discovery Center A4
4 Wonderland Amusement Park F1

Sleeping

5 Ambassador Hotel D4
6 Hampton Inn F4
7 Microtel Inn & Suites G4
8 Parkview House E4

Eating

9 806 .... B1
10 Cowboy Gelato B1
11 Golden Light Cafe & Cantina B1
12 Stockyard Cafe G3

Shopping

13 6th Street Antique Mall B2
14 Boots 'n Jeans D4

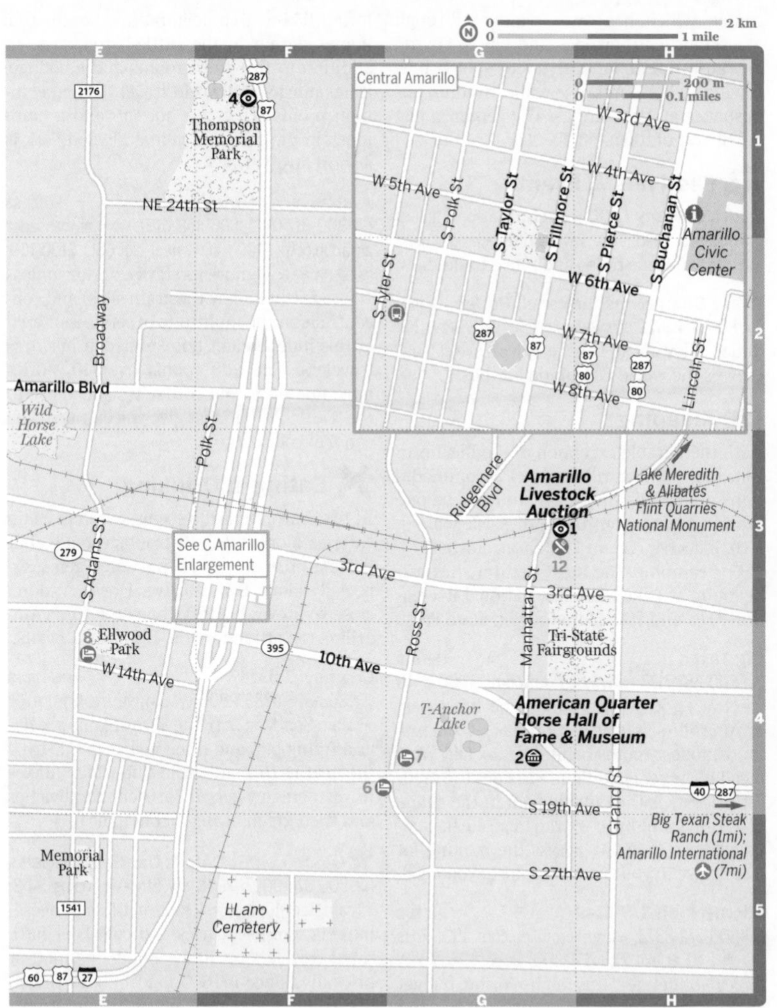

but all are welcome. Grab lunch at the Stockyard Cafe.

★ American Quarter Horse Hall of Fame & Museum MUSEUM
(☎806-376-5181; www.aqha.com; 2601 I-40 E exit 72A; adult/child $6/2; ⊙9am-5pm Mon-Sat) Quarter horses, favored on the Texas range, were originally named for their prowess at galloping down early American racetracks, which were a quarter-mile long. These beautiful animals are celebrated at this visually striking museum, which fully explores their roles in ranching and racing.

Don Harrington Discovery Center MUSEUM
(☎806-355-9547; www.dhdc.org; 1200 Streit Dr; adult/child $10/7; ⊙9:30am-4:30pm Tue-Sat, from noon Sun; 👪) Sadly you can't inhale any helium and talk like Donald Duck, but the lighter-than-air gas that was an Amarillo industry is honored at the Don Harrington Discovery Center. Aquariums, a planetarium and science exhibits (including a good one on birds of prey) round out a visit.

Wildcat Bluff Nature Center NATURE RESERVE
(☎806-352-6007; www.wildcatbluff.org; 2301 N Soncy Rd; adult/child $7/2; ⊙dawn-dusk) Stretch those road legs at this 600-acre nature

center, which has trails winding through grasslands, cottonwoods and bluffs. Spy on a prairie dog town and try to spot a burrowing owl or porcupine while avoiding rattlesnakes and tarantulas. The center is just northwest of town, off TX 335.

Festivals & Events

Coors Cowboy Club Ranch Rodeo RODEO
(806-378-3096; www.coorsranchrodeo.com; early Jun) Huge rodeo and ranch trade show.

World Championship Ranch Rodeo RODEO
(806-374-9722; www.wrca.org; early Nov) No dudes allowed at this real-deal event that crowns the world-champion cowboy.

Sleeping

With the notable exception of the Big Texan Inn, most of Amarillo's motel accommodations are chains (in fact there can't be one brand missing from the endless slew along I-40. Exits 64, 65 and 71 all have clusters.

For camping, the most natural sites can be found at Lake Meredith National Recreation Area and Palo Duro Canyon State Park.

Big Texan Inn MOTEL $
(800-657-7177; www.bigtexan.com; 7700 I-40 E exit 74; r $50-90;) The hotel part of Amarillo's star attraction has 54 surprisingly modest rooms behind a faux Old West facade. The real highlight – besides the modest prices – is the outside pool in the shape of Texas. Should you try the huge steak challenge, even crawling across the parking lot to collapse in your room may be beyond you.

Microtel Inn & Suites MOTEL $
(806-372-8373; www.microtelinn.com; 1501 Ross St, off I-40 at exit 71; r $70-100; @) A typical outlet for this high-scoring budget chain. Rooms are spread over two stories and have interior hallways. 'Suites' are really just larger rooms, but for a small rate increase (often just $10) you get a room that sleeps four easily plus has a fridge and microwave.

Hampton Inn MOTEL $$
(806-372-1425; www.hamptoninn.com; 1700 nI-40 E, east of exit 71 on south side; r $80-140;) A standard outlet of the always comfortable and reliable midrange chain. There are 116 rooms in a two-story building. Guests enjoy a full breakfast.

Parkview House B&B $$
(806-373-9464; www.parkviewhousebb.com; 1311 S Jefferson St; r $85-135;) This old Victorian B&B is in a neighborhood of historic homes dating to the cattle-baron days. In addition to five guest rooms and a cottage, it has music- and world-travel themed common rooms. There's a hot tub and a hammock in the yard and genial Elwood Park is a short stroll away.

Ambassador Hotel HOTEL $$
(800-817-0521, 806-358-6161; www.ambassadoramarillo.com; 3100 I-40 W near exit 68; r $100-160; @) Ignore its stark exterior (unless you're fascinated by the grain silos) and concentrate on the multitude of services offered at this independent hotel aimed at business travelers. The 263 rooms over 10 stories have numerous plush touches and those in the 'Cattle Baron' class give you extras so you can feel your oats.

Eating & Drinking

At first burp, Amarillo seems awash in chain eateries along the I-40 frontage roads, but delve a little deeper to find some gems, especially along SW 6th Ave. However, don't close your eyes to everything on I-40, as Amarillo's top attraction, the Big Texan, awaits.

Cowboy Gelato AMERICAN $
(806-376-5286; 2806 SW 6th Ave; treats from $2; 11am-8pm Mon-Sat) The Texas plains are flat as a frying pan and often just as hot. Escape the heat in this cute little cafe which makes its own creamy gelati. Barbecue sandwiches and fried green beans fill out a meal.

★**Golden Light Cafe & Cantina** BURGERS $
(806-374-0097; 2908 SW 6th Ave; mains $4-8; cafe 11am-10pm, bar 4pm-2am) Classic cheeseburgers, home-cut fries and cold beer have sated travelers on Route 66 at this modest brick dive since 1946. On most nights there's live country and rock music in the atmospherically sweaty cantina next door.

806 CAFE $
(806-322-1806; www.the806.com; 2812 SW 6th Ave; mains from $5; 8am-midnight;) Wobbling, mismatched chairs define the funky vibe at this coffeehouse, where local hipsters ponder moving to New York. Beer in bottles plus lots of tasty, healthy snacks such as chili and hummus provide fuel for thought. It has live acoustic music some nights.

Stockyard Cafe AMERICAN $
(806-374-6024; 100 S Manhattan St; mains $5-15; 9am-2pm Mon-Thu, to 8pm Fri) This cafe in the Amarillo Livestock Auction building is

where the cattlemen sit down for some beef. The steaks are ideal – thick and perfectly charred – but most have the plate-swamping chicken-fried steak. Follow your nose here, past corrals and railroad tracks.

★**Big Texan Steak Ranch** STEAKHOUSE **$$**
(www.bigtexan.com; 7701 I-40 E, exit 74; mains $10-40; ⏲7am-10:30pm; 👪) A classic, hokey Route 66 roadside attraction, the Big Texan made the move when I-40 opened in 1971 and has never looked back. Stretch-Cadillac limos with steer-horn hood ornaments offer free shuttles to and from area motels, marquee lights blink above, a shooting arcade pings inside the saloon, and a big, tall Tex road sign welcomes you (after taunting billboards for miles in either direction).

The legendary come-on: the 'free 72oz steak,' a devilish offer as you have to eat this enormous portion of cow plus a multitude of sides in under one hour, or you pay for the entire meal ($72). Contestants sit at a raised table to 'entertain' the other diners and you can watch anytime via a live webcam (we watched one beefy guy who started out all cocky but by the 45-minute mark was less than half done and staring glumly at the door).

Less than 20% pass the challenge, although one lunatic wolfed it all down in 8 minutes 52 seconds in 2008. Insane eating aside, the ranch is a fine place to eat, the steaks are excellent – and still huge – and we had a very fine prime rib. Adding to the fun are strolling cowboy troubadours, a beer garden with 11 superb house-brewed beers, a buzzing bar and the willfully schticky vibe. In a word, it's a hoot!

ROUTE 66: GET YOUR KICKS IN TEXAS

The Mother Road arrows across Texas for a mere 178 miles. The entire route has been replaced by I-40, but through frontage and access roads plus detours through towns such as Amarillo, you can re-create most of the old route.

Given the featureless landscape, one can only imagine the road ennui suffered by scores of travelers as they motored past the brown expanses. As always, there were plenty of entrepreneurs ready to offer diversions for a buck or two. Going east to west, here's some Route 66 highlights in Texas.

Follow old Route 66 which runs immediately south of I-40 from the Oklahoma border through barely changed towns such as **Shamrock**, with its restored 1930s buildings.

About 33 miles from the border, cross I-40 to the north side and the battered town of **McClean**. There, the **Devil's Rope Museum** (www.barbwiremuseum.com; 100 Kingsley St; ⏲9am-5pm Mon-Fri, 10am-4pm Sat Apr-Nov) FREE has vast barbed-wire displays (where hipsters look for new tattoo patterns) and a small but homey and idiosyncratic room devoted to Route 66. The detailed map of the road in Texas is a must. Also worth a look are the moving portraits of Dust Bowl damage and the refugees from human-made environmental disaster.

You'll have to join I-40 at exit 132, but just west of here on both sides of the freeway are Route 66–themed rest stops.

The next sights will appear on the horizon long before the hamlet of **Groom** and Exit 113 appear in your windshield: the famous **Leaning Water Tower** and (one of) the **World's Tallest Cross**. The former was an eye-catching gimmick by a long-gone gas station; the latter tops out at 190 ft.

At exit 78 leave I-40, which runs just south of Amarillo, and follow SE 3rd Ave and SW 6th Ave through town. Here you'll find a plethora of Route 66 sites: the Big Texan Steak Ranch (p203), the historic livestock auction and the San Jacinto District, which still has original Route 66 businesses such as the Golden Light Cafe (p202).

Just west of Amarillo after exit 62, look for the Cadillac Ranch (p199), where 10 road veterans have met a colorful end.

Use the old highway north of I-40 or exit 36 to reach **Vega**, an old road town that seems little changed in decades, but which still has some decent cafes. Some 14 miles west, **Adrian** clings to fame as the purported historic Route 66 midpoint, with LA and Chicago each 1139 miles distant.

Just at the New Mexico border, tiny **Glenrio** makes the moniker 'ghost town' seem lively.

Shopping

The stretch of SW 6th Ave west of Georgia St has numerous antique and junk shops that recall the old Route 66 beat.

6th Street Antique Mall ANTIQUES
(☎806-374-0459; 2715 SW 6th Ave; ⏲10am-6pm Mon-Sat) Anchors a strip of antique stores.

Boots 'n Jeans WESTERN WEAR
(☎806-353-4368; 2225 S. Georgia St; ⏲9am-6pm Mon-Sat, 11am-6pm Sun) A one-store-only local legend (although it is now owned by retail giant Sheplers), Boots 'n Jeans leaves little about its inventory to the imagination. Some Panhandle locals will only shop here.

Information

The *Amarillo Independent* is a frisky free weekly with full local event info and an alternative viewpoint.

Amarillo Convention and Visitor Council (☎806-374-1497, 800-692-1338; www.visitamarillotx.com; Amarillo Civic Center, 401 S Buchanan St; ⏲9am-5pm Mon-Fri, noon-4pm Sat Sep-May, 9am-5pm Mon-Fri, 10am-4pm Sat & Sun Jun-Aug) The staff will be mighty glad you stopped.

Texas Travel Information Center (☎806-335-1441; 9700 E I-40 exit 76; ⏲8am-5pm, to 6pm summer; wi-fi) Excellent resource, with vast amounts of info.

Getting There & Around

Rick Husband Amarillo International Airport (AMA; ☎806-335-1671; http://airport.amarillo.gov) is located on the eastern edge of town north of I-40 via exit 76. It's served by American Eagle (Dallas–Fort Worth), Continental (Houston) and Southwest (Dallas and Denver).

Greyhound (☎806-374-5371; www.greyhound.com; 700 S Tyler St) runs buses east and west on I-40 plus to major cities in Texas such as Dallas ($92, seven hours).

Around Amarillo

The best sights near Amarillo are Palo Duro Canyon and the little towns along Route 66. But you can also find some natural escapes to the north.

Sights & Activities

Lake Meredith National Recreation Area PARK
(☎806-857-3151; www.nps.gov/lamr; off TX 136; ⏲24hr) FREE Some 35 miles northeast of Amarillo, this recreation area is a result of the Sanford Dam water project on the Canadian River. It's a popular spot for boating and fishing.

Boat rentals are available at marinas in Meredith. **Shep Brown's Boat Basin** (☎603-279-4573; www.shepbrowns.com; 31 Lovejoy Sands Rd; boats from $225 per half day; ⏲9am-5pm) has a variety of boats for rent.

For fishing, Lake Meredith is home to large-mouth, small-mouth and white bass, catfish, white crappie, sunfish, carp and walleye.

Camping at Lake Meredith is free, mainly because amenities are limited: it offers no reservations, hookups or showers, but it does have picnic tables, grills and pit toilets. Sites include spots overlooking the reservoir and more remote locations back in the canyons.

Alibates Flint Quarries PARK
(☎806-857-3151, 806-857-6680; www.nps.gov/alfl; Cas Johnson Rd, off TX 136; ⏲Contact Station 8am-4.30pm) FREE It's not every day you can pick up a hammer stone used to make tools 10,000 years ago or hold discarded shards of beautifully colored flint left behind by ancient peoples. But at Alibates Flint Quarries visitors can touch the past and learn what it was like to live off the land when mammoths roamed the plains.

Tours, which are the main way to visit, involve 1.5 miles of walking. You must call to reserve these trips in advance. Otherwise there is a short self-guided walk you can do.

Canadian

POP 2800

Named for the local river, Canadian has few links with the cheery country far to the north (although with locally popular Coors being owned by Molsen, you could say the convenience stores are filled with Canadian beer). Rather, it is a once-dying Texas plains town (one of dozens) that, thanks to the leadership of the local Abraham family, has uniquely saved itself by embracing tourism.

Main St – often a place to watch out for falling bricks in other small Texas towns – has been much-restored; stores, cafes and a beautifully renovated movie theater are among the highlights.

There's also an excellent museum, the **River Valley Pioneer Museum** (☎806-323-6548; 118 N 2nd St; admission free; ⏲9am-4pm Tue-Fri, 1-3pm Sat) and an art gallery, the **Citadelle** (www.thecitadelle.org; 520 Nelson Ave;

adult/child $10/free; ⌚11am-4pm Thu-Sat, 1-4pm Sun), housed in a 1910 mansion.

Outside of town, a series of nature trails wander through the fertile countryside. In spring people come from all over to see the rather comical mating habits of the prairie chicken – antics worthy of an *Animal Planet* special.

Canadian is 100 miles northeast of Amarillo on US 60/83.

Sleeping & Eating

Canadian Inn MOTEL $
(☎806-323-6402; www.thecanadianinn.com; 502 N 2nd St; r $40-70;) Rest yourself from the excitement of prairie-chicken mating at this restored motor court. The 29 rooms are basic but clean and have fridges and microwaves.

City Drug CAFE $
(☎806-323-6099; 224 Main St; mains $6; ⌚9am-5pm Mon-Fri, 1-3pm Sat) Located in an old drugstore, the soda fountain lends scoopfuls of charm to this excellent cafe. The coffee is the best for miles, as are the baked goods such as the chocolate cream pie. It has a small and changing lunch menu each day.

Information

Canadian Visitors' Center (☎806-323-6234; www.canadiantx.org; 119 N 2nd St; ⌚9am-5pm Mon-Fri) Has maps for driving tours, walking tours of the historic downtown and hikes in the region. Look for the excellent visitor's guide online or pick one up outside the office after hours.

Houston & East Texas

Includes ➡

Best Places to Eat

- ➡ Oxheart (p224)
- ➡ Haven (p226)
- ➡ Royers Café (p238)
- ➡ Larry's French Market & Cajun Kitchen (p253)

Best Museums

- ➡ NASA Space Center Houston (p234)
- ➡ Houston Museum of Natural Science (p211)
- ➡ Menil Collection (p211)
- ➡ Museum of Fine Arts Houston (p214)

Why Go?

More down-home than Dallas, more buttoned-up than Austin: Houston has money and culture, but wears them like a good ol' country boy come to town. What's that mean? Award-winning, chef-run restaurants where ties are rarely required. Attending world-class museum exhibits followed by cheap beer at patio bars. Enclaves of attraction spread all across the state's largest – and widest – city.

When you get sick of the concrete maze of interstates, it's easy to escape. Within day-tripping distance, Galveston calls to beach lovers and Washington County entices antique-hunters. Further afield, Northeast Texas *is* the Piney Woods, with towering forests, winding roads, natural attractions and Southern belle historic towns. To the east, Beaumont and the Golden Triangle may be a little oil-and-gas industrial, but the Cajun influence there has appeal. Come for the city, stay for the country; Houston & east Texas has both.

When to Go

Houston

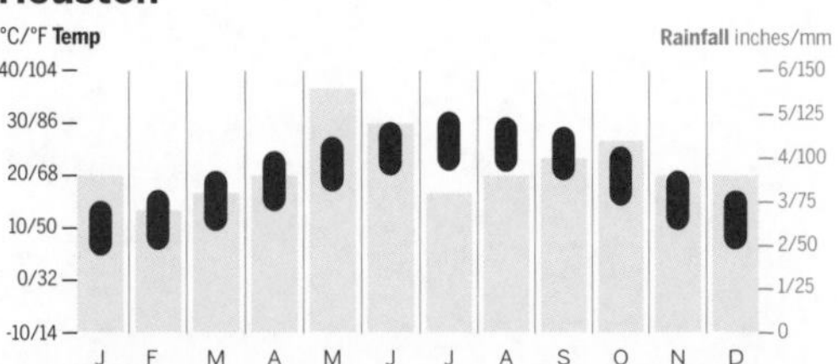

Mar–Apr Azaleas and bluebonnets in bloom; not-too-hot weather with lower humidity.

Oct Temperatures crawl down from summer highs; it's small-town festival time.

Dec Towns go all out for Christmas with light shows, festivals, even outdoor ice-skating.

Advance Planning

Generally speaking, Houston and East Texas do not require a lot of advance planning. The exception is if you are staying anywhere during Texas' spring break, which covers the entire month of March; then you should book as far in advance as possible. In Houston, make reservations in top-end ($$$) restaurants at least a week ahead; for Oxheart you should book more than a month before. Boat and other tours should be reserved at least two days before departure.

TRANSPORTATION

You gotta love your car in East Texas, otherwise you'll never get anywhere. Other than the light rail corridor on Main St in Houston, public transportation is all but useless – if it exists at all. Inside downtown Houston, parking is plentiful, but you'll have to pay. Everywhere else in the region parking is abundant, and mostly free. Gas prices are generally higher in small towns, so fuel up before you hit the road.

Off the Beaten Path

- National Museum of Funeral History (p215) See a crab-shaped coffin and learn a new embalming technique.
- Beer Can House (p211) An estimated 50,000 flattened cans cover this, um, artistic home.
- Art Car Parade (p221) No, you're not hallucinating, it's an 8ft papier-mâché rabbit rolling down the road.
- Big Thicket National Preserve (p252) Hike among the towering pines and swampy cypress... Yes, there are trees in Texas.
- Discovery Green's Ice Skating Rink (p210) No, December is not really freezing in Houston, but that doesn't stop locals from having an outdoor ice rink.

FIRST TIMERS

From June through September, Houston and east Texas are hot and humid; drink plenty of water. If you plan to spend time in the outdoors, be prepared with sunscreen and mosquito repellent.

Fast Facts

- **Houston metropolitan population** 6.22 million
- **Upper East Texas population** 117,000
- **Beaumont & Golden Triangle population** 388,745
- **Washington County population** 34,093
- **Houston area** 656 sq miles

For Kids

- Discovery Green (p210)
- Children's Museum of Houston (p222)
- Kemah Boardwalk (p235)
- Stewart Beach (p243)
- Gator Country (p251)

Resources

- **Houston Tourist Board** (www.visithoustontexas.com)
- **Washington County Chamber** (www.visitbrenhamtexas.com)
- **Texas Forest Trails Region** (http://texasfortstrail.com)
- **Galveston** (www.galveston.com)

Houston & East Texas Highlights

1 Kicking back on a shady patio, drink at hand, in an atmospheric neighborhood like **the Heights** (p226) in Houston.

2 Touring a historic mansion, then lazing on the beach in **Galveston** (p241).

3 Eating ice cream from the source at Brenham's **Blue Bell Creameries** (p237).

4 Ghost hunting in the former riverboat town of **Jefferson** (p258).

5 Eating fried shrimp and watching the sailboats go by from the deck at Seabrook's **Outriggers Seafood Grill & Bar** (p235).

6 Boating among the mysterious cypress trees on the

labyrinthine **Caddo Lake** (p260).

7 Browsing, and maybe buying, at a ginormous antiques fair in **Round Top** (p238).

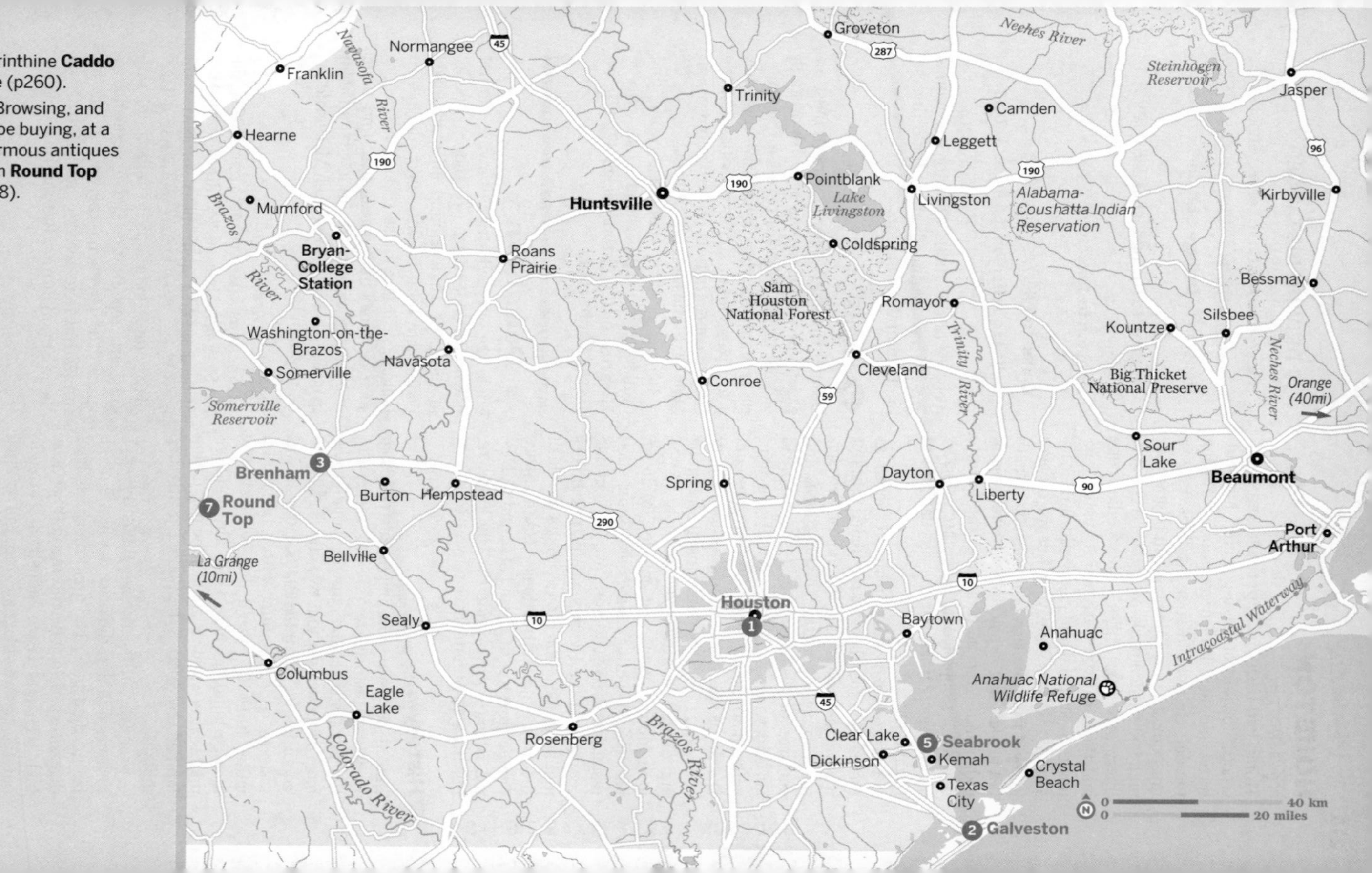

HOUSTON

POP 2.14 MILLION

Think laid-back, pickup truck and boot-scootin' town meets high-powered, high-cultured and high-heeled metropolis. During the day, chill out in your flip-flops, take in museums and shopping, and hit happy hour on a leaf-shaded deck. At night, revel in culinary or cultural bliss – the foodie scene and theater district are both nationally renowned. Sure, oil-and-gas wealth underlies a lot of the city's endeavors, but you'd never know it from the lack of pretension. What's not to like about a place where a weeks-long rodeo and barbecue cook-off is the favorite reason for stepping out? Here starched jeans are *de rigeur* in all but the very fanciest of restaurants.

Houston may rank behind Chicago as the nation's fourth most populated city, but it covers a greater area than all of New Jersey. Diverse residential neighborhoods and enclaves of restaurants and shops spread far and wide. You'll miss out if you limit yourself to Downtown. The leafy Museum District is the city's cultural center; Upper Kirby and River Oaks have upscale shopping and dining; Montrose contains cute bungalows, quirky shops and eateries; Midtown has up-and-coming condos and some good restaurants; Washington Ave is nightlife central and the Heights has historic homes and boutiques. Don't forget that a couple of the town's main attractions – NASA's Space Center Houston in Clear Lake, and Galveston Island – are outside the city limits, requiring a 45-minute drive down I-45.

DRIVING DISTANCES

Houston to Austin 161 miles, 3 hours

Houston to Dallas 242 miles, 4 hours

Houston to College Station 98 miles, 1¾ hours

Houston to Nacogdoches 145 miles, 2¾ hours

Houston to Jefferson 242 miles, 4¼ hours

Dallas to Tyler 98 miles 1½ hours

Dallas to Jefferson 164 miles, 3 hours

History

Indeed the two most important words in Houston's history are 'oil' and 'cattle.' But the city's spectacular growth would never have happened without two others: 'air' and 'conditioning.' Until the 1930s, Houston was a sleepy regional center with a population under 100,000 – you'll find relatively few historic buildings here. Once air-conditioning became widely available, the population jumped: by 1960 it numbered nearly one million.

From the 1970s through 1990s the city's fortunes followed the price per barrel of oil: boom, then bust. The area's business base diversified to include the medical services, high tech and space industries. Throughout the nationwide recession and gradual recovery of the 2000s, Houston's economic growth has continued, attracting a diverse, multicultural population.

Sights

Despite Houston's general sprawl, most areas of interest for visitors lie north or south of I-59, in the 10 miles between the Galleria area and the city center. Downtown has a few parks and outdoor activities, but the largest concentration of attractions is off Main St, in the Museum District.

Remember that shopping, eating and drinking in neighborhoods like eclectic Montrose or the historic Heights (p231) are also local attractions.

Downtown

You'll see few pedestrians braving the hot downtown sidewalks. No, they're not all at the pool. Underground air-conditioned pedestrian tunnels link most downtown buildings. In fact, those seeking necessities such as water and snacks may find them more easily within the tunnel system than in streetside shops. (Yes, even McDonald's is underground.)

Discovery Green PARK

(Map p216; www.discoverygreen.com; 1500 McKinney St; 6am-11pm; ; METROrail station Main St Square) FREE Your place to play right downtown. This 12-acre park has a lake, playground, fountains to splash in, outdoor art, restaurants and a performance space. The Green has become a hub for fun festivals and activities such as ovies on the green, nighttime flea markets – even a

Christmas-time ice rink. Check the online calendar for more.

Market Square Park PARK

(Map p216; www.marketsquarepark.com; cnr Congress & Travis Sts) FREE You'll notice how the 19th-century buildings on Market Sq, the historical center of Downtown, sharply contrast with their modern surroundings. A few restaurants line the square and there's a cafe in the park. In summer the small green space plays host to concerts and outdoor movies.

Allen's Landing Park PARK

(Map p216; 1001 Commerce St) FREE Named after Houston's founders, Allen's Landing marks the spot on Buffalo Bayou where Houston's settlement began. The original wharf has been improved with concrete paths and grassy lawns, and in the next few years an outdoor plaza with a cafe and bike and boat rentals is slated to follow.

Heritage Society at Sam Houston Park MUSEUM

(Map p216; ☎713-655-1912; www.hertiagesociety.org; 1100 Bagby St; museum free; tours adult/child $15/6; ⏲museum 10am-4pm Tue-Sun; tours 10am, 11:30am, 1 & 2pm Sat & Sun) Take a free cell-phone tour around the few historic homes that have been relocated to this park. Among them, the Yates House (1870) is home of a freed slave who became a prominent local preacher, and the Old Place (1823) is a log cabin thought to be the town's oldest. Guided tours get you inside, but you need to reserve your place in advance.

Montrose & Museum District

Museum-lovers, you've hit the jackpot in the area north around Hermann Park. To get a full list of museums or to plot your route, check out the map at the **Houston Museum District** (www.houstonmuseumdistrict.org).

Houston Museum of Natural Science MUSEUM

(Map p218; ☎713 639 4629; www.hmns.org; 5555 Hermann Park Dr; general admission adult/child $20/15, butterfly conservatory/special exhibits $5 extra per person; ⏲9am-6pm; 👪; METROrail station Hermann Park/Rice) World-class traveling exhibits - on everything from Medici gems to Mayan civilization - have always been a big part of the attraction at this stellar museum. With the $30 million addition of an impressive dino-focused paleontology wing and the opening of an Ancient Egyptian hall there are even more permanent reasons to visit.

Kiddos love the hands-on learning in the chemistry, energy and other science exhibits. In addition to the IMAX theater, there are planetarium shows and a giant glass butterfly conservatory. Special exhibits, films, shows and the butterfly house add an additional $5 to $8 per ticket.

Menil Collection MUSEUM

(Map p218; www.menil.org; 1515 Sul Ross St; ⏲11am-7pm Wed-Sun) FREE The late local philanthropists John and Dominique de Menil collected more than 17,000 works of

QUIRKY HOUSTON: ART CARS & BEER CAN HOUSES

Conservative Houston has a quirky, creative streak - one the **Orange Show Center for Visionary Art** (☎713-926-6368; www.orangeshow.org) fosters with a few oddball museums and one fabulous parade.

The late Jeff McKissack spent decades molding his house into a junk-art tribute to his favorite fruit. Today the giant, welded-steel oranges and plastic flower art takes up a mazelike 300 sq ft outside the **Orange Show Monument** (http://orangeshow.org/orange-show-monument; 2401 Munger St; admission $1; ⏲10am-2pm Mon-Fri, noon-5pm Sat & Sun Jun-Aug; noon-5pm Sat & Sun Sep-May). Seek out the informational posters which illustrate his vision, and tour the house. Next door, a new art park is under construction.

Is it a house, is it a sculpture? More than 50,000 aluminum cans cover the **Beer Can House** (Map p218; www.beercanhouse.org; 222 Malone St, off Memorial Dr; admission $2; ⏲noon-5pm Sat & Sun) as siding, as edging, as wind chimes. It's worth buying a self-guide booklet or taking a tour to learn more. Either way, don't miss the film on the house's history.

If you're not in town for the fabulous Art Car Parade (p221) in May, the next best thing is to view a few of the decorated vehicles at the **Art Car Museum** (www.artcarmuseum.com; 140 Heights Blvd; ⏲11am-6pm Wed-Sun) FREE. The cars have been tricked out into anything from a stiletto shoe to a Mad Max-esque wonder. Cool rotating art exhibits at the museum have included themes like road refuse and bone art.

Greater Houston

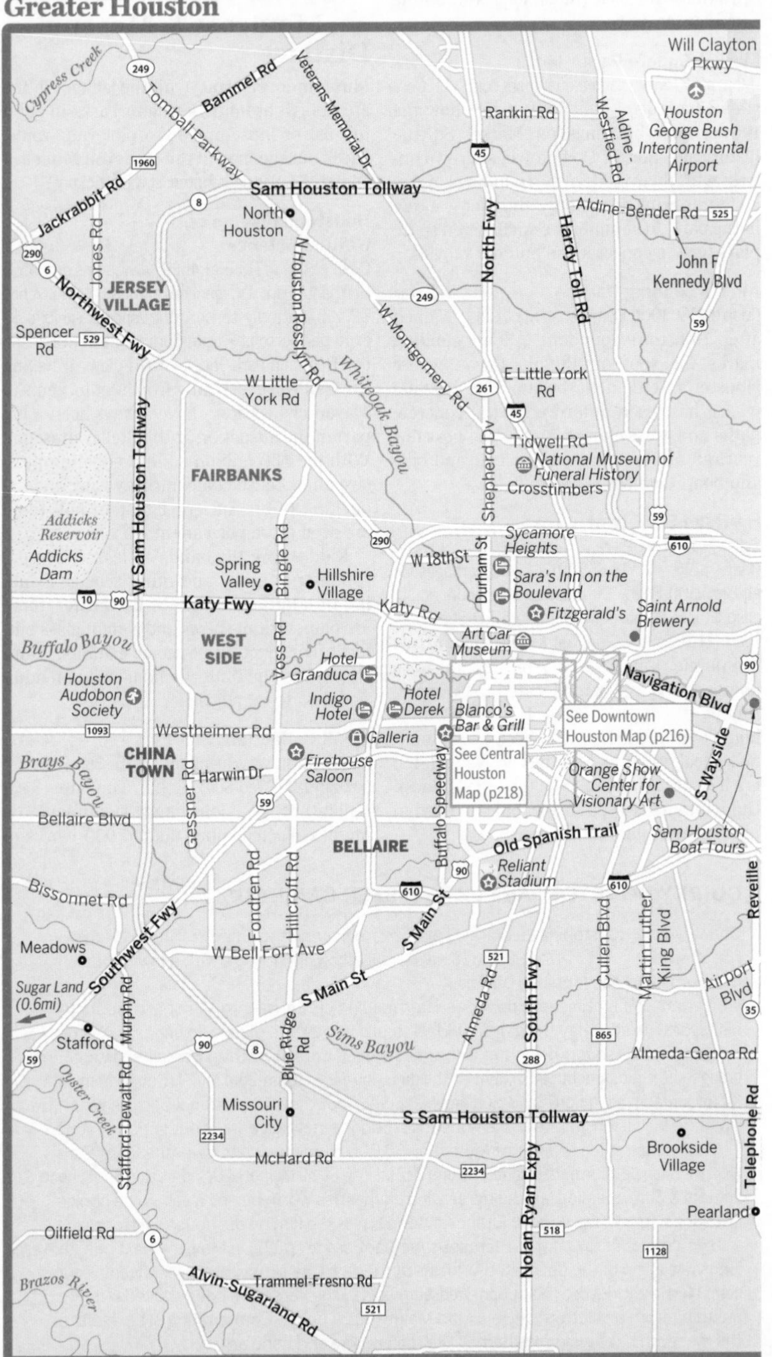

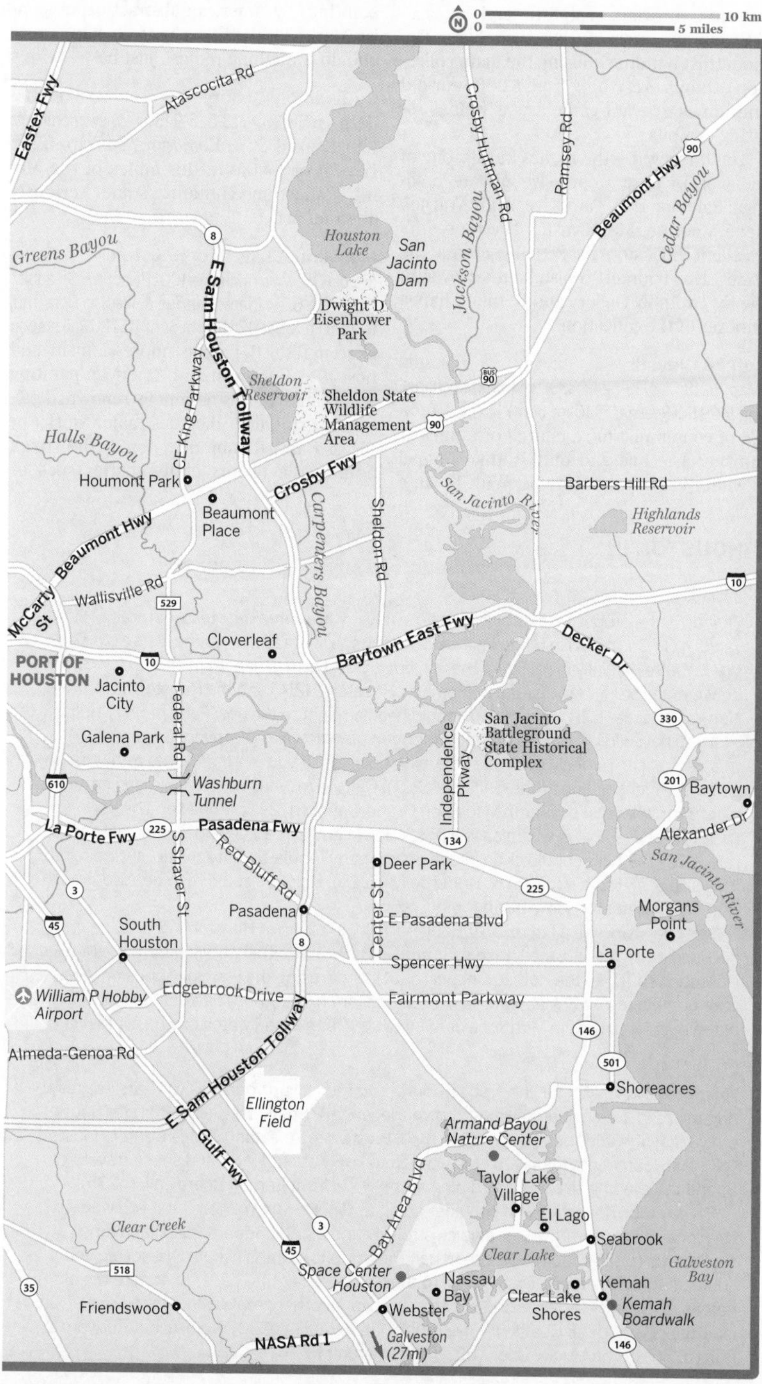

0 10 km
0 5 miles
Atascocita Rd
Eastex Fwy
Crosby Huffman Rd
Ramsey Rd
Beaumont Hwy
90
Cedar Bayou
8
Houston Lake
San Jacinto Dam
Greens Bayou
E Sam Houston Tollway
Jackson Bayou
Dwight D Eisenhower Park
CE King Parkway
Sheldon Reservoir
Sheldon State Wildlife Management Area
Halls Bayou
Houmont Park
Crosby Fwy
Beaumont Place
Carpenters Bayou
Sheldon Rd
San Jacinto River
Barbers Hill Rd
Highlands Reservoir
Beaumont Hwy
McCarty St
Wallisville Rd
529
10
Cloverleaf
Baytown East Fwy
Decker Dr
PORT OF HOUSTON
Jacinto City
Federal Rd
San Jacinto Battleground State Historical Complex
330
Galena Park
Independence Pkway
610
Washburn Tunnel
201
Baytown
La Porte Fwy
225
Pasadena Fwy
S Shaver St
Red Bluff Rd
134
Alexander Dr
Deer Park
San Jacinto River
3
45
Pasadena
Center St
E Pasadena Blvd
Morgans Point
South Houston
La Porte
Spencer Hwy
William P Hobby Airport
Edgebrook Drive
Fairmont Parkway
146
Almeda-Genoa Rd
501
Shoreacres
Ellington Field
Armand Bayou Nature Center
Gulf Fwy
Bay Area Blvd
Taylor Lake Village
El Lago
Clear Creek
Seabrook
Clear Lake
518
Space Center Houston
Galveston Bay
35
Nassau Bay
Clear Lake Shores
Kemah
Kemah Boardwalk
Friendswood
Webster
NASA Rd 1
Galveston (27mi)

painting, drawing, sculpture, archeological artifacts and more during their lives. The modernist building housing the main collection exhibits everything from 5,000-year-old antiquities to avant-garde art, as well as rotating exhibits.

You'll recognize the names in this, one of the world's most impressive private holdings: Salvidor Dali, Paul Klee, Andy Warhol, René Magritte, Max Ernst.... The museum's excellent bookstore is actually across the street. Don't forget to also saunter over to the Cy Twombly Gallery and Rothko Chapel, annexes of the collection.

Rothko Chapel MUSEUM
(Map p218; ☎713-524-9839; www.rothkochapel.org; 1409 Sul Ross St; ⏰10am-6pm) FREE A temple of contemplation, a church or a nuclear bunker? The one and only Rothko Chapel is whatever you want it to be. With 14 large paintings by American abstract expressionist Mark Rothko, it's a perfect place to sit and do something radical: just be.

Cy Twombly Gallery MUSEUM
(Map p218; ☎713-525-9450; www.menil.org; 1501 Branard St; ⏰11am-7pm Wed-Sun) FREE Love it or loathe it, this annex of the Menil Collection contains some seriously abstract art.

Museum of Fine Arts Houston MUSEUM
(Map p218; www.mfah.org; 1001 Bissonnet St; adult/child $13/6; ⏰10am-5pm Tue & Wed, to 9pm Thu, to 7pm Fri & Sat, 12:15-7pm Sun; METRORail station Museum District) French impressionism and post-1945 European and American painting really shine in this nationally renowned palace of art, which includes major works by Picasso and Rembrandt. Across the street, admire the talents of luminaries such as

HOUSTON IN...

Two Days

First up is the proper Texan way to start the day – with a breakfast taco, naturally. Hit up Tacos A Go Go (p224) in Midtown, before taking the light rail over to the **Museum District**. You're officially in museum mecca, but it's overload to see them all in a day. Choose between the stunning Museum of Fine Arts Houston (p214) and the Houston Museum of Natural Science (p211), where you should head straight to the new Paleontology Hall.

If you have kids in tow, spend the afternoon downtown at Discovery Green (p210); this central city park always has something going on. If you'd prefer a little retail therapy, go for the high fashion at the Galleria (p231). Culture mavens will have already gotten tickets for whatever's on at the Houston Grand Opera (p229) or the Alley Theatre (p229) that evening, in which case a post-show nightcap can be had at candlelit La Carafe (p227). Others should choose one of the many foodie-favorite restaurants, such as Indika (p225), Hugo's (p225) or Underbelly (p225). Hipsters could then head to **Washington Avenue** for some bar-hopping.

Start day two with a big meal at Baby Barnaby's (p225) in Houston's coolest neighborhood, **Montrose**. Sated, take your time in the area – either strolling from the Menil Collection (p211) to the Rothko Chapel (p214), or perusing the clothing shops on Westheimer or antiques on W Alabama. When it's time for an afternoon refreshment, choose one of the open-air patios in Montrose or leafy **Rice Village**, and watch day turn into night.

Four Days

Follow the above plan for the first 48 hours, and then fill up your tank with gas: we're hitting the road. Begin your day at Midtown's legendary Breakfast Klub (p224) for Southern wings 'n' waffles before driving to the **Clear Lake Area** and Space Center Houston (p234) to learn everything you ever wanted to know about NASA and space travel. Spend the evening strolling and dining at the waterfront Kemah Boardwalk (p235).

On day four, honestly, we'd consider going to **Galveston** (p241). But If you want to stay local, head downtown for a quick stroll around Market Square (p211) and lunch at Treebeards (p223). You haven't seen half the exhibits in the Museum District, so you could double back there. Or go north to the Houston Heights (p231) to admire the old homes, browse the eclectic shops and end up on another great patio, like the one at Onion Creek Cafe (p228). Later, for live music, Fitzgerald's (p230) is close, but Rudyard's Pub (p230) or the Mucky Duck (p230) really aren't far.

WHAT THE...? FUNERAL MUSEUM

'Any day above ground is a good one.' That's the trademark of the **National Museum of Funeral History** (www.nmfh.org; 415 Barren Springs Dr; ⏲10am-4pm Mon-Sat, noon-5pm Sun). If you've ever wanted to see a coffin collection that includes a casket made of money, literally, or one that's crab-shaped, now's your chance. Exhibits include those on embalming, famous memorials and historical hearses. Halloween would seem a good time to check out the Day of the Dead festival room.

Rodin and Matisse in the associated **Cullen Sculpture Garden** (Map p218; cnr Montrose Blvd & Bissonnet St; ⏲dawn-dusk) FREE which is freely accessible from dawn until dusk.

Holocaust Museum Houston MUSEUM
(Map p218; ☎713-942-8000; www.hmh.org; 5401 Caroline St; suggested donation $7; ⏲9am-5pm Mon-Fri, noon-5pm Sat & Sun) A superbly curated and presented museum offers an in-depth education on the context, history and aftermath of not only the Holocaust itself but of the Nazi's terrifying rise to power. Other exhibits trace the lives of Houston-connected European Jews and focus on the rescue efforts made by the Danish.

Contemporary Arts Museum MUSEUM
(Map p218; ☎713-284-8250; www.camh.org; 5216 Montrose Blvd; ⏲10am-5pm Tue-Sat, 10am-9pm Thu, noon-5pm Sun) FREE One of Houston's epicenters of what's cool, new and seriously cutting edge. Immerse yourself in the works of just one or two artists at a museum that's strength lies in its lack of permanent collection.

Asia Society Texas Center ARTS CENTER
(Map p218; http://asiasociety.org/texas; 1370 Southmore St; building entry free, exhibits $5; ⏲10am-6pm Tue-Sun) The contemporary architecture of the Asia Center building, complete with infinity pool and hourly misty fog, is as impressive as its changing exhibits. Check the schedule for Asian community–related events.

Museum of Printing History MUSEUM
(Map p218; ☎713-522-4652; www.printingmuseum.org; 1324 W Clay St; ⏲10am-5pm Tue-Sun) FREE This often-missed gem traces the history of printing from its advent until the early newspaper era. Rare and unusual printed works include the *Dharani Scroll* (dating from AD 764) and newspapers printed on historical dates – the *Titanic* disaster, JFK's assassination, the invasion of Pearl Harbor, etc.

Further Afield

Saint Arnold Brewery BREWERY
(www.saintarnold.com; 2000 Lyons Ave; admission $8; ⏲Tap room 3-4:15pm Mon-Fri, 11am-2pm Sat & Sun) An $8 admission gets you a brewery tour and four tokens to swap for tastings in the beer hall. (Tip: buy a larger glass at the gift shop and you get larger 'tastes'.) Tours depart at 3:30pm weekdays and on the hour during weekends.

Bayou Bend Collection & Gardens MUSEUM
(Map p218; www.mfah.org; 6003 Memorial Dr; tours adult/child $12/6, gardens-only $5; ⏲10am-5pm Tue-Sat, 1-5pm Sun) The Museum of Fine Arts Houston curates the impressive historical decorative arts collection (1600s to 1850s) displayed here. The 1928 home once belonged to Ms Ima Hogg, a well-known Houston civic leader and philanthropist. (As the joke goes, you know you're from Houston if you can say Ima Hogg without laughing.) Tours include admission to 14 acres of gardens.

Activities

Downtown's Discovery Green (p210) and the Museum District's **Hermann Park** (Map p218; www.hermannpark.org; Fannin St & Hermann Park Dr; ⏲6am-11pm) provide a good amount of room for little ones to run.

Buffalo Bayou Shuttle Service KAYAKING
(☎713-538-7433; http://bayoushuttle.com; ⏲10am-5pm Tue-Sun) Explore Buffalo Bayou by kayak. Rentals and shuttles are available. For the uninitiated we recommend taking a kayak tour of the Houston skyline area or one further afield and more extreme. Advance reservations required.

Houston Audobon Society BIRD-WATCHING
(www.houstonaudubon.org; Edith L Moore Nature Sanctuary, 440 Wilchester Blvd; ⏲9am-5pm Mon-Fri) FREE The Houston Audobon society website has loads of information about birding around the region. They also offer classes and field trips.

Downtown Houston

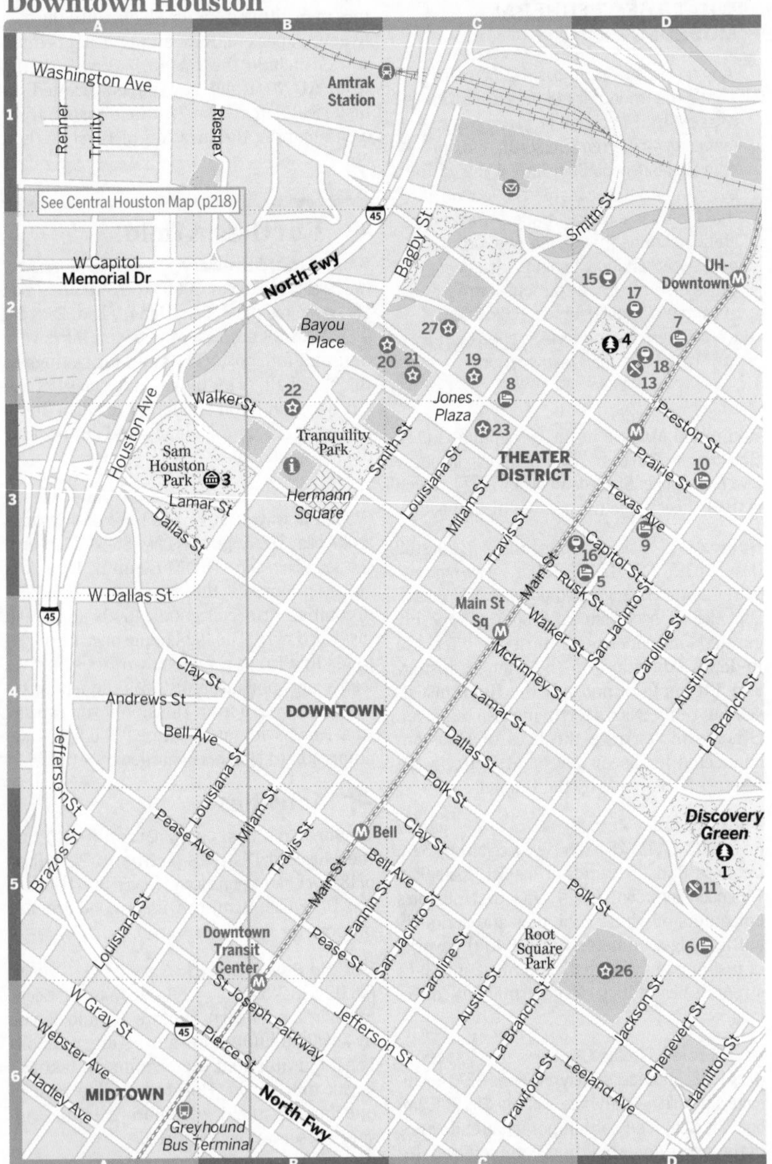

☞ Tours

★Houston Culinary Tours CULTURAL TOUR

(☎281-444-8636; www.houstonculinarytours.com; tour $180) Offerings change constantly, but many of these foodie adventures are led by local chefs and food celebrities. You may join Hugh Ortega for a Day of the Dead, Mexican excursion; Monica Pope for a farm-to-table tour; or Robb Walsh on the barbecue trail. Culinary tours take off from Central Market, 3315 Westheimer Rd, at Weslayan. Expect to eat well.

Downtown Houston

Top Sights
1 Discovery Green D5

Sights
2 Allen's Landing Park E2
3 Heritage Society at Sam Houston Park B3
4 Market Square Park D2

Sleeping
5 Club Quarters D3
6 Hilton Americas D5
7 Hotel Icon D2
8 Lancaster Hotel C2
9 Magnolia Hotel D3
10 Sam Houston Hotel D3

Eating
11 Grove Restaurant & Bar D5
12 Oxheart F1
13 Treebeards D2
14 Vic & Anthony's Steakhouse E4

Drinking & Nightlife
15 Eagle D2
16 Flying Saucer Draught Emporium D3
17 La Carafe D2
18 Warren's Inn D2

Entertainment
19 Alley Theatre C2
20 Angelika Film Center & Cafe C2
21 Bayou Music Center C2
22 Hobby Center for the Performing Arts B3
23 Jones Hall for the Performing Arts C3
24 Last Concert Cafe F1
25 Minute Maid Park E4
26 Toyota Center D5
27 Wortham Center C2

Tickets must be purchased in advance and on the website. Over 21 only.

Segway Tours of Houston GUIDED TOUR
(☎866-673-4929; http://segwaytoursofhouston.com; 2hr tour $80) Discover Houston's history or cruise along Buffalo Bayou on guided tours on Segways, the slightly geeky self-balancing personal transporters. Reservations required; tours launch from Wortham Plaza, 501 Texas Ave.

Sam Houston Boat Tours BOAT TOUR
(☎713-670-2416; www.portofhouston.com; 7300 Clinton Ave; ⏰tours 10:30am & 2:30pm) FREE Departing twice daily are three 90-minute tours of one of the largest ports in the USA; call to reserve 24 hours in advance.

Houston Urban Adventures GUIDED TOUR
(☎832-7689255; www.houstonurbanadventures.com; tour $30) Eclectic tour offerings include a trip through Houston's tunnel system and

Central Houston

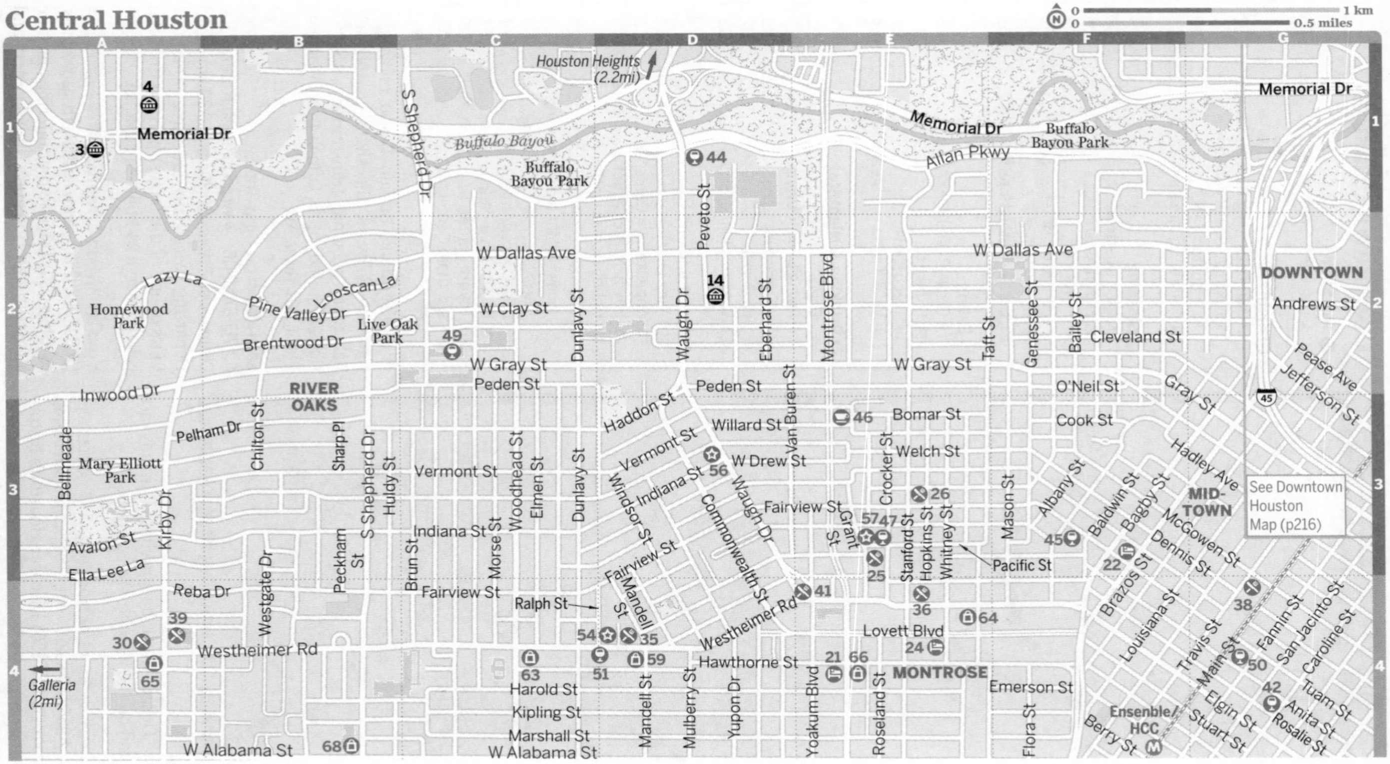

0 — 1 km
0 — 0.5 miles

A B C D E F G
1 2 3 4

Houston Heights (2.2mi)
Memorial Dr
Buffalo Bayou
Buffalo Bayou Park
Allan Pkwy
S Shepherd Dr
W Dallas Ave
DOWNTOWN
Andrews St
Lazy La
Homewood Park
Pine Valley Dr
Looscan La
Live Oak Park
Brentwood Dr
W Clay St
Dunlavy St
Waugh Dr
Peveto St
Eberhard St
Montrose Blvd
Taft St
Genessee St
Bailey St
Cleveland St
Pease Ave
Jefferson St
W Gray St
Peden St
Inwood Dr
RIVER OAKS
Van Buren St
O'Neil St
Gray St
Haddon St
Willard St
Bomar St
Cook St
Pelham Dr
Chilton St
Sharp Pl
S Shepherd Dr
Huldy St
Bellmeade
Mary Elliott Park
Vermont St
Woodhead St
Elmen St
W Drew St
Crocker St
Welch St
Hadley Ave
Windsor St
Indiana St
Commonwealth St
Fairview St
Grant St
Stanford St
Hopkins St
Whitney St
Mason St
Albany St
Baldwin St
Bagby St
MID-TOWN
McGowen St
Dennis St
See Downtown Houston Map (p216)
Kirby Dr
Avalon St
Ella Lee La
Peckham St
Brun St
Morse St
Westgate Dr
Reba Dr
Mandell St
Pacific St
Brazos St
Louisiana St
Ralph St
Westheimer Rd
Lovett Blvd
Travis St
Main St
Fannin St
San Jacinto St
Caroline St
Hawthorne St
MONTROSE
Galleria (2mi)
Harold St
Kipling St
Marshall St
W Alabama St
Mulberry St
Yupon Dr
Yoakum Blvd
Roseland St
Emerson St
Flora St
Ensemble/HCC
Berry St
Elgin St
Stuart St
Tuam St
Anita St
Rosalie St

3 4 14 21 22 24 25 26 30 35 36 38 39 41 42 44 45 46 47 49 50 51 54 56 57 59 63 64 65 66 68

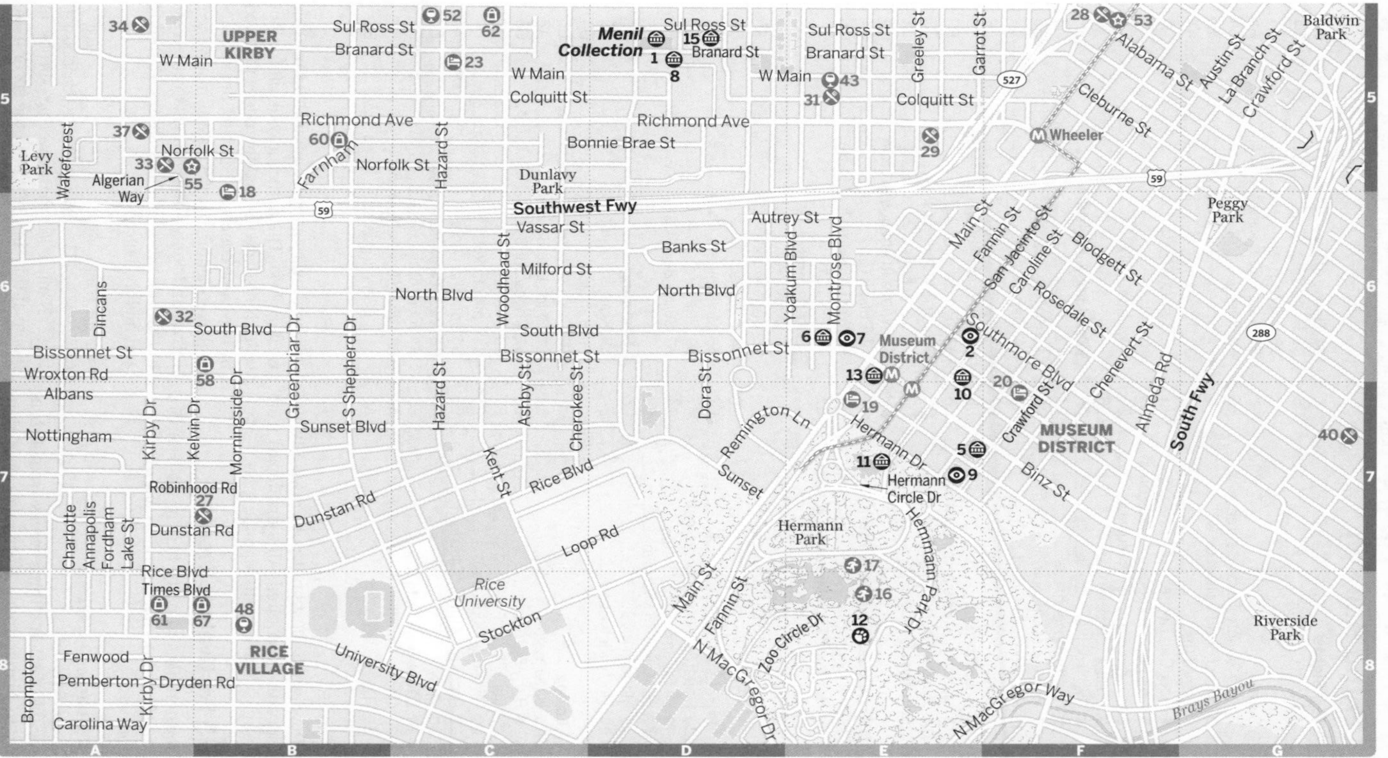
UPPER KIRBY
Menil Collection
MUSEUM DISTRICT
RICE VILLAGE
Museum District
Wheeler
Baldwin Park
Peggy Park
Dunlavy Park
Levy Park
Hermann Park
Riverside Park
Rice University
Brays Bayou
South Fwy
Southwest Fwy
Sul Ross St
Branard St
W Main
Colquitt St
Richmond Ave
Bonnie Brae St
Norfolk St
Farnham
Algerian Way
Wakeforest
Hazard St
Garrot St
Greeley St
Alabama St
Austin St
La Branch St
Crawford St
Cleburne St
Blodgett St
Rosedale St
Chenevert St
Almeda Rd
Caroline St
San Jacinto St
Fannin St
Main St
Southmore Blvd
Binz St
Hermann Dr
Hermann Circle Dr
Hermann Park Dr
N MacGregor Way
N MacGregor Dr
Zoo Circle Dr
Montrose Blvd
Yoakum Blvd
Autrey St
Banks St
North Blvd
Bissonnet St
Dora St
Remington Ln
Sunset
Vassar St
Milford St
South Blvd
Cherokee St
Ashby St
Rice Blvd
Loop Rd
Woodhead St
Kent St
Stockton
University Blvd
S Shepherd Dr
Sunset Blvd
Dunstan Rd
Greenbriar Dr
Morningside Dr
Kelvin Dr
Kirby Dr
Robinhood Rd
Times Blvd
Dincans
Wroxton Rd
Albans
Nottingham
Lake St
Fordham
Annapolis
Charlotte
Fenwood
Pemberton
Dryden Rd
Carolina Way
Brompton
288
527
59
A
B
C
D
E
F
G
5
6
7
8
1
2
5
6
7
8
9
10
11
12
13
15
16
17
18
19
20
23
27
28
29
31
32
33
34
37
40
43
48
52
53
55
58
60
61
62
67

Central Houston

Top Sights
1 Menil Collection........D5

Sights
2 Asia Society Texas Center........E6
3 Bayou Bend Collection & Gardens........A1
4 Beer Can House........A1
5 Children's Museum of Houston........E7
6 Contemporary Arts Museum........E6
7 Cullen Sculpture Garden........E6
8 Cy Twombly Gallery........D5
9 Health Museum........E7
10 Holocaust Museum Houston........E6
11 Houston Museum of Natural Science........E7
12 Houston Zoo........E8
13 Museum of Fine Arts Houston........E6
14 Museum of Printing History........D2
15 Rothko Chapel........D5

Activities, Courses & Tours
16 Hermann Park........E8
17 Hermann Park Miniature Train........E7

Sleeping
18 Extended Stay America – Greenway Plaza........B5
19 Hotel ZaZa........E7
20 Houston International Hostel........F7
21 La Colombe d'Or Hotel........E4
22 La Maison in Midtown........F3
23 Modern B&B........C5
24 Morty Rich Hostel........E4

Eating
25 Baba Yega........E3
26 Baby Barnaby's........E3
27 Benjy's........B7
28 Breakfast Klub........F5
29 Brooklyn Athletic Club........E5
30 Chuy's........A4
31 Eatsie Boys Cafe........E5
32 Goode Co BBQ........A6
33 Haven........A5
34 House of Pies........A5
35 Hugo's........D4
36 Indika........E4
37 Kata Robata Sushi & Grill........A5
38 Reef........G4
Sparrow Bar & Cookshop........(see 28)
39 Taco Milagro........A4
Tacos A Go Go........(see 53)
40 This Is It........G7
41 Underbelly........E4

Drinking & Nightlife
42 13 Celsius........G4
43 Black Labrador........E5
44 Élan........D1
45 F Bar........F3
46 Inversion Coffee House........E3
47 JR's Bar & Grill........E3
48 Little Woodrow's........B8
49 Local Pour........C2
50 Nouveau Antique Art Bar........G4
51 Poison Girl........D4
52 West Alabama Ice House........C5

Entertainment
Cézanne........(see 43)
53 Continental Club........F5
54 EJ's Bar........D4
55 McGonigel's Mucky Duck........A5
56 Rudyard's Pub........D3
57 South Beach........E3

Shopping
58 Brazos Bookstore........B6
59 Buffalo Exchange........D4
60 Cactus Music........B5
61 Chloe Dao Boutique........A8
62 Chocolate Bar........C5
63 Domy........C4
64 Folk Market........E4
65 Jonathan Adler........A4
66 M2M Fashions........E4
67 Rice Village........B8
68 Whole Earth Provision Company........B4

a Downtown ghost hunt/pub crawl. Advance reservations required. All tours depart from Georgia's Market, 410 Main St.

Festivals & Events

Houston likes to party, heat or no heat. For a full list of events, log on to www.visithouston.org.

★ Houston Livestock Show & Rodeo — RODEO

(www.hlsr.com) For three weeks from February to March, rodeo fever takes over Houston and everyone gets gussied up in their western best. The barbecue cook-off is a hot seller but so are the nightly rodeos followed by big-name concerts – starring Bruno Mars to Blake Shelton. Buy tickets way in advance. Fairgrounds-only admission gets you access to midway rides, livestock shows, shopping and nightly dances.

Azalea Trail — GARDEN

(☎713-523-2483; www.riveroaksgardenclub.org) FREE Named for the flowering shrubs in bloom at this time of year in the six or more historic homes and gardens opened for tours on one weekend in March.

Bayou City Art Festival FESTIVAL
(☎713-521-0133; www.bayoucityartfestival.com) FREE Hundreds of artists sell their wares, and there's a festive array of musicians and food. This popular biannual festival takes places in Memorial Park each March, and Downtown each October.

Houston International Festival CULTURE
(☎713-654-8808; www.ifest.org) A multicultural celebration of food, art and music lights up the city two weekends in April. Save money on concert tickets by purchasing ahead.

Art Car Parade & Festival PARADE
(www.orangeshow.org) FREE Wacky, arted-out vehicles (think Mad Max or giant rabbits) hit the streets en masse the second Sunday in May. The parade itself is complemented by weekend-long festivities, including concerts.

Juneteenth CULTURE
(☎832-429-4432; www.houstonculture.org/juneteenth) This celebration of African American culture, with plenty of gospel, jazz and blues, takes place at Miller Outdoor Theater around June 19 – the day in 1865 when word reached Texas that slaves had been emancipated.

Pride Houston PARADE
(www.pridehouston.org) FREE One of the largest GLBT parades in the southwest. A Saturday in late June, 1000-plus participants entertain with colorful floats, costumes and music. Events spill over into an entire Pride week.

Houston Shakespeare Festival THEATER
(☎713-926-2277; http://houstonfestivalscompany.com/hsf) FREE Star-crossed lovers and mistaken identities prevail at the Miller Outdoor Theatre for two weeks beginning in late July. To get a seat reserve free tickets online, or picnic on the lawn.

Fiestas Patrias CULTURE
(☎713-926-2636) FREE This September 16 festival features a parade, a ball, street music and dance performances in celebration of Mexican Independence Day.

Sleeping

A few Houston hotels stand out, but the vast majority of sleeping spots belong to the chain gang. Options off I-610 near the Galleria tend to be the newest and priciest. The further out you get, the cheaper the chain motels. Budget digs are hard to find near the center.

Stay downtown and you'll be walking distance to the Theater District, Market Square or the light rail. Around the I-59 corridor between Downtown and the Galleria, in Midtown, Montrose and the Museum District, you're well located for museums, shops and restaurants.

Downtown

Magnolia Hotel BOUTIQUE HOTEL **$$**
(Map p216; ☎713-221-0011; www.magnoliahotelhouston.com; 1100 Texas Ave; r $130-230; P ❄ @ 🛜 ≋) Layered in luxurius velvet and damask, with pops of modern color, rooms in this downtown hotel are both stylish *and* comfortable. Don't miss the free happy hour at the Lounge from 5pm until 7pm daily.

Sam Houston Hotel BOUTIQUE HOTEL **$$**
(Map p216; ☎832-200-8800; www.thesamhoustonhotel.com; 1117 Prairie St; r $145-200; P ❄ @ 🛜; METROrail station Preston) Sleek yet low-key, the smallish rooms at this historic 1923 property have a contemporary decor done in all-gray. Luxe linens, Keurig coffee makers and Aveda bath products dress things up.

Lancaster Hotel HOTEL **$$**
(Map p216; ☎713-228-9500; www.lancasterhotel.com; 701 Texas Ave; r $99-240; P ❄ @ 🛜 🐾) Original marble and old-fashioned decor make this gracious hotel feel more like London than Houston. Say cheers with a gimlet in the Lancaster Bistro, where old-school bartenders preside over a chatty post-theater crowd.

Club Quarters HOTEL **$$**
(Map p216; ☎713-224-6400; www.clubquarters.com; 720 Fannin St; r $105-130; P ❄ @ 🛜) When members don't fill them, you can snag reduced-rate business hotel rooms here. Some have kitchenettes.

Hilton Americas HOTEL **$$**
(Map p216; ☎712-739-8000; www.americashouston.hilton.com; 1600 Lamar St; r $150-250; P ❄ @ 🛜 ≋) Location, location, location. At the contemporary convention-center Hilton hotel you're only steps from Discovery Green, the Toyota Center and Minute Maid baseball park.

Hotel Icon HISTORIC HOTEL **$$$**
(Map p216; ☎713-224-4266; www.hotelicon.com; 220 Main St; r $180-290; P ❄ @ 🛜) You can feel the history in this hotel's ornate red-and-gold lobby with a 1911 bank vault reception area, soaring marble columns and coffered

HOUSTON FOR KIDS

Young 'uns gettin' restless? There's a great place to play right downtown, Discovery Green (p210). Think playgrounds, play fountains, fun art and a kid-friendly restaurant.

In the museum district, Hermann Park (p215) is home to playgrounds, a lake with paddleboats and the **Hermann Park Miniature Train** (Map p218; ☎713-529-5216; www.hermannpark.org/railroad.php; 6104 Hermann Park Dr, Kinder Station, Lake Plaza; per ride $3; ⏰10am-5:30pm Mon-Fri, 10am-6pm Sat & Sun;). More than 4500 animals inhabit the semitropical, 55-acre **Houston Zoo** (Map p218; www.houstonzoo.org; 6200 Hermann Park Dr; adult/child $14/10; ⏰9am-6pm), also in the park. Activities include wildlife talks catering to different age groups and summertime zoo sleepovers.

Walking distance from the park you'll find the high-octane, stupendously fun **Children's Museum of Houston** (Map p218; www.cmhouston.org; 1500 Binz St; admission $9; ⏰9am-6pm Tue-Sat, noon-6pm Sun), where little ones can make tortillas in a Mexican village, or draw in an open-air art studio. A few blocks away, future brain surgeons will like checking out the huge organs on display at the interactive **Health Museum** (Map p218; ☎713-521-1515; www.mhms.org; 1515 Hermann Dr; adult/child $8/6; ⏰9am-5pm Mon-Sat, noon-5pm Sun).

Looking for a way to beat the summer heat? Take the kids to the **Galleria Skating Rink** (☎713-621-1500; 5015 Westheimer Rd, Galleria Mall; admission $8, skate rental $3.50; ⏰10am-5pm & 8-10pm Mon-Thu, 10am-10pm Fri, 12:30-10pm Sat, 1-7pm Sun;). Yes, that's right, there's an ice rink right in the center of the city's biggest mall.

ceilings. Take the antique elevator up to modern-chic rooms.

Midtown, Montrose & Museum District

Morty Rich Hostel HOSTEL **$**
(Map p218; ☎713-636-9776; www.hiusa.org/houston; 501 Lovett Blvd; dm $22-27; P ❄ @ 📶 ≋) A classic Montrose home hosts this Hosteling International member. Most of the bright, clean, four- to eight-bed dorms are co-ed, but there is a single-sex option. Hang out in the billiard room or chill in the backyard pool after a hard day's sightseeing. Accessible via public transport.

Extended Stay America – Greenway Plaza MOTEL **$**
(Map p218; ☎713-521-0060; www.extendedstayamerica.com; 2330 Southwest Fwy (I-59); ste $89-105; P ❄ 📶) Sure this is a multistory, interior-access chain motel on the freeway. But it's a decent one, in a great location. Nothing is a far drive, and the restaurants of Upper Kirby and those of Rice Village are just a couple miles away. Rooms are all-suite so you get a kitchenette in each – bonus.

Houston International Hostel HOSTEL **$**
(Map p218; ☎713-523-1009; www.houstonhostel.com; 5302 Crawford St; dm/d/q $16/50/110; P ❄ @ 📶) A mix of semipermanent residents and backpackers. A friendly, eccentric staff and worn '70s furnishings lend the place a throwback hippie feel. It's an easy walk to Houston's major museums and light rail.

La Maison in Midtown INN **$$**
(Map p218; ☎713-529-3600; http://lamaisonmidtown.com; 2800 Brazos St; r $160-219, ste $330; P ❄ 📶) Relaxing on the wraparound porch with skyline view or enjoying a breakfast feast, you'll feel the Southern hospitality at this purpose-built, urban inn. Upscale rooms are individually decorated, and all have elevator access. Includes breakfast.

Modern B&B B&B **$$**
(Map p218; ☎832-279-6367; http://modernbb.com; 4003 Hazard St; r incl breakfast $100-225; P ❄ @ 📶) An architect's dream, this mod, solar-powered, 11-room inn is rife with airy decks, spiral staircases and sunlight. Think organic mattresses, in-room Jacuzzi tubs, private decks and iPod docking stations. Owners also rent two nearby apartments.

Hotel ZaZa BOUTIQUE HOTEL **$$**
(Map p218; ☎713-526-1991; www.hotelzaza.com; 5701 Main St; r $205-270; P ❄ @ 📶 ≋; METRO-rail station Hermann Park/Rice) Hip, flamboyant and fabulous. From the bordello-esque colors to zebra-accent chairs, everything about Hotel ZaZa is good fun – and surpris-

ingly unpretentious. Our favorite rooms are the concept suites such as the eccentric Asian Geisha, or the space age 'Houston We Have a Problem.' You can't beat the location overlooking the Museum District's Hermann Park, near the light rail.

La Colombe d'Or Hotel LUXURY HOTEL **$$$**
(Map p218; ☎713-524-7999; www.lacolombedor.com; 3410 Montrose Blvd; ste $295-400; P ❄ ᯤ) Each of the five exquisite, one-bedroom suites were inspired by the colors and styles of a painting master – Cezanne, Van Gogh, Renoir ... Suitably so, as the rare oils and antiques decorating this 1923 Montrose mansion are museum quality. Standards at the intimate, on-site French restaurant are in keeping with such refined tastes. It's one mile west of Ensemble/HCC metrorail station.

Galleria

Hotel Derek BOUTIQUE HOTEL **$$**
(☎713-961-3000; www.hotelderek.com; 2525 West Loop St; r $115-260; P ❄ @ ᯤ ≋ 🐾) After shopping at the Galleria, you can lay your head in high-fashion style. Urban chic or accessible elegance: call it what you like, famous guests such as Faith Hill and Tim McGraw seem to appreciate it.

Indigo Hotel BOUTIQUE HOTEL **$$**
(☎713-621-8988; www.uptownhoustonhotel.com; 5160 Hidalgo St; r $130-235; P ❄ @ ᯤ) A cool place to refresh and recharge in this big hot city. Hotel Indigo brings the casual fun of the seaside to the Galleria area with beachy appeal and vibrant colors.

Hotel Granduca LUXURY HOTEL **$$$**
(☎713-418-1000; www.granducahouston.com; 1080 Uptown Park Blvd; r $220-350; P ❄ @ ᯤ ≋) Expect Italian elegance with a warm Texan welcome. Granduca was modeled after a Duke's *palazzo*, so rooms are suitably rich and the pool area is a garden oasis. In Uptown Park, the hotel is close enough to the Galleria (with free transport to it), yet a bit removed from the mad traffic.

Houston Heights

Sycamore Heights B&B **$$**
(☎713-861-4117; www.sycamoreheights.com; 245 W 18th St; r incl breakfast $120 ; P ❄ ᯤ) Stay within walking distance to the fun shops and restaurants of the Historic Heights. The three rooms at in this large Arts and Crafts–era bungalow are all classically comfortable.

Sara's Inn on the Boulevard INN **$$**
(☎713-868-1130; www.saras.com; 941 Heights Blvd; r incl breakfast $115-180; P ❄ @ ᯤ) A Victorian feels right at home among the historic houses of the Heights. Eleven airy rooms say 'boutique hotel' more than 'frilly B&B.' But the the inn still has the kind of sprawling Southern porch that makes you want to gossip over mint juleps.

Eating

Houston's restaurant scene is smokin' hot – and we don't just mean the salsa. In fact, Houstonians eat out more than residents of any other US city; the *New York Times* and *GQ Magazine* have both touted the city's offerings. To keep abreast of what's in and what isn't, we recommend **Cook's Tour Blog** (www.29-95.com/alison-cook) by Alison Cook, a favorite local food writer. The razor-tongued **Fearless Critic** (www.fearlesscritic.com) isn't bad either. Twitterites can follow @eatdrinkhouston.

Downtown

Downtown dining caters mainly to the business-lunch crowds, with a few noteworthy exceptions.

Treebeards SOUTHERN **$**
(Map p216; http://treebeards.com; 315 Travis St; specials $8-11; ⌚11am-2pm Mon-Fri) Locals flock here at lunchtime to chow down on great Cajun gumbos and jambalaya, but don't discount the appeal of daily changing specials like jerk chicken and stuffed pork chops.

Grove Restaurant & Bar AMERICAN **$$**
(Map p216; ☎713-337-7321; http://thegrovehouston.com; 1611 Lamar St; lunch & brunch mains $13-21, dinner mains $15-29; ⌚11am-10pm Sun-Thu, to 11pm Fri & Sat; METROrail station Main Street Square) Free-range chicken potpie, pork belly sliders…the American classics get a metropolitan update at the Grove. The modern, glass-filled dining room overlooks Discovery Green park.

Original Ninfas MEXICAN **$$**
(www.ninfas.com; 2704 Navigation Blvd; mains $10-21; ⌚11am-10pm Mon-Fri, 10am-10pm Sat & Sun) The original, where generations of Houstonians have come since the 1970s for shrimp *diablo*, *tacos al carbón* (tacos cooked over charcoal) and handmade tamales crafted

with pride. Hopefully the recent new ownership will not change anything vital.

★ Oxheart MODERN AMERICAN **$$$**
(Map p216; ☎832-830-8592; www.oxhearthouston.com; 1302 Nance St; menus $49-79; ⏲5:30-11pm Thu-Sun) Houstonians Jeff Hu and Karen Man delight foodies and critics alike with the inventive flavor pairings on the four- to seven-course tasting menus. In the ever-changing line-up you may find ginger and lemongrass-spiked guinea hen or caramelized chocolate cake with tomato jam.

The obscure warehouse that houses this award-winning restaurant is north of town, off N San Jacinto St. Reserve a month or more in advance.

Vic & Anthony's Steakhouse STEAKHOUSE **$$$**
(Map p216; ☎713-228-1111; www.vicandanthonys.com; 1510 Texas Ave; mains $25-55; ⏲5-10pm Sun-Thu, 5-11pm Fri & Sat) Sink into one of the nail-trimmed leather chairs or enveloping booths for an intimate evening at this clubby steakhouse.

Midtown & Museum District

Midtown has up-and-coming and diverse dining options spread out around Travis and W Gray Sts.

Tacos A Go Go TEX-MEX **$**
(Map p218; ☎713-807-8226; http://tacosagogo.com; 3704 Main St; tacos $2, meals $6-10; ⏲7am-10pm Mon-Thu, 8am-2am Fri & Sat, 9am-3pm Sun; METROrail station Ensemble/HCC) Everyone has their own favorite of the served-all-day, scrambled-egg breakfast tacos here: we like bacon, bean and potato – with jalepeño, of course. But we also seek out this funky, fun place for spicy margaritas and late-night noshing.

This Is It SOUTHERN **$**
(Map p218; ☎713-659-1608; http://houstonthisisit.com; 2712 Blodgett St; meals $6-11; ⏲7-10am & 11am-8pm Mon-Sat, 11am-6pm Sun) Soul food served cafeteria style in the Museum District: think oxtails, ham hocks and ribs - served from the heart.

Breakfast Klub SOUTHERN **$**
(Map p218; www.thebreakfastklub.com; 3711 Travis St; dishes $8-15; ⏲7am-2pm Mon-Fri, 8am-2pm Sat; P 📶) Come early; devotees line up around the block for down-home breakfast faves like fried wings 'n' waffles. Lunch hours are only slightly less crazy at this coffeehouse-like eatery favored by local girl Beyonce and her boy, Jay-Z. Coffee is great and there's wi-fi.

TOP FIVE MEXICAN MEALS

Mexican food means a lot more than tacos in Texas.

- Original Ninfas (p223) Classic Mexican served by waiters wearing traditional guayabera shirts.
- Hugo's (p225) Master chef Hugo Ortega's restaurant is interior-Mexican cuisine at it's finest.
- Tacos A Go Go (p224) The go-to place for breakfast tacos.
- Taco Milagro (p225) Music, margaritas and a salsa bar – olé!
- Chuy's (p225) Tex-Mex fun and 'burritos as big as yo' face.'

Sparrow Bar & Cookshop MODERN AMERICAN **$$$**
(Map p218; ☎713-524-6922; www.sparrowhouston.com; 3701 Travis St; mains $16-32; ⏲11am-3pm & 5-10pm Tue-Sat) Nationally renowned chef Monica Pope brings top-quality local and organic ingredients to life in her new American cuisine. Share plates might include shiitake mushroom dumplings with a blue cheese sauce or wild boar. On a nice night, patio dining is a must.

Reef SEAFOOD **$$**
(Map p218; ☎713-526-8282; www.reefhouston.com; 2600 Travis St; lunches $12-26, dinner mains $20-29; ⏲11am-10pm Mon-Fri, 5-11pm Sat; METRO-rail station McGowen) Gulf Coast seafood is creatively prepared and served in a sleek and sophisticated dining room – with a skyline-view raw bar. Chef Bryan Caswell has has won oodles of national awards for himself and his restaurant.

Montrose

Mixed among the area's funky boutiques and bars, Montrose eateries (radiating out from the intersection of Westheimer and Montrose Blvd) are some of the most creative in town.

★ Eatsie Boys Cafe CAFE **$**
(Map p218; http://eatsieboys.com; 4400 Montrose Blvd; dishes $6-12; ⏲8am-10pm Mon-Sat, brunch

9am-3pm Sun; 📶) The Eatsie Boys intergalactic food truck has landed. Owners now operate out of a fun cafe, and all the better for it. Order your matzo-ball *pho* (trust us, it's good) or a Gulf shrimp po'boy with jalepeño tatar sauce, then sidle up to one of the shady picnic tables to enjoy. The brew their own craft beers, too. Mmmmmm...

Baby Barnaby's BREAKFAST **$**
(Map p218; ☎713-522-4229; www.barnabyscafe.com; 604 Fairview St; breakfast $6-9; ⏰7am-noon Mon-Fri, 8am-2pm Sat & Sun; 👪) We suspect that Montrosians are playing hooky for the chicken apple sausage, pancakes and strong coffee here, where the atmosphere is always friendly. A Houston original, Barnaby's Cafe has several locations that also serve lunch and dinner: one here, next door to Baby Barnaby's, one downtown, and one – with a patio – on Kirby.

Taco Milagro TEX-MEX **$**
(Map p218; ☎713-522-1999; http://taco-milagro.com; 2555 Kirby Dr; mains $7-11; ⏰11am-10pm Sun-Tue, to 11pm Wed, to 1am Thu, to midnight Fri & Sat; 🥗) Modern Tex-Mex in a sexy, upscale setting. We're big fans of the fresh ingredients, bountiful salsa bar and killer margaritas. But it's the huge patio with gurgling fountain – and live music Thursday through Saturday evenings – that really brings us back.

Chuy's TEX-MEX **$**
(Map p218; ☎713-524-1700; www.chuys.com; 2706 Westheimer Rd; mains $7-12; ⏰11am-10pm Sun-Thu, 11am-11pm Fri & Sat; 👪) What's not fun about burritos 'as big as yo' face,' a shrine to Elvis and a party atmosphere that's kid friendly? It's so popular, in fact, that this Texas chain has gone national.

Underbelly NEW AMERICAN **$$**
(Map p218; ☎713-528-9800; www.underbellyhouston.com; 1100 Westheimer Rd; dishes $14-40; ⏰11am-3pm & 5-10pm Mon-Fri, 5-11pm Sat) Chef Chris Shepherd set out to fuse Houston's multicultural influences. He succeeds with dishes like cornbread-crusted oysters in *kimchi* butter and Vietnamese meatballs with gravy. The man even rears his own pigs and goats these days. Bring a group; plates are meant for sharing. It's a 20-minute walk from Ensemble Metrorail station in the Montrose neighbourhood.

Indika INDIAN **$$**
(Map p218; ☎713-524-2170; www.indikausa.com; 516 Westheimer Rd; lunch & brunch $12-18, dinner mains $17-35; ⏰11am-2pm & 6-10pm Tue-Sat, brunch 11am-3pm Sun) OK, we'll fess up – we have a crush on Indika. The alluring dining room sets the tone for the sublime Indian food, a fusion of authentic tastes and adventurous preparations, such as crabmeat samosas with papaya-ginger chutney. Great happy hour and Sunday brunch.

Baba Yega AMERICAN **$$**
(Map p218; ☎713-522-0042; www.babayega.com; 2607 Grant St; meals $8-16; ⏰11am-9pm Mon-Thu, 11am-10pm Fri & Sat, 10am-9pm Sun; 🥗) A pretty garden bungalow cafe provides plenty of TLC for vegetarians – think veggie meatloaf with garlic mashed potatoes – plus good burgers and homemade peanut-butter pie. Brunch served Sunday.

★Hugo's MEXICAN **$$$**
(Map p218; ☎713-524-7744; www.hugosrestaurant.net; 1600 Westheimer Rd; lunch & brunch $14-19, dinner mains $22-30; ⏰11am-10pm Mon-Thu, 11am-11pm Fri & Sat, 10am-9pm Sun) Chef Hugo Ortega's inspired, interior-Mexican regional cuisine tastes like nothing else in town. You might try squash-blossom crêpes or Veracruz snapper with tomatoes, olives and capers. Brunch is not to be missed. Book ahead for any meal.

Rice Village

Rice Village's bustling shopping area near the university is home to numerous casual restaurants. North of I-59 Kirby gradually blends into the ritzy River Oaks area. Houston's heavy hitters are found here and in the Galleria area.

Goode Co BBQ BARBECUE **$$**
(Map p218; www.goodecompany.com; 5109 Kirby Dr; plates $10-16; ⏰11am-10pm) Belly up to the beef brisket, smoked sausage and gallon ice teas in a big ol' barn or out back on picnic tables.

Benjy's NEW AMERICAN **$$**
(Map p218; ☎713-522-7602; www.benjys.com; 2424 Dunstan Rd; lunch & brunch $12-16, dinner mains $15-25; ⏰11am-9pm Sun & Mon, to 10pm Tue-Thu, to 11pm Fri & Sat) Local ingredients star at this fashionable Rice Village restaurant. Saturday and Sunday brunch is the week's highlight for many. Think nut-crusted challah French toast and chorizo fritattas.

Upper Kirby, River Oaks & Galleria

North of I-59 Kirby gradually blends into the ritzy River Oak area.

House of Pies AMERICAN $
(Map p218; ☎713-528-3816; www.houseofpies.com; 3112 Kirby Dr; breakfast & sandwiches $5-9, dinner mains $10-12; ⏲24hr) Classic diner fare served 24/7. The pie's really the thing here: banana cream, lemon ice box, buttermilk, German chocolate, wild blueberry... But the place is also a late-night breakfast hit with post-clubbing hipsters.

★ **Haven** SOUTHERN $$$
(Map p218; ☎713-581-6101; http://havenhouston.com; 2502 Algerian Way; lunch & brunch $12-20, dinner mains $25-38; ⏲11am-10pm Mon-Fri, 5-10pm Sat, 11am-2pm Sun) Dedicated to our rural roots, this self-billed 'seasonal kitchen' prides itself on its site-grown herbs and veggies and locally sourced meats. Heck, they even raise their own bees for honey.

What's not to love about Texas-inspired dishes like shrimp corn dogs, quail with jalapeño-and-sausage stuffing, or farm-grown fried egg sandwiches with heirloom tomato salad. Brunch served Sunday.

Kata Robata Sushi & Grill SUSHI $$$
(Map p218; ☎713-526-8858; http://katarobata.com; 3600 Kirby Dr; sushi $5-18, small plates $12-19; ⏲11:30am-3pm & 5-10:30pm Mon-Fri, noon-10pm Sat & Sun) Foodies' local fave for Houston's freshest sushi. Specialty rolls and super *toro* tuna aren't the only options that shine on this eclectic menu, which includes fusion noodle and grill dishes. We dare anyone to dislike the miso mac-and-cheese.

Tiny Boxwoods CAFE $$$
(☎713-622-4224; http://tinyboxwoods.com; 3614 W Alabama; breakfast, brunch & lunch $10-20, dinner mains $22-45; ⏲7am-10pm Tue-Sat, brunch 9am-2pm Sun) Set among blooming flowers in a River Oaks garden shop, this lovely cafe is a natural respite for ladies who lunch. With food this good (aged Gouda grilled cheese and pesto sandwiches at noon, buffalo tenderloin with mushroom risotto at night), guys secretly love it too.

Philippe Restaurant & Lounge FUSION $$$
(☎713-439-1000; www.philippehouston.com; 1800 Post Oak Blvd; lunch mains $16-28, dinner mains $19-45; ⏲11am-3pm & 5:30-10:30pm Mon-Thu, 11am-3pm & 5-11:30pm Fri, 5-11:30pm Sat; P) French sophistication meets Southern comfort. The buttermilk-fried calamari here are every bit as exquisite as the gnocchi with chanterelles and truffle oil. A multicourse, master chef–set lunch is quite the deal at $20. Unfortunately the lounge menu is nowhere near as inspired as the restaurant's.

Houston Heights & Washington Avenue

Washington Ave is known for its nightlife, but you can find plenty to eat too. Several Houston restaurant chains, such as Benjy's and Blue Fish, have outlets here.

ON THE GO: HOUSTON FOOD TRUCKS

Unlike in some other cities food trucks in Houston really move. You might see the same one in two or three places the same day. Check online for their latest locations, but they're often near bars and cafes in Montrose. The Menil Collection (p211) and Museum of Fine Arts (p214) parking lots are also frequent stopovers. Note: you'll rarely see them downtown because of parking regulations.

Good Dog (www.gooddogfoodtruck.com) Our guilty pleasure, selling things like gourmet guac dogs and tofufurters with homemade toppings and sides.

Waffle Bus (www.thewafflebus.com) Waffles and waffle sammiches, one topped with site-fried chicken and ancho-chili mayo. Need we say more?

BAC Mobile Takeaway versions of **Brooklyn Athletic Club** (Map p218; www.thebrooklynathleticclub.com; 601 Richmond Ave; ⏲11am-2pm & 5-10pm Tue-Sun) faves; parked beside the restaurant's patios, bocce ball and croquet fields.

Oh My Gogi! (www.ohmygogi.com) A fusion of two local cultures: try Korean barbecue tacos or kimchi quesadillas.

Hubcap Grill & Beer Yard BURGERS $
(www.hubcapgrill.com; 1133 W 19th St; burgers $5-10; ⏲11am-9pm Mon-Thur, 11am-10pm Fri & Sat) Maybe Hubcap is popular because everything's homemade, from the freshly formed beef patties to the site-baked buns and hand-cut fries. Or maybe it's the crazy topping choices: Cheetos burger, anyone?

Les Givral's VIETNAMESE $
(www.lesgivrals.com; 4601 Washington Ave; dishes $3-8; ⏲9am-6pm Mon-Thu, to 10pm Fri & Sat) *Banh mi*, oh my! Food bloggers go crazy for this sleek but cheap eatery. Here they keep it simple and sweet – *pho*, a smattering of rice and meat dishes, and the aforementioned, to-die-for Vietnamese sandwiches.

Gatlin's BARBECUE $$
(www.gatlinsbbq.com; 1221 W 19th St; sandwiches $6, mains $10-15; ⏲11am-7pm Tue-Sat) Houston's best barbecue. The *Houston Press* says so, and we wouldn't argue otherwise. Buy your slow-smoked brisket and baby backs - and pulled pork, and turkey – by the pound or by the plate. But watch your timing; not only are their hours limited, their sometimes sell out.

Down House NEW AMERICAN $$
(http://downhousehouston.wordpress.com; 1801 Yale St; sandwiches $10-15, mains $12-20; ⏲9am-midnight) Take a break from the hip shopping of the Heights. Craft beer and creative sandwiches are on the daily menu, but so are larger evening dishes like a bone-in pork chop with cider reduction. If it weren't in Houston, we'd be tempted to call this a gastro pub.

Drinking & Nightlife

Houston's subtropical climate means that a drink on an open-air patios is practically mandatory. The Montrose neighborhood is the classic hangout, but you'll also find great outdoor spaces concentrated in Rice Village and the Heights.

Hard-partying bars and clubs are scattered around town, but to the youngish set, Washington Ave defines all that is hip and happening in Houston nightlife. Do ask around, the club scene changes frequently and what was hot five minutes ago might not be today. Note that some of Houston's most popular dance clubs are also GLBT venues.

A great way to avoid drinking and driving is by riding the Houston Wave (p234), a shuttle service that transports revelers on fixed routes around town.

Downtown

Radiating out from the 300 block of Main St is a good place to start looking for Downtown's emerging nightlife scene. Don't forget Saint Arnold Brewery (p215), just north of town. You can forgo the tour and line up on weekends at 11am, like locals do, to bring a picnic lunch and enjoy four supercheap 'tasting' glasses of their sudsy brews ($8) in the massive beer hall.

La Carafe BAR
(Map p216; 813 Congress St; ⏲1pm-2am) In an 1860 building, this intimate downtown place claims title to the 'oldest bar in Houston.' Expect well-priced wines by the glass and an ancient wooden bar lit by candles.

Warren's Inn BAR
(Map p216; ☎713-247-9207; 307 Travis St; ⏲11am-2am Mon-Sat, 2pm-2am Sun) The jukebox at this lovable downtown dive bar has been officially voted best in town, while the cheap drinks have been unofficially voted the stiffest.

Flying Saucer Draught Emporium PUB
(Map p216; 705 Main St; ⏲11am-1am Mon-Thu, noon-2am Fri & Sat, noon-midnight Sun) At this big beer bar there are more than 200 types of suds, including drafts from all of the local Houston craftworks and many more Texas brews.

Midtown

Nouveau Antique Art Bar BAR
(Map p218; ☎713-526-2220; 2913 Main St; ⏲4:30pm-2am Tue-Fri, 9pm-2am Sat) Full of stunning Tiffany lamps and actual art nouveau decorations, this romantic hideaway in Midtown is where they play Frank Sinatra and Cat Power low enough to have a conversation.

13 Celsius WINE BAR
(Map p218; ☎713-529-8466; 3000 Caroline St; ⏲4pm-midnight Sun-Wed, to 2am Thu-Sat) The only bar in Houston to keep a completely temperature-controlled wine cellar has an earthy Italian *enoteca* (wine bar) feel. Knowledgeable bartenders offer friendly guidance to oenophiles and the clueless alike.

Montrose

Inversion Coffee House CAFE
(Map p218; ☎713-523-4866; 1953 Montrose Blvd; ⏲6:30am-10pm Mon-Fri, 7:30am-10pm Sat & Sun;

) A great indie coffee house. Even if you're not in the neighborhood, the casual local vibe, decent baked goods and a rotation of food trucks outside make it worth a detour.

West Alabama Ice House BAR
(Map p218; 713-528-6874; 1919 W Alabama St; 10am-midnight Mon-Fri, until 1am Sat, noon-midnight Sun) Texas' oldest 'ice house' (where people really used to come to get their ice; now open-air drinkeries) draws the crowds, from bikers to lawyers. We think it's because of the cheap beer and huge dog-friendly yard with picnic tables. Wear sunscreen, and buy someone a beer.

Black Labrador PUB
(Map p218; 713-529-1199; http://blacklabradorpub.com; 4100 Montrose Blvd; 11am-11pm Mon-Thu, 11am-midnight Fri & Sat, 11am-10pm Sun) English pubs in this town are commonplace, but not ones in gorgeous brick buildings with lovely patios and giant outdoor chess games. Brilliant.

Poison Girl LOUNGE
(Map p218; 1641 Westheimer Rd; 4pm-2am) Add a killer back patio with a Kool Aid man statue to an arty interior with vintage pinball games and you get one very cool, dive-y bar. Nice eclectic crowd, too.

Rice Village

The tall trees along Morningside Dr provide a cool and leafy location for several pub patios. Start in the 5100 block and wander south. Note that parking is tight in the area.

Little Woodrow's PUB
(Map p218; http://littlewoodrows.com; 5611 Morningside Dr; 3pm-2am Mon-Fri, noon-2am Sat & Sun) You really can't get more kicked-back than a giant shaded deck with sports on the TVs and so many beers on tap. The Rice Village Woodrow's attracts a university crowd more than the other locations (in Midtown and the Heights) do.

Upper Kirby & River Oaks

Élan CLUB
(Map p218; www.elanhouston.net; 526 Waugh Dr; 9:30pm-2am Thu-Sat) A sophisticated dance club with plenty of loungy seats, Élan caters to 30- and 40-somethings who remember the '80s tunes they often play.

Local Pour BAR
(Map p218; www.localpourhouston.com; 1952 W Gray St; 4pm-2am Mon-Sat, 11am-2pm Sun) Trendy and upscale, yes, but don't be put off by the polished professionals and valet parking. Service here may be refined, but with 48 Texas beers on tap and live music weekends, the vibe is defintely relaxed.

Houston Heights & Washington Avenue

The Heights corner of White Oak and Studemont is home to four great hangouts, including a roadhouse, a tiki bar and a live-music club, Fitzgerald's (p230) – all with big patios. Washington Ave, meanwhile, is Houston at its hippest. Venues frequently change but you'll find plenty of places to party between TC Jester and Heights Blvd: bars, sports pubs, DJ-ed dance clubs...

★ **Onion Creek Cafe** CAFE
(3106 White Oak; 7am-midnight Sun-Wed, 7am-2am Thu-Sat) Open from early-morning coffee and eggs *verde* (with green chili sauce) to late-night cocktails and 'Frenchy' hot dogs with sauteed onions and Dijon. Onion Creek is the quintessential neighborhood hangout. Weekends every table on the sprawling, ultra-chill patio is taken. Great daily specials, Saturday morning farmer's market.

Porch Swing Pub PUB
(65 Heights Blvd; 11am-2am;) One of the biggest and best patios on Washington. Picnic tables are close together, so you'll get to know your neighbors as you tip back a local Houston brew.

Pearl Bar CLUB
(713-868-5337; 4216 Washington Ave; 2pm-2am) Start out on the chill back patio with ping-pong tables; after midnight when the DJ comes on, migrate to the dance floor where you can show off your moves for that hottie you've been eyeing.

☆ Entertainment

Houston's cultural heart lies downtown in the Theater District (www.downtownhouston.org/district/theater), at the intersection of Smith St and Texas Ave. The numerous venues here attract the well-heeled. In nice weather, concerts are often held in front of Jones Hall for the Performing Arts (p229), as well as at Discovery Green (p210) and Market Square Park (p211), also downtown.

You have plenty of local choices for live music at clubs and concert halls around town, though Texas country music is surprisingly scarce.

Look for event listings in the widely available, and free, independent weekly **Houston Press** (www.houstonpress.com). The Thursday edition of the **Houston Chronicle** (www.chron.com) lists nightlife and Sunday's paper has a performing arts section, 'Zest'.

Cinema

Angelika Film Center & Cafe CINEMA
(Map p216; ☎713-225-5232; www.angelikafilmcenter.com; 510 Texas Ave, Bayou Place) Movie buffs will thrill over this Southern outpost of Manhattan's famed Angelika, which shows art-house films in an upscale setting.

Theater & Performing Arts

Alley Theatre THEATER
(Map p216; ☎713-220-5700; www.alleytheatre.org; 615 Texas Ave) Houston's heavy-hitter theater is one of the last in the nation to keep a resident company of actors. From classics to modern plays, the magic of this experienced ensemble is palpable.

Hobby Center for the Performing Arts THEATER
(Map p216; ☎713-315-2525; www.thehobbycenter.org; 800 Bagby St) Hobby Center for the Performing Arts is home to the acclaimed **Theatre Under the Stars** (www.tuts.com), which produces big-budget, Broadway-style musicals (actually inside and in air-conditioned comfort, despite the company's name).

Jones Hall for the Performing Arts THEATER
(Map p216; www.houstonfirsttheaters.com; 615 Louisiana St) Jones Hall hosts the **Houston Symphony Orchestra** (☎713-224-7575; www.houstonsymphony.org) and the **Society for the Performing Arts** (☎713-227-4772; www.spahouston.org), which brings world-class dance troupes to town. Contact the organization, rather than the theater, for tickets.

Wortham Center THEATER
(Map p216; www.houstonfirsttheaters.com; 501 Texas Ave) Wortham Center is an impressive, multi-venue complex that is home to the **Houston Ballet** (☎713-227-2787; www.houstonballet.org) and the **Houston Grand Opera** (☎tickets 713-228-6737; www.houstongrandopera.org), both highly regarded nationally.

GAY & LESBIAN HOUSTON

Despite Houston's conservative streak, the town has a thriving gay scene, which centers in Montrose. The neighborhood has changed a bit in recent years, but you still have a great mix of gay and straight, arty and eclectic residents in the area.

To take the pulse on the local Gay, Lesbian, Bisexual and Transgender (GLBT) community, **OutSmart** (www.outsmartmagazine.com) is the go-to news source that also has a bar guide. Every June, the community sponsors a huge Pride Parade (p221).

Houston has no less than 20 bars and clubs in the gayborhood. The largest and loudest is **South Beach** (Map p218; ☎713-529-7623; www.southbeachthenightclub.com; 810 Pacific St; ⊙9pm-2am Fri & Sat), where young guys and high-tech dance music keep things hot. **F Bar** (Map p218; www.fbarhouston.com; 202 Tuam St; ⊙9pm-2am Tue-Sat, 5pm-2am Sun), a 'boutique nightclub,' has a slightly more mature crowd – plus award-winning DJs. Off the beaten path in Downtown, the **Eagle** (Map p216; http://eaglehouston.com; 213 Milam St; ⊙9am-5am Fri & Sat, 6pm-2am Sun) dance club aims to attract the manliest of men; Sundays are country and western.

With a stylish but low-key vibe and cheap drinks, **JR's Bar & Grill** (Map p218; http://jrsbarandgrill.com; 808 Pacific St; ⊙noon-2am) consistently rates among the best in Houston – especially with reigning drag queen champion Kofi as emcee. Laid-back, local hangout, **EJ's Bar** (Map p218; ☎713-527-9071; 2517 Ralph St; ⊙11am-2am) puts some hunky eye candy on display during frequent shows such as amateur striptease.

Way out west off I-10, the **Usual** (http://theusualpub.com; 5519 Allen St; ⊙4pm-2am Mon-Fri, 3pm-2am Sat & Sun) has been voted the number-one women's bar for several years running. Sure the girls come for the company (especially during Wednesday specials), but there's also karaoke and a great skyline patio view.

Recovering from a late night? Enjoy a tasty cup o' Joe at Inversion Coffee House (p227), which attracts a mix of Montrose neighbors.

Bayou Music Center THEATER
(Map p216; ☎713-230-1666; http://bayoumusic-center.com; 520 Texas Ave, Bayou Place) This massive venue lures an interesting array of entertainers, from Sesame Street Live to LL Cool J to the Houston Roller Derby girls.

Live Music

Houston Music News (www.houstonmusicnews.net) can keep you up to date on country music happenings. When it's time to rock out, visit **Space City Rock** (www.spacecityrock.com). Both are also free monthly newspapers available at venues.

Rudyard's Pub LIVE MUSIC
(Map p218; ☎713-521-0521; www.rudyards.com; 2010 Waugh Dr; ⊙11:30am-2am) Host to eclectic – OK, sometimes downright kooky – theatrical fare as well as good local band concerts. Hipsters just love to hang at Rudyard's.

McGonigel's Mucky Duck LIVE MUSIC
(Map p218; ☎713-528-5999; www.mcgonigels.com; 2425 Norfolk St; ⊙11am-11pm Mon-Thu, 11am-2am Fri & Sat, 5:30-9pm Sun) Acoustic, Irish, folk and country performers play nightly in pub-by surrounds. Tickets are cash-only. Arrive early if you want supper before the show.

Continental Club LIVE MUSIC
(Map p218; ☎713-529-9899; www.continentalclub.com; 3700 Main St; ⊙8pm-midnight Mon, 8pm-2am Tue-Wed & Sat, 6pm-2am Thu & Fri) Not everyone loves the close quarters at Continental Club. But you can't beat the top-notch rock, rockabilly and theme events five nights a week. Convenient to the light rail in Midtown.

Blanco's Bar & Grill LIVE MUSIC
(www.blancosbarandgrill.com; 3406 W Alabama St; ⊙11am-2am Mon-Fri) One of the few places to hear country music within the city limits. Blanco's is every bit the old-fashioned honky-tonk, complete with a tight dance floor. Note the weekday-only hours; live music Wednesday through Friday.

Cézanne LIVE MUSIC
(Map p218; ☎713-522-9621; www.cezannejazz.com; 4100 Montrose Blvd; ⊙9pm-midnight Fri & Sat) Simply Houston's best place to hear jazz. Above the Black Labrador this classy, intimate venue mixes some of the best Texas and international jazz with a very cool piano bar.

Last Concert Cafe BAR
(Map p216; ☎713-226-8563; www.lastconcert.com; 1403 Nance St; ⊙11am-2am Tue-Sat, 10:30am-9pm Sun) For a real local original, find your way to the warehouse district northeast of Downtown. After you knock on the red door (there's no sign), you can hang out drinking cheap suds at the bar or dig into cheap Tex-Mex and listen to live music evenings in the courtyard.

Firehouse Saloon LIVE MUSIC
(www.firehousesaloon.com; 5930 I-59 S; ⊙4pm-2am Tue-Sat) Live Texas music with a twang. Though you can catch the odd rock or rockabilly band playing at this big barnlike place, most of the acts are pure country. It's worth the trip southwest of town on I-59.

Fitzgerald's LIVE MUSIC
(www.fitzlivemusic.com; 2706 White Oak Blvd; ⊙7pm-2am) When the Fitz first opened in the late '70s everyone from Stevie Ray Vaughn to the Ramones played here. Today you might catch a grunge rock or heavy metal show.

Sports

While Houston teams don't get quite the rabid following as, say, the UT Longhorns or the San Antonio Spurs, there's plenty of sports action to be found.

Reliant Stadium FOOTBALL
(www.reliantpark.com; 1 Reliant Park) The **Houston Texans** (www.houstontexans.com) play at this high-tech retractable roof stadium. They draw plenty of raucous crowds, especially since their sucessful 2012 season.

Minute Maid Park BASEBALL
(Map p216; ☎713-259-8000; 501 Crawford St) The **Houston Astros** (http://houston.astros.mlb.com) play pro baseball right downtown. The first retractable roof in town still attracts attention, or maybe it's the real steam train that chugs along every homerun. See the website for ballpark tour times.

Toyota Center BASKETBALL
(Map p216; www.houstontoyotacenter.com; 1510 Polk St) Basketball fans can follow the NBA's **Houston Rockets** (www.nba.com/rockets/) here.

Shopping

Whole neighborhoods are named for their shopping centers in Houston – the Galleria, Rice Village, etc. Montrose has good shops but they're spread out: fashionistas searching for a bargain should start in the 1600 to 1800 block of Westheimer St, near Dunalavy Rd, where they'll find a mix of used- and new-clothing stores selling everything from vintage to punk to Tokyo mod.

West Alabama, between Kirby Dr and Timmon St, is a good place to look for high-end art and antiques. **Art Houston** (www.arthouston.com) produces a guide to the town's scattered galleries. **Paper City Magazine** (www.papercitymag.com) can help you keep current on local design trends.

For bluebonnet-covered, Texasy souvenirs, just about every mall has a **Y'all's Texas Store** (www.yalls.com), and **Cavender's Boot City** (www.cavenders.com) stores abound. Seeking somehing different? The shops of Little India, on Harwin Dr southwest of town off I-59, sell saris galore.

Galleria MALL
(www.simon.com; 5075 Westheimer Rd; ⏰10am-9pm) Welcome to THE mall, Houston's Valhalla of shopping. The sprawling Galleria is Texas' biggest indoor shopping center, with 2.4 million sq ft, 400 stores, 30 restaurants, two hotels – oh, and an ice-skating rink.

Just about every upscale national department and chain store you can think of is represented here, plus exclusive design houses and boutiques. This place is so iconic to Houston that 'the Galleria' refers to the whole surrounding neighborhood, which has many more shopping and dining plazas.

Rice Village NEIGHBORHOOD
(Map p218; www.ricevillageonline.com; btwn Kirby & Morningside Drs, & University & Rice Blvds) One of the few parts of town best explored on foot, Rice Village buzzes with a hip student energy thanks to neighboring Rice University. Though upscale chains are well represented in a mall-like plaza, many of the smart shopping options on outlying streets are one of a kind.

Houston Heights NEIGHBORHOOD
(www.houstonheights.org; 19th St, btwn Yale St & Shepherd Dr) Funky vintage shops, eclectic homewares, an antique outlet or two and artsy clothing boutiques – including one specializing in *Mad Men*, '60s-era togs – concentrated along a short stretch of 19th St in the Heights. On the first Saturday of every month, 19th St takes on a carnival-like air with outdoor booths and entertainment.

The eclectic old neighborhood's bungalow homes add to the charm of shopping here, as does the odd cafe or two.

Chloe Dao Boutique BOUTIQUE
(Map p218; ☎713-807-1565; http://chloedao.com; 6127 Kirby Dr, Rice Village; ⏰11am-7pm Mon-Sat) Try on *Project Runway* winner Chloe Dao's fashionable wares in this Rice Village gem that's all about local design, looking good and having fun.

Buffalo Exchange CLOTHING
(Map p218; ☎713-523-8701; www.buffaloexchange.com; 1618 Westheimer Rd; ⏰10am-8pm Mon-Sat, noon-7pm Sun) Houston's definitive and most selective buy-sell-trade clothing store. Yes, they're picky, and that's a good thing.

Jonathan Adler HOMEWARES
(Map p218; www.jonathanadler.com; 2800 Kirby Dr; ⏰10am-7pm Mon-Sat, noon-6pm Sun) Design-driven homewares star at Jonathan Adler's flagship store, but his fashion accessories also exemplify his 'happy chic.'

Folk Market HANDICRAFTS
(Map p218; www.avantgardenhouston.com; 411 Westheimer Rd; ⏰noon-6pm Sun) Local independent artists sell their handmade and crafty wares the third Sunday of every month at the AvantGarden cafe-bar-lounge. Look for miniature markets Friday evenings during the summer months.

Whole Earth Provision Company OUTDOOR EQUIPMENT
(Map p218; ☎713-526-5226; www.wholeearthprovision.com; 2934 S Shepherd Dr; ⏰10am-9pm Mon-Fri, to 8pm Sat, noon-6pm Sun) Along with lots of sporty shoes, clothes and gadgets for the outdoorsy set, Whole Earth has essential travel merchandise such as guide books and high-tech gadgets.

M2M Fashions CLOTHING
(Map p218; ☎713-521-0804; www.m2mfashion.com; 3400 Montrose Blvd; ⏰11am-8pm Mon-Thu, until 9pm Fri & Sat, noon-6pm Sun) Gay or straight, frat boy or professional, this menswear store isn't about a demographic so much as about whatever's hottest (Zachary Prell, Diesel, Z Brand...).

Domy GIFTS
(Map p218; ☎713-523-3669; www.domystore.com; 1709 Westheimer Rd; ⏰noon-8pm Mon-Fri, 11am-8pm Sat, 11am-7pm Sun) A fun-spirited store that features a mod mix of architecture, design, art and style – plus weird Japanese toys. After shopping, retreat to the back patio cafe.

Brazos Bookstore BOOKS
(Map p218; ☎713-523-0701; www.brazosbookstore.com; 2421 Bissonnet St; ⏰11am-8pm Mon-Sat, noon-6pm Sun) Houston's independent

bookseller since 1974. Browse local titles or meet authors at their many monthly events.

Cactus Music MUSIC
(Map p218; ☎713-526-9272; www.cactusmusictx.com; 2110 Portsmouth St; ⏰10am-9pm Mon-Sat, noon-7pm Sun) Off Richmond Ave in Upper Kirby, Houston's original indie-music store has been rocking out for more than 30 years, pleasing hippies, punks and country fans alike.

Chocolate Bar FOOD
(Map p218; ☎713-520-8599; www.theoriginalchocolatebar.com; 1835 W Alabama St; ⏰10am-10pm Mon-Sat, noon-10pm Sun) Resistance is futile. The handcrafted chocolate here – in all of its forms: bar, confectionary, cake, pie, ice cream – is irresistible.

Information

EMERGENCY

For all emergencies, dial ☎911.

Houston Police (☎nonurgent 713-884-3131) Call to report nonurgent issues.

INTERNET ACCESS

Most Houston coffee shops provide free wi-fi. Most hotels and motels have in-room wired or wireless internet. At more expensive hotels, this service may incure a fee ($10 to $20 per day). Some do offer wi-fi free in the lobby.

Not dragging your laptop around? Internet cafes are an endangered species, instead look for copy shops and libraries.

Copy.com (☎713-528-1201; www.copydotcom.com; 1201 Westheimer Rd; per hr $7.50; ⏰7am-9pm Mon-Fri, 11am-7pm Sat) Montrose copy center where you can check your email and print documents.

Houston Public Library (www.hpl.lib.tx.us; 500 McKinney St; ⏰10am-8pm Mon-Thu, 10am-5pm Sat; wi-fi) Free internet computers and wi-fi.

CITY PASS

Seeing all the major sights and traveling with children? Then the **City Pass** (www.citypass.com; adult/child $46/36) can help you save about 40%. With it you get admission to the Houston Museum of Science, the Houston Zoo, the Children's Museum or the Museum of Fine Arts, and Johnson Space Center. Buy it online, at the visitor center or at attractions.

MEDIA

Houston Chronicle (www.chron.com) The major daily newspaper and online resource. 'Nuff said.

Houston Press (www.houstonpress.com) Alternative weekly offering political comment and loads of dining and entertainment info; widely available at cafes, bookstores and street kiosks.

KUHT 88.7 Classical music and National Public Radio (NPR) from the University of Houston.

Semana News (www.semananews.com) Houston's biggest Spanish-language news source.

MEDICAL SERVICES

For minor problems, urgent care clinics are cheaper than hospital emergency rooms. Countless CVS and Walgreens pharmacies dot Houston; some have 24-hour prescription services.

Memorial Hermann Hospital (☎713-704-4000; www.memorialhermann.org; 6411 Fannin St; ⏰24hr) Emergency room in Texas Medical Center megacomplex.

River Oaks Emergency Center (☎713-526-2320; www.rediclinic.com; 2320 S Shepherd Dr; ⏰24hr) Urgent-care clinic treating minor illnesses and injuries on a walk-in basis.

MONEY

You'll find numerous ATMs all around town - in banks, gas station convenience stores and at airports, among other places.

Chase Bank (www.chase.com; 712 Main St) Currency exchange and ATM.

POST

Main Post Office (Map p216; 401 Franklin St; ⏰10am-5pm Mon-Fri) Plenty of parking, at the north edge of Downtown.

SAFE TRAVEL

The usual advice for American big cities applies in Houston. Lock your car, keep valuables out of sight, beware of dark and lonely streets. Areas to the immediate east and southeast of downtown Houston can be sketchy at any time, but that description is by no means universal.

TELEPHONE

When making phone calls you must dial both the area code and the number. Three area codes serve the greater Houston area: ☎281, ☎713, and ☎832.

TOURIST INFORMATION

Greater Houston Convention & Visitors Bureau (Map p216; ☎713-437-5200; www.visithoustontexas.com; City Hall, 901 Bagby St; ⏰9am-4pm Mon-Sat) As much a giant souvenir shop as an info center. Note that the office closes Saturdays during downtown

AIRPORT HOTEL

Late arrival or early departure? Skip the hassle and stay at George Bush Intercontinental Airport. The **Marriott Houston Airport** (☎281-443-2310; www.marriott.com; 18700 JFK Blvd; rooms $149-249; P ⊖ @ 🛜 🏊) is between terminals A and B.

events (festivals, marathons, etc). Free parking on Walker St.

USEFUL WEBSITES

The city's newspaper and tourist bureau websites are really the town's most useful.

www.houston.com Links to city resources, from golf courses to airport info to festivals.

www.downtownhouston.org Events guide, listings and great maps for the Downtown area.

Getting There & Away

AIR

Houston Airport System has two airports; free wi-fi is available at both facilities. Twenty-two miles north of the city center, the largest, **George Bush Intercontinental Airport** (IAH; www.fly2houston.com/iah; Will Clayton Parkway or JFK Blvd, off I-59, Beltway 8 or I-45) serves cities nation- and worldwide through many carriers, including United. Two inter-terminal train systems connect passengers to all five terminals. Southeast of town, **William P Hobby Airport** (HOU; www.fly2houston.com/hobby; Airport Blvd, off Broadway or Monroe Sts; 🛜) is a major hub for Southwest Airlines and for domestic travel. At the time of writing an international expansion wing was under consideration.

BUS

Greyhound Bus Terminal (Map p216; www.greyhound.com; 2121 Main St) Long-distance buses depart for cities across Texas. Terminal is located two blocks from the Downtown Transit Center light rail stop.

TRAIN

Ah, train travel. Such a romantic idea, yet still such a pain in Texas.

Amtrak Station (☎800-872-7245; www.amtrak.com; 902 Washington Ave) The chronically late *Sunset Limited* train stops here three times a week en route between New Orleans and Los Angeles.

Getting Around

Houston is a sprawling metropolis, poorly served by public transportation. You will need a car. The exception being if you plan to stay in the light rail corridor and only travel between Downtown, Midtown, the Museum District, the Medical Center and on to Reliant Park.

TO/FROM THE AIRPORT

A shuttle is the most convenient and cost effective way to get downtown. **SuperShuttle** (☎800-258-3826; www.supershuttle.com) provides regular service from both Bush ($25) and Hobby ($20) airports to hotels and addresses around town.

All major rental cars are available at both Houston airports; decent prices make Houston an ideal departure point for a Texas road trip.

Taking a bus will cost time but save money; a cab, vice versa. The Metropolitan Transit Authority (p233) runs bus 102 between George Bush Intercontinental and Downtown stops, including the light rail Downtown Transit station (one hour) from 5:30am to 8pm. Bus 88 operates between Hobby and Downtown (30 minutes) from Monday to Saturday, 6am to 11pm. The fares are $1.25.

Taxis are readily available at both airports. Airport rates are determined by zone. Expect to shell out $50 to get from George Bush Intercontinental to Downtown; from Hobby it's about $25.

CAR & MOTORCYCLE

Downtown, metered streetside parking is made easier by numerous vending machines that sell timed tickets that are not site specific. Lots are plentiful, if not cheap (upwards of $20 a day).

Outside Downtown, parking is usually free. Don't be put off by valet parking at restaurants and malls; if it costs at all, it's cheap, and it can be easier than finding a space.

PUBLIC TRANSPORTATION

Houston's public transportation is run by the **Metropolitan Transit Authority** (METRO; ☎713-635-4000; www.ridemetro.org; one-way $1.25). Bus transit is geared toward weekday, downtown commuters. The light rail train, METRO Rail, however, is exceptionally useful for travelers. It has only one simple line, but that line links most sights – and some restaurants – along its Downtown–Museum District–Reliant Park corridor. Look for maps, including downloadable smartphone ones, online. The METRO Rail operates from 5am until midnight Sunday through Thursday, and until 2:20am on Friday and Saturday. A single-ride ticket is $1.25.

TAXI

Taxis are easy to hail within Downtown, where they charge a flat $6 rate to go anywhere. Relying on taxis further afield is unreasonable. Given Houston's sprawl, a cab tab could quickly surpass limo rental rates.

Yellow Cab (☎713-236-1111; www.yellowcabhouston.com) Call a taxi to come to you, or download their 'Hail a Cab' app.

Houston Wave (☎713-863-9283;www.thehoustonwave.com; single/multiple routes $10/15; ⏰6pm-1am Thu, 6pm-3am Fri & Sat, 4pm-1am Sun) Houston's on-call jitney service runs shuttle buses on fixed routes for bar-hopping around Midtown, Montrose, Washington Ave, the Heights, Rice Village and Downtown. Phone and you'll be picked up promptly, or 'wave' them down en route. A free park-and-ride lot is at the corner of Houston St and Memorial Blvd.

AROUND HOUSTON

Some of Houston's most interesting attractions are actually out of town. Those we list here are within 50 miles of downtown Houston. But don't forget that so are the historic homes and sandy beaches of Galveston (p241).

The **Bay Area Houston Convention & Visitors Bureau** (☎281-474-9700; www.visitbayareahouston.com; 913 N Meyer Rd, Seabrook; ⏰9am-5pm Mon-Fri, 10am-5pm Sat & Sun) provides regionwide information online or in person.

Clear Lake & Around

Less than 30 miles south of downtown Houston is the Clear Lake area, Houston's recreational boating port of call. In addition to astronaut-central, Space Center Houston along NASA Rd 1, you'll find a harbor with water sport rental and a beachy bar-restaurant or two.

At the lake's outlet, look out for the communities of Seabrook and Kemah; the latter, an entertaining waterfront village with amusements and eateries. You could definitely visit the whole area as a day trip, but the number of things to do – and the traffic to and from Houston – makes an overnight worthwhile.

Sights & Activities

Space Center Houston MUSEUM
(☎281-244-2100; http://spacecenter.org; 1601 NASA Pkwy 1; adult/child $23.50/19.50 with audio guide; ⏰9am-7pm) Dream of a moon landing? You can hardly get closer than at the official visitor center and theme park–esque museum of the National Air & Space Admistration's (NASA) Johnson Space Center. The 90-minute tram tour of the center itself includes the historic Mission Control (you know, the 'Houston' as in the *Apollo 13* transmission, 'Houston, we have a problem.').

While manned US space missions such as the Apollo and shuttle programs have their high-profile launches from the Kennedy Space Center in Florida, the planning and most of the training happens here. When the Johnson Space Center first opened with the Mercury Missions in 1961, it helped put Houston on the map. Today it's one of the town's biggest tourist attractions.

Interactive exhibits let you try your hand at picking up an object in space, landing a space shuttle, and experincing 3Gs in a gyroscope. Be sure to enter and watch the short theater films, because you exit past exhibits. For a more in-depth experience, reserve ahead to lunch with an astronaut (noon Fridays, adult/child $50/20) or to take a Level 9 Tour (10:45am daily, tour $90) that gets you behind the behind-the-scenes at the center.

Pinky's Kayak Rental WATER SPORTS
(☎713-510-7968; www.pinkyskayakrental.com; 4106 NASA Pkwy; kayak rental 1hr $25) Rent kayaks for adjacent Taylor Lake or take a kayak tour. Pinky's also has jetski rental ($50 for a half hour), and half-hour banana-shaped innertube rides (per person $25).

Windsong Charters SAILING
(☎281-332-3108; www.windsong-charters.com; cruises from $150) Private sunset sails, dinner cruises – even boat & breakfast overnight packages are available aboard a 57ft, double masted sailing vessel.

Sleeping & Eating

More atmospheric eats and sleeps are to be found around Kemah. That said, there are plenty of chain options on NASA Rd 1. The various Marriott sub-brands are among the newer hotels. **Opus Bistro** (☎281-334-5225; http://opusbistro.net; 1002 Aspen Rd, off FM 2094; ⏰5-10pm) stands out among the area's casual seafood shacks and slick commercial chains, offering upscale dishes like shrimp-and-crab-topped snapper with a view of the marina.

Seabrook

There's blessedly little to do here in this laid-back community. Live like a local at one of two fully furnished guest houses for rent from **Old Parsonage Guest House** (☎713-206-1105; www.seabrookaccommodation.com; 1113 Hall St; 2br house $150-185). From there it's a short walk to the couple of shops and restaurants in Old Seabrook (1st and 2nd Sts, off Hwy 146). **Tookie's** (www.tookiesburgers.com; 1202 Bayport Blvd; dishes $6-8; ⏲11am-10pm) is as casual as it gets inside, and out on the back patio, where the regular following is chowing down on homemade hamburgers and hand-cut onion rings.

Our favorite area restaurant is a little harder to find, under the Kemah Bridge on the north side access road. **Outriggers Seafood Grill & Bar** (www.facebook.com/outriggersSeafoodGrillBar; 101 Bath St) is worth the search. You can't beat the Gulf-caught fried shrimp, and the sunburned sailor crowd. Locals know to stake out a deckside waterfront table early on weekend afternoons, to watch the boats come and go and listen to the live music downstairs.

Kemah

On the edge of Galveston Bay, Kemah waterfront is a grotesque carnival of commercialism to some, a keep-the-family-busy blessing to others. Weekends expect to wait before you can turn off Hwy 146.

The **Kemah Boardwalk** (www.kemahboardwalk.com; 215 Kipp Ave, off Hwy 146; admission free, all-day ride pass adult/child $20/18; ⏲10:30am-10pm; 👪) is the reason most people come. Its carnival-like atmosphere comes complete amusements including a serious ferris wheel, roller coaster and tower ride, plus step-right-up-and-try-your-luck games. If you decide to book a ride on the Beast (adult/child $17/$14), a 70ft, 70mph jetboat – you WILL get wet.

Kitschy souvenirs are available on the Boardwalk, but more interesting are the quirky boutiques on **Bradford and 6th Sts**. There you can by a handcarved pelican statue before or after you have your tarot reading.

If you want to overlook all get a room with a balcony at the **Boardwalk Inn** (☎281-334-9880; www.kemahboardwalkinn.com; 8 Kemah Boardwalk; r $129-329; ❄📶). There are also a number of B&Bs around; the visitor center has a full list. You can't beat the bayfront location at **White Pelican Inn B&B** (☎281-538-3900; www.awhitetexaspelican.com; 408 Bay Ave; r incl breakfast $125-250; ❄📶), where you can fish from a private 250ft pier or watch the sunset from the guest-use hot tub.

Landry's restaurant group owns the Boardwalk, literally, so you'll find waterfront, boardwalk dining at their chains with names likes Bubba Gump Shrimp Co and Cadillac Bar. Our 8- and 11-year old nieces/restaurant critics give the **Aquarium** (☎281-334-9010; 11 Kemah Boardwalk; mains $15-30; 👪) four stars – because there they can eat surrounded by a filled-to-the-gills, multistory, 50,000-gallon fish tank. (The food isn't bad, either.)

Locals tend to hang a little further inland. **T-Bone Tom's** (http://tbonetoms.com; 707 Hwy 146 ; dishes $7-20; ⏲dining room 11am-10pm; backyard 5pm-2am Mon-Fri and 11am-2am Sat & Sun) has been a Kemah classic for generations, popular for the site-made smoked sausage and barbecue, plus steaks and seafood. Its backyard hosts bands and singer-songwriter showcases most evenings. For something a bit more intimate, try the tiny **Tabella at Clear Creek Winery** (☎281-957-9090; http://dineattabella.com; 709 Harris Ave; mains $20-36; ⏲11am-2pm & 5-9pm Tue-Thu, to 10pm Fri & Sat) which emphasizes farm-to-market ingredients on its tasting menu – paired with its own wines, of course.

The fun doesn't go down with the sun here. Check out the widely available, free monthly entertainment magazine, **Scene** (http://thescenemagazine.com), for area events and live music.

San Jacinto Battleground State Historic Site

In the late afternoon on April 21, 1836, General Sam Houston and his ragtag Texan army caught up with the Mexican forces of General Antonio López de Santa Anna that were resting on the banks of the San Jacinto River. Fighting was fierce, as Houston's men 'remembered the Alamo,' and the massacre at Goliad. Santa Anna's surrender came relatively quickly. The final tally: 630 Mexicans dead and hundreds more wounded, but only nine Texan casualties. Victory was total. The Mexican army retreated; Texas had won its independence.

More than 1100 acres of the battleground are now preserved as the **San Jacinto Battleground State Historical Site** (www.tpwd.state.tx.us; 3523 Hwy 134; admission free; ⏲9am-6pm). The independence monument itself strongly resembles the Washington Monument in DC, except that it has a concrete star on top, making the Texas version 12ft taller. Tour the museum, watch the movie, then ride up to the observation deck to look over the field. Also part of the historic site is the docked 1912 battleship, USS *Texas*, one of the first steel-plated ships of its era.

The park lies 22 miles east of downtown Houston, via I-10 E. Exit at Crosby-Lynchberg Rd, turn south and take the small car ferry across to the site. **Monument Inn** (www.monumentinn.com; 4406 Independence Pkwy S; meals $12-26; ⏲11am-9pm Sun-Thu, 11am-10pm Fri & Sat) has great Gulf seafood with ship channel views next to the ferry.

Spring

Historic buildings, boutiques and cafes galore, **Old Town Spring** (www.oldtownspring.com; ⏲shops: 10am-5pm Tue-Sat, noon-5pm Sun) is a browser-and-buyers delight. Set up like a large village, many of the old houses and storefronts moved here date to the early 1900s. Each of the shops is unique, some more so than others. Shop at the hat store or the one dedicated solely to birdhouses and you'll see what we mean. Crafts, gifts, antiques, even Texas wines, are all to be had here. When you get hungry, food stands, tea houses and restaurants offer nourishment. **Puffabelly's** (www.puffabellys.com; 100 Main St; dishes $6-18; ⏲11am-3pm Tue & Sun, 11am-3pm & 6-9pm Wed, 11am-9pm Thu-Sun), in an old railroad depot, not only has free peanuts and big country-style main dishes, they serve up a Texas country singer-songwriter showcase every Wednesday night.

Sam Houston National Forest

East Texas has four national forests, the largest being **Sam Houston National Forest** (☎ranger station 936-344-6205; www.fs.fed.us/texas; 394 FM 1375 W, New Waverly), covering 255 sq miles just north of Houston between I-45 and I-59. Recreational facilities include lakes, camping, mountain biking and hiking trails. At the time of writing, sections of the 128-mile **Lone Star Hiking Trail** (www.lonestartrail.org) are closed indefinitely due to tree damage; maps and section openings are posted online. Exercise extreme caution during deer-hunting season (November to early January); call the ranger's office for exact dates.

Huntsville

Thick, shady forests of tall pine trees: only 70 miles north of Houston, Huntsville feels far removed from city life. Driving I-45 north, you'll know you've found the spot when you see the humongous, 67ft-tall Sam Houston statue. The **Statue Visitor Center & Gift Shop** (http://samhoustonstatue.org; 7600 Hwy 75 S, exit 109 off I-45; admission free; ⏲9am-5pm Mon-Fri, 11am-5pm Sat & Sun) also has information about the area.

The town's dubious claim to fame is its seven state prisons that contain more than 13,000 prisoners at any given time. As disturbing as it is fascinating, the **Texas Prison Museum** (☎936-295-2155; 1113 12th St; adult/child $2/1; ⏲noon-5pm Tue-Fri & Sun, 9am-5pm Sat) doesn't sugarcoat its exhibits, such as 'Old Sparky,' the electric chair once used to dispatch the condemned.

One of east Texas' best barbecue joints is also here. If you visit on a weekend, don't pass up a chance to eat the slow-smoked 'Q' served by **New Zion Missionary Baptist Church** (☎936-294-0884; 2601 Montgomery Rd; all-you-can-eat $12; ⏲11am-7pm Thu-Sat). Some say it's a revelation. If that's closed, the country cuisine at **Farmhouse Cafe** (☎936-435-1450; 1004 14th St; meals $7-9; 👪) ain't bad either.

WASHINGTON COUNTY

Have you seen those iconic photos of a lone live oak tree on a small rise overlooking an endless field of bluebonnets? It may well have been snapped in Washington County. With old courthouse squares alive with shops and cafes, frequent town festivals, and historic Texas-independence sites, you can't get more stereotypically small-town Texas than this. Sitting equidistant from Houston and Austin (about 70 miles from either), Washington County makes an easy country escape from the city. No town is more than 40 miles from the region's main center, Brenham. Note that the county has loads of small but special lodgings; the Round Top Chamber of Commerce (p238) curates the most comprehensive list.

Brenham

No wonder downtown Brenham is listed on the National Register of Historic Places - it's darn cute. Wandering the atmospheric streets full of boutique and antique shops is a good day's diversion. Since 1907 this community has also been the home of Blue Bell Creameries, producer of the unofficial state ice cream of Texas. As the largest town in the region, Brenham serves as a good base for exploring.

Sights & Activities

Pick up a historic building, scavenger hunt walking tour brochure at the visitor center.

★Blue Bell Creameries FACTORY
(979-830-2179; www.bluebell.com; 1101 S Blue Bell Rd; tour adult/child $6/4; 8am-5pm Mon-Fri, 10am-2pm Sat; tours 8:30am-3pm Mon-Fri;) Explore the museum-like welcome center before heading to the gift shop and ice cream parlor (scoop $1). On the 45-minute production tour you'll see 180 pints made per minute, and get a free cupful at the finish. Entertaining, long-time-employee tour guides are true ice-cream lovers, proving they really 'Eat all they can, then sell the rest.'

Of the 53 permanent and seasonal flavors produced annually, we like the fancier concoctions such as Lemon Bliss (with vanilla cream cookies) or Moo-llenium Crunch (with chocolate chunks, caramel and pecans). The tried and true, top three favorites across the 20 states they serve remain the same: Homemade Vanilla, Cookies 'n' Cream and Dutch Chocolate.

Brenham Heritage Museum MUSEUM
(www.brenhamheritagemuseum.org; 105 S Market St; adult/child $3/free; 1-4pm Wed, 10am-4pm Thu-Sat) Kiddos love the antique fire engine collection, and everyone can dig special events like Archaeology Day at this town history museum.

Toubin Park PARK
(208 S Park St) Duck into Belle's Alley, between Alimo and Commerce Sts, on your downtown wanderings. There little Toubin Park has illustrated signs that show the story of the devastating 1866 fire. You can also see below ground to one of the private cisterns built to combat water troubles.

Pleasant Hill Winery WINERY
(www.pleasanthillwinery.com; 1141 Salem Rd; tour free, tastings $2-10; 11am-6pm Sat, noon-5pm Fri) Take a weekend drive to this lovely little vineyard in the country. The light crisp whites are a 'pleasant' surprise. Three to four tours offered weekends.

Sleeping & Eating

Brenham House B&B B&B $$
(979-251-9947; www.thebrenhamhouse.com; 705 Clinton St; r incl breakfast $129-148;) Multicourse, gourmet breakfasts always include a delicious bread or pastry product, making it clear that the proprietors were bakers in another life. Comfortable rooms in the rambling 1900s home are as gracious as your hosts.

Ant Street Inn INN $$
(800-481-1951; www.antstreetinn.com; 107 W Commerce St; r incl breakfast $135-245;) You'll get a full dose of 19th-century Texas rustic elegance in the rooms of this historic inn. Complimentary breakfasts are served at the adjoining grill restaurant.

Must Be Heaven CAFE $
(http://mustbeheaven.com; 107 W Alamo St; dishes $4-10; 8am-5pm Mon-Sat, 11am-3pm Sun) At lunch or for an afternoon snack, go for the delish sandwiches and homemade desserts at the aptly named Made In Heaven.

Volare Italian Restaurant RESTAURANT $$
(979-836-1514; www.volareitalianrestaurant.com; 102 Ross St; lunch mains $7-9 dinner mains $11-19; 11am-2pm & 5-9:30pm Tue-Sat) Rustic Italian meals are served in a lovely wooden house. This is the local favorite for a night out.

Shopping

For many, wandering and window shopping are the main attractions in Brenham. Start on Alamo St near the courthouse, where there are singular specialty clothing, gift and

SCENIC DRIVE: EAST CENTRAL TEXAS

Brenham and Round Top may be the most well-known destinations in east central Texas, but don't stop there. Washington County, and Fayette and Austin counties to the south, are riddled with small town attractions and scenic vistas. Get a good map and take to the rural roads. You might happen upon a ranch restaurant and B&B in Cat Spring, a Friday night shindig at the Chicken Ranch Hall in Nechanitz, or an old town cafe in Fayetteville. At the very least expect to see bucolic farms and, in spring, bluebonnets. The **Central Texas Bluebonnet Council** (877-426-6763; www.texasbluebonnets.org) keeps tabs on which areas are in full bloom. For road-tripping tunes, we especially like FM 2161 north of Brenham. Or tune your radio to 95.9 FM's all-Texas country music, all the time.

homeware stores. Antiques also abound, though prices can be high.

American Man Cave ANTIQUES
(214 E Alamo St; ⏲10am-6pm) Need an old Harley Davidson, a stoplight or a Pachinko machine in your rec room? You've come to the right place; this is a guy's guy antique store, offering complimentary beer or coffee while you shop.

Information

Washington County Chamber of Commerce (☎979-836-3696; www.visitbrenhamtexas.com; 115 W Main St; ⏲9am-5pm Mon-Fri, 10am-2pm Sat) Look for the visitor center inside the 1925 Simon Theater, where you can pick up info on the entire county. The visitor booklet and emaps are also available online.

Burton

Just a hop and a skip from Brenham, this little town was where much of the area's cotton used to be processed. To see how it was done, visit the **Burton Cotton Gin & Museum** (www.cottonginmuseum.org; 307 N Main St; adult/child $6/4; ⏲10am-4pm Mon-Sat). If you're out and about, you might want to stop for a taste of Barn Red, a rich berry blend, from the ranch vineyards **Saddlehorn Winery** (www.saddlehornwinery.com; 958 FM 1948 N; tasting free; ⏲11am-6pm Tue-Sat). The French chef behind the stove at the weekend-only **Brazos Belle Restaurant** (http://brazosbellerestaurant.com; 600 Main St; mains $12-28; ⏲5:30-9pm Fri & Sat, 11:30am-2pm Sun) is quite the surprise in such a tiny town. Across the street, **Knittel Homestead Inn** (☎979-289-5102; http://knittelhomestead.com; 520 N Main St; r incl breakfast $105-175; ❄📶) has six rooms in two comfortably restored historic homes.

Round Top

The tiny rural outpost of Round Top (population 90) has several big claims to fame. The old town square, if it's big enough to even call it that, is home to one of Texas' landmark cafes. Winedale historic complex is nearby. And two weeks a year one of the country's top 10-rated antiques markets takes over not only the town, but the county.

What started out as Ms Emma Lee Turney's private little antiques fair in 1968 has morphed into **Round Top Antiques Weekend** (www.roundtop.org; Hwy 237, btwn Burton & La Grange), encompassing more than 30 miles, six small towns and thousands of dealers. Though it officially takes place one weekend in April and one in October, in actuality events run for about 10 days. This is not one show, but MANY. Your best bet is to get a guide from www.showdaily.us and scope out where you want to go ahead of time. Some of our favorite venues include Zapp Hall, for treasures repurposed by the local **Junk Gypsies** (http://gypsyville.com); the Original Big Red Barn, for European antiques; and anything in Warrenton – if we're bargain hunting.

When you get hungry during the events, there are plenty of ad-hoc bars and eateries around. You'd have to book months ahead to grab a seat at **Royers Cafe** (☎979-249-3611; www.royersroundtopcafe.com; 105 Main St; sandwiches $7-12, mains $12-28; ⏲11am-2pm Wed, 11am-9pm Thu-Sat, noon-3pm Sun) during the fairs. The cafe is almost as famous for its great sandwiches (grilled shrimp BLTs) and mains (center-cut pork chops with raspberry chipotle reduction) as it is for their pies (Texas Trash, with chocolate chips, pecans, pretzels, coconut and caramel – oh my!). The decor is a crazy collection of memorabilia and fun T-shirts covering every inch of the old clapboard walls.

'Downtown' Round Top is a collection of small old buildings set up to house arts and craft galleries and other small shops, open year-round, 11am-5pm Wednesday through Sunday. Because of the antiques fair, there are numerous area B&Bs and cottage rentals; the **Round Top Chamber of Commerce** (☎979-249-4042; www.roundtop.org; 102 E Mill Street; ⏲10am-4pm Tue-Sat) has a comprehensive list. Set on a hill above town, the two-story covered porches on the 1874 **Belle of Round Top B&B** (☎936-521-9300; www.belleofroundtop.com; 230 Days End Lane; r incl breakfast $150-195; ❄📶) lend it all the grace and Southern charm of an old plantation home.

In the countryside northeast of Round Top look for the **Winedale** (www.cahutexas.edu/museums/winedale; 3738 FM 2714; ⏲by appointment) historic village, part of the University of Texas at Austin. Tours are by appointment only; the best way to see the historic homes and storefronts are during festivals throughout the year. During **Shakespeare at Winedale** (www.shakespeare-winedale.org; Winedale, 3738 FM 2714; tickets adult/child $10/5; ⏲mid-July–Aug), loyal fans drive for miles and miles to watch university students perform the Bard's plays in a rustic setting redolent of his more ribald comedies.

Nearby, the queen of shabby chic herself designed the stylish places to slumber at **The Prairie by Rachel Ashwell** (☎979-836-4975; http://theprairiebyrachelashwell.com; 5808 Wagner Rd; cottage incl breakfast $200-500; ❄📶). Whether a king suite studio or a two-bedroom bungalow, each individual cottage is straight out of a magazine – one surrounded by a pastoral landscape to rival any painting.

La Grange

Technically, La Grange lies in Fayette County, 40 miles south of Brenham, but we think it's close enough to count. The **La Grange Chamber of Commerce** (www.lagrangetx.org; 171 S Main St; ⏲9am-5pm Mon-Fri, 10am-2pm Sat) has a free walking tour brochure of the largish main square (the town does have a population of 4,400, after all). But the real attraction is the **Texas Quilt Museum** (www.texasquiltmuseum.org; 140 W Colorado St; adult/child $8/4; ⏲10am-4pm Thu-Sat, noon-4pm Sun), opened by the organizer of the annual Houston quilt show. Two refurbished mid-19th-century buildings make an excellent home for permanent and special exhibits. While you're in town, be sure to stop by **Weikel's Bakery** (http://weikels.com; 2247 W Hwy 71; pastries $1-3; ⏲5am-9pm) for some site-baked *kolaches* (Czech-inspired rolls stuffed with sweets or savories, such as fruit jam or jalepeño sausage and cheese); they serve barbecue, too.

Less than two miles north of town you and the little ones can take a hay ride, milk a cow and meet the herd that has starred in Blue Bell Creameries TV commercials at the **Jersey Barnyard** (www.texasjersey.com; 3117 Hwy 159; tours adult/child $8/6.50; ⏲10am-6pm Mon-Sat, 1-6pm Sun; 👪). The tastings of the sweet and spicy honey wines at **Rohan Meadery** (www.rohanmeadery.com; 6002 FM 2981 ; tastings $6; ⏲noon-6pm Wed-Sun) may be for adults, but there is a picnic area outside for families to enjoy.

Note that Shiner (p122), home of Shiner Bock beer, is only 40 miles to the south.

Chappell Hill

Talk about a one horse town. The historic area on Main St is hardly three blocks long. But that is where you'll find **Bever's Kitchen** (www.bevers-kitchen.com; 5162 Main St; dishes $7-14; ⏲11am-5pm Mon-Thu, 11am-8pm Fri, 11am-5pm Sat), another classic country cafe. On weekends a picker plays on the front porch while you eat your burgers and pie. Chappell Hill is known for its locally made smoked sausage, which you can pick up at any one of the barbecue joints along the highway.

Eight miles northeast of town, spring smells awfully sweet at the **Chappell Hill Lavender Farm** (www.chappellhilllavender.com; 2250 Dillard Rd; admission free; ⏲10am-2pm Fri, 9am-5pm Sat & 11am-5pm Sun Mar-Oct), Here you can picnic, roam the fields and cut your own lavender – or shop for related products in the gift shop.

Washington-on-the-Brazos

Nicknamed 'the Birthplace of Texas,' this Washington is where Texas declared its independence from Mexico on March 2, 1836. The **Washington-on-the-Brazos State Historic Site** (www.tpwd.state.tx.us/state-parks; 12300 Park Rd 12; admission free, tours adult/child $5/3; ⏲Visitor center 10am-5pm; park 8am-dusk) preserves and recreates parts of the original settlement. Make sure to watch the visitor center film before you take a tour of Independence Hall and the town-site grounds.

Also on the property: the **Star of the Republic Museum** (www.starmuseum.org; 23200 Park Rd 12 ; adult/child $5/3; ⏲10am-5pm), run by Blinn College, tells the story of early Texas through artifacts and exhibits. **Barrington Living History Farm** (www.tpwd.state.tx.us; 12300 Park Rd 12; adult/child $5/3; ⏲10am-4pm) was originally the home of the last president of the Republic of Texas. Today costumed docents, and real sheep and cows, recreate farm life in the 1850s.

Weekends-only, **R Place** (☎936-878-1925; www.rplacetexas.com; 23254 FM 1155 E; dishes $5-9, dinner $18; ⏲11am-6pm Fri, 11am-9pm Sat, 11am-6pm Sun) serves sandwiches and barbecue and Saturday night cooks up one main dish at dinner for patrons to enjoy family style.

Head across the Brazos River from here and the topography changes to endlessly flat floodplains and agricultural fields, with Bryan-College Station 30 miles to the north. Brenham is 20 miles south; Houston, 80 miles southeast.

BRYAN-COLLEGE STATION

POP 172,463

'Welcome to Aggieland.' Texas A&M University is the reason for being, not only for College Station but for neighboring Bryan, which was long ago subsumed into one metro area. Each school year the town's combined permanent population gets a whopping 46,000 student boost. Then all the businesses on College Station's main drag, University Blvd, really bustle. A few miles north of the university, the downtown Bryan area is a bit quieter but still has some bars and eateries.

Sights & Activities

At 5200 acres, Texas A&M (which originally stood for Agricultural and Mechanical) is one of the nation's largest college campuses. While the buildings comes off as more corporate than picturesque, the school is steeped in tradition – in fact, students claim it's more like a religion.

Texas A&M Appelt Aggieland Visitor Center UNIVERSITY
(979-845-5851; http://visit.tamu.edu; Rudder Tower; 8am-5pm Mon-Fri) You have to book ahead for a free walking tour offered by the visitor center. If you plan to explore the campus on your own, stop here first to pick up a map. Otherwise, how will you find the 6500lb of bronze 'Aggie' class ring at the Haynes Ring Plaza?

Kyle Field STADIUM
(tickets 979-845-5129; www.aggieathletics.com; 198 Joe Routt Blvd) Having packed in a record 90,000 fans, behemoth Kyle Field is one of the largest football stadiums in this football-crazed state – one notorious for successfully intimidating visiting teams. With that many fans standing and chanting in unison the entire game, it's not hard to understand why.

Catching an Aggie game is an unforgettable experience of 'maroon madness,' and *the* way to see the interior of Kyle Field. After the 2013 season a $450-million renovation of the stadium began and is forecast to be completed in 2015.

George Bush Presidential Library & Museum MUSEUM
(979-691-4000; http://bushlibrary.tamu.edu; 1000 George Bush Dr W, off FM 2818; adult/child $7/3; 9:30am-5pm Mon-Sat, noon-5pm Sun) Whether they agree with the former president's politics or not, Republican and and Democrats alike would have a hard time arguing that this is anything but one darn fine museum. The well-curated exhibits trace the elder President Bush's life and career, and serve as an interesting primer on American history from WWII through the 1990s.

Follow the statesman's rise from Texas oil prospector through his virtual tour of national politics: from Ambassador to the UN, to Republican National Committee (RNC) chairman, to CIA director, to the White House, to becoming the first American president to see his own offspring occupy the Oval Office. (Yes, that's 'Dubya,' or America's 43rd president, George W Bush.) Family moments, and Barbara Bush's contributions are also included. The story is told with compelling videos throughout, making the additional audio wand superfluous.

TEXAS A&M FOOTBALL: THE 12TH MAN

Who is the 12th man? You are. Well, you, me and all the other A&M fans standing to support the team at Kyle Field during a home game. The tradition started way back in 1922 during a difficult Dixie Classic game (precursor to the Cotton Bowl). So many injuries were sustained that coach DX Bible thought he might not have enough players to finish. So former player E King Gill was pulled from the stands and suited up. At game end he was the last player standing on the sidelines, and though he never touched the ball, his willingness was well noted.

Today the student body and fans stand throughout the game to show that they are the 12th man, ready to help. And they aren't quiet about it either. Yell leaders on the field use an elaborate set of hand and body gestures to call the response-chants – which everyone knows, and SHOUTS. Thirty thousand students, all dressed in maroon, shouting, swaying and gesturing in unison is quite the sight to see. Even if you're not an Aggie fan, we recommend you don't wear orange (that's rival University of Texas' color).

Sleeping

Chain motels line Hwy 6 on the eastern edge of Bryan-College Station, but on football weekends, all lodgings sell out. Book ahead.

Rudder-Jessup Bed & Breakfast B&B $$
(☎866-744-2470; www.rudderbandb.com; 115 Lee Ave; r incl full breakfast $169-209;) Stay in the old college president's stately home, just across George Bush Dr from A&M. Rooms have a comfortable country feel. The hosts will charm your socks off; as they wryly state, 'Children with well-behaved parents are welcome.'

Abigaile's Treehouse B&B $$
(☎979-823-6350; www.abigailestreehouse.com; 1015 E 24th St, Bryan; r incl breakfast $129-229;) Architecture- and design-lovers will dig the uniquely shaped Abigaile's, which does indeed resemble a tree. Four deluxe rooms look out onto leafy, manicured gardens; the Eagle's Nest has a great deck. Spa services available.

Vineyard Court Hotel HOTEL $$
(☎888-846-2678; www.vineyardcourt.com; 1500 George Bush Dr E; ste incl breakfast $109-179;) Gurgling fountains, a wisteria arbor and a coutyard pool makes this all-suite hotel feel worlds removed from school. Each room has a full kitchen but you'll hardly need it, what with the free wine-and-cheese happy hour and continental breakfast.

Eating & Drinking

Come nightfall, head to Northgate District (University Dr, between Wellburn Rd and S College Ave), the most happenin' – and only walkable – stretch of restaurants and nightlife in College Station. Early on it's a sociable area to grab a drink and dinner; later it turns into a spectacle of collegiate sport-drinking. For a more mature evening, head to **downtown Bryan** (www.downtownbryan.com).

On Thursdays, the Bryan-College Station newspaper, **The Eagle** (www.theeagle.com), publishes and posts a list of live music and other events.

Dixie Chicken BAR $
(☎979-846-2322; www.dixiechicken.com; 307 University Dr; burgers $6-10; ⊙10am-2am) An Aggie tradition since 1974, you can't say you've seen A&M if you didn't drink at the Dixie Chicken. Burgers and beer are the usual fare. Expect live country music and loud crowds on weekends.

Village CAFE
(www.thevillagedowntown.com; 210 W 26th St, Bryan; sandwiches $6-11; ⊙8am-5pm Sun & Mon, to 10pm Tue-Thu, to midnight Fri, to 2am Sat) Relaxed, artsy cafe by day; swinging scene by night. Local bands play weekend evenings, followed by a salsa dance party every Saturday night. Thursday is for singer-songwriters.

Madden's Casual Gourmet NEW AMERICAN $$$
(☎979-779-2558; www.pmaddens.com; 202 N Bryan Ave, Bryan; lunch $9-11, dinner mains $19-27; ⊙11am-2pm & 5-9pm Mon-Wed, 11am-9pm Thu-Sat;) With rustic elegance and gracious service, Madden's specializes in adventurous dishes such as a chocolate, coffee and chile-rubbed beef tenderloin with cheddar polenta, but it also offers vegetarian, gluten-free and children's options. During the day, you can browse the antique shops in the adjacent marketplace.

Veritas Wine & Bistro FUSION $$$
(☎979-268-3251; www.veritaswineandbistro.com; 830 University Dr E; lunch $15-20, dinner mains $25-50) Chef Tai Lee puts a creative twist on everything he touches, whether it's the sea bass with miso sauce or a barely seared steak, served sushi-style. Daily specials are a standout.

Information

Bryan-College Station Convention & Visitors Bureau (☎800-777-8292; www.visitaggieland.com; 715 University Dr E, off Hwy 6; ⊙8am-5pm Mon-Fri, 10am-2pm Sat) The visitor bureau puts out a comprehensive guide to eating, drinking, playing and staying in Bryan-College Station, with detailed maps, too. Also available online.

GALVESTON

POP 48,444

Part genteel Southern belle, part sunburned beach bunny: Galveston Island is Houston's favorite playmate. The old gal took a pretty severe beating by Hurricane Ike in 2008, but she's battled back. Sitting on a barrier island near the northern end of a 600 mile-long Texas coastline, Galveston may not have the state's best beaches, but nowhere else in-state will you find such sun-drenched historic charms.

This sandy playground is only 51 miles southwest of downtown Houston. Traveling further south from Galveston, you can skirt the coast 215 miles to Corpus Christi (see boxed text, p267). To the north the Galveston–Port Bolivar Ferry, an attraction in itself, takes you to the isolated Bolivar Peninsula.

History

History and Mother Nature have not always been kind to Galveston Island. Jean Lafitte, the notorious pirate, founded the first European settlement here in 1817 (albeit a lawless and bacchanalian one). The party ended when Lafitte was chased off and the town burnt. Needless to say, stories of buried treasure still abound... Developers arrived in the mid-1830s, and Galveston quickly became the nation's third-busiest port, a jumping-off point for setters heading west. By the beginning of the 20th century, it was the largest city in Texas, boasting a long list of state firsts: first opera house (1870), first electric lights (1883) etc, etc.

All that changed on September 8, 1900, when a hurricane devastated the island. The town never regained its status, ceding port traffic and population to nearby Houston. It took until the 1970s for the beaches' potential to bring back large-scale investment. The local economy was humming along in the 2000s. Then Hurricane Ike hit in September of 2008.

Sights

Galveston stretches 30 miles in length but is no more than 3 miles wide. The main attractions – the historic districts and beaches – lie at the northeastern end of the island, bordered by Seawall Blvd and the Gulf to the southeast and Harborside Dr and the port to the northwest.

A thin strip of freely accessible beaches line Seawall Blvd. But there's more sand and services – and less concrete wall – at organized beaches. Fewer people frequent the southwestern beaches along FM3005. Look for the large amusement parks on the west end, southwest of 61st St.

The Strand NEIGHBORHOOD
(Btwn 25th and 19th Sts, Strand & Church Sts) Stroll the historic Strand District to get an appreciation for the city's glory days of the late 19th century. The commercial horse-drawn carriages seem right at home clip-clopping over historic trolley tracks, past elaborate brick facades that now contain shops and restaurants. Informative historical markers identify buildings around the district.

Look for the Grand 1894 Opera House (p248), still in operation. The old dock area just north off Harborside Dr has been converted to house waterfront restaurants and museums.

Pier 21 Theater THEATER
(☎409-763-8808; www.galvestonhistory.org; Pier 21; adult/child $6/5; ⏲10am-6pm) Pirate Jean Lafitte and Galveston itself are the subject of two of the interestingly informative films shown here. The third, the *Great Storm*, is the best of the bunch. This 30-minute multimedia documentary recounts the 1900 hurricane through photos, eyewitness accounts and various special effects.

Texas Seaport Museum & Tall Ship Elissa MUSEUM
(www.galvestonhistory.org; cnr Harborside Dr & 21st St; adult/child $8/5; ⏲10am-4:30pm) This vast museum explains every facet of life around Galveston's port during its heyday in the 19th century. Outside, clambor aboard to tour the *Elissa,* a beautiful 1877 Scottish tall ship that is still seaworthy.

East End Historic District NEIGHBORHOOD
(www.eastendhistoricdistrict.org; btwn 11th & 19th Sts, & Mechanic St & Broadway Ave) Bordering the Strand, the residential East End Historic District has scores of pretty old houses, from simple cottages to Greek Revival mansions, some of which may be featured on the annual Historic Homes Tour (p246). A good driving and cycling guide and map is available at the visitor center and on the district's website.

Moody Mansion & Museum HISTORIC SITE
(☎409-762-7668; www.moodymansion.org; 2618 Broadway Ave; adult/child $10/8; ⏲tours 11am, 1pm & 3pm Mon-Fri; hourly 11am-3pm Sat & Sun) The grandest on the island, this home dating from 1895 still shines with splendor. Original family furnishings fill the nearly 28,000-sq-ft mansion. Tours take in 20 rooms and last about an hour. Discounted entry is available on the website.

Bishop's Palace HISTORIC SITE
(☎409-762-2475; www.galvestonhistory.org; 1402 Broadway Ave; adult/child $10/5; ⏲11am-5pm) Built between 1886 and 1893, this ornate stone mansion has hidden back stairs and other fun features. Self-guided audio tours

explain the home's history. Docent-led tours depart daily at 12:30pm and 3:30pm. Discount coupons and tickets are widely available.

Ocean Star Offshore Drilling Rig & Museum MUSEUM
(409-766-7827; www.oceanstaroec.com; Harborside Dr, Pier 19; adult/child $8/5; 10am-5pm) From 1969 to 1984, this offshore rig drilled for oil in up to 173ft of water out in the gulf. Now moored off the end of 19th St, it has been converted into a three-level museum that explains offshore oil exploration for people who want to know more about both benefits and dangers.

Galveston Railroad Museum MUSEUM
(409-765-5700; www.galvestonrrmuseum.com; 2602 Santa Fe Pl, cnr 25th St & Strand; adult/child $7/5, train ride $4; museum 10am-5pm; train rides 11am-2pm Sat;) Housed in the beautiful former Santa Fe Railroad Station, this little museum has exhibits on train history as well as model railroads. Saturday you can all-aboard for a 15 minute train ride on the tracks out back.

East Beach BEACH
(1923 Boddecker Dr, off Seawall Blvd; per vehicle $16; dawn-dusk Mar-Oct) Also called Apffel Park, this vast expanse of hard-packed sand is at the very far northeastern end of the island. On summer weekends, it hosts live concerts and becomes one vast outdoor party (large signs proclaim 'drinking permitted').

There is beach parking for a mere 7000 cars here. Per-vehicle admission is discounted weekdays; you can also park before the entrance and walk the roughly 500ft in for free.

Stewart Beach BEACH
(201 Seawall Blvd, at 6th St; dawn-dusk Mar-Oct;) Galveston's family-friendly beach offers summer weekend activities like sand castle building contests as well as a snack bar, chair rental and the all-important bath house with restrooms.

Sea Life Facility WILDLIFE RESERVE
(409-766-3670; www.tamug.edu/sealife; 200 Seawolf Parkway, TAMUG, Bldg 3029; 10am-4pm Wed-Sat) FREE Texas A&M University at Galveston runs a state-of-the-art marine research and rehabilitation facility largely dedicated to endangered sea turtles. From its outreach observation center, you can see the main lab and recovering turtles. Volunteers are on hand to answer questions.

Pleasure Pier AMUSEMENT PARK
(409-766-4950; www.pleasurepier.com; 2501 Seawall Blvd; admission only adult/child $10/8, with ride day pass adult/child $27/20; 10am-10pm Jun-Aug, 11am-10pm Sat & Sun Sep-May;) Sixteen rides, two roller coasters, carnival games, and souvenir and snack kiosks: Landry's restaurant group packs a lot into its post-Ike redo of Galveston's historic, 1130ft Pleasure Pier. For a lower-key but similar set up – with a no-admission, a la carte option – we prefer their Kemah Boardwalk (p235).

Galveston County Beach Pocket Parks BEACH
(FM 3005; per vehicle $16; dawn-dusk Mar-Sep) Several crescent-shaped beaches run by the county are found southwest of town off FM 3005 (the continuation of Seawall Blvd). Their names are taken right off the odometer: 7 Mile Rd, 9 Mile Rd and 11 Mile Rd. All have bathrooms and showers, and the latter two have concession stands. Parking rates are reduced on weekdays.

Moody Gardens AMUSEMENT PARK
(www.moodygardens.com; 1 Hope Blvd; day pass $50; 10am-6pm;) Three colorful glass pyramids form the focus of one entertainment complex. The Aquarium Pyramid showcases king penguins, fur seals and the largest array of sea horses in the world. The 10-story Rainforest Pyramid is a lush tropical jungle full of plants, birds, butterflies and a wonderful creepy-crawly bug exhibit. The Discovery Pyramid hosts traveling exhibits and some so-so space-related stuff.

Elsewhere on-site there are the requisite IMAX, 3D and ride-film theaters. Outside, you can swim up to the artificial Palm Beach or take a boat ride on a replica paddle wheeler. Attraction tickets can be purchased a la carte (with adult/child price differences), a good idea if you don't think you'll do everything in a day pass. If you buy passes online you'll save $5 over the gate price. To reach Moody Gardens, take 81st St from Seawall Blvd to Jones Rd, then turn left onto Hope Blvd.

Schlitterbahn Waterpark AMUSEMENT PARK
(409-770-9283; www.schlitterbahn.com; 2026 Lockheed St; adult/child $40/32; 10am-8pm Jun-Aug) Close to Moody Gardens, this ginormous, indoor-outdoor water park has slides and indoor beaches among 32 watery

Galveston

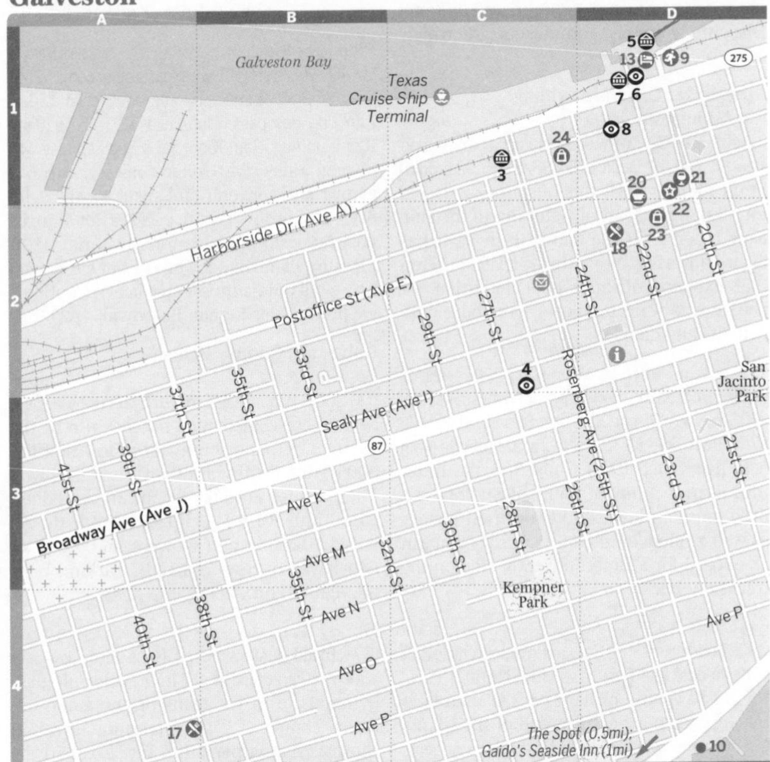

delights. Except for February, when it closes, the indoor part of the park is open weekends year round.

Lone Star Flight Museum MUSEUM

(☎409-740-7722; http://lsfm.org; 2002 Terminal Dr; adult/child $10/5; ⊙9am-5pm) Inside the hangers at Galveston Municipal Airport you can watch the ongoing restoration of storm damage to the impressive historic airplane collection here. For just a bit more ($375) you can take a ride on one of the historic planes like the B-25.

Galveston Island State Park STATE PARK

(☎409-737-1222, reservations 512-389-8900; www.tpwd.state.tx.us; 14901 FM 3005; adult/child $3/free) Some 10 miles southwest of downtown, swimmers will find a hard-packed white-sand beach far from the vacation rentals and tourists of town. This state park also has nature trails through the coastal dunes, salt marshes, bayous and mudflats. Facilities are few and shade is rare, but it's a lovely spot.

Activities

Many stores along Seawall Blvd rent bicycles ($25 to $40 per day) and four-seater, pedal-operated surreys ($20 per hour). Both are excellent ways to roll on down the beachfront seawall path. Water-sports gear like surfboards ($45 per day) and kayaks are also usually for rent.

Red snapper is the fish most prized by people fishing offshore from Galveston, though limits are often enforced. You have your pick of fishing charters and party boats from Pier 19; the visitor center keeps a full list.

In the winter months especially, birders will have no trouble spotting waterbird friends and fowl here. For a list of the area's best sites, log onto www.galvestonnaturetourism.org.

Galveston

Sights
1 Bishop's Palace E2
2 East End Historic District F1
3 Galveston Railroad Museum C1
4 Moody Mansion & Museum C2
5 Ocean Star Offshore Drilling Rig & Museum D1
6 Pier 21 Theater D1
7 Texas Seaport Museum & Tallship Elissa D1
8 The Strand D1

Activities, Courses & Tours
9 Fishing Boat Information Booths D1
10 Galveston Island Duck Tours D4
11 Island Bicycle Company E3

Sleeping
12 Grace Manor E1
13 Harbor House D1
14 Hotel Galvez E4
15 Victorian Bed & Breakfast Inn E1

Eating
16 Farley Girls F1
17 Shrimp N Stuff A4
18 Star Drug Store D2
19 Sunflower Bakery & Cafe E1

Drinking & Nightlife
20 Mod Coffeehouse D1
21 Old Quarter Acoustic Cafe D1

Entertainment
22 Grand 1894 Opera House D1

Shopping
23 Galveston Art League Gallery D2
24 La King's Confectionery C1

Island Bicycle Company ADVENTURE SPORTS
(409-762-2453; www.islandbicyclecompany.com; 1808 Seawall Blvd; 9:30am-6pm Sun-Wed, 9:30am-8pm Thu-Sat) Centrally located, Island Bicycle is a convenient choice for renting most activity gear: surreys, bicycles, surfboards, stand-up paddle boards, boogie boards, kayaks etc. You can even rent fishing poles ($30 per day) or metal detectors for beachcombing ($40 per day).

Tours

Numerous tours ply the islands. For a full list, see the visitor center (p248) in person or online.

Artist Boat Kayak Adventures BOAT TOUR
(409-770-0722; www.artistboat.org; per person 2/4hr tours $25/50) Guides meld science and art during these creative and fascinating kayak tours of the natural sights around Galveston Island; advance reservations required. Ask about discounted tours that support the Coastal Heritage Preserve area off the West Bay.

Historic Harbor Tours BOAT TOUR
(409-763-1877; www.galvestonhistory.org; Pier 21, Texas Seaport Museum; adult/child $10/8; 11:30am, 1pm, 2:30pm & 4pm) Patrons often spot dolphins on these very reasonable, one-hour tours of the boat- and oil-rig-filled harbor. Call to ensure tours are going that day.

Galveston Island Duck Tours TOUR
(409-621-4771; www.galvestonducks.com; cnr 25th St & Seawall Blvd; adult/child $18/12; 9:30am-7pm Jun-Aug) Tour the island's land and water sights in this amphibious vehicle.

Festivals & Events

Galveston puts on a parade of special events; log on to www.galveston.com for a calendar. Be warned: though not an organized event, the weeks of spring break in Texas (varying throughout March) get CRAZY here.

Mardi Gras STREET CARNIVAL
(www.mardigrasgalveston.com) For the 12 days before Ash Wednesday, Galveston does its best New Orleans impression, with parades, pageants, parties and more. At least one Sunday is dedicated to families. Make lodging reservations far, far in advance.

★**Historic Homes Tour** CULTURE
(409-765-7834; www.galvestonhistory.org) The Galveston Historical Foundation puts the island's finest privately owned old houses on display the first two weekends in May. In addition to tours of historic homes, other events include organized evening strolls, bicycle and bus tours, and a jazz brunch.

Dickens on the Strand CULTURE
(409-765-7834; www.dickensonthestrand.org) The first weekend in December the historic Strand District morphs into Victorian London. Costumed jugglers and musicians take to the street as peddlers vend their old timey wares and Queen Vic herself makes a special appearance.

Sleeping

Rates for hotel/motel rooms vary widely, from the lows of midweek winter to the high-highs of June and July weekends. During special events, two-night stays may be required and everything books up months in advance. Note that because of the heat in August, sometimes late summer rates are reasonable.

Be wary of budget motels that we haven't listed. Some are fine, but all are definitely not created equal here. Note that most of Galveston's 'beachfront' lodgings are actually across busy Seawall Blvd from the sand. Reliable chain properties, like La Quinta, are well represented.

The island's official website, www.galveston.com, compiles a complete list of lodgings, including the many rentable condominiums that line FM 3005 southwest of town.

Beachcomber Inn MOTEL $
(800-733-7133; www.galvestoninn.com; 2825 61st St; r $35-120;) A block removed from the beach, this basic two-story motel provides a neat-and-clean budget break. Minifridges and microwaves in every room.

Gaido's Seaside Inn MOTEL $
(409-762-9625; http://gaidosseaside.com; 3802 Seawall Blvd; r $60-120;) This older motel behind the famous, eponymous restaurant has simple but comfortable, well-maintained rooms. Exterior corridors let you ponder the surf and make new friends.

★**Harbor House** BOUTIQUE HOTEL $$
(409-763-3321; www.harborhousepier21.com; Pier 21, off Harborside Dr; r incl breakfast $90-270;) Stay among the shops and museums of the Pier 21 complex in the heart of the historic Strand District. Rustic touches accent the 42 large, comfy rooms occupying a recreated, wharfside warehouse. You have good views of the harbor through smallish windows.

Grace Manor B&B $$
(409-621-1662; www.gracemanor-galveston.com; 1702 Postoffice St; r incl breakfast $140-200;) Built in 1905, this grand, stucco-facade home has colonnades inside and out. The four guest rooms are decorated period-plush with king-size beds and either claw-foot or Jacuzzi tubs.

Victorian Bed & Breakfast Inn B&B $$
(409-762-3235; www.vicbb.com; 511 17th St; r & apt incl breakfast $160-200;) Stay in a sprawling 1899 brick Victorian that survived the 1900 hurricane. Rooms either have king-size beds and a shared hall bathroom, or private bathrooms and one or two bedrooms. We like the Garden Apartment, with private entry, kitchen and access to gorgeous gardens.

Hotel Galvez LUXURY HOTEL $$$
(409-765-7721; www.galveston.com/galvez; 2024 Seawall Blvd; r $160-400;) Bask in palm-fringed Spanish-colonial luxury at this 1911 historic hotel. The full-service spa services – muscle soaking milk bath or seaweed contour wraps, anyone? – are renowned, and the pool deck has a lovely gulf view. Ask about spa special package deals.

Eating

The locals' favorite way to eat fish may be fried, but that doesn't mean they don't have discriminating taste. The dining scene here is a mix of independent eateries and seafood chains run by Landry's restaurant group. A cluster of the latter can be found at the waterfront Pier 21 complex off Harborside in the Strand District.

Star Drug Store DINER $
(☎409-766-7719; 510 23rd St; meals $6-9; ⏱8:30am-3pm) Not retro because it's never changed. This 1923 drug store serves soda fountain treats and classic diner faves (big breakfasts!). Belly up to the counter and order a banana split.

Shrimp N Stuff SEAFOOD $
(3901 Ave O; mains $6-12; ⏱10:30am-8:30pm Mon-Thu, to 9:30 Fri & Sat) Simply good fried shrimp – and catfish, and oysters – served casually. Order at the counter and then head out to eat with the locals at the courtyard tables.

★**Farley Girls** AMERICAN $$
(www.farleygirls.com; 901 Postoffice St; dishes $9-13; ⏱10:30am-3:30pm Mon-Fri, 8:30am-3:30pm Sat & Sun) The historic building may be elegant, with fern-studded colonnades and high wood ceilings, but the tasty comfort food and counter service are down-home casual. Eclectic offerings include both Latin American–spiced *chimichurri* steak salad and mac-and-cheese. At weekend brunch they reinterpret breakfast classics, serving eggs Benedict Texas-style with melted Mexican cheese, or pairing scrambled eggs with their saucy Gouda-and-mushroom grits.

Sunflower Bakery & Cafe AMERICAN $$
(www.thesunflowerbakeryandcafe.com; 512 14th St; sandwiches $7-12, mains $11-22; ⏱7am-7pm Mon-Fri, 8am-9pm Sat & 8am-3pm Sun) Made from scratch, as it should be: site-baked breads, daily made desserts – even fresh local seafood. Piled-high sandwiches are an expected staple at this husband-and-wife team's cafe. That they also serve mouthwatering mains like smoked pork chops, and parmesan-crusted snapper is a bonus.

Clary's SEAFOOD $$$
(☎409-740-0771; http://clarysgalveston.com; 8509 Teichman Rd; mains $18-30; ⏱4:30-10pm Tue-Sat) On Offatts Bayou, this nondescript building has serene water views in the rear. Clary's has been serving fresher-than-fresh seafood dishes for years, though lately service has been a little hit-or-miss. It's just as you enter the island off I-45 at Harborside Dr

Gaido's SEAFOOD $$$
(☎409-762-9625; www.gaidos.com; 3800 Seawall Blvd; mains $20-35; ⏱11am-9pm) Run by the

A TALE OF TWO HURRICANES

During the night of September 8, 1900, the **Great Storm** – a hurricane with winds of 120mph – drove a surge that submerged much of the island under 20ft of water. Where Galveston had been, there were now only the waters of the Gulf of Mexico. Back then there was no weather tracking, and no warning. Of the town's 37,000 people, it's estimated that as many as 8000 died, but no one will ever know the exact toll. The storm struck in the dead of night and survivors recounted the horrifying screams and dying out of lights. To this day it is still the nation's deadliest natural disaster. Learn more at the Great Storm film at Pier 21 Theatre (p242), which uses actual photos and survivor diary entries to recount the tale.

To prevent another such a catastrope, in the 1900s the city constructed a 10-mile-long, 17ft-high seawall. At the same time they raised the grade of the land – from a few inches to seawall height – in a roughly 500 sq block area. Private property owners had to pay to have their own buildings jacked up to the required height. You'll notice the difference at Ashton Villa, one of the few buildings that was allowed to be partially buried.

Both the seawall and technological weather-watching advances likely saved many lives when **Hurricane Ike** made landfall September 13, 2008. Roughly 110mph winds and a 13ft storm surge caused $29 billion in damage, making Ike the third costliest hurricane in the nation's history. More than 125 lives were lost locally.

Reconstruction has taken time – beaches were swept out to sea and much of the downtown area was not only flooded but deluged by sludge as sewage lines burst. (This author's sister-in-law waited two years to get back into her affected offices.) Beach restoration projects have pumped sand from the gulf back onto the shore, and rebuilding will continue indefinitely. Not all the previous businesses reopened, but new restaurants and shops have come in. Some of the BOI ('born on islanders') think the mix is better than it ever was.

same family since 1911, Gaido's is easily the best-known and best-loved restaurant in Galveston. Expect vast platters of no-compromise seafood (oh, the oysters...) served on white tablecloths and with hushed tones. They have a more casual sister restaurant, **Nick's Kitchen & Beach Bar** (☎409-762-9625; http://nicksgalveston.com; 3800 Seawall Blvd; dishes $13-22; ⏰11am-9pm Sun-Thu, to 10pm Fri-Sat), next door.

Drinking

The walkable Strand District provides bar-hopping potential with a couple of great old boozers, plus one or two trendy clubs, along both Postoffice St and the Strand. Several classic beach bars stretch out along Seawall Blvd.

Mod Coffeehouse CAFE
(☎409-765-5659; 2126 Postoffice St; ⏰7am-10pm; 📶) The de facto Strand District community center, this warehouse-based coffeehouse serves fine espressos and swell iced teas. At tables out front you'll hear all the local gossip.

Old Quarter Acoustic Cafe BAR
(☎409-762-9199; http://oldquarteracousticcafe.com; 413 20th St; ⏰8pm-2am Wed-Sat) A long-time, local-favourite bar, which features lots of live music and is prone to festivals honoring Dylan.

The Spot BAR
(☎409-621-5237; www.thespotgalveston.com; 3204 Seawall Blvd; ⏰11am-11pm Sun-Thu, to midnight Fri & Sat) This rollicking and boisterous bar overlooking the gulf is the best of many competitors (with classic names of the genre like 'The Poop Deck'). Good burgers and sandwiches help absorb the vast array of fancy cocktails on offer. Live music at least on weekends.

☆ Entertainment

Grand 1894 Opera House THEATER
(☎409-765-1894; www.thegrand.com; 2020 Postoffice St; ⏰box office 9am-5pm Mon-Sat) The beautifully restored 1894 Opera House well illustrates Galveston's turn-of-the-20th-century culture and wealth. Popular concerts, broadway shows and humorous theatrical productions are staged here.

Shopping

You can find all the sea shells and swim gear you could want along Seawall Blvd. The Strand itself has more than its share of beachy kitsch merchants. For more interesting shopping head to Postoffice St, which has been dubbed the Postoffice Arts & Entertainment District by the city. The blocks between 21st & 24th are especially rich with artist galleries, antiques and curio shops.

La King's Confectionery FOOD
(☎409-762-6100; 2323 Strand (Ave B); ⏰10am-7pm) Watch the saltwater taffy, peanut brittle and chocolates being made at this Strand classic, an old-fashioned candy store and ice-cream parlor.

Galveston Art League Gallery ARTS & CRAFTS
(☎409-621-1008; http://galvestonartleague.com; 2117A Postoffice St; ⏰noon-6pm Thu-Sat) Start exploring the vibrant local art scene at this gallery that shows league members' work. Every six weeks they sponsor an art walk evening, when galleries stay open late and serve refreshments. See the website for the schedule, and for art workshop dates.

Information

Galveston Island Visitors Center (☎409-797-5145; www.galveston.com; Ashton Villa, 2328 Broadway; ⏰10am-5pm Mon-Sat, 9am-4pm Sun) After Hurricane Ike, Ashton Villa (1851) did not reopen to the public, but the visitor center took up residence on a lower level. Pick up a map and the island's 'official guide,' which has coupons, or buy a **Galveston Island Pass** (www.galvestonislandpass.com) here. The latter gets you 40% off big-name attractions like Moody Gardens.

Getting There & Around

From Houston, follow I-45 southeast for 51 miles. On the island, the highway morphs into Broadway Ave and travels toward the historic districts. Turn off onto 61st St to reach Seawall Blvd.

Hurricane Ike knocked the Galveston Island Trolley, run by **Island Transit** (☎409-797-3900; www.islandtransit.net; adult/child $1/0.50), off the rails. Until it's restored – at some far distant, undetermined date – you really need a car to get around. The island's bus service caters to local commuters, not tourists.

Galveston Limousine Service (☎409-744-5466; www.galvestonlimousineservice.com) Three buses a day travel both to and from Houston Hobby Airport (adult/child $45/20, one hour) and Houston Intercontinental Airport (adult/child $55/25, two hours). Advance reservations required.

Galveston–Port Bolivar Ferry (☎409-763-2386; http://traffic.houstontranstar.org/ferry

> **CRUISE SHIP PARKING**
>
> Cruising out? Some accommodations in the area will let you leave your car parked for free if you stay over at least one night before departure. Otherwise, the visitor bureau's website (www.galveston.com/cruiseparking) acts as a consolidator of sorts for area cruise ship parking lots. Rates run $40 to $70 per week, shuttle included.

times; 1 Ferry Rd; ⏲24hr) Linking Galveston Island and the much less populated Bolivar Peninsula, this 20-vehicle ferry runs 24/7, weather permitting. The 20-minute, one-way ride is an attraction in itself.

Get out of your car and climb the platform for better views of freighters from all over the world, and sometimes, dolphins. Note that on summer weekends the boat wait can easily be an hour or longer.

Around Galveston

Bolivar Peninsula

After arriving by ferry (p248) from Galveston, the drive north along this windswept peninsula passes through areas that were hard hit by Hurricane Ike in 2008. There are no real sights to see, but if you're looking for an ain't-nothin'-fancy, local beach getaway that's a world apart from Galveston, **Crystal Beach** (www.crystalbeach.com) has numerous vacation rentals and two laid-back, island-style bar-restaurants.

TX 87 continues 30 miles north to **High Island** (www.birdinghighisland.com), a bird-watcher's delight. The scrubby forests of this area serve as a stopping point for fall and spring migratory birds. When inclement weather hits, fall-outs may fill the trees with the birdsong of thousands. The Houston Audobon Society (p215) runs four small sanctuaries here, with detailed site maps online and at each site. The **Boy Scout Woods** (www.houstonaudubon.org; 2088 5th St, High Island; admission $7; ⏲dawn-dusk) is one of the most well-regarded, for its wooded trail, ponds and observation tower.

Northeast of High Island, the TX 87 coastal road is closed. To reach Sabine Pass and Port Arthur, you have to cut inland at Hwy 124.

Anahuac National Wildlife Refuge

Of the three national wildlife refuges along the Gulf Coast from Galveston to Louisiana, **Anahuac** (☎409-267-3337; www.fws.gov/refuge/Anahuac; 4017 FM 563, Anahuac; ⏲visitor center 10am-5pm Thu-Sun) has the best access – 50 miles northwest of Galveston and 80 miles southeast of Houston – and is therefore the most popular. Due to repeated hurricane damage, the visitors center and bookshop are inland at the park's headquarters, off I-10. Stop there first to get a map to the refuge's main section, which is off FM 1985, 10 miles west of FM 1985's juncture with TX 124. From the high bridge on the latter, the refuge unfolds like one vast green carpet.

The outhouse and main park entrance is 3 miles south of FM 1985. There gravel and dirt roads traverse deep marsh, ponds, prairie and bayous. During the winter, up to 80,000 Canadian snow geese can gather at one time – a truly spectacular sight. Year-round you will see a variety of water fowl and some shore birds. Other wildlife includes alligators and what just may be the largest mosquitoes you ever encounter. In spring, **Friends of Anahuac** (www.friendsofanahuacnwr.org) organize walks in search of the elusive yellow rail ground bird.

> **BIRDING THE UPPER TEXAS COAST**
>
> The uper Texas coast from Galveston to Port Arthur is prime bird-watching territory. It's a stopover for numerous migratory birds (March and September), and a wintering ground for many, many others (December through February). For more information on the region, **Texas Parks & Wildlife** (☎800-792-1112, 512-389-8900; www.tpwd.state.tx.us) is a great help. They produce a full-color *Great Texas Coastal Birding Trail - Upper Texas Coast* map and have birdlists and area info online. The Houston Audobon Society (p215) runs sanctuaries, holds events and is another keen source of information in the region. Local visitor bureaus often have extensive resources as well; the Port Arthur Convention & Visitor Bureau (p253), for example, produces an excellent detailed booklet on all the birding sites around Sabine Pass.

CAJUN CULTURE

The Golden Triangle is also referred to as the Cajun Triangle due to the large number living in the area. French-speaking settlers exiled from l'Acadie (now Nova Scotia), sought refuge in adjacent southwestern Louisiana in the mid- to late-18th century (the term ' Cajun' is a corruption of 'Acadian'). In the early 20th century many Cajuns moved across the border to Beaumont and Port Arthur to find work in the oil fields.

Cajun culture is famed for its cuisine, music and spirit. Let the *bons temps roulée!* Their influence is felt in in Houston and towns along the coast, but nowhere more strongly than here. Don't pass up this opportunity to eat Cajun specialties such as *boudin* (sausage made from spicy pork and rice), seafood gumbo (a roux-based soup) and *etoufées* (seafood in a creamy but spicy sauce), or try the classic red beans and dirty rice (with pork sausage). On menus you'll also see po'boys (loaf sandwiches filled with such fried treats as oysters, shrimp or catfish).

Locals can't wait for crawfish season to come around. If you're in town between March and May, you have to try a crawfish boil. The miniature-lobsterlike shellfish (also called 'mudbugs') are dropped live into the pot simmering with spicy cayenne seasonings. Corn on the cob, new potatoes, sausage or sometimes shrimp, go in too. *Oooh, chér,* now that's passing a good time. Make sure you wear a bib.

A second, smaller section of the park, the Skillern Track, lies 7 miles east of the main on FM 1985. The pond boardwalk is nice and you can follow a 2-mile round-trip trail through the grasses. As intimated above, *always* bring mosquito spray to either.

BEAUMONT & GOLDEN TRIANGLE

The cities of Beaumont, Port Arthur and Orange – roughly 20 miles apart each – make up the three points of the Golden Triangle in the southeastern most corner of the state. First settled by French and Spanish trappers in the early 19th century, the area has more in common culturally and environmentally with neighboring Louisiana than it does with the rest of Texas. Among the cypress trees, swamps and coastal wetlands, you can find a few natural adventures – for example in the Big Thicket – but most of the area's attractions are tied to the oil-and-gas industry.

When black gold gushed skyward from a site called Spindletop in 1901, it set the stage for the region's development. Companies that later transmogrified into giants such as Chevron, Texaco, Mobil and Exxon got their starts here. Some of the largest petrochemical works in the world are still found near Port Arthur and Beaumont. Which is to say, the area is not necessarily the world's prettiest. Especially as hurricanes seem to regularly rack this coast (Rita in 2005, Ike in 2008...).

Taken separately, the cities of Beaumont, Port Arthur and Orange may not be the most compelling tourist destinations. But together they could warrant a day or two spent exploring the few good museums and interesting oil-related sights. The Ben J Rogers Regional Visitor Center (p252) in Beaumont services the entire Golden Triangle area.

Beaumont

POP 118,548

Besides the petrochemical industry, Beaumont has developed a busy port on the Neches River that services offshore oil-drilling platforms. At local museums you can learn most everything you ever wanted to know about local oil and gas. Living here largely takes place along the interstate. Downtown is pleasant, but mostly quiet apart from a block of upscale bars. Beaumont lies 80 miles east of Houston on the I-10.

Sights & Activities

Texas Energy Museum MUSEUM

(☎409-833-5100; www.texasenergymuseum.org; 600 Main St; adult/child $5/3; ⏰9am-5pm Tue-Sat, 1-5pm Sun) Downstairs, animated movies and interactive exhibits explain the science of hydrocarbons, petrochemicals and oil extraction in a fairly entertaining fashion; upstairs exhibits cover the Spindletop discovery and the growth of the state's oil industry – these are well done, with movie-action mannequins.

Spindletop & Gladys City Boomtown Museum MUSEUM
(http://spindletop.org; 5550 Jimmy Simmons Blvd, off US 69; adult/child $5/3; 10-5pm Tue-Sat, 1-5pm Sun) Several prospectors saw promise in the salt dome named Spindletop, but it took nearly a decade before an exploratory well leased by Anthony Lucas blew a fountain of oil. Almost overnight Gladys City, full of wildcat oil explorers, sprang up. Soon wooden oil derricks crowded together like trees in a forest. This intriguing, open-air museum recreates part of the original boomtown.

A local photo studio in business at the time is to thank for much of the amazing documentation at the museum. Only one thing is missing – add 800,000 barrels of spilled oil and then you'd really know what it felt like back then.

McFaddin-Ward House HOUSE
(409-832-2134; www.mcfaddin-ward.org; 1906 McFaddin Ave, visitor center 1906 Calder St; tours $3; 10am-2:30pm Tue-Sat, 1-3pm Sun) Visit this fabulous 1906 mansion to see the excess made possible by the Spindletop oil boom. Members of the McFaddin family lived in the house until 1984; their rich antique furnishings fill the lavish rooms.

Gator Country WILDLIFE RESERVE
(409-794-9453; www.gatorrescue.com; 21159 FM 365, at I-10 exit 838; adult/child $14/11; 10am-8pm daily Jun-Aug, 10am-6pm Sat & Sun Sep-May) Feed the gators, photo-op with small reptiles and watch a live edutainment show put on by this local animal rescue outfit. You may have seen the Gator Country crew in one of their roles on cable TV shows like River Monsters and Gator 911. The park is 15 miles west of downtown Beaumont.

Cardinal Neches River Adventures BOAT TOUR
(409-651-5326; www.nechesriveradventures.org; Beaumont Riverfront Park, 801 Main St; adult/child $15/10; weekly Mar-Nov) Once a week a two-hour cruise on the flat-bottomed boat *Cardinal* takes passengers through the Neches River ecosystem, which has more than 200 trees, countless birds and, yes, alligators.

Sleeping

Lodging options are not the greatest in Beaumont. Chain motels and hotels are numerous on I-10, but many venues are older. The largest concentration is near the US 69/96/287 interchange.

Sleep Inn & Suites MOTEL $
(409-892-6700; www.sleepinn.com; 2030 N 11th St, at I-10 exit 853B; r $55-90;) This budget motel has 53 rooms over three floors with interior halls. It's basic but there are business services and a small pool.

La Quinta Inn - Beaumont West MOTEL $$
(409-842-0002; www.lq.com; 5820 Walden Rd; r incl breakfast $99-120;) A well-maintained La Quinta with attentive staff. Amenities include microwaves and mini-fridges in the rooms, hot breakfast, a nice outdoor pool and hot tubs.

Holiday Inn & Suites - Parkdale MOTEL $$
(409-892-3600; www.ihg.com; 7140 Hwy 69 N, at Rte 105; r incl breakfast $110-140;) Welcoming staff and modern rooms make this a top choice among the chain gang. The location just north of town is ideal for those heading toward the Big Thicket.

Eating & Drinking

Don't forget to roam the Golden Triangle to maximize your food fun. There's a strip of bar-restaurants and dance clubs downtown in the **Crockett St District** (www.crockettstreet.com). Ok, it's really one side of one short block, but they do pack 'em in Wednesday through Saturday 8pm until 2am.

Willy Burger BURGERS $
(5635 Calder Ave; dishes $5-12; 6am-8pm Mon-Sat, 11am-8pm Sun) The retro diner appeal here comes complete with a silver Airstream trailer and an 'eat-here' neon arrow sign. The burgers and shakes are as good as you'd expect, plus they do breakfast.

Floyd's Cajun Seafood CAJUN $$
(www.floydscajun.com; 2290 I-10 S; lunch $9-11, dinner mains $16-24; 11am-10pm) All your Cajun faves, and lots of lively fun, are available at this beloved southeast Texas chain. Expect a wait weekends, especially during spring crawfish season.

Suga's Deep South Cuisine & Jazz Bar SOUTHERN $$
(409-813-1808; http://sugasdeepsouth.com; 461 Bowie St; lunch & brunch $8-14, dinner mains $18-32; 11am-10pm Mon-Fri, 5-10pm Sat, 10:30am-3pm Sun) Set in a sleek, circa 1914 building, Suga's gives off a sexy, speakeasy vibe.

Southern dishes like blackened shrimp with remolade and grits definitely speak Texan with a Creole accent.

Information

Ben J Rogers Regional Visitor Center (800-392-4401; 5055 I-10 S, Beaumont; 10am-5pm) Pick up a copy of the comprehensive visitor guide to the entire Golden Triangle at this welcome center 15 miles west of downtown Beaumont.

Beaumont Convention & Visitors Bureau (800-392-4401, 409-880-3749; www.beaumontcvb.com; 505 Willow St; 8am-5pm Mon-Fri) In addition to an information office, the CVB has a great website and mobile app. Regional visitor guides can be requested online.

Getting There & Around

You really need a car to get around, but **Amtrak** (800-872-7245; www.amtrak.com; 2555 W Cedar St) does run the often-late and very slow *Sunset Limited* going west to LA via Houston (a lethargic three hours for 80 miles) and east to New Orleans (seven hours).

Big Thicket National Preserve

Until the mid-19th century, the Big Thicket was a dense and mysterious forest where Civil War draft dodgers hid out. Today the **National Preserve** (www.nps.gov/bith) is the crossroads of Texas' most interesting ecosystems: where coastal plains meet desert sand dunes, and cypress swamps stand next to pine and hardwood forests. Growing here are 145 different tree and plant species, plus 20 rare (and hard to find) orchids.

The park is broken into nine widely separated units that together total more than 105,000 acres. Several of the units are linked by narrow, sinuous corridors that follow creeks and rivers. The **Big Thicket Preserve Visitor Center** (409-951-6700; www.nps.gov/bith; 6102 FM 420, Kountze; 9am-5pm), 30 miles north of Beaumont on US 69/287, has maps and trail info, which is also available online.

About 3 miles east of the visitor center on FM 420, the interpretive **Kirby Trail** (1.7 to 2.5 miles round trip) is a good area introduction, cutting through swampy land that supports magnolias and cypress communities, as well as slope forest with beach and tall, tall, tall loblolly pines. You can continue on to see cacti on the **Sandhill Loop Trail** (2-mile round-trip extension). About 5 miles northwest off US 69/287, the **Sundew Loop Trail** (1 mile round trip) provides a look at bizarre carnivorous plants (four of North America's five species grow here). Look for wildflowers on this trail in late spring to summer.

Orange

POP 18,744

The smallest of the Triangle cities, Orange may have been named for citrus trees that once grew here or for some Dutch settlers; no one is certain. A widely scattered Cajun population lives along the secluded bayous and tributaries of the Sabine River, which forms the border with Louisiana.

Prominent turn-of-the-20th-century local businessman WH Stark and his philanthropic son HL Stark have greatly influenced the cultural offerings in Orange. You can tour the **Stark Museum of Art** (409-883-6661; www.starkmuseum.org; 712 W Green Ave; 10am-5pm Tue-Sat) FREE, which has collections of native wildlife and bird art, including works by John J Audubon. Or visit **WH Stark House** (409-883-0871; http://starkculturalvenues.org; 610 W Main St; tours $5, no children under 10yr; 10am-3pm Tue-Sat), a museum itself. But our favorite family-funded attraction is the **Shangri La Botanical Gardens & Nature Center** (http://starkculturalvenues.org; 2111 W Park Ave; adult/child $6/4; 9am-4pm Tue-Sat). Though it's not totally isolated, you can still get a good feel for the area's environment by peering through the bird blind at the heron rookery on Ruby Lake, or by taking a boat ride on Adam's Bayou.

If you get hungry while in town, stop at **Old Orange Cafe** (http://oldorangecafe.com; 914 Division St; dishes $7-15; 11am-2pm Mon-Fri & Sun), inside what used to be a dairy. Everything from the fresh salads and sandwiches to the seafood crêpes is good here. **E House Inn** (409-886-0122; www.ehouseinn.com; 205 College St; r incl breakfast $95;), a simple B&B in a rambling Victorian with great balconies, is just a few blocks away.

The state-operated **Texas Travel Information Center** (800-452-9292, 409-883-9416; www.traveltex.com; 1708 I-10 E; 8am-5pm) just inside the Texas–Louisiana border has loads of statewide information and a 600ft boardwalk over the swamp out back. See if you can spy the resident gators and snapping turtles. From the Texas side, take the last I-10 access road exit before the Sabine River Bridge and U-turn, or else you'll be miles into Louisiana before you can reverse course.

Port Arthur

POP 53,937

After the Spindletop oil well blew, Port Arthur prospered, growing into a pretty little town – eventually home to a young Janis Joplin. The oil-and-gas industry is still strong here and you can't miss the refineries along Hwy 82. At night the tower lights oddly resemble a city skyline at night. And huge deep-sea drilling rigs wait in gulfside maintenance yards. Authentic Cajun food and the town's one great museum are reason enough to visit.

Port Arthur is 20 miles southwest of Orange on Hwy 87 and 17 miles south of Beaumont on US 69/96/287; the parallel TX 347 is a slower but a more interesting road.

Sights & Activities

Lakeshore Dr near the center of Port Arthur has good views from the tall levee and a few beautiful old homes from the region's glory days that have managed to survive the hurricanes. The visitor bureau provides a free historic driving tour map, as well as a booklet about birding hotspots in the region.

Museum of the Gulf Coast MUSEUM
(409-982-7000; www.museumofthegulfcoast.org; 700 Procter St; adult/child $4/2; 9am-5pm Mon-Sat, 1-5pm Sun) This is a splendid museum that covers the natural, geological and cultural history of the region, 'from Jurassic to Joplin.' A large section is devoted to Janis, who remained a hometown girl until her death in 1970. The area's other musicians covered include blues great Clarence 'Gatemouth' Brown and Jiles Perry Richardson Jr, aka 'the Big Bopper.'

Sleeping

Port Arthur has numerous older, unremarkable chain motels found along US 69/96/287. Consider spending the night elsewhere in the Golden Triangle.

Eating & Drinking

The staple of local cuisine is shrimp supplied by the scores of fishing boats that call Port Arthur home. Some of the best eats are actually in the neighborhoods of Nederland (north) and Groves (east).

Boudin Hut CAJUN $
(409-962-5079; www.boudinlink.com; 5714 Gulfway Dr, Groves; dishes $6-10; 8am-2am Mon-Sat) The cheap, tasty Cajun dishes – and beer – are hugely popular with gregarious refinery workers getting off shift. Don't pass up the deep fried boudin balls. Live music some evenings and Sunday afternoons.

★**Larry's French Market & Cajun Restaurant** CAJUN $$
(409-962-3381; http://larrysfrenchmarket.com; 3701 Atlantic Hwy/FM 366, Groves; lunch dishes $6-10, mains $17-26, buffet $29; 11am-2pm Mon-Wed, to 9pm Thu, to 10pm Fri, 5-10pm Sat) Larry's is the real Louisiana deal. You can't get more authentic than this rustic restaurant and dance hall. During lunch the local specialties – including shrimp creole, fried crawfish and gumbo – are served cafeteria style. Come Friday and Saturday nights at 8pm, the hot tables turn into an incredible all-you-can-eat buffet. (There's always a menu as well.)

From Thursday to Saturday evenings the dance floor fills with dancers shuffling to upbeat Cajun two-step, swamp pop and zydeco bands. The regulars couldn't be friendlier. But get there early on weekend evenings, or you'll find you're in for a long wait.

Sartin's Seafood SEAFOOD $$
(http://sartinsnederland.com; 3520 Nederland Ave; mains $15-20; 11am-9pm Mon-Thu, to 10pm Fri & Sat, to 3pm Sun) Although owned by an ex-daughter-in-law of the original Sartin restaurant family in Sabine Pass, this casual Nederland outlet is still famous for its barbecued crabs. Those and other grilled or fried seafood, with a Cajun spice, are offered alone and in combo platters.

Information

Port Arthur Convention and Visitors Bureau (800-235-7822, 409-985-7822; www.visitportarthurtx.com; 3401 Cultural Center Dr; 8am-5pm Mon-Fri) Area visitor guides are available in person, or by request online.

Around Port Arthur

Driving through the refineries from Port Arthur the 12 miles south along TX 87 to Sabine Pass and beyond offers an interesting look at the area's historic past, its economy and its nature today. During the Civil War, the pass was vital to the Confederacy if it hoped to continue its lucrative cotton

NATIONAL FORESTS OF NORTHEAST

Pining for a walk in the woods? East Texas has four large national forests (including Sam Houston (p236), near Huntsville) filled with more than 300 kinds of trees, rivers, lakes, camping, hiking, canoeing...yep, they've got it all.

Detailed maps and information about each forest and its recreational areas are available online from the **US Forest Service** (USFS; ☎936-639-8501; www.fs.fed.us/r8/texas). Most campsites ($10 to $20) in and nearby the parks are available on a first-come, first-served basis. A few can be reserved at www.recreation.gov. Avoid hiking during hunting season each fall and winter; contact the ranger station for dates.

The 251 sq miles of **Davy Crockett National Forest** (☎936-655-2299; Ranger Station, 18551 TX 7, Kennard) lie 45 miles southwest of Nacogdoches between Lufkin and Crockett. It contains the **Ratcliff Lake Recreation Area**, and the picturesque, 20-mile **Four C National Recreation Trail** overlooking the Neches River. Canoers will dig the **Big Slough Canoe Trail**, part of a 3000-acre wilderness area which contains some of the biggest old-growth timber in Texas.

The smallest of the bunch is **Angelina National Forest** (☎936-897-1068; Ranger Station, 111 Walnut Ridge Rd, Zavalla), 49 miles southeast of Nacogdoches. The **Sawmill Hiking Trail** is a 5½-mile-long gem along the Neches River. For the area's best boating and fishing, head to the **Sam Rayburn Reservoir**.

Along the Texas–Louisiana border, 47 miles east of Nacogdoches, **Sabine National Forest** (☎409-625-1940; Ranger Station, 5050 Hwy 21 E, Hempell) lines the west bank of **Toledo Bend Reservoir**, where you'll find recreational, boating and camping sites onshore. Inside the park, **Indian Mounds Recreation Site & Wilderness Area** offers several hiking trails.

trade with England and France. The small fort that was built there is now offshore, but detailed outdoor displays at **Sabine Pass Battleground State Historic Site** (☎409-971-2451; www.visitsabinepassbattleground.com; admission free; ⏲8am-5pm) recall the conflagration in which 47, mostly drunk, Irish-Texans held off 4000 Union Troops. The 57-acre park offers great views of passing ships, plus idle oil rigs, and has good picnic areas.

After Sabine Pass, TX 87 theoretically continues for 50 miles southwest to Bolivar Peninsula and Galveston Island. But much of the road has been closed for years because of hurricane damage. The furthest you can get from this end is **Sea Rim State Park** (☎800-792-1112; www.tpwd.state.tx.us; TX 87), a bird-watching favorite. Blinds have been built in key areas around the more than 15,000 treeless acres that include marshlands north of TX 87 and 5 miles of beaches south of the road. Services are limited to the occasional earth-friendly outhouse.

NORTHEAST TEXAS

Tall pine forests in Texas? You're darn tootin'. This region northeast of Houston and east of Dallas is so filled with mixed hardwood and conifer forests, in fact, that it is known as the 'Piney Woods.' And that's not all that's a bit of a surprise in this part of the state. The Northeast was the area in Texas most attached to the ways of the Old South, and subsequently affected by the Civil War. You'll find a traditional Southern influence in accents, antebellum architecture and fine Southern food here.

Though lacking in jaw-dropping superlatives, the gently rolling wooded terrain provides plenty of low-key thrills for nature lovers, especially around Caddo Lake. Pretty, small towns, such as Kilgore and Nacogdoches, are enough to beguile any visitor with their classic central squares and stately brick buildings. Jefferson was once a riverboat town, and is undeniably still the biggest draw in the area. Slightly cooler air and more rain mean that roses and azaleas bloom gloriously up here. So slow down, explore an unexpected region, and enjoy life's little, Southern, charms.

ℹ Information

The **North East Texas Visitor & Events Guide** (www.northeasttexasguide.com) is widely available at visitor centers, and is online. The Texas tourist board has dubbed this the 'Texas Forest

Trail Region,' and provides more information at www.texastimetravel.com.

Nacogdoches

POP 33,405

Whether Nacogdoches (nack-uh-*doe*-chuss) is really the oldest town in Texas (as it claims) might be debated, but you can't argue it's recent, that's for sure. The first European settlement here dates from 1716, when a mission was established as a remote outpost of the Spanish empire. Most of the historic brick buildings on the cobblestone downtown square date to the mid-1800s. Today's town has a remarkably genteel sensibility balanced by a college-town buzz from the local Stephen F Austin State University. Come spring, the area's true colors show with the proliferation of azaleas, the focus of a favorite local festival.

Sights & Activities

The visitor information center (p256) contains a small, free museum and provides historic self-walking tour maps both for the old town center and of the Oak Grove cemetery. Interesting antiques shops occupy many of the old storefronts on Main St.

Sterne-Hoya House HOUSE
(www.ci.nacogdoches.tx.us/departments/shmuseum.php; 211 S Lanana St; 10am-4pm Tue-Sat) FREE The Sterne-Hoya House, built in 1828, is a good example of a refined town house of the era, and was the site of Sam Houston's baptism (sites visited by Sam Houston are the Texas equivalent of 'George Washington slept here').

Durst-Taylor House & Gardens HOUSE
(www.ci.nacogdoches.tx.us/departments/dtmuseum.php; 304 North St; 10am-4pm Tue-Sat) FREE Get a sense of the simple life led by less-affluent farmers at the circa 1830 Durst-Taylor house. Docents grow gardens appropriate to the period here.

Stone Fort Museum MUSEUM
(936-468-2408; www.sfasu.edu/stonefort; cnr Clark & Griffith Blvds, Stephen F Austin State University; 9am-5pm Mon-Sat, 1-5pm Sun) FREE Don Antonio Gil Y'Barbo's 1789 stone house subsequently served as a grocery store, a saloon and a fortification. Exhibits in the reconstructed 'fort' serve as an overview of east Texas history.

Millard's Crossing HISTORIC SITE
(936-564-6631; www.millardscrossing.org; 6020 North St; tour adult/child $6/5; 9am-4pm Mon-Sat, 1-4pm Sun;) Tour a slightly ragtag collection of 12 old buildings dating from 1820 to 1905, including a schoolhouse and a log cabin. Weekends, hands-on activities include plowing and writing with a quill pen.

Festivals

Azalea Trail FLOWER
(www.nacogdochesazaleas.com) The month of March is an azalea extravaganza, with three different mapped routes to follow and events like home tours, plant sales and downtown shopping strolls. Check with the visitor center to estimate when blooms will peak.

Sleeping

Contact the visitor center for a full list of area B&Bs and countryside lodgings.

Hardeman House B&B $$
(936-205-5280; www.hardemanhouse.com; 316 N Church St; r incl breakfast$100-140) What gorgeous woodwork and well-decorated rooms there are in this 1872 Victorian. Expect a warm welcome from proprietors who live here with their family. Children welcome.

Brick House Inn B&B $$
(936-564-7428; www.thebrickhouseinn.biz; 522 Virginia Ave; r incl breakfast $115-130; P) Three comfy rooms in one of the oldest (brick, obviously) houses in town. Hope that orange pecan French toast is for breakfast.

Hotel Fredonia BOUTIQUE HOTEL $$
(936-564-1234; www.hotelfredonia.com; 200 N Fredonia St; r $100-150; P) Gurgling fountains and crooning Frank Sinatra muzak lend an air of 1950s glamour to this hotel. Too bad the slightly dated rooms haven't all caught up with the fab lobby renovation. Ask for a cabana room out by the lushly landscaped saltwater pool.

Eating & Drinking

★ **Shelley's Bakery Cafe** CAFE $$
(936-564-4100; www.shelleysbakerycafe.com; 112 N Church St; dishes $9-14; bakery 10am-3pm & restaurant 11am-2pm Tue-Sat) A certain breezy Southern charm here makes your cares, or at least your diet, fade away. Eat one of the excellent salads or homemade soups and you can afford to splurge on the luscious éclairs.

Clear Springs Cafe SOUTHERN **$$**
(☎936-569-0489; www.clearspringscafe.com; 211 Old Tyler Rd; sandwiches $7-9, mains $10-22; ⏰11am-9pm Sun-Thu, 11am-10pm Fri & Sat; 👪) In a cavernous old warehouse, exposed brick and hanging memorabilia lend a rustic air to this Southern restaurant. The fried catfish is a fave.

Banita Creek Hall CLUB
(☎936-462-8000; http://banitacreekhall.com; 401 W Main St; ⏰8pm-midnight Wed-Fri, 8pm-1am Sat) Grab a guy or gal and two-step around the floor to live local country music. Wednesday night offers country & western dance lessons.

ℹ Information

Nacogdoches Convention & Visitors Bureau (☎936-564-7351; www.visitnacogdoches.org; 200 E Main St; ⏰9am-5pm Mon-Fri, 10am-4pm Sat, 1-4pm Sun) This remarkably thorough visitor center has pamphlets on just about any area subject that might interest you.

Around Nacogdoches

Remnants of Texas' Native American history are few and far between. So the 1200-year-old ceremonial mounds at **Caddoan Mounds State Historic Site** (☎936-858-3218; www.visitcaddomounds.com; 1649 Hwy 21 W, Alto; adult/child $2/1; ⏰8:30am-4:30pm Tue-Sun; 👪), just 25 miles east of Nacogdoches, are worth noting. Learn more from the small museum's exhibits and interpretive trail. It's a nice picnic spot, too.

El Camino Real, the royal road connecting missions between Mexico City and current-day Louisiana, ran right through Nacogdoches. At **Mission Tejas State Park** (☎info 800-792-1112, reservations 512-389-8900; www.tpwd.state.tx.us/missiontejas; 105 Park Rd 44, Grapeland; adult/child $2/free; ⏰8:30am-4:30am Tue-Sun), 32 miles east of town, you can see a replica of the 17th-century Mission San Francisco de los Tejas, tour a 19th-century log cabin and hike in the footsteps of Davy Crockett on a part of the road itself. The pleasant, 660-acre park also has shady, reservable campsites ($10 to $15).

Thirty-five miles north of Nacogdoches, relive the glory days of the steam engine on the **Texas State Railroad** (☎877-726-7245; www.texasstaterr.com; Hwy 84; adult/child $32/23; ⏰11am Sat & Sun Mar-Apr & Sep-Nov, 11am Fri-Sun May-Aug; 👪). Four-hour, round-trip train rides travel through dogwood bloom–filled forests between Rusk and Palatine. Either direction you go, the train stops long enough for a picnic lunch before returning.

WHAT THE...? TIGERS IN TEXAS

Tiger Creek Wildlife Refuge (www.tigercreek.org; FM 14, exit 562 off I-20; adult/child $10/6; ⏰10am-5pm Mon-Sat), 13 mile north of downtown Tyler, is home to 50 big cats that have been rescued from accross the country. Tour the wooded enclosures on the ever-expanding, 30-acre-plus site and meet the lions, leopards, cougars – and tigers.

Tyler

POP 98,546

Romantics, be prepared to swoon: the country's biggest domestic supplier of roses, Tyler is also home to the 14-acre **Tyler Municipal Rose Garden** (☎903-531-1212; www.texasrosefestival.com; 420 Rose Park Dr; ⏰dawn-dusk) FREE, which is in full bloom from May through October. Flowers are also the focus of two annual festivals in 'Rose City': the **Azalea & Spring Flower Trail** (www.tylerazaleatrail.com) in late March, and the **Rose Festival** (www.texasrosefestival.com) in October. Contact the **Tyler Convention & Visitors Bureau** (☎800-235-5712; www.visittyler.com; 315 N Broadway; ⏰8:30am-5pm Mon-Fri) for seasonal variation in dates.

Given the size of the city and the services available, Tyler makes a good base for exploring the area. **Rosevine Inn** (☎903-592-2221; www.rosevine.com; 415 S Vine; r incl breakfast $129-199; P❄📶) is a gracious brick home with five sweet, comfy rooms that enjoy use of the outdoor hot tub and the red barn rec room, which has a pool table. Otherwise, because of nearby Tyler University, numerous upscale chain hotels line the highways: our favorite among them is the **Fairfield Marriott** (☎903-561-2535; www.marriott.com; 1945 W SW Loop 323; r incl breakfast $104-130; ❄📶), because of its friendly staff and Loop 323 location.

Tyler's old courthouse square is kinda dead in the daytime, but a couple of bars and restaurants bring it to life at night. For a fancy date night of dining, and maybe dancing, try **Rick's on the Square** (☎903-

WORTH A TRIP

EDOM & BEN WHEELER

Itchin' for a Sunday drive? The stretch of FM 279 between **Edom** (www.edomevents.com) (pop 375) and **Ben Wheeler** (http://benwheelertx.com) (pop 400) holds a surprising number of diversions.

The **Shed Cafe** (www.theshedcafe.com; 8337 FM 279; dishes $4-11, steaks $18-24; 6:30am-8pm Mon-Thu, to 9pm Fri & Sat, 7am-1pm Sun) routinely makes Texas Monthly's list of top country cafes, serving great lemon icebox pie and chicken fried chicken. Live pickin' and grinnin' music plays Wednesday night. And just down the road you can hear acoustic music concerts at the **Old Firehouse** (903-852-2781; www.jeffreylancephotography.com/theoldfirehouse; 8241 FM 279, Edom ; 7pm Sat Sep-May).

The other old buildings in Edom have been turned into galleries filled with handmade arts and crafts (pottery, original photography, jewelry...). They're part of the **Farm Road 279 Artisan Trail** (http://279artisanstrail.com), which stretches the 8 miles northeast to Ben Wheeler, where the 1930s-era false front buildings contain gift shops, galleries – even a cowboy hat store. **Scoots 'n' Scoops** (1560 FM 279, Ben Wheeler; 11am-5pm Thu & Fri, 11am-6pm Sat, Wed & Sun 11am-3pm) is a vintage motorcycle/ice cream shop, what else?

A mix of country, blues and Cajun music bands play Friday through Sunday night at **Moore's Store** (www.benwheelertx.com; 1551 FM 279, Ben Wheeler; dishes $5-12; 10:30am-2:30pm Sun, Tue & Wed, 10:30am-10pm Thu, 10:30am-11pm Fri & Sat), a 1933 mercantile. Their burgers and beers are quite popular with the weekend Harley hog-riding crowd. The **Forge Bistro** (http://theforgebenwheeler.wordpress.com; 1610 FM 279, Ben Wheeler; dishes $7-18; 11am-10pm Wed, to 11pm Thu, to midnight Fri & Sat, 11am-5pm Sun) serves pizza, and singer-songwriter folk music Thursday through Saturday.

For a list of area lodging, including B&Bs and cabin rental, check the town and the Trail web sites. FM 279 is 20 miles west of Tyler, 72 miles east of Dallas.

531-2415; www.rix.com; 104 W Erwin St; lunch $7-12, dinner mains $20-40; 11am-midnight Mon-Fri, 5pm-1am Sat). Their live music Wednesday through Saturday is usually jazzy, but may be rockin' instead. Other local favorite restaurants are spread all around town. **Wasabi** (www.wasabityler.com; 5617 Donnybrook Ave; sushi $5-15, mains $9-12; 11:30am-9:30pm Sun-Thu, 11:30am-10:30pm Fri & Sat) serves sushi rolls and suprisingly inventive Asian fusion dishes, and has a great patio.

KE Cellars (http://kiepersol.com; 54574 S Broadway Ave; 11am-9pm Wed-Sat), the in-town store for the local boutique winery, morphs into a tasting bar with live music evenings from 6pm to 9pm. If you have time, it's well worth visiting **Kiepersol Estates Winery** (903-894-8995; www.kiepersol.com; 4120 FM 344 E; tastings $1, tours $5; tasting room 11am-5pm, tours 2pm & 4pm Sat) itself, 15 miles southeast of downtown. Walk the mile-long vineyard trail, take a taste or a tour. On Saturday their restaurant is open, above which two luxe B&B rooms perch.

Tyler is 90 miles east of Dallas, 205 miles northeast of Houston and 70 miles west of Jefferson.

Canton

First Monday Trade Days (http://firstmondaycanton.com; admission free; dawn-dusk) have been taking place in Canton since the 1850s. Today more than 5000 vendors gather the Thursday through Sunday before every first Monday of the month. Peak summer weekends, more than 100,000 visitors may attend this, the state's largest flea market. Exploring the more than 100 acres can be daunting. Pick up or download a visitors guide, available from the **Canton Visitor Bureau** (www.visitcantontx.com; 119 N Buffalo St; 9am-5pm Mon-Fri), for a festival map and service list.

Note that the many area B&Bs are usually booked up during Trade Days. Tyler is only 20 miles east and Dallas is 60 miles west.

The rest of the month, Canton is a sleepy little town with a pleasant courthouse square and a few full-time shops. Our favorite is the **Canton Dish Barn** (208 W Dallas; 9am-4pm Mon-Sat) selling Fiestaware exclusively. We've never seen so much colorful dishware in one place.

Kilgore

POP 13,110

Twenty miles east of Tyler, Kilgore's old downtown recalls the kind of place you might imagine James Dean roaming around circa Giant movie era. An old theater, the brickfront buildings and dusty streets, the oil wells rising in the distance... Indeed, many of the buildings date to the boomtown era after oil was discovered here in 1930.

Trace the town's boom – and bust – at the evocative **East Texas Oil Museum** (903-983-8295; www.easttexasoilmuseum.com; Kilgore College Campus, cnr Hwy 259 & Ross St; 9am-4pm Tue-Sat, until 5pm Apr-Sep) FREE, with vivid exhibits that do an admirable job re-creating the pre-oil discovery town. The **World's Richest Acre Park** (cnr E Main & Commerce St), has 70 recreated, light-topped oil derricks to commemorate the wells that gave this site its name. This patch of real estate yielded 2.5 million barrels of oil during a 30-year run. At the height of the boom the number of oil wells everywhere in town numbered 1200, even on street corners.

But oil is not the only kind of drilling Kilgore is famous for; the town also claims bragging rights as home to the world's oldest women's precision drill teams, the Kilgore Rangerettes. These ladies – in their nifty red shirts, blue skirts and white hats and boots – have performed at several presidential inaugurations and every Cotton Bowl since 1950. Don't skip the film at the **Rangerette Showcase & Museum** (www.rangerettes.com; 1100 Broadway; admission free; 9am-4pm Mon-Fri, 10am-4pm Sat), it's your chance to see the Rockette-like, high-kicking action. Every April the Rangerette's showcase their more diverse dance talents at a variety showcase, called the Revels.

Before you leave, make sure to take a turn around the art deco downtown (corner of Kilgore & E Main Sts), where several boutique western-wear shops sport names like Calamity Jane's and Crystal Spur. You'll find a cafe or two there, but we recommend getting out of town. The **Country Tavern** (903-984-9954; www.countrytavern.com; 1526 FM 2767; dishes $8-25; 11am-9pm Mon-Thu, 11am-10pm Fri & Sat), 5 miles west on Hwy 31, is known statewide for its mind-blowingly tender barbecued ribs and other smoked meats. In town, the super casual, Texas-rustic Back Porch does a good job on buffalo burgers, chicken-fried steak and fried green tomatoes. Live country music on the patio Wednesday, Friday and Saturday evening.

Kilgore is just the kind of small town where we'd like to slow down and stay a spell. Pity that the lodging is limited to nice-enough, but characterless chains such as Holiday Inn Express. For more town information, contact the **Kilgore Chamber of Commerce & Visitor Bureau.** (903-984-5022; www.kilgorechamber.com; 813 N Kilgore St; 9am-5pm Mon-Fri).

Jefferson

POP 2110

With gracious architecture, a perfectly preserved old town, charismatic locals and a superb natural setting, Jefferson is the kind of town tourist boards dream about. Once the largest inland river port in the USA, pre-Civil War Jefferson was a mini New Orleans: the stomping grounds of a wild bunch of gamblers, riverboat men and madams. Since then, Jefferson has calmed down considerably. (What else can you say about a place that boasts it's the B&B capital of Texas?) But it still has a few ghosts in the closet, maybe literally.

The town is relatively small, but don't even think of stopping for just an afternoon. The old streets beg to be strolled, with a requisite stop at one of the soda fountains, of course. Then there are the antique shops to browse, historic homes to tour, ghosts to hunt... Make sure you take a boat ride on the Big Cypress Bayou, part of Caddo Lake. Jefferson's a seductive Southern belle with a checkered past, don't be suprised if you fall under her spell.

Sights

The first thing to do is to take a stroll around town. Jefferson is visitor driven so not everything will be open on weekdays. The visitor center has a full list of all the small museums and house tours that keep irregular hours. Don't forget that Caddo Lake (p260) is little more than 15 miles away.

Jefferson Historical Museum MUSEUM
(903-665-2775; www.jeffersonmuseum.com; 223 W Austin St; adult/child $7/4; 9:30am-4:30pm) For a bitty place, the town's museum is mighty big. The three-story, 1888 brick courthouse contains interesting exhibits on early life in east Texas and the original Caddo Indian tribe.

Excelsior House HISTORIC SITE

(903-665-2513; www.excelsior@jeffersontx.com; 211 W Austin St) FREE This central, historic hotel was built in the 1850s by a riverboat captain. Famous guests have included US presidents Ulysses S Grant and Rutherford B Hayes, as well as poet Oscar Wilde. Inquire about free daily tours of the hotel.

The Atlanta HISTORIC SITE

(903-665-2513; 208 W Austin St; tours $5) Rail baron Jay Gould once offered to bring the railroad to Jefferson, but the town (inauspiciously) turned him down, deciding to bet its future on river traffic. Gould's ultraluxe private 1888 railroad car, the *Atlanta*, now sits near the center of town. Contact the Excelsior House (p259) about tours, usually, but not always available 10am to 3pm.

The Grove HOUSE

(903-665-8018; www.thegrove-jefferson.com; 405 Moseley St; tour $5; tours 2pm Sat, 11am Sun) The Grove, a private home built in 1861, had reports of hauntings way back in 1882. Take an hour-long tour with owner and author Michael Whittington, who has written numerous books about Jefferson and the town's ghosts.

Tours

Turning Basin Tours BOAT TOUR

(903-665-2222; www.jeffersonbayoutours.com; 200 Bayou St; adult/child $8/6; Tue-Sat Apr-Oct) You'll hear plenty of local lore on the narrated, hour-long flat-bottom boat rides on Big Cypress Bayou. The launch point is just across Polk St bridge from downtown. Call for varying departure times, and for the required reservations.

Historic Jefferson Ghost Walk WALKING TOUR

(903-665-6289; http://jeffersonghostwalk.com; cnr Austin & Vale Sts; adult/child $12/6; 8pm Fri & Sat) Learn about the town's tragedies and legends as you walk in and among the old buildings. Ghost tours last about an hour and a half, departing from the vacant lot next to the Atlanta rail car.

Historic Jefferson Railway TRAIN

(866-398-2038; www.jeffersonrailway.com; 400 E Austin St; adult/child $12/8; 9pm Fri, 2:30, 4:30 & 9pm Sat Jun-Aug;) Summer weekends, take a narrated open-air train-car ride during the day, or a ghost tour at night. Theme trains (Great Train Robbery, Halloween, Christmas) operate other weekends during the year.

Festivals

Throughout the year, Jefferson holds numerous events – Railroad Days, Old West plays, car shows, Christmas-time tours, etc. Log into the visitor center website for more.

Pilgrimage Tour of Homes CULTURAL

(www.jeffersonpilgrimage.com; adults/children $20/3; May) One weekend in May the influential local garden club hosts a home tour of historic properties. It's the event of the year, with accompanying balls, plays and a parade.

Sleeping

Far more B&Bs operate locally than we could list, everything from one-room cabins to Victorian mansions. The visitor center posts them all online. Note that the town's active train tracks run near everything – *woo-woo*!

Delta Street Inn B&B **$$**

(903-665-2929; www.deltastreetinn.com; 206 E Delta St; r incl breakfast $99-145;) With the restrained mix of gorgeous English antiques and comfortable reproductions, owners here have created the ideal B&B. This painstakingly restored 1920s four-square combines a classic feel with modern convenience. Amenities include a game room, daily sweet treats, and an upstairs coffee bar for early mornings.

Benefield House B&B **$$**

(903-665-9366; http://benefieldhouse.com; 1009 S Line St; r incl breakfast $99-149;) All the frills you'd expect of a Victorian 'painted lady.' Deep, rich colors and period-appropriate American antiques fill this Queen Anne home. Except for the kingsize beds and wi-fi, you might think you were back in the 1800s.

White Oak Manor B&B B&B **$$**

(903-665-8185; www.bedandbreakfastjeffersontx.com; 502 E Benners St; r incl breakfast $89-150;) Make yourself at home, relax on the wraparound porch or pop popcorn and watch a DVD in your room at this welcoming Greek Revival house, a short walk from downtown.

Jefferson Hotel HISTORIC HOTEL **$$**

(903-665-2631; www.historicjeffersonhotel.com; 124 W Austin St; r $99-120;) Fans of paranormal activity are advised to stay at this historic, if dated, hotel. Rooms 19 and 20 have been known to freak out eye-rolling skeptics (even Stephen King is rumored to have been spooked).

OFF THE BEATEN TRACK

TEXAS COUNTRY MUSIC HALL OF FAME

Carthage, Texas, 50 miles south of Jefferson and 40 miles east of Kilgore, is barely a spot on the map. But it was the birthplace of legendary cowboy singer Tex Ritter, and home to the museum where he stars, the **Texas Country Music Hall of Fame** (☎903-693-6634; www.carthagetexas.com/HallofFame/museum.htm; 310 W Panola, Carthage; adult/child $5/3; ⏲10am-4pm Mon-Sat). Browse the exhibits about the radio and silver-screen star, and other legends of Texas country, then sit back and listen to them sing from the free juke box. Saturday evenings the **Country Music Hayride** (☎903-622-4390; http://hayridecarthage.com; Esquire Theater, 114 W Sabine St, Carthage; admission $6; ⏲7pm Sat) harks back to the early days of the Grand Ol' Opry and other country variety shows.

Eating & Drinking

Jefferson has more restaurants than you'd expect for a town its size. Many are situated around Austin St in the old downtown core.

★ **Joseph's Riverport BBQ** BARBECUE $
(☎903-665-2341; 201 N Polk St; dishes $5-11; ⏲11am-7pm Tue-Sat, 11am-2pm Sun) Texas barbecue done right. Order at the counter and retreat to the long wooden tables with your groaning plate of brisket, turkey breast, fried okra, plus sweet iced tea – if you can grab a space from the locals.

Austin Street Bistro NEW AMERICAN $$
(☎903-665-9700; www.austinstreetbistro.com; 117 E Austin St; sandwiches $8-12, mains $13-17; ⏲11am-8pm Wed-Thu, to 9pm Fri & Sat, to 3pm Sun) What an authentic, unpretentious place. The tiny, fully visible kitchen turns out artfully presented mains, such as pecan-and-maple crusted salmon, as well as good vegetarian options. All breads, pastries, sauces and such are site-made.

Five D Cattle Co STEAKHOUSE $$
(http://fivedcattle.com; 9 N Main St, Avinger; mains $11-22) Reasonable steaks and the friendly, down-home atmosphere is worth the drive 15 miles west to Avinger. Everybody knows everybody eating in here in these converted old wooden store buildings; you soon will, too.

Shopping

Look for antiques stores lining the western end of Austin and Lafayette Sts, and also on S Polk, S Vale and S Walnut Sts.

Jefferson General Store SOUVENIRS
(☎903-665-8481; www.jeffersongeneralstore.com; 113 E Austin St; ⏲9am-6pm Sun-Thu, to 10pm Fri & Sat) A kitschy delight: the old general store is crammed with a wacky array of Texas-themed souvenirs. When you're done shopping, cool off with an ice cream or soda at the counter.

Information

Jefferson is small, but Marshall TX (population 24,000) is only 15 miles south; it has all the services you could need. Pick up your copy of the free seasonal town guide, the *Jeffersonian Magazine* at area restaurants or the visitor center.

Jefferson Visitor Center (☎903-665-3733; www.visitjeffersontexas.com; 305 E Austin St; ⏲9am-5pm Mon-Fri, 11am-4pm) Helpful staff with comprehensive information; they even have a binder with pictures and descriptions of every B&B or rental within a 50-mile radius.

Around Jefferson

A cottage wine industry has grown up in east Texas; four vineyards lie within an hour's drive of Jefferson. Locals favor **Enoch's Stomp** (☎903-240-1587; www.enochsstomp.com; 871 Ferguson Rd, Harleton; tasting $5, restaurant mains $12-28; ⏲winery noon-6pm Wed & Thu, noon-10pm Fri & Sat, noon-6pm Sun; restaurant 11am-10pm Fri & Sat) for its beautiful 35-acre grounds with grassy hills (great for picnicking) an orchard and two ponds. The winery holds frequent events and their restaurant is top-notch.

Caddo Lake

Picture craggy, partly submerged bald cypress trees covered with low-hanging moss swaying in the breeze. Imagine floating quietly past 3ft-tall herons and egrets on labyrinthine waterways. Envision the occasional alligator eyes gliding by... You've got the scene: evocative, intoxicating, and OK, we admit it, a little eerie. Texas' largest freshwater lake snakes off into narrow bayous and tributaries that cover more than 26,000 acres that are well worth exploring by boat. If you can, get up early to watch as the steam rises off the bayous.

Caddo Lake State Park (☎903-679-3351; www.tpwd.state.tx.us; FM 2198, off Hwy 43; admission $2, tent/RV sites $10/20, cabins $75-115; ⏰office 8am-5pm, park 24hr) is a good place to start your adventure. Take an interpretive hike through the cypress forest on the lake's western edge. Or, in summer, rent a canoe from the on-site concession, **Old Port Caddo** (☎903-930-0075; www.oldportcaddo.com; 2670 Blairs Landing Rd, Caddo Lake State Park; rental per day $35, tours adult/child $18/10; ⏰8am-5pm May-Sep). They also offer hour-long pontoon boat tours, reservations required. The park itself has some great little cabins built by the Civilian Conservation Corps and the riverside tent sites are pretty sweet. Don't forget bug spray.

The lake's de facto headquarters is the community of **Uncertain** (www.cityofuncertain.com), which is a funky (some might say junky) meandering area of fishing shacks, tour companies, cabins, groceries and a few casual restaurants and small cafes. For even more information log onto www.caddolake.info. Note that at the time of writing, most online GPS maps are WRONG for this area, including those on iPhones and from Bing!

Local authorities call affable local-boy John Winn when someone gets lost on the lake. You should, too; his private, one-hour to full-day **Caddo Outback Backwater Tours** (☎903-789-3384; www.caddolaketours.com; 1869 Pine Island Rd; tours per couple $40-160) take you by 18ft swamp boat to places other outfitters can't reach. Ask about nighttime tours. You'll be transported back to Jefferson's heyday aboard the steam-powered paddle steamer, the **Graceful Ghost** (☎903-789-2238; www.gracefulghost.com; 510 Cypress Dr, Uncertain; adult/child $20/18; ⏰noon, 2pm & 4pm Tue-Sat, Mar-Nov), which offers 90-minute lake tours during summer months.

When you're ready for a repast, you have two main choices for waterfront fried catfish and other swamp seafood: rustic **Big Pines Lodge & Watering Hole** (http://bigpineslodge.com; 747 Pine Island Rd, Karnack; dishes $6-15; ⏰4pm-9pm Wed-Fri, 6:30am-9pm Sat & Sun), a 60-year Caddo Lake classic that was rebuilt after a 2009 fire, or go a little upscale at **River Bend Restaurant** (☎903-679-9000; 211 FM 2422, Karnack; mains $18-28; ⏰5pm-9pm Tue-Thu, to 10pm Fri, 11am-10pm Sat, noon-7pm Sat), which has a glass-enclosed patio.

Hodge Podge Cottages (☎903-789-3901; www.hodgepodgecottages.com; 724 Cypress Dr, Uncertain; cottage $125) is true to its name, offering everything from a mobile home to a regular house to a dry-docked houseboat for overnight rental next to the river. Free canoe use included.

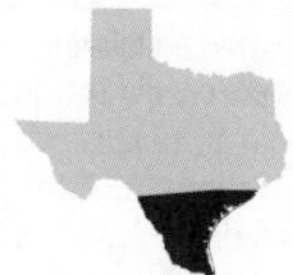

Gulf Coast & South Texas

Includes ➡

Why Go?

America's 'Third Coast,' as it's dubbed itself, is a place of many contrasts. The mellow beach-town scene of Port Aransas is a sea of calm compared with the frenetic hedonism of South Padre Island (SPI), for one. Yet they also have much in common. At both Aranasas National Wildlife Refuge and Padre Island National Seashore, you can get lost in nature. Much of the coast is undeveloped.

Besides SPI, there's fun to be had in Corpus Christi (and even Port Aransas can kick up its heels for some merriment). Inland you'll find reminders of the state's dramatic history from the Palo Alto Battlefield National Historic Site to the legacies found in stone around Goliad.

History is still being made in the very south along the Rio Grande. Border politics affect all aspects of life and Mexican culture accents the towns and remote stretches from Brownsville to Laredo and beyond.

Best Places to Eat

- McMillan's BBQ (p271)
- King's Inn (p281)
- Joe's Oyster Bar Restaurant (p283)

Best Natural Places

- Aransas National Wildlife Refuge (p266)
- Padre Island National Seashore (p279)
- Sabal Palm Sanctuary (p290)

When to Go

Corpus Christi

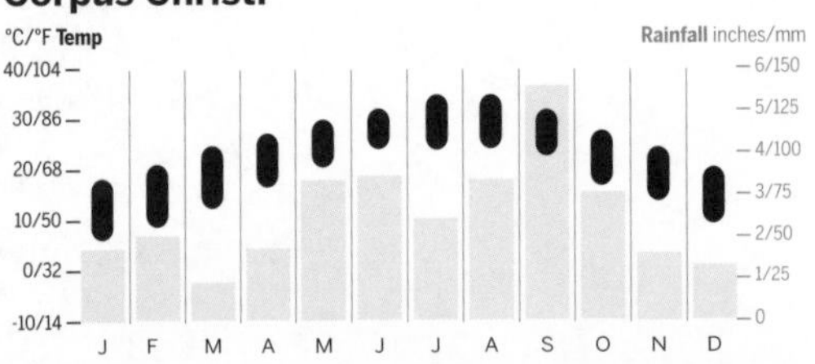

Mar Spring Break! Hordes of partying teens may appeal or cause you to go scurrying.

Apr–May & Sep–Oct The weather is reliably balmy but crowds are few.

Dec–Feb In the very south, mild weather brings 'Winter Texans' but don't expect too much.

THE COASTAL BEND

The name 'Coastal Bend' can rather amorphously apply to communities from Galveston to South Padre Island. But its heart is the rural stretch running from the southern tip of Galveston Island to Corpus Christi. Here small towns, many forgotten by time, lie Gulf-side at the end of long and quiet roads. Many shelter in the profusion of inlets and bays, protected by more than 100 miles of uninhabited barrier islands. The only visitors to the islands are birds, which flock here by the score.

The region just south of Galveston, around the Brazos River, doesn't get much respect despite the clever marketing moniker that has been dreamed up for it: 'Brazosport.' Or maybe that's the reason for it. South of here, the countryside is rural and often bucolic. Natural areas such as Aransas National Wildlife Refuge and Goose Island State Park should be your focus along with the towns of Fulton and Rockport.

It's more than possible to drive from Galveston south along the confusing maze of roads to Corpus Christi or Port Aransas in a day and still see the best sights.

Brazosport Area

POP 92,000

Nine towns – Brazoria, Clute, Freeport, Jones Creek, Lake Jackson, Oyster Creek, Quintana, Richwood and Surfside Beach – are part of a confused hodgepodge crisscrossed by industry railroads, highways, creeks, lakes and channels and surrounded by chemical plants, collectively known as Brazosport.

This area has been the focus of many arguments between the federal Environmental Protection Agency (EPA) and the state of Texas over pollution regulations and their enforcement.

Sights

Sea Center Texas AQUARIUM

(979-292-0100; www.tpwd.state.tx.us/seacenter; 300 Medical Dr, Lake Jackson; 9am-4pm Tue-Sat, 1-4pm Sun;) FREE One attraction worth tracking down in the tangle of Brazosport is this fun aquarium. Learn about Texas salt marshes, the surf zone and coastal bays. A large tank holds gulf stars like huge groupers and slithery eels. Out back are 35 acres of fish hatcheries which you can tour at certain times. A walkway extends across 5 acres of wetlands.

Varner-Hogg Plantation HISTORIC SITE

(979-345-4656; www.visitvhp.com; 1702 N 13th St; adult/child $6/4; 8am-5pm Tue-Sun) This plantation dates to the early 1800s and includes a grand mansion built by slaves. Amidst beautiful pecan and magnolia trees, visitors learn how past owners made money growing, drilling and distilling – often with indentured help. It's located 18 miles northwest of Lake Jackson.

Matagorda

POP 1300

Place-names in this area must have been hard to come by, because authorities decided to confuse everybody by christening a bay, a town, a county, a peninsula and an island with the same name – Matagorda. The tiny town offers a link to the peninsula (Matagorda Peninsula, not to be confused with Matagorda Island, the remote state park off Port O'Connor), a popular spot for fishing.

The town still has a vintage feel to it and has a few stores. Head south on TX 60 over the grand new bridge which arches high above the busy Intracoastal Waterway (views from the top show the land seeming to dissolve into water), and drive 6 miles to the end of the road to meet the gulf.

There are 22 miles of lonely white-sand **beaches** out here. With a permit ($10; buy it at any gas station in Matagorda), you can drive out and onto the beach and stake out your claim. **Matagorda Bay Nature Park** (979-863-2603; www.lcra.org; 8am-5pm) FREE is a great resource with numerous programs where you can learn about the

> **DRIVING DISTANCES**
>
> **Austin–Corpus Christi** 192 miles, 3 hours
>
> **Brownsville–Laredo** 204 miles, 3½ hours
>
> **Corpus Christi–Brownsville** 159 miles, 2½ hours
>
> **Corpus Christi–South Padre Island** 172 miles, 3 hours
>
> **Houston–Beaumont** 86 miles, 90 minutes
>
> **Houston–Corpus Christi** 211 miles, 3¼ hours
>
> **Laredo–San Antonio** 154 miles, 2½ hours

Gulf Coast & South Texas Highlights

1. Spot majestic and rare – but recovering – whooping cranes at **Aransas National Wildlife Refuge** (p266).
2. **Mustang and Padre Islands** (p279) have endless white-sand beaches, some purely for fun, others carefully protected.
3. Feel the past in the evocative historic sites in and around **Goliad** (p270).
4. **Port Aransas** (p276) has goofy old places to stay, goofy seafood joints for chow, and laid-back bars in which to be a goof.

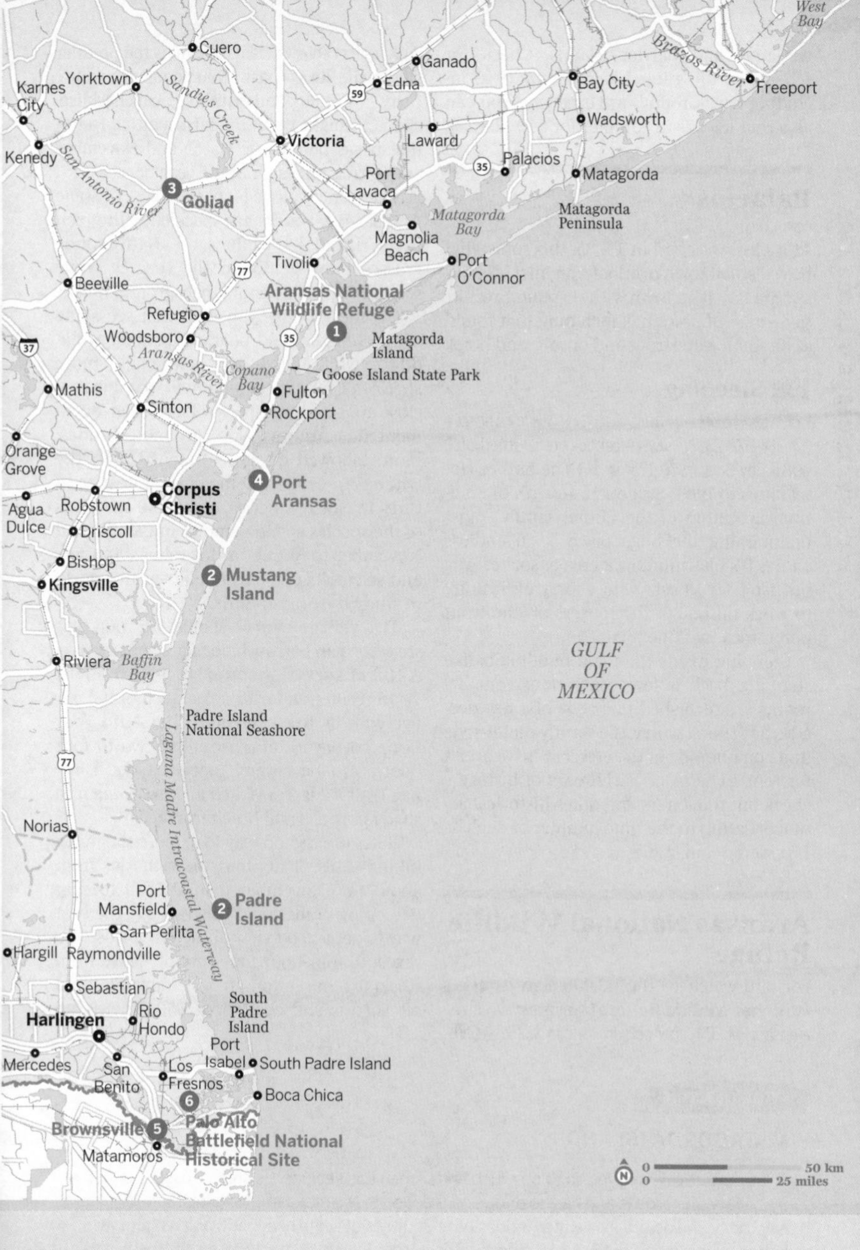

❺ Wander **Brownsville** (p289) and its downtown with buildings dating back to 1848 and shops that are pure Mexico.

❻ Learn how today's politics were shaped on the sunburned expanse of the **Palo Alto Battlefield National Historic Site** (p292).

❼ Feel the lush! **Bentsen-Rio Grande Valley State Park** (p295) has beautiful trails for finding feathered friends.

wetlands and barrier islands. Check for schedules; the guided kayak tours ($40 including kayak rental) are excellent. You can also rent kayaks in summer for $20 per day.

Palacios

POP 4800

At a pleasant bend in TX 35, this somewhat frayed small town overlooks an inlet off Matagorda Bay. It's a town with – a realtor would say – a lot of potential, including that found at its small waterfront and once-grand hotel.

Sleeping

Luther Hotel HISTORIC HOTEL **$**
(361-972-2312; www.facebook.com/lutherhotel; 408 S Bay Blvd; r $70-125;) The Luther Hotel dates to 1904. Still operating, it's the full-time avocation of the Luther family – just maintaining the huge place is an endless chore. It's charming in a creaky sort of way but isn't for guests who expect everything to work (although the rockers on the front porch rock just fine, thank you).

Stepping inside the main building is like stepping back a few generations. The 29 rooms are furnished in a style of a few decades ago (don't worry, the scruffy motel-style units on one side of the crescent drive aren't for rent). The place fairly reeks of history – check out the letters and other historical artifacts dating to the time luminaries such as LBJ were regular guests.

Aransas National Wildlife Refuge

For bird-watchers, the 115,000-acre **Aransas National Wildlife Refuge** (www.fws.gov/refuge/aransas; FM 2040; per person/carload $3/5; 6am-dusk, visitor center 8:30am-4:30pm) is the premier site on the Texas coast. Even people who don't carry binoculars and ornithological checklists can get caught up in the bird-spotting frenzy that peaks here every March and November and is great throughout the year.

The scenery alone is spectacular – the blue Aransas Bay waters are speckled with green islets ringed by white sand. Native dune grasses blow gently in the breezes while songbirds provide choral background music.

On the ground, you may well see some of the refuge's wild boars, alligators, armadillos, white-tailed deer and many more species. Everywhere you will see birds – close to 400 bird species have been documented at Aransas. None are more famous, more followed or more watched than the **whooping cranes**. Some of the rarest creatures in North America, about 250 survivors of the species spend summer in Canada and November to March in this refuge. Spotters and scientists come from all over the world to study the 5ft-tall birds.

The **visitor center** should be your first stop. You can borrow binoculars here for free. A 40ft **observation tower** is 5 miles from the visitor center and overlooks much of the refuge with its free telescopes. The **Auto Tour Loop** covers 16 miles, so allow two to four hours. Among several looped walks, **Birding Trail #2** is less visited and has some nice shady portions and beach frontage.

Bikes are a good way to explore the many hiking trails. Boats tour the estuaries from about mid-November to mid-April to spot whooping cranes, and this is easily the best way to get a good view of the rare birds. The three- to four-hour tours usually leave from Rockport or Fulton in the mornings and afternoons and cost about $50. There's no

WORTH A TRIP

MATAGORDA ISLAND

To escape civilization, you can't do much better than this secluded island accessible only by boat. Matagorda Island has no bridge connection to the mainland, no telephone, no electricity and no drinking water. It does have 80 miles of white beaches along its 38-mile length, plus almost limitless hiking possibilities. More than 320 species of birds drop by throughout the year; deer, coyotes, raccoons, rabbits, alligators and more call it home.

Most people visit just for the day. To use one of the 12 primitive camping sites, see the **Texas Parks & Wildlife website** (www.tpwd.state.tx.us/matagordaisland) for the island. The only way out to the island is by boat across the 8 miles of Espiritu Santo Bay from Port O'Connor. Check out the local **chamber of commerce website** (www.portoconnorchamber.org) and look under 'Guides/Outfitters' for suppliers.

WORTH A TRIP

SCENIC COASTAL DRIVE: GALVESTON TO CORPUS CHRISTI

Following the coast between Galveston and Corpus Christi is not a straightforward adventure – roads and highways that jog in and out seem to change names and numbers with every turn. But it's worth the effort for the timeless coastal towns and natural backwaters that see little traffic diverted from busy US 59 and US 77 inland. You can cover this route easily in a day, but if you plan on spending time in any of the nature areas and beaches, make it two.

The Route

After the upscale beach houses that extend to the southern tip of Galveston Island, the sudden lack of development once you cross the San Luis Pass bridge to the emptiness of Follets Island can be a pleasant surprise.

Surfside Beach, 13.5 miles southeast, is a workmanlike party town, where few pass the convenience store at the main crossroad without stopping for a case of beer.

Fans of oil refineries will appreciate the 11-mile drive inland on TX 332. Watch for signs for the delightful Sea Center Texas (p263) in **Lake Jackson**.

From Lake Jackson, take FM 2004, which becomes FM 2611 when it crosses TX 36. This a lovely drive through lush lands laced with rivers and peppered with wildflowers. Turn north when you hit FM 457, go 6 miles and turn west on FM 521 for 15.5 miles to TX 60, then turn south to **Matagorda** (p263) and the beaches, a total of 55 miles from Lake Jackson.

From Matagorda, drive back north 9 miles to FM 521 and turn west. You make a big loop to the north around a nuclear power plant – watch out for lobsters the size of Godzilla – and after 19 miles you turn south on TX 35 for 5 miles to **Palacios** (p266).

Continue on TX 35 for 50 miles through Port Lavaca (avoiding any temptation to detour to uninteresting Port O'Connor) until just past tiny Tivoli, where you should turn southeast on TX 239. Follow the signs for 18 miles through humdrum corn farms until you reach the wonders of Aransas National Wildlife Refuge (p266).

Leaving Aransas NWR, take FM 774 through a series of turns 12 miles west to TX 35. Turn south and go 13.5 miles to Lamar and the charms of Goose Island State Park (p267).

From here, it's only 6 miles south on TX 35 to the fun twin coastal towns of **Fulton** and **Rockport** (p268). Port Aransas, a good place to bed down, is only 20 miles beyond while Corpus Christi is another 30 miles further on.

camping anywhere in the park, but Goose Island State Park is a good option.

Aransas Refuge is easily reached: coming from the south (it's 31 driving miles north of Goose Island State Park), take curving FM 774 off of TX 35 and continue on to FM 2040. From the north, take TX 239 off of TX 35 and continue via the tiny town of Austwell and FM 2040.

Rockport Birding & Kayak Adventures BIRD-WATCHING
(☎877-892-4737; www.whoopingcranetours.com; 202 N Fulton Beach Rd, Fulton Harbor; 3½hr tours $50; ⏰7:30am & 1pm) Estuaries tour leaves from Fulton. Also rents kayaks (from $60 per day).

Wharf Cat BIRD-WATCHING
(☎361-729-4855, 800-782-2473; www.texaswhoopers.com; tours adult/child from $50/25; ⏰10am mid-Dec–Mar) Tours leave from Rockport Harbor (Wednesday to Sunday) and Port Aransas's Fisherman's Wharf (Tuesday).

Goose Island State Park

The main part of **Goose Island State Park** (☎361-729-2858; www.tpwd.state.tx.us; adult/child $5/free; ⏰8am-10pm), where admission is charged, is right on Aransas Bay (although there's no swimming). The namesake marshy island is a mere 140 acres, linked to another 174 acres on the mainland. The busiest times at the park are during the summer and in whooping crane season (November to March). It's worth booking **campsites** in advance. Walk-in sites away from RVs are $10 while sites with utilities are $22. A word of caution: the phrase 'bring insect repellent' appears more frequently in this park's official brochure than in any other. Kayaking along the calm inlets is popular here.

The oldest tree on the coast is an oak more than 1000 years old near the main part of the park. Stuck with the prosaic moniker of **Big Tree** (the trunk is more than 35ft in diameter), this grand specimen is in an idyllic spot amid a sea of wildflowers, near the sea, and surrounded by panels with poetry. It is near 12th St and outside the gated park area. Both lie at the end of a sweet little drive from TX 35 and the village of **Lamar**, with the drive passing under an entire thicket of live oaks that shade the road.

The park is 12 miles north of Rockport, off E Main St, which runs east from TX 35, just north of the bridge over Copano Bay. Big Tree is 1.5 miles north of the park along the water.

Rockport & Fulton

POP 10,200

A pedestrian-friendly waterfront, numerous worthy attractions, fishing boats plying their trade and cute little downtown Rockport make the adjoining towns of Rockport and Fulton an enjoyable stop on the coast.

The side streets between TX 35 and Aransas Bay are dotted with art galleries, especially in the center of Rockport; the towns claim to be home to the Texas' highest percentage of artists.

Sights & Activities

Coming from the north, leave TX 35 after you cross the LBJ Causeway and follow shoreline-hugging Fulton Beach Rd south first through Fulton and then into Rockport, where Austin St is the main drag of the walkable downtown. In either direction, avoid strip-mall-lined TX 35.

Rockport Harbor HARBOR

Crescent-shaped Rockport Harbor is one of the prettiest on the Gulf Coast. It's lined with all manner of boats (shrimp, fishing charter, tour and pleasure craft) and a series of rustic peel-and-eat shrimp joints and bait shops.

Texas Maritime Museum MUSEUM

(361-729-1271; www.texasmaritimemuseum.org; 1202 Navigation Circle, Rockport; adult/child $8/3; 10am-4pm Tue-Sat, 1-4pm Sun) Everything from fishing boats to offshore oil rigs to the story of the short-lived Texas Navy is covered at this large museum on the harbor. Displays emphasize the human aspects of the Texas seacoast. Several old boats that were used to rescue people caught in storms are displayed outside.

Aquarium at Rockport Harbor AQUARIUM

(361-727-0016; www.rockportaquarium.com; 702 Navigation Circle; admission free; 1-4pm Thu-Mon) This small volunteer-run aquarium has crabs and other local sea critters, including most of the fish avidly sought by local fishers. You'll often see local artists just outside capturing the colors of the sea.

Rockport Center for the Arts CULTURAL CENTER

(361-729-5519; 902 Navigation Circle; 10am-4pm Tue-Sat, 1-4pm Sun) It's worth popping into this cheery center, housed partly in a charming 1890s building, to see what's going on with the lively local arts scene. It offers painting classes and is right on the water.

Fulton Mansion State Historical Park HISTORIC BUILDING

(361-729-0386; www.visitfultonmansion.com; 317 S Fulton Beach Rd; adult/child $6/4; 9:30am-4:30pm Tue-Sat, 12:30-4:30pm Sun) This imposing 1870s mansion comes as a surprise amid other more modern – and modest – shorefront buildings. It was built by George Fulton, who was clever with the design. On the outside, it looks like an imposing French Second Empire creation, right down to the mansard roofs.

Inside those walls, however, are concrete foundations and walls more than 5in thick. Although other contemporary buildings have been blown away, the mansion has withstood several hurricanes.

An education and history center offers interactive exhibits, presentations and Victorian craft activities. Tours of the mansion itself depend on ongoing restoration work; call to book.

Slowride KAYAKING

(361-758-0463; www.slowrideguide.com; 821 S Commercial, Aransas Pass; 4hr kayak rental $40) The estuaries of the coast are ideal for kayaking. You can rent kayaks at this shop just south of Rockport or arrange for guided fishing and ecotours.

Sleeping & Eating

The Fulton waterfront by the mansion has a few modest motels and there is another good patch down by Rockport harbor.

Bayfront Cottages & Pier MOTEL, CABIN $

(361-729-6693; www.rockportbayfrontcottages.com; 309 S Fulton Beach Rd, Fulton; r $50-100;) A nicely updated old motor court is next to the mansion and across from the water. Use

BIRDERS OF A FEATHER FLOCK TOGETHER

The Texas coast and border comprise many of the world's finest bird-watching areas.

➡ Sea Rim State Park (p254) Near Port Arthur; vast and suited to explorations by water.

➡ Aransas National Wildlife Refuge (p266) Home to whooping cranes.

➡ Nature preserves of Port Aransas (p276) Easily accessed right in town.

➡ Padre Island National Seashore (p279) Seventy miles of sand and dunes sheltering shorebirds.

➡ Laguna Atascosa National Wildlife Refuge (p282) Has over 400 species of birds.

➡ South Padre Island Birding & Nature Center (p285) Features boardwalks amidst the birds.

➡ Bentsen-Rio Grande Valley State Park (p295) Right on the Rio Grande.

➡ Resaca de la Palma State Park (p292) Some 1200 acres in a beautiful subtropical setting.

➡ Roma Bluffs (p296) Includes an observation deck looking across the Rio Grande.

its pier to catch a fish, then cook it up in the small kitchen that comes with each unit.

Hoope's House HISTORIC HOTEL **$$**
(☎361-729-8424; www.hoopeshouse.com; 417 N Broadway St, Rockport; r $110-175; ❄📶🏊) This landmark mansion overlooks the Rockport Harbor, and has four rooms in the main house and another four in a modern wing. It's plush without being fussy and there's a large pool and a fab breakfast on offer.

Apple Dumpling CAFE **$**
(☎361-727-2337; 118 N Magnolia St, Rockport; mains from $5; ⏲8am-5pm Mon-Sat) Don't let the plain-Jane exterior deter you from this locally loved deli and cafe in downtown Rockport. The homemade ice cream is creamy and dreamy and the sandwiches are just the thing for picnics amidst the local natural splendor.

Boiling Pot SEAFOOD **$$**
(☎361-729-6972; 2015 Fulton Beach Rd, Fulton; meals $18; ⏲4-10pm Mon-Thu, 11am-11pm Fri & Sat, 11am-10pm Sun) This is a rustic classic, and a lot of fun. Mountains of shellfish plus potatoes, sausage and corn are put in a pot full of spicy boiling water; then dumped on your paper-covered table and you dive in (no cutlery, no crockery – bibs provided).

Latitude 2802 SEAFOOD **$$$**
(☎361-727-9009; www.latituderockport.com; 105 N Austin, Rockport; mains $15-33; ⏲5-10pm Tue-Sun) The finest dining in the area. Look for creative takes on seafood at this stylish little place that includes an art gallery. The local special, grouper, is prepared several ways; sides vary seasonally. Shrimp and oyster dishes are also excellent.

ℹ Information

Rockport-Fulton Area Chamber of Commerce (☎800-826-6441, 361-729-9952; www.rockport-fulton.org; 319 Broadway St, Rockport; ⏲9am-5pm Mon-Fri, 9am-2pm Sat) This very helpful office is near Rockport Harbor.

COASTAL PLAINS

Goliad is worth a detour from the coastal bend; it's a charming small town steeped in history. You might consider a circle route that takes in the coast one way and the plains the other.

Victoria

POP 62,600

Victoria has some 100 historic buildings near its downtown. Many have been restored by owners drawn to deeply shaded, oak-lined streets. The **Victoria Convention and Visitors Bureau** (☎361-485-3116; www.visitvictoriatexas.com; 700 Main St; ⏲8.30am-5pm Mon-Fri) has tour information.

The granite and limestone **Old Victoria County Courthouse** (101 N Bridge St) dates from 1892, when towns took pride in such places. It fronts the picturesque **DeLeon Plaza**. Note, however, that much of the city is just urban sprawl, so you can easily take in the historic charms and then be on your way.

Like a side of good food to go with your history? Reputedly the oldest deli in Texas, **Fossati's Delicatessen** (☎361-576-3354; 302 S Main St; mains from $5; ⏰9am-5pm Mon-Sat) is a good accompaniment to a historic tour of Victoria. Make friends at the bar.

Victoria is at the junction of US 77 and US 59, 125 miles south of Houston and 85 miles north of Corpus Christi. It is a good base for exploring the historical parks in Goliad, 25 miles to the south on US 59. Chain motels for every budget are found along the highways.

Goliad

POP 2000

'Remember the Alamo!' is the verbal icon of the Texas revolution, but it should also be 'Remember Goliad!' Here, on Palm Sunday, March 27, 1836, Mexican general Antonio López de Santa Anna ordered 350 Texan prisoners shot. The Texan death toll was double that at the Alamo and helped inspire the Texans to victory over Santa Anna at San Jacinto the following month.

There is a wealth of historic sites in and around the lovely town of Goliad, making it a must-see stop. It's 25 miles off US 77 and Victoria.

Sights

The hub of Goliad, **Courthouse Square**, features – surprise! – a grand old 1894 courthouse. Among the many stately oaks on the square is one labeled the 'Hanging Tree,' for self-explanatory reasons. A historical marker recalls the Regulators, 50 vigilantes who 'pursued criminals with vigor and often with cruelty' from 1868 to 1870.

Goliad State Park HISTORIC SITE

(☎361-645-3405; www.tpwd.state.tx.us; 108 Park Rd 6, off US 183; adult/child $3/free; ⏰8am-5pm, gates close 10pm except to overnight guests) The focus of this park just south of town is the huge and restored **Mission Espiritu Santo**. Dating to the 18th century, this was an important site during the Spanish colonial era. Massively rebuilt, you can get a sense of that time in the echoey chapel.

Don't miss the museum in the old school and workshop building. The lush surrounding park has quiet riverside hiking trails.

Presidio La Bahia HISTORIC SITE

(☎361-645-3752; www.presidiolabahia.org; US 183; adult/child $4/1; ⏰9am-4:45pm) Built in 1749 by the Spanish to deter the French (who were then sniffing around the eastern edges of their empire), Presidio La Bahia played a role in six revolutions and wars. Texas revolutionaries seized the fort – now faithfully restored by the church – in October 1835.

The following year, Colonel Fannin and his men were held inside the walls by Mexican forces for two weeks before they were executed (their graves are nearby). The presidio is 2 miles south of Goliad and close to Mission Espiritu Santo.

Fannin Battleground State Historic Site HISTORIC SITE

(☎512-463-7948; www.visitfanninbattleground.com; 734 FM 2506, off US 59) FREE On March 20, 1836, Col James W Fannin fought Spanish forces here at the Battle of Coleto Creek. The men were overwhelmed and surrendered. Two weeks later most were executed at the Presidio La Bahia in nearby Goliad. The site, 9 miles east of Goliad, is quiet today. Look for the gin screw, a relic of early efforts to commemorate the battle.

THE CURSED COLUMBUS FLEET

In 1992, the government of Spain built replicas of Columbus' ships, the *Niña*, the *Pinta* and the *Santa María*, to commemorate the 500th anniversary of Columbus' voyage to the New World. After sailing them around the Atlantic, Spain agreed to lease them to the city of Corpus Christi for 50 years. Shortly after they arrived to huge fanfare in 1993, a rogue barge went out of control on the ship channel and rammed all three, causing huge damage. The **Niña** stayed afloat (and can be seen today at the Lawrence St T-Head), while the **Pinta** and **Santa María** were moved to a concrete dry dock behind the Museum of Science and History, looking quite the worse for wear. Of the latter two, the *Pinta* is still in decent shape.

After Spain made several offers to restore the boats met with hassles from Corpus Christi, it realized that no good deed goes unpunished and washed its hands of the ships in 2006. Meanwhile wrangling over the ships' futures continues.

Sleeping & Eating

Courthouse Square has cafes; on the second Saturday of each month Market Day lures vendors of all types.

Goliad State Park CAMPGROUND $
(☎361-645-3405; www.tpwd.state.tx.us; 108 Park Rd 6, off US 183; sites $10-22) There are well-shaded camping areas in the park, including many along the San Antonio River. Reserve in advance.

★**McMillan's BBQ** BARBECUE $
(☎361-645-2326; www.mcmillansbbq.com; 9913 US 59, Fannin; mains from $6; ⏱10am-3pm Mon-Wed, 10am-8pm Thu-Sun) Close to the Fannin battleground site, this small roadhouse is loved for its sweet and savory barbecue. Don't miss the buttery, tender beef brisket.

Information

Goliad Chamber of Commerce (☎361-645-3563; www.goliadcc.org; 231 S Market St; ⏱9am-5pm Mon-Fri) Offers a good walking-tour brochure for the town.

CORPUS CHRISTI AREA

Corpus Christi is the bull's-eye of its namesake region and bay. Its museums and attractions can fill a day or more while the pull of the beaches on Mustang and Padre Islands is irresistible – Port Aransas is easily the most charming beach town in Texas. But it's not all sand and sea – it can be cowboys and cattle too, if you like: an easy day trip from Corpus Christi takes you to Kingsville, home of the King Ranch, one of the largest and oldest working ranches in the world.

Corpus Christi

POP 308,000

Known simply as Corpus, this city by the placid bay is a growing and vibrant place. Its attractions are worth a visit and its perpetually sunny location on its namesake bay is beguiling.

The Spaniards named the bay after the Roman Catholic holy day of Corpus Christi in 1519, when Alonzo Álvarez de Piñeda discovered its calm waters. The town established here in the early 1800s later took the name as well. Growth was slow, however, due to yellow fever in the 19th century and a hurricane in 1919. Construction of Shoreline Blvd and the deepwater port between 1933 and 1941, combined with a boom brought on by WWII, caused rapid growth. Although the downtown is sleepy away from the water, the city does a good business attracting large conventions and meetings at the vast American Bank Center.

DRIVING THE BAY LOOP

You can do a loop of Corpus Christi Bay in two hours, without stops. In the south, Padre and Mustang Islands are joined to the mainland via the John F Kennedy Causeway across Laguna Madre. The causeway in turn is reached from Corpus Christi by either Ocean Dr from downtown or by TX 358 (S Padre Island Dr, often called just SPID), which links to the other highways and passes by an ocean of shopping malls. In the north, a car ferry links Port Aransas to TX 361, which leads to Aransas Pass where TX 35 links with US 181 and Corpus itself.

Sights

Downtown Corpus lies behind Shoreline Blvd, a wide seafront boulevard that was designed by Gutzon Borglum, the sculptor of Mt Rushmore.

North Beach, the closest beach to downtown, lies across the ship channel to the north. The soaring US 181 Harbor Bridge spans the channel between the downtown and beach areas. You can make the dizzying walk up and over the span; on the south side start near Beldon St.

★**USS Lexington Museum** HISTORIC SHIP
(www.usslexington.com; 2914 N Shoreline Blvd; adult/child $14/9; ⏱9am-5pm, to 6pm Jun-Aug) The second sight you are likely to notice in Corpus (after the bay) is this 900ft-long **aircraft carrier** moored just north of the ship channel. The ship served in the Pacific during WWII and was finally retired in 1991. High-tech exhibits give visitors a chance to experience a taste of wartime, without actually dying in a kamikaze attack.

During the evening, the ship is eerily lit with blue lights that recall its WWII nickname, 'the Blue Ghost.'

Texas State Aquarium AQUARIUM
(☎361-881-1200; www.texasstateaquarium.org; 2710 N Shoreline Blvd; adult/child $18/13; ⏱9am-5pm, to 6pm summer; 👪) Learn about marine

Corpus Christi

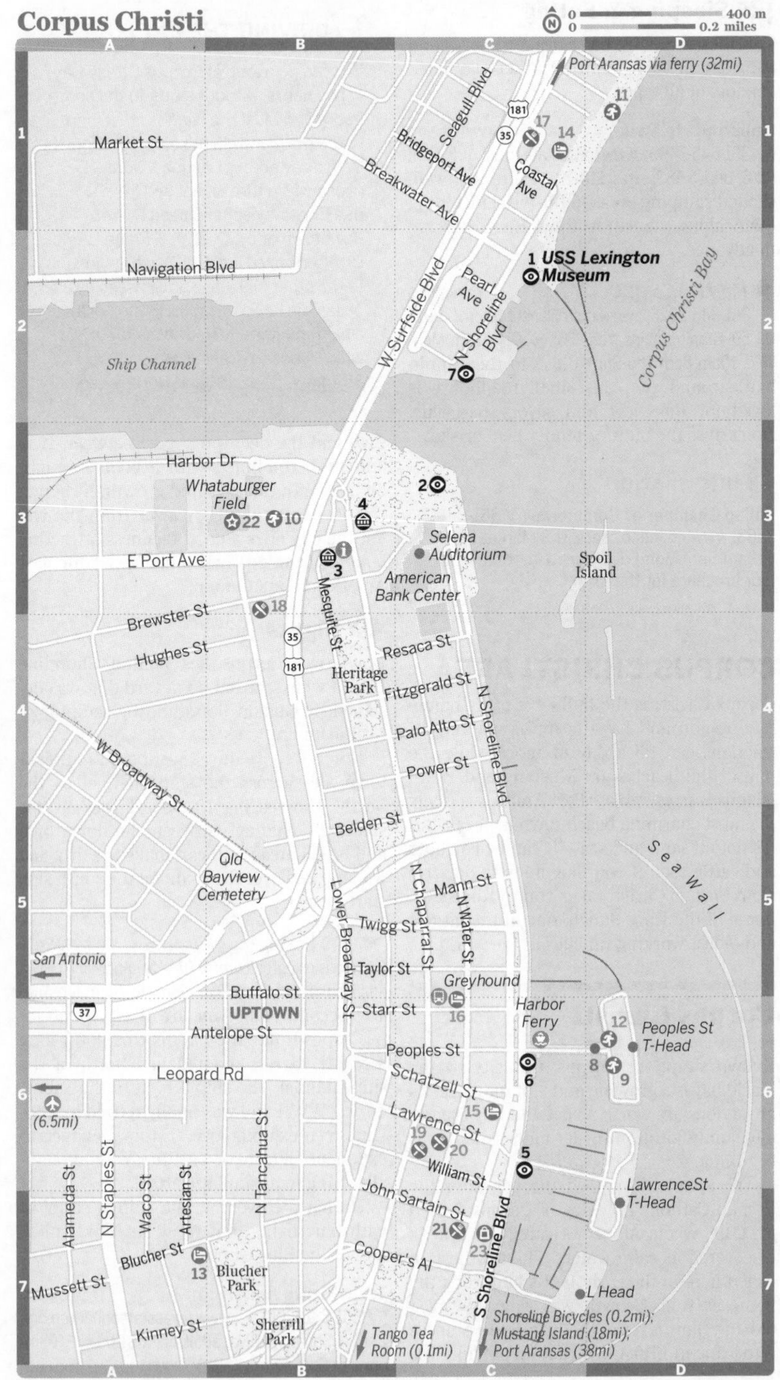

0
400 m
0.2 miles
Port Aransas via ferry (32mi)
Seagull Blvd
Bridgeport Ave
Breakwater Ave
Coastal Ave
Market St
Navigation Blvd
1 USS Lexington Museum
Corpus Christi Bay
Pearl Ave
N Shoreline Blvd
W Surfside Blvd
Ship Channel
Harbor Dr
Whataburger Field
Selena Auditorium
American Bank Center
Spoil Island
E Port Ave
Brewster St
Hughes St
Mesquite St
Resaca St
Heritage Park
Fitzgerald St
Palo Alto St
Power St
W Broadway St
Belden St
Old Bayview Cemetery
Sea Wall
Mann St
N Chaparral St
N Water St
Lower Broadway St
Twigg St
Taylor St
San Antonio
Greyhound
Buffalo St
UPTOWN
Starr St
Harbor Ferry
Antelope St
Peoples St
Peoples St T-Head
Leopard Rd
Schatzell St
(6.5mi)
Lawrence St
William St
LawrenceSt T-Head
John Sartain St
S Shoreline Blvd
Alameda St
N Staples St
Waco St
Artesian St
N Tancahua St
Blucher St
Blucher Park
Cooper's Al
Mussett St
L Head
Kinney St
Sherrill Park
Tango Tea Room (0.1mi)
Shoreline Bicycles (0.2mi); Mustang Island (18mi); Port Aransas (38mi)

Corpus Christi

Top Sights
1 USS Lexington Museum C2

Sights
2 Art Museum of South Texas................C3
3 Museum of Asian Cultures..................B3
4 Museum of Science & History.............B3
5 Niña Columbus Ship Replica............. C6
6 Selena Memorial & Statue................. C6
7 Texas State Aquarium C2

Activities, Courses & Tours
8 Bay Cruise.. D6
9 CC Fun Time Rentals.......................... D6
10 Hurricane Alley Waterpark..................B3
11 North Beach D1
12 Yachting Center of Corpus Christi D6

Sleeping
13 George Blucher House.........................A7
14 Radisson Beach Hotel......................... C1
15 Super 8 Motel...................................... C6
16 V Boutique Hotel................................. C6

Eating
17 Blackbeard's... C1
18 Brewster Street Icehouse....................B3
Cafe Hesters................................ (see 2)
19 Executive Surf Club C6
20 Water Street Seafood Company C6
21 Whataburger C7

Entertainment
22 Whataburger Field...............................B3

Shopping
23 Art Centre of Corpus Christi C7
Surf Club Records .... (see 19)

life along the Gulf Coast at this vast, flashy attraction. The main exhibits, on a circular course, include a huge tank replicating the environment around offshore oil rigs, complete with sharks, grouper and red snapper (but no leaks). Other popular critters include turtles, otters, alligators and dolphins. A new 'stingray lagoon' is a big hit.

Museum of Science & History MUSEUM
(www.ccmuseum.com; 1900 N Chaparral St; adult/child $12.50/6; 10am-5pm Tue-Sat, noon-5pm Sun;) Explore shipwrecks at this fun museum, right on the south side of the ship channel. Learn how Texas proved to spell doom for French explorer La Salle and see the moldering remains of reproductions of two of Columbus' ships (p270).

Art Museum of South Texas MUSEUM
(361-825-3500; www.artmuseumofsouthtexas.org; 1902 N Shoreline Blvd; adult/child $8/free; 10am-5pm Tue-Sat, 1-5pm Sun) Rotating exhibits of contemporary art are the main feature at this dramatic museum, across the plaza from the Museum of Science & History. It also houses a permanent collection of American art.

Selena Museum MUSEUM
(361-289-9013; www.q-productions.com; 5410 Leopard St; adult/child $3/1; 10am-4pm Mon-Fri) Selena's studio is still a working music and production house, presided over by her still-proud father Abraham Quintanilla Jr. It includes numerous displays dedicated to the life of Selena (p274), including her awards, her red Porsche and many of her stage costumes. On a tour, you can visit the studios where she recorded her music.

The studios and museum are 5 miles west of the downtown waterfront in a vaguely industrial area.

Museum of Asian Cultures MUSEUM
(361-882-2641; www.asianculturesmuseum.org; 1809 N Chaparral St; adult/child $6/3; 10am-4pm Tue-Sat) This small museum is worth a look if you have an interest in Japanese and other Asian art. There are some interesting masks and kabuki figures, plus a tranquil bamboo garden.

Heritage Park HISTORIC SITE
(N Chaparral St, at Resaca St) Originally a neighborhood of old homes, Heritage Park has morphed into an old-home theme park. A dozen Corpus houses, from humble to grand and dating back as far as 1851, have been relocated to this area, bounded by Mesquite, N Chaparral, Hughes and Fitzgerald Sts.

Activities

For truly awesome beaches, head east out to Mustang Island and Port Aransas.

Cycling

If the wind's not too fierce, a very pleasant afternoon can be spent cycling along the bayfront. **Shoreline Bicycles** (361-883-8888; 555 S Shoreline Blvd; 9am-5pm Mon-Sat) rents bikes (from $20 per day).

Fishing

Most of the skippers who charter boats are based in Rockport or Port Aransas because it puts them closer to the gulf.

Water Parks

Mega-water-park-operator Schlitterbahn (www.schlitterbahn.com) is set to make a splash with a new park due to open at the east end of the intersection of TX 358 and the JFK Causeway onto Padre Island. Opening is set for summer, 2014.

Hurricane Alley Waterpark WATER PARK
(☎361-883-9283; www.hurricanealleycc.com; 702 E Port Ave; admission $20-25; ⏰11am-6pm daily Jun–mid-Aug, weekends only mid-Aug–Oct & Mar-May; 👪) Water slides, including a towering one called the 'Cat 5', are the highlights of this seasonal water park near Whataburger Field.

Water Sports

Laguna Madre, west of Padre Island, is a prized windsurfing location thanks to the unusually calm waters and the nearly constant breezes. The alphabetically shaped T and L docks downtown are home to large marinas.

CC Fun Time Rentals WATER SPORTS
(☎361-443-0707; 600 N Shoreline Blvd at People St T-Head; ⏰10am-4pm Mar-Oct) Rent power boats ($80 per hour), kayaks ($15 for one hour) and enjoy other adventures at this small port-side shop.

Wind & Wave Surf Shop WATER SPORTS
(☎361-937-9283; 10721 S Padre Island Dr/TX 358; ⏰10am-5pm Mon-Sat) A good place to get information on local conditions, it rents boogie boards, surfboards for the terminally optimistic ($30 per day) and kayaks (from $50 per day).

Yachting Center of Corpus Christi BOATING
(☎361-881-8503; www.yachtingcc.com; Harrison's Landing, 108 Peoples St, T-dock; ⏰10am-5pm) Offers an introduction to yachting ($60), which includes two hours of hands-on sailing.

Tours

Bay Cruise BOAT TOUR
(☎361-881-8503; Harrison's Landing, 108 Peoples St, T-dock; adult/child $10/5; ⏰sailing times vary) One-hour cruises on Corpus Christi Bay at various time through the year.

Sleeping

Dare we say it: you may want to opt for the beach-town charms of Port Aransas for your slumber and visit Corpus as a day trip. But there are also good options near the water here, and the parks on Padre and Mustang Islands all have camping facilities.

Super 8 Motel MOTEL $$
(☎361-884-4815; www.super8.com; 411 N Shoreline Blvd; r $70-140; ❄📶🏊) No surprises here, but you will find decent, budget rooms in an excellent downtown location, smack bang between the T-heads and the nightlife of

SELENA

Selena Quintanilla Perez, easily the most famous person Corpus Christi has produced, was almost single-handedly responsible for the crossover of Tejano music to the mainstream. She had a charismatic stage presence and, since her murder in 1995, has been considered a martyr by many. Images of her can be found behind cash registers in shops and restaurants all over town.

Selena was 23 when Yolanda Saldivar, the president of her fan club, shot her dead in the parking lot of the Days Inn near the Corpus Christi airport. At the trial prosecutors successfully argued that Saldivar shot the singing star because Selena had discovered that the fan-club president was stealing her money. Saldivar got life in prison.

In death, Selena's music still sells and many devotees make the pilgrimage to Corpus. Her story has been embraced by fans because it is one with which they can empathize. Selena's parents tried and failed at running a Mexican restaurant in Corpus, and it fell to their plucky daughter and her crowd-pleasing talents to save the family from ruin. Along the way, she ran afoul of her father, an authoritarian who objected to her revealing stage clothes. Plus she married her lead guitarist in a secret ceremony. It was great melodrama, as seen in 1997's *Selena,* which made a star of the then relatively unknown Jennifer Lopez.

In Corpus Christi, the **Selena Memorial & Statue** stands at the entrance to the Peoples St T-head on Shoreline Blvd – but to really celebrate Selena and feel tangible links to her life, don't miss the Selena Museum (p273).

Water St. The pool is probably more inviting than the limpid waters across the street.

Radisson Beach Hotel HOTEL $$
(☎361-883-9700; www.radisson.com; 3200 Surfside Blvd; r $100-200;) The 139 rooms are comfortable (and have balconies, microwaves and fridges) at this 1970s beachfront hotel. Get a 7th-floor room facing the Lexington and imagine you're coming in for a landing.

George Blucher House B&B $$
(☎361-884-4884; www.georgeblucherhouse.com; 211 N Carrizo St; r $120-190;) A large wood-and-brick 1904 mansion near the center of town, the George Blucher House has six bedrooms, each with a bathroom. All are decorated in what could be described as 'period plush.' Sit on the covered porch and listen to the pecan trees grow.

V Boutique Hotel BOUTIQUE HOTEL $$$
(☎361-883-9200; www.vhotelcc.com; 701 N Water St; r $150-250;) Absolutely adored by its guests, this small hotel in the heart of downtown offers a high level of service, including 24-hour concierge. Rooms come in eight styles, from studios to one-bedroom loft suites.

Eating & Drinking

Bars and restaurants cluster on the streets surrounding Chaparral and Water Sts downtown.

Whataburger BURGERS $
(www.whataburger.com; 121 N Shoreline Blvd; mains from $3; 10am-late) Corpus Christi's own entry in the burger wars, Whataburger, got its start in town in 1950. This location, with its view of the marina, eschews much of the 1970s orange theme found in the chain's 700 other outlets, but the trademark big-diameter (and wafer-thin) burger is the classic loved locally.

Don't miss the statue of the chain's founder, Harmon Dobson.

Cafe Hesters CAFE $
(☎361-885-0151; www.hesterscafe.com; 1902 N Shoreline Blvd; mains from $5; 10am-3pm Tue-Sat) Nestled artfully in the Art Museum of South Texas, Hesters has the kind of baked goods that make you order one for now and another for 'Ron (later on). Sandwiches, omelets, quiches and more highlight the fresh, creative menu.

Hamlin Pharmacy and Fountain CAFE $
(☎361-853-7303; 3801 S Staples St, at Weber Rd; mains $4-6; 9am-5pm Mon-Sat) A character-filled throwback to the days when drug stores all had lunch counters, this place is the real deal. Sit on a stool at the counter or in a tiny booth and have a grilled cheese plus something luscious from the soda fountain. The surrounding store has more candy and toys these days than medicinals.

Hamlin is in a vintage strip mall about 5 miles south of the marinas.

Blackbeard's TEX-MEX $
(☎361-884-1030; 3117 Surfside Blvd; meals from $8; 11am-10pm Sun-Thu, to 11pm Fri & Sat) Near North Beach, this rollicking place serves up tasty Mexican and American cuisine. Wash it down with cheap margaritas while sitting back for the live music.

Executive Surf Club SOUTHERN $
(309 N Water St; mains $6-10; 11am-11pm Sun-Wed, to midnight Thu-Sat) Eat a fried-shrimp po'boy from a surfboard table at this long-time fave, which has tables inside and out plus live music. It's just divey enough that you can forget you're downtown.

Tango Tea Room CAFE $$
(☎361-883-9123; 505 S Water St; mains from $8; 10am-7pm Mon-Thu, to 9pm Fri & Sat, noon-6pm Sun;) Amid a coven of little alternative shops offering herbal healing and belly-dancing lessons, this funky vegetarian cafe has a long menu of fresh sandwiches, salads and baked goods, plus all the teas implied by the name.

Brewster Street Icehouse BURGERS, SEAFOOD $$
(1724 N Tancahua St; mains $7-16; 11am-2am;) Has fried everything, cold brews, live music (Thursday to Saturday night) and a huge deck. This old warehouse really rocks after baseball games at nearby Whataburger Field. Kids love the playground.

Water Street Seafood Company SEAFOOD $$
(☎361-882-8684; 309 N Water St; mains $12-25; 11am-10pm Sun-Thu, to 11pm Fri & Sat) Busy all week, this high-ceilinged restaurant has a huge and changing selection of fresh seafood, much of it not deep-fried. It also has a very popular oyster bar, big with the after-work crowd. It's the best option for higher-end fare downtown.

✪ Entertainment

Whataburger Field BASEBALL
(☎361-561-4665; www.cchooks.com; N Port Ave; admission $5-10; ⊙Apr–early-Sep;) Corpus Christi's minor league baseball team, the Hooks, are a AA affiliate of the Houston Astros. Games at Whataburger Field are fun-filled family affairs; many picnic on the lawns overlooking outfield.

Shopping

Art Center of Corpus Christi ARTS & CRAFTS
(☎361-884-6406; 100 Shoreline Blvd; ⊙10am-4pm Tue-Sun) Galleries and studios for local artists are housed in this grand old building downtown. The cafe is good for lunch.

★**Surf Club Records** MUSIC
(☎361-882-2364; 309 N Water St; ⊙10am-8pm Mon-Sat, 11am-5pm Sun) Part of the Water St Market, there is a great selection of hard-to-find CDs with surf music, country and rock. There's a small surfing museum area with displays on the history of surfing in Texas.

Information

Corpus Christi Convention & Visitors Bureau (☎800-766-2322; www.visitcorpuschristitx.org; 1823 N Chaparral; ⊙10am-4pm Mon-Sat, also noon-4pm in summer) Near the museums.

Getting There & Around

Corpus Christi International Airport (CRP; ☎361-289-0171; www.corpuschristiairport.com) You'll find Corpus Christi International Airport 6 miles west of downtown at International Dr and TX 44. American Eagle serves Dallas–Fort Worth, United Express serves Houston IAH and Southwest serves Houston Hobby. Cabs from the airport to downtown cost at least $35; many motels and hotels run shuttles.

Greyhound (☎361-882-2516; www.greyhound.com; 702 N Chaparral St) Has regular services to Houston ($32, 4½ hours), Brownsville ($32, three hours) and San Antonio ($35, 2½ hours).

The B (☎361-289-2600; www.ccrta.org; adult/child $0.75/0.25, day pass $1.75) The jaunty name for the local buses. Buses on most routes run about 6:30am to 7pm, although few run on Sunday. A useful route for travelers is the 78 CC Beach/Bayfront Connector, which links the downtown and marinas with the North Beach area.

Harbor Ferry (☎361-289-2600; www.ccrta.org; single ride $1.50; ⊙10am-6:30pm Wed-Mon Jun-Aug, weekends only mid-Mar–May & Sep-Nov) Run by the T, this seasonal ferry links the Peoples St T-Head with North Beach. It's the most scenic way to to make the link.

Port Aransas

POP 3500

Port Aransas (ah-*ran*-ziss), or Port A, on the northern tip of Mustang Island, is in many ways the most appealing beach town on the Texas coast. It is small enough that you can ride a bike or walk anywhere, but large enough that it has lots of activities and nightlife. The pace is very relaxed, and activities are dominated by hanging out on the beach, fishing and doing nothing.

Sights

Port A can be your base, or a stop on a looping drive around the bay.

★**Beaches** BEACH
Port A has 18 miles of silvery white beaches on the gulf side of Mustang Island. You can drive and park on the sand, thought you may require a permit; the main access point is via Beach St (try to remember that) to the county-run **IB Magee Beach Park** (☎361-749-6117; www.nuecesbeachparks.com; Beach St). The park has rest rooms, the Horace Caldwell fishing pier and seasonal concession stands.

Port Aransas Museum MUSEUM
(☎361-749-3800; www.portaransasmuseum.org; 101 E Brundrett St; ⊙1-5pm Thu-Sat) FREE Volunteers make this small museum a delightful place to learn the history of Port A, from sand (when this was just a barrier island) to sea (when the residents were professional fishers) to sand and sea (when the economy was based on fishing and beachgoing for fun).

University of Texas Marine Science Institute MUSEUM
(☎361-749-6806; www.utmsi.utexas.edu; 750 Channelview Dr; ⊙8am-5pm Mon-Fri year-round, 10am-5pm Sat May-Aug) FREE The tiny school's visitor center has views of the busy shipping channel and exhibits about dunes, sand, fish and of course the myriad local bird species.

Nature Preserves NATURE RESERVE
(☎361-749-4158; Ross Ave & Port St; ⊙dawn-dusk) FREE The city runs two birding centers that share views over the bird-filled marshes and salt flats on the east side of town. There are two points of access and you can wander over 2 miles of boardwalks and partake in the feathery spectacle from observation decks and towers.

BEACH PARKING PERMITS

You can drive your vehicle right onto the sand at many points in Port Aransas and Mustang Island. In fact the beaches are usually so hard that even a regular car will have no problem – just look to see what others are doing. At city and county beaches, you'll need a **beach parking permit** ($12). These are easily purchased at convenience stores, supermarkets and at the Port A tourist office (p278).

San José Island ISLAND

A privately owned island, known as St Jo to locals, is just across the ship channel from Port Aransas. This desert island is popular for fishing and beachcombing, although users are advised to bring over virtually everything they will require, including water. The **jetty boat** (☎361-749-5448; www.wharfcat.com; 900 N Tarpon St; adult/child $12/6; ⏰hourly boats 7am-6pm) runs many times daily.

Activities

There are myriad places offering water adventures and gear for surfing, kiteboarding and more. Fishing is big business in Port A, and there are dozens of boats offering trips and private charters. The tourist bureau has listings. Rates vary widely, somewhere between $50 and $1000 or more, depending on whether you're going to the bay or gulf, the length of the trip and what exactly you're trying to catch.

Woody's Sports Center ADVENTURE SPORTS

(☎800-211-9227, 361-749-5252; www.woodysonline.com; 136 Cotter Ave) Fishing trips, dolphin watches and nature tours offered; also rents jet skis ($100 an hour).

Island Surf Rentals WATER SPORTS

(☎361-749-0822; www.islandsurfrentals.com; 124 E Ave G; ⏰10am-5pm) Per day rentals: surfboards ($25), boogie boards ($10), bikes ($20) and kayaks ($45 to $60).

Texas Surf Camps SURFING

(☎361-749-6956; www.texassurfcamps.com; ⏰Jun-Aug) Surf lessons in Port A for $70 per day.

Kiteboard Corpus WATER SPORTS

(☎361-244-5402; www.kiteboardcorpus.com; lessons per hr from $60) Legendary kiteboarder Adam 'A-Bomb' DelVecchio offers lessons on the windy waters in and around Port A, Mustang Island and Padre Island.

Deep Sea Headquarters FISHING

(☎800-705-3474, 361-749-5597; www.deepseaheadquarters.com; 440 Cotter Ave) The name says it all. Daily five-/eight-hour fishing trips cost $40/60, including equipment and bait.

Sleeping

There are more motel/condo rooms in Port A than there are permanent residents, so there are plenty of options and something to meet most budgets. Not surprisingly, summer weekends are when rooms are at their dearest; book in advance. Lots of options let you wander the walkable part of Port A; avoid the unsightly large condo developments south of town.

You can camp at both IB Magee Beach Park (p276) and Mustang Island State Park (p279). At the former, primitive beach camping is $12 per night while a tent site with utilities costs $25.

Port A has scores of locally owned motels that are filled with character, if not characters. All the ones listed here are close to nightlife. Rates often drop in low season.

★ **Amelia's Landing** MOTEL $$

(☎888-671-8088; www.ameliaslanding.com; 105 N Alister St; r $95-200; ❄📶🏊) This centrally located motel has an aviation theme, with each unit decorated for a different bit of flying lore (star in the *Top Gun* room, blast off in the Apollo room etc). All are loaded with amenities (fridges, DVDs, microwaves) and some have kitchens. It books up early in high season.

Sea Shell Village CABINS $$

(☎361-749-4294; www.seashellvillage.com; 502 E Ave G; r $100-260; ❄📶🏊) These bright, colorful units are close to the beach and can each sleep two to six people. Floor plans differ, but all come with kitchens or kitchenettes and are ideal for a longer stay (weekly rates are also available).

Sea Breeze Suites HOTEL $$

(☎361-749-1500; www.seabreezeportaransas.com; 407 Beach St; r $100-220; ❄📶🏊) Close to both the beach and the center of town, the building won't win any architecture awards but the 24 rooms are large and have balconies with views of the gulf and channel. Each has a full kitchen.

★Tarpon Inn HISTORIC HOTEL $$

(☎361-749-5555, 800-365-6784; www.thetarponinn.com; 200 E Cotter Ave; r $90-220; ❄📶) Dating from 1900, this charming, rickety place has been rebuilt several times after hurricanes, most extensively after the 1919 big blow. The lobby has more than 7000 of the huge silver scales that come from tarpon, the 6ft-long namesake fish. Most of the 24 rooms are small and have no TVs or phones, but do have lots of character and rocking chairs on the verandah.

Dancing Dunes CABINS $$

(☎361-749-3029; www.5dancingdunes.com; 1607 S 11th St; r $120-225; ❄) Five funky beach apartments in a small compound have two or three bedrooms each. Flotsam, jetsam and wrecked rowboats decorate the grounds and decor like a holiday episode of *Laverne & Shirley*. Guaranteed fun.

Condo Agents

A large proportion of the lodging around Port A is in condos. They range from simple units in town and away from the water to imposing high-rises on the beach (11th St is known as Condo Row). Many developments are south of town, beyond easy walking distance. There are units for virtually all budgets. Agents include:

CCMS ACCOMMODATION SERVICES

(☎361-749-4141, 800-598-2267; www.portaransastexas.com; 200 S Alister St) Represents many of the large condo buildings.

Coastline Adventures ACCOMMODATION SERVICES

(☎361-749-7635, 800-656-5692; www.coastadv.com; 107 N Cutoff Rd) Has a variety of accommodations listings.

Eating & Drinking

Port A has a great selection of restaurants and divey bars, almost all as casual as a bunch of sand in your shorts. Many have the kind of goofy vibe that helps make Port A the cool beach town that it is. Note that there're a lot of humdrum seafood places that fry up frozen fish: beware.

★Avery's Kitchen CAFE $

(☎361-749-0650; www.averyskitchen.com; 200 W Ave G; mains from $6; ⏲7am-9pm) With a large sunny deck, this cheap and cheerful cafe stays crowded by offering up excellent breakfasts, sandwiches and daily seafood specials. The onion rings are superb and everyone gets free Jello. The shrimp in all its variations is good.

The Gaff BAR $

(☎361-749-5970; 323 Beach St; mains from $8; ⏲11am-late) Out by the beach, this shacky bar is perfect for one aspiring to arrested development. Fun includes belt sander races and chicken-poop bingo (come on bird, come on!). There's decent pizza and subs plus live music that includes blues and country. Most days are 'talk like a pirate day' here.

Roosevelt's SEAFOOD $$

(☎361-749-5555; 200 E Cotter Ave; mains from $15; ⏲5-10pm Wed-Sat, 10am-1pm Sun) The fine dining room at the Tarpon Inn is worth getting spiffed up for. Reserve a table on the verandah and settle back to enjoy a seasonal menu of seafood and steaks, simply and creatively prepared. Brunch will have you snoozing for the rest of the day.

★Tarpon Ice House BAR

(☎361-749-2337; 321 N Allister St; ⏲around 4pm-late) A top local choice for drinking, carousing, mellowing out on the terrace or bursting into song. Kind of the prototypical beach town bar.

Shorty's BAR

(☎361-749-8077; 821 Tarpon St; mains from $7; ⏲11am-2am) The town's 'oldest and friendliest' watering hole is filled with real local seadogs and characters, both inside and out on the battered porch. It has dartboards and pool tables, and the ceiling is adorned with hundreds of caps from around the world. You can bar-hop around the block here, down by the docks.

Port Aransas Brewing BREWERY

(☎361-749-2739; www.portabrewing.com; 429 N Alister St; ⏲11am-10pm Thu-Tue) The microbrews are darn tasty at this small bar and grill in the center (we like the Island Pale Ale) and they get points for also stocking bottles of some of the best microbrews from around the US. The burgers are thick, juicy and lauded (mains from $9). There's a small deck out front.

Information

Port Aransas Chamber of Commerce and Tourist Bureau (☎361-749-5919, 800-452-6278; www.portaransas.org; 403 Cotter Ave; ⏲9am-5pm Mon-Fri, 9am-3pm Sat) Has stacks of brochures, maps and information. Loans out binoculars for bird-watching.

Getting There & Around

A highlight of getting to Port A is the constantly running, free **ferries** (☎361-749-2850; ⏰24hr) which connect with TX 361 and Aransas Pass on the mainland. The ride takes 15 minutes and the wait is usually under 10 minutes, except at busy times when it can be 45 minutes.

The public transit option for Port Aransas is operated by The B (p276). Route 65 runs twice daily June to August from the transit mall on the south side of Corpus Christi. From here you can transfer to buses to the airport and downtown. Route 94 ($0.75, hourly 10am to 5pm) shuttles around much of Port Aransas.

Golf carts for cruising the streets and beaches are all the rage. **Cars & Carts** (☎361-749-1655; www.carsandcarts.com; 325 E Ave G; cart rental per hr/day $29/160; ⏰9am-5pm) rents oodles.

Mustang & Padre Island Beaches

The gulf side of Mustang and Padre Islands is one 131-mile-long beach. The notable parks are Mustang Island State Park and Padre Island National Seashore. The rest of the beach is administered by Nueces County.

There are beach access roads every few miles, and most have a parking area; parts of the beach are blocked off so that yahoos in SUVs can't mow you down. Camping is permitted anywhere, but limited to three days in any one location. Sand dunes back most of the beach area. Only since the 1970s have some monstrous condo developments appeared on Mustang Island near Port Aransas, otherwise most of the sand is blissfully undeveloped.

For most of the beaches you'll need a permit (p277) to drive on the sand. However a 6-mile stretch just north of Padre Island National Seashore is free to drivers.

Mustang Island State Park PARK
(☎361-749-5246; www.tpwd.state.tx.us; adult/child $5/free; ⏰gates close 10pm except to overnight guests) This well-equipped park covers 4000 acres and has 5.5 miles of beach. It is popular with surfers, but given the normally calm nature of the gulf, you may have to wait for storms to see any surfable waves. Some picnic areas have shade. There are 300 nonreservable campsites on the beach ($10) that have access to water, showers and rest rooms.

The campsites (a 1.5-mile hike to the facilities from the furthest sites) are a good compromise for people who want to wake up to the sound of waves but don't want to dig a hole to poop. A more formal – and reservable – site with utilities costs $20 per night.

Padre Island National Seashore

One of the longest stretches of undeveloped seashore in the US, the southern part of **Padre Island** (www.nps.gov/pais; Park Rd 22; 7-day pass per car $10; ⏰visitor center 9am-5pm) is administered by the National Park Service. Its main feature is 65 miles of white sand and shell beaches, backed by grassy dunes and the very salty Laguna Madre.

The island is home to all the coastal wildlife found elsewhere along the coast and then some. There's excellent birding, of course, plus numerous coyotes, white-tailed deer, sea turtles and more. It offers a delightful day's outing for anyone who wants to try a little natural beauty, or a major adventure for anyone who wants to escape civilization.

Note that Padre Island National Seashore is separated from South Padre Island by the Mansfield Channel and there is no transport across this gap. South Padre Island, the resort town, is only accessible from the very south of the state.

The first 6 miles of road into the park are paved. After that are 5 miles of beach to the south, which has very hard-packed sand suitable for driving most cars. After milepost 5 on the beach, only 4WDs can continue the trip.

The excellent park map is free at the entrance. Besides showing the island in great detail, it has good information about flora, fauna and various activities such as fishing and beachcombing. If you're visiting in summer, you might be able to take part in a turtle release; call the **Hatchling Hotline** (☎361-949-7163) for information.

Activities

Hiking & Fishing

The rangers advise campers and hikers to apply common sense in trekking south on the island. Bring at least 1 gallon of water per person per day, along with sunscreen, insect repellent, good shady hats and other sensible attire. Shore fishing is permitted with a Texas state fishing license.

Windsurfing

Bird Island Basin faces the Laguna Madre and has been voted as one of the best windsurfing spots in North America. **Worldwinds** (☎800-793-7471, 361-949-7472; www.worldwinds.net)

has a base here, offering equipment and gear rental ($50 to $65 per day) and lessons.

Tours

Padre Island Safaris (☎361-937-8446; www.billysandifer.com) goes to remote parts of the park for nature-watching and fishing. Respected fisherman and unofficial local historian Captain Billy Sandifer will take you the length of the park; a four- to six-hour birding trip costs $400 for two. You can also view turtles and hunt for shells.

Sleeping

Reservations are not accepted for any of the facilities. Primitive camping on the beaches is free but requires a permit (available from the visitor center).

The **Malaquite Campground** is a developed camping area close to the beach and about half a mile from the visitor center. It's suitable for tents and RVs, but it doesn't have any hookups. It does have rest rooms and showers, and camping here costs $8 a night. Many people park their RVs and trailers along the first 5 miles of beach, where driving is fairly easy.

There is primitive camping (pit toilets only) at Bird Island Basin, on the Laguna Madre about 4 miles from the visitor center. It's suitable for RVs and tents and costs $5 a night.

Information

Entrance to the park costs $10 per vehicle, which is good for seven days.

The **Malaquite Beach Visitor Center** (☎361-949-8068; www.nps.gov/pais; visitor center 9am-5pm, park 24hr) is on the beach just before the end of the paved road. It has showers, rest rooms and picnic facilities and offers excellent information. Check the schedule for interpretive walks (there's usually one at 11am along the beach).

A small store with convenience foods and souvenirs is also here. There is very little past the visitor center except beautiful beaches and dunes where the only sounds you'll hear are the wind and water, punctuated by the occasional bird's cry.

Corpus Christi to Harlingen

US 77 is the main southbound route from the Corpus Christi to the semitropical south. Except for a few diversions like Kingsville, there's 120 miles of scrubland before you reach Harlingen.

Kingsville

POP 24,800

King is the name of the game in this company town that is the direct result of the fabled 825,000-acre King Ranch, the largest of its kind in the world. Former riverboat captain Richard King established the ranch in 1853 on land that others saw as a scrub-covered semidesert. King instead saw semidesert with the only natural springs for hundreds of miles. Today the ranch is bigger than Rhode Island, a state that the ranch's fences would reach if they were laid end to end.

Sights & Activities

Kingsville is on US 77 and the ranch makes an interesting stop while passing by or as a day trip from Corpus Christi. Sadly, the historic downtown has been decimated by chain stores on the garish strip by the highway, although there's some life on weekdays.

King Ranch HISTORIC SITE

(☎visitor center 361-592-8055; www.king-ranch.com; 2205 W Hwy 141; ranch tours adult/child $12/6; 9am-4pm Mon-Sat, noon-5pm Sun) Much of the King Ranch is not open to the public, but there are 60,000 head of cattle, 400 horses and dozens of cowboys here – many are fifth- and sixth-generation descendants of Mexicans who moved to the ranch in the 1860s.

On the tour's 10-mile loop you will see the horse and cattle breeds that made the ranch famous, plus some native wildlife. You'll pass the lavish main building (33,000 sq feet), and with any luck you'll get to hear some excellent commentary and personal anecdotes from the tour guides, who are often retired ranch employees.

Tours depart from the visitor center (p281), which is just inside the rather modest entrance to the ranch on the west side of Kingsville at the end of Santa Gertrudis Ave.

In addition to the standard tours, there are guided bird-watching and wildlife-spotting tours across the unspoiled expanses of the ranch, lasting from 2½ to nine hours ($45 to $300). Schedules change seasonally.

King Ranch Museum MUSEUM

(☎361-595-1881; www.king-ranch.com; 405 6th St; adult/child $6/3; 10am-4pm Mon-Sat, 1-5pm Sun) Housed in a renovated ice-storage house downtown, the King Ranch Museum covers the history of the ranch. Be sure to follow the minor family dramas of the first generation; it's just like a movie (foreman marries King's daughter etc).

1904 Train Depot HISTORIC BUILDING
(☎361-592-3212; 104 E Kleberg Ave; ⏰10am-4pm Mon-Fri, to 1pm Sat) FREE Downtown, the old train depot has been beautifully restored and is filled with historical items, especially those relating to a time when you could board a train here and connect to the rest of the nation.

Eating

Harrel's CAFE $
(☎361-592-3354; www.harrels.com; 204 E Kleberg Ave; mains from $5; ⏰9am-5pm Mon-Fri, to 3pm Sat) Besides capsules with cold and flu remedies, this pharmacy serves up a time-capsule in the form of a soda fountain that hasn't changed in decades. The hash browns at breakfast are real, the burgers juicy and cheap and the soda sweet and tasty.

Shopping

The downtown has a few antiques shops.

King Ranch Saddle Shop CLOTHING
(☎800-282-5464; 201 E Kleberg Ave; ⏰10am-6pm Mon-Sat) The upmarket King Ranch Saddle Shop has expensive clothing and gear branded with the distinctive King Ranch logo, which looks like a squiggly snake.

Information

Kingsville Visitor Center (☎361-592-8516, 800-333-5032; www.kingsvilletexas.com; US 77, at Corral St; ⏰9am-5pm Mon-Fri, 10am-2pm Sat) Right near the freeway exit on the north side of town.

Loyola Beach

This unassuming Texas coastal village, 24 miles southeast of Kingsville, is home to another one of those restaurants that causes people to detour in droves. **King's Inn** (☎361-297-5265; 1116 E County Rd 2270; mains from $10; ⏰11am-10pm Tue-Sat) is a legendary place known for its vast platters of fresh seafood, onion rings, avocado salad and more. About 15 miles south of Kingsville look for FM 628 and go east 9 miles. Make reservations for dinner.

Sarita

This unassuming town 21 miles south of Kingsville on US 77 was once home to a family empire that for a brief period rivalled that of the Kings. At the **Kenedy Ranch Museum** (☎361-294-5751; www.kenedymuseum.org; 200 E La Parra Ave; adult/child $3/2; ⏰10am-4pm Tue-Sat, from noon Sun) you can see how an empire was created and then lost between the 1850s and the 1960s. It's housed in the stout old ranch HQ.

LOWER GULF COAST

Palm trees and hot humid weather are but one sign you've hit the subtropical southern Gulf Coast. Ribbons of traffic zipping along TX 100 to South Padre Island mean that you've come within the gravitational pull of the state's favorite beach resort.

Harlingen

POP 70,900

Harlingen just isn't what it used to be, and that's a good thing. In 1910 it was called Six-Shooter Junction because of the explosive stew of lawless bands, Mexican raiders, Texas Rangers and US National Guardsmen who prowled its streets. Today, most permanent residents are more occupied with agriculture than lawlessness. Look for fields of large, spiky aloe plants, which produce the soothing substance used in lotions, shampoos and ointments. It has a couple of diversions worthy of a pit stop on your way to South Padre Island or the Rio Grande Valley. Mostly, though, this is a land for Winter Texans (see box, p295).

Sights

Harlingen Arts & Heritage Museum MUSEUM
(☎956-216-4906; www.myharlingen.us; Boxwood & Raintree Sts, off Loop 499; ⏰10am-4pm Tue-Sun) FREE Return to the days of Six-Shooter Junction at this modern facility which combines several museums in one. An 1870s stagecoach inn recalls the hot, dusty conditions of the old trail, where the only friend you were likely to make at the end of a long day was a bedbug. The region's colorful and violent past is extensively documented. The museum is located near the airport.

Sleeping & Eating

Harlingen has so many chain hotels that some brands have more than one location. Rates are rather cheap but note that the drive to South Padre Island's beaches can take an hour or more from here.

Foodwise, it's more chains, except for lots of cheap and cheerful Mexican joints scattered amidst the motels.

Information

Texas Travel Information Center (956-428-4477; 2021 W Harrison St; 8am-5pm) This excellent visitor center at the junction of US 77 and US 83 has maps, brochures and other information about the region and the entire state.

Getting There & Away

Valley International Airport (HRL; 956-430-8600; www.flythevalley.com; Loop 499) The airport is 3 miles east of downtown and has service from United Express to Houston and Southwest to and from Houston and Dallas. It's a popular link for South Padre Island and the Rio Grande Valley.

Laguna Atascosa National Wildlife Refuge

From the moment you step out of your car at this 70-sq-mile federal **preserve** (956-748-3607; www.fws.gov; per vehicle $3; gates dawn-dusk, visitor center 8am-4pm), northwest of Port Isabel, you are surrounded by birdcalls. You may think you've stepped into the Hitchcock movie or are trapped in a hellish version of the old Woolworth's parakeet department, but you haven't. The calls soon blend into a mélange of melodies that cause you to stop and just listen.

The land is a veritable avian playground (more than 400 species have been spotted); wetlands, thorn brush, trees and grasses offer something for everything with feathers. The refuge is also home to the rare, but rather cute, ocelot, a relative of the jaguar.

Wildlife Tours (956-748-3607; www.friendsofsouthtexasrefuges.org; tours $4-25; schedules vary) are a great way to spot and learn about the park's abundant wildlife. Run by volunteers, they are much recommended. Tours include ones by tram and kayak in addition to guided walks.

The roads to the refuge are not well marked. From Harlingen, take FM 106 east 18 miles until it dead-ends, then turn left and drive 3 miles to the refuge entrance. If you're coming from the east, take FM 510 from TX 100 at Laguna Vista and then Buena Vista Rd for a total of 15 miles north to the refuge.

Los Fresnos

Strung out along TX 100, the South Padre Island road, there are two good reasons to pause in Los Fresnos.

Bobz World (956-554-4540; 36451 TX 100; 9am-6pm, longer during holidays) is a souvenir store that is so over the top as to be literally unmissable. Outside, enormous plaster dinosaurs and sea creatures beckon. Inside, every kind of shell, trinket and beach toy imaginable await. There's fudge too.

Excellent Texas barbecue awaits at **Wild Blue BBQ** (956-233-8185; 31230 TX 100; mains from $8; 11am-9pm Mon-Sat), a splendid roadside joint where the little things matter. Even the sides are just so and the sweet potato flan is sublime. It's somewhat hidden on the south side of the road.

Port Isabel

POP 5200

In the days before inexpensive hurricane insurance made South Padre Island (SPI) viable as a town, Port Isabel was the focus of life near the southern end of Texas. Records show that Spaniards and pirates both made frequent landfalls here in the 16th, 17th and 18th centuries.

Today Port Isabel is a must-stop just before SPI. Its small old town covers the waterfront for a couple of blocks on either side of the base of the TX 100 Queen Isabella Causeway. It is served by the free Wave shuttle to/from SPI.

Sights

The three main sights are all close to each other and to the cute waterfront. You can buy combined tickets for all three (adult/child $7/2).

Port Isabel Lighthouse HISTORIC BUILDING
(956-943-7602; www.portisabelmuseums.com; TX 100 & Tarnava St; adult/child $3/1; 9am-5pm) The Port Isabel Lighthouse was built between 1852 and 1853. A climb up its 70 steps yields great views of the surrounding area, SPI and the gulf. It is also the source of local tourist info.

Port Isabel Historical Museum MUSEUM
(956-943-7602; www.portisabelmuseums.com; 317 Railroad Ave; adult/child $3/1; 10am-4pm Tue-Sat) Built sturdily in 1899 of bricks to resist storms, the home of the history museum

served at various times as the town's railroad station, post office and general store. You'll find it one block south of TX 100, near the lighthouse.

Treasures of the Gulf Museum MUSEUM
(☎956-943-7602; www.portisabelmuseums.com; 317 Railroad Ave; adult/child $3/1; ⌚10am-4pm Tue-Sat) Sunken treasure! That's the focus of this fun museum which has artifacts from three Spanish galleons that went down nearby in 1554. It does a good job of telling the stories of the hapless crews.

Eating

The waterfront is predictably lined with popular seafood joints and bars with decks overlooking the water. But go a few blocks inland for some of the best eats in the area.

Manuel's Restaurant MEXICAN $
(☎956-943-1655; 313 Maxan St; mains from $6; ⌚7am-2pm Mon-Sat) That steady 'patting' sound you hear comes from the ladies in the back room making flour tortillas. Everything is dead-simple here, including the decor, but the classic Mexican fare is excellent. Get a side of avocado with anything you order, including the huevos rancheros at breakfast.

★**Joe's Oyster Bar Restaurant** SEAFOOD $$
(☎956-943-4501; 207 Maxan St; mains from $8; ⌚11am-7pm) Delight in seafood direct off the boats at this simple joint. They make a mean crab cake and the oysters are renowned. You can get anything to go for picnics or packed fresh for cooking later in the condo.

BEACH GUIDE

SPI is beaches, but there is great variety along the 34 miles of bright white, hard-packed Gulf sand. You can enjoy the company of a few thousand of your best friends you haven't met yet, go for a drive, get lost in the dunes or shed virtually everything far from another soul.

SPI's spine, Padre Blvd, extends 12 miles from the south to a point where the pavement literally ends. Within the city limits, roughly the area south of the SPI Convention Center, there are 23 free beach access points between the condos, motels and houses that line the sand. These have very limited parking and seldom have toilets.

North of here it gets increasingly undeveloped and there are several access points where you can drive your vehicle out onto the sand, sometimes for a fee. On summer weekends, many of these areas are tailgating paradises.

Need an umbrella to shade from the energetic sun and some beach loungers to rest your weary bones? Most beach access points have vendors that will rent you gear. Among the largest is **Beach Service** (☎956-761-5622; www.padrebeachservice.com; rentals from $25; ⌚Mar-Nov) with 20 locations. You can reserve in advance (vital on busy weekends) or have your gear delivered.

From south to north, here are some SPI beach highlights:

Isla Blanca County Park (☎956-761-5494; 1/2 Park Rd 100; per vehicle $5) Just south of the causeway, this county park is the most popular beach on SPI thanks to various concessions and facilities.

Andy Bowie County Park (Beach Access #2; ☎956-761-2639; per car $5; ⌚dawn-dusk) Across from South Padre Island Convention Center, this pleasant beach park is now surrounded by condo developments. It has a shaded picnic building with views, real toilets and is 5.5 miles north of Isla Blanca.

Edwin King Atwood County Park (Beach Access #5; per car $5; ⌚dawn-dusk) Two miles north of Bowie, Atwood sports towering sand dunes backing the beach. This is a beautiful, unspoiled area where sand often obscures Padre Blvd; however, real estate agent signs suggest a different future.

North End Padre Blvd ends 12 miles north of Isla Blanca. North of here there's 20 miles of nothing but sand and dunes all the way to Port Mansfield Pass. Nude sunbathers, anglers, bird-watchers and other outdoorsy types can find a sandy acre to call their own; vehicles can drive on the beach.

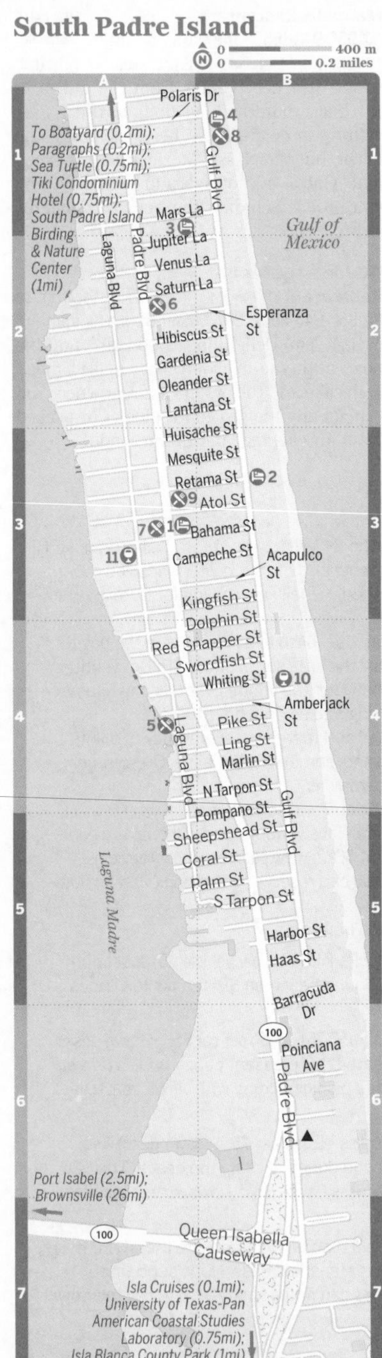

South Padre Island

POP 3100

Covering the southern 5 miles of South Padre Island, the town of South Padre Island (SPI) works hard to exploit its sunny climate and beaches. The water is warm for much of the year, the beaches are clean, and the laid-back locals are ready to welcome each and every tourist who crosses the 2.5-mile Queen Isabella Causeway from the mainland. (The permanent population is augmented by 10,000 or more visitors at any given time.) SPI is a mix of beach overdevelopment, charming cottages and long stretches of open sand.

Until 1962, there was no South Padre Island, only the 147-mile Padre Island, a barrier island that was the longest of its kind in the world. However, the pleas of Port Mansfield for direct access to the gulf shipping lanes were finally heeded, and a channel was cut through the island, creating 34-mile South Padre Island.

January and February, when the weather can be either balmy or a bit chilly, are the quietest months to visit SPI. The busiest (and most expensive) periods are spring break (all of March except the first week) and summer, when the moderating gulf breezes make the shore more tolerable than the sweltering inland areas.

Sights

The beach is the first and last thing many visitors wish to see but there are various

South Padre Island

Sleeping
1 Flamingo Inn......A3
2 Palms Resort......B3
3 South Beach Inn......A1
4 Wanna Wanna Inn......B1

Eating
5 Amberjack's Bayside Bar & Grill......A4
6 Blackbeard's......A2
7 Daddy's Seafood & Cajun Kitchen......A3
Padre Island Brewing Company......(see 1)
8 Wanna-Wanna Beach Bar & Grill......B1
9 Zeste Cafe & Market......A3

Drinking & Nightlife
10 Boomerang Billy's Beach Bar & Grill......B4
11 Coconuts......A3
Louie's Backyard......(see 11)

other attractions that allow you to engage with SPI's natural beauty.

★ **South Padre Island Birding & Nature Center** NATURE RESERVE
(☎956-243-8179; www.spibirding.com; 6801 Padre Blvd; adult/child $5/2; ⌚9am-5pm) Part of the World Birding Center, this 50-acre nature preserve has boardwalks through the dunes, bird blinds, spotting towers and much more. Learn the differences between a dune meadow, a salt marsh and an intertidal flat – and there won't even be a quiz after. The exhibit hall is in a posh, new building.

You can also access some of the site for free from a boardwalk at the **SPI Convention Center** just to the north. Look for egrets, alligators, turtles, crabs and much more.

★ **Sea Turtle Inc** NATURE RESERVE
(www.seaturtleinc.com; 6617 Padre Blvd; suggested donation adult/child $3/2; ⌚10am-4pm Tue-Sun) The late Ila Loestcher started Sea Turtle Inc in 1977, after sea turtles had almost vanished from the Texas coast. Today more than a dozen Kemp's ridley sea turtles are nesting again on SPI and her organization is thriving thanks to a dedicated cadre of volunteers and benefactors.

Visits to the center are a fascinating change from SPI's commercialism; you can see rescued turtles and learn firsthand about the slow growth of local turtle populations.

Schlitterbahn Beach Resort WATER PARK
(☎956-772-7873; www.schlitterbahn.com; 90 Padre Blvd; adult/child $55/44; ⌚10am-8pm summer, shorter hours other times, outdooor features closed Oct-Mar; 👪) Just north of Isla Blanca County Park, this vast waterpark offers water slides and pools of every description, including the Seablaster. The park now has a hotel and indoor slides.

University of Texas-Pan American Coastal Studies Laboratory AQUARIUM
(☎956-761-2644; Isla Blanca Park; ⌚1:30-4:30pm Mon-Fri) FREE This working lab is open for self-guided tours of its fish tanks and various wall displays. If you can get past its meager utilitarian charms, you'll find lots of information about local marine life. Grapefruit-sized conch show you how the popular fritters look while still in the water.

Activities

There are so many activities on SPI that you may be exhausted before you start.

Fishing

More than 50 fishing boats leave from the piers on the lagoon. To find a guide and/or boat charter it's best to just wander the docks and talk to the skippers to find one who seems in sync with what you want. Group trips start at $40. You may catch flounder or speckled trout close to SPI. Longer trips head into the gulf for prime game fish such as wahoo.

Horseback Riding

About a mile north of the convention center, **South Padre Island Adventures** (☎956-761-4677; www.horsesonthebeach.com; Padre Blvd; 1hr rides from $50) rents horses for all levels of riders and leads tours of the beaches.

Water Sports

You'll find outfits offering parasailing and other rides over and on the water along the beaches in the developed part of SPI. The lagoon side is renowned for wind-powered water sports like windsurfing. There are

SAND CASTLES

If you've always dreamed of having your own castle, you can build one on South Padre Island – out of sand. And not just some humdrum, upended-bucket-and-garnished-with-a-seagull-feather affair either, but an honest-to-goodness castle, standing about 8ft tall, with towers, moats, a keep and anything else your heart desires.

Of course, such a creation doesn't come easy – that's where a gaggle of longtime SPI residents come in. They've carved out a lucrative living teaching people how to build vast creations that survive only until the next dawn – or whenever the tide comes in. All you need is a shovel, a bucket and a few household tools.

Two recommended schools are **Sons of the Beach** (☎956-761-6222; www.sonsofthebeach.com; lessons from $75) and **Sandy Feet** (☎956-459-2928; www.sandcastleworkshops.com; group lessons from $40). Both offer fun-filled lessons across the island at times of your own choosing.

SPRING BREAK: A PARTY FOR 100,000

Like other second-tier beach resorts, such as Florida's Panama City Beach, South Padre Island has struck gold with spring break, the period in March when hordes of college students (and high-school students with lax parents) congregate at beaches for a week or more of pleasurable excess that's limited only by the capacity of their livers, loins and billfolds. Resorts such as Fort Lauderdale, in Florida, now turn up their noses at spring break, but SPI does everything possible to welcome this free-spending mob.

During the last three weeks of March, when various US colleges and universities have their breaks, more than 100,000 students descend on the island for days of drinking, swimming, sunbathing, frolicking and more, followed by nights of drinking, skinny-dipping, frolicking and more. Major sponsors, such as beer and soda companies, stage concerts and games on the beaches. MTV is usually there broadcasting live.

During spring break, it's hard to escape the mobs of students cruising the developed part of town. If the idea of spending a week at a beach party with thousands of young people on their first real bender appeals to you, you will have a wonderful time. Otherwise you should avoid the island for the entire month.

Ground zero for SPI's spring break is the area near the end of the causeway, where the largest condos and hotels, including the Isla Grand Beach Resort and the Sheraton South Padre Beach Condominiums, are located. Major clubs catering to the spring break crowds include Chaos and Louie's Backyard. Apart from these hot spots, any place on SPI that sells beer will see spring-break action, with many serving locally popular drinks such as The Whammy and Charlie's Cherry.

The best accommodations – meaning those closest to the action – usually book up six months or more before March. The web is awash with offers.

dozens of operators; we've listed two of the best (offering lessons and rental).

Boatyard WATER SPORTS
(☎956-761-5061; www.windsurftheboatyard.com) Rents windsurf boards (half-day $60) and also kayaks and mountain bikes. Lessons are available.

Windsurf, Inc WINDSURFING
(☎956-761-1434; www.windsurfinc.com) Specializes in windsurfing (individual lessons from $279 for three hours), kiteboarding, surfing, kayaking and wakeboarding.

Tours

Bottlenose dolphins love the lagoon and SPI visitors love looking at them. Among a slew of operators, **Isla Cruises** (☎956-761-4752; www.islatours.com; 1 Padre Blvd; tours from $18) offers two-hour boat rides to see the finned friends. You can bring your own beer on board, which gives you the opportunity to invent new drinking games that involve Flipper.

Festivals & Events

SPI schedules events year-round, including weekend fireworks through the summer. In addition to spring break in March, some of the major events and their usual dates include **Sand Castle Days** in mid-October and the **Kite Festival** in early November. The CVB (p288) has details.

Sleeping

Options for bedding down are myriad. Obviously without advance reservations you'll be left bedless during spring break and on busy weekends. Of course you can always claim a free patch of sand on the north end of the island. You can save money by staying on the mainland in Port Isabel or even as far as Harlingen but the commute may sour your mood.

Hotels & Motels

Hotels and motels on SPI come in three broad categories: big glitzy resorts, regular chain motels and funky places with lots of beach atmosphere. Some of the resort places are nice, while others look like the result of a five-year plan. Rates vary hugely between warm-weather weekends (when it pays to seek out quiet neighbors) and the middle of January.

Flamingo Inn MOTEL $
(☎956-761-3377; www.flamingo-spi.com; 3408 Padre Blvd; r $50-150;) It looks like a chain motel but the managers live right here and there are delightful quirks (like the colonnaded Jacuzzi suites) that make it pure indie.

Needless to say, the Flamingo is painted pink. All 29 rooms have fridges and microwaves.

★Palms Resort MOTEL $$
(☎800-466-1316, 956-761-1316; www.palmsresortcafe.com; 3616 Gulf Blvd; r $70-200; 📶🏊) This tidy two-story motel looks right over the grass-covered dune to the gulf. Units are large and have fridges and microwaves; some have granite wet bars and showers for two (no more dirty backs). The beachfront cafe/bar is fun.

Wanna Wanna Inn MOTEL $$
(☎956-761-7677; www.wannawanna.com; 5100 Gulf Blvd; r $80-200; ❄📶) Much remodeled, the low-rise Wanna Wanna has but 15 rooms, some with excellent views of the gulf from this beachfront location. Units have either microwaves and fridges or kitchenettes. Murals in the rooms include one with a spunky Flipper that is bound to be inspirational. The beachside bar is fun.

South Beach Inn MOTEL $$
(☎956-761-2471; www.southbeachtexas.com; 120 E Jupiter Lane; r $100-200; ❄📶🏊) This 19-unit motel is vintage 1961 but has been colorfully kept and exudes a fun vibe. It is a half-block from the beach and has a pool, barbecue area and rooms with kitchens.

Tiki Condominium Hotel RESORT $$
(☎800-551-8454, 956-761-2694; www.thetiki.com; 6608 Padre Blvd; r $100-350; ❄📶🏊) It's Ginger or Mary Ann time at this wonderful Polynesian-themed veteran that plays the tiki-cliché to the max. Large, two-story blocks cover the beachfront site at the north end of developed SPI. Units have full kitchens and range in size from one to three bedrooms.

Camping

Camping is popular on SPI. You can choose an organized park with all the amenities or a pristine, nearly deserted beach with no facilities whatsoever.

Isla Blanca County Park CAMPING $
(☎956-761-5494; 1/2 Park Rd 100; tent sites $15, sites with amenities from $25; 📶) Popular because of its proximity to the action, this park has a variety of camping facilities, including sites with beach views. Long-term rates are available. Reservations may only be made for stays of seven or more days.

Condo Agents

More than 4000 apartments are available for rent on SPI. They can be ugly – notable examples being the Saida Towers and the thoroughly god-awful Bridgepoint – or nice. They come with one, two or three bedrooms and always have kitchens. Most of the larger complexes have pools and other facilities such as tennis courts and whirlpools.

Often just off the beach, you can rent part of a house or cottage that may not have the ocean view but will have plenty of beach-town charm.

Rates run the gamut. Some places offer daily rentals; others require a week minimum. For the peak summer season, reservations are recommended three months in advance. During the winter, you can often bargain for substantial discounts.

The website www.vrbo.com is a good source of interesting properties being rented by their owners. The CVB (p288) has links to rental agents.

Service 24 ACCOMMODATION SERVICES
(☎956-761-1487, 800-828-4287; www.service24.com) Represents scores of big condo resorts as well as holiday homes.

South Padre Beach Houses & Condos ACCOMMODATION SERVICES
(☎956-761-6554; www.sopadrerentals.com) The name says it all.

Eating

Except for the peak periods, South Padre Island closes early so unless noted otherwise, plan on dining by 9pm. Condo dwellers will find plenty of markets for all those essential foods you'd never eat at home.

Farmers Market MARKET
(8605 Padre Blvd; ⏲11am-1pm Sun Mar-Nov) Check out the size of the grapefruits and give other local produce a squeeze at this market held at the Shores condominium resort.

★Zeste Cafe & Market MEDITERRANEAN $$
(☎956-761-5555; 3508 Padre Blvd; meals from $8; ⏲hours vary, usually 11am-8pm) *The* place to assemble that beach picnic that will cause great envy among the weenie-scarfing masses. The deli section has a huge assortment of fine food stuffs. The cafe has Med-accented salads and mains. On some weekend nights they have a long tapas menu until 10pm.

★Padre Island Brewing Company BREWERY $$
(☎956-761-9585; www.pibrewingcompany.com; 3400 Padre Blvd; mains from $10; ⏲11am-late) A

microbrewery treat on an island where the national breweries sponsor constant promotions emphasizing quantity over quality. Burgers and other bar foods are popular. There is also a longer and more complex list of seafood. You can stop here for a drink or a meal.

Wanna-Wanna Beach Bar & Grill CAFE **$$**
(956-761-7677; www.wannawanna.com; 5100 Gulf Blvd; mains from $8; 10am-11pm) Everybody's idea of the laid-back beach bar and restaurant. Lounge barefoot in plastic chairs on the (at times) shaded deck and take in the surf and sights. Burgers and other basics go down a treat with large cold drinks.

Daddy's Seafood & Cajun Kitchen CAJUN **$$**
(956-761-1975; www.daddysrestaurant.com; 3409 Padre Ave; mains $10-25; 11am-9pm Sun-Thu, to 10pm Fri & Sat) You'll love making a mess with New Orleans–style seafood that includes spicy boiled shrimp and crawfish. Corn, potatoes, oysters and a lot more offer diversions. Lunch specials for $10 are popular.

Blackbeard's SEAFOOD **$$**
(956-761-2962; www.blackbeardsspi.com; 103 E Saturn Lane; mains $8-25; 11:30am-10pm) Year after year crowds flock here for an ocean of seafood cooked in countless ways. Enormous platters have so many options that it may drive you to drink – fortunately the excellent margaritas are cheap. The vast terrace makes the inevitable waits a pleasure.

Amberjack's Bayside Bar & Grill SEAFOOD **$$**
(956-761-6500; 209 W Amberjack St; mains $12-30; 11am-11pm) Lagoonside Amberjack's has a popular bar that's more classy than a lot of its neighbors – drinks even come in vessels made of real glass. The long menu concentrates on fresh seafood and steaks. Romantic platters for two are best enjoyed on the huge covered patio. It gets rollicking on weekends.

Drinking & Nightlife

There's a long stretch of bars and clubs on the lagoon side along Laguna Blvd between Tarpon and Red Snapper Sts.

Coconuts BAR
(956-761-4218; www.coconutsspi.com; 2301 Laguna Blvd; 11am-late) The clichés start with the thatched roof over the deck, but that doesn't stop the mixed crowd of tourists and locals from cutting loose from before the sun sets until well after midnight. Live music rocks the house.

Louie's Backyard CLUB
(956-761-6406; www.lbyspi.com; 2305 Laguna Blvd; 5pm-2am) Spring break central, Louie's serves a mere 3000 to 4000 every night. There are multiple stages, big name rappers, a dance floor overlooking the water, cheap booze and snacks, and a minimalist dress code that allows for just about anything.

Boomerang Billy's Beach Bar & Grill BAR
(956-761-2420; www.boomerangbillysbeachbar.com; 2612 Gulf Blvd; 11am-late) Billy's is behind the shambolic Surf Motel and is one of the few bars right on the sand on the gulf side. Mellow sounds a bit too energetic for this ultimate crash pad. On weekend afternoons, listen to the talented singing of Leslie Blasing, who belts her tunes out over the sand.

Shopping

Paragraphs BOOKS
(956-433-5057; 5505 Padre Blvd; 10am-5pm Mon & Wed-Sat, noon-4pm Sun;) An excellent indie bookstore with a nice patio.

Orientation

South Padre Island is only a half-mile wide at its widest point. Laguna Madre, the shallow inland waterway between the island and the mainland, is ideally suited for windsurfing and bird-watching.

The southern, developed end of Padre Blvd is the main traffic artery, so it tends to be crowded and noisy. In fact the stretch north from Dolphin St is a pedestrian nightmare, with families trying to cross around SUVs doing 60mph. One block west, Laguna Blvd is a more peaceful road for walking or cycling. To the east, running parallel to the beach, is Gulf Blvd, which is mostly lined with large developments.

No ferry or bridge crosses Port Mansfield Pass. To reach Padre Island National Seashore from South Padre Island you must either have your own boat or make the long drive all the way around the mainland via Harlingen and Corpus Christi.

Information

South Padre Island Convention & Visitors Bureau (956-761-4412; www.spichamber.com; 600 Padre Blvd; 9am-5pm)

Getting There & Around

If you can get out to SPI, you won't necessarily need a car. The developed area is fairly compact, easy for walking or cycling, and there's a shuttle.

TO/FROM THE AIRPORTS

Brownsville South Padre Island International Airport is 26 miles southwest. You can catch **Rio Gulf Express** (☎800-574-8322; www.flybrownsville.com; fare $1; ⏰shuttles about every 90 minutes 6am-8pm) to Port Isabel and transfer to the Wave for a journey time of just under 90 minutes.

Harlingen's Valley International Airport is 43 miles northwest. The **South Padre Shuttle** (☎877-774-0050; www.southpadreshuttle.com; one-way/return $25/40) offers door-to-door service; book in advance.

BUS

The **Wave** (☎956-761-1025; www.sopadre.com; ⏰7am-9pm), a shuttle service, serves the island as far north as the convention center and all the way south to Isla Blanca County Park and over the causeway to Port Isabel. Buses on three routes run every 30 to 60 minutes.

TAXI

SPI cab companies include **BB's Taxi** (☎956-761-7433; www.bbstaxi.com), charging $40 to $45 to Brownsville airport, $50 to $60 to Harlingen airport.

RIO GRANDE VALLEY

The semitropical southern border area of Texas is much wetter than the arid west, thanks to the moisture-laden winds off the Gulf of Mexico. This lush environment is perfect for farming; much of the winter produce sold in the USA comes from Texas.

The temperate winter climate attracts hordes of migratory creatures. A breed known as 'Winter Texans' – American retirees from the north – arrives in flocks, as do more than 500 species of birds, who in turn attract flocks of bird-watchers to scores of natural spots.

The valley begins at the mouth of the Rio Grande, which meets the gulf in vast palm-studded wetlands, lagoons and remote beaches.

Further west in the valley, most of the land is given over to farming. In the lands west of McAllen, the gulf winds diminish and the land becomes more arid and unpopulated.

History

The Laredo border area was sparsely populated with nomadic Native American groups until Don Tomás Sánchez, a captain in the Spanish royal army, was given a grant of land here in 1775.

The first non-Indian settlers were ranchers, and missionaries passed through the area, heading into the interior of Texas.

In 1836 Texas seceded from Mexico, an act that inspired the Rio Grande Valley and much of what is now northeastern Mexico to declare itself a separate republic – the Republic of the Rio Grande – in 1840. With its capital at Laredo, the republic lasted just 283 days, until the Mexican army regained control.

The Treaty of Guadalupe Hidalgo, which ended the Mexican War, established the new border of the USA down the Rio Grande. Like much of Texas, the next century was largely about cattle and then oil.

The valley began a new boom in 1994 with the passage of the North American Free Trade Agreement (Nafta), which opened up trade across the border.

Brownsville

POP 172,500

Matamoros, Brownsville's Mexican counterpart across the Rio Grande, grew to prominence in the 1820s as the Mexican port closest to then-booming New Orleans. After the Mexican War (1846–8), American merchants and traders thought it wise to cross the Rio Grande to Texas, where they established Brownsville. The town was named for Major Jacob Brown, the US commander of Fort Taylor (later renamed Fort Brown), who died during a Mexican raid.

During the rest of the 19th century, the fast-growing town was filled with ornate brick structures that drew their architectural inspiration from Mexico and New Orleans. Many survive today and help make Brownsville an atmospheric stop. Its slightly gritty culture makes it an excellent day trip from South Padre Island (SPI).

Sights

Brownsville lies at the southern end of US 77, the spine of the southern Gulf Coast. The downtown area, near the Gateway International Bridge/Puente Nuevo, E Elizabeth St and International Blvd is a busy place.

One of the best things you can do in Brownsville is simply go wandering around the downtown area. Streets such as E Washington and E Elizabeth are still busy with the kinds of small shops that once lined main streets across the USA, although ironically,

DAY TRIPS TO MEXICO: SHOULD YOU VISIT?

Time was when no visit to the Rio Grande Valley was complete without a jaunt across the border into a Mexican town such as Nuevo Laredo, which is twinned with Laredo on the US side. Good and cheap Mexican food (and tequila), mariachis, cheap tatty souvenirs as well as cut-rate dental work and prescription drugs were just some of the lures. Plus there was the thrill of entering a dramatically different culture, just by strolling across a bridge spanning the Rio Grande.

But several years of lurid headlines outlining the carnage of Mexico's drug wars have put a big question mark over border-town day trips. Although tourists are not targets, fear of getting caught up in the violence is a real concern. Meanwhile, businesses that have delighted generations of Americans (or simply sold them cheap pharmaceuticals) have suffered greatly.

Should you visit? The best answer is to ask locally on the Texas side of the border; conditions change constantly. No matter what, you'll probably be safest by going during the day. You can also check with the US State Department (http://travel.state.gov) for travel advisories. While on the other side, look out for images of La Sante Muerte (Holy Death), an iconic figure of a skeleton with a scythe dressed in robes. It's the symbol of a fast-growing religious cult popular with Mexican gangs.

most of the customers are now day-trippers from Mexico.

★Sabal Palm Sanctuary NATURE PRESERVE
(☎956-541-8034; www.sabalpalmsanctuary.org; Sabal Palm Rd; adult/child $5/3; ⏲7am-5pm) The only palm tree native to Texas grows at this 557-acre sanctuary, operated by a foundation for the National Audubon Society. It sits in a bend of the Rio Grande River that was never plowed under. It's a lush, beautiful and peaceful place with excellent nature hikes.

Although closed for several years by border politics, an agreement keeps the US border fence open during the day so that you can access this lost oasis on US soil. A highlight is the **Rabb Plantation House**, the 1892 mansion of the original owner. It's being restored and will house a visitors center. Among the good hikes is the 0.4-mile-long **Forest Trail**.

Sabal palms reach 20ft to 48ft high and have feathery crowns and thick, bristly trunks. They once lined the Rio Grande, covering an area of nearly 63 sq miles. In the past 150 years, most have been cut down, first by early settlers who needed lumber and later by those clearing land for agriculture.

The sanctuary is 6 miles east of Brownsville off FM 1419 (also called Southmost Rd).

Gladys Porter Zoo ZOO
(www.gpz.org; 500 Ringgold St; adult/child $9.50/6.50; ⏲9am-5:30pm Mon-Fri, to 6pm Sat & Sun; 👪) This 31-acre zoo displays more than 1500 animals in large areas that replicate their natural habitats. Among the crowd-pleasing exhibits are pink flamingos flanking the entrance; Butterflies, Bugs and Blooms, a walk-through, up-close greenhouse; and a large new aquatic centre with sharks, sting-rays and more.

Historic Brownsville Museum MUSEUM
(☎956-548-1313; www.brownsvillemuseum.org; 641 E Madison St; adult/child $5/2; ⏲10am-4pm Tue-Fri, to 2pm Sat) Housed in the grand Spanish Colonial–style 1928 Southern Pacific Railroad Depot, this small museum houses historical artifacts and an 1872 steam locomotive. The museum is part of the Mitte Cultural District. Other nearby facilities include an art gallery and a children's museum.

Fort Brown HISTORIC SITE
The University of Texas at Brownsville and Texas Southmost College share a downtown campus that includes the site of Fort Brown, a former US army outpost dating from 1846. It is named for Jacob Brown who died here that year fighting the Mexicans. Several buildings from 1868 are restored and used by the campus (older ones were lost in an 1867 hurricane), including the post hospital (Gorgas Hall) and the 1848 Neale Home.

Historic Buildings

Downtown Brownsville still has dozens of 19th-century buildings, many of which are slowly moldering away. Be sure to get a copy of the excellent *Guide to Historic Brownsville* at the museums or at the CVB (p291). This free brochure details the city's heritage and has superb walking tours. The sites listed can all be visited on a one-hour stroll.

★**Brownsville Heritage Complex** HISTORIC SITE
(956-541-5560; www.brownsvillehistory.org; 1325 E Washington St; adult/child $4/2; 10am-4pm Tue-Sat, 1-5pm Sun) The 1850 home of Brownsville founder Charles Stillman now houses the Brownsville Heritage Complex about his life. This is a good place to learn about the downtown area.

Old Market Place HISTORIC BUILDING
(12th & Market Sq, btwn E Adams & E Washington Sts) Among the scores of structures downtown is one of the oldest city halls in continuous use in the US, the Old Market Place. Built in 1850, it now also serves as the city's transit center.

Immaculate Conception Cathedral CHURCH
(1218 E Jefferson St, at E 12th St) A late-19th-century Gothic-style example of the artistry of local brick masons.

Gem HISTORIC BUILDING
(400 E 13th St) The Gem, between E Levee St and E Elizabeth St, is the city's oldest building, dating from 1848. Its projecting balconies once sheltered a saloon.

Russell/Cocke Residence HISTORIC BUILDING
(602 E St Charles St) An 1872 house that shows the wealth of the local traders. Like many downtown buildings it has an interesting historical marker.

V Fernandez Complex HISTORIC BUILDING
(1106 E Adams St) The old trade links to New Orleans are clearly visible in this 1877 building.

Sleeping

Most motels are along US 77/83. Unless you are getting an early start for bird-watching, you might want to stay amid the beachy charms of South Padre Island, an easy 28 miles northeast.

University Inn MOTEL $
(956-546-0381; 55 Sam Perl Blvd; r $40-60;) An older two-story motel built around a large parking lot and pool, it is close to downtown and the border. Service, decor and frills are dead simple but it's well located for soaking up the town's atmosphere.

Holiday Inn Express MOTEL $$
(956-550-0666; www.hiexpress.com; 1985 N Expwy, exit US 77/83 at Ruben Torres Sr Blvd; r $120-200; @) Fairly comfortable but also generic, the HI has 74 rooms across three floors with inside corridors. The pool is outside near nascent palms. Guests enjoy a large breakfast buffet.

Eating

Fans of Mexican food will need a week to sample just some of the excellent local eateries.

★**Taco Palenque** MEXICAN $
(956-546-8172; 1803 Boca Chica Blvd; mains from $4; 7am-10pm) This is the flagship restaurant of a small Rio Grande Valley chain run by a famous local family; you may find yourself here more than once. Order tacos at the counter and then start drooling over the best salsa bar ever. Ten kinds of salsas, cilantro, cabbage, chilies and much more await.

Vermillion TEX-MEX $
(956-542-9893; 115 Paredes Line Rd; mains from $8; 11am-10pm) It may seem to be as old as Brownsville, but actually this venerable family-run restaurant dates back to 1934. Both the Tex (sublime chicken-fried steak) and the Mex (amazing fajita nachos) are good.

Information

Brownsville Convention & Visitors Bureau (956-546-3721; www.brownsville.org; 650 Ruben M Torres Sr Blvd, at FM 802 exit; 8am-5pm Mon-Fri, 9am-4pm Sat & Sun) On the west side of US 77/83 is this excellent source of information on the entire area.

Getting There & Away

Brownsville South Padre Island International Airport (BRO; 956-542-4373; www.flybrownsville.com; 700 S Minnesota Ave), 4 miles east of downtown, has service on American Eagle to Dallas–Fort Worth and United Express to Houston. For details on ground transport to South Padre Island, see p291.

Greyhound (956-546-7171; www.greyhound.com; 1134 E St Charles St) has a station just three blocks west of the Gateway International Bridge. There is frequent service to McAllen ($26, 70 minutes) and several busses daily to Corpus Christi and beyond ($35, 3½ hours). Buses also fan out across Mexico.

Around Brownsville

US 281 hugs the border and is an interesting route to see sugar cane, the Rio Grande and the vast border fence. This 60-mile route to McAllen goes via Hidalgo.

MEXICAN BORDER TOWNS

Matamoros

While Matamoros (population 440,000) could hardly be described as a cultural mecca, it has the most to offer of all the gritty Mexican border towns that dot the frontier with Texas. You'll find a cluster of historic buildings, a decent contemporary art museum and some stylish restaurants. The touristed areas here are generally safe during the day.

Reynosa

Reynosa (population 510,000) is more attractive and less intimidating than Nuevo Laredo but has less appeal than Matamoros. The tourist trade is geared to Texan day-trippers, many of whom come to visit the city's surfeit of dentists, doctors and pharmacists.

Reynosa is 9 miles south of the center of McAllen via US 281. The easiest way to visit is to park in a guarded lot on the US side and then make the short walk over the bridge.

Nuevo Laredo

Nuevo Laredo (population 350,000) is Mexico's busiest border town, and a significant percentage of Mexico–US trade passes through, but it's much more famous as 'Narco' Laredo, a reference to brazen violence between rival drug cartels that has sullied the city's reputation. But it isn't the fear of getting caught in the crossfire that should cause you to reconsider a visit; it's that the city has little to offer other than the usual cheap trinkets, tequila and tricks found in most border towns. The city's greatest landmark, the huge **flag** (164ft x 94ft flag on a 320ft-tall pole) just across the border, is an arresting and at times mesmerizing sight. It's easily seen from much of Laredo, especially when heading south on San Bernardo Ave.

Two international bridges link the Laredos. You can do the short walk (or drive) over Puente Internacional No 1 from Convent Ave and Laredo's old town right onto the north end of Avenida Guerrero. Puente Internacional No 2 is vehicle only.

Piedras Negras

The border crossing between Piedras Negras (population 140,000) and Eagle Pass is a major commercial route. Piedras Negras is not an attractive city and not somewhere you'll want to linger long. It has that small-border-town roughness to it.

Walking there is popular – it's just four short blocks from downtown Eagle Pass to downtown Piedras Negras on the main international bridge.

Palo Alto Battlefield National Historic Site PARK

(☎956-541-2785; www.nps.gov/paal; ⏰8am-5pm) FREE On May 8, 1846, General Zachary Taylor and his troops defeated a larger Mexican army on this site in the first major battle of the Mexican War. The visitor center does an excellent job of putting the battle into context: were the Americans invaders or defenders?

The 3400-acre site has been preserved from developers (just in the nick of time) and the result is a surprisingly evocative and moody place. It's easy to imagine the soldiers of both sides toiling in the heat, firing cannons and wondering how they ended up in such a desolate place. (Note the display showing what conservative Texas commentators of the day called Abraham Lincoln – a war and slavery critic – and contrast it to the politics of today.)

The site is near the intersection of FM 1874 (Paredes Line Rd) and FM 511, 5 miles north of Brownsville, 2 miles east of US 77/83 and 3.5 miles south of TX 100, the main road to SPI.

Resaca de la Palma State Park PARK

(☎956-350-2920; www.worldbirdingcenter.org; 1000 New Carmen Rd; adult/child $4/free; ⏰dawn-dusk, visitors center 8am-5pm Thu-Sat) Part of the World Birding Center, this new 1200-acre park is not far from the border. Old courses of the Rio Grande have left several coil-shaped lakes which are ideal for birds and their spotters. Trails wander through this semitropical landscape making this a lovely – and bug-filled – stop, even if your interest in birds is flighty.

You can rent bikes ($5 to $8) and binoculars ($3). The park is 7 miles northwest of Brownsville and is easily reached via US 77/83 or US 281.

McAllen

POP 132,400

McAllen is not just near the Mexican border, it is also near a natural border. To the east are the lush green lands of the Rio Grande Valley, with its farms, palm trees and fast-growing population. To the west is the beginning of the Chihuahuan Desert, where the land becomes more barren due to the increasingly arid climate.

McAllen is the center of two Texas industries: grapefruits and Winter Texans. The former are picked when ripe and juicy, the latter are, well, ripe. The highlight of the season for many is the huge Texas Square Dance Jamboree held each February.

Although McAllen may be short on attractions, its many hotels and restaurants plus its central location make it a good base for exploring the natural delights of the surrounding area, including the sites of the World Birding Center (www.worldbirdingcenter.org).

Sights

US 83 passes south of the center as a freeway; the business route is more interesting. The main retail spine is 10th St, running north and south. The downtown still has lots of little shops and is an interesting place to stroll.

Museum of South Texas History MUSEUM
(956-383-6911; 200 N Closner Blvd, Edinburg; adult/child $7/4; 10am-5pm Tue-Sat, 1-5pm Sun) Just 7 miles north of McAllen in Edinburg, the Museum of South Texas History covers cross-border history from the Ice Age when mammoths roamed the area to the 19th century when soldiers and settlers fought for the region's future.

Sleeping

Fast-growing McAllen has myriad chain motels along 10th St and the two iterations of US 83. For camping, try the lovely natural lands at Bentsen-Rio Grande Valley State Park.

La Copa Inn MOTEL $
(956-686-1741; www.lacopamcallen.com; 2000 S 10th St; r $50-90;) A modest motel that is part of a small local chain, the La Copa is an older 150-room motel that's had a faux-Spanish makeover. It's clean, tidy and good value.

★ **Alamo Inn** INN $
(956-782-9912; www.alamoinnsuites.com; 801 Main St, Alamo; $60-120;) A brilliant find for birders and travelers of all sorts. This historic inn is lovingly operated by Keith Hackland, who has oodles of info on local sights and attractions. A birder himself, Keith can advise on the best sites. Many of the rooms

PLEASE FENCE ME IN

After spending close to $3 billion since 2005, the US Department of Homeland Security has a fence along the Mexican border that is still far from complete. But travelers to the eastern end of the Rio Grande Valley will see plenty of tax dollars at work. From the Gulf of Mexico, a 20ft-tall fence runs along the Rio Grande for over 200 miles. Built of heavy steel and with slats to allow small animals through (but certainly not people!) it is impossible to miss as you drive US 281.

The fence has caused plenty of controversy. Some ranchers have complained that it runs too far inland from the border and the river, cutting off vital access. You'll see protest signs from residents cut off from their own country on the drive out to the Sabal Palm Audubon Center and Sanctuary.

Environmentalists' fears that it would disrupt bird migratory paths are still not proven, but areas of natural beauty in some places along the river have suffered greatly.

Meanwhile, no one is sure if the wall is even restricting the flow of immigrants and drugs into the US (or if drops in border crossings have been the result of reduced economic activity stateside). Tunnels, ladders and other exotic schemes have all been used to circumvent it. Repairs are constant, even as the arguing over how – or if – it should be finished continues. Wall or no wall, you will constantly see border patrols when you drive near the border. And checkpoints are common, even relatively far inland.

WHAT THE...? KILLER BEE

The **World's Largest Killer Bee statue** (704 E Texano Dr) is in Hidalgo. A classic example of a town's efforts to make lemonade from lemons – or in this case honey from imminent peril – the statue dates to the early 1990s. Hidalgo spent $20,000 on this statue. You might say they got stung as 'killer bees' turned out not to represent a grave threat to society.

are suites and some have kitchens. There are good places to eat close by.

The inn is 7 miles east of McAllen on Business US 83/E Center Ave.

Renaissance Casa de Palmas Hotel HISTORIC HOTEL **$$**
(956-631-1101; www.marriott.com; 101 N Main St; r $100-160;) The classiest place in town dates from 1918 and is lovingly managed by Marriott's upscale brand. Right downtown, the restored Spanish-style hotel is perfectly elegant without being pretentious. The 165 rooms surround a beautiful central courtyard and pool.

Eating & Drinking

As elsewhere throughout the borderlands, Mexican food is the most common cuisine here, but there are good alternatives. North 10th St is lined with eateries.

★**Ms G's Tacos n' More** MEXICAN **$**
(956-668-8226; 2263 Pecan Blvd; mains from $3; 6:30am-8pm Mon-Fri, 7am-3pm Sat) Ms G herself arrives every morning at 4:30am to make the region's best flour tortillas for her deceptively simple tacos. Options are many, but you'll never go wrong with *carne guisada* (spicy beef), beans and avocado. There's no place to sit, so either picnic or enjoy this fine fare in your car.

Costa Messa MEXICAN **$**
(956-618-5449; 1621 N 11th St; mains from $8; 11am-10pm) With a menu that crosses the border and gets away from Tex-Mex standards, this casual sit-down place is a great place to explore dishes you might not have had, such as various hearty soups and a bevy of shrimp creations. The fiery guacamole is not to be missed.

Roosevelt's at 7 CAFE **$**
(956-928-1994; 821 N Main St; mains from $8; 11am-2am;) In a land where miserable watery domestic beers rule, the over 40 taps here are like a vision, a glorious vision. In the midst of a modest arts district, Roo's has a large patio with a pool table and lots of casual food like excellent pizza, sandwiches and salads.

Patio on Guerra STEAKS **$$$**
(956-661-9100; www.patioonguerra.com; 116 S 17th St; mains $18-42; 5pm-late Mon-Sat) In the midst of a small nightlife district in the old downtown, the Patio is popular for after-work drinks on its namesake architectural feature. The wine list is superb and diners feast on some of the finest steaks in the valley. There's regular live entertainment.

Information

McAllen Convention & Visitors Bureau (956-682-2871; www.mcallencvb.com; 1200 Ash Ave; 8am-5pm Mon-Fri) Just off US Business 83, the CVB is focused on business rather than tourist needs.

Getting There & Away

Busy **McAllen Miller International Airport** (MFE; 956-681-1500; www.mcallenairport.com) is just south of US 83, off S 10th St. American flies to Dallas–Fort Worth, Continental serves Houston, and Delta Connection links to its hub in Memphis.

Greyhound (956-686-5479; www.greyhound.com; 1501 W US Business 83) has frequent service to Brownsville ($26, 70 minutes) and San Antonio ($48, 4½ hours). There's one bus daily up the valley to Laredo ($29, 3½ hours).

Around McAllen

There are a number of natural sights along the Rio Grande that are reason enough to make McAllen your base.

Sights & Activities

Santa Ana National Wildlife Refuge NATURE RESERVE
(956-787-3079; www.fws.gov; off US 281; per vehicle $3; dawn-dusk, visitor center 8am-4pm) A birder's heaven, this 2088-acre refuge run by the US Fish and Wildlife Service is one of the valley's most beautiful spots. Lakes, wetlands, thorny bushes and palms combine for a bucolic setting where the only noises come from birds. The refuge is the seasonal home

to almost 400 avian species. Hundreds of butterfly species have been spotted here as well.

Tram tours (adult/child $4/2; ⏲9am, noon & 2pm Dec-Apr, other times call for schedules) are popular, but to really experience the place, head out on foot on some of the 12 miles of trails. Short, looping wooden boardwalks are a breeze for the time-challenged; Spanish moss–draped ash, cedar and elm trees shade the lovely trail, which leads to Willow Lakes. Don't miss the rope bridge to an observation tower. Note that bugs here can make vultures seem tame.

Bentsen-Rio Grande Valley State Park PARK
(www.tpwd.state.tx.us; 2800 S Bentsen Palm Dr; adult/child $5/free; ⏲park 7am-10pm, center 8am-5pm) Spot some of over 300 bird species in this serene 760-acre park, which is headquarters for the World Birding Center. Much of the park surrounds several *resacas* – water-filled former river channels that support lush foliage. The visitor center offers excellent trail guides and many bird books. You can rent binoculars and inquire about special programs like bird walks and tram tours.

The site is good for bikes (per day $5 to $12), which make getting to key attractions, like the 1.8-mile Rio Grande loop trail, easy. The park's 10 widely spaced **tent sites** (per site $12) rarely fill up and have water. Surrounded by thorny brush and shaded by trees, the pastoral experience is described as 'waking up with the birds.' The neighboring **Bentsen Palm Village RV Resort** (☎956-585-5568; www.bentsenpalm.com; 2500 S Bentsen Palm Dr; RV sites from $40, cabins from $90; 📶🏊) is part of a growing retirement village.

To get here, take the Bentsen Palm Dr (FM 2062) off Business US 83, 3 miles west of Mission. Drive south 5 miles to the park.

National Butterfly Center NATURE RESERVE
(☎956-583-9009; www.nationalbutterflycenter.org; adult/child $5/2.50; ⏲8am-5pm Sep-Mar, 9am-4pm Apr-Aug) Who isn't enchanted by butterflies? This park is both a learning center and a sanctuary for butterflies and endangered plants. More than 300 species of the little winged jewels have been spotted amidst its 5 acres laced with walking trails. It is only 1 mile east of Bentsen-Rio Grande State Park along Military Rd.

Parts of the site are still being developed but many of the trails are complete as is the cheery visitor center.

WINTER TEXANS

Every fall, 160,000 creatures begin their annual migration to the Rio Grande Valley from points throughout the US and Canadian Midwest. But they aren't wildlife. Not even close. They're retired folks drawn to the south end of Texas by the bone-warming climate and the low prices.

Affectionately dubbed 'Winter Texans' by grateful civic boosters, they add at least $450 million to the local economies during the prime season from October to March. They come in huge slow-moving RVs, SUVs or large sedans and stay in the more than 500 senior-citizen parks from Brownsville to McAllen, where they find accommodations for both RVs and mobile homes.

Most Winter Texans return to the same parks every year, where they are part of a close and friendly seasonal society. The communities bustle with activity, including square dancing, cycling, water sports, bingo, craft classes and much, much more. While many folks engage in sedate matches of shuffleboard, others indulge in rougher pursuits, such as water polo.

Many make regular treks to Mexico, where they can obtain economical medical and dental care as well as cheap pharmaceuticals. Most restaurants do a big dinner business from 4pm to 6pm, which is the traditional suppertime in the Midwestern towns that are home to many of these retirees.

The valley's museums, parks and attractions benefit from the Winter Texans who volunteer in droves to staff information desks in visitor centers. They are invariably well informed and anxious not only to help but also to chat for a while. Residents and tourists also benefit from the value-conscious Winter Texans, who know a good deal when they see it and know how to stretch fixed incomes. Prices are generally low everywhere.

Come spring, when the snow-blanketed lands they hail from begin to thaw, the Winter Texans head back north for the summer.

WHAT THE...? GRAPEFRUIT

So unattractive it's compelling, the bizarre **World's Largest Grapefruit** (La Placita Park, 801 Conway Ave) could be a model for a fatal internal growth if it weren't a highly stylized citrus fruit. It's 6 miles west of McAllen in Mission, just south of US Business 83.

The Upper Valley

The semi-arid scrublands between McAllen and Laredo are sparsely populated northwest of Rio Grande City and have a certain desolate beauty. Falcon International Reservoir is favored by fishers.

The **Los Ebanos Ferry** (956-485-2855; car with driver $3.50; 8am-3:45pm), the only hand-pulled ferry across the Rio Grande, carries people over an isolated section of the river west of McAllen. The ferry can carry three cars and several people on each five-minute journey.

Privately operated since 1742, the ferry isn't a vital transportation link. Note that the US side of the river has been militarized with an overwhelming new inspection facility, fences and frequent patrols. The local village is quite poor and tourists are the only real color. It's 6 miles south of US 83 on FM 886.

Rio Grande City

POP 14,500

Fifty-two miles west of McAllen in arid Starr County, Rio Grande City is in the heart of border patrol efforts to stem drug- and people-smugglers. The territory to the west is desolate, although to the east Winter Texans and other developments are spreading from McAllen.

The town was once a busy trading center, and several brick buildings dating from the 19th century do a slow burn in the sun around town.

La Borde House (956-487-5101; www.labordehouse.com; 601 E Main St; r $70-90) is an 1893 villa designed by a French architect; it has been restored and converted into a small B&B. It has a pleasant, shady courtyard and a small restaurant serving Mexican food. The rooms are filled with period furniture and seem like a time capsule. Nothing here is posh, and service and details can be rather ragged, so stay here for the adventure. Among the local lore: tunnels once led from the hotel to the border to expedite smuggling.

Stop in at the hotel if only to pick up one of the brochures detailing the town's historical buildings.

Roma

POP 11,700

Unlike neighboring Rio Grande City, Roma has actively preserved its heritage, which dates back to 1770. The downtown, one block south of US 83, was designated a National Historic Landmark and is such a perfect representation of an early-1900s border town that the 1952 movie *Viva Zapata* was filmed here.

The small downtown dates to 1751 and you can still get a real sense of the past along a couple of blocks of Convent St. Historical plaques add context.

Birds, however, are the real draw in Roma. The **Roma Bluffs** (956-849-4930; www.worldbirdingcenter.org; Lincoln Ave; dawn-dusk) FREE observation deck is right downtown and overlooks 3 acres of lush nature preserve along the banks of the Rio Grande. It has great views of birdlife, Mexico and the thinly populated countryside.

Falcon International Reservoir

This 136-sq-mile lake was formed by the Falcon Dam (1953) on the Rio Grande. The 500-acre **Falcon State Park** (956-848-5327; www.tpwd.state.tx.us; adult/child $3/free; 6am-10pm), 3 miles west of US 83 off FM 2098, lines the US side of the lake, which is popular for fishing. The land is mostly covered by cactuses and shrubs – no trees – so the park has shaded shelters and picnic areas.

Although seemingly tranquil, the lake has also suffered from the border tensions: fishing boats have been beset by pirates. Like so much of the region, there's a pervasive sense of desolation.

On the lake's northeast side are the hamlets of **Zapata** and **San Ygnacio**. Zapata was named for Emiliano Zapata, land reformer and freedom fighter during the Mexican Revolution (1911–17). Six miles west of town, a scenic overlook off US 83 provides views of an archetypal Western landscape, complete with mesas on the horizon. San Ygnacio, 30 miles southeast of Laredo on US 83, was founded as a ranching outpost in 1830.

Laredo

POP 226,200

Even more than other Texas border towns, Laredo has always been tightly entwined with its sister city to the south, the fittingly named Nuevo Laredo. So drug violence and tight border controls have severely crimped a place where Mexico and the US seemed to blend the most seamlessly, even just a decade ago.

While the border situation remains unsettled, Laredo makes for a good stop on any Rio Grande itinerary. Its historic old downtown is evocative and has two good museums. And in many ways, starting with its strong Hispanic culture, Laredo's like a trip south of the border without the customs inspection.

Sights

Historic downtown Laredo occupies a compact area on the Rio Grande's north bank, at International Bridges Nos 1 and 2. I-35 ends right at the border.

★San Agustín Plaza HISTORIC SITE

Parts of this plaza, right downtown and the oldest in town, date from 1767. The streets surrounding it are cobblestoned and lined with ancient oaks where you can escape the sun. For details about the historic buildings throughout downtown, pick up a copy of the brochure *Heritage Walking Tour of Historic Laredo* at the CVB (p298) or at area hotels.

Nearby streets are interesting for the traditional shops catering to day-tripping Mexicans. Step behind the La Posada Hotel for views of the fortified border area, the trickle of the Rio Grande and the omnipresent huge Mexican flag.

San Agustín Church CHURCH

(San Agustín Plaza; hours vary) This is the third church that has stood on this site at the plaza's east end. Vaguely Gothic-Revival, the church was erected in 1872 and has thick whitewashed walls. The decoration inside and out is simple, and the church hops with large, traditional weddings all weekend long.

Republic of the Rio Grande Museum MUSEUM

(956-727-3480; www.webbheritage.org; 1005 Zaragoza St; admission $2; 9am-4pm Tue-Sat) Housed in the 1840 capitol of the short-lived Republic of the Rio Grande, this excellent museum brings that turbulent period to life with displays about the confused politics plus items from everyday life. Be sure to head (or rather, stoop) to the back, where the oldest part of the building dates to the 1830s.

Nearby, and also operated by the Webb County Heritage Foundation, the **Border Heritage Museum** (810 Zaragoza St) may be open with a special exhibition; check at the main museum. The Border Heritage Museum is housed in the restored 19th-century Villa Antigua.

Sleeping

Most of Laredo's lodgings are on San Bernardo and Santa Ursula Aves, which run parallel with I-35 right to downtown and the border.

Super 8 Motel MOTEL $

(956-722-6321; www.super8.com; 2620 Santa Ursula Ave, at I-35 exit 2; r $50-95;) The better of the two properties of this ubiquitous budget chain is also closer to the center. The 71 rooms are off outside corridors over two floors and all come with microwaves and fridges.

Courtyard by Marriott MOTEL $$

(956-725-5555; www.marriott.com; 2410 Santa Ursula Ave, at I-35 exit 3; r $100-170; @) Two miles north of downtown, this motel's amenities include a health club and whirlpool (after a day touring in 100°F weather, there's nothing like relaxing in a vat of near-boiling water). The 110 rooms reflect an upscale business motif, with large desks and easy chairs.

★La Posada Hotel & Suites HISTORIC HOTEL $$

(956-722-1701; www.laposada.com; 1000 Zaragoza St, San Agustín Plaza; r $110-200; @) Far and away the best choice in Laredo, this hacienda-style hotel occupies a complex of buildings dating from 1916. (It was originally a high school.) The stylish rooms surround two large pools and gardens; the deeply shaded verandahs are a world away from the city bustle just outside. Some rooms have patios overlooking the action of the river and border area.

Eating

During the day, street vendors ply the streets of Laredo, offering tacos, ice cream and other cart-distributed treats. Mexican food fans will want to stay multiple nights here.

Taco Palenque MEXICAN $
(☎956-725-9898; www.tacopalenque.com; 4515 San Bernardo Ave, off I-35 at exit 3; mains from $4; ⊙24hr) This outlet of the phenomenally fast-growing Rio Grande Valley chain is ready to please around the clock. The vast salsa bar awaits and there's beer available.

La Unica De Nuevo Laredo MEXICAN $
(☎956-717-4089; 4500 San Bernardo Ave; mains from $6; ⊙8am-9pm) It's sit-down simple at this family-run classic that got its start across the border in Nuevo Laredo. Fans of Mexican food will find all the standards, it's just that they're better here. The *flautas* come with a guacamole that will spoil you for others although the cream topping is also pretty damn seductive.

★**El Meson De San Augustin** MEXICAN $
(www.elmesondesanagustin.com; 908 Grant St; mains from $6; ⊙11am-4:30pm Mon-Sat) Six days a week, superb food issues forth from this tiny, uber-nondescript family-run restaurant. It's almost like going to someone's house for lunch, especially given the paucity of signage outside. Seemingly humdrum fare like enchiladas and chips and salsa reach heights few thought possible.

★**Palenque Grill** MEXICAN $$
(☎956-728-1272; www.palenquegrill.com; 7220 Bob Bullock Loop; mains $10-18; ⊙11am-11pm) The upscale branch of the Taco Palenque empire features an open and airy main dining room and a spacious terrace. The menu is ambitious and features regional cuisine from around Mexico. Just the chips, salsa and toppings that arrive with your menus foretell the great eats that await.

Zaragoza Grill MEXICAN FUSION $$$
(☎956-753-4444; La Posada Hotel, 1000 Zaragoza St; dinner mains $20-30; ⊙9am-10pm) In the beautiful lobby of the La Posada Hotel, the Zaragoza offers some of Laredo's finest dining. Needless to say there's a long list of vintage tequilas and wines, as well as a creative menu that starts with Mexico then ranges far afield. Chef Alberto Gutierrez specializes in Mexican fusion fare that varies with the season.

Shopping

Prowl San Bernardo Ave heading north from downtown for scores of Mexican shops selling everything from housewares to outdoor sculpture to your basic, albeit colorful, junk.

Basket & Pottery Alley ARTS & CRAFTS
(☎956-724-2415; 3519 San Bernardo Ave; ⊙10am-6pm Mon-Sat) An exuberant cliché selling everything from pots to piñatas in a fiesta-like setting.

Bruce's Pottery ARTS & CRAFTS
(3008 San Bernardo Ave; ⊙10am-6pm Mon-Sat) Yes there's pottery but there's also all manner of strange and wonderful metalworks here.

Information

Laredo Convention & Visitors Bureau (☎800-361-3360, 956-795-2200; www.visitlaredo.com; 501 San Agustín Ave, at Lincoln St; ⊙8am-5pm Mon-Fri) Basic but useful.

Texas Travel Information Center (☎956-417-4728; I-35 & US 83 exit 18; ⊙8am-5pm) About 16 miles north of Laredo, this comprehensive center is a showplace and worthy of a stop just for the Southwestern architecture and gardens.

Getting There & Around

Laredo International Airport (LRD; ☎956-795-2000; www.ci.laredo.tx.us/airport) has service by American Eagle and United Express to and from their respective hubs at Dallas–Fort Worth and Houston. The airport is off Bob Bullock Loop, 1.2 miles north of US 59 on the town's northeast side.

Greyhound (☎956-723-4324; www.greyhound.com; 610 Salinas Ave) operates right downtown. It offers frequent service to San Antonio ($32, from 2¾ hours) and Houston ($40, 6½ hours) plus once daily down the Rio Grande Valley to McAllen ($29, 3½ hours).

Carrizo Springs

A little burst of life amid the empty lands of the Central Rio Grande, Carrizo Springs is an important junction on Rio Grande journeys. Laredo is 80 miles of sagebrush south on US 83, while Eagle Pass is 44 miles northwest on US 277. There's a smear of fast-food joints and you can admire the stolid 1927 limestone **Dimmit County Courthouse** as you drive past.

Eagle Pass

POP 22,300

Eagle Pass may be the most Mexican town in the USA. About 97% of its residents are of Mexican origin, and Spanish is spoken far more often than English. In fact, the main reason most travelers come to Eagle Pass is to get to its sister city – Piedras Negras, in Mexico – and beyond. The town itself is almost immediately forgettable. Most people on the streets seem to be on their way to someplace else.

From the downtown area, US 277 swings north along Ceylon St (an area of a few beautiful homes), 2nd St and Del Rio Blvd.

For centuries, the favored crossing of the Rio Grande in this area was 30 miles south at Guerrero, Coahuila. The route was used by everyone from 17th-century Spanish explorers to Antonio López de Santa Anna as he led his troops to the Alamo. After the Texas War for Independence, the Mexican government prohibited direct trade with Texans, but Mexican villagers near the Rio Grande continued to use a clandestine road that ran north of the old San Antonio Rd. It crossed the river near what was called Paso del Águila (Eagle Pass) for the many eagles' nests perched in the nearby pecan trees. The US Army established Fort Duncan at the Paso del Águila in 1849 to protect emigrants heading west in the California gold rush, as well as the flow of trade from Mexico.

Sights

Fort Duncan Museum MUSEUM
(830-773-1714; Fort Duncan Park, Bliss St; admission by donation; hours vary) Fort Duncan Museum, housed in the old fort headquarters building, has exhibits and artifacts from the Spanish colonial period through the early 20th century. Note that the museum's hours may be erratic.

Sleeping & Eating

There's no good reason to spend the night in Eagle Pass, however should Del Rio or Laredo seem too far you'll find a half-dozen chains at either end of town along US 277. Not surprisingly, the best food here is Mexican.

Best Western Eagle Pass MOTEL $
(830-758-1234; www.bestwestern.com; 1923 Veterans Blvd; r $85-110;) This older motel has a pleasant outdoor pool area surrounded by palm trees. The 40 rooms are in two-story wings with outside corridors so you can park outside your door. The property has been much improved of late and guests receive a full breakfast.

Parilla de San Miguel MEXICAN $
(830-757-3100; 408 S Texas Dr; mains from $6; 11am-9pm) Many customers at first think they have discovered a new upscale Mexican chain when they walk into this well-polished restaurant that evokes a sidewalk cafe. Salsas are varied and are good over the various marinated steaks. It's two blocks southwest of where E Garrison St meets E Main St.

Information

Eagle Pass Chamber of Commerce (830-773-3224; www.eaglepasstexas.com; 400 Garrison St; 9am-5pm Mon-Fri) has information on both Eagle Pass and Piedras Negras.

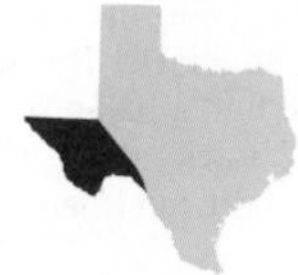

Big Bend & West Texas

Includes ➡

Best Places to Eat

- Reata (p320)
- Starlight Theater (p311)
- Cochineal (p318)
- Crave (p330)

Best Places to Stay

- Holland Hotel (p320)
- La Posada Milagro (p311)
- Indian Lodge (p315)
- El Cosmico (p317)

Why Go?

Welcome to the land of wide open spaces. Along I-10 there's not much to look at – just scrub brush and lots of sky – but dip below the interstate and you'll find vistas that are as captivating as they are endless. Sometimes the rugged terrain looks like the backdrop in an old Western movie; other times it looks like an alien landscape, with huge rock formations suddenly jutting out of the desert.

But what is there to do? Plenty. Exploring an enormous national park that's nearly the size of Rhode Island. Stopping in small towns that surprise you with minimalist art, planet-watching parties or fascinating ghost-town ruins. Chatting with friendly locals whenever the mood strikes you. And letting the delicious slowness of west Texas get thoroughly under your skin.

When to Go

El Paso

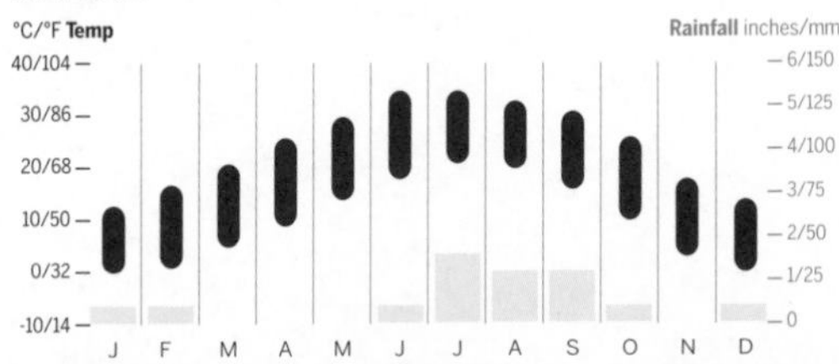

Jan & Feb Forget winter weather – the desert is moderate and dry.

Mar–May Prime time: the weather is still cool and wildflowers are in bloom.

Jul & Aug If you can take the heat, you'll avoid a lot of the crowds.

BIG BEND NATIONAL PARK

Everyone knows Texas is huge. But you can't really appreciate just how big it is until you visit this **national park** (www.nps.gov/bibe; 7-day pass per vehicle $20), which is almost the same size as Rhode Island. When you're traversing Big Bend's 1252 sq miles, you come to appreciate what 'big' really means. It's a land of incredible diversity, vast enough to allow a lifetime of discovery, yet laced with enough well-placed roads and trails to permit short-term visitors to see a lot in two to three days.

Like many popular US parks, Big Bend has one area – the Chisos Basin – that absorbs the overwhelming crunch of traffic. The Chisos Mountains are beautiful, and no trip here would be complete without an excursion into the high country. But any visit to Big Bend should also include time in the Chihuahuan Desert, home to curious creatures and adaptable plants, and the Rio Grande, providing a watery border between the US and Mexico.

When to Go

Most travelers consider spring and fall the best times to visit Big Bend National Park. Summer (June through August) is very hot, with typical daytime temperatures around 100°F; late summer can be rainy too. Spring means moderate temperatures and lots of wildflowers (and lots of people), and fall is also quite pleasant, especially for white-water rafting.

Some park-fanciers believe winter is the best time of all to come; it's usually relatively mild, although temperatures in the Chisos can fall below freezing and Basin Rd typically closes two or three times each winter, sometimes for several days. But the snow is never deep enough to preclude hiking, and the touch of frost makes the trees and cacti a beautiful sight. At all times of the year, it's wise to layer your clothes in the morning and peel off the top layers as you warm up.

BEAR IN MIND...

There's a slim chance you'll encounter a black bear in the park. If you do, don't run away; instead make lots of noise and look as big as possible by waving your hands above your head. If you see cubs, back away slowly so the mother won't fear an attack. To keep bears from joining you for dinner, store all food, coolers, cooking utensils and toiletries in the trunk of your car or in the special bear-proof lockers, and discard trash in the bear-proof containers provided at campsites and near trailheads.

Geology

For millions of years Big Bend lay at the bottom of the sea, part of a trough that extended into what is now Arkansas and Oklahoma. Over time the sea became shallower and eventually disappeared, leaving a wondrous fossil record of marine life and beds of limestone, both thick (the Sierra del Carmen and Santa Elena formations) and thin (the Boquillas formation). Once the sea was gone, the dinosaurs took over; Big Bend was especially favored by pterosaurs, the largest flying creatures ever with a wingspan of 35ft or more.

About 65 million years ago, the Cenozoic era began, and tectonic forces produced the Rocky Mountains and the Sierra Madre. Volcanic activity followed, spreading ash and lava over thousands of miles in the region. Increased tensions in the earth's crust created faulting, dropping the central portion of the park while further elevating the Chisos Mountains. Meanwhile, the Rio Grande carved the great canyons that define the river today.

Sights

Sam Nail Ranch HISTORIC SITE

A short walk from the Ross Maxwell Scenic Drive, just five minutes or so in, you'll find the ruins of the Sam Nail Ranch. The windmill still pumps for no one's benefit, and the ruins of the house and shed can feel vaguely haunted, especially at dusk.

Castolon Historic District HISTORIC SITE

Dwarfed by the looming Sierra Ponce, the cluster of buildings that make up the Castolon Compound were built in 1920. A half-mile historic stroll offers a brief look at life on the frontier in the Castolon Historic District. Start at the famous La Harmonia Store, which is a mainstay for locals on both sides of the river as well as an ice-cream vending oasis for tourists. A pamphlet ($1) sold in the store serves as a guide.

Activities

Scenic Drives

Big Bend National Park has 110 miles of paved road and 150 miles of dirt road, and

Big Bend & West Texas Highlights

1. Enjoying music, margaritas and mixing with the locals at the **Starlight Theater** (p311) in Terlingua ghost town.
2. Window shopping at the **Prada Marfa** (p319) – a surreal art installation on the side of the road just before Valentine.
3. Getting up early to hike the Grapevine Hills Trail and find the Balanced Rock in **Big Bend National Park** (p301).
4. Stargazing and planet-peeping at a late-night star party at **McDonald Observatory** (p313) in Fort Davis.
5. Catching a glimpse of the **mystery lights** (p317) outside of Marfa.
6. Exploring the many free museums in downtown El Paso, including the excellent **El Paso Museum of Art** (p323).

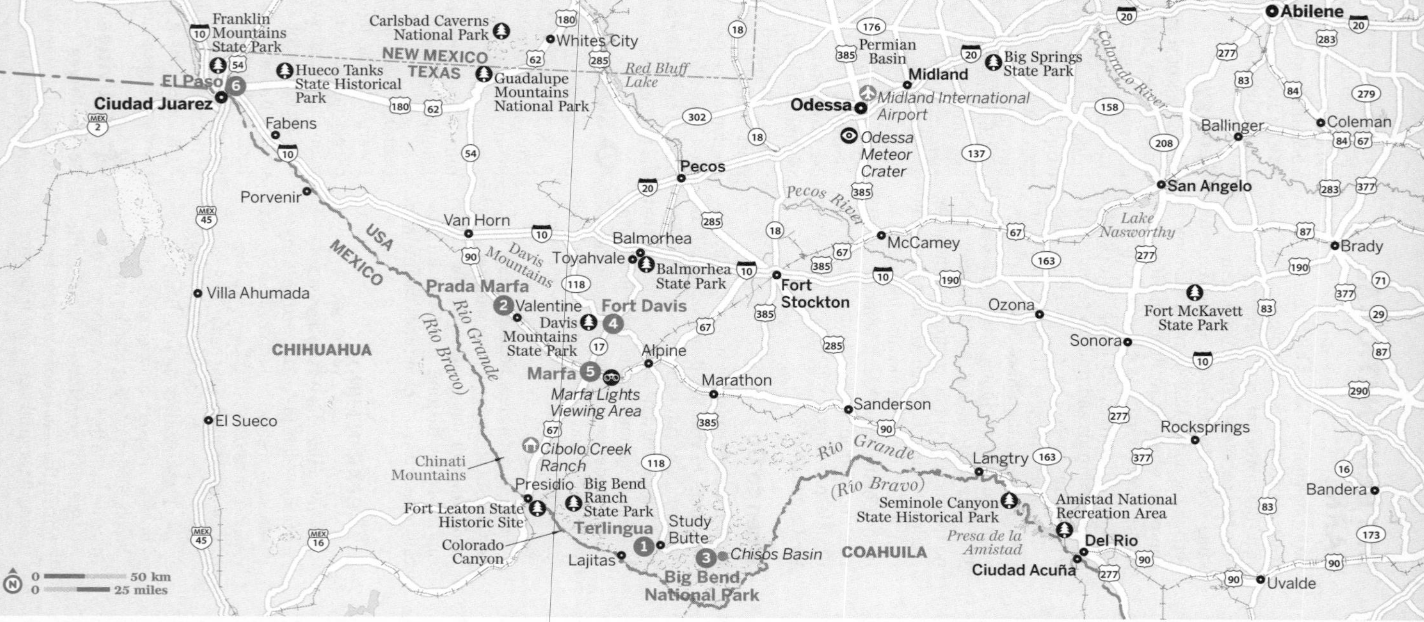

scenic driving is easily the park's most popular activity. Booklets are available for $1.95 from the visitor centers to help you make the most of it.

Maverick Drive The 22-mile stretch between the west entrance and park headquarters is notable for its desert scenery and wildlife. Just west of Basin Junction, a side trip on the gravel Grapevine Hills Rd leads to fields of oddly shaped, highly eroded boulders.

Ross Maxwell Scenic Drive This 30-mile route leaves Maverick Dr midway between the west entrance and park headquarters. The Chisos Mountains provide a grand panorama, and the big payoff is the view of Santa Elena Canyon and its 1500ft sheer rock walls.

Rio Grande Village Drive This 20-mile drive leads from park headquarters toward the Sierra del Carmen range, running through the park toward Mexico. The best time to take this drive is at sunrise or sunset, when the mountains glow brilliantly with different hues.

Backpacking

Big Bend's primitive backpacking routes range from well-traveled desert washes to the truly challenging limestone uplifts of Mesa de Anguila and the Dead Horse Mountains. Rangers say that because of the constantly changing trail and spring conditions, it's pretty much impossible to plan an extended backpacking trip before you actually get to the park. What you can do instead is figure out how much time you have and the distance you'd like to cover and, based on that information, park staff will help you plot a trip. Many trails require use of topographical maps and a compass.

Bird-Watching

Over 450 bird species have been spotted in the park; prime sites include Rio Grande Valley, the Sam Nail Ranch, the Chisos Basin and Castolon near Santa Elena Canyon. The Big Bend region may be best known for its peregrine falcons, which, while still endangered, have been making a comeback. A dozen known nests are found within or near the park.

Among other Big Bend bird celebrities, the Colima warbler has its only US nesting spot in the Chisos Mountains, where it lives from April through mid-September. More common Big Bend species include golden eagles, cactus wrens, ravens, Mexican jays, roadrunners, acorn woodpeckers, canyon towhees and a whole bunch of warblers and hummingbirds.

River Trips

The Rio Grande has earned its place among the top North American river trips for both rafting and canoeing. Rapids up to class IV alternate with calm stretches that are perfect for wildlife viewing, photography and just plain relaxation.

Trips on the river can range from several hours to several days. **Boquillas Canyon** is the longest and most tranquil of the park's three canyons and is best for intermediate to advanced boaters and canoeists with camping skills. **Colorado Canyon** is just upriver from the park and, depending on the water level, has lots of white water. **Mariscal Canyon** is noted for its beauty and isolation, and **Santa Elena Canyon** is a classic float featuring the class IV Rock Slide rapid.

Guided floats cost about $120 per person per day, $70 for a half day, including all meals and gear (except a sleeping bag for overnighters). These three companies have been in business a long time and have solid reputations:

Big Bend River Tours (☎800-545-4240, 432-371-3033; www.bigbendrivertours.com; Rte 170) offers saddle-paddle tours with half a day each rowing and horseback riding.

Desert Sports (☎888-989-6900, 432-371-2727; www.desertsportstx.com; Rte 170) is tops with bikers for its bike-canoe combo trips.

Far Flung Adventures (☎800-839-7238; www.bigbendfarflung.com; Terlingua) puts together fun outings like a wine-tasting river trip.

Want to go it alone? Any of the above companies will rent you equipment and provide shuttle service. Just remember to obtain your free permit at Panther Junction within 24 hours before putting in. Permits for the lower canyons of the Rio Grande are available at the Persimmon Gap visitor center and the Stillwell Store on FM 2627.

Horseback Riding

Although horses are permitted on many trails at Big Bend, they can't be rented inside the park. If you bring your own, get the required permit, available for free at any visitor center, and be aware of the many

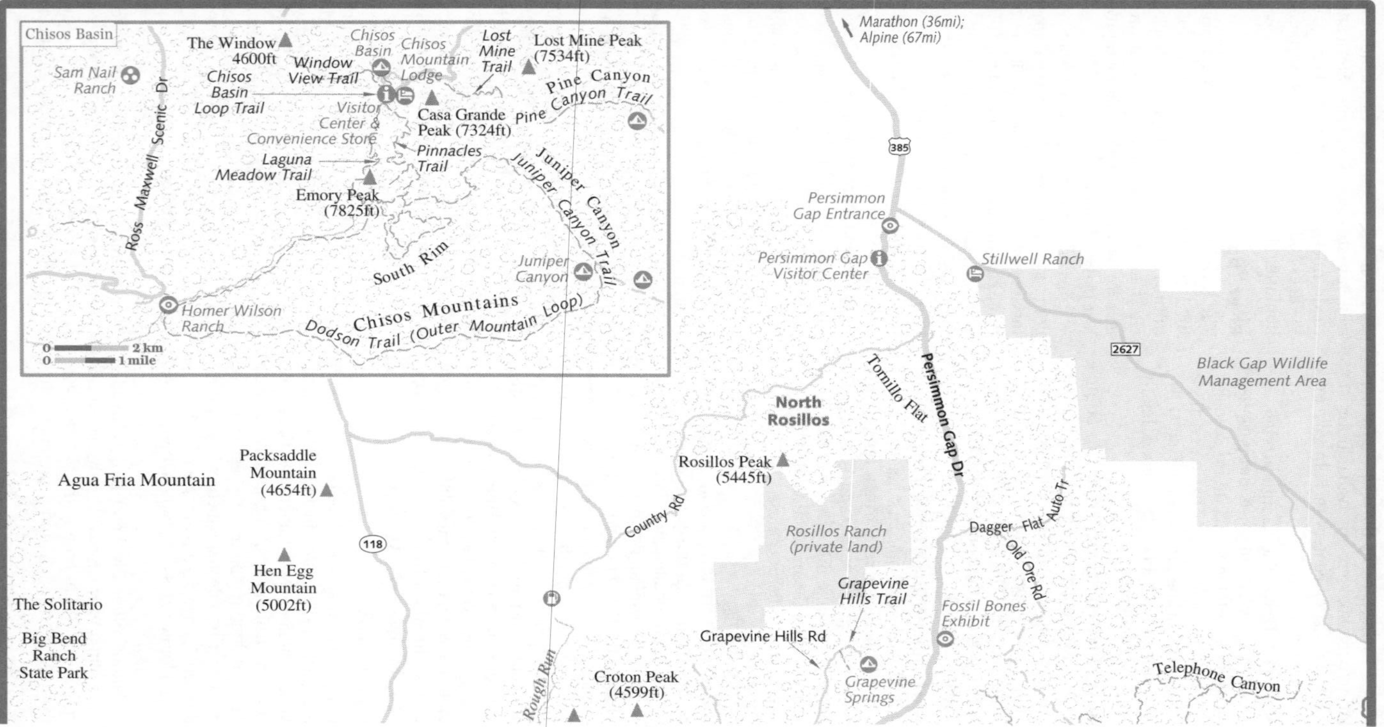
Big Bend National Park
0 20 km
0 12 miles
Chisos Basin
The Window 4600ft
Sam Nail Ranch
Chisos Basin
Chisos Mountain Lodge
Window View Trail
Chisos Basin Loop Trail
Lost Mine Trail
Lost Mine Peak (7534ft)
Pine Canyon
Pine Canyon Trail
Visitor Center & Convenience Store
Casa Grande Peak (7324ft)
Pinnacles Trail
Laguna Meadow Trail
Emory Peak (7825ft)
Juniper Canyon
Juniper Canyon Trail
Ross Maxwell Scenic Dr
South Rim
Juniper Canyon
Chisos Mountains
Homer Wilson Ranch
Dodson Trail (Outer Mountain Loop)
0 2 km
0 1 mile
Marathon (36mi); Alpine (67mi)
385
Persimmon Gap Entrance
Persimmon Gap Visitor Center
Stillwell Ranch
2627
Black Gap Wildlife Management Area
Persimmon Gap Dr
Tornillo Flat
North Rosillos
Rosillos Peak (5445ft)
Packsaddle Mountain (4654ft)
Agua Fria Mountain
118
Country Rd
Rosillos Ranch (private land)
Dagger Flat Auto Tr
Old Ore Rd
Hen Egg Mountain (5002ft)
Grapevine Hills Trail
Fossil Bones Exhibit
The Solitario
Grapevine Hills Rd
Big Bend Ranch State Park
Rough Run
Croton Peak (4599ft)
Grapevine Springs
Telephone Canyon

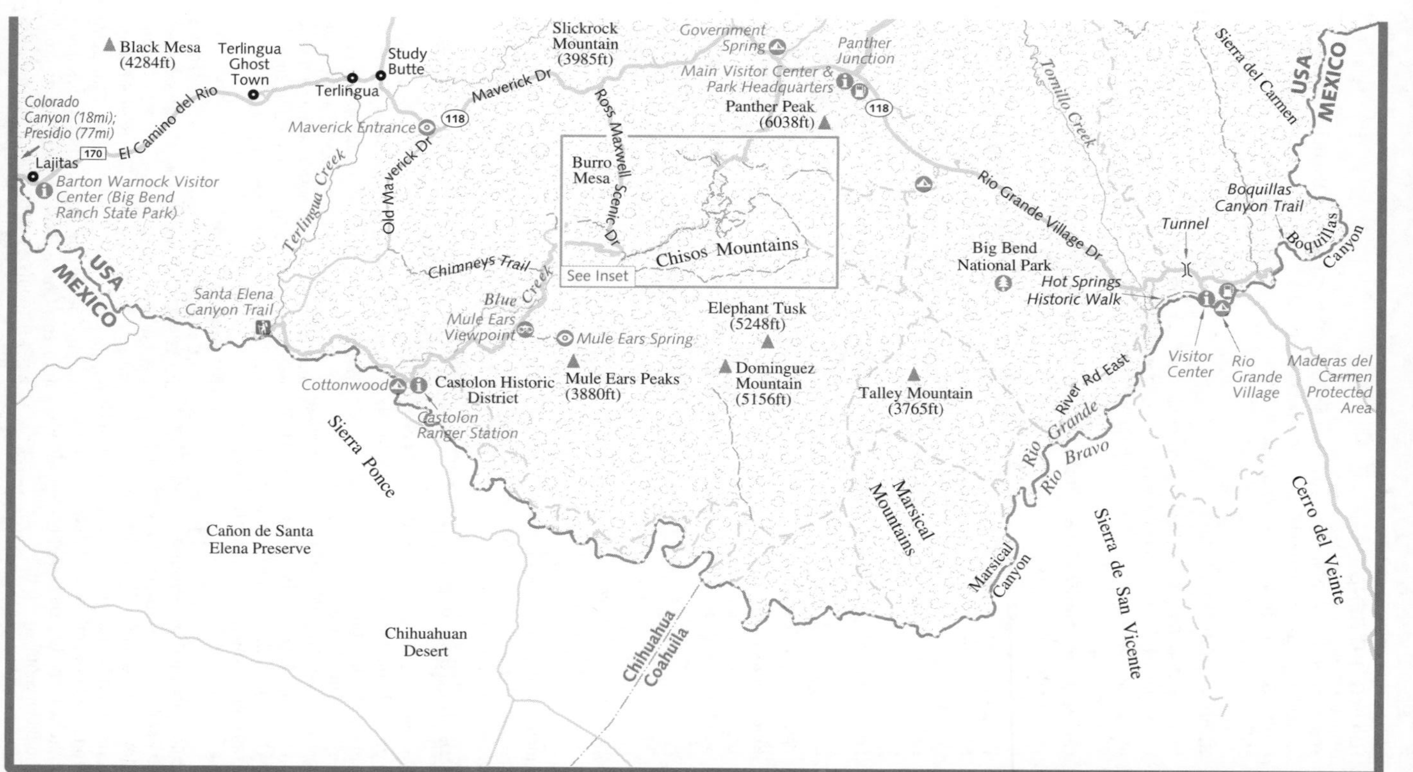
Black Mesa (4284ft)
Terlingua Ghost Town
Study Butte
Terlingua
Slickrock Mountain (3985ft)
Government Spring
Panther Junction
Main Visitor Center & Park Headquarters
118
Panther Peak (6038ft)
Colorado Canyon (18mi); Presidio (77mi)
El Camino del Rio
170
Lajitas
Barton Warnock Visitor Center (Big Bend Ranch State Park)
Maverick Dr
Maverick Entrance
Old Maverick Dr
Terlingua Creek
Ross Maxwell Scenic Dr
Burro Mesa
Chisos Mountains
See Inset
Tornillo Creek
Rio Grande Village Dr
Sierra del Carmen
USA
MEXICO
Boquillas Canyon Trail
Boquillas Canyon
Tunnel
Big Bend National Park
Hot Springs Historic Walk
Chimneys Trail
Blue Creek
Santa Elena Canyon Trail
Mule Ears Viewpoint
Mule Ears Spring
Elephant Tusk (5248ft)
Cottonwood
Castolon Historic District
Mule Ears Peaks (3880ft)
Dominguez Mountain (5156ft)
Talley Mountain (3765ft)
Castolon Ranger Station
Visitor Center
Rio Grande Village
Maderas del Carmen Protected Area
River Rd East
Rio Grande
Rio Bravo
Sierra Ponce
Marsical Mountains
Cañon de Santa Elena Preserve
Marsical Canyon
Sierra de San Vicente
Cerro del Veinte
Chihuahuan Desert
Chihuahua
Coahuila

HIKING BIG BEND

With over 200 miles of trails to explore, it's no wonder hiking is big in Big Bend. Here are some of the most popular hikes; get specifics from the visitor center or pick up the *Hiker's Guide to Trails of Big Bend National Park* ($1.95 at park visitor centers) for more choices.

Chisos Mountains Hikes

Window View Trail (0.3 miles) The absolute lowest amount of commitment is this short trail that leaves from behind the basin's convenience store. It's paved and wheelchair-accessible – perfect for nonhikers or for anyone who wants to watch the sunset over the Window.

Chisos Basin Loop Trail (1.6 miles) Also leaving from the basin store, this trail offers nice views of the basin and a relatively large amount of shade provided by the Mexican piñons and alligator junipers.

Window Trail (4.4 miles) This popular trail has a great payoff: after descending into scrub brush, you enter a shady canyon and scramble around on some rocks, then the trail suddenly ends with a narrowed pass and a 200ft drop-off. Leave from the campground trailhead to shave more than a mile off the hike. The return is steep and unshaded; this trail is best done in the morning.

Lost Mine Trail (4.8 miles) Another really popular trail, this one is all about views, which just get better and better as you climb over 1000ft in elevation. If you're not up for the full climb, which ends with a series of switchbacks, you can get a pretty good payoff with impressive views just a mile in.

Emory Peak (9 miles) Sturdy hikers can bag the highest peak at Big Bend on the 9-mile portion of the Pinnacles Trail complex. Be prepared to climb at the finish: it ends with a short scramble up a sheer rock wall.

regulations you'll have to adhere to, just to make sure it's worth the trouble. Government Spring, a primitive campsite near Panther Junction, caters to parties with between four and eight horses. It can be reserved up to 10 weeks in advance by calling ☎432-477-1158.

Sleeping & Eating

For tent campers or smaller RVs that don't require hookups, there are three main campgrounds, some of which can be reserved, some of which are first-come, first-served. Sites typically fill up during spring break, Thanksgiving and Christmas. When everything's full, rangers direct tent campers to primitive sites throughout the Big Bend backcountry.

Chisos Basin Campground CAMPGROUND $
(☎877-444-6777; www.recreation.gov; campsites $14) The most centrally located of the main campgrounds, this 60-site campground has stone shelters and picnic tables. It's located right near the Chisos Lodge Restaurant and the Basin Store.

Cottonwood Campground CAMPGROUND $
(campsites $14) Located beneath cottonwood trees near Castolon, the 31-site Cottonwood Campground provides a subdued and shady environment along the river with no generators or idling vehicles to ruin the ambience. No reservations.

Rio Grande Village Campground CAMPGROUND $
(☎877-444-6777; www.recreation.gov; campsites $14) On the southeastern edge of the park, this campground offers 100 sites with water and flush toilets. Generators may only be used from 8am to 8pm; mercifully, there is also a no-generator zone available.

Rio Grande Village RV Campground CAMPGROUND $
(☎432-477-2293; per 2 people $33, per extra person $3) If you have a larger RV, Rio Grande Village is the only facility with hookups within the park. (Trailers over 25ft have trouble navigating the winding roads down into the Chisos Basin.) Since there aren't any restrooms, your rig will need water and

South Rim (13 to 14.5 miles) Many serious hikers say this is their favorite trek, mainly because of the view at the end: from the South Rim, the vista includes Santa Elena Canyon and the Sierra del Carmen. Consult with the visitor center for your best plan of attack.

Desert Hikes

Grapevine Hills Trail (2.2 miles) The highlight of this fascinating desert hike near Panther Junction is Balanced Rock, a much-photographed formation of three acrobatic boulders that form an inverted-triangle 'window.' After hiking almost a mile in, you'll climb a quarter of a mile over some rocks to reach the window.

Mule Ears Spring (3.8 miles) Bring your hat for this pretty desert hike that crosses several arroyos before leading you to a small spring, a rock corral and a small adobe house.

The Chimneys (4.8 miles) With no shade, the sun can be brutal, but the trail is mercifully flat. Your reward is rock formations and Native American pictographs and petroglyphs.

Riverside Hikes

Rio Grande Village Nature Trail (0.75 miles) Beginning at campsite 18 at the Rio Grande Village campground, the trail passes through dense vegetation before emerging into the desert for a view of the Rio Grande. This is a good short trail for birding and photography.

Hot Springs Historic Walk (1 mile) On the way to the hot springs – a stone tub brimming with 105°F spring water at the river's edge – you'll pass historic buildings and Native American pictographs painted on rock walls.

Boquillas Canyon Trail (1.4 miles) After a short climb, you'll descend a sandy path to the river. Leave time to play on the sand slide and enjoy the sunlight dancing on the canyon walls.

Santa Elena Canyon Trail (1.7 miles) At the end of Ross Maxwell Scenic Dr (a long drive from most of the park) is a short trail into a photogenic river canyon. You start by crossing Terlingua Creek, which could be wet or muddy, so plan accordingly.

electrical hookups, as well as a 3in sewer connection.

Chisos Mountains Lodge MOTEL **$$**
(☎877-386-4383, 432-477-2291; www.chisosmountainslodge.com; lodge & motel r $123-127, cottages $150) This concessionaire-operated complex in the basin gets good, if not great, marks for accommodations and food service. You can do better on both counts if you stay outside the park, but the scenery here is a lot better, and it's nice not to have to drive 45 minutes to rest up after your hike.

The lodge offers three overnight options. **Roosevelt Stone Cottages** are the choice accommodations in the park. Each has three double beds, so you could sleep six people semi-comfortably. There are only four of these cottages, though, so they're hard to come by.

Casa Grande Lodge and **Rio Grande Motel** both have modest, motel-style rooms with private balconies and good views of the basin and surrounding mountains. Most rooms have two double beds; a few have one double and one single. The guest rooms here don't have TVs or telephones. Reservations are a must, but management says there are often cancellations.

Chisos Basin Store MARKET **$**
(☎432-477-2291; ⏲8am-9pm) Snacks, camping supplies, cold beer, suntan lotion, sun hats and even some souvenirs can all be found at the convenience store in the Chisos Basin right next to the visitor center. You can find a similar selection at the **Rio Grande Village Store** (☎432-477-2293; ⏲8am-7pm, to 5pm summer) and in the **La Harmonia** (⏲10am-6pm, to 4pm summer) store at Castolon.

Chisos Lodge Restaurant AMERICAN **$$**
(Lodge Dining Room; Chisos Mountains Lodge; ⏲7-10am, 11am-4pm & 5-8pm) Talk about a captive audience: it's a 45-minute drive to the next-closest restaurants in Study Butte and Terlingua. Still, the food here is decent, there are plenty of options, and the staff, for the most part, is surprisingly cheery and attentive. Try to get a window table, since the

WORTH A TRIP

EAST OF BIG BEND

For all but the southernmost towns in Texas, I-10 is the fastest way in and out of Big Bend, but if you want to take the meandering route home, the area east of Big Bend has some interesting stops along the way, including some of the oldest rock art in North America.

Del Rio

This atmospheric town on the Mexican border has a lovely downtown lined with historic buildings from the 1800s, including an imposing limestone courthouse built in 1887. Ask the **chamber of commerce** (830-775-3551; www.drchamber.com; 1915 Veterans Blvd; 8:30am-5pm Mon-Fri) for *A Guide to Historic Del Rio*, a free walking tour of historic downtown and a driving tour of the rest of town. While you're there, check out the **Whitehead Memorial Museum** (830-774-7568; www.whiteheadmuseum.org; 1308 S Main St; adult/child $5/2; 9am-4:30pm Tue-Sat, 1-5pm Sun), an idiosyncratic place where Judge Roy Bean happens to be buried.

Seminole Canyon State Historical Park

The best art galleries in south central Texas are right here, featuring works of rock art that have been on view for at least 4000 years. The most famous is the Fate Bell Shelter, a cave dwelling with pictograph-lined walls. **Tours** (888-762-5278; www.rockart.org; 10am & 3pm Wed-Sun, no afternoon tours Jun-Aug) FREE led by the Rock Art Foundation (which also organizes Saturday tours to other more remote sites) last up to 90 minutes and include a fairly strenuous hike down and up a canyon. You can also hike to Panther Cave from here; this cave is known for its 9ft-long drawing of a mountain lion accompanied by many other animal and human figures.

Amistad National Recreation Area

With 850 miles of shoreline, boating, water-skiing, swimming, fishing and bird-watching are all reasons to visit this reservoir formed by a 6-mile dam on the Rio Grande. The **Visitor Information Center** (830-775-7491; www.nps.gov/amis; 8am-5pm) will set you up with the information you need. You can use your boat to access Panther Cave as well as Parida Cave, assuming water levels are high enough.

Langtry

Practically a ghost town, Langtry (population 45) has turned its principal claim to fame into a major tourist attraction on US 90: the **Judge Roy Bean Visitor Center** (432-291-3340; www.traveltex.com; US 90; 8am-5pm, to 6pm Jun-Aug). Displays cover the life of the legendary Lone Star lawman and include the .41-caliber Smith & Wesson revolver he used as his gavel.

Where Not to Go

Sadly, two of the best reasons to take this route have undergone big changes in recent years:

Ciudad Acuña The US State Department recommends you avoid this dangerous detour for now.

Alamo Village John Wayne's full-scale reproduction of the Alamo in Bracketville is closed to visitors.

sublime Chisos Basin view is the best thing about this place.

Orientation

Park headquarters and the **main visitor center** (432-477-2251; 8am-6pm) are at Panther Junction, which is on the main road 29 miles south of the Persimmon Gap entrance and 22 miles east of the Maverick entrance near Study Butte. A Chevron station offers fuel, repairs and a small stock of snacks and beverages.

From Panther Junction, it's a (relatively) short 10-mile drive to the Chisos Basin. Sharp curves and steep grades make Basin Rd unsuitable for recreational vehicles longer than 24ft and trailers longer than 20ft.

Another major road leads 20 miles southeast to Rio Grande Village, where you can find the only other fuel pumps within the park (good to know because you're a long way from anywhere).

Two other principal roads, the 7-mile Basin Rd and 30-mile Ross Maxwell Scenic Dr, take off from the main park road west of Panther Junction.

Information

DANGERS & ANNOYANCES

Big Bend National Park is one of the most remote spots in North America, set amid wild country with all kinds of potential hazards. This doesn't mean it's an inherently dangerous place, but it does mean precautions should be taken.

Don't take the heat for granted; this is the desert, after all. Drink lots of water, and take plenty with you when you hike. To protect against sunburn, wear a hat, sunscreen, long pants and a long-sleeved shirt. And take a cue from the animals: do your hiking early in the morning or in the evening, not at midday when the unrelenting sun turns Big Bend into one big Easy-Bake Oven.

Big Bend's poisonous snakes and tarantulas won't attack unless provoked. Simple rule of thumb? Don't provoke them. Most snakes keep a low profile in daylight, when you're unlikely to see them. Night hikers should stay on the trail and carry a flashlight. Big Bend's scorpions are not deadly, but you should still get prompt attention if you're stung. Shake out boots or shoes before putting them on.

EMERGENCY & MEDICAL SERVICES

To report an emergency day or night in the park, call the **main park number** (☎432-477-2251; ⌚8am-6pm). After the automated telephone system answers, press 4. If there's no answer, hang up and dial ☎911.

Big Bend is no place to get seriously injured or gravely ill. The closest hospital is in Alpine, 108 miles from Panther Junction. However, the nonprofit **Terlingua Fire & EMS** (☎432-371-2536; 23250 FM 170) has a first-aid station that's 26 miles west of Panther Junction, where trained paramedics can offer some assistance.

MAPS

Readily available at the entrances and visitor centers, the free National Park Service *Big Bend* map is adequate for most visitors to the park. The visitor centers also stock a handy booklet ($1.95) that describes the developed trails. Serious backpackers or anyone looking to hike the less-developed trails will want to pick up a topographic map at the visitor centers or gateway-town bookstores.

MONEY

This is one of the few parts of the country where you can drive a couple of hours and not find a bank. There is, however, an ATM at the convenience stores in Chisos Basin and Rio Grande Village.

TOURIST INFORMATION

In addition to the park headquarters at Panther Junction, visitor centers are found in **Chisos Basin** (⌚8:30am-4pm) and at **Persimmon Gap** (⌚9am-4:30pm). There are also seasonal visitor centers open November through April at Castolon and the Rio Grande Village. Find out how to make the most of your visit from park rangers, and check bulletin boards for a list of upcoming interpretive activities. You'll also find a variety of free leaflets on special-interest topics, including biological diversity, hiking and backpacking, geology, archaeology and dinosaurs.

Getting There & Away

There is no public transportation to, from or within the park. The closest buses and trains run through Alpine, 108 miles northwest of Panther Junction. The nearest major airports are in Midland (230 miles northeast) and El Paso (325 miles northwest).

Please note that the border patrol has checkpoints for vehicles coming from Big Bend. If you're not a US citizen, presenting your passport will help avoid delays (ie prove you're not coming from Mexico).

WEST OF BIG BEND NATIONAL PARK

Small towns. Ghost towns. Towns that aren't even really towns. Throw in lots of dust and a scorching summer heat that dries out the stream of visitors until it's just a trickle. This isn't everyone's idea of a dream vacation. But if you can't relax out here, then you just plain can't relax. Whatever concerns you have in your everyday life are likely to melt away (along with anything you leave in your car). With rugged natural beauty and some offbeat destinations, you can see why this unlikely corner of the country is actually fueled almost entirely by tourism.

This is the land that public transportation forgot. You'll need a car, not just to get to Terlingua, but to get around once you're there.

Terlingua & Study Butte

POP 267

A former mining boomtown in the late 19th and early 20th centuries, Terlingua went bust when they closed down the cinnabar

THE CHAMPIONS OF CHILI

Every November, Terlingua is invaded by thousands of visitors with a hankering for homemade chili. This is no small-town festival; the **Terlingua Chili Cookoff** is such a big deal that they actually have two events to accommodate the hundreds of entrants:

International Chili Championship Held by the Chili Appreciation Society International (CASI; www.chili.org).

Original Terlingua International Frank X Tolbert-Wick Fowler Championship Chili Cookoff (www.abowlofred.com) Less competitive and more like a big, delicious party.

Don't expect to enjoy quality time with the locals during these events; they mostly go into hiding.

mines in the 1940s. The town dried up and blew away like a tumbleweed, leaving buildings that fell into ruins and earning Terlingua a place in Texas folklore as a ghost town.

But slowly the area has become repopulated, thanks in large part to its proximity to Big Bend National Park, to which it supplies housing for park employees, as well as services to the more than 300,000 park visitors each year. Several businesses make their homes in and around the ghost town; many of the old adobes have been reclaimed by river guides, artists and others who relish the solitude of the outback.

You'll hear people talk about Terlingua, Study Butte (pronounced 'stoody byoot'), and Terlingua ghost town as if they're three different towns, but the only real town here is Terlingua; the other two are just areas of the town. Addresses are a relative and fluid thing out here; have patience if you're using a GPS, but take comfort knowing the town's not all that big.

Sights & Activities

For many locals and laid-back travelers, the main activity in Terlingua is sitting on the porch of the Terlingua Trading Co, drinking a beer and shooting the breeze while watching the sunset, an activity we highly recommend.

There's not a lot to see 'round here, except some stone ruins and an old cemetery from the early 1900s. Many of the ruins are on private land, so remember: 'uninhabited' does not equal 'open to the public.' The cemetery, however, is open to visitors, and it's one of the most fascinating final resting places in the US. No manicured lawns or tasteful headstones here: these graves are piled high with local rocks that reflect the style of the nearby ruins.

For more active types, Terlingua sits amid prime mountain-biking territory. Desert Sports (p303) provides rental bikes, along with advice on the best places to ride. It also offers raft, canoe, bike and combo trips throughout the Big Bend area.

If you'd like to explore the countryside on horseback, call **Big Bend Stables** (☎800-887-4331, 432-371-3064; www.bigbendstables.com; Hwy 118 & FM-170), where rates run $40 for one hour, $60 for two hours and $75 for three hours. (They don't actually go into Big Bend, which doesn't allow commercial outfitters, but they do host a trail ride in the Terlingua area.)

Sleeping

You'd think lodging would be inexpensive out here; quite the opposite. Expect to pay a little more than you think you ought to.

Big Bend Resort & Adventures MOTEL, CAMPGROUND **$**
(☎432-371-2218, reservations 877-386-4383; www.bigbendresortadventures.com; Hwy 118 & FM 170 junction; d $60-90, RV sites $24-29, tent camping $16; 📶🐾) This place has all sorts of sleeping options, including serviceable motel rooms in the Motor Inn and Mission Lodge, duplex units, apartments, tent camping and RV sites.

BJ's RV Park CAMPGROUND **$**
(☎432-371-2259; www.bjrvpark.com; FM 170; RV sites $25; 📶🐾) Sure it's dry and dusty. The whole town is dry and dusty. At least they've got showers. This utilitarian park, 5 miles west of Hwy 118, provides a handy alternative when everything's full up in Big Bend.

Chisos Mining Co Motel MOTEL **$**
(☎432-371-2254; www.cmcm.cc; 23280 FM 170; s/d $60/78, cabins from $101; ❄) You'll

recognize this quirky little place less than a mile west of Hwy 118 when you spot the oversized Easter eggs on the roof. The rooms are minimalist but as cheap as you'll find.

Big Bend Holiday Hotel HOTEL **$$**
(☎432-201-1177; www.bigbendholidayhotel.com; d $130-140, ste $160, houses $185, Perry Mansion $245) Located spittin' distance from the famous Starlight Theater and Terlingua Porch are three wonderful rooms done up in ranch-style decor with a Spanish influence. They're fairly fancy, for a ghost town, but without putting on airs.

Under the same management company are a suite, a house or the two surprisingly nice bedrooms in the ruins of the Old Perry Mansion. Let 'em know what you want and they'll make you feel right at home.

★**La Posada Milagro** INN **$$**
(☎432-371-3044; www.laposadamilagro.net; 100 Milagro Rd; d $185-210; ❄📶) Built on top of and even incorporating some of the adobe ruins in the historic ghost town, this guesthouse pulls off the amazing feat of providing stylish rooms that blend in perfectly with the surroundings. The decor is west-Texas chic, and there's a nice patio for enjoying the cool evenings. Budget travelers can book a simpler room with four bunk beds for $145 a night.

Eating

Espresso...Y Poco Mas CAFE **$**
(☎432-371-3044; 100 Milagro Rd; food $2.50-6.50; ⏲8am-2pm, to 1pm summer; 📶) We love this friendly little walk-up counter at La Posada Milagro, where you can find pastries, breakfast burritos, lunches and what might just be the best iced coffee in all of west Texas. Like the *casitas* (cottages), the cafe incorporates stone ruins for an authentic ghost-town feel, and the shady patio is a great place to soak up the ambience, make friends, fuel yourself up and use the wi-fi.

Roadrunner Deli DELI **$**
(☎432-371-2364; Study Butte Mall; menu items $3.50-7; ⏲7:30am-2pm Tue-Sat) This deli, east of the Hwy 118 and FM 170 intersection, specializes in packing tasty picnics for the Big Bend–bound, and they also serve breakfast and lunch. There's a grocery store next door if you need to supplement your supplies.

★**Starlight Theatre** AMERICAN **$$**
(☎432-371-2326; www.thestarlighttheatre.com; 631 Ivey St; mains $9-25; ⏲5pm-midnight) You'd think a ghost town would be dead at night (pardon the pun), but the Starlight Theatre keeps things lively. This former movie theater had fallen into roofless disrepair (thus the 'starlight' name) before being converted into a restaurant. Monday nights are famous for two-for-one burgers.

There's live music nearly every night in spring and fall, and if there's no entertainment inside, there's usually someone strumming a guitar outside on the porch. To get there, take Hwy 170 to the ghost town turnoff and follow the road to the end.

La Kiva Restaurant & Bar BARBECUE **$$**
(☎432-371-2250; Hwy 170; mains $10-20; ⏲5-10pm) Talk about your underground restaurants. This quirky place specializing in barbecue and grilled meat is, literally, underground. There's frequent live music, and a ridiculous happy hour from 5pm to 6pm where you can score a draft beer for a buck. Although the kitchen closes at 10pm, the bar is open till midnight. It's about 3 miles west of Hwy 118.

Tivo's Restaurant MEXICAN **$$**
(☎432-371-2133; Hwy 118; meals $8-14; ⏲5-9pm Wed-Sun) This family-run Mexican restaurant gets nothing but kudos from locals. Try the spicy chile rellenos. They also serve gringo fare.

Shopping

Terlingua Trading Co GIFTS
(☎432-371-2234; 100 Ivey St; ⏲11am-8pm) This store in the ghost town has great gifts, from hot sauces and wines to an impressive selection of books. Pick up a brochure on the walking tour of historic Terlingua, or buy a beer inside the store and hang out on the porch with locals at sunset.

Information

Study Butte refers to a cluster of buildings on Hwy 118 immediately outside the west gate of Big Bend. One mile up the road, at the junction of Hwy 118 and FM 170, things pick up a bit; that's where you'll find the Terlingua **post office** (☎432-371-2269) and a 24-hour ATM at **West Texas National Bank** (☎432-371-2211). Head west on FM 170 for more of the town's business district. And keep going 5 miles to reach the historic area called the **Terlingua ghost town**, where you'll find old ruins and new businesses built on top of old ruins.

To get more information on the area, visit the **Big Bend Chamber of Commerce** (☎432-317-3949; www.bigbendchamberofcommerce.org).

WORTH A TRIP

SCENIC DRIVE: RIVER ROAD

West of Lajitas, Rte 170 (also known as River Rd, or El Camino Del Rio in Spanish) hugs the Rio Grande through some of the most spectacular and remote scenery in Big Bend country. Relatively few Big Bend visitors experience this driving adventure, even though it can be navigated in any vehicle with good brakes. Strap in and hold on: you have the Rio Grande on one side and fanciful geological formations all around, and at one point there's a 15% grade – the maximum allowable. When you reach Presidio, head north on US 67 to get to Marfa. Or, if you plan to go back the way you came, at least travel as far as Colorado Canyon (20 miles from Lajitas) for the best scenery.

Lajitas Golf Resort & Spa

About half an hour west from the junction in Terlingua, you can trade funky and dusty for trendy and upscale (but still dusty) at **Lajitas Golf Resort & Spa** (☎432-424-5000; www.lajitasgolfresort.com; d from $169;). What used to be small-town Texas got bought up and revamped into a swanky destination. The old trading post is gone and in its place is a new general store. (The former trading post was the stuff of folk legend, as it was the home of a beer-drinking goat who got elected mayor of the town. Alas, no more.)

The resort has a pool, lighted tennis courts and an 18-hole golf course called **Black Jack's Crossing**. There are also some well-run stables that are open to local visitors whether they're staying at the resort or not. The **Lajitas Equestrian Center** offers horseback trail rides by the hour ($50), sunset rides ($115), and overnight rides to the Buena Suerte Mine and Ghost Town ($400).

As for lodging, you can choose from a range of different experiences around the resort, from motel rooms to condos to RV camps. Among the nicest guest rooms are those in the high-ceilinged **Officers' Quarters**, a complex modeled after the original at Fort Davis.

Big Bend Ranch State Park

At 433 sq miles, **Big Bend Ranch State Park** (☎432-358-4444; www.tpwd.state.tx.us; off Rte 170; adult peak/nonpeak $5/3, child under 12yr free) takes up almost all the desert between Lajitas and Presidio, reaching north from the Rio Grande into some of the wildest country in North America. As massive as it is, this former ranch is one of the best-kept secrets in Big Bend country. It's full of notable features, most prominently the Solitario, a geological formation that sprang up 36 million years ago in a volcanic explosion. The resulting caldera measures 8 miles east to west and 9 miles north to south.

Access to the park is limited and a permit is required, even for hiking along the well-traveled FM 170. If you're coming from Big Bend, you can learn all about the region when you buy your permit at the **Barton Warnock Visitor Center** (☎432-424-3327; www.tpwd.state.tx.us; FM 170; ⌚8am-4:30pm), located at the eastern entrance of the park, 1 mile east of Lajitas on FM 170. This interpretive center is staffed by some of the most knowledgeable folks in the region and offers tons of information on the region's history, geology and landscape. Call for a schedule of interpretive programs ranging from desert wildflowers to the habits of bats.

If you're coming from the west, pick up your permit at **Fort Leaton State Historic Site** (☎432-229-3613; FM 170; ⌚8am-4:30pm), 4 miles southeast of Presidio. This restored adobe built in 1848 once served as a trading post but is now the western entrance to the park.

Since the park has few facilities and much fewer visitors, you should come prepared. Make sure you have spare tires, a full tank of gas, a gallon of water per day per person, sunscreen, a hat, mosquito repellent and a well-stocked first-aid kit.

CENTRAL WEST TEXAS

The small towns of west Texas have become more than just the gateway to Big Bend National Park. Fort Davis, Marfa, Alpine and Marathon have a sprawling, easy-going charm and plenty of ways to keep a road-tripper entertained.

Fort Davis & Davis Mountains

POP 1201

More than 5000ft above sea level, Fort Davis has an altitudinal advantage over the rest of Texas, both in terms of elevation and the cooler weather it offers. That makes it a popular oasis during the summer, when west Texans head towards the mountains to escape the searing desert heat.

The area is part of both the Chihuahuan Desert and the Davis Mountains, giving it a unique setting where wide-open spaces are suddenly interrupted by rock formations springing from the earth. As for the town of Fort Davis, it sprang up near the actual fort of the same name, built in 1854 to protect the pioneers and gold rushers who were heading out west from the attacks of Comanche and Apache warriors. The town retains an Old West feel befitting its history.

Of the towns in this region, Fort Davis is the closest to I-10. The main street through town is a stretch of Hwy 118 that's officially named State St, but everyone around here calls it Main St. The town is so small that, when you turn off Main St, you might well end up on a dirt road. Just a few miles west of town on Hwy 118 is Davis Mountains State Park.

Sights

★McDonald Observatory OBSERVATORY

(☎432-426-3640; www.mcdonaldobservatory.org; 3640 Dark Sky Dr; daytime pass adult/child 6-12yr/under 6yr $8/7/free, star parties adult/child $12/8; ⏲visitor center 10am-5:30pm; 👪) Away from all the light pollution of the big cities, the middle of west Texas has some of the clearest and darkest skies in North America, making it the perfect spot for an observatory. They have some of the biggest telescopes in the world here, perched on the peak of 6791ft Mt Locke and so enormous you can spot them from miles away.

A day pass gets you a guided tour (11am and 2pm) that includes close-up peeks at – but not through – the 107in Harlan J Smith Telescope and the 430in Hobby-Eberly Telescope, as well as a solar viewing, where you get to stare at the sun without scorching your eyeballs. On Tuesday, Friday and Saturday nights, the star parties help you see the night sky in a whole new way.

The observatory is 19 miles northwest of Fort Davis. Allow 30 minutes to drive from town, and get there early because tours fill up fast – especially in March, when they're packed with spring breakers.

Fort Davis National Historic Site HISTORIC SITE

(☎432-426-3224; www.nps.gov/foda; Hwy 17; adult/child $3/free; ⏲8am-5pm except major holidays) A remarkably well-preserved frontier military post with an impressive backdrop at the foot of **Sleeping Lion Mountain**, Fort Davis was established in 1854 and abandoned in 1891. More than 20 buildings remain – five of them restored with period furnishings – as well as 100 or so ruins.

It's easy to picture the fort as it was in 1880, especially with bugle calls sounding in the background. It's even easier in the summer months, when interpreters dressed in period clothing are on hand to describe life at the fort.

The fort is strategically located at the foot of Sleeping Lion Mountain and **Hospital Canyon**. The site serves as trailhead for several hikes, ranging from the 1-mile **Tall Grass Loop** to the more ambitious 3-mile trek to **Davis Mountains State Park**. Ask for a trail map in the fort's visitor center.

Davis Mountains State Park PARK

(☎432-426-3337; http://www.tpwd.state.tx.us; Hwy 118; adult/child under 12yr $6/free) Just a few miles northwest of Fort Davis on Hwy 118, set amid the most extensive mountain range in Texas, is Davis Mountains State

A STAR-STUDDED EVENT

On Tuesday, Friday and Saturday nights, about half an hour after sunset, McDonald Observatory shows off its favorite planets, galaxies and globular clusters at its popular **star parties**, where professional astronomers guide you in some heavy-duty stargazing. Using ridiculously powerful laser pointers, they give you a tour of the night sky, and you'll get to use some of the telescopes to play planetary peeping Tom. Remember: it gets cold up there at night, even in the summer, so wear layers you don't think you'll need – lest you find yourself plunking down $30 for a hoodie from the gift shop.

WORTH A TRIP

DETOUR: BALMORHEA STATE PARK

Swimming, scuba diving and snorkeling are the attractions at the 46-acre **Balmorhea State Park** (☎432-375-2370; www.tpwd.state.tx.us; Hwy 17; adult/under 12yr $7/free; ⏲8am-sunset), a true oasis in the west Texas desert. The swimming pool covers 1.75 acres, making it the largest spring-fed swimming facility in the US, 25ft deep and about 75°F year-round. The park is at Toyahvale, 5 miles south of the town of Balmorhea (pronounced bal-mo-ray), which itself is just off I-10.

Park. Hiking, mountain biking, horseback riding (BYO horse) and stargazing are all big attractions here, as is bird-watching. Pick up a bird checklist from park headquarters so you know what you're looking at, or, if you already know what you're looking at, use it to impress your bird-watching friends.

With mountains come views, and there's no better place to enjoy your position than at an overlook at the top of Skyline Dr. In daylight, you can check out the surrounding area and neighboring mountain ranges. Dusk brings majestic sunsets, and after dark – and boy does it get dark – you can test your knowledge of the constellations.

Overnighters can camp within the park or bunk down at Indian Lodge (p315).

Overland Trail Museum MUSEUM
(☎432-426-3904; Fort & 3rd Sts; donations accepted; ⏲1-5pm Tue-Sun) Pioneer doohickeys and Old West thing-a-majigs are on this display in the former home of early settler Nick Mersfelter, located right along the stagecoach route known as the Overland Trail. And it's not just personal whatnots you'll find; there are larger displays like the original switchboard from nearby Valentine.

Rattlers & Reptiles MUSEUM
(☎432-426-2465; 1600 N State St; adult/child under 10yr $4/1; ⏲10am-dark) Snakes, spiders, scorpions...all the things you should check your boots for before you put them on can be seen on display at the funky little Rattlers & Reptiles. Sure, the critters on display give some people the willies, but better to run into them here than out on the trail or, worse yet, in your tent.

Chihuahuan Desert Nature Center NATURE RESERVE
(☎432-364-2499; www.cdri.org; 43869 Hwy 118; adult/child under 12yr $6/free; ⏲9am-5pm Mon-Sat) Four miles south of town, the Chihuahuan Desert Nature Center exhibits the region's flora in gardens and on trails. Take a 2-mile hike down into a canyon, watch butterflies flitting around wildflower gardens, check out a permanent exhibit on mining, or visit the cactus greenhouse.

Activities

Scenic Drive

Pack up the kids or hop on your bikes and head out for 75 miles of paved splendor on this scenic drive through the Davis Mountains. First you go up, up, up, then you come down, down, down. The countryside is so gorgeous, it's no wonder this is considered one of the most scenic drives in the US. It's also tops among cyclists – at least, the ones who can handle the climb.

Head out on Hwy 118 northwest from town, then turn left on Hwy 166, which loops you back to town. Or go the opposite route; both afford equally appealing views, although the former is better in the morning so you're not driving or riding into the sun, while the latter is better in the afternoon.

Cycling

Fort Davis is one of Texas' best areas for road cycling. In addition to the aforementioned Scenic Loop Dr, which is as challenging as it is dramatic, there's some nice, gentle terrain just outside of town for casual cyclists. Unfortunately, there's no place in town that rents bikes, so you'll have to bring your own either from home or from another town.

Horseback Riding

Going for a horseback ride is a natural in the Old West setting of Fort Davis. If you find yourself without a trusty steed, try out one of the one-hour guided horseback tours at **Prude Ranch** (☎432-426-3202; www.prude-ranch.com; Hwy 118; 1hr rides $30), 6 miles northwest of town. Choose from a one-hour trail ride or a half-day ride with sack lunch.

Sleeping

Stone Village Tourist Camp MOTEL $
(☎432-426-3941; www.stonevillagetouristcamp.com; 509 N State St; camp r $44, d $69-99; 📶🏊) This renovated motor court is a fun little bargain. The 14 regular rooms are cheery and comfortable, and the six camp rooms are perfect for the budget traveler. Located in the former garages, they have concrete floors, stone walls, a roof, electricity, a sink and even wi-fi. The only catch? One end of the room has a screen and privacy curtain instead of a wall. If you're looking for more room, inquire about a suite or house rental.

Old Schoolhouse Bed & Breakfast B&B $
(☎432-426-2050; www.schoolhousebnb.com; 401 Front St; r incl breakfast s $84-93, d $96-105; ❄📶) You can't really tell it used to be the town's schoolhouse, but you can tell the owners put a lot of work into being great hosts, from the comfy rooms to the wonderful homemade breakfasts.

Davis Mountains State Park CAMPGROUND $
(☎park office 432-426-3337, reservations 512-389-8900; www.tpwd.state.tx.us; Hwy 118; tent sites $8-15, RV hookups $20-25) Pitch your tent here and the stargazing can go on till the wee hours. The campsites are in a lush, tree-shaded environment and include picnic tables and grills. Backcountry camping and RV hookups are also available.

★**Indian Lodge** INN $$
(☎lodge 432-426-3254, reservations 512-389-8982; Hwy 118; d $95-125, ste $135-150; ❄📶🏊) Located in the Davis Mountains State Park, this historic 39-room inn has 18in-thick adobe walls, hand-carved cedar furniture and ceilings of pine *viga* and *latilla* that give it the look of a Southwestern pueblo – that is, one with swimming pool, gift shop and restaurant. The comfortable and surprisingly spacious guest rooms are a steal, so reserve early.

When the lodge is full, the on-site restaurant often does a breakfast buffet. Don't pass it up; it's an amazing spread.

Hotel Limpia HOTEL $$
(☎800-662-5517, 432-426-3237; www.hotellimpia.com; 101 Memorial Sq; r $95-119; ste $129-149; 🚭📶🏊) Built in 1912, this historic hotel leans heavily on antiques and floral prints, in a Victorian-meets–Old West kind of way, like the womenfolk came along and gussied up the place. There are few finer places to kick back than on the rocking chairs on the back porch.

Eating & Drinking

Local liquor laws mean you can't order an adult beverage with your dinner; however, almost every place in town is cheerfully BYOB, with the exception of the Black Bear (where it's forbidden) and Blue Mountain Bistro (which has a bar). There aren't a ton of restaurant choices in Fort Davis. Keep in mind that Marfa is only 22 miles away.

Cueva de Leon MEXICAN $
(☎432-426-3801; 100 W 2nd St; mains $6-11; ⏲11am-3pm & 5-9pm Mon-Sat) While El Paso has a Mexican restaurant on practically every street corner, they're harder to find in central west Texas, so grab some decent enchiladas and chile rellenos while you can at this local favorite. Remember, this is a dry county, so pick up some cerveza at a grocery store if you'd like to imbibe.

Fort Davis Drug Store AMERICAN $$
(☎432-426-3118; www.fortdavisdrugstore.net; 113 N State St; mains $6-19; ⏲7am-9pm daily; 📶👪) Part diner, part old-fashioned soda fountain – but no 1950s nostalgia here. The theme is pure cowboy, with corrugated metal, big wooden chairs and lots of saddles providing the backdrop. Dine on country-style breakfasts, diner-style lunches and full entrees at dinner. But whatever you do, save room for a banana split (or at least a milkshake).

Black Bear Restaurant AMERICAN $$
(☎432-426-3254; 16453 Park Rd 3 at Indian Lodge; breakfast $8-10, dinner mains $12-17; ⏲7am-8pm Sun-Thu, to 9pm Fri & Sat) What could have been a perfunctory restaurant at the Indian Lodge within Davis Mountains State Park is actually a more-than-decent dining option. We can't speak for all the meals – the evening menu has limited options – but we were lucky enough to enjoy a breakfast buffet (served most weekends) that was laden with hot, delicious treats. More biscuits and gravy? Yes please!

Murphy's Pizzeria & Café PIZZERIA $$
(107 Musquiz Dr; mains $7-13; ⏲11am-9pm Mon & Wed-Sat) Plenty of choices, including thin-crust pizza, sandwiches and salads, make this casual cafe an easy sell when you need to grab a bite.

Blue Mountain Bistro AMERICAN $$$
(www.blue-mountain-bistro.com; 101 Memorial Sq; mains $18-29; ⏲11am-2pm & 5-9pm Tue-Fri, 9am-noon & 5-9pm Sat, 9am-noon Sun) Located next to the Hotel Limpia – and ostensibly taking the place of their much-missed dining room – Blue Mountain Bistro seems to be the only upscale dining option in town. We don't know how they did it, but they also have the only bar in Jeff Davis County – and it's a full bar at that! Good to know when a six pack from the grocery store just won't do.

Information

On Sundays this sleepy little town takes a full day of rest; most of the businesses are closed till Monday. To find out what's going on, visit the **Fort Davis Chamber of Commerce** (☎432-426-3015; www.fortdavis.com; 4 Memorial Sq; ⏲9am-5pm Mon-Fri) at the junction of Hwys 118 and 17.

You can get cash (even on Sunday) at **Fort Davis State Bank** (☎432-426-3211; 100 S State St), which has a 24-hour ATM. Hook up to free wi-fi at the **Jeff Davis County Library** (☎432-426-3802; 100 Memorial Sq; ⏲10am-6pm Mon-Fri) – housed in the former county jail between the town square and the courthouse – or at the Fort Davis Drug Store (p315).

Getting There & Around

No regularly scheduled public transportation serves Fort Davis or the Davis Mountains. You can get to nearby Alpine (24 miles away) by train or bus, then rent a car. The closest airports are Midland International Airport (about 160 miles away) and El Paso International Airport (194 miles away).

Marfa

POP 1981

The first thing you might wonder about Marfa is, 'Where did all these New Yorkers come from?' and the second, 'What's the deal with James Dean?' Founded in the 1880s, Marfa's two major cultural influences came in the latter part of the 20th century. It got its first taste of fame when Rock Hudson, Elizabeth Taylor and, yes, James Dean came to town to film the 1956 Warner Brothers film *Giant*, and has since served as a film location for movies such as *There Will Be Blood* and *No Country for Old Men*.

And as for those New Yorkers: tiny, dusty Marfa has become a bit of a pilgrimage for art lovers, thanks to one of the world's largest installations of minimalist art. This, in turn, has attracted a disproportionate number of art galleries, quirky lodging options and interesting restaurants. Throw in some mysterious lights that may or may not be aliens (OK, probably not, but it's fun to pretend) and Marfa has become a majorly buzzed-about destination.

Sights & Activities

Yep, it's small. One mile in any direction from the center of town, and you've just left town. Also? Marfa is on its own schedule, which is pretty much made up according to whim. Plan on coming late in the week or on a weekend, because more than half the places you'll want to visit are closed early in the week.

If you didn't come to Marfa for the art, you might be surprised to find the amazing concentration of galleries in town. We're not talking about rustic cowboy art framed in barbed wire and old barn wood. And we're not just talking about Donald Judd–esque minimalism, either. The town has all sorts of art to explore, most of it contemporary; you can pick up a list of galleries at the **visitor center** (☎432-729-4942; www.visitmarfa.com; 302 S Highland Ave; ⏲9am-5pm Mon-Fri & on event weekends).

★**Ballroom Marfa** GALLERY
(☎432-729-3600; www.ballroommarfa.org; 108 E San Antonio; ⏲10am-6pm Wed-Sat, to 3pm Sun) Be sure to find out what's happening at Ballroom Marfa, a nonprofit art space located in a former dance hall. The focus is on offbeat, interesting projects, including film installations and excellent monthly concerts. They're also working on an ambitious new project: a drive-in theater and outdoor venue slated for 2015.

Chinati Foundation Museum MUSEUM
(☎432-729-4362; www.chinati.org; 1 Calvary Row; adult/student $25/10; ⏲by guided tour only 10am & 2pm Wed-Sun) This is it. This is what all the fuss is about. Minimalist artist Donald Judd single-handedly put Marfa on the art-world map when he created the Chinati Foundation on the site of a former army post, using the abandoned buildings to create and display one of the world's largest permanent installations of minimalist art.

This is great news if you like minimalist art. But the tour draws equal numbers of people who look like they're gazing upon works of genius and people who look like they're going to say 'What the hell was that about?' as soon as they get in their car. (It's also a bit of a commitment, taking up the better part of a day: the tour is broken into two parts and goes from 10am to noon and 2pm to 4pm).

Not sure if you're in their demographic? It's worth a gander at the website to be certain you're a fan.

Marfa Mystery Lights LOOKOUT
Ghost lights, mystery lights…call them what you want, but the Marfa Lights that flicker beneath the Chinati Mountains have captured the imagination of many a traveler over the decades. On many nights, the mystery seems to be whether you're actually just seeing car headlights in the distance.

However, there are convincing enough accounts of mysterious lights that appear and disappear on the horizon – accounts that go all the way back to before there was such a thing as cars. In fact, the cowboy who first reported seeing them in 1883 thought they were Apache signal fires.

Try your luck at the **Marfa Lights Viewing Area** about 9 miles east of Marfa on Hwy 90/67. Look to the south and find the red blinking light. That's where you will (or won't) see the lights doing their ghostly thing. This phenomenon is best enjoyed if you can channel your inner pre-teen (all the better if you actually are a pre-teen) and simply choose to believe something really exciting has just happened.

Marfa & Presidio County Museum MUSEUM
(432-729-4140; 110 W San Antonio St; donations accepted; 2-5pm Tue-Sat) Wandering around this homegrown museum is kind of like exploring your grandmother's attic: lots of old stuff to look at that gives you a glimpse into the past but isn't necessarily organized in any strikingly prescriptive way. The one area where the museum beats out grandma is with its excellent collection of black-and-white photography documenting west Texas in the early 19th century.

GODDESS OF JUSTICE

High atop the **Presidio County Courthouse** dome is the Goddess of Justice, one hand holding a sword and the other holding – hey, wait, where are her scales? Her empty left hand, which lingers in the air almost like she's checking her watch, probably did once hold a set of scales, as Goddesses of Justice so often do. But legend has it that a gun-slinging cowboy back in the late 1800s shot them out of her hand with a rifle, saying, 'There is no justice in Presidio County.' One way or the other, it makes a good story, and when the courthouse was restored in 2001 no attempt was made to restore the scales.

Festivals & Events

Every May or June, Marfa puts on the **Marfa Film Festival** (www.marfafilmfestival.org), screening features and shorts – including some of the Texas-centric films that have used Marfa as a location. And September brings the **Marfa Lights Festival** – which has little to do with the lights and is really just a good excuse to throw a town-wide street party.

Sleeping

Riata Inn MOTEL $
(432-729-3800; www.riatainnmarfa.com; 1500 E Hwy 90; d $71-82;) With all the interesting choices in town, the main reason to choose this motel is the low price – but the super-sized rooms and super-friendly manager are a nice plus. The parking lot is also a prime viewing area for the Marfa Lights.

★**El Cosmico** CAMPGROUND $$
(432-729-1950; www.elcosmico.com; 802 S Highland Ave; tent camping per person $12, safari tents $65, teepees $80, trailers $110-180;) One of the funkiest choices in all of Texas, El Cosmico lets you sleep in a stylishly converted travel trailer, a teepee or a safari tent. It's not for everyone: the grounds are dry and dusty, you might have to shower outdoors, and there's no AC (luckily, it's cool at night). But, hey, how often do you get to sleep in a Kozy Coach? The cool and colorful community lounge and the hammock grove make particularly pleasant common areas.

Thunderbird BOUTIQUE HOTEL $$
(877-729-1984; www.thunderbirdmarfa.com; 601 W San Antonio St; d $120-150;) This classic 1950s motel was reopened in 2005 as a small boutique with a spiffy new look. The rooms are hip and minimalist, and the grounds and common areas are as cool as the desert air at night.

Stay Marfa APARTMENT $$
(888-627-3246; www.marfaretreat.com; San Antonio & Dean Sts; 1-bedroom apt $89-109,

2-bedroom apt $139; ❄📶) For the price of a room, you can enjoy a whole apartment decorated in a cool, modern style that's one part Ikea, one part art gallery. The apartments come about their aesthetic rightly: they're owned and decorated by the fellows at local gallery Inde/Jacobs.

Hotel Paisano HOTEL **$$**
(☎432-729-3669; www.hotelpaisano.com; 207 N Highland Ave; d $99-149, ste $159-220; ❄@📶🏊) Marfa's historic hotel has a unique claim to fame: it's where the cast of the movie *Giant* stayed. Some of the rooms could stand a little updating, but the place does have a dignified charm, along with a snazzy indoor pool and a touch of taxidermy for good measure.

Cibolo Creek Ranch RANCH **$$$**
(☎432-229-3737; www.cibolocreekranch.com; d $250-345, ste $500; ❄📶🏊) If you just really want to get away from it all, this luxurious private ranch is definitely *away*. Marfa is the closest town, but it's still a 45-minute drive (part of the reason the ranch offers a meal plan for an additional $75 a day). They even have a private airstrip, and, if for some reason you don't have your own plane, arrangements can be made.

Eating & Drinking

Restaurant schedules tend to be fickle around here, so call ahead if you want to double-check hours, or be prepared to be flexible.

Food Shark FOOD TRUCK **$**
(105 S Highland Ave; meals $5-8; ⏲noon-3pm Thu-Sat) See that battered old food trailer pulled up under the open-air pavilion where the weekend farmers market is? If you do, that means Food Shark is open for business. If you're lucky enough to catch them, you'll find incredibly fresh food like pulled-pork tacos and their specialty, the Marfalafel. Daily specials are excellent, and sell out early.

Future Shark AMERICAN **$**
(☎432-729-4278; www.foodsharkmarfa.com; 120 N Highland Ave; mains $7-13; ⏲11am-7pm Mon-Fri) Hooray! The Food Shark truck finally has a bricks-and-mortar restaurant serving up similarly awesome fare as the popular truck, but cafeteria style. The additional days and hours Future Shark is open are a boon to hungry travelers, who sometimes line up out the door waiting to get hold of the Shark's Mediterranean-influenced dishes.

The Get Go MARKET **$**
(208 S Dean St; ⏲9am-8pm) This fancy-pants grocer caters to Marfa's sophisticated world travelers' highly developed palates. Because one must have access to one's Nicolas Feuillatte champagne, organic goats-milk yogurt and yerba mate tea when one is traveling in the desert, *n'est ce pas*? All kidding aside, it's kind of amazing what wonderful treats you can find in the aisles of this small-town grocery.

Squeeze Marfa CAFE **$**
(☎432-729-4500; www.squeezemarfa.com; 215 N Highland Ave; mains $5-8; ⏲8am-4pm Tue-Sat, to 2pm Sun) This cute little cafe across from the courthouse serves fresh and healthy breakfasts, lunches and smoothies, all the better to enjoy on the pleasant, shady patio. The address is on Highland, but the entrance is on Lincoln.

★**Cochineal** AMERICAN **$$$**
(☎432-729-3300; 107 W San Antonio St; breakfast $4-10, small plates $5-15, dinner $24-28; ⏲brunch 9am-1pm Sat & Sun, dinner 6-10pm Thu-Tue) This is where foodies get their fix at dinnertime, with a menu that changes regularly due to a focus on local, organic ingredients. Portions are generous, so don't be afraid to share a few small plates in lieu of a full dinner. Weekend brunch is also a treat. Reservations are recommended.

★**Planet Marfa** BAR
(☎432-386-5099; 200 S Abbott St; ⏲2pm-midnight Fri-Sun) Nightlife, Marfa style, is epitomized in this wonderfully funky open-air bar. There's usually live music at night, and shelters are scattered about to protect you from the elements. If you're lucky, someone will have saved you a spot inside the teepee.

Padre's BAR
(209 W El Paso St; meals $3-8; ⏲4pm-midnight Wed-Fri, noon-1am Sat, 2-10pm Sun) Padre's makes sense when there's live music playing; otherwise it just seems like a cavernous dive bar (not that there's anything wrong with that). The kitchen stays open until 9pm serving up bar food like burgers and Frito pie, which is a welcome find in a town where many restaurants close early.

Shopping

Marfa Book Company BOOKS
(☎432-729-3906; 105 S Highland Ave; ⏲10am-7pm Wed-Sat, 11am-5pm Sun) A book lover's oasis in the middle of desolate west Texas, Marfa Book Company stocks art books,

guidebooks and a large selection of Texas literature.

Information

To get started and pick up some handy maps, stop by the Marfa Visitors Center (p316). Get free internet access at the **Marfa Public Library** (☎432-729-4631; 115 E Oak St), and if you need to restock your wallet, **Marfa National Bank** (☎432-729-4344; 301 S Highland Ave) has a 24-hour ATM.

Getting There & Away

There is an airport in Marfa, but you can't catch a flight there unless you actually charter one. Closest airports for the non–Howard Hughes set are Midland (156 miles away) and El Paso (190 miles away). You can, however, catch a Greyhound. The **bus station** (☎432-729-8174; 3988 Hwy 90 W) is at the old Jimenez Chevron Station, and Amtrak serves nearby Alpine (26 miles away).

Alpine

POP 5905

Centrally located as the hub between Fort Davis, Marfa and Marathon, Alpine is about a half-hour drive from any of them. And it's not just a hub, geographically speaking: it's the seat of Brewster County and the biggest of the four towns, offering services and amenities the others don't. The only city in the area with more than 5000 people, it also has the area's sole four-year college and its only modern hospital.

Sights & Activities

Museum of the Big Bend MUSEUM

(☎432-837-8143; www.sulross.edu/museum; 400 N Harrison St; donations accepted; 9am-5pm Tue-Sat, 1-5pm Sun) This interesting little museum has been around since 1937, but a complete renovation in 2006 has made it a great place to brush up on the history of the Big Bend region. Learn about how Big Bend was once under the sea, and find out how camels fit into the region's history.

The museum is designed for maximum visual appeal, incorporating broad and impressive re-creations rather than cases full of relics. Reading is kept to a minimum, but, when called for, the beautifully designed signage draws you right in.

Most impressive? The enormous wing bone of the Texas pterosaur found in Big Bend National Park – the largest flying creature ever found, with an estimated wing span of more than 50ft – along with the intimidatingly large re-creation of the whole bird that's big enough to snatch up a fully grown human and carry him off for dinner.

WHAT THE...? PRADA

So you're driving along a two-lane highway in dusty west Texas, out in the middle of nowhere, when suddenly a small building appears in the distance like a mirage. As you zip past it you glance over and see...a Prada store? Known as the **Prada Marfa** (although it's really closer to Valentine), this art installation doesn't sell $1700 handbags, but it does get your attention as a tongue-in-cheek comment on consumerism.

Woodward Ranch ROCK HUNTING

(☎432-364-2271; www.woodwardranch.com; adult/child under 6yr $5/free; 9am-5pm Mon-Sat) Hunt for red plume and pom-pom Texas agate, jasper, labradorite feldspar, calcite, opal and other minerals at the Woodward Ranch. This 100-year-old cattle ranch is 16 miles south of town on Hwy 118 and has nearly 3000 acres open to rock hounds. It's $3 a pound for whatever you keep, or, if you prefer easy pickings, visit the **rock shop** (9am-5pm).

They also have camping ($20) and RV sites ($35) if you care to bunk down for the night.

Festivals & Events

Preserving the oral tradition of the American West, the annual **Cowboy Poetry Gathering** (www.texascowboypoetry.com) is held every year in late February or early March. This down-home event takes over most of town, from university classrooms to Kokernot Park. Poetry recitations, gun-twirling pistolero demonstrations and chuck-wagon breakfasts are just some of the activities.

Sul Ross State University is the birthplace of intercollegiate rodeo, and many members of the Sul Ross Rodeo Club have gone on to win national championships. Watch these collegiate cowboys strut their stuff each fall at the **Sul Ross National Intercollegiate Rodeo Association Rodeo**.

Sleeping

You must book hotel rooms several months in advance if you plan on attending the

Cowboy Poetry Gathering. Visit the chamber of commerce website at www.alpinetexas.com for more lodging options.

Antelope Lodge CABIN $
(☎432-837-2451; www.antelopelodge.com; 2310 W Hwy 90; s $53-75, d $58-80, ste $105-120;) You'd think from the name you were getting a hunting lodge, but it's nothing like that. Rustic stucco cottages with Spanish-tile roofs – each one holding two guest rooms – sit sprinkled about a shady lawn. There's a casual, pleasant vibe, and the rooms have kitchenettes, making this great value for your money.

★Holland Hotel HISTORIC HOTEL $$
(☎432-837-3844, 800-535-8040; www.thehollandhoteltexas.com; 209 W Holland Ave; d $99-120, ste $120-220;) Some renovations suck all the charm out of a historic property, and some don't go far enough. But sometimes they get it just right. Built in 1928 and beautifully renovated in 2009, the Holland is a Spanish Colonial building furnished with an understated, hacienda-style decor that retains all of its 1930s charm, but with just the right contemporary touches.

Add in a lovely (and free!) breakfast, and you'll feel downright pampered. Fair warning: the train tracks go right by here, so wear the provided earplugs lest you hear a friendly *woo-woo* in the night.

Maverick Inn MOTEL $$
(☎432-837-0628; www.themaverickinn.com; 1200 E Holland Ave; r $96-117;) The maverick road-tripper will feel right at home at this retro motor court that's been smartly renovated to include luxury bedding and flat-screen TVs. We can't help but love this place, from the west Texas–style furnishings to the cool neon-art sign to the resident cat. Plus, the pool is mighty nice after a hot, dusty day.

Eating

Alicia's Burrito Place MEXICAN $
(☎432-837-2802; 708 E Ave G; mains $4-11; ⏲8am-8:30pm Mon, Tue & Thu-Sat, to 3pm Wed, to 4pm Sun) Alicia's is known for its quick and hot breakfast burritos, which, yes, is a Texas thing. Eggs, bacon and the like get rolled up in a portable meal you can eat with your hands – known to cure a hangover or two in their time. The Mexican cheeseburger is also a favorite.

Murphy St Raspa Co. ICE CREAM $
(100 W Murphy St; ⏲noon-7pm Sun, Mon & Wed, to 8pm Thu-Sat;) Part Mexican *tienda* (store), part ice-cream shop, this colorful place sells Mexican handicrafts and nearly 50 flavors of shaved ice. There's ice cream on the menu too, if you'd rather, plus drinks, of course – the perfect place to cool off on a hot summer afternoon.

Bread & Breakfast CAFE $
(☎432-837-9424; 114 W Holland Ave; mains $5-9; ⏲7am-2pm Wed-Mon) The name is kind of misleading in that they also have lunch, but that's just not as alliterative. This pleasant little bakery-cafe is adept at the baked goods; if nothing else, stop in for a brownie.

La Casita MEXICAN $
(☎432-837-2842; 1104 E Ave H; mains $5-10; ⏲11am-8:30pm Mon-Sat) This Mexican restaurant is one of the most popular places in town. If you can get a seat, join the locals over a plate (and be careful, the plate is hot) of spicy, cheesy specialties.

★Reata STEAKHOUSE $$
(☎432-837-9232; www.reata.net; 203 N 5th St; lunch $9-14, dinner $10-25; ⏲11:30am-2pm & 5-10pm Mon-Sat, 11:30am-2pm Sun) Named after the ranch in the movie *Giant,* Reata does turn on the upscale ranch-style charm – at least in the front dining room, where the serious diners go. Step back into the lively bar area or onto the shady patio and it's a completely different vibe, where you can feel free to nibble your way around the menu and enjoy a margarita. (The tortilla soup brought us back the next day for seconds.)

Century Bar & Grill AMERICAN $$
(☎432-837-1922; 209 W Holland Ave; mains $13-34; ⏲11am-2:30pm Wed-Sun, dinner 6pm-close nightly) Located inside the Holland Hotel, this place has the same vibe as the rest of the building: historic but fashionable, like a ranch done in dark woods with splashy touches. The excellent food – American, but leaning toward Texan – is a nice addition to the Alpine dining scene.

Reservations recommended. Be sure to at least check to make sure they're open, if for no other reason than the schedule seemed to be in flux at time of research.

Entertainment

It may be a small town, but it's a college town, which means Alpine does have a thing or two going on after dark.

Harry's Tinaja LIVE MUSIC

(☎432-837-5060; 412 E Holland Ave; ⏲noon-2am) This locals' watering hole is fun, a little divey, and occasionally even boisterous. You're likely to find friendly old-timers hanging out and telling stories till the wee hours, but if not, there's also a pool table and sometimes there's live music. Posted hours are till 2am, but if you find 'em closed, it's 'cause no one showed up that night.

Railroad Blues LIVE MUSIC

(☎432-837-3103; www.railroadblues.com; 504 W Holland Ave; ⏲4pm-2am) This is the place to go in Alpine for live music and the biggest beer selection in Big Bend country. The club has hosted an impressive list of musicians, and sometimes draws Austin-based bands heading west on tour. Happy hour is 4pm till 7pm if you'd rather just enjoy some friendly conversation.

Shopping

Kiowa Gallery ARTS & CRAFTS, GIFTS

(☎432-837-3067; 105 E Holland Ave; ⏲10am-5pm Tue-Sun) Paintings, folk art, cool crafts and jewelry fill this space floor to ceiling. Offerings range from real art to just fun stuff to hang on the wall, all with a uniquely west Texas take on things.

Front Street Books BOOKS

(☎432-837-3360; www.fsbooks.com; 121 E Holland Ave; ⏲9am-6pm Mon-Fri, 10am-6pm Sat, 1-6pm Sun) The best bookstore in town is open daily and has a smart selection of new, used and out-of-print titles – as well as the *New York Times* and *Wall Street Journal,* which are rare commodities out this way. With a surprising number of well-known authors living in the area, this bookstore has some pretty big-city book signings too.

Information

In addition to providing lots of local information, Alpine's **Chamber of Commerce** (☎432-837-2326; www.alpinetexas.com; 106 N 3rd St; ⏲8am-5pm Mon-Fri, to 4pm Sat) has put together a *Historic Walking & Windshield Tour* brochure featuring 39 stops in the downtown area plus a few notable spots further out. Get a copy of the brochure at the chamber office.

Alpine Post Office (☎432-837-9565; 901 W Holland Ave; ⏲8am-4pm Mon-Fri, 10am-1pm Sat)

Alpine Public Library (☎432-837-2621; 203 N 7th St; ⏲9:30am-5:30pm Mon-Sat, 10am-1pm Sun) Free internet access.

FIRST THANKSGIVING

We all know that the first Thanksgiving was celebrated in 1621 at Plymouth, right? Not so fast, says El Paso. In 1598, while traveling from Mexico to Santa Fe with an eye toward settling the Southwest, Don Juan de Oñate led 500 followers to the banks of the Rio Grande at what is now San Elizario, Texas. There, the Spanish colonists met with Native Americans for what many El Pasoans say was the real first Thanksgiving, 23 years before the Pilgrims feasted at Plymouth Rock in Massachusetts. Anyone who loves their traditional Thanksgiving feast should give thanks that we celebrate the 1621 version, since the 1598 event occurred on April 30. (Just try finding fresh pumpkin in April.)

Big Bend Regional Medical Center (☎432-837-3447; 2600 Hwy 118 N) One of the region's most state-of-the-art hospitals, offering basic care and a 24-hour emergency room.

Fort Davis State Bank (☎432-837-1888; 1102 E Holland Ave) A 24-hour ATM service near Sul Ross State University.

West Texas National Bank (☎432-837-3375; 101 E Ave E) A 24-hour ATM service right in the middle of town.

Getting There & Around

There are no scheduled flights round these parts, but Alpine's airport, north of town along Hwy 118, can accommodate charter flights.

There is, however, an **Amtrak station** (☎800-872-7245; www.amtrak.com; 102 W Holland Ave). The train frequently runs anywhere from one to eight hours late in both directions, so it's important to call Amtrak to get an update before setting out for the station. Check the website for prices and schedules.

Alpine is served by **Greyhound** (☎432-837-5497; 2305 E Hwy 90) with service to and from El Paso, San Antonio and beyond.

Rental cars are available from **Alpine Auto Rental** (☎432-837-3463; www.alpineautorental.com; 2501 E Hwy 90; ⏲8am-6pm Mon-Sat).

Marathon

POP 430

Just don't show up and call it 'Mar-a-THON' like it's a race. If you want to fit in 'round these parts you have got to say 'Mar-a-thun,' and it helps if you're wearing a hat and give a friendly nod each time you say it.

This tiny railroad town has two claims to fame: it's the closest town to Big Bend's north entrance, providing a last chance to fill up your car and your stomach before immersing yourself in the park. And it's got the Gage Hotel, a true Texas treasure that's a worthwhile reason to stay awhile – at least overnight.

Sights & Activities

There's not a whole lot do in Marathon for the average tourist. If you're into birdwatching or feel in the mood for a picnic, you could head 5 miles south of town on Ave D, west of Hwy 385, to **Fort Peña Colorado** – a former military outpost that's now a public park known locally as 'the Post.'

Festivals & Events

With a name like Marathon – pronunciation aside – this was bound to happen. The **Marathon2Marathon** (www.marathon2marathon.net) is a 26.2-mile run through the desert from Alpine to Marathon, and it's a qualifying race for the Boston Marathon, which, after west Texas, should be a cinch. Runners and nonrunners alike mark the occasion with a street festival.

Sleeping

For such a small town, there are actually several interesting lodging options, including rental houses. Check out the listings on www.marathontexas.com.

Marathon Motel & RV Park CABIN $
(432-386-4241; 701 US Hwy 90; d $65-100, RV hookups $25;) A lot of places in Texas seem to have their claim to fame, and this renovated 1940s motor court got its 15 minutes when it was used as a location for the filming of Wim Wenders' film *Paris, Texas*. The cabins are rustic but cute, and a lovely central courtyard surrounded by an adobe wall makes a nice place to hang out.

Gage Hotel HISTORIC HOTEL $$
(432-386-4205; www.gagehotel.com; 102 NW 1st St/Hwy 90; d with shared bathroom $97, with private bathroom $136-156;) This Old West hotel has a fabulous style that's matched only by its love of taxidermy. Each room at this property is individually (though similarly) decorated with Indian blankets, cowboy gear and leather accents. The original building was designed by Henry Trost and built in 1927, and the Los Portales annex has more expensive rooms that surround the lovely pool.

Eating & Drinking

The main drag has a couple of restaurants that are open till early afternoon. After 3pm, your choices are extremely limited.

Marathon Coffee Shop CAFE $
(301 NW 1st St; mains $4-10; 7am-3pm;) Breakfast enchiladas? Don't mind if we do! This stylin' coffee shop serves up breakfast, lunch, coffee and wi-fi – all essential 'gets' for the Big Bend–bound.

French Co. Grocer MARKET $
(432-386-4522; www.frenchcogrocer.com; 206 N Ave D; 7:30am-9pm Mon-Fri, from 8am Sat, from 9am Sun) Stock up on picnic supplies for the road or enjoy them at the tables outside at this charming little grocery – formerly the WM French General Merchandise store, established in 1900. They also stock toothbrushes, fresh-baked cookies, wine, cookout necessities, hats – things you might need if, oh, say, you were about to go camp in a remote national park.

12 Gage AMERICAN $$$
(432-386-4205; 101 US 90 W; dinner mains $17-37; 6-8:45pm Sun & Mon-Thu, to 9:45pm Fri & Sat) This restaurant at the Gage serves up upscale Western comfort food in a ranch-fabulous setting. Menus change seasonally, but it's safe to expect some meat on the menu. Cowskin-covered chairs, chandeliers made of horns and a modicum of taxidermy add to the atmosphere, which is remarkably elegant.

White Buffalo Bar BAR
(432-386-4205; 101 US 90 W; 5pm-midnight) Guess what's on the wall of this upscale bar located in the Gage Hotel? Not just taxidermy but *rare* taxidermy. Enjoy a margarita, and try to ignore his glassy stare.

Information

If you want to know more about Marathon, you can get in touch with the **Marathon Chamber of Commerce** (432-386-4516; www.marathontexas.com; 105 Hwy 90 W) in Front Street Books and they'll help you explore all your options.

Getting There & Away

There is no public transportation to Marathon. Amtrak serves Alpine, 32 miles west on Hwy 90.

EL PASO

POP 800,647

Well, you've made it. You're just about as far west in Texas as you can go. Surrounded mostly by New Mexico to the north and Mexico to the south, El Paso is wedged between the two like a splinter. In fact, at times the city seems to have more in common with its non-Texas neighbors than it does with Texas itself.

Sadly, El Paso and its sister city – Ciudad Juárez, Mexico, which is right across the river – have had a bit of a falling out. At one time, the two cities were inextricably linked, with tourists streaming back and forth across the Good Neighbor International Bridge all day long. But with the rise in gang- and drug-related violence, Juárez has become so dangerous that there is now little traffic between the two sides.

Even with Mexico out of the equation, there's still plenty to do. Outdoorsy types can enjoy cycling in the largest urban park in the US, with over 24,000 acres to explore, and the warm weather makes nearby Hueco Tanks an ideal destination for wintertime rock climbing. Or you can go the culture route and enjoy some of El Paso's excellent museums, most of which are free. Ride the gondola to a mountain peak, buy handcrafted boots and, by all means, eat some of the city's famous red enchiladas.

History

Native Americans had already settled the El Paso area for thousands of years when Spanish explorers first arrived in the 1530s. What is now the Mexican city of Juárez was founded in 1659 as 'El Paso del Norte,' but it wasn't until 1827 that the first permanent settlements were established on the northern banks of the Rio Grande on the site of what we now know as El Paso.

By 1873, El Paso had been incorporated as a Texas city, and the Southern Pacific Railroad came to town in 1881, bringing with it gunfighters like John Wesley Hardin and kicking off El Paso's Wild West era.

In 1911, the Mexican Revolution, led by Pancho Villa, sent many Mexicans fleeing from Juárez to safety in El Paso, but it also stirred up controversy over the precise location of the US–Mexico border. The Chamizal Convention of 1963 settled it once and for all, and the two cities sit on opposite banks of the Rio Grande, together but separate.

WHAT TIME IS IT?

When it comes to time zones, El Paso sides with New Mexico, conforming to Mountain Time rather than Central Time like the rest of Texas. Confusing? Occasionally. If you're telling someone in neighboring Van Horn or Fort Stockton what time you'll meet them, be sure to add on the extra hour you'll lose just by leaving El Paso.

Sights

Many of El Paso's museums are free or by donation. Visit www.freeelpaso.com/exhibits.html for a list of free things to do.

El Paso is a sprawling city of 240 sq miles, but much of that space is taken up by Fort Bliss and the enormous Franklin Mountains State Park. The Franklin Mountains divide the city into a west side and an east side, with downtown sitting due south of the mountains, and the I-10 serving as the primary through-route. Just south of downtown is the Rio Grande and, across the river, Juárez, Mexico.

Downtown

★El Paso Museum of Art MUSEUM

(Map p328; ☎915-532-1707; www.elpasoartmuseum.org; 1 Arts Festival Plaza; special exhibits charge admission; ⏰9am-5pm Tue-Sat, to 9pm Thu, noon-5pm Sun) FREE This thoroughly enjoyable museum is in a former Greyhound station. They'd want us to brag about their *Madonna and Child* (c 1200), but the Southwestern art is terrific, and the engaging modern pieces round out the collection nicely. All this, and it's free?! Well done, El Paso, well done.

El Paso Holocaust Museum MUSEUM

(Map p328; www.elpasoholocaustmuseum.org; 715 N Oregon St; ⏰9am-4pm Tue-Fri, 1-5pm Sat & Sun) FREE It may seem a little anachronistic in a predominately Hispanic town, but the Holocaust Museum is as much a surprise inside as out for its thoughtful and moving exhibits that are imaginatively presented for maximum impact.

El Paso Museum of History MUSEUM

(Map p328; ☎915-351-3588; www.elpasotexas.gov/history; 510 N Santa Fe St; ⏰9am-5pm Tue, Wed, Fri

Greater El Paso

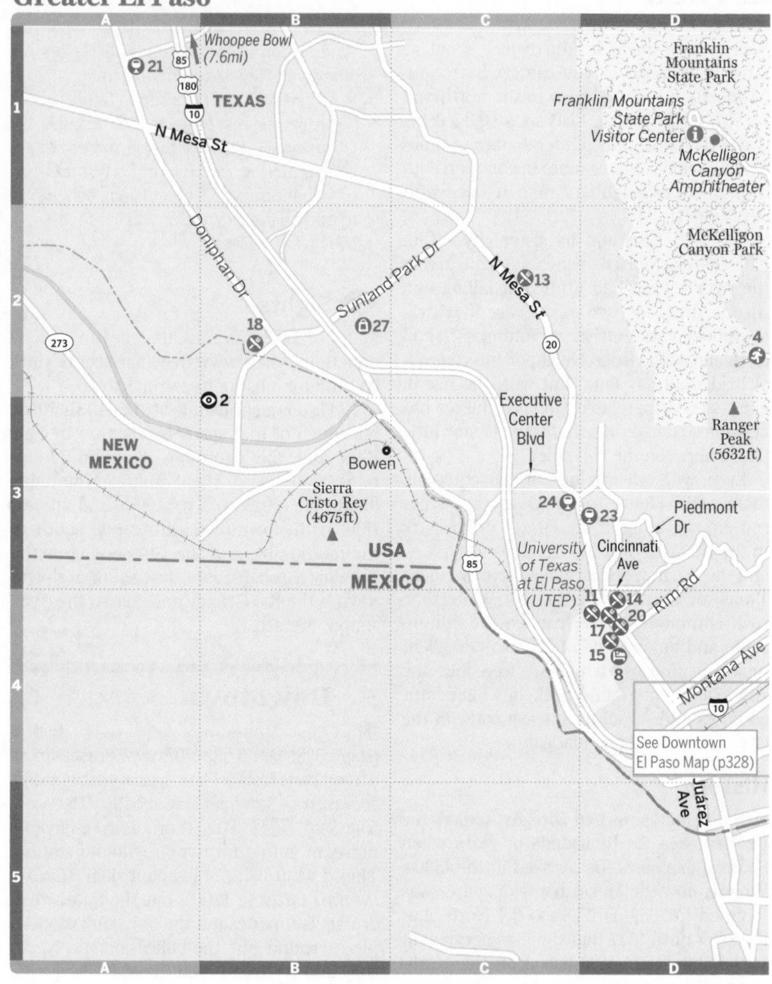

& Sat, to 8pm Thu, noon-5pm Sun) FREE This museum has a shiny new location in the heart of the downtown museum district. It's not huge and sometimes there seems to be a lot of reading, but it's an easy stop-off if you're already at the Museum of Art.

Magoffin Home HISTORIC BUILDING
(Map p328; 915-533-5147; www.visitmagoffinhome.com; 1120 Magoffin Ave; adult/child 5yr & under $4/free; 9am-5pm Tue-Sun, tours on the hour) One of Texas' best-kept secrets, this El Paso landmark was built in 1875 for Joseph Magoffin, an early El Paso politician and businessman. With 4ft-thick adobe walls and many original furnishings, the home is a fine example of the Southwest Territorial style of architecture prevalent during the late 19th century.

Railroad & Transportation Museum MUSEUM
(Map p328; 915-422-3420; www.elpasorails.org; 400 W San Antonio Ave; 11am-5pm Tue-Sat, 1-5pm Sun) FREE The main reason to visit is to see 'Old No. 1' – a huge 1857 locomotive that fills most of this tiny museum near the convention center.

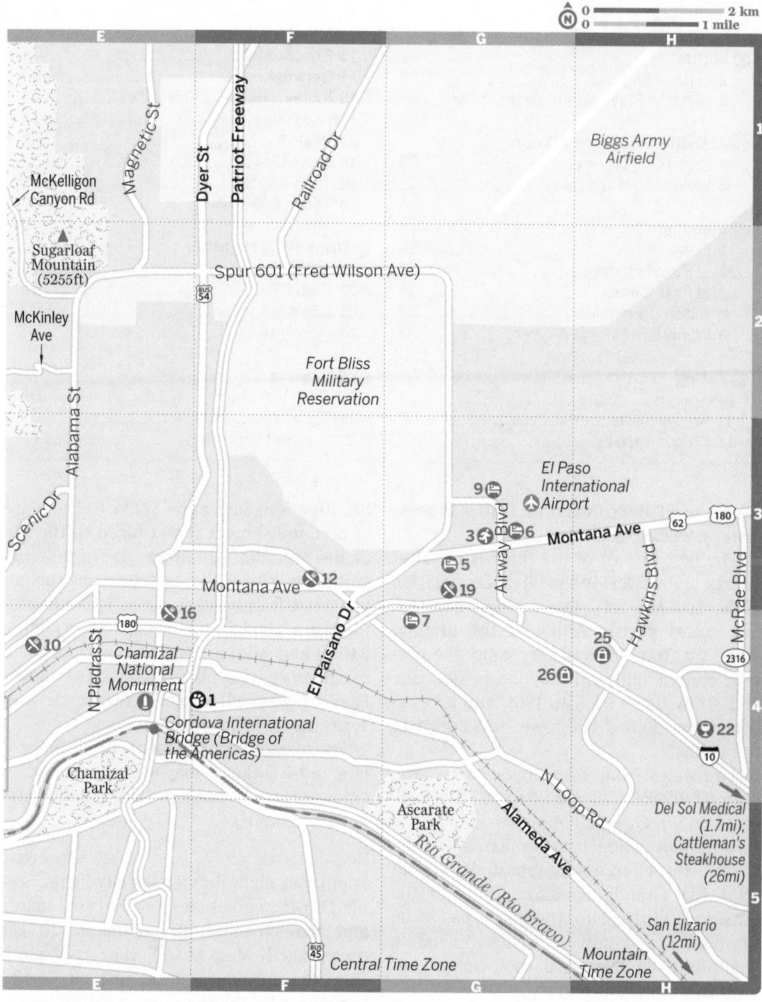

North

Franklin Mountains State Park PARK

(www.tpwd.state.tx.us; Transmountain Rd; adult/child $5/free; 8am-5pm Mon-Fri, 6:30am-8pm Sat & Sun) At 23,863 acres, this is the largest urban park in the US. Although it's in the middle of a city, it's home to ringtail cats, coyotes and a number of other smaller animals and reptiles, and it's capped by 7192ft North Franklin Peak.

Head to the **visitor center** (Map p324; 915-566-6441; 1331 McKelligon Canyon Rd) to get a basic park map, written descriptions of the hiking trails, mountain-bike trail maps, or route maps of the 17 different rock-climbing routes.

East

Mission Trail HISTORIC SITE

Ready for some local history? This 9-mile trail links two mission churches and a presidio chapel, all of which are on the National Register of Historic Places. Privately owned by the Catholic Diocese, they're not always as visitor-friendly as you might like, but you can arrange a tour or get more information

Greater El Paso

Sights
1 El Paso Zoo F4
2 Western Playland Amusement Park B3

Activities, Courses & Tours
3 Crazy Cat Cyclery G3
4 Wyler Aerial Tramway D2

Sleeping
5 Coral Motel G3
6 El Paso Marriott G3
7 El Paso Suites G4
8 Hilton Garden Inn D4
9 Wyndham El Paso Airport G3

Eating
10 Amigos E4
11 Aroma Restaurant D4
12 Chicos Tacos F3
13 Crisostomo C2
14 Geogeske D4
15 Kinley's House Coffee & Tea D4
16 L&J Cafe E4
17 Rib Hut D4
18 State Line B2
19 Taco Cabana G3
20 Tom's Folk Cafe D4

Drinking & Nightlife
21 Aceitunas A1
22 Club 101 .... H4
23 Hope & Anchor D3
24 Hoppy Monk C3

Shopping
25 Cielo Vista Mall H4
26 El Paso Saddleblanket G4
27 Sunland Park Mall B2

from the **El Paso Mission Trail Association** (www.elpasomissiontrail.com).

The best known of the three is **Mission Ysleta** (915-859-9848; 131 S Zaragoza Rd; 7am-5pm Mon-Sat), Texas' oldest continually active parish. Although the original structure from 1682 is long gone, the current church built from adobe bricks, clay and straw dates back to 1851, and a beautiful, silver-domed bell tower was added in the 1880s.

Two miles from Ysleta is **Socorro Mission** (915-859-7718; 328 S Nevarez Rd; 8am-4pm Mon-Fri). Originally built in 1681 by the Piro Indians, who later assimilated into the Tiguas, the church was repeatedly rebuilt after Rio Grande flooding. Although the outside is fairly plain, the inside has some impressive decorative touches, including beautifully hand-painted roof beams rescued from the 18th-century mission.

Though not open to the public, the last stop is the presidio chapel of **San Elizario** (915-851-2333; 1556 San Elizario Rd, San Elizario), located on a military fort established for the Spanish government in 1684. Today, peaceful San Elizario is notable for its 1882 church and the adjacent town plaza where de Oñate issued his 1598 proclamation claiming the region for Spain.

Activities

Wyler Aerial Tramway TRAMWAY

(Map p324; 915-566-6622; 1700 McKinley Ave; adult/child 12yr & under $8/4; noon-7pm Fri & Sat, 10am-5pm Sun) Sure, you'd feel a sense of accomplishment if you hiked to the top of the Franklin Mountains. We're not suggesting you take the easy way out (or are we?), but it only takes about four minutes to take a gondola to the top. After gliding 2400ft and gaining 940ft in elevation, you'll reach the viewing platform on top of Ranger Peak, where you'll enjoy spectacular views of Texas, New Mexico and Mexico.

For maximum enjoyment, bring binoculars and a jacket – maybe even a picnic to enjoy at the top (but leave alcohol and glass bottles at home).

Scenic Drive SCENIC DRIVE

Popular at night for viewing city lights, Scenic Dr offers great views of El Paso, Juárez and the surrounding mountains. To get there, take N Mesa St to Kerbey Ave (across from the university), head east till Kerbey becomes Rim Rd, then turn right on Scenic Dr. En route, keep an eye out for little Murchison Park – at 4222ft, it's a fine spot for sunrises.

Crazy Cat Cyclery BIKE RENTAL

(Map p324; 915-772-9666; 6625 Montana Ave; overnight rental $40; 10am-8pm Mon-Sat, to 6pm Sun) The best source of local cycling information and equipment. Some of the city's best mountain biking is five minutes away, and they'll point you in the right direction and sell you a map if you'd like one. They also offer scheduled group rides led by enthusiastic cyclists.

Rio Bosque Wetlands Park PARK
(915-747-8663; Ave of the Americas at Pan American Dr; dawn-dusk) This park offers walking tours several times a month. A network of natural surface trails weave through the wetlands, and a fully paved loop trail is in the works. It is really hard to find, so call to get directions, but it's worth the adventure because of the bird life available.

Tours

Border Sights Tours TOUR
(915-533-5454; www.bordersights-tours-of-elpaso.com; pick-up at your location; adult $45) Tours of the city, Mission Trail and more, as well as specialty tours (extra charge) like wine-tasting – all north of the border.

El Paso Convention & Visitors Bureau WALKING TOUR
(Map p328; 915-534-0601; www.visitelpaso.com; 1 Civic Center Plaza; 8am-5pm Mon-Sat) The CVB has some good walking tours available on its website or in its office. The excellent, self-guided 'El Paso Downtown Historic Walking Tour' takes about 90 minutes to complete.

Si El Paso Tours TOUR
(915-541-1308; www.sielpasotours.com) Offers tours of the town and sometimes sponsors tours led by special guests.

Festivals & Events

Don Juan de Oñate's First Thanksgiving CULTURE
(www.sanelizariohistoricartdistrict.com) A reenactment is staged on the last weekend of April, with festivities at Chamizal National Monument and San Elizario.

Southwestern International PRCA Rodeo RODEO
(www.elprodeo.com) Held in September, this long-running tradition has kept broncs a-buckin' in El Paso since 1929.

Amigo Airsho AIR SHOW
(www.amigoairsho.org) Flying performers of all sorts gather in Biggs Field for this October event. Most of the action takes place up in the air, but there's also entertainment down on the ground.

Sun Bowl College Football Classic SPORTS
(800-915-2695; www.sunbowl.org) Takes place the last week in December at Sun Bowl Stadium, with many pre-game events held throughout the holiday season.

Sleeping

Almost every hotel in El Paso is a chain, and you have to cross over into New Mexico to find a bed and breakfast. There are two main clusters of budget motels; one on N Mesa St around the university and the other on Montana Ave near the airport and Fort Bliss.

Most of the top-end hotels cater to the business world. This makes weekday stays at these places rather pricey, but most offer good deals Friday through Sunday.

Downtown

Gardner Hotel/El Paso International Hostel HOSTEL $
(Map p328; 915-532-3661; www.gardnerhotel.com; 311 E Franklin Ave; dm $24 s/d $35, with bathroom $60/70;) El Paso's oldest continually operating hotel is also the only real downtown bargain. It probably hasn't changed a whole lot since John Dillinger stayed here in the 1930s, but it has a certain ragtag charm, and the dormitory rooms are an economical choice, although they're only available for students and international guests.

Camino Real Hotel HOTEL $$
(Map p328; 915-534-3000, 800-769-4300; www.caminorealelpaso.com; 101 S El Paso St; d $72-109, ste from $132;) The only US location of an upscale Mexican hotel chain, the historic Camino Real – which has been in operation for over 100 years – has a prime

LOS MURALES

They're not always mentioned in guidebooks – maybe because they're primarily in the poorest areas of town – but Los Murales, the murals of El Paso, are perhaps the city's preeminent cultural treasure. Of the more than 100 murals in the city, the greatest concentrations are south of downtown between Paisano Dr and the Border Hwy and north of Paisano Dr near Douglass Elementary School. There are also more than 40 murals painted on the freeway columns around Durazno St between Copia and Raynolds Sts. Stop by the convention center and visitors bureau for a map.

Downtown El Paso

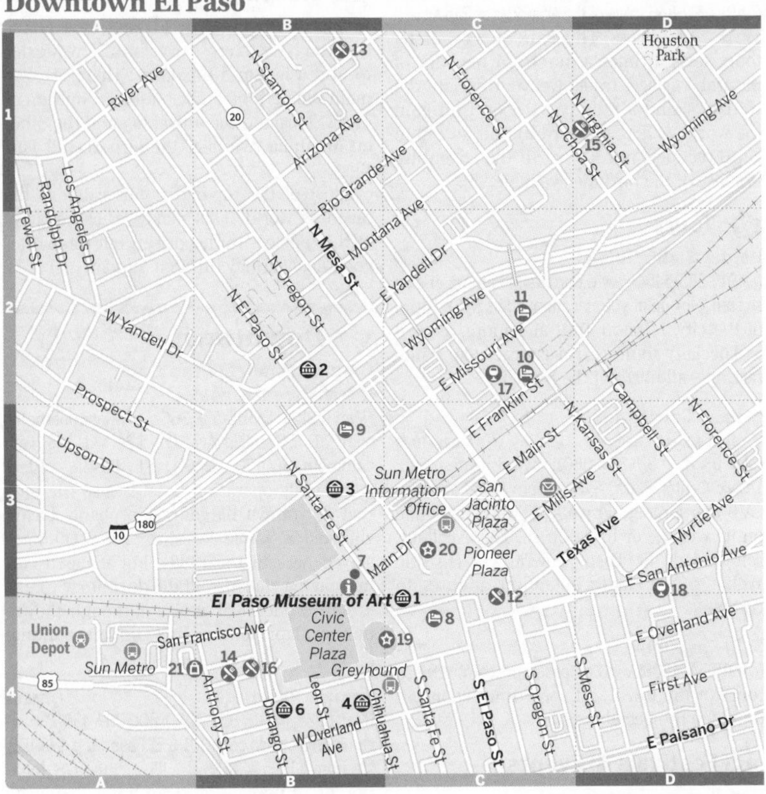

Downtown El Paso

Top Sights

1 El Paso Museum of Art C4

Sights

2 El Paso Holocaust Museum B2
3 El Paso Museum of History B3
4 Exploreum B4
5 Magoffin Home F2
6 Railroad & Transportation Museum B4

Activities, Courses & Tours

7 El Paso Convention & Visitors Bureau B3

Sleeping

8 Camino Real Hotel C4
9 Doubletree El Paso Downtown B3
10 Gardner Hotel/El Paso International Hostel C2
11 Holiday Inn Express C2

Eating

12 Cafe Central C4
13 G&R Restaurant B1
14 Garden B4
15 H&H Coffee Shop D1
16 Tabla B4

Drinking & Nightlife

17 Briar Patch C2
Dome Bar .... (see 8)
18 Tap Bar & Restaurant D3

Entertainment

19 Abraham Chávez Theatre C4
20 Plaza Theatre C3

Shopping

21 Rocketbuster Boots A4

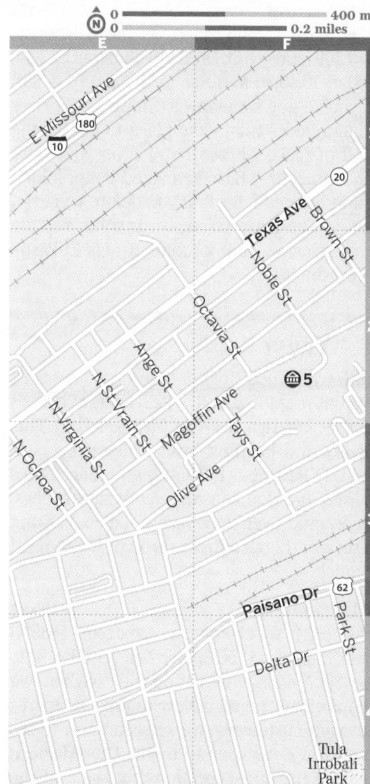

location steps from the convention center and downtown museums; a gorgeous bar with an art glass dome; large, comfortable rooms; and pretty friendly service, even when it's swamped.

Holiday Inn Express HOTEL **$$**
(Map p328; ☎915-544-3333; www.hiexpress.com; 409 E Missouri Ave; d $63-125; @ 📶 🏊) Sure, it's wedged between a freeway and train tracks, but it still manages to be surprisingly quiet and calm inside. The rooms are cheerful and up to date, and breakfast is included.

Doubletree El Paso Downtown HOTEL **$$**
(Map p328; ☎915-532-8733; 600 N El Paso St; d $95-189; 📶 🏊) Freshly remodeled from top to bottom in 2009, the former International Hotel is one of the nicest places in town. The rooms are luxuriously smart, with pleasing color palettes and all the little niceties you could want.

West

Hilton Garden Inn HOTEL **$$**
(Map p324; ☎915-351-2121; www.hiltongardeninn.com; 111 W University Ave; r $89-169; ❄ @ 📶 🏊) Opened at the edge of the University of Texas in El Paso (UTEP), the Garden Inn was built to blend with campus architecture. So, of course, it resembles a Bhutanese *dzong* (religious fortress) – what else? (Architects thought the style would fit the desert-mountain landscape.) The interior is more nice chain hotel than exotic monastery.

Casa de Suenos B&B **$$**
(☎575-874-9166; www.casaofdreams.com; 405 Mountain Vista Rd S, La Union, NM; d $98-110; 📶) El Paso may not have a bed-and-breakfast, but New Mexico does, and it's just 20 miles from downtown. The decor is uber-Southwestern, but it's a serene retreat from the city.

East

Coral Motel MOTEL **$**
(Map p324; ☎915-772-3263; fax 915-779-6053; 6420 Montana Ave; s/d $45/55; ❄) Anyone who loves 1950s roadside nostalgia will feel right at home at this funky little motel that mixes genres wildly, from the Spanish-style barrel-tile roof to the Jetsons-esque sign to the mishmash interiors.

★ **El Paso Suites** HOTEL **$**
(Map p324; ☎915-779-6222; www.elpasosuiteshotel.com; 6100 Gateway Blvd E; ste $80-120; P ❄ 📶 🏊) This is the only independent hotel in town – but it used to be an Embassy Suites, so the rooms still have that generic chain-hotel feel. Still, it's a bargain, especially considering you get two full rooms. Each suite opens onto an eight-story skylit atrium with iron balconies, which does actually make up for the rooms quite a bit.

Wyndham El Paso Airport HOTEL **$$**
(Map p324; ☎915-778-4241; 2027 Airway Blvd; d $105-145, ste $125-175; @ 📶 🏊) Late arrival? Early departure? Staying 200yd from the airport has its advantages. But this place has more to offer than just proximity: it also has the biggest and best hotel pool in town.

El Paso Marriott HOTEL **$$**
(Map p324; ☎915-779-3300; www.marriott.com; 1600 Airway Blvd; d $90-205; 📶 🏊) Just down the street a few blocks from the airport, the Marriott has the plushest rooms outside of

downtown, although they're on the generic side of lovely.

Eating

El Paso has long proclaimed itself the Mexican-food capital of the US, and there certainly are dozens of good restaurants in that category. Ask three different El Pasoans who serves the best Mexican cuisine and you'll get three (or maybe six!) different answers. The area is also known for its steak houses, several of which are just far enough out of town to make dinner feel like an adventure.

Downtown

H&H Coffee Shop MEXICAN **$**

(Map p328; 915-533-1144; 701 E Yandell Dr; mains $5-8; 9am-5pm Mon-Fri, to 6pm Sat) It doesn't look like much, but sometimes good things come in weird packages. This hole in the wall – which, curiously, is attached to a car wash – is a well-known breakfast hangout that's authentic and friendly.

G&R Restaurant MEXICAN **$**

(Map p328; 915-546-9343; 401 E Nevada Ave; mains $5-10; 8am-8pm Mon-Thu, to 9pm Fri & Sat) Family-owned since 1960, G&R is a local favorite. The colonial-style dining room is fun and colorful, all the better to enjoy the authentic and super-affordable enchiladas, rellenos and burritos.

★ **Tabla** TAPAS **$$**

(Map p328; 115 Durango St; small plates $6-15) Get ready to share all sorts of awesomeness. The small plates here are less Spanish-style tapas and more like an excuse to try a little bit of everything, like a big buffet of fun. The stylish warehouse space has tall ceilings, an open kitchen and the requisite pig motif sprinkled about, which make the vibe refreshingly current.

Garden AMERICAN **$$**

(Map p328; 915-544-4400; www.thegardenep.com; 511 Western St; mains $9-19; 10:30am-10pm Mon-Thu, to 11pm Fri & Sat;) Decisions, decisions. This place has hamburgers, sushi, salads and pizza – something for almost everyone, including good vegetarian options. Located inside a converted warehouse, the cool space has three distinct seating areas to choose from too: the lofty dining room, the breezy bar area or the sunny outdoor patio.

The bar stays open to 2am on weekends, so you can finish your night here, as well.

Cafe Central AMERICAN **$$$**

(Map p328; 915-545-2233; www.cafecentral.com; 109 N Oregon St; lunch $10-36, dinner $23-44; 11am-10:30pm Mon-Thu, to 11:30pm Fri & Sat) If you've got someone to impress – prices be damned – this is *the* place to go. It's the kind of place where, if you drop your napkin, someone will have picked it up, folded it and handed it back to you before you even notice. The seasonal cuisine is solid, and the small, elegant dining room attracts El Paso's finest diners.

West

Kinley's House Coffee & Tea CAFE **$**

(Map p324; 915-838-7177; 2231 N Mesa St; meals $3-8; 7am-11pm Mon-Sat, from 8am Sun) This cheery and bustling little coffee shop near the UTEP campus has lattes and macchiatos galore, and you can also score sandwiches, crepes and even Japanese noodles. Parking is scarce; there's a drive-through if you need it quick.

Crisostomo MEXICAN **$**

(Map p324; www.burritocrisostomo.com; 5658 N Mesa St; burritos $1.50-3.75; 7am-9pm Mon-Fri, to 8pm Sat, to 4pm Sun) What do you do when you run a hugely popular burrito joint in Juárez but your customers stop crossing over to see you? You cross over to them. This Mexican favorite has three locations this side of the border, serving up tasty, filling and inexpensive burritos and quesadillas. Cash only.

Crave AMERICAN **$$**

(915-351-3677; www.cravekitchenandbar.com; 300 Cincinnati Ave; mains $9-28; 7am-11pm Mon-Sat, to 6pm Sun) Winning extra points for style – from the cool sign to the forks hanging from the ceiling – this hip little eatery serves up comfort food and classics with a little extra flair. Although dinner goes up to $30, there's still plenty to munch on in the $15-and-under category. There's also a newer location on the **east side** (915-594-7971; 11990 Rojas Dr; 7am-11pm Mon-Sat, to 6pm Sun).

Aroma Restaurant AMERICAN **$$**

(Map p324; 915-532-4700; 2725 N Mesa St; mains $17-28, lunch $12; 11am-10pm Mon-Thu, to 11pm Fri & Sat) Upscale entrees – think sesame seared tuna or New York strip steak – are what you'll find in this intimate restaurant that's surprisingly stylish given its strip-mall location. The prix-fixe lunch is a bargain:

$12 gets you soup or salad, main course and dessert.

Geogeske AMERICAN $$
(G2; Map p324; ☎915-544-4242; www.g2geogeske.com; 2701 Stanton St; mains $9-24; ⏲11am-10pm Mon-Thu, to 11pm Fri & Sat) It's hard to describe the strip-mall location: pleasingly neutral? Not at all strip mally? No matter, the food is the draw, both in quality and variety, with everything from sandwiches to Chilean sea bass on the menu.

Tom's Folk Cafe AMERICAN $$
(Map p324; www.tomsfolkcafe.com; 204 Boston Ave; mains $10-22; ⏲11am-9pm Tue-Sun) This tiny, unassuming place wins lots of fans for its creative takes on Southern cooking made with fresh, locally sourced food. There are only six tables inside and a few more on the patio, and the casual atmosphere belies the sophisticated preparation.

State Line BARBECUE $$
(Map p324; ☎915-581-3371; 1222 Sunland Park Dr; mains $9-23; ⏲11:30am-9:30pm Mon-Thu, to 10pm Fri & Sat, to 9pm Sun) Vegetarians, plug your ears: it's hard to say what we like better, the groovy roadhouse-style decor, or the mounds and mounds of delicious, steaming brisket, sausage and ribs.

Rib Hut BARBECUE $$
(Map p324; ☎915-532-7427; 2612 N Mesa St; mains $8-20; ⏲11am-10pm Mon-Sat, noon-9pm Sun) Go all caveman-like and join the UTEP crowd over a serious plate of ribs in this funky little A-frame building with typical campus-adjacent decor. Wednesday night is packed for rib night, when ribs are $1.95 each.

East

Chicos Tacos MEXICAN $
(Map p324; 5305 Montana Ave; tacos $1-4; ⏲9am-1:30am Sun-Thu, to 3am Fri & Sat) With several locations, Chicos Tacos specializes in its namesake fare – with lots of garlic. Expect a crowd from about 10pm to midnight, when El Pasoans citywide experience a collective craving.

Taco Cabana MEXICAN $
(Map p324; ☎915-775-1460; 6345 Gateway Blvd W; tacos $1-3, plates $3-7; ⏲24hr) In El Paso, even the fast-food Tex-Mex is great. In addition to this central location on I-10, this chain has locations all over town; keep an eye out for the big, pink neon sign. El Paso's not a late-night kind of town, so you'll especially appreciate it in the wee hours.

L&J Cafe MEXICAN $
(Map p324; ☎915-566-8418; www.landjcafe.com; 3622 E Missouri Ave; mains $7-12; ⏲10am-9pm) This El Paso staple is located next to the Concordia Cemetery. It's a great place to cure a hangover on Saturday morning, when it serves its famous menudo. If the outside looks divey, it's because it's been open since 1927. Don't be scared; the inside is much more inviting.

Amigos MEXICAN $
(Map p324; ☎915-533-0155; 2000 Montana Ave; mains $8-11; ⏲6:30am-3pm Mon, to 8pm Tue-Fri, 7am-8pm Sat & Sun) This sunny spot on Montana is a reliable favorite that will jolt your taste buds from their ennui. The friendly owner can let you know which dishes really bring on the *fuego* (fire), or help you pick something suited for a more moderate palate.

★**Cattleman's Steakhouse** STEAKHOUSE $$$
(☎915-544-3200; Indian Cliffs Ranch; mains $16-38; ⏲5-10pm Mon-Fri, 12:30-10pm Sat, 12:30-9pm Sun; 👪) This place is 20 miles east of the city, but local folks would probably drive 200 miles to eat here. The food is good, and the scenery is even better. Portions are huge, and for just $6 extra you can share an entree and gain full access to the family-style sides.

Come early and wander around the grounds of Indian Cliffs Ranch, where you'll see everything from bunnies to buffalo waiting for you in their pens, then catch the sunset either before or after your meal.

To get there, exit at Fabens then follow the signs to 4.7 miles northeast of the freeway.

Drinking & Nightlife

Dome Bar BAR
(Map p328; ☎915-534-5012; Camino Real Hotel, 101 S El Paso St; ⏲3-11pm) Gaze up at the elegant stained-glass dome, sip a martini and enjoy an intimate conversation at this low-key place inside downtown's Camino Real Hotel.

THE BEST BLOCK IN EL PASO

Not sure what you're in the mood for? Head to the always-lively Kern Pl district near UTEP, where you can restaurant hop and bar crawl to your heart's delight; the epicenter is Cincinnati Ave between Stanton St and Mesa St.

Hoppy Monk BAR
(Map p324; 4141 N Mesa St; ⏲3pm-2am Mon-Thu, from 11am Fri-Sun) We love this place up off Mesa on the west side, not just for its beer selection, which is ponderous and includes – no surprise – some great Belgians, but for its nice patio and better-than-usual pub food.

Hope & Anchor BAR
(Map p324; www.hopeandanchorelpaso.com; 4012 N Mesa St; ⏲3pm-2am Mon-Sat, from 4pm Sun) Too crowded inside? That's okay, we were heading to the beautiful patio to enjoy the nice weather anyway. This is a great place to unwind just down the street from the Hoppy Monk. Pub crawl, anyone?

Tap Bar & Restaurant BAR
(Map p328; 408 E San Antonio Ave; ⏲9am-2am Mon-Sat, noon-2am Sun) If you prefer dive bars, duck in to the Tap. Located right downtown, it's also a Mexican restaurant, so you can scarf down some nachos to soak up the booze.

Aceitunas BAR
(Map p324; 5200 Doniphan Dr; ⏲3pm-2am) A unique spot in El Paso, this open-air beer garden is a great place to wind down after a long day. The folks here are some of the friendliest you will meet. Extra points for its T-shirt: 'The liver is evil and must be punished!'

Club 101 CLUB
(Map p324; ☎915-544-2101; www.club101.com; 9515 Viscount Blvd; ⏲8pm-2am Tue-Sat) A new location for *the* reigning dance club in town, where you might find anything from '80s music to comedians. Check the website or call to see what's happening.

☆ Entertainment

El Paso has a lively fine-arts scene and plenty going on in the bars and nightclubs too, though compared to Austin, there's little in the way of local original music. But if you look hard enough and ask around, you can find live music almost any night of the week. To learn what's going on in town, try the *Tiempo Friday* supplement to the *El Paso Times* (http://calendar.elpasotimes.com).

Performing Arts

The sombrero-shaped **Abraham Chávez Theatre** (Map p328; ☎915-534-0609; 1 Civic Center Plaza) is host to most of El Paso's major performing organizations and many touring concerts and plays. These include **El Paso Symphony Orchestra** (☎915-532-3776; www.epso.org), **Showtime! El Paso** (☎915-544-2022; www.showtimeelpaso.com) and **El Paso Opera Company** (☎915-581-5534; www.epopera.org).

Opened in 1930, the grand **Plaza Theatre** (Map p328; www.theplazatheatre.org; 125 Pioneer Plaza) is a downtown landmark and a fabulous place to catch a play, concert or show.

Sports

The **El Paso Diablos** (☎915-755-2000; www.diablos.com) play Double A Texas League baseball April to September at **Cohen Stadium** (9700 Gateway Blvd N), but at time of research, a brand-new stadium was being built

EL PASO FOR KIDS

El Paso Zoo (Map p324; ☎915-521-1850; www.elpasozoo.org; 4001 E Paisano Dr; adult/child 3-12yr/senior $10/6/7.50; ⏲9:30am-5pm) Home to a large number of endangered animals, including the Asian elephant, Sumatran orangutan, Malayan tiger and the rare Amur leopard. All told, 700 animals represent 220 species packed into 35 acres. It's not the biggest or most impressive zoo you've ever seen, but it's worth a visit. And it's mercifully shady for both the animals and you.

Exploreum (Map p328; ☎915-533-4330; www.lynxexhibits.com; 300 W San Antonio Ave; child or adult/senior/child under 2yr $8/6/free; ⏲10am-6pm Mon-Sat, from noon Sun; P) This interim children's museum is meant to bridge the gap between the Insights Museum that was torn down to build the ballpark and the new children's museum slated to open in 2016. It does feel a little makeshift, but the kids don't seem to mind much.

Four separate areas invite interactive play: the Old El Paso Village, High Tech Hot Spot, Airport Adventure, where kids run the airport, and STEAM Ahead, which focuses on scientific theories.

Western Playland Amusement Park (Map p324; ☎575-589-3410; www.westernplayland.com; 1249 Futurity Dr, Sunland Park, NM; admission $5, per ride $2, full access $18; ⏲hours vary, check website) Small but fun, this old-school amusement park is just over the border in New Mexico, and it's a great way to burn off the pent-up kid energy.

downtown that was slated to open in time for the 2014 season.

Shopping

Like most major US cities, El Paso has its share of malls where the shopper can find anything from books to socks. **Cielo Vista Mall** (Map p324; ☎915-779-7070; 8401 Gateway Blvd W; ⏲10am-9pm Mon-Sat, noon-6pm Sun) is located off I-10 on the east side; **Sunland Park Mall** (Map p324; 750 Sunland Park Dr; ⏲10am-9pm Mon-Sat, noon-6pm Sun) is the major westside shopping center. Savvy shoppers can hunt for deals at the **Outlet Shoppes at El Paso** (7051 S Desert Blvd, Canutillo; 10am-9pm Mon-Sat, to 7pm Sun), 20 minutes northwest of town on I-10.

Feel like you're missing out on south-of-the-border bargains? For an experience not altogether unlike shopping in Juárez, head to the **Golden Horseshoe** area between Stanton and El Paso Sts and San Antonio Ave in El Paso's downtown area, where cheap clothing, jewelry and housewares abound. It's fairly scruffy, but it avoids the danger of crossing over.

Whoopee Bowl ANTIQUES

(☎915-886-2855; 9010 N Desert Blvd, Canutillo) This isn't the kind of antique store where you find authentic Chippendale pieces or a rare Fabergé egg. This is the kind of place where you pull up your Dodge Ram to haul home an enormous fiberglass chicken or a wooden Indian from a cigar store. Sure, there are smaller items too, but the real fun is exploring the huge front yard full of ridiculous treasures.

Located on the I-10 access road just before the New Mexico border.

El Paso Saddleblanket ARTS & CRAFTS

(Map p324; ☎915-544-1000; www.saddleblanket.com; 6926 Gateway Blvd E) 'Incredible 2-acre shopping adventure!' the billboards scream. This place is indeed huge, and it's chock full of all things Southwestern. Stuff your suitcases with pottery, blankets, turquoise jewelry, even a sombrero if you must. They've got mounted steer horns, but we can tell you right now you're not going to be able to carry them onto the plane.

GAY & LESBIAN EL PASO

The scene is certainly more under-the-radar than in cosmopolitan Dallas or laid-back Austin, but there are still some organizations and bars ready to welcome you to town.

Travelers can find gay-friendly businesses, including bars, shops, restaurants and hotels, at **GayCities** (http://elpaso.gaycities.com). (The most gay-friendly businesses are downtown near the Camino Real Hotel.)

If you're looking for nightlife, the **Briar Patch** (Map p328; ☎915-577-9555; 508 N Stanton St) is a good place to start. The patio is a nice place to knock back some drinks with like-minded new friends.

Information

DANGERS & ANNOYANCES

El Paso is among the safest cities of its size in the US. This is due in part to Operation Hold the Line, an effort to crack down on illegal immigration into El Paso. Green-and-white Border Patrol vehicles are highly visible all along the El Paso side of the Rio Grande, and the police presence has had the side effect of quelling crime.

Crossing over into Juárez is a different story. While El Paso is one of the safest cities, Juárez has become one of the most dangerous, due to gruesome violence – some of it random – resulting from drug wars. For now, just say no.

EMERGENCY & MEDICAL SERVICES

El Paso Police (☎911, non-emergency 915-832-4400; 911 N Raynor St)

Del Sol Medical Center (☎915-595-9000; 10460 Vista Del Sol) Provides acute care and emergency services on the east side.

Providence Memorial Hospital (☎915-577-6011; 2001 N Oregon St) West-side hospital with a 24-hour emergency room.

INTERNET ACCESS

El Paso Public Library (☎915-543-5433; www.elpasolibrary.org; 501 N Oregon St; ⏲10am-7pm Mon-Thu, 11am-6pm Fri, 10am-6pm Sat, noon-6pm Sun) Free internet access. Check the website for additional branches.

MONEY

Bank of America (☎915-532-5356; 330 N Mesa St; ⏲9am-5pm Mon-Fri) ATM and currency exchange available.

WestStar Bank (☎915-532-1000; 500 N Mesa St) Has a 24-hour drive-up ATM.

POST

Post Office (Map p328; ☎915-532-8824; 219 E Mills Ave; ⏲8:30am-5pm Mon-Fri, to noon Sat) Call ☎800-275-8777 to locate other branches.

CUSTOM BOOTS

It's the ultimate west-Texas souvenir: a gorgeous pair of cowboy boots made just for you. As boot maker to the stars, **Rocketbuster Boots** (Map p328; ☎915-541-1300; www.rocketbuster.com; 115 S Anthony St; ⏰showroom 8am-4pm Mon-Fri, personalized service by appointment) has shod such celebrities as Julia Roberts, Dwight Yoakum, Emmylou Harris and Oprah Winfrey. Its over-the-top designs include everything from wild floral prints to 1950s-era pin-up cowgirls to Day of the Dead skeletons.

Sure, you could just pick up a pair of mass-produced boots like most people do – after all, these beauties start at $850 and go up to $3500 or more for a one-of-a-kind design – but it's not the same as having something created just for you. Your feet will know the difference, and besides, you'll be much less likely to get stopped on the street by awestruck admirers.

One visit to the showroom and you might be a little awestruck yourself. It's not a shop, per se, but there are lots of samples so you can get some inspiration. Call first if you'd like some personalized attention from owner-designer Nevena Christi. Otherwise, poke your head in for a visual treat, both from the boots and from the whimsical shop that's decorated with both space-age gadgets and cowboy memorabilia.

TOURIST INFORMATION

El Paso Visitors Center (Map p328; ☎800-351-6024, 915-534-0600; www.visitelpaso.com; 1 Civic Center Plaza; ⏰8am-5pm Mon-Fri, 10am-3pm Sat) Stocks racks and racks of brochures, and the staff is quite helpful. It also has a well-populated website for planning.

 Getting There & Away

AIR

El Paso International Airport (ELP; Map p324; www.elpasointernationalairport.com) is 8 miles northeast of downtown El Paso. It's accessible by bus, taxi and shuttles.

Southwest Airlines (☎800-435-9792; www.southwest.com) is the biggest carrier at El Paso International, with about 60% of the domestic flights. Other airlines include **American Airlines** (ww.aa.com), **Delta** (www.delta.com) and **New Mexico Airlines** (www.pacificwings.com/nma/nm), for which El Paso is a hub.

BUS

The terminal for **Greyhound** (Map p328; www.greyhound.com; 200 W San Antonio Ave) is four blocks from the center of downtown.

CAR

El Paso is on the I-10 just 12 miles from the New Mexico line, but a long day's drive or more from any other major city in Texas. Stay on I-10 eastbound for San Antonio or Houston; I-20, the route to Fort Worth and Dallas, leaves I-10 about 150 miles east of El Paso. The only other major highways are Hwy 54, which runs north to I-40, and Hwy 62/180, the route to Guadalupe Mountains and Carlsbad Caverns National Parks and eventually to Lubbock.

TRAIN

You can catch Amtrak at **Union Depot** (www.amtrak.com; 700 San Francisco Ave), which serves both the *Texas Eagle,* which runs from Los Angeles to Chicago with stops in San Antonio, Austin and Dallas, and the *Sunset Limited,* which runs from Los Angeles to New Orleans with stops in San Antonio and Houston. Check the website for fares and schedules.

 Getting Around

TO/FROM THE AIRPORT

Many hotels and motels provide free shuttles from the airport; call to see if yours does. All the major car-rental companies, as well as ground-transportation options, can be found near baggage claim. Sun Metro's bus 33 will get you from the airport to downtown, which is about an 8-mile trip. A taxi to downtown costs between $23 and $25.

BUS

Sun Metro (Map p328; ☎915-533-3333; www.sunmetro.net; Union Depot, 700 San Francisco Ave) is El Paso's bus service, operating 47 routes citywide. Routes are extensive, but most services stop running early in the evening, including

 DOWNTOWN CIRCULATOR BUS

Sun Metro (p334) operates three free circulator buses around downtown from early morning till 5pm or 6pm. Check online, call or stop at the visitor center to find out where its services can take you.

the airport bus (the last one leaves around 9pm). Exact change is required. Check the website for route maps and schedules.

Bus fares are $1.50 for adults and $1 for children aged six to 18. Transfers are free but should be requested when you board your original bus.

CAR

Downtown can be tricky, because there are one-way streets laid out at weird angles, but the outlying commercial areas and neighborhoods are easy to find via I-10 and the major surface streets.

TAXI

Look for taxi stands at the airport and the Greyhound and Amtrak depots. Rates are $1.65 at flag fall, $2.25 each additional mile. We've been warned about unscrupulous cabbies charging extortionate rates downtown, so double-check rates before boarding and make sure the meter's on. Larger companies include **Yellow Cab** (915-532-9999; www.yellowcabelpaso.com) and **United Independent Cab** (915-590-8294; www.elpasotaxicab.com).

Around El Paso

About 32 miles east of El Paso is **Hueco Tanks State Historical Park** (park 915-857-1135, reservations 512-389-8900; www.tpwd.state.tx.us; 6900 Hueco Tanks Rd/FM 2775; adult/child $7/free; 8am-6pm). The 860-acre park contains three small granite mountains pocked with depressions that capture rainwater – *hueco* is Spanish for 'hollow' – creating an oasis in the barren desert. The area has attracted humans for as long as 10,000 years, as evidenced by more than 2000 pictographs found within the park, some dating back as much as 5000 years.

To minimize human impact, a daily visitor quota is enforced; make reservations 24 hours in advance to gain entry. At park headquarters you'll find a small gift shop, an interpretive center and 20 campsites ($12 to $16). You can explore the North Mountain area by yourself, but to hike deeper into the park – where the more interesting pictographs are – you have to reserve and join one of the **pictograph, birding** or **bouldering-hiking tours** (915-857-1135; per person $2; call for schedule).

If you're a rock climber, chances are you already know about the park. Hueco Tanks ranks among the world's top rock-climbing destinations during the winter months (October through early April), when other prime climbs become inaccessible. During the summer, however, the desert sun generally makes the rocks too hot to handle.

Van Horn

POP 2064

Van Horn is notable mainly as a travelers' overnight spot on the long desert that is I-10 in west Texas, sitting at the crossroads of the interstate, Hwy 54 (which runs north to Guadalupe Mountains National Park) and Hwy 90 (a major route to Big Bend country).

Most people on the interstate truck on through to El Paso, which is just two more hours away, but if you're ready to bunk down for the night, there are a few motels right off the interstate. Better yet, try the historic **Hotel El Capitan** (877-283-1220; www.hotelinvanhorn.com; 100 E Broadway; d $99-119, ste $139-175;), a richly decorated Spanish hacienda–style lodging which has considerably more charm than the chains.

Hungry? Stop off for a little Tex-Mex at **Chuy's Spanish Inn** (915-283-2066; www.chuys1959.com; 1200 W Broadway St; Mexican plates $7-12; 10am-10pm). It's right on the highway, so you can't miss it. Chuy's has earned a place in 'Madden's Haul of Fame,' so named by US football broadcaster John Madden. Because he won't fly, the well-traveled Madden spends a lot of time crossing the US by bus, and he named this as one of his favorite restaurants.

If you're looking for a good place to stretch your legs, wander over to Fancy Junk, right next to Chuy's on Broadway. It's a junkyard that has taken the shape of an art exhibit.

Fort Stockton

POP 8311

Although short on charm, Fort Stockton snags a spot on many Texas travelers' itineraries by virtue of its location. Despite having fewer than 10,000 people, it is by far the biggest town on I-10 between El Paso, 238 miles west, and San Antonio, 310 miles east. It's also a major gateway to Big Bend National Park, which is 100 miles south.

Sights

Historic Fort Stockton HISTORIC SITE
(432-336-2400; www.historicfortstockton.com; 300 E 3rd St; adult/child 6-12yr $3/2; 9am-5pm Mon-Sat, to 6pm summer) You can view several original and reconstructed buildings of a 19th-century fort on the Texas frontier

WORTH A TRIP

DETOUR: CARLSBAD CAVERNS

If you've made it all the way out to the Guadalupe Mountains, you're not too far from another excellent natural attraction: **Carlsbad Caverns National Park** (575-785-2232; www.nps.gov/cave; 3225 National Parks Hwy; cave entry adult/child under 15yr $6/free; visitor center 8am-5pm, to 7pm summer). Although the park is over the border in New Mexico, it's only 40 miles from the Guadalupe Mountains National Park, making it closer than, well, almost everything else in the state of Texas.

Cave entrance fees are good for three days and get you access to the one-hour self-guided tour of the Big Room, the seventh-largest cave chamber in the world. There are additional fees, and reservations are required, for six different ranger-led tours, including the King's Palace and the Hall of the White Giant. Please note that each of the guided tours has an age limit of anywhere from four to 12 years, depending on difficulty (of the route, not the child), so plan accordingly if you're traveling with a little one.

at Historic Fort Stockton. The site includes Barracks No 1, a reconstructed building housing the **Fort Museum**, where exhibits and a short video describe the post's history. Living History days are held the first weekend of each November, with demonstrations, encampments and entertainment.

Annie Riggs Memorial Museum MUSEUM
(432-336-2167; 301 S Main St; adult/child 6-12yr $3/2; 9am-5pm Mon-Sat, to 6pm summer) Housed in a former hotel and boarding house, this museum is named for the frontier woman who owned and ran the hotel for many years. The building is a documented example of Territorial architecture and is featured in some trade books. It is unusual in that the walls are made only of adobe and no stucco has ever been added to preserve it. Historic photographs and Texas memorabilia line the walls.

Sleeping & Eating

We'll keep this brief. While there are plenty of options, they're fairly interchangeable. Nothing glamorous, just lots of chains. In fact, we found the rooms to be surprisingly expensive for what you get: $100 for a motel room? No thanks. There are better deals to be found further down the highway.

Atrium West Inn Hotel & Suites HOTEL $
(432-336-6666; www.atriumwestinn.com; 1305 US 285 N; s/d $70/80;) One of the more reasonable options in town is this just-the-basics hotel, which does indeed have an atrium with a pool, making it a decent place to stop if you want to splash around a bit.

Bienvenidos MEXICAN $
(432-336-3615; 405 W Dickinson Blvd; plates $6-10; 11-9pm Mon-Sat) This local favorite is there to welcome you with heaping plates of Tex-Mex. The food is average, but the staff is friendly, and it beats resorting to the International House of Pancakes.

Guadalupe Mountains National Park

We won't go so far as to call it Texas' best-kept secret, but the fact is that a lot of Texans aren't even aware of the **Guadalupe Mountains National Park** (915-828-3251; www.nps.gov/gumo; US Hwy 62/180; 7-day pass adult/child under 16yr $5/free). It's just this side of the Texas–New Mexico state line and a long drive from practically everywhere in the state.

Despite its low profile, it is a Texas high spot, both literally and figuratively. At 8749ft, Guadalupe Peak is the highest point in the Lone Star State. The fall foliage in McKittrick Canyon is the best in west Texas, and more than half the park is a federally designated wilderness area.

The National Park Service has deliberately curbed development to keep the park wild. There are no restaurants or indoor accommodations and only a smattering of services and programs. There are also no paved roads within the park, so whatever you want to see, you're going to have to work for it. But if you're looking for some of the best hiking and high-country splendor Texas can muster, you should put this park on your itinerary.

History

Until the mid-19th century, the Guadalupe Mountains were used exclusively by Mescalero Apaches, who hunted and camped in the area. Members of this tribe, who called themselves Nde, became the hunted starting in 1849 when the US Army began a ruthless three-decade campaign to drive them from the area. The mid-19th century also marked the brief tenure of the Butterfield Overland Mail Route. Guadalupe Mountains National Park was established in 1972.

Geology

A geologist's dream, Guadalupe Mountains National Park sits amid the world's most extensive exposed fossil reef. In fact, the mountains contain the world's best example of a 260- to 270-million-year-old exposed rock layer, the Guadalupian Global Stratotype. The reef began to grow 250 million years ago when an immense tropical ocean covered parts of Texas, New Mexico and Mexico. Over a period of five million years, lime-secreting marine organisms built the horseshoe-shaped reef to a length of 400 miles. After the sea evaporated, the reef was buried in sediment for millions more years, until a mountain-building geological uplift revealed part of it as the Guadalupe Mountains.

Sights

The Pinery HISTORIC SITE

Check out the ruins of a Butterfield Overland Mail stagecoach stop via an easy and wheelchair-accessible 0.75-mile round-trip trail leading from the Pine Springs visitor center. Despite its remote location, the Pinery is the only remaining Butterfield station ruin standing close to a major highway. The ruins are fragile and climbing on them is forbidden.

Frijole Ranch & Museum MUSEUM

(museum 8am-4:30pm) FREE The Frijole Ranch & Museum, a mile or so northeast of Pine Springs, has historical exhibits inside an old ranch house that give some good insight into what it must have been like to live in such a remote location. A tiny, one-room schoolhouse nearby might just make your kids appreciate how good they've got it.

Activities

Interpretive programs are held on summer evenings in the Pine Springs campground amphitheater, as well as several times a week during the spring. Topics depend on the rangers' interests, but they have included everything from stargazing to geology.

Hiking

With more than 80 miles of trails and no real designated scenic drives through the park, Guadalupe Mountains National Park is a hiker's oasis, with trails ranging from short nature walks to strenuous climbs. The weather can be unpredictable out here. Thunderstorms are likely on summer afternoons, and winds frequently blow 40mph to 50mph in spring and early summer.

To find the hike that's right for you, try the visitor center, but here are a few good ones to get you started:

McKittrick Canyon Trail is among the park's most popular trails, and deservedly so. The 6.8-mile round-trip is level and scenic any time of year, though never so scenic as in the fall. The **Pratt Cabin** (4.8 miles round-trip) is a highlight. The cabin was built in 1932 by petroleum geologist Wallace Pratt, who later donated the land to the Park

THE MAIL COACHES

Although it operated for only 2½ years or so between 1858 and 1861, the Butterfield Overland Mail Company spurred a revolution in American communications and transportation. Before that time, a letter bound for California from the east was sent via steamship around Cape Horn. The Butterfield Overland Mail Company's stagecoaches made it possible for a letter to move 2700 miles from St Louis to San Francisco via El Paso, Tucson and Los Angeles in a then-breathtaking 25 days. (Take that, FedEx.)

The Butterfield Overland's legacy is well known throughout west Texas, but it's especially well preserved here at Guadalupe Mountains National Park. At 5534ft, the Pinery stagecoach station – one of 200 on the route – was the highest in the system. Four times a week, a bugle call would herald the arrival of the stagecoach and its cargo of mail and passengers.

The Pinery station operated for 11 months, until the original route was abandoned for a new road through Fort Stockton and Fort Davis – a thoroughfare better protected from Native American attacks. But the Pinery station lived on for decades after as a refuge for emigrants, trail drivers and outlaws.

Service. The cabin remains furnished as the Pratt family left it. Big Adirondack chairs beckon on the porch, and picnic tables and rest rooms make this a good lunch spot.

Want to stand on the highest spot in Texas? Needless to say, you'll have to work for it on the 8.5-mile round-trip hike up **Guadalupe Peak**. No rock climbing is necessary, but there's a 3000ft elevation gain, so go easy if you've just driven in from the lowlands.

If you're looking for something a little easier, try the **Smith Spring Trail** starting at Frijole Ranch. This path, shaded by Texas madrone and alligator juniper, is a perfect spot to get out of the desert heat without too much exertion. The 2.3-mile loop takes you to Manzanita Spring and gradually climbs up to the refreshing Smith Spring, both precious watering holes for wildlife.

Other Activities

Bird-watchers flock to the park, especially McKittrick Canyon, for excellent viewing opportunities. There are no formal programs, but a checklist of the park's 260 species is available at the park headquarters.

Although many park trails are open to **horseback riding**, no horses are available in or near the park, and no overnight pack trips are permitted. For people bringing their own horses, corrals and campsites are available at Dog Canyon and Frijole Ranch; reserve them by calling the visitor center.

Sleeping & Eating

If you're planning on sticking around for a night or two, there aren't a lot of options. You can drive 45 minutes to Whites City, NM, or you can camp in the park and bring your own food. Aaaaand…that's it.

The park **campgrounds** (☎915-828-3251; per night $8) are first come, first served, unless you have a group of 10 or more, in which case you can reserve a group camping spot up to 60 days in advance for $3 per person.

The campsites fill up during spring break as well as several nights a week in the summer, although visitors arriving by early afternoon will usually find a site. The most convenient campgrounds are at Pine Springs, right along Hwy 62/180 near the visitor center; if it looks full, look for the 'campground host' sign for directions to overflow spots. If all the sites are full, RVs are permitted to park overnight at the nearby state-highway picnic areas.

There are even fewer eating options than sleeping options – in other words, zero. Plan on bringing food, either to hold you over till you can get to Whites City, or to sustain you throughout your stay without having to cross state lines. And just to make it even more challenging, there are no wood or charcoal fires allowed within the park. (Bring on the trail mix!)

Information

Information, rest rooms and drinking water are available at McKittrick Canyon and Dog Canyon, in addition to the **Pine Springs Visitor Center** (☎915-828-3251; www.nps.gov/gumo; ⏲8am-4:30pm, to 6pm summer). Visit the website to download a map of the park before you visit.

McKittrick Canyon's fall colors are glorious from early October through mid-November, and while nights can be chilly, daytime is warmly sublime. But be aware that autumn weekends are by far the busiest time and there may be a several-hour wait to enter the canyon.

There are no restaurants, accommodations, gas or other supplies in the park, so some planning is in order. Keep your gas tank full and your cooler stocked. The closest gas stations are 35 miles in either direction on Hwy 62/180 and the closest services are in Whites City, NM, 45 minutes northeast of the park entrance on Hwy 62/180. If camping is not appealing and you want to spend more than a day exploring the park, this resort town with over 100 motel rooms, two RV parks and a couple of mediocre restaurants is your best bet.

DANGERS & ANNOYANCES

Dehydration is the park's main danger. Carry and drink plenty of water – the park recommends one gallon per person per day. Five rattlesnake species live in the park, but rangers say no one has ever been bitten in the park's almost 50-year history. If you're camping, keep your tent flaps closed to keep out snakes, scorpions and desert centipedes.

Getting There & Away

Guadalupe Mountains National Park is on Hwy 62/180, 110 miles east of El Paso and 55 miles southwest of Carlsbad, NM. Although there is no scheduled public transportation to the park, **Greyhound** (☎in El Paso 915-542-1355; www.greyhound.com) bus drivers on the El Paso–Carlsbad route will drop you off or make a whistle-stop pickup if you make arrangements in advance.

Understand Texas

Texas Today

Oil set the pace for the state's early development, but today's Texas is both diversified and evolving. The economy has been one of the strongest in the nation for the last decade, and it just keeps growing. But, then, so too does the population. Demographics seem ready to shift toward a young, Hispanic majority. And immigration reform is as hot a topic as they come.

Best on Film

Giant (1956) The life of an oil and ranching family, starring Elizabeth Taylor, Rock Hudson and James Dean.
Lonesome Dove (1989) Miniseries about two retired Texas Rangers, a small town and a long cattle drive; based on Larry McMurtry's eponymous book.
The Alamo (1960) John Wayne's epic masterpiece.
Urban Cowboy (1980) Starring John Travolta and a mechanical bull at Gilley's honky-tonk outside Houston.

Best in Print

Texas: A Novel (James A Mitchner; 1985) Historical fiction of mammoth proportion.
In a Narrow Grave (Larry McMurtry; 2001) Classic essays from the state's most iconic author.
Drinker with a Writing Problem (Kinky Friedman; 2011) Compilation of *Texas Monthly* articles by an outrageous humorist.
Looking for Texas (Rick Vanderpool; 2001) Follows the author's 20,500-mile journey photographing Texas.
A Natural State (Stephen Harrigan; 1994) Natural history that evokes the landscapes of Texas.

Conservative-Liberal Divide

Texas is a red state with a blue heart. There's no denying the state has a conservative streak. During the 2012 presidential election, and in the three before it, the state's 38 electoral votes went for Republican candidates, with a 56% to 61% majority. Looking county by county, the notable and consistent exceptions to the red-state rule are Travis County (Austin) and Harris County (urban Houston). There is also a liberal majority in the growing Mexican American–dominated counties along the rural southwestern border.

Republicans have dominated the Texas Legislature and the governor's office for more than 10 years. Governor Rick Perry leads the conservative charge and many expect he's considering another presidential run. Of the divisive conservative-liberal topics that regularly resurface, the ground seems to be shifting on one – gay marriage rights. Despite a 2005 law banning gay marriage, a 2013 University of Texas poll indicates that 28% now support civil unions and 37% support gay marriage. That's 65% in favor of some sort of increase in gay rights. Texas seems to be moseying along the same direction as the rest of the country.

The Economy & Oil

Historically oil and gas exploration and production was the only factor in the success or failure of Texas fortunes. But the boom-and-bust cycle of the 1980s taught the state a thing or two about diversifying. Today the Texas economy is based on numerous breadwinners – including a strong tech sector around Austin and a large bio-medical industry in Houston. Oil no longer tops the list.

During the global recession and slow national recovery, the Texas economy continued to expand, with an average growth rate of 3.1% compared to the nation's 1.6%. Texas has created more private-sector jobs than any other state over the past decade and of the 10 largest states has the lowest unemployment rate. So the mood tends to be justifiably upbeat about the future.

Reasons cited for Texas' success include the absence of income tax, low average housing prices and strong consumer-protection laws that prevented a 'housing bubble' crisis. Meanwhile, the oil industry still plays a big role. Among the 52 top Fortune 500 companies calling Texas home, in addition to Dell and AT&T you'll find names like Exxon-Mobile and Chevron. And the development of Eagle Ford Shale in south-central Texas is setting all kinds of records. So while the majority of people may no longer work directly in the oil industry, it'd be impossible to say it's not a factor.

Population Growth

Texas has been the fastest-growing state in the USA during the 2000s, adding more than five million people during the first 13 years of the decade. According to the US Census Bureau, eight of the nation's 15 fastest growing cities and towns are in Texas. While some of the population growth is attributable to the strong economy and domestic immigration, a portion is due to natural increase. A shrinking and aging Anglo (or Caucasian) population and a growing and young Hispanic one has produced a marked demographic change, especially in urban areas. The Texas State Data Center estimates a shift to a Hispanic majority will happen between 2015 and 2020.

And that's only discussing the population that's been counted. Illegal immigrants in Texas, mostly Hispanic, number approximately 1.65 million according the Pew Hispanic Research Center. Many provide manual labor as a part of the Texas workforce. Critics argue that the population is a drag on state resources such as social services for the poor and tuition assistance. Immigration reformers cite the United States' historical tradition of welcoming all. Phrases like 'seal the border' or 'path to citizenship (amnesty)' can send normally polite Texans over the edge. With no solution in sight and a shifting population, the only thing certain in Texas is change.

POPULATION: **26.06 MILLION**

AREA: **261,232 SQ MILES**

GROSS STATE PRODUCT (GSP): **1.35 BILLION**

ANNUAL GROWTH RATE: **3.1%**

UNEMPLOYMENT: **6.4%**

if Texas were 100 people

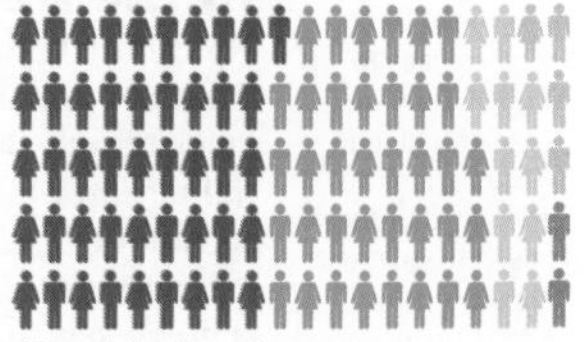

46 would be Caucasian
37 would be Hispanic
11 would be African American
4 would be Asian
2 would be Other

belief systems

(% of population)

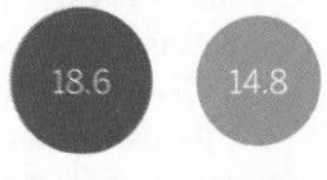

Catholic
Baptist
non-denominational Christian (Evangelical)

Methodist
other
no affiliation

population per sq mile

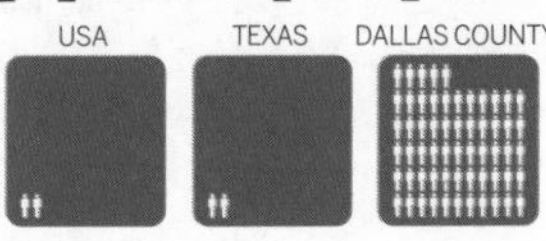

≈ 45 people

History

The Lone Star State was a cultural and political hotbed from the start, belonging to several different colonial powers – and becoming its own country – before joining the USA. Perhaps because of this, legend looms large in Texas history. Mention the Alamo or the JFK assassination and you're bound to hear a variety of tales told, a mix of fact and exaggerated fiction. Not surprising, really, in a state where the history is as iconic as it is actual.

The word 'Texas' goes back to 1691. Spanish explorers found the Caddos so friendly that they began to call their new territory *tejas* ('tay-has'), a corruption of the Caddo word for 'friend.'

In the Beginning...

Texas hasn't always been Texas. Or Mexico, for that matter. Or the United States, or Spain, or France, or any of the six flags that once flew over this epic state in its eight changes of sovereignty. The earliest evidence of humans in what is now Texas exists in the *llano estacado* ('staked plain') section of Texas and New Mexico. Little is known about the various indigenous peoples, but by the time the first Europeans arrived in the 16th century, several distinct groups of Native Americans were settled in the region. One of these tribes, the Caddos, still figures strongly as a namesake and cultural influence in east Texas, where the Caddo Mounds State Historic Site commemorates their unique history.

Spanish Acquisition

Spanish explorers first arrived in Texas territory during the 1500s, mapping the gulf coast and searching for gold. During one failed incursion, Cabeza de Vaca and his Moroccan-born slave, Esteban (likely the first black person to explore the New World) were stranded and held by the Karankawa Indians. His diaries spurred on exploration for years to come.

By the mid-17th century, the Spaniards' tack was more 'please read this pamphlet' than 'take me to the riches.' The conquistadores had triumphed in lands from Florida through present-day Mexico and beyond. Spain set about constructing a series of *misións* (missions) and *presidios* (forts) to convert Native Americans to Christianity and, not incidentally, into Spanish subjects. The earliest mission constructed in Texas was in the 1680s, near what is now El Paso.

TIMELINE

Pre-history

More than 16 species of dinosaurs roamed the to-be-Texas landscape until they became extinct more than 65 million years ago.

c 1400 BC

The Caddo Indians establish a sedentary society, based on agriculture, in east Texas. They construct ceremonial mounds outside present-day Nacogdoches.

1539

Half of those on Franciscan friar Marcos de Niza's greed-fueled expedition die during Indian attacks. The friar flees back to Mexico – hastily claiming the ground he'd covered for Spain, of course.

The French Threat?

Meanwhile, the French were also sniffing around North America. In the 1680s, they laid claim to the territory they called Louisiana and to a piece of east Texas. This hardly amused the Spanish, who constructed Mission San Francisco de los Tejas, outside present-day Nacogdoches (the site is a state park today), and other fortifications. Due to disease, hostile native attacks and Spanish settlement, French 'rule' in the east dissipated a scant five years later.

East Texas cypress trees are hundreds of years old. The moss that hangs off them was nicknamed 'Spanish Beards' by early French settlers in an attempt to insult their Spanish rivals.

Mission Impossible

In 1718 the Spanish began building missions and forts in south-central Texas to reduce the distances crossed by supply trains. Mission San Antonio de Valero, which later became known as the Alamo, and sites along the present-day Mission Trail were constructed around this time. In 1731, the settlement of Villa de Bexar was established by Spanish colonists imported from the Canary Islands, and a civil government was set up in the area. The Spanish Governor's Palace still lies at the heart of San Antonio.

More than 30 missions were eventually built here. During the heyday of the missions, from 1745 to 1775, they became successful enough to attract the rather unpleasant attention of Apache and Comanche Indians. While the missionaries and native tribes who lived within the system learned to defend themselves against physical attack, the failure of the Spanish colonial system itself was a major factor in the missions' eventual undoing.

Mexican Independence

Concurrent with the American, French and Spanish squabbling over North America at the end of the 18th century, a growing movement in Mexico sought freedom from Spain. Sporadic fighting took place from 1810 until 1821, when Spain agreed to Mexican independence. An opportunistic soldier, Antonio López de Santa Anna, eventually helped establish a Mexican Republic, of which he was elected president in 1833.

Newly independent Mexico administratively grouped Texas with the Mexican state of Coahuila. To the north, Mexico included much of what is now Southwestern USA.

Americans Horn In

Before 1820, settlers moving to Texas from the USA were mainly relocated Native Americans, who were being forcibly removed from newly acquired US territories in the southeast.

The first large group of Anglo-American settlers in Texas arrived as the result of a deal brokered by Moses Austin. He negotiated for the Spanish government to allow him and 300 families from the USA to move into central Texas but he died before the move could begin. His son, Stephen Fuller Austin, who is credited in Texas folklore as the 'Father of Texas,'

1598

Spanish explorer Juan de Oñate stopped to feast with Native Americans on the banks of the Rio Grande. Some Texans believe it to be the first real Thanksgiving.

1718

The Mission San Antonio de Valero, aka the Alamo, is founded in present-day San Antonio.

1800

Napoléon Bonaparte forces the Spanish to cede Louisiana to France. Yet three years later France turns around and sells the entire Louisiana Territory to the USA for $15 million.

1810

Miguel Hidalgo y Costilla, parish priest of the town of Dolores, issues his now-famous call to rebellion, the *Grito de Dolores*, demanding 'death to bad government.'

The Six (Count 'Em!) Flags Of Texas

Spanish *1519–1685; 1690–1821*

French *1685–90*

Mexican *1821–36*

Republic of Texas *1836–45*

United States *1845–61*

Confederate States *1861–65*

United States *1865 to the present*

carried out his father's plans in 1821, immediately attracting more than 5000 Americans and creating a bustling trade with Mexico.

The word 'Texian' was coined to describe the region's residents, who were beginning to form a separate identity. By 1830, with more than 30,000 settlers in the Texas territory, the situation was becoming, well, revolting. In that year, a Mexican decree banned further American settlement and limited the importation of slaves. Around that time political unrest in Mexico led to the imposition of martial law and banning of weapons in many Mexican territories, including Texas.

Texas War for Independence

Stephen F Austin traveled to Mexico City to plead the settlers' case for independence, but was arrested and detained. William B Travis led a group of hot-headed Texians who'd rather fight than allow more Mexican troops to arrive. Armed skirmishes throughout 1835 sparked the Texas War for Independence, which officially ran from September 30, 1835, to April 21, 1836.

At the outbreak of war in December 1835, Texian troops (composed of Americans, Mexicans and a fair number of English, Irish, Scottish, Germans and other European settlers) captured San Antonio, and occupied and further fortified the Alamo.

Remember the Alamo!

'You may all go to hell, and I will go to Texas.' Davy Crockett, 1835

It's hard to tell the story of the Battle of the Alamo. There's hot debate about the number of defenders and of Mexican troops and casualties, among many other details. Objective, first-hand accounts are to date impossible to find.

Alamo Movies

The Immortal Alamo (1911) *Silent film.*

The Alamo (1960) *John Wayne directed and starred.*

The Alamo: Thirteen Days to Glory (1987) *Starring Brian Keith.*

The Alamo (2004) *Starring Dennis Quaid.*

It is generally agreed that on February 23, 1836, Mexican general Antonio López de Santa Anna led anywhere from 2500 to 5000 Mexican troops in an attack against the Alamo. The 160 or so men inside the fortress included James Bowie (of Bowie knife fame), who was in command of the Alamo until pneumonia rendered him too sick; William B Travis, who took command of the troops after Bowie's incapacity; and perhaps most famous of all, David Crockett, called 'Davy' by everyone. Crockett, a three-time US congressman from Tennessee with interesting taste in headgear, first gained fame as a frontiersman and then for his public arguments with President Andrew Jackson over the latter's murderous campaigns of Native American 'removal' in the southeastern USA. Less well known were Bowie's and Travis' African American slaves, who fought alongside their masters during the battle and were two of the only male survivors.

Travis dispatched a now-famous letter to other revolutionaries pleading for reinforcements, saying that his men would not stand down under any circumstances – his call was for 'Victory or death.' Because of slow

1819

The USA acquires Florida in exchange for Spanish control over Texas; the USA will control all territory east of it.

1825

The first skirmish in the Texas War for Independence took place on October 2, when Texians raised a flag daring Mexican troops to 'Come and take it'; it being the local cannon.

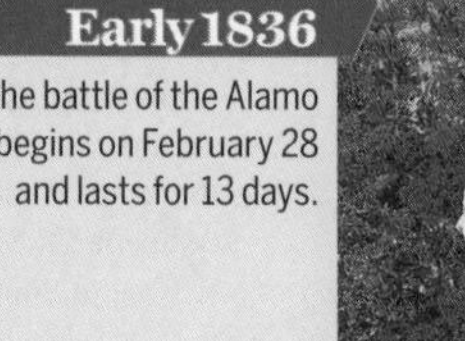

Early 1836

The battle of the Alamo begins on February 28 and lasts for 13 days.

➡ Sam Houston statue (p236)

communications, the only reinforcements that arrived in time were a group of about 30 men from Gonzales, Texas, bringing the total number of Alamo defenders up to 189 – at least according to literature from the Daughters of the Republic of Texas (DRT), which lists the names of all but one, an unidentified African American man.

Santa Anna's troops pounded the Alamo for 13 days before retaking it. Mexican losses were devastating; estimates run as low as 1000 and as high as 2000. When the Alamo was finally recaptured, the advancing troops executed almost all of the surviving defenders. The few who were spared, mostly women, children and slaves, were interrogated and released.

Remember Goliad!

Colonel James Fannin and more than 400 volunteers who had set out too late to assist at the Alamo encountered Mexican troops north of Goliad. After a daylong battle, the Texians surrendered and were taken to the *presidio*, which was occupied by the Mexican army. On March 27, Palm Sunday, Santa Anna ordered between 300 and 350 prisoners shot – a death toll about twice the number lost at the Alamo. The two events, instantly labeled 'massacres' by Texians, galvanized the troops, who continued fighting under the rallying cry of 'Remember the Alamo! Remember Goliad!'

Perhaps as a result of losses suffered and supplies spent at the battles of the Alamo and Goliad, Santa Anna's troops simply were not prepared when, on April 21, they ran into troops commanded by Samuel Houston. The Texian general was a former major general in Tennessee's militia and an 'Indian fighter' under US general Andrew Jackson. At the Battle of San Jacinto, outside modern-day Houston, Santa Anna's forces were finally and completely routed. Texas' war for independence was won.

The Lone Star Republic

The 54 delegates who gathered at Washington-on the-Brazos on March 1, 1836, literally wrote the Texas Declaration of Independence overnight – while the Alamo was under siege. Though Texas declared itself a 'a free and independent republic,' neither the USA nor Mexico recognized it as such. In its early years the new republic's main business was forging trade and political ties and trying hard to establish a government and a capital city.

In 1839, the central Texas village of Waterloo was renamed Austin, in honor of Stephen F, and the capital was established there. That same year, the Republic of Texas' policy toward the Native Americans who lived within its borders changed drastically, and a ruthless and thorough campaign of removal began, leading to an increase in raiding parties. The turn of the decade was also marred by continual harassment from Mexican troops in the south.

EL CAMINO REAL

El Camino Real was a trail between Mexico and Louisiana that was well traveled by the Spanish, and later by incoming US settlers. Historical markers along 34 miles of northeast Texas' Hwy 21, outside Alto, mark part of the route.

April 1836

April 21, Sam Houston's Texian army wins a decisive battle against Mexican General Santa Anna. Texas becomes a republic.

1846

Texas' annexation by the USA leads directly to the Mexican-American War, a total rout in which US troops capture Mexico City from Santa Anna.

1848

At the end of the Mexican-American War, Mexico cedes modern Texas, California, Utah, Colorado and most of New Mexico and Arizona to the USA. *¡Ay, caramba!* Talk about a loss.

1900

The (first) Great Storm hits populous Galveston Island, killing an estimated 6000 to 8000 people the night of September 8.

President Sam Houston and the republic lobbied Washington for annexation as a territory in order to gain assistance in settling both the border dispute with Mexico and issues with Native Americans. A country for less than 10 years, Texas was annexed to the USA during a state constitutional convention in 1845.

Until 1839 the city of Austin was called Waterloo. (It's still the name of Austin's best-known music shop, Waterloo Records.)

Civil War & Reconstruction

The US Civil War (1861–65) was brought on by a number of issues, including states rights, but standing in the foreground was the moral and economic debate over slavery. Settlers poured into Texas from slave-owning states in the South, but Governor Sam Houston was firmly against the South-favored secession. Popular opinion and a referendum defeated him, and he was forced to resign.

Texas seceded from the USA and joined the Confederate States of America on March 16, 1861. Aside from providing an estimated 80,000 troops, Texas' role in the Civil War was mainly one of supplying food to the Confederate war machine. Even if Texas soil did not play a large part in the war, the wounds ran incredibly deep for years afterward.

President Andrew Johnson, the Southerner and former slaveholder who succeeded Lincoln, devised a Reconstruction plan. While his plan granted many concessions, it was absolutely firm that the states' constitutions ratify the 13th Amendment, abolishing slavery, before re-admittance. The Texas Constitution of 1866, hastily drawn up to assure re-admittance to the Union, granted African Americans some measure of civil rights, but it did not give them the right to vote until martial law imposed it. Hyper-restrictive Black Codes, later to be expanded to what became known as Jim Crow laws, were introduced, making it illegal for African Americans to be unemployed, restricting freedom of movement and segregating much of Southern life into white and African American camps.

In 1519, Alonzo Avarez de Piñeda mapped the coast of the Gulf of Mexico from Florida to Mexico, creating the first cartographic record of present-day Texas. He camped at the mouth of the Rio Grande (which he called the 'river of palms').

On the Cattle Trail

During the Civil War, the Confederate forces' need for food had increased Texas cattle production. Ranching in Texas became an enormous business, and cattle drives – the herding of up to 200,000 head of longhorn steers northward – were born.

Of all the trails that ran through Texas, the evocatively named Goodnight-Loving Trail to Pueblo and Denver, Colorado, and Cheyenne, Wyoming, and the Sedalia Trail to Sedalia, Missouri, are the most famous. But it was the Chisholm Trail – through San Antonio to Abilene, Kansas, at the western terminus of the Kansas Pacific Railroad – that really spurred the business of bringing Texas cattle to market. By 1873, the railroad had reached Fort Worth, and cattle could also be transported the newfangled way.

1909

After being jailed for six weeks at Fort Sam Houston, Apache leader Goyathlay (aka Geronimo) dies a prisoner of war. The US military has still not repatriated his remains.

1913

Mexican revolutionary Pancho Villa is a darling of the American media, portrayed as a dashing freedom fighter. Eventually, the US turns against him and Villa is mysteriously assassinated in 1923.

WWI

Four major military bases are established in Texas for training – Camp Travis (San Antonio), Camp Logan (Houston), Camp MacArthur (Waco) and Camp Bowie (Fort Worth).

1920s

Twenty-eight bars and two breweries line the party-hearty streets of Brenham, Texas. Prohibition comes to town, bars close, and the parties go underground.

RECONCILIATION BARBECUE

On the eve of WWI the central Texas town of Brenham was heavily German; kids of different heritages all studied German in school. Then the Ku Klux Klan rode into town, tarring and feathering those of German descent, beating up prominent town businesspeople, and torching the German newspaper print shop. People began avoiding the mean streets of Brenham, and businesses withered.

The city decided to solve the problem Texas-style: by throwing a giant barbecue to which they would invite all sides. On the day of the festivities, October 29, 1923, more than 10,000 people – German speakers, African Americans, Czechs, Mexicans, you name it – gathered at the firefighters' park to eat smoked meat cooked over giant pits, plus German potato salad and peach cobbler with Brenham Creameries' (later Blue Bell) ice cream. The German community agreed to stop publicly speaking or teaching in their native tongue in exchange for an antiviolence truce. Soon after that the KKK – at least in Brenham – disbanded.

Though immortalized in many old Western movies, the cattle-drive days barely lasted two decades. By the early 1880s, with the invention of barbed wire, fences stretched across much of Texas. Disputes naturally arose. In 1883 Texas banned the cutting of fences, legislating a new way of life throughout the state. (In Austin it's still illegal to carry and conceal wire cutters in your pocket.) The Texas Rangers, once mere border guards, were reinstated as a state police force to enforce the new law. This was, effectively, the end of what most of us think of as the cowboy era.

The first barbed fence, then known as 'thorny wire' was patented by Michael Kelley in 1868. The Devil's Rope Museum in McLean today recognizes 2000 types of barbed wire.

Black Gold

As early as 1866, oil wells were striking in east Texas. At the time, oil was being put to a number of uses, including the sealing of dirt roads. But speculators bet that oil, found in sufficient supply, could replace coal as an energy mainstay.

Everything changed on January 10, 1901, when a drilling site at Spindletop, east of Houston in Beaumont, pierced a salt dome, setting forth a gusher of oil so powerful that it took days to bring it under control. Spindletop began producing an estimated 80,000 barrels of oil per day. As automobiles and railroads turned to the oil industry for fuel, discoveries of 'black gold' financed the construction of much of modern Texas.

San Antonio's early-20th-century growth was also due to the military; Fort Sam Houston was joined by Kelly Air Force Base, now the nation's oldest air force base, in 1917, followed by Lackland, Randolph and Brooks Air Force Bases.

1930s

WPA workers begin to restore and renovate San Antonio's old Spanish missions, which have fallen into disrepair since Texas' independence from Mexico.

MICHAEL DEFREITAS / GETTY IMAGES ©

➡ Mission Espada (p104)

WWII

The government creates a dozen new military bases and activates more than 40 airfields in Texas.

1963

On November 22, as his motorcade passes by, President John F Kennedy is shot from a sixth floor window in the Book Depository in Dallas.

Texas History Online

Handbook of Texas History *(www.tshaonline.org)*

Lonestar Junction *(www.lsjunction.com)*

Daughters of the Republic of Texas *(www.drtl.org.)*

Texas Almanac *(www.texasalmanac.com)*

The Great Depression

Following the end of WWI in 1918, Texas' economic machine, as well as the nation's, was humming right along. The surge in private automobiles made for an enormous Texas oil boom, and people were dancing the Charleston in the streets.

Then, on Black Thursday, October 24, 1929, the New York Stock Exchange hiccuped and the bottom fell out of the economy. The crash, the result of unchecked Wall Street trading practices, led the US and the world into the Great Depression. Northern Texas was part of the region that became known as the 'dust bowl,' as former farmland was destroyed by overuse and lack of rain. Increased oil production caused a market glut that further depressed prices.

As part of Roosevelt's New Deal, the Works Progress Administration (WPA) and Civilian Conservation Corps (CCC) were created. The WPA sent armies of workers to construct buildings, roads, dams, trails and housing. The CCC worked to restore state and national parks. The cabins and other lodging in state parks such as Caddo Lake and Davis Mountain date from this time.

WWII & Postwar

New Deal or not, some felt what the country really needed to break out of the Depression was a good war. The Japanese attack on Pearl Harbor, Hawaii, on December 7, 1941, finally brought the USA into the fighting that had been going on throughout the world since 1939.

The Texas war machine was brought back to full capacity. With the activation of all its bases, the creation of more than a dozen new ones and more than 40 airfields, Texas became a major preparing ground for WWII soldiers – almost 1.5 million were trained in the state.

The economic prosperity in the USA after WWII was unprecedented. The wartime economy had created a powerhouse, and when the fighting stopped in 1945, industry didn't want to stop with it. For the next 15 years, the US economy surged, fueled by low consumer credit rates and a defense-based economy that plowed money into manufacturing military hardware (as well as ever more automobiles and household appliances). Most people were feeling pretty good. So good, in fact, that a whole passel of Texans was born in this period: the baby boomers.

Recent Texas Governors

Rick Perry (2000 to present)

George W Bush (1995–2000)

Ann Richards (1991–95)

Bill Clemens (1987–91)

Mark White (1983–87)

1960s

Native son Lyndon Baines Johnson was from Stonewall, east of Austin, in south-central Texas. Johnson, affectionately known as LBJ, had a well-deserved reputation for being a hard-nosed Southern Democrat. He was as stubborn as a barn full of mules, as dirty a political fighter as he needed to be, and fiercely loyal to Texas in the fight for pork-barrel

1960s

LBJ's administration sees the USA through the invasion of North Vietnam, civil protest at home and 'the Great Society,' an unprecedented flurry of social legislation.

1969

Neil Armstrong transmits the first words from the surface of the moon: 'Houston, the Eagle has landed,' on July 20.

1978

Dallas, the prime-time soap opera following the oil-rich Ewing clan, premieres to an adoring audience. Fans storm the real Southfork Ranch.

1970s

Gas prices quadruple. Texans – who are the biggest domestic oil supplier and have many of the nation's largest refineries – profit and profit some more.

HOUSTON & THE SPACE RACE

Upon his election as vice president, one of the first things Lyndon Johnson did was to work on instituting well-funded federal programs back home in Texas. The most notable of these was the relocation of the National Aeronautics and Space Administration's (NASA) Mission Control from Florida to Texas. At the time, the Mercury space missions were just getting under way. As the 'space race' between the USA and the USSR heated up, the forward-thinking vice president realized the enormous financial potential. He lobbied congress mercilessly and in 1961 was victorious. Although launches continued to leave from Cape Canaveral, Mission Control and the astronaut training program were moved to the Manned Space Flight Center (now, cozily enough, called the Johnson Space Center) near Houston.

government contracts. As majority leader of the US Senate, Johnson accepted the vice-presidential nomination in 1960.

On November 22, 1963, President John Fitzgerald Kennedy and Vice President Johnson rode in separate open limousines through downtown Dallas. At 12:30pm, JFK was shot. Texas governor John M Connally, riding in the seat in front of the president, was also injured by gunfire. The president died at 1pm; Connally survived. Later that day, as Kennedy's body was being transported to Washington, DC, Vice President Johnson took the oath of office aboard Air Force One, the presidential airplane, with Jacqueline Kennedy standing at his side. LBJ defeated Barry Goldwater in the presidential election of 1964, and his administration oversaw some of the USA's most tumultuous, tragic, and socially catalyzing events, including the Vietnam War and Civil Rights Movement.

Boom then Bust

The energy crisis in the 1970s brought Sultan-of-Bruneian wealth to Texas. The crisis began when members of the Organization of the Petroleum Exporting Countries (OPEC) imposed a major reduction in oil sales to the USA and its allies to punish the country for its pro-Israel policy. Texans found themselves the biggest domestic suppliers of oil, and laughed all the way to the bank.

The oil shortage created a class of nouveaux riches, who played the part as if they had been supplied by central casting. Newly wealthy Texans bought British titles outright from debt-ridden members of the British aristocracy, creating legions of Lady Jane Billy Bobs and Duke Zachary Jims. Ranches became practically passé in the move to bigger and better spreads for oil barons, who also built skyscrapers, hotels, casinos and pleasure domes. The original *Dallas*, a prime-time soap opera

NASA's space shuttle fleet – Columbia, Challenger, Discovery, Atlantis and Endeavour – flew a total of 135 missions between 1979 and July 2011.

1984

PC revolutionary Michael Dell creates a little computer company from his University of Texas dorm room. The billions come later.

1993

Federal agents storm the Branch Davidian compound outside Waco. Cult leader David Koresh and 85 of his followers, along with four law officers, are killed.

Late 1990s

The dot-com boom hits. Laid-back college town and capital, Austin, becomes a hotbed for technology companies, earning the nickname 'Silicon Hills'.

2000

On November 2, Governor George W Bush becomes the second George Bush to be elected president of the United States.

following the high jinks of that wacky, oil-rich Ewing clan, premiered in 1978 and showed off Texas excess for all the world, which lapped it up.

By the close of the energy crisis, the country had developed new sources of oil (mainly in Texas and Central and South America, as well as in Alaska) and new types of energy (nuclear, hydroelectric and others that had existed for years, but had yet to be put to large-scale use).

When Iran ceased sales to the US in 1979, other oil producing nations flooded the market. As OPEC argued, oil prices halved; by 1986, it was down to a paltry $10 a barrel, and Texas was hurting. Oil extraction and exploration became unprofitable. Downtown Houston became little more than a ghost town, with unoccupied office towers filling the streets in what looked like a post-apocalyptic nightmare.

During the 1990s the Texas economy diversified. Trade with Mexico began booming with the 1994 passage of the North American Free Trade Agreement (NAFTA). Technology was another big story in the 1990s; Austin, with its highly educated populace, became a powerhouse of high-tech companies and innovation.

LIQUID GOLD

Texas produces 30% of the oil in the US. Production has doubled since 2005, largely due to the development of Eagle Ford shale.

Double Feature: The George Bushes

Though originally from Massachusetts, Republican George HW Bush, the senior, moved his young family to west Texas in 1948, where he worked in the oil industry. By the 1960s he had turned to politics, representing a Houston district in the House of Representatives before he later became CIA director and Ronald Reagan's vice-president in 1981. He ran and won one term as president in 1988.

His son George W Bush grew up in Midland and Houston. He'd worked on others' campaigns, as a business owner in oil and gas exploration and production, and as managing partner of the Texas Rangers baseball team, but he'd never held public office before winning the Texas governorship in 1994 and again in 1998.

In January 2001, Bush, the junior, became only the second son in American history (after John Quincy Adams in 1824) to follow his father to the White House. The election was a bitterly contested one involving recounted votes in Florida and a landmark Supreme Court case. In the end, although Al Gore received more popular votes than Bush, he lost by electoral votes. Bush defied his critics by winning the presidency again in 2004.

Not All That Long Ago

Those still involved in the oil industries had long joked: 'Lord, give me just one more boom and I promise I won't piss it away.' Crude-oil prices rose dramatically in the early 2000s, and it looked like their dreams just may have come true. Texas took a hit along with the rest of the nation during the global economic crisis, but the state economy remained strong.

2006

Longhorn quarterback Vince Young leads the University of Texas to a second, back-to-back Rose Bowl victory. The streets of Austin 'bleed orange' – the school's colors.

2008

In September 1, Hurricane Ike makes landfall at Galveston, devastating the island and knocking out power in parts of Houston for 21 days.

2011

NASA's Mission Control at Johnson Space Center in Houston guides the last space shuttle launch before decommissioning the spacecraft.

2013

On April 17, 2013, a fertilizer plant explosion killed 15 and wounded at least 160, devastating the tiny town of West, Texas (population 2800).

Life in Texas

There are about as many ways to live in this giant state as there are fleas on a farm dog. Sure, pickup trucks, cowboy boots and country songs are a part of the puzzle, but so are *quinceañeras* (15th-birthday, coming-of-age parties) and Tejano-conjunto music. That said, a few constants remain: faith, family and Friday night football all still run deep to the heart of Texas.

Who are Texans?

Texan First

'Don't mess with Texas' was the bumper-sticker slogan of a famous anti-litter campaign, but the sentiment speaks volumes about the fiercely independent spirit of Texas. After all, this is the only state in the union that was once its own republic – and locals from Longview to Laredo won't let you forget it. Texans, in general, are mighty patriotic and proud to be Americans, but they are Texans first.

Why, you say? Maybe it's left over cowboy cockiness. Or maybe it's because Texas is as big as a country. As a sovereign nation, the state's economy would be the 14th largest in the world, and one of the few that kept on growing during the global recession. Fifty-two of the top Fortune 500 companies call Texas home; Houston is the nation's second busiest port; the state has one of the top-10 lowest costs of living... If all this sounds like bravado, it is. And as they say here, 'it ain't braggin' if it's true.' Newcomers may find the home-state pride equal parts obnoxious and endearing. Locals (and quite a few recent transplants, too) wouldn't have it any other way.

Great Texas Town Names

- *Happy*
- *Utopia*
- *Earth*
- *Paris*
- *Bacon*
- *Turkey*
- *Notrees*
- *Cut and Shoot*

Talkin' Texan

Howdy, y'all... Say that to a single person and they'll know you ain't from around here, are ya. 'Y'all' is a conjunction of 'you' and 'all', making it plural. Everybody knows that.

The way Texans talk is mighty particular, and it ain't to be mistaken with any old Georgia boy's drawl. Them smart folks who study this say the accent's influences draw from the Lower South (Louisiana, Alabama) and South Midland (Tennessee, Kentucky) dialects mixed in with Mexican Spanish and Central European influences.

What's all that mumbo jumbo mean? It's a Southern accent, sure 'nough, but it's not quite as lilting (some might say as mushy) as those in the Deep South (though you hear that a bit in East Texas). The main sound characteristic is the flattened vowels, which is what makes 'right' sound 'raht', as in 'I'll be *raht 'chere* when you get back.' There's also a tendency to elongate words. We know some who can stretch an affirmative *yea-a-as* into mighty near three syllables. And that's another thing, here two-word adjectives and verbs are used to add emphasis: *fixin' to* (about to), *might oughtta* (maybe should), *cotton to* (take a liking to).

But it's not just about the *way* Texans say thangs, it's *what* they say. Though usage might be fading a bit, colorful metaphors and similes still spice up conversations. This author's personal favorite is when her

95-year-old mother-in-law says something is 'so soft it makes her ass laugh.' A few more fun ones (avert your eyes if you're easily offended):

- *More nervous than a cat in a room fulla rockin' chairs.*
- *Hotter than a jalpeña fart.*
- *Purdy as a speckled pup.*
- *Slicker 'n owl sheee-it.*
- *He was on that like white on rice.*
- *He doesn't have sense 'nough to pour piss out-ov-a boot.*
- *She was hit with the ugly stick.*
- *This ain't my first rodeo.*
- *Dance with the one that brung ya*

Light Texas Reading

Kinky Friedman's Guide to Texas Etiquette (Kinky Friedman)

Just a Guy: Notes from a Blue Collar Life (Bill Engvall)

There's Nothing in the Middle of the Road but Yellow Stripes & Dead Armadillos (Jim Hightower)

Fixin' to be Texan (Helen Bryant)

Regional Differences

All inadequate, of course, but it is possible to make some vast generalizations about the different personalities you'll find in the cities and regions around the state.

If Texas is a 'Whole Other Country,' as the tourist board claims, then Austin is another country within that country. The progressive politics and creative inhabitants of the capital city are just way too far out there for many Texans. Hippies moved in during the 1970s and their legacy lives on. Green is not an idea here, it's a way of life. Even the dot-commers who came next were totally cool. Today, the high-tech workforce pool (and favorable tax structures) continues to attract employers like Facebook and eBay. Downtown especially, the population is youngish, hip, athletically outdoorsy, and probably has the highest number of tattoos per capita. Other-city dwellers are likely to admit Austin's a great place to visit, they just don't want to live there. Austinites are more than OK with that.

In the Big D you'll find more shoppers and socialites – it's the see-and-be-seen set of the Texas crowd. And it's not all show. Dallas is sixth on the list of cities that house the most billionaires (with a 'B') in the world – 14 live in Dallas, to be exact. That's not to say people aren't friendly – this *is* Texas after all. Folks here will smile and call you sweetie-pie along with the best of 'em. Thankfully the big hair and

THE COWBOYS

Perhaps no other figure in literary or cinematic history has been so romanticized as the cowboy. The image has become a symbol of the freedom of wide open spaces and the industrious and untamable nature of the Texan people themselves.

Mexican *vaqueros* (wranglers) brought their methods to Texas and passed them on. The cowboys caught calves using a lariat (from the Spanish *la reata*), and imprinted them for identification using the heated-iron design of the owner's brand. When the cowboys got bored they strengthened their skills by competing with one another; events that have evolved into the rodeos you see all over the state come springtime.

But it's the cattle drive that most captured the cinematographer's vision of Texas. Around the end of the Civil War, cowboys would herd thousands of cattle up the Chisolm Trail to Kansas City railroads. The pack was led by a scout and chuckwagon, who would prepare food in advance of the arrival of the herd. To filter the dust, cowboys used bandanna handkerchiefs tied over their noses and mouths.

While horses would be changed in relays along the trail, the cowboy always kept his own masterfully crafted saddle. By the 1880s the railroads had come to Fort Worth and most of the land was fenced. Cattle driving was a hardscrabble life, one that didn't last more than a couple of decades, but the cowboy legacy in Texas endures today.

rhinestone-studded style days passed with the '80s (OK, the '90s). This is the new *Dallas*, complete with a new TV show.

In Dallas the money's new, and everyone flaunts it. In Houston the money's old, and nobody gives a damn. This is the kind of town where the guy in old cowboy boots drinking a Lone Star at the bar might be an oil-company millionaire. Or he might just be a guy in old cowboy boots. Wearing jeans to a fancy restaurant is not frowned upon, as long as they're starched. Although completely casual, Houston retains a strong conservative streak. Even though the city has a large gay and lesbian population and parade, you're unlikely to see much PDA on the street.

San Antonio is probably the most Tex-Mexican of the bunch, and locals are proud of their Hispanic art and culture. Town-wide festivals, or fiestas, are common, and you can hear mariachis on the Riverwalk nightly. These festivities are just a natural out-growth of the warm, extended-family get-togethers that happen every weekend all around town. If you're lucky enough to be invited, you'll be calling the matriarch *abeula* (grandmother, or beloved older woman) before long.

El Paso is closer to California than to east Texas, and it shows. In many ways the residents (and the food) have a lot more in common with New Mexico than with the Texas Hill Country heartland.

West Texans, in general, are a rural lot. Living with that blazing sun and desert drought isn't easy. It's a hardy, well-tanned soul that chooses such an isolated life; that's probably why there's a certain stubborn, determined-to-go-my-own-way spirit here. Artists and outdoorsmen and women are drawn to outposts such as Marfa and Fort Davis

Ethnic Identities

Hispanic

According to the census bureau, just under 40% of Texas' population is of Hispanic descent. But that statistic is misleading, and not just because everyone might not have been counted. Tex-Mex is a way of life here. Mexican culture, foods and traditions are inextricably interwoven in the Texas tapestry – whether people are conscious of it or not. Office workers order out breakfast *taquitos* (tacos) for breakfast, Spanglish peppers everyone's conversations and school kids study 'the first Thanksgiving' when Don Juan de Oñate and 500 followers broke bread with Native Americans on the banks of the Rio Grande in 1598.

Understandably, the influence is more pronounced the farther south you get. But there are pockets in any city where it's no trouble at all to get around if you don't speak English. Unfortunately, the state's prosperity has not extended evenly to all quarters. Texas has the highest proportion of minimum-wage workers in the USA, and the lowest percentage of citizens who hold a high-school diploma. Areas of the state with the highest numbers of Hispanics are often the poorest. Bringing family members over officially is a complicated process that can take years and years. It's not uncommon to hear of those who hired coyotes, the often exploitative 'guides' that help some circumvent the system.

European

Of the many European immigrant groups that arrived at the turn of the 20th century, it's the Germans and the Czechs who have had the longest lasting cultural affects on the state. Most settled in the Hill Country and central-east Texas counties like Washington, where today you can see signs asking *Jak sa maš*? (How are you?) A surprising number of residents still speak the language of their forebears. Both the small-town dance halls and meat-market barbecue that Texas is famous for grew out of traditions these Europeans brought with them. Local festivals in central areas celebrate the polka and favorite foods, such as sausage and *kolache* (sweet-bread pastries stuffed with savories or sweets.)

Asian

Although making up only between 4% and 7% of any city's population, Asian immigration to urban Texas has been increasing, especially from Vietnam. Houston has the largest melting pot, with Korean neighborhoods and a little India, in addition to large Vietnamese and Chinese communities. This has meant an expanded array of authentic foods have entered the local lexicon. Don't be surprised when a *bánh mì* (Vietnamese sandwich) food truck pulls up next to you.

Native American

There's a notable absence of Native Americans in Texas. The small population is a result of several factors, including disease. But much of it can be attributed to the mass exile way back during the end of the Republic of Texas and beginning of statehood. There are three state-recognized tribes with reservations in Texas. The Alabama-Coushatta Reservation, and its casino, is in east Texas, near Livingston. The Ysleta del Sur Pueblo has its reservation outside El Paso, and the Kickapoo Tribe occupies land in southwest Texas, near Eagle Pass. Of the east Texas tribe whose language gave Texas its name, the Caddo Indians, only a dozen or so native speakers remain.

HOWDY

If a Texan passes you on a country road in a truck, they'll likely raise a few fingers off the steering wheel in greeting or give a nod of their head. That's code for 'Howdy,' so nod back and smile.

Way of Life

So you want to know about life in Texas? Pull on some boots, get in the truck, cruise the farm-to-market (FM) backroads, eat hole-in-the-wall barbecue, jump in a swimming hole, buy someone a beer, sweet-talk your waiter, burn your tongue with salsa, witness the madness of a high-school football game, say 'ma'am' to young girls and old ladies alike, wave to a stranger, curse in Spanish, and two-step all night in a honky-tonk. In other words, live it.

Kicking-back

Texas is a work-hard, play-hard kind of state. Kicking-back is serious business around here. Come weekend, you'll usually find folks in the great outdoors: off at their hunting camp, attending their tike's football game, throwin' some meat on the pit (which could be any kind of barbecue, even a gas grill), or just rockin' on the neighbor's porch.

In the summer heat water plays a big role – anyone who can get to some usually does. Lakes fill with recreational boaters and swimmers, and those close enough to hit the beaches, do. Rivers seem to hold a special place in Texan hearts. Many a young one grew up floating in an innertube down the Guadalupe, or the Frio, or the Comal, or the San Marcos... Whether riding over mild white water, shoes flying, kids squealing, or drifting peacefully for hours with beer in the cooler bobbing next to you, it's a big party – one that's not to be missed if you can help it. Locals don't even worry if the river's not running, they'll set their camp chair – or their bottoms – down in the water and stay a spell anyway.

Weather is a big topic of conversation in Texas. When it rains a lot, it can be a *gully-washer*, a *toad-strangler* or *turd-floater*. But until it rains like *a cow pissin' on a flat rock*, it's hardly coming down at all.

Hunting & Gun Ownership

Yes, there are a lot of guns in Texas. And no, Texas gun laws are not especially strident. Beyond saying that, it's hard to pin down many specifics about gun ownership in the state. Wild guestimates conclude that there are about 51 million guns here, for a population of 26 million. Most owners here firmly believe that they have a right to protect their property and those they love; that having a gun, and knowing how to use it, is not just a crime deterrent, but a crime stopper. Not to mention that hunting is as much a Texas tradition as the pickup truck. Boys get their first pellet guns at eight or 10, and they're accompanying their fathers on dove and deer hunts soon after. Girls are more than welcome to come along if they want to. Gun owning is a way of life in Texas, and despite increasing gun-control legislation in other states, that's not something likely to change any time soon.

Though not enforced, according to the Texas Bill of Rights, one must acknowledge a supreme being before being able to hold public office.

Religion

Texas is considered to be the 'buckle' in the Bible Belt – a swath of states across the Southern USA associated with conservative protestantism and evangelical Christianity. Roughly 57% of the population claims some religious affiliation. Surprisingly, Catholicism is actually the largest denomination, due to the significant Hispanic population.

The evidence is in the good number of churches you'll see as you drive along. Lubbock is rumored to have the highest number per capita in the US, but that's hard to pin down. Abilene has three Christian universities in a town of 118,117 people. In Houston, charismatic church leader Joel Osteen bought out the former Rockets basketball stadium when his Lakewood Church needed to expand (that's 16,300 seats filled twice on Sunday).

In east Texas, this also means many of the counties are 'dry' – you can order drinks in restaurants, but you can't buy liquor at stores there. And nowhere in the state can you by beer before noon on a Sunday. Go out to a restaurant lunch midday and you'll find all the tables full with families come straight from church in their Sunday best.

Stars from Texas

- *Jennifer Love Hewitt*
- *Eva Longoria*
- *Jamie Foxx*
- *Matthew McConaughey*
- *Renee Zellweger*
- *Steve Martin*
- *Tommy Lee Jones*

Culture

Reading & Writing

Writing has deep roots in Texas. In the 1880s, famed short-story writer William Sidney Porter, whose pen name was O Henry, lived and wrote in a Victorian cottage in Austin that's now the O Henry Museum. Born in 1890, Pulitzer Prize–winning novelist Katherine Anne Porter, who grew up in Kyle, won critical acclaim for her penetrating short stories.

There are hundreds of notable Texas writers, and more are coming up all the time. We've listed a sampling of the best that Texas has to offer

PICK-UP MAN

There's just something women like about a pick-up man. Joe Diffie

Joe Diffie's classic 1990s country song captures the pick-em-up truck–lovin' spirit here when he says 'You could set my truck on fire and roll it down the hill, and I still wouldn't trade it for a coupe de ville...' Texans may be mighty attached to their trucks, but how come? Well, the plain and simple truth is that they're darned usefui – for loadin', haulin' or pullin' just about anything. It's the state's long distances, bumpy country roads and rural ranchin' traditions that originally made trucks a necessity, but now they're a way of life. Texans buy 14% of trucks sold in the nation, far more than their fair share. Here, a pickup isn't just transportation – it's an extension of one's self, a symbol of freedom and independence, and of status. Drive a Ford F150 Platinum Edition and you'll have heated and cooled leather seats, automatic fold-down running boards, an extendable bed and cargo holder, Sirus XM satellite radio and a 6.2 liter V8 engine for only $52K. Sidlin' up next to your boy- or girlfriend on the front bench seat is almost a right of passage in the country. As a gal, if you drive up in a polished red, one-ton Dodge dually (with four rear tires), you're bound to attract attention from some good ol' boy (trust this author on that one).

ICONIC TEXAS FILMS

Giant (1956) This film's as sprawling as the King Ranch that was its inspiration. Elizabeth Taylor, Rock Hudson and James Dean are superb in this big-ticket yarn tracing the life of an oil and ranching family.

The Last Picture Show (1971) This engaging film is based on a Larry McMurtry novel that follows the coming of age of two high-school football players in a deader-than-dirt small Texas town in the 1950s.

The Thin Blue Line (1988) Director Errol Morris' powerful documentary tells the story of Randall Adams, who was given a life prison sentence for murdering a Dallas policeman but who turned out to be innocent. The film got Adams released – no small feat – and captured the confession of the real killer.

El Mariachi (1992) Robert Rodriguez's little movie shot on the Texas–Mexico border for $7000 became an icon for film-school students everywhere when it was shown across the USA. It is a charming fable about an unlucky traveling mariachi.

Hands on a Hard Body (1997) SR Bindler's hilarious documentary follows four sleep-deprived contestants as they vie to win a new Nissan hardbody pickup truck.

Hope Floats (1998) Sandra Bullock and Harry Connick Jr play former school mates falling in love when she returns to her small Texas hometown after a messy divorce. Does a good job showcasing life in little Smithville.

Friday Night Lights (2004) Predating the TV series, the movie is based on Buzz Bissinger's true story about the role the local Permian Panthers High School football team played in uplifting the depressed west Texas town of Odessa.

No Country for Old Men (2007) Cormac McCarthy's bleak Western landscapes meet the Coen Brothers' morbid humor in this rapturously terrifying flick. It's a harrowing, tightly paced film about a welder in west Texas who finds a bundle of drug money and decides to keep it. (Guess what? *Bad* idea.)

to give you an overview. An honorable mention goes to vampire author Anne Rice, who lived in Texas for a time.

Larry McMurtry (1936–) The Wichita Falls–born icon whose many Texas-set books and screenplays have entered into the realm of legend. *Lonesome Dove, The Last Picture Show* and *Terms of Endearment* are just a few of his novels.

Sandra Cisneros (1954–) A San Antonio resident who grew up straddling the Mexican–American cultural line. Her first novel, *House on Mango Street*, is a must-read.

James A Mitchner (1907–1997) A Texas transplant, Mitchner is known for his epic fictionalized histories of regions and countries, including, of course, *Texas.*

Molly Ivins (1944–2007) Nobody beat syndicated columnist Molly Ivins on pure acerbic wit and the exposure of Texisms big and small. Her books were even better; start with *Molly Ivins Can't Say That, Can She?*

Cormac McCarthy (1933–) El Paso–born McCarthy has written numerous brooding, dark and masterfully crafted novels. *All the Pretty Horses* won the US national book award.

Mary Karr (1955–) Known for her best-selling, shoot-from-the-hip memoir *The Liar's Club*, which brought her gritty Texas girlhood to vivid life. *Cherry* was the follow-up.

James Lee Burke (1936–) Best known for his series of Dave Robicheaux detective novels, such as *Purple Cane Road*. Burke also wrote *Two for Texas*, a historical novel covering the Texas War for Independence.

Rick Riordan (1964–) His page-turning thrillers have wonderfully twisted plots; look for *The Devil Went Down to Austin*, *The Last King of Texas* or *The Widower's Two-Step*.

On the Big & Little Screen

Hundreds and hundreds of films have been shot in Texas, including cult favorites *Dazed and Confused* and *Office Space*, and the original slasher flick, *Texas Chainsaw Massacre*.

In recent years Austin's film-making has blossomed into an industry spearheaded by directors Richard Linklater, Robert Rodriguez and Quentin Tarantino, and actor Sandra Bullock, all of whom either live or own property in Austin. Of the state's many film festivals, the town boasts two of the heavy hitters: the Austin Film Festival (p69) in October and the South by Southwest (SXSW) Film Festival (p68) in March.

Any number of TV shows have included Texas in some capacity, including *Reba, King of the Hill, The Client List*, even *Storage Wars Texas*, a reality show on A&E. But *Dallas* (1978-1989) is undoubtedly the most recognized Texas TV show of all times. The soap opera resumed as the new *Dallas* in 2012, continuing to follow the filthy-rich oil family, the Ewings. Several original cast members returned; unfortunately Larry Hagman passed away during the filming of the second season.

Coming in a close second for illustrating iconic Texas stereotypes is *Friday Night Lights* (2006–2011), based on the film and the book of the same name. It was originally based on life and football in the small west Texas town of Odessa. Though garnering critical acclaim and cult-like status in-state, it was never universally popular and was cancelled. You can still catch it on iTunes and Netflix.

The Searchers (directed by John Ford; 1956) is one of the finest roles for John Wayne – the ultimate silver-screen cowboy. A pioneer family is murdered on their Texas ranch, and their daughter Natalie Wood is kidnapped, setting off a decade-long search by her uncle, the Duke.

Music Scene

Country and western crooners dusty from the trail, western swing artists mixing it up, outlaws creating their own kind of music – whatever subgenre of country you want to discuss, you can bet it ties back to Texas. That's not to say there aren't rockers from the Lone Star state; Austin has long been a hub of the alternative scene.

Musical Museums

Tex Ritter's Texas Country Music Hall of Fame (p260)

Bob Wills Museum (p195)

Buddy Holly Center (p190)

Museum of the Gulf Coast (p253)

Early Cowboy Country

The musical roots for country and western trace back to Anglo-Irish folk songs. But it was the singing cowboys of the silver screen that first brought the sound to national attention in North America. Classic singers like Gene Autry and Tex Ritter, both Texas-born boys, first played the musical hero on radio shows in the 1930s, then on TV; combined they also starred in more than 100 movies.

About the same time, Bob Wills was playing his violin at ranch dances in west Texas. He learned frontier fiddlin' from his grand-pappy and jazzy blues from African Americans in the cotton fields. He mixed that with other sounds he heard around – mariachi, Tejano, polka – and the result was western swing, a Texas original. 'San Antonio Rose' became the signature song of his band, the Texas Playboys. This enduring new style of country music continues to be popular today.

The Classics

The 1950s and '60s saw the emergence of Nashville and the Grand Ole Opry as an epicenter of the country sound, which included everything from ballads to rockabilly, an offshoot of western swing. Some of the classics in country music from this era had Texas connections: Earnest Tubbs, Jim Reeves, Buck Owens, Johnny Horton, Lefty Frizzell, Johnny Rodriguez, George Jones, Don Williams, Ray Price, Roger Miller, Willie Nelson... The latter three toured Texas' small clubs and honky-tonks together for a good many years. Country music variety hours were all the rage on television at the time. If you haven't seen the straight-laced, short-hair photos of Willie in the western dress of the era, you really ought to. Even if all the stars weren't from Texas, many were crooning about it. Marty Robbin's 'El Paso' is perhaps the most classic country ballad of all time.

Outlaw Country & Austin's Influence

Whether it was Willie Nelson leaving Nashville or the Armadillo World Headquarters club opening that had more influence on what happened next in Texas country is hard to say. But either way, it had to do with Austin.

The Armadillo of the 1970s was a hippie haven. The club's owners included Eddie Wilson, former band manager for Shiva's Head Band, and Jim Franklin, a local muralist and poster artist. They created a place that quickly became known as a counterculture hangout. It was a bar where bikers, cowboys, hippies and college kids could all hang out. They played a wide variety of music, but it was here that Texas singer-songwriters pioneered what would be called 'outlaw country'.

Willie had come home to Texas looking for more creative freedom than Nashville allowed. He, Waylon Jennings and Kris Kristofferson started writing music that mixed softer, traditional Nashville country with blues and rock, rhythms reminiscent of honky-tonks' early days. Though there was an edge to the music, the term 'outlaw' had a lot more to do with the singers' personal lives than with the music.

Tunes such as 'Luckenback, Texas' and 'Mammas Don't Let Your Babies Grow Up to be Cowboys' forced the industry to take notice. Musicians and bands who had been hard-pressed to find an audience for their country-rock songs began to flock to the Armadillo. Bands like Asleep at the Wheel and Kinky Friedman regularly played to packed crowds. In 1976, Austin City Limits, a live Texas public radio music program still on-air, debuted with Willie Nelson playing the pilot episode.

Though the Armadillo as it was closed its doors in the 1980s, Threadgill's World Headquarters restaurant, opened in 1996 in a building next door, continue to book live acts five nights a week.

Popular Country & George Strait

Little did the San Marcos college band Ace in the Hole know that in 1981 when they hired George Strait as lead singer they'd be launching a superstar. At the time of writing, Strait has had 60 number one hit singles – the most of any musician, in any genre, on record. His signature neo-traditional sound, and those starched Wrangler jeans and boots, are the reason for much of his success. George Strait is a real cowboy: one with a ranch and who participates in team-roping events. In fact, what started as a little family affair with him and his brother Buddy catchin' calves has morphed into the George Strait Team Roping Classic (www.gstrc.com) in San Antonio, during which more than 650 teams compete for $700,000 in prizes.

Not just George Strait, but numerous country artists from Texas have garnered popular, mainstream country success from the 1980s to today. Perhaps you've heard a few of their names: Gatlin Brothers, Barbara Mandrell, Kenny Rogers, Tanya Tucker, Reba McEntire, Brooks & Dunn (well, OK, one of them), Leanne Rimes, Dixie Chicks, Blake Shelton, Miranda Lambert, Sugarland... Should we go on? Of the up-and-comers, Morgan Frazier, a John Lennon Songwriter Contest winner, is one to watch – at 19 she's already played the Grand Ole Opry several times.

URBAN COWBOY

Loosely based on a now-defunct bar called Gilley's in a Houston suburb, John Travolta's *Urban Cowboy* (1980) struck a chord. For the next few years there were country-and-western bars with mechanical bulls all across the country.

ROCK IN TEXAS

There are those who say that Lubbock-born Buddy Holly (p191) invented rock and roll. While that may be strechin' the truth a little, it's true that Texan musicians have been at the forefront of rock since its inception.

Other notable Lone Star rockers you may have heard of include Roy Orbison, Roky Erickson of the 13th Floor Elevators, Janis Joplin, ZZ Top, the Steve Miller Band, the Fabulous Thunderbirds and the Butthole Surfers. Possibly the biggest name to come out of Texas lately is rock-pop diva Beyoncé, who has won an armful of Grammys with her 3½-octave range.

Texas also has proven a hotbed for indie-rock talent, and the best place to see it – other than every night of the week at clubs throughout Austin, Denton and Dallas – is at the SXSW and Austin City Limits festivals. Austin-based alternative bands that have achieved some success include the Spoon and White Denim. For more on the current scene, check out http://austin.thedelimagazine.com.

Texas Country Today

Meanwhile, back at the ranch... Texas continued producing singer-songwriters who didn't quite fit the Nashville country mold. Following close behind Waylon and Willie were artists like David Allen Coe, Lyle Lovett, Jimmie Dale Gilmore, Robert Earl Keen, Lucinda Williams, Rodney Crowell and Jerry Jeff Walker (admittedly a transplant).

And yet another sub-genre was created. When you hear someone talking about 'Texas country,' they're talking about a sound as well as describing the fact that the musicians hail from the state. Think of it as a progressive continuation of the outlaw phase. Radio stations across the state host daily or weekly Texas-country hours; some have even changed their format to be all Texas country, all the time. When tuning in, listen for Roger Creager, Pat Green and Gary P Nunn, in addition to those we've listed above.

Dance Hall Resources

Dance Halls and Last Calls *By Geronimo Treviño*

Texas Dance Hall Preservation Inc *www.texasdancehall.org*

Honky Tonk Texas, USA *www.honkytonktx.com/dancehalls*

Dance Halls & Honky-Tonks

Czech and German immigrants brought more than barbecue to the central part of the state when they arrived in the late 1800s. They also brought their dance hall tradition. At one time there may have been thousands of cavernous wooden dance halls in the country, but few remain today. Though they originally hosted polka bands, today they're all country. Most are old, but some, like Cheatham Street Warehouse (p123) are newer, or made from metal. We've listed the top venues in the destination chapters, including places like Gruene Hall (p121), one of the oldest dance halls in Texas. But many halls are in tiny towns too small to mention or they only hold dances once a month, for example **Twin Sisters Dance Hall** (www.twinsistersdancehall.com) in Blanco. If you're interested, it's worth searching out venue info and schedules on dance hall web sites. Hint: Schroeder Hall, Kendalia and Anhalt are classics, but not always open.

Honky-tonks may be a bit more like bars than dance halls, but many have that same great old-timey Texas feel to them: Broken Spoke (p77) in Austin being the perfect example. You'll find these in towns and cities rather than way out in the country; they may be anything from a tiny basement bar to a huge *Urban Cowboy*-esque night club like Billy Bob's (p170) in Fort Worth. Bandera has several (p135). We love the ones that are in old grocery stores or other businesses, such as **John T**

TEXAS ROAD TRIP SOUNDTRACK: TOP 25 ESSENTIALS

- 'New San Antonio', Rose Bob Wills and his Texas Playboys
- 'Luckenback, Texas', Waylon Jennings
- 'On the Road Again', Willie Nelson
- 'Truckstop in La Grange', Dale Watson
- 'Amarillo by Morning', George Strait
- 'What I like about Texas', Jerry Jeff Walker & Gary P Nunn
- 'Miles and Miles of Texas', Asleep at the Wheel
- 'El Paso', Marty Robbins
- 'Texas (When I die)', Tanya Tucker
- 'Waltz Across Texas', Ernest Tubbs
- 'Corpus Christi Bay', Robert Earl Keen
- 'God Blessed Texas', Little Texas

Floore's Country Store (www.liveatfloores.com; 14492 Bandera Rd; tickets $10-30; ⏲11am-1am Fri & Sat, to 10pm Sun) and **Coupland Inn** (www.couplanddancehall.com).

When you're ready to head out two-stepping, what music will you be hearing? The clubs and halls in and around Austin and Hill Country especially have an incredible array of talent to choose from. Some of the old-timers occasionally still play in the area, so you may catch Willie Nelson or Ray Price if you're lucky. Cornell Hurd, the Derailers and Dale Watson are all great country crooners with tunes you can boot-scoot to. Mickey & the Motor Cars have a primarily Americana, rockabilly sound. And we love the bluesy-rock sensibility that Kelly Willis brings to her shows, usually performed with her husband Bruce Robison. For a list of the top Texas dance halls and honky-tonks, see p22.

Football!

What's the official religion in the state of Texas? Football. The word alone will incite passion, a smile and plenty of opinions in many Texans. Boys in Texas are raised to play when they're barely out of the cradle. And come game day – any game at any level – all else is set aside to watch and, often, to party.

Texas Football Facts

Dave Campbell's Texas Football *(www.texasfootball.com) Team previews*

Texas High School Football *(www.texashsfootball.com)*

Texas Preps Football *(www.txprepsfootball.com) More high school stats*

Growing Up with Football

A football as a baby gift may seem strange elsewhere, but not here. Kids start throwing the ball around as soon as they can. Then follows the pee-wee leagues (ages 4 to 13) before high-school ball.

Texan parents have been known to delay their sons' initial school enrollment by a year (or even two); by the time these boys graduate from high school, logic goes, they'll be older – but most importantly, bigger and brawnier – than their grade-level cohorts. Does it guarantee that these boys will be NFL stars? No. But don't tell that to true believers.

High School Ball

If you are in Texas on a Friday night from September to November, you should absolutely attend a high-school football game. HG Bissinger's book about Odessa, *Friday Night Lights*, and the subsequent movie and TV series, nail it. Texas high-school ball takes on mythic proportions and meanings, especially in small towns. At stake in games are local pride, reputations and other intangibles that fuel the mania. The team's quarterback is the local hero, every bit as popular as a mayor when things are going well.

Increasingly, 16- to 19-year-olds are expected to be facsimiles of the pros. Roughly 48,000 fans attended the Texas State High School Championships in 2012, held in the Dallas Cowboys' Stadium. This author knows a certain eight-year-old who follows each state high school play-off game and can recite all the stats. Following local teams is not hard to do given the numerous websites on the subject. Many games are now also televised.

How seriously games are taken can be seen by the trappings that surround them. Coaches are not as well paid here as in the pros, but they definitely do better than regular teachers. Then there are legions of students supporting the team's effort: assistants and trainers; varsity cheerleaders who ascend to the squad through competitions as ruthless as those on the field; vast marching bands; dancing and drill teams; honor guards for the flags; and many more. That's not to mention the enthusiastic parents who cheer, scream and raise more and more money.

College Games

High school games are great, but college football really makes Texas tick. Graduates are unfailingly loyal to their alma mater. But many rabid fans have never set one academic foot on their favorite team's campus. State school rivalries go back decades. The bitterest contest in Texas college football? Hands down, it's the University of Texas (UT) Longhorns and the Texas A&M Aggies. Next is the University of Oklahoma Sooners and

OH, THERE ARE OTHER SPORTS IN TEXAS?

Contrary to how it may seem, Texas has all the same sports available as any other state. Soccer is quite a common activity for young boys and girls first taking to a field. Softball, baseball and basketball are all played in intramural and school leagues.

On the national level, Dallas' Texas Rangers and the Houston Astros baseball teams have nice stadiums and draw some crowds. The Dallas Stars hockey team, draws less of a crowd, but there's still some turn out.

Houston Rockets and Dallas Mavericks, pro National Basketball Association (NBA) teams, hold their own in terms of attendance and fan base. But Texans really go crazy for the San Antonio Spurs – a basketball team that has won four NBA championships, giving them a perfect record unmatched by any team except for the Chicago Bulls, proving there is more to Texas sports than football.

the UT Longhorns. As the reorganization of the conferences that determine what teams play each other threatened to end some long-held series, lawmakers intervened. Yes, the classic Thanksgiving morning UT versus A&M football game deserves state legislature's attention – it's that important.

Each school has an elaborate set of traditions surrounding the game. UT fans 'bleed orange,' in reference to the school colors. A&M has 'yell' instead of 'cheer' leaders, and those boy do stir up some noise in the stands with call-and-response chants that everybody knows. Various incarnations of the Texas Tech Red Raider's primary mascot, the Masked Rider, have been galloping into the stadium (on real horseback) since 1954.

College football's not just fun and games either: it's an industry. UT head coach Mack Brown's salary is a cool $5.19 million (plus incentives), making him the country's highest paid coach. A&M's head coach Kevin Sumlin reportedly makes a measly $2 million. The rationale for such salaries is that a successful team brings in huge revenue for the university. Needless to say, a coach's performance is a hot topic all season.

In 2012 Johnny Manziel (Texas A&M) became the fourth Heisman Trophy winner from Texas and the first ever to win it as a freshman. His freewheeling attitude and skill both contributed to his nickname 'Johnny Football.' Manziel garnered a lot of press and fan attention.

ROLLER DERBY

Austin is home to the Texas Roller Derby (www.txrd.com); the Lonestar Rollergirls team are tough athletes who also know how to put on a fun and flashy show.

National Teams & Tailgating

The Dallas Cowboys are the most famous football team not only in Texas but the USA as a whole; in fact, their nickname is 'America's Team' which is only reinforced by the blue and white star-spangled outfits of their nearly equally famous cheerleaders. Though their glory days may have been in the 1980s, no one seems to notice.

Houston still mourns the loss of their original NFL team, the Oilers (now the Tennessee Titans), back in 1996. The town got a new team, the Texans, in 2000, which hasn't been as popular. When the Texans made the play-offs for the first time in 2011, it helped residents outside Houston find some interest in the team.

Tailgating, the practice of partying in the parking lot before kick-off, is almost a requirement before game attendance. Heck, some people tailgate and then watch the game on satellite TVs in the parking lot. Though this pre-game party takes place nationwide, Texans do it up big. Expect to see pop-up 12ft-by-12ft awnings and guys painted in team colors kicking back in comfortable camp chairs next to a spread of food worthy of a top catering company. Preparations may be the most elaborate at pro games, but college fans get in on the act, too. Though most college stadiums do not sell beer, they allow it – on game day only – out in the parking lot and at campus picnic spots nearby.

Land & Wildlife

Let the Texas landscape surprise you. No less than 35 ecoregions exist here, and not one of them is called 'hot and flat as a pancake'. OK, maybe the northern Panhandle Plains should be... In any case, contrary to stereotypes, white-sand beaches, soaring pine forests and snow-capped mountains are all part of the picture. Indigenous birds, mammals and alligators outnumber the head of cattle here. Which means the nature of the state is a major reason to visit.

Land

Texas Parks & Wildlife (www.tpwd.state.tx.us) is an incredible resource for information on land use and wildlife in Texas. Their downloadable *Young Naturalist* series is recommended for kiddos.

Texas, as everyone here will tell you, is big. The second-largest state in the union has an area more than 261,000 sq miles. While that's less than half the size of Alaska, Texas is larger than all of Germany, the UK, Ireland, Belgium and the Netherlands combined. But those Western movies lie: Texas is not all dry desert, tumbleweeds and oil wells. In fact, with the natural boundaries of the Gulf of Mexico at the east and the Rio Grande at the west and south, Texas ranks as the ninth-largest state for total water area.

Within each major natural region of Texas there is a remarkable range of terrain. In northeast Texas, the Piney Woods is the southwestern edge of the southern coniferous forest belt and is characterized by a mix of pine and hardwood growth. The Gulf Coastal Plains, which run along the coast from Port Arthur to Brownsville, contain bays, lagoons, sandy barrier islands, saltwater marshes and flat grasslands. Yes, in the furthest southern reaches, palm trees do grow here naturally.

Verdant hills and meandering rivers make up central Hill Country, which is part of the Edward Plateau, a limestone karst region. The Southern Texas Plains, from Hill Country south to the Rio Grande Valley, is brush country, with scrubby vegetation and abundant prickly pear cacti. Spreading north of Austin there are several regions of prairies and plains. The land in the Panhandle is the highest and driest of these. Tablelands spread east of Lubbuck and Amarillo, containing red rock canyons, badlands and mesas.

In west Texas, the basin-and-range terrain is home to the Guadalupe Mountains, with elevations of more than 8000ft, as well as to Chihuahuan Desert lands. South of the Guadalupe Mountains, the Big Bend region follows the Rio Grande through dramatic canyons and sheer wall beyond the Chisos Mountains.

Parks & Land Protection

Texas has two national parks, Big Bend and Guadalupe Mountains, as well as 16 national preserves (www.nps.gov), 55 state parks (www.tpwd.state.tx.us) and four state forests. Oil drilling and natural gas exploration is allowed, but managed, in some of the natural preserves and on public lands. As well as providing opportunities for recreational activities, many of the preserves offer interpretive activities and educational programs.

Wildlife

Texas' sheer size and environmental diversity mean that it's home to a startling array of wildlife: over 5000 species of plants, 600 different birds (more than any other state) and 125 vertebrate animals are found here.

Mammals

To the eternal shame of early settlers, American bison, or buffalo, were hunted to the brink of extinction and today exist only in remnant populations. These days, the two most famous Texas animals are the armadillo and longhorn steer, respectively the state's official smallest and largest mammals. The armadillo, whose bony carapace is unique among mammals, resembles an armored vehicle. Many homeowners are annoyed when the armadillo digs up their lawns in its search for grubs. Speeding drivers are a hazard for the armadillo, which you may first encounter as an inevitable sight on a long Texas drive: road kill. Deer are also populous (and potential road dangers) in Hill Country.

Once the most common mammals found in west Texas, another (unofficial) mascot of the state is the black-tailed prairie dog – essentially a fat, friendly squirrel that lives off prairie grasses. Highly sociable, the prairie dog lives in large colonies called 'towns' and hibernates in winter. Natural and human-caused environmental changes have vastly reduced the prairie-dog population over the years, but protected prairie-dog towns can be found in west Texas and the Panhandle Plains.

It's a big old mammal party in Big Bend: a whopping 75 species call the region home. The black bear, all but gone from the region by the mid-20th century, made an amazing comeback about 20 years ago. More than 200 sightings are now reported in a typical year, most in the national park's Chisos Mountains. Mountain lions (sometimes called panthers) are seen fairly rarely, but about two dozen live in the Chisos. And that

TEXAS GEOLOGY & BLACK GOLD

The most exciting geological aspect of Texas is why there's oil. The sticky black stuff sits beneath Texas, southern Mississippi and Alabama, and Louisiana; there is heaps of it under the Gulf of Mexico near all these states, as well as the Mexican states of Tamaulipas, Veracruz and Tabasco – all areas surrounding the huge sedimentary basin that forms the Gulf of Mexico.

Evolving for more than 100 million years, the basin consists of a thick sequence of sedimentary rocks. As the sedimentary material makes its way deeper into the earth, it's subjected to a great deal of pressure and heat – enough to convert much of the organic debris (the remains of plants and animals that are always part of sedimentary material) into petroleum. You know, to refine for gasoline, to fill up those ubiquitous Texas trucks needed to traverse these great distances... See, every issue here comes back, inexorably, to the land.

Petroleum flows freely, but tends to collect into large masses that migrate into traps – so named because rocks or other impermeable materials catch the oil – where it forms pools. Pools are what oil explorers are after. Under Texas, salt domes (which are just what they sound like) act as traps; when they're pierced, oil that has been trapped beneath gushes forth. That's what happened when early 1900s prospectors first struck oil at Spindle Top in Beaumont, and at the World's Richest Half Acre in Kilgore. Gushers, however, are rare these days, as oil exploration has become extremely sophisticated.

These days it's the Eagle Ford shale, found south of Hill Country, that's making news. This late Cretaceous rock formation is mineral rich, with oil and gas deposits. The high percentage of carbonate makes the formation more brittle, and therefore responsive to hydraulic-fracturing (or fracking), which is used to extract it. This somewhat controversial process is fueling a growing economy in once moribund south-central Texas.

blur you just saw streaking across the desert? No, it's not a lost Austin hippie running towards a mirage. It's probably a jackrabbit. Big Bend's full of the critters.

Bats

Thirty-one species of bats – those flying mammals that populate horror movies, Halloween decorations and attics – call Texas home. But bats are actually Texans' friends; they eat large amounts of mosquitoes and insects nightly, and rarely bother humans.

You'll hear references to 'Mexican free-tailed bats', these are the ones you'll see streaming out from caves and from underneath the Congress Ave Bridge in Austin just before dusk. This is actually a migratory subspecies of Brazilian free-tailed bats (*Tadarida brasiliensis*).

The endangered Mexican longnosed bat has its only US home in the Chisos Mountains, where it summers. A total of 20 bat species live at Big Bend, ranking it top among national parks in bat diversity.

Bluebonnet Festivals

Burnet *(www.bluebonnetfestival.org)*

Chappel Hill *(www.chappellhillmuseum.org/bluebonnet.html)*

Ennis *(www.visitennis.org)*

La Vernia *(www.lavernialions.org/bluebonnetfest.html)*

Birds

An image in many a traditional and blues song, the mockingbird – a long-tailed gray bird that can mimic other birds' songs – is the official bird of Texas.

Texas has more than 600 documented bird species – over 75% of all species reported in the US. Several on that list are threatened species. The endangered golden-cheeked warbler, which exclusively nests in central Texas, is best identified by the male's distinctive song heard during late spring. Delisted, but still protected, bald eagles nest in the eastern part of the state from October to July, and overwinter in the Panhandle Plains and central-east Texas. Aransas Pass on the Gulf Coast is the wintering home to the endangered whooping crane, the tallest bird in North America – males approach 5ft in height and have a 7ft wingspan.

More than 50% of species spotted in Texas are just passing through. The Central Flyway for annual bird migrations cuts right through Texas. Some avian navigators use this path to commute from the Arctic Circle all the way down to Patagonia. Spring migration starts as early as February, when ospreys are seen in great numbers near Houston, and continues through May. Fall migration runs roughly from September through November.

Shorebirds and water fowl – roseate spoonbill, ibis, heron, egret, and of course, ducks and geese – can commonly be found in coastal areas year round, though their numbers increase come winter. For information about bird-watching in Texas, see Outdoor Activities (p39).

Field Guides

Birds of Texas, Keith Arnold

Texas Wildflowers, Campbell Loughmiller

Trees of Texas, Stan Tekiela

Animal Tracks of Texas, Ian Sheldon

Marine Life

You don't have to drag the kids to SeaWorld in San Antonio to spot dolphins. Several species of dolphin call the Gulf of Mexico home, including rough-toothed, common, bottle-nosed, striped, pantropical, Atlantic spotted and Risso's dolphins. Take a boat ride along the coast and you'll likely see them playing in your wake.

Game fish are common throughout the state, especially bass and trout, and sport fishing is very popular in the gulf. Most of the Big Bend region's native fish are tiny. One species, the Big Bend mosquito fish, lives in only one pond inside Big Bend National Park and nowhere else in the world. At one time, the population sadly had dwindled to two males and one female.

American Alligator

The name 'alligator' derives from the Spanish *el lagarto*, 'the lizard,' and you'll find these reptiles in east Texas swamps and along the Gulf Coast.

They are usually (but not exclusively) found in freshwater – shallow lakes, marshes, swamps, rivers, creeks, ponds and human-made canals. Caddo Lake and Anahuac National Wildlife Refuge are two likely places to catch a sighting.

Gators are carnivorous: even hatchlings eat insects, frogs, small fish, snails and the like. But they prefer prey that can be swallowed whole, such as fish, birds and snakes. Cold-blooded gators are warm-weather fans and are rarely active when the temperature dips below 68°F – cold comfort to anyone who likes to swim the bayous come winter. Their metabolism slows considerably in cold weather, but they can die when the temperature is more than 100°F. To cool themselves, they sit on riverbanks or in the shade with their mouths wide open, which dissipates heat.

Horror movies aside, alligators generally eat only when they're hungry, not as a punitive measure – unless they're feeling attacked. A great place to catch a gator sighting is Caddo Lake.

Snakes

There are snakes in Texas, hundreds of varieties of 'em. Thankfully the vast majority are not harmful. Walking through tall grass anywhere, especially Big Bend, do keep an eye out for the 11 poisonous kinds of rattlers. The very common western diamondback is the most dangerous; it can grow to be 8ft long and has a big, heavy, brownish body marked with dark (almost black) diamond shapes, set off by yellowish white borders. Look where you're going and listen up: it will usually rattle before attacking.

The coral snake's poison is the most potent of any North American snake. It looks very pretty – a slim body with sections of black and red divided by thin orange-yellow stripes – and it can easily be mistaken for the harmless scarlet king snake. To tell them apart, remember this cheerful little rhyme: 'Red touch yellow, kill a fellow; red touch black, good for Jack.' Fortunately, the coral snake is very shy and generally nocturnal, and on the whole it rarely bites people.

When traveling in high-risk areas, such as Big Bend or any place where there are tall grasses or shrubs, you can reduce the risk of being bitten by using basic common sense: wear boots and long pants, for example.

BATS

Texas' official flying mammal is the Mexican free-tailed bat. For a list of the best places to spot them, download the Texas Parks & Wildlife's bat-watching brochure at www.tpwd.state.tx.us/publications.

Plants

Wildflowers

Wildflowers are to Texas what fall foliage is to Vermont: they're a way of life. Wildflower tourism is so entrenched in the state that highway and local visitor centers can help you plan entire trips around watching them bloom. So what's the best time to see the crimsons and the blues in all their glory? Diehard wildflower enthusiasts would tell you that the time to see the best and widest range is from mid-March to mid-April, when roadsides and fields throughout central and west Texas, and especially the Hill Country, become explosions of color – blankets of wonderful reds, rusts, yellows and blue. For more on finding spring sightings, search http://texas.wildflowersightings.org.

A sighting of Texas' official state flower, the bluebonnet, means that spring has officially sprung. While this wildflower – whose name derives from its small, blue, bonnet-shaped petals – comes in several species of North American lupine, the most beloved and iconic in Texas culture is the *Lupinus texensis*: that's right, the Texas bluebonnet. Other beloved wildflower species include Indian blankets, also known as firewheels, the petals of which possess a red-orange-yellow pattern that looks almost woven. Indian paintbrushes share the same palette, but are shorter

TEXAS GOES GREEN

Austin has lead the way towards a greener future for Texas. The environmentally progressive city has garnered national and international awards for its initiatives, including the Green Building Program which offers practical workshops on sustainable building practices. Numerous private, grassroots groups such as Save Our Springs Alliance, protector of the the Edwards Aquifer zone and the the endangered Barton Springs salamander, act as watchdogs restraining over-development.

Even the city government is getting green. Carbon-neutral buses and bike lanes have been around seemingly forever. Since 2000, all new municipal buildings in Austin are built to Leadership in Energy & Environmental Design (LEED) standards. As of 2012, municipal departments buy 100% of their energy from renewable sources through GreenChoice. And the town passed legislation banning plastic bags in 2013.

Buy-local-first, home growing veggies and farmers markets have long been traditions with many Austin residents. But today we're seeing environmentally dedicated mixed-use, green communities pop up: complete with community gardens and green space, recycled art and green-energy use. We could go on, and on..

Austin may be leading the way, but other Texas towns are following suit. Houston constructed and continues to expand its light rail system. Bike sharing stations number 21 in town, and the Bikeways program is developing shared and single use bike lanes. Dallas has likewise undertaken development of an extensive bikeway system. Several new gardens and green spaces have opened that town. And all new municipal buildings (and those larger than 10,000 sq ft) are held to silver LEED standards, including the Perot Museum of Nature and Science that opened in 2012. For the SUV- and one-ton-Dually-pick-up-loving populace, it ain't always easy being green. But towns have made a start.

and often grow in fields of bluebonnets. Mexican hats, which belong to the sunflower family, do resemble nodding sombreros, and they're easily found growing alongside highways. The pink-blossomed buttercups have a blush of yellow at the center.

Flower-crazed tourists make the epic drive to Big Bend region specifically to see the wildflowers. The blooms peak early March to April in the lowlands and May to July in the Chisos Mountains, but it's possible to find flowers year-round; there's often a second bloom in late summer after the season's heavy rains. Big Bend bluebonnet, a 2ft tall relative of the Texas state flower, blooms from December through June in the lowlands. Other varieties you may see include prickly poppy, sweet William, snapdragon, cardinal flower, silverleaf, bracted paintbrush, rock-nettle and desert verbena.

Spider phobia? Tarantulas are common in rural Texas, as are scorpions – 11 species of stinging scorpions live in the Big Bend region. Spot one? Give it room.

Desert Dwellers

The creosote bush is among the most prevalent desert species in Texas, with dark-green leaves and a 30ft taproot that searches for underground water. The ocotillo, sometimes called coachwhip, is a woody shrub with long, slender wands that produce scarlet flowers. Lechuguilla, a fibrous-spined agave, is unique to the Chihuahuan Desert and may grow 15ft tall. Candelilla has long been used by the area's indigenous people to produce wax.

Prickly pear is the most common kind of cactus, with several varieties: Engelman, purple-tinged, brown-spine and blind (so-called because it looks like it has no thorns – but it does, so beware.) Other cactus species include fishhook, cholla, claret cup, rainbow, eagle's claw and strawberry pitaya. One species you *won't* find is the saguaro cactus, which – although often used by New York City ad agencies as a symbol for west Texas – actually is found in the Sonoran Desert of Arizona. After spring rains, look for claret cup and other cacti in Big Bend to be in brilliant bloom.

Survival Guide

Directory A–Z

Accommodations

From B&Bs to Bandera dude ranches, Texas does have some interesting accommodations. Unfortunately, the vast majority of the state's sleeping options are chain motels and hotels. Budget travelers beware: motel rates have increased dramatically in recent years and there are only a few hostels, which are in the major cities. If you want to sleep on the cheap, campgrounds are an option, but then you absolutely need a car.

Hotel and motel rates vary by day and by season:

- Business-oriented town hotels cost more weekdays; leisure-oriented ones cost more on weekends.
- Summer high-season and school holidays have the highest rates, but an event in town can send prices soaring at any time.
- Book ahead, but still expect to pay more, during Texas' spring break (all of March).
- B&B room prices tend to stay the same year round.

Amenities

Beverages Mid-range motels and hotels may have microwaves and small refrigerators in the rooms. Top-end properties usually stock the minibar with mini liquors and pricey snacks.

Internet Wired or wireless internet is almost always available at lodgings. In top-end hotels, expect to pay $15 to $20 per day; elsewhere, it's free.

Nonsmoking/smoking Unless otherwise noted, all lodgings we list offer at least some nonsmoking rooms. More and more hotels and motels are going completely smoke free. B&Bs never allow smoking in the building itself, and some may not even allow smoking outside on the porch or in the garden.

Parking In the downtown core of major cities, you'll pay $15 to $35 per night for parking; otherwise it is usually freely available.

B&Bs

Texas B&Bs are not super casual or cost effective. These are traditionally well-established businesses, not just a spare room in someone's home. They might be in rambling old houses, or newer and purpose built. Owners usually live on-site, but in separate quarters; though some have professional innkeepers that sleep away.

The best are family-run places with involved owners who are ready and willing to chat about the area, themselves – anything. Communal breakfasts are served at a set hour, at a big dining table, allowing guests to get to know one another and compare travel notes. But this is not always the case. Breakfast may be delivered to your door, or weekdays it might just be a gift certificate to a local restaurant or a light continental. Off-site innkeepers will generally provide the requisite restaurant recommendations but may be scarce outside breakfast and check-in hours.

In addition to some sort of breakfast, amenities often include baked goods in the afternoons and beverage stations available all day. Most B&Bs have common areas for guests to gather. Private, en suite bathrooms are the rule rather than the exception. Each B&B has its own policies, but almost all prohibit smoking, pets and children under the age of 12. Cancellations of less than a week may forfeit a night's pay. Two-day stays may be required.

Camping

Tent site rates range from $10 to $20 per night. Most campgrounds are set up

> **BOOK YOUR STAY ONLINE**
>
> For more accommodations reviews by Lonely Planet authors, check out http://lonelyplanet.com/hotels/. You'll find independent reviews, as well as recommendations on the best places to stay. Best of all, you can book online.

SLEEPING PRICE RANGES

The following prices refer to a room with a bathroom; rates do not include a 6% occupancy tax or any city taxes (up to an additional 7%).

$	less than $100
$$	$100–$200
$$$	more than $200

for recreational vehicles (RVs) with electricity and water at sites ($20 to $50 per night). Facilities almost always include water, toilets and showers. Private campgrounds may have club rooms, pools and internet access. State parks host some of Texas' best campgrounds, for more see Outdoors (p35).

Hostels

The Texas hostel network is very small. Austin has several good ones, and Houston has two. Check www.hostelz.com to see if any others have popped up.

Hotels & Motels

Chain hotels and motels rule the state; relatively few places are independently owned.

BARE-BONES BASIC

- Chains such as Motel 6, Red Roof Inn, Econo Lodge.
- Synthetic comforters, fake veneer furnishings: expect that they'll all look oddly similar.
- Hard to find nice ones under $70 a night.

MID-RANGE

- Brands include La Quinta, Best Western, Hilton Garden Suites, Marriott Courtyard.
- From $90 to $140 per night.
- Changeable duvets, coffee makers are usually standard.
- Rarely have an on-site restaurant.

TOP-END

- Four Seasons, Westin, St Regis etc.
- Boutique hotels in Houston, Dallas and San Antonio fall into this category.
- Stylish surrounds, posh public areas.
- Numerous dining and drinking outlets on-site.
- Rates start at $190; some basic amenities (eg internet) may cost extra.

HISTORIC HOTELS

Texas has some excellent historic hotels. Two of the best are the **Menger** (Map p96; ☎800-345-9285, 210-223-4361; www.mengerhotel.com; 204 Alamo Plaza; d from $125; P⊖❄📶🏊🐾) in San Antonio and the **Driskill** (Map p64; ☎800-252-9367, 512-474-5911; www.driskillhotel.com; 604 Brazos St; r $199-299, ste $300-900 ; P❄📶) in Austin. You'll also find a few out in the far west Texas towns of Fort Davis and Marathon.

Ranches

Guest ranches, also called dude ranches, can be fun places to stay, but they are few and far between. The exception is in the countryside around Bandera, west of San Antonio, where a dozen or more dude ranches offer horseback riding and cowboy activities as part of the daily rate, which also includes full board (from $120 per person, per day). For more information, log on to www.banderacowboycapital.com or contact the **Bandera County Convention & Visitors Bureau** (CVB; ☎800-364-3833; www.banderacowboycapital.com; 126 Hwy 16; ⏲9am-5pm Mon-Fri, 10am-3pm Sat).

Guest ranches elsewhere may provide you an opportunity to interact with animals, or they may just be a pretty place to stay in the country.

Resorts

- Generally located in ideal landscapes such as Hill Country.
- A few may be found in cities.
- Enhanced grounds and facilities may include several pools, trails or sports options.
- Resort fee of $10 to $20 per night.

Discounts

AAA Membership in the American Automobile Association provides access to hotel room discounts and some reduced admission, as well as roadside assistance.

Seniors If you are over the age of 65, discount rates on hotel rooms and attractions may be available. Having an American Association of Retired Persons (AARP) card is not usually required.

Students An ISIC or official school ID card often gets you discounts on admission to museums and other attractions.

PRACTICALITIES

- **Newspapers** *Austin-American Statesman* (www.statesman.com), *Dallas Morning News* (www.dallasnews.com), *Houston Chronicle* (www.chron.com), *San Antonio Express-News* (www.mysanantonio.com)
- **Periodicals** *Texas Monthly* (www.texasmonthly.com), *Texas Highways* (www.texashighways.com)
- **Radio** National Public Radio (NPR; www.npr.org)
- **Weights & Measures** Imperial (feet, miles, ounces, pounds etc)

Electricity

Food

Dinner reservations are essential at all top-end ($$$) restaurants in this book. Smoking is not allowed indoors at most restaurants, in some places it may be OK on the patio.

EATING PRICE RANGES

The following prices refer to a standard main course. Tips and taxes are not included.

$	less than $10
$$	$10–$20
$$$	more than $20

Gay & Lesbian Travelers

Texas is generally conservative. The larger cities have gay, lesbian, bisexual and transgender communities, but outside of Pride days and Austin in general, you won't see sexual preference being flaunted. In rural areas, displays of affection may draw negative attention from locals. We wouldn't advise trying it.

Resources

Gay & Lesbian Yellow Pages (www.glyp.com) Directories to Austin, Dallas, Galveston, Houston and San Antonio.

National Gay and Lesbian Task Force (☎202-393-5177; www.thetaskforce.org) Advocacy group with great national news coverage.

This Week in Texas (www.thisweekintexas.com) Statewide publication with business directories and bar guide.

Insurance

Taking out a travel insurance policy to cover theft, lost tickets and medical problems is a good idea in the USA, where some privately run hospitals refuse care without evidence of insurance. These are offered by travel agencies, your airline and others. Different policies cover different circumstances, always check the fine print. Worldwide travel insurance is available at www.lonelyplanet.com/travel_services. You can buy, extend and claim online anytime – even if you're already on the road.

Internet Access

Many, many cafes offer free wi-fi service for your personal computer or tablet (or phone, or iPod...). Airports usually have hot spots, but it's not always free. Most hotels have wi-fi in the lobbies and wired or wi-fi access in the rooms.

Not traveling with your own device makes finding access trickier. Your best bet is the local library (free), or a copy center like FedEx Office (from $7 per hour).

Legal Matters

Aside from it being against the law to carry wire clippers in your pocket in Austin, or shoot a buffalo from any 2nd-story window, the laws in Texas are similar to the rest of the states. It's illegal to possess controlled substances and to drive under the influence (with more than .08% blood alcohol level). If you are arrested, you are assumed innocent until proven guilty; you have a right to make one phone call and you will be assigned an attorney if you cannot afford one.

Do note that speed limits are strictly enforced, especially in small towns trying to make their budget. There is no provision for on-the-spot fine payment. (So don't offer!) For more on road rules, see p379.

Maps

As phone and tablet GPS become more widely used, maps become less necessary, but in rural areas and some small towns in Texas these GPS options are inaccurate. Maps are available at bookstores and at gas stations; you can order ahead of time at **Texas Map Store** (www.texasmapstore.com). Helpful maps include:

Delorme Texas State Atlas & Gazzetter Detailed atlas, good for rural roads.

Mapsco City maps covering all the main Texas towns.

Texas Official Travel Map Available free at many visitor centers and tourist offices.

Money

The US dollar ($) is divided into 100 cents (¢). Coins come in denominations of 1¢ (penny), 5¢ (nickel), 10¢ (dime), 25¢ (quarter). Quarters are the most commonly used coins in vending machines and some parking meters, so it can be handy to have a stash of them. Bills (banknotes) come in $1, $2, $5, $10, $20, $50 and $100 denominations – $2 bills are rare, but perfectly legal. In smaller places, cashing $100 can be difficult. Carry some small bills, especially for tips.

ATMs

➡ Common everywhere: airports, banks, grocery stores, malls, gas station convenience stores...

➡ Both your bank and the ATM owner you use will typically charge a small fee for each transaction (from $1.50 up to 5%).

➡ Local ATMs must display fees; check how much your bank charges before you leave home.

Credit Cards

➡ MasterCard or Visa are accepted at most places of business in Texas. A few eateries take cash only.

➡ American Express, Discover and other major cards are less universal, but still widely accepted.

➡ A credit card is usually required for car rental, hotel reservation and advance transportation ticket purchasing.

Tipping

Tipping is not optional. Service employees make minimum wage and rely on tips for their livelihoods.

Anyone delivering anything $2 to 15% for food, pizza, flowers, extra pillows in the hotel, your car from valet parking; really, anything.

Baggage services $2 per bag.

Bartenders 15% to 20%, or at least $1 per round if bill is small.

Hotel and B&B housekeeping $5 per stay is nice, though not as widely expected as other tips.

Hotel concierge $10 to $20 if they do a lot for you, such as procuring difficult tickets.

Restaurant servers 15% to 20% depending on level of service.

Taxi drivers 10% to 15%

Traveler's Checks

Traveler's checks from American Express or Thomas Cook offer protection from theft or loss, but they have fallen out of use in the US. Some places may not accept the checks at all, causing you to exchange them in a bank. Using a mix of ATM withdrawals and some cash is easier.

Opening Hours

We've listed opening hours for individual businesses in the destination chapters; below are general guidelines. Note that tourist attractions often keep longer hours during summer. Some such as amusement and water parks may also close in the winter. Super-center grocery stores stay open 24 hours. A good number of restaurants do not close between lunch and dinner. While places are only allowed to serve liquor until 2am, a few dance clubs stay open until 4am.

Banks 9am to 5pm Monday to Friday

Bars 11am to 2am

Cafes 7am to 8pm

Grocery stores 6am to midnight Monday to Saturday, until 10pm Sunday

Night clubs 8pm to 2am

Post offices 9am to 5pm Monday to Friday

Restaurants 11am to 2pm and 5pm to 10pm

Shops 9am to 6pm Monday to Saturday, 11am to 6pm Sunday

Public Holidays

Banks, schools and government offices (including post offices) are closed on major holidays. Public holidays that fall on a weekend are often observed on the following Monday.

New Year's Day January 1

Martin Luther King Jr Day third Monday in January

President's Day third Monday in February

Texas Independence Day March 2

Easter Sunday March/April

Memorial Day last Monday in May

Independence Day July 4

Labor Day first Monday in September

Columbus Day second Monday in October

Veterans Day November 11

Thanksgiving fourth Thursday in November

Christmas Day December 25

Safe Travel

Travel, including solo travel, is generally safe in Texas. As anywhere you should exercise more vigilance in large cities than in rural areas.

Guns

Texas does allow personal gun ownership, including the permitted carrying of concealed hand guns. You will see signs forbidding firearms in some public places, and that will likely be your closest encounter with a gun.

In Texas metro areas, as in all all big cities, there are some neighborhoods that are less safe than others. Exercise a normal amount of caution. Aggravated theft (with the use of a weapon) is not common.

We don't recommend getting involved in road rage incidents (no swearing or making rude gestures at another motorist), whether or not the other person may have a gun.

Recreational Hazards

In wilderness areas the consequences of a getting lost or having an accident can be very serious. Off main trails always travel with a hiking partner. Even on established routes, if going it alone inform someone of your destination and expected return – at the very least leaving a note in your car.

JELLYFISH

Jellyfish can be present year round in the mild waters of the Gulf of Mexico. Two varieties pack powerful stings: the Portuguese man-of-war, which is a translucent blue with long tentacles dangling from the center; and the sea nettle, which is also translucent but has tentacles attached to the edge of its bell-shaped central mass. Do not touch these even if you see one dead on the beach.

If you are stung, a supermarket-bought unseasoned meat tenderizer can ease the pain. For serious reactions, seek medical attention.

MOSQUITOES

Year round in the great Texas outdoors you may see mosquitoes that deserve inclusion in the boast that 'everything is bigger here.' The best way to combat these bugs is to keep yourself covered (wear long sleeves, long pants, hats and shoes rather than sandals) or apply a good insect repellent. Repellents containing DEET are the best, but children under two should not be exposed to DEET and children aged 2 to 12 years should not be allowed to use repellant containing more than a 10% solution.

Telephone

Cell Phones

In the USA, cell phones operate on different frequencies from other countries. You'll need a multiband GSM phone in order for an international phone to work here. If your phone is unlocked, a prepaid rechargeable SIM card is usually cheaper than roaming charges on your own network. SIM cards and inexpensive prepaid phones are sold at telecommunications and electronics stores.

Pay Phones & Phone Cards

With the prevalence of cell phones, pay phones have become hard to find. Airports and some gas stations may have them. Coins may sometimes be used (minimum of 50¢).

For long-distance and international calls, whether at a pay phone or on a hotel's land line, use a prepaid phonecard, which are sold at gas station convenience stores and some supermarkets.

Phone Codes

In many areas, local calls have moved to a 10-digit calling system. This means you must dial the area code even when making a local call.

Country code ☎1

International dialing code ☎011

Time

Central Standard Time Most of Texas is an hour behind New York (Eastern time), two hours ahead of Los Angeles (Pacific time), and five hours behind Greenwich Mean Time (GMT).

Daylight Savings Time In effect in the US from early spring to late fall; clocks 'spring forward' one hour in March and 'fall back' one hour in November.

Mountain Standard Time El Paso and Hudspeth counties in far west Texas; one hour behind Central, six behind GMT.

Tourist Information

Larger cities and towns have tourist information centers run by local convention and visitor bureaus. In smaller towns, local chambers of commerce often perform the same functions.

The *Texas State Travel Guide* (www.traveltex.com) is a comprehensive glossy guidebook that lists almost every city and town in the state. You can request one online, where most of the information is also posted, or at the Texas Travel Centers located on major interstates near the state line.

Travelers With Disabilities

Texas has gone a long way toward ensuring accessibility at attractions, in hotels and on public transit.

Communication

Braille Many ATMs and elevators have instructions in braille.

Telephone Companies are required to provide relay operators for the hearing impaired.

Public Spaces & Accessibility

Guide dogs May legally be brought into restaurants, hotels and other businesses.

Lodging Most hotels and motels have rooms set aside for disabled guests.

Public buildings Hotels, restaurants, theaters, museums etc. Required by the Americans with Disabilities Act (ADA) to be wheelchair accessible and have accessible restroom facilities

Road crossings In major cities at main intersections there are audible crossing signals as well as dropped curbs at busier roadway intersections.

Resources

Mobility International USA (www.miusa.org)

Access-able Travel Source (www.access-able.com)

Society for Accessible Travel & Hospitality (www.sath.org)

Transportation

Note that in general public transportation is not extensive or overly useful in Texas.

Airlines Will provide assistance for connecting, boarding and deplaning the flight, but you need to request when making your reservation.

Buses Both buses and trains must have wheelchair access available.

Parking Disabled parking sites with blue-colored demarcation is by permit only.

Standard car rental companies Some standard companies have hand-controlled vehicles or vans with wheelchair lifts by reservation.

Wheelchair Accessible Vans (www.txwheelchairvans.com) Hires vans in several Texas cities.

Visas

Note that visa rules change frequently and travelers should always double-check current requirements at the **Department of State** (http://travel.state.gov/visa), where downloadable forms are also available.

Visa Applications

All foreign visitors that need to obtain a temporary visitor visa (B-2) must do so from a US consulate or embassy abroad. Consult that embassy website for forms and procedures, which vary by country. In general:

- Your passport must be valid for at least six months longer than your intended stay in the USA.
- You will need to make an appointment, and likely have an interview.
- You'll need to submit a recent photo (2in by 2in) with the application.
- There is a $160 processing fee, which is sometimes required in advance.

Visa Waiver Program

Currently, under the US Visa Waiver Program (VWP), visas are not required for citizens of 37 countries, including the United Kingdom, Australia, New Zealand, EU countries, South Korea and Japan. VWP regulations state:

- You must have a machine-readable passport (MRP). If you don't have one, you'll need a visa to enter the USA.
- Visa waiver is good for 90 days, no extensions.
- VWP visitors must register only with the **Electronic System for Travel Authorization** (ESTA; https://esta.cbp.dhs.gov) at least 72 hours before their trip begins. Once approved, ESTA registration is valid for up to two years.
- Note that though not a part of the VWP, citizens from Canada do not require a visa for 90-day stays.

Transportation

GETTING THERE & AWAY

Most travelers arrive in Texas by air or by car. Flights, tours and rail tickets can be booked online at www.lonelyplanet.com/travel_services.

Air

Unless you live in or near Texas, flying to the region and then renting a car is the most time-efficient travel option. Entering Texas as your first port of call in the US is fairly easy; the following are just a few points to consider:

Customs If you're arriving from outside the USA, you must clear customs and immigrations at the first airport where you land. Retrieve your luggage and return it to the belt after customs, even if it is checked through to Texas.

Digital Registration Almost all international visitors will be digitally photographed and have their electronic (inkless) fingerprints scanned upon entry to the country; it takes just a minute.

Exemptions Currently many Canadian visitors, children under 14 and seniors over 79 are exempt from digital registration; for details contact the US Department of Homeland Security (DHS; www.dhs.gov).

Prohibitions Transportation Security Administration (www.tsa.gov) prohibits pocket-knives and liquids and gels on airplanes, unless they are stored in 3oz or smaller bottles placed inside a quart-sized clear plastic zip-top bag. Check its website for additional, ever-changing prohibitions.

Airports & Airlines

The main international gateways to Texas are Dallas/Fort Worth International Airport (www.dfwairport.com), American Airline's hub, and Houston's George Bush Intercontinental Airport (www.fly2houston.com/iah), United Airlines Hub. San Antonio (www.sanantonio.gov/sat), Austin (www.austintexas.gov/airport) and El Paso (www.elpasointernationalairport.com) have flights to and from Mexico.

Numerous domestic airlines have flights to the major international airports. Additionally, Dallas Love Field (www.dallas-lovefield.com) and Houston's William P Hobby Airport (www.fly2houston.com/hobby) service numerous destinations throughout the US, primarily through Southwest Airlines.

Land

Border Crossings

There are 14 official crossing points along the Texas–Mexico border, most of them are open 24 hours daily. US Customs and Border Protection (http://apps.cbp.gov/bwt) lists open hours, and estimated border waiting times for drivers

CLIMATE CHANGE & TRAVEL

Every form of transportation that relies on carbon-based fuel generates CO_2, the main cause of human-induced climate change. Modern travel is dependent on airplanes, which might use less fuel per kilometer per person than most cars but travel much greater distances. The altitude at which aircraft emit gases (including CO_2) and particles also contributes to their climate change impact. Many websites offer 'carbon calculators' that allow people to estimate the carbon emissions generated by their journey and, for those who wish to do so, to offset the impact of the greenhouse gases emitted with contributions to portfolios of climate-friendly initiatives throughout the world. Lonely Planet offsets the carbon footprint of all staff and author travel.

If you are not a Mexican national arriving from down south, whether to cross the Texas–Mexico border or not, given gang violence in recent years, is a serious question. Check with the US State Department (http://travel.state.gov/travel) for travel advisories. For more, see Day Trips to Mexico: Should You Visit?, p290. If you should decide to day trip into Mexico, be aware of the following:

International taxis You may find international taxis near border crossings. Fares are from $10 to $30 – bargaining expected.

Mexican tourism permit (*forma migratoria para turista*, or FMT) Required unless you are staying within the border zone (about 15 miles in) and not staying more than 72 hours.

Motor vehicles Taking a vehicle into Mexico is not advised, but if you do, you must obtain Mexican motor insurance and a temporary vehicle importation permit; look for booths at crossings. Bridge tolls cost $3 per vehicle.

Passports Everyone, even US tourists visiting Mexico on a day trip, must carry a passport to enter the US.

Returning A stop at US Customs is required; be prepared to state your nationality and declare any purchases made in Mexico. Note that it is not legal to bring back many prescription drugs.

Walking Most people crossing into Mexico for a day trip from Texas walk across the bridge (most of the Mexican cities are a few steps from the Rio Grande); bridge tolls $1 per pedestrian.

TRAVELING IN TEXAS BORDERLANDS

Note that the US Border Patrol maintains several checkpoints at scattered locations throughout the Texas interior. If you are traveling within 50 miles of the border, be sure to carry your international passport or domestic drivers license/photo ID with you. You may be asked to pull over and produce it.

Bus

Greyhound (☎800-231-2222; www.greyhound.com), the nationwide bus company, has reduced its services considerably but still runs cross-country.

- Buses are generally comfortable and safe; but they are slow and do not always represent a substantial cost savings over advance airfares or car rental.
- Fixed routes stop in major cities only, not always in the best part of town.
- Reserve tickets at least two weeks in advance, or more, and travel at off-peak hours for best fares.
- Reduced carbon emissions are a benefit to bus riding.

Car & Motorcycle

Interstate 35 runs south from Oklahoma into the Dallas–Fort Worth metro area. The transcontinental interstate for the southern USA is I-10, and it runs from Florida to California, passing through much of Texas. For further information on traveling around Texas by car or motorcycle, see p378.

Train

Amtrak (☎800-872-7245; www.amtrak.com) provides two cross-country passenger services that stop in a several cities across Texas. Services are fairly comfortable, even in the reclining coach seats, and dining or snack cars available. However, the trains run at a slow speed, with frequent service delays and late arrivals, and tickets are not always reasonably priced; booking as far in advance as possible helps. The two cross-country services are as follows:

Sunset Limited Runs between New Orleans and Los Angeles, stopping in Houston and San Antonio and El Paso.

Texas Eagle Travels between Los Angeles and Chicago, stopping in Dallas, Fort Worth, Austin, San Antonio, Alpine and El Paso.

GETTING AROUND

The best way to see the state is to rent a car and drive, but distances add up if you're not staying in one or two regions. To cover more ground in a shorter time, you can fly. Southwest Airlines serves many towns in Texas and, if you book ahead, usually has good fares. In the four major cities – Dallas, Houston, San Antonio and Austin – you may be able to get away without a car if you stay in the core areas. Otherwise you need to rent a car at each airport. Public transportation in Texas is limited.

Air

It is possible to go far by air around Texas. Corpus Christi, Brownsville, Harlingen, McAllen, Laredo Midland-Odessa, Lubbock and Amarillo all have primarily regional airports served by flights from within Texas. Book in advance for the best deals; signing up for airlines' online weekly sales newsletters can be a help.

Southwest Airlines (SWA; ☎800-435-9792; www.southwest.com) Has the state's most comprehensive – and usually the cheapest – internal flights. Serves all regional airports listed above through Dallas Love Field and Houston's William P Hobby Airport. Additional service connects San Antonio, El Paso, Lubbock and Midland-Odessa directly with other regional airports.

American Airlines (AA; ☎800-433-7300; www.aa.com)

Connects to regional airports through Dallas–Fort Worth International Airport.

United Airlines (www.united.com) Regional flights go through Houston's George Bush Intercontinental Airport.

Bus

Greyhound Bus Lines (☎800-231-2222; www.greyhound.com) is the main company serving Texas. Bus travel generally has a cost edge over flying, but not necessarily over car rental if booked ahead. Greyhound has eliminated services to smaller communities it once served, so your only real option is busing it between big cities. Service is slow and you will still need a car to get around in most towns in Texas – making it quite inconvenient to arrive in town by bus.

Car & Motorcycle

Having a car during at least some portion of your trip is all but a necessity. Texans love their vehicles and most cities are well spread out as a result. Public transportation is limited even within big metro areas and it's non-existent in small towns.

Exiting Highways in-state may come together for a while and branch off each other; note that exits are not always on the right.

Interstates Posted speed limits may be as much as 85mph, and traffic can move even faster. Lanes multiply in cities; don't be surprised to find yourself in traffic that is 12 lanes across.

Rural Roads Posted speed limits are often still high (as much as 70mph) on rural roads. Some locals like this, and will pass you going a million miles an hour, whizzing past trailer homes. Others will take their sweet time no matter what the speed limit; be prepared to slow down if you get stuck behind a slow driver.

Rush Hour From 7am to 9am and 4:30pm to 6:30pm; major city driving is to be avoided at these hours. Also expect a mini lunch rush between noon and 1:30pm.

Petty Theft In metro areas do not leave valuables in sight on the car seat; petty theft does happen.

Size Matters Pickup trucks and SUVs dominate in Texas; if driving a compact, get used to being the smallest thing on the road.

Automobile Associations

American Automobile Association (AAA; ☎800-765-0766; www.aaa-texas.com; annual fee $54) membership provides emergency road-side service in the event of an accident, breakdown, running out of fuel or locking your keys in the car.

- Consider joining if you plan on doing a lot of driving in the USA.
- Membership also helps with hotel discounts.
- Car rental programs may offer alternative road-side assistance plans.
- AAA has reciprocal agreements; members of some foreign auto clubs are entitled to local services. Check in advance and bring your membership card.

Driver's License

Texas has reciprocity agreements with 83 countries, meaning your driver's license is likely good in Texas if you plan to stay less than a year.

- Some of the countries included are: Canada, Mexico, United Kingdom, most of Europe, Australia, New Zealand, Japan and South Korea.
- To make sure your country is on the reciprocal list, do a general online search for 'Texas driver's license, international reciprocity' to reach the Texas Secretary of State's Administrative Code page, or contact their office at register@sos.state.tx.us.
- It never hurts to carry an International Driving Permit (IDP) in addition to your domestic license; for foreign nationals not on the list, this is a must. IDPs are available from your local automobile association and are usually valid one year.

Fuel & Fix-it

Car Rental Problems In the event of a mechanical problem or break-down in a rental car, contact the rental agency immediately (the number is likely on the key chain); they will make provision to help.

ROAD DISTANCES (M)

	Amarillo	Austin	Big Bend National Park	Corpus Christi	Dallas	El Paso	Fort Worth	Galveston	Houston	San Antonio
Austin	510									
Big Bend National Park	470	395								
Corpus Christi	655	220	590							
Dallas	365	200	575	415						
El Paso	440	580	370	695	640					
Fort Worth	340	190	570	405	35	610				
Galveston	660	220	590	225	290	800	320			
Houston	600	160	555	220	240	745	270	55		
San Antonio	510	80	395	145	280	550	265	250	195	
South Padre Island	805	365	650	180	565	845	550	410	370	290

Gas Stations They're everywhere, usually open 24 hours. Pay at the pump with a credit card or pay in advance with cash.

Roadside Assistance Having an automobile association membership or other roadside assistance can be a big help with minor problems.

Service Stations Full automotive service is not generally available at gas stations. If you need an oil change or to fix a flat, national chains such as Jiffy Lube (www.jiffylube.com) and Discount Tire (www.discounttire.com) are widely represented in Texas.

Insurance

Note that in Texas (as well as the United States as a whole) you must have liability insurance for any car you drive.

- Liability insurance means that you won't have to pay for damages if you hit someone.
- If you're renting a car, the liability insurance is called Loss/Damage Waiver (LDW), or Collision/Damage Waiver (CDW), and is not automatically included in rates.
- If you have your own private vehicle insurance elsewhere in the US, it may extend to vehicles you rent; ask ahead and bring your insurance card.
- In some cases, your major credit card may offer insurance coverage if you reserve and pay for the rental with that card.
- When you rent a car, adding LDW coverage ($10 to $25 per day extra) will always be offered as an option.
- Uninsured motorists in Texas account for less than 13% of drivers. Note that LDW does not cover damages and medical injuries caused by the uninsured, but your personal policy might. You can add supplemental Personal Accident Insurance to your rental if you are concerned.

Rental

All major car-rental companies in the USA have offices throughout Texas. Airports are the most common rental location, but city and suburban offices also exist.

- In general, reserve as far ahead as possible for the best rates. But if price is a big concern, keep checking for sales afterwards. Bookings are entirely changeable.
- Rates for a compact to mid-size car generally range from $25 to $45 per day, $170 to $250 per week.
- Note that in addition to the base rate, there will be heaps of local, state and airport concession taxes (15% to 20%); most companies now quote the total, tax-included price online.
- Weekend-only rentals can be super cheap ($5 to $20 per day).
- Unlimited mileage is usually included, but check to be sure. (Have we mentioned Texas is big?)
- Consolidators like Hotwire (www.hotwire.com) and Priceline (www.priceline.com) can sometimes save you money, especially if you're willing to accept whatever rental company they choose.
- Car Rental Express (www.carrentalexpress.com) is a clearing house for independent car rental agencies; note that there aren't many in Texas and they're usually off-airport.
- If you plan to drop off the car somewhere other than where you picked it up, be aware that additional fees can be hefty ($100 or more).
- Enterprise (www.enterprise.com) has the most suburban locations in Texas.

AGE & CREDIT REQUIREMENTS

- Most rental agencies require that you have a major credit card in your own name, both for reserving ahead and at the counter.
- Some companies require operators to be at least 25 years old; those allowing 18- to 25-year-olds to drive charge high supplemental fees.
- Some companies will allow a spouse to legally drive a rental without paying the second driver fee (from $25).

Road Rules

- The minimum age for driving a car in Texas is 16.
- Drive on the right side of the road and pass on the left.
- Right turn on a red light is permitted after a full

DRINKING & DRIVING

The drinking age is 21, and you need an ID (driver's license or other identification with your photograph and date of birth on it) to prove your age. Undercover agents from the Texas Alcoholic Beverage Commission may pose as employees or consumers in shops that sell alcohol, trawling for underage buyers. You could incur stiff fines, jail time and penalties if caught driving under the influence of alcohol. Statewide the blood-alcohol limit is 0.08%, which is likely to be reached after just two 12oz bottles of beer for a 135lb woman or three for a 175lb man. If you're younger than 21 years old it is illegal to drive after you have consumed any alcohol – zero tolerance. Roads near notorious bars may be watched. During holidays and special events, roadblocks are sometimes set up to check for (and deter) drunk drivers.

stop unless signs indicate otherwise. Speed limits are posted and enforced.

- Unless otherwise posted, speed limits are 70mph daytime, 65mph nighttime on interstates and freeways.
- Speed limits in cities and towns vary (25mph to 55mph).
- School zones have strictly enforced speed limits as low as 15mph during school hours.
- Speeding fines are expensive – as much as $165 for between 1mph and 5mph over in Houston. That said, driving 5mph over the speed limit on highways is common.
- Driving while intoxicated (defined as not having the normal use of faculties, or .08% blood alcohol level) is illegal; penalties are severe, starting with a minimum 72 hour confinement.
- Texas requires the use of seat belts for drivers and front-seat passengers. Child safety seats are also required for those under eight years old or 4ft 9in.
- Texas requires motorcycle riders under age 21 to wear helmets; over age 21 it is not required if a rider has completed a safety training course or has medical insurance coverage (greater than $10,000) that includes motorcycle accidents. Police cannot stop a helmetless rider solely to see if they qualify for exemption.

ACCIDENTS DO HAPPEN

If you get in a fender-bender, take the following steps:

- Do not drive away. Move your car out of traffic, but remain at the scene; otherwise you may spend some time in the local jail.
- Call 911 to reach the police (and an ambulance, if needed); provide as much specific information as possible (your location, if there are any injuries involved etc).
- Get the other driver's name, address, license number, license plate number and insurance information. Be prepared to provide similar documentation.
- Tell your story to the police. It's your right under the law to have a lawyer present when answering questions, but unless a death is involved, cases where this is necessary are rare.
- Always comply with an alcohol breathalyzer test. If you take the option not to, you'll almost certainly find yourself with an automatic suspension of your driving privileges.
- If you're driving a rental car, call the rental company promptly.

Local Transportation

Local public transportation including buses, trollies and trains, is available only in major cities, and then it is not comprehensive or necessarily traveler friendly. Operating hours differ from city to city, but in general services run from about 6am to 10pm. Basic fares average between $1.25 and $2.

Austin Buses can be handy for getting around downtown and to S Congress Ave; the light rail primarily heads out of town.

Dallas The light rail system connects several downtown stops with outlying suburbs; McKinney Ave Trolley great for traveling between uptown and downtown. Weekdays, Trinity Express trains connect Dallas with Fort Worth.

Houston Has a limited light rail system, good for connecting from downtown to museums, but not for going further; buses are not very useful here.

San Antonio Four 'street car' (bus-like trolley) routes cater to city visitors, connecting all major downtown sights (Alamo, Market Square, HemisFair Park, etc)

Train

Amtrak (☎800-872-7245; www.amtrak.com) has two national routes that connect through Texas towns. Unless you just love the romance of train travel and want to take your time getting places, the service is fairly impractical. Scheduled arrivals may be in the middle of the night and service is often late. For more on train routes in Texas, see Getting There & Away p377.

Behind the Scenes

SEND US YOUR FEEDBACK

We love to hear from travelers – your comments keep us on our toes and help make our books better. Our well-traveled team reads every word on what you loved or loathed about this book. Although we cannot reply individually to postal submissions, we always guarantee that your feedback goes straight to the appropriate authors, in time for the next edition. Each person who sends us information is thanked in the next edition – the most useful submissions are rewarded with a selection of digital PDF chapters.

Visit **lonelyplanet.com/contact** to submit your updates and suggestions or to ask for help. Our award-winning website also features inspirational travel stories, news and discussions.

Note: We may edit, reproduce and incorporate your comments in Lonely Planet products such as guidebooks, websites and digital products, so let us know if you don't want your comments reproduced or your name acknowledged. For a copy of our privacy policy visit lonelyplanet.com/privacy.

OUR READERS

Many thanks to the travelers who used the last edition and wrote to us with helpful hints, useful advice and interesting anecdotes:
Joachim Bergmann, Jules & Harry Clinton, Doreen Coppens, Mikael Lypinski, John Malone, Iwona Mielnik, Angelika Neudecker, Peter O'Neill

AUTHOR THANKS

Lisa Dunford

I can't thank all my family and friends in Texas enough. Billy, I wouldn't want to take this, or any journey, without you. To George and Carol Springs: thanks for traveling the backroads with us. To my parents and my sister's family, thanks for eating, seeing and reviewing. My beloved mother-in-law, Helen Dickman, says I've learned to talk (or at least write) Texan real well. This is for her.

Mariella Krause

Thanks to Angela Otey for the fun night at the Cove; Pat Fowler for putting me up in El Paso; Leigh Ann Schmidt for welcoming me back to Austin; Gene Brenek for taking that epic road trip through west Texas with me; and Spoetzl Brewery, for the obvious reasons. I'd like to wish a permanent and ongoing thank you to my husband Tim Bauer, who I met the first day I moved to Texas three million years ago.

Left to Right: Mariella Krause, commissioning editor Suki Gear, Ryan Ver Berkmoes, Lisa Dunford.

Ryan Ver Berkmoes

Thanks to Lonely Planet's Suki Gear in Oakland for giving me the chance to continue living a Texas adventure that started in 1997. I also want to thank my coauthors Mariella Krause and occasional beer buddy Lisa Dunford for keeping me honest. Huge thanks go to my dear friend Justin Marler and Laura. And just like the multipurpose onion ring, I love all things Golden.

ACKNOWLEDGMENTS

Cover photograph: Cowboy at the Stockyards cattle drive, Fort Worth. Jill Hunter / Alamy ©

Climate map data adapted from Peel MC, Finlayson BL & McMahon TA (2007) 'Updated World Map of the Köppen-Geiger Climate Classification', Hydrology and Earth System Sciences, 11, 163344.

THIS BOOK

This 4th edition of Lonely Planet's *Texas* guidebook was researched and written by Lisa Dunford, Mariella Krause and Ryan Ver Berkmoes. The previous edition was also written by Sarah Chandler.

This guidebook was commissioned in Lonely Planet's Oakland office, and produced by the following:

Commissioning Editor Suki Gear

Coordinating Editors Kate Mathews, Ross Taylor

Senior Cartographer Alison Lyall

Coordinating Layout Designer Carol Jackson

Managing Editors Sasha Baskett, Bruce Evans

Senior Editor Karyn Noble

Managing Layout Designer Chris Girdler

Assisting Editors Sarah Bailey, Judith Bamber, Barbara Delissen, Jodie Martire, Charlotte Orr, Erin Richards

Assisting Cartographers Fatima Bašić, Jeff Cameron, Mark Griffiths, Valentina Kremenchutskaya

Cover Research Naomi Parker

Internal Image Research Aude Vauconsant

Thanks to Anita Banh, David Carroll, Nicholas Colicchia, Lauren Egan, Ryan Evans, Larissa Frost, Jane Hart, Genesys India, Jouve India, Andi Jones, Elizabeth Jones, Trent Paton, Mazzy Prinsep, Kerrianne Southway, Tasmin Waby, Gerard Walker

Index

Map Pages **000**
Photo Pages 000

Map Pages **000**
Photo Pages **000**

N

O

P

Map Pages **000**
Photo Pages **000**

Map Legend

Sights

- Beach
- Bird Sanctuary
- Buddhist
- Castle/Palace
- Christian
- Confucian
- Hindu
- Islamic
- Jain
- Jewish
- Monument
- Museum/Gallery/Historic Building
- Ruin
- Sento Hot Baths/Onsen
- Shinto
- Sikh
- Taoist
- Winery/Vineyard
- Zoo/Wildlife Sanctuary
- Other Sight

Activities, Courses & Tours

- Bodysurfing
- Diving
- Canoeing/Kayaking
- Course/Tour
- Skiing
- Snorkeling
- Surfing
- Swimming/Pool
- Walking
- Windsurfing
- Other Activity

Sleeping

- Sleeping
- Camping

Eating

- Eating

Drinking & Nightlife

- Drinking & Nightlife
- Cafe

Entertainment

- Entertainment

Shopping

- Shopping

Information

- Bank
- Embassy/Consulate
- Hospital/Medical
- Internet
- Police
- Post Office
- Telephone
- Toilet
- Tourist Information
- Other Information

Geographic

- Beach
- Hut/Shelter
- Lighthouse
- Lookout
- Mountain/Volcano
- Oasis
- Park
- Pass
- Picnic Area
- Waterfall

Population

- Capital (National)
- Capital (State/Province)
- City/Large Town
- Town/Village

Transport

- Airport
- Border crossing
- Bus
- Cable car/Funicular
- Cycling
- Ferry
- Metro station
- Monorail
- Parking
- Petrol station
- Taxi
- Train station/Railway
- Tram
- Other Transport

Note: Not all symbols displayed above appear on the maps in this book

Routes

- Tollway
- Freeway
- Primary
- Secondary
- Tertiary
- Lane
- Unsealed road
- Road under construction
- Plaza/Mall
- Steps
- Tunnel
- Pedestrian overpass
- Walking Tour
- Walking Tour detour
- Path/Walking Trail

Boundaries

- International
- State/Province
- Disputed
- Regional/Suburb
- Marine Park
- Cliff
- Wall

Hydrography

- River, Creek
- Intermittent River
- Canal
- Water
- Dry/Salt/Intermittent Lake
- Reef

Areas

- Airport/Runway
- Beach/Desert
- Cemetery (Christian)
- Cemetery (Other)
- Glacier
- Mudflat
- Park/Forest
- Sight (Building)
- Sportsground
- Swamp/Mangrove

OUR STORY

A beat-up old car, a few dollars in the pocket and a sense of adventure. In 1972 that's all Tony and Maureen Wheeler needed for the trip of a lifetime – across Europe and Asia overland to Australia. It took several months, and at the end – broke but inspired – they sat at their kitchen table writing and stapling together their first travel guide, *Across Asia on the Cheap*. Within a week they'd sold 1500 copies. Lonely Planet was born.

Today, Lonely Planet has offices in Melbourne, London and Oakland, with more than 600 staff and writers. We share Tony's belief that 'a great guidebook should do three things: inform, educate and amuse'.

OUR WRITERS

Lisa Dunford

Coordinating author; Houston & East Texas Does living in a state for 22 years, marrying a native and learning to speak the language mean someone can become a naturalized Texan? Lisa sure hopes so. Over the years she's logged tens of thousands of miles exploring her adopted home. She loves cruising the country roads seeing what there is to see – a cow in a bluebonnet field, or an old barnlike dance hall. She's bought boys drinks at the Continental Club in Austin, ridden the rides at the State Fair in Dallas and sailed on Corpus Christi Bay.

Before becoming a freelance writer, Lisa was a restaurant reviewer and an editor in the features department at the *Corpus Christi Caller-Times* newspaper. Now no matter where she roams, she always returns to the patch of riverfront east of Houston that she, her husband and their dogs call home.

Lisa also wrote the Welcome to Texas, Texas' Top 25, Need to Know, If You Like, Month by Month, Itineraries, Outdoor Activities, Travel with Children and Regions at a Glance chapters, as well as the Understand and Survival sections.

Mariella Krause

Austin; San Antonio & Hill Country; Big Bend & West Texas Mariella first fell in love with Austin when she checked out the UT campus during her junior year of high school. After college, she intended to live 'everywhere,' but felt so at home in Austin that she accidentally stayed for 15 years. Mariella will always consider Texas home, and she still sprinkles her language with Texanisms whenever possible, much to the amusement of those who don't consider 'y'all' a legitimate pronoun.

Mariella also wrote the Texas BBQ & Cuisine chapter.

Ryan Ver Berkmoes

Dallas & the Panhandle Plains; Gulf Coast & South Texas Ryan grew up in Santa Cruz, California, the sort of goofball beachtown place that made him immediately love Port Aransas. An itinerant wanderer, he was most at home on the hundreds of miles of Texas backroads he traversed for this book. Whether it was discovering a forgotten town on Texas Hwy 70 or driving to the literal end of the road to (happily!) check out yet another empty Gulf Coast beach, he relished every click on the odometer.

Published by Lonely Planet Publications Pty Ltd
ABN 36 005 607 983
4th edition – Jan 2014
ISBN 978 1 74220 199 3

10 9 8 7 6 5 4 3 2
Printed in China